WHAT'S SO

WRONG

WITH BEING ABSOLUTELY

RIGHT

WHAT'S SO
WRONG
WITH BEING ABSOLUTELY
RIGHT

The Dangerous Nature of Dogmatic Belief

JUDY J. JOHNSON

 Prometheus Books

59 John Glenn Drive
Amherst, New York 14228–2119

Published 2009 by Prometheus Books

Inquiries should be addressed to
Prometheus Books
59 John Glenn Drive
Amherst, New York 14228–2119
VOICE: 716–691–0133, ext. 210
FAX: 716–691–0137
WWW.PROMETHEUSBOOKS.COM

13 12 11 10 09   5 4 3 2 1

Library of Congress Cataloging-in-Publication Data

Johnson, Judy J., 1943–
    What's so wrong with being absolutely right : the dangerous nature of dogmatic belief / by Judy J. Johnson.
        p. cm.
    Includes bibliographical references and index.
    ISBN 978–1–59102–657–0 (pbk. : alk. paper)
    1. Dogmatism. I. Title.

BF698.35.D64J64 2008
153.4—dc22

2008049648

Printed in the United States of America on acid-free paper

*For my mother, Jan Johnson, and
my sons, Marc and Jay Shandro*

CONTENTS

1

PART II PORTRAITS OF DOGMATISM

PART III CONTEMPORARY MODELS

PART IV INFLUENTIAL FACTORS: DEVELOPMENTAL AND PERSONALITY THEORISTS

ACKNOWLEDGMENTS

I could not have written this book without the generous financial and sabbatical support of Mount Royal College, Calgary, Alberta. Nor could I have successfully completed this book without the initial editorial services of Richard Collier, who deserves an honorary degree in psychology for his patience in teaching me how to concisely organize my thoughts and words. Thanks also to my Prometheus editor, Kristine Hunt, whose thoughtful, meticulous editing was always given with respectful, open-minded collaboration that was the very antithesis of dogmatism.

I am grateful to all of my colleagues in the Department of Psychology who supported my sabbatical applications and willingly provided me with resource material. Many other colleagues and friends, too numerous to mention, made helpful comments that, unbeknownst to them, sparked my thinking and helped me fine-tune my ideas. I especially want to thank Monica Baehr for her patient help with technology and incisive probes about dogmatism and existentialism. Avril Torrence edited segments of my writing (particularly my use of metaphors) and asked insightful questions all along the way. Thanks also to Janet Sissons for her assistance with early philosophers' contributions to an analysis of dogmatism.

Words cannot convey my gratitude for the support and suggestions from my open-minded friends who never failed to encourage me and stimulate my thinking about dogmatism. Long walks and lunches with Joan Taylor, Gayl Benedict, Jean Shafto, Avalon Roberts, Gillian Steward, Donna Michael, and Corrine Frick helped me clarify my thoughts and maintain an enthusiasm that brought this book to fruition. In addition, every member on the Calgary Board of Friends of Medicare urged me on and stimulated my thinking, as did Mel and Joan Teghtmeyer, Ted Woynillowicz, and Donna Ingwersen of the Council of Canadians, Calgary branch.

Closer to my heart, special thanks to my brother Dale Johnson, who patiently ploughed through badly written initial drafts of this book. His critiques of my chapters on Adler and Buddhism were invaluable. Indeed, they were given with Adlerian encouragement and Buddhist loving-kindness, as were the challenging questions raised by my son Marc Shandro and his partner, Debbie Brooks, who both spent many hours mulling over drafts, particularly the chapter on Buddhism. My mother, Jan Johnson, was my empathic sounding board for the entire writing and publishing process—it seems her every phone call began, "How's the book coming, honey?" Dale, Marc, and Mom championed this book and gave me what I most needed to complete it. For their ongoing love and support, this book is dedicated to them, with more love than I can convey on these simple pages. And Jay, you too are always in my heart.

PREFACE

I've been thinking a lot about dogmatism over the past twenty-five years, and as far as I can tell, it isn't going away anytime soon. Disrupting the best intentions of science, politics, and religion, dogmatism alters the course of human history. Sarcastically described as pigheaded, hidebound rednecks who never met a bigot they didn't like, dogmatists give momentum to ideological radicalism that jeopardizes democracy and human rights. In some cases, their pursuit of dogmatic goals may be as subtle as the *b* in subtle, but the effects of their efforts are as blatant as the *b* in blatant. What, then, is the nature of implacable Truth, and what's so wrong with being absolutely right?

Despite its ubiquitous presence among people we live and work with, in politicians of the highest order, in priests, educators, policymakers, and leaders of various stripes, no scholarly theory has advanced an explanation of the psychological forces that give dogmatism its momentum. The description and effects of fanatical idealism have recently been given considerable attention, and there is abundant research on the measurement of dogmatism, but no comprehensive theory of the *origins* of dogmatic, ideological extremism exists. Despite scientific advances in the areas of cognitive psychology, social and personality development, and cognitive neuroscience, no explanation is forthcoming about the causes and effects of dogmatism in the domains of family, marriage, politics, religion, business, and academia, where its continued influence is so damaging. This book fills that gap in theory. It weaves a causal tapestry of influences and characteristics that depict a mind like the bed in the guest room: always made up, but seldom used.[1]

In the chapters that follow, we will familiarize ourselves with the thirteen characteristics of dogmatism that derive from key deficiencies in childhood and adolescence. These deficiencies are central to a closed-minded approach to knowledge and the rigid certainty of beliefs one considers to be true and unalterable. The theory draws from perceived relationships that, in many cases, have yet to be tested; however, such perceptions are based on observations, readings, and research, rather than ideas that were simply fabricated along the way. Yet it is important to emphasize that the model of dogmatism contained within these chapters is not a causal model; it is based on informed assumptions—some of which have been tested in the literature, some not. It is therefore impossible to draw definitive conclusions about the theory developed here.

We can, however, safely conclude that the closed- or narrow-mindedness of dogmatism damages people's careers, erodes their friendships, and limits their potential for intimacy. In the public domain, meanwhile, dogmatism is the bottleneck on freedom's horn of plenty. Dogmatic people who occupy positions of influential power destabilize existing democracies and prevent progressive political, scientific, and cultural transitions. Because questioning their established beliefs threatens their deep psychological needs for certainty and safety, dogmatists sidestep the duties of responsible citizenship—duties that demand transparency and accountability.

Equally dangerous are dogmatic followers. Adrift in a sea of ideological dependency and oblivious to the motives of dogmatic leaders who colonize their minds, dogmatic followers naively support authoritarian leaders who rule the marketplace of ideas and deny free speech.

In this dogmatic tango, both leaders and followers are chained by the dogma they proudly endorse as true and inviolate. With closed-minded certainty and unyielding arrogance, they waste their imaginative potential and injure their integrity.

§§

Little did I know that in 1975, a serendipitous reading of Milton Rokeach's *Open and Closed Mind*[2] would become the inspiration for two graduate theses and subsequent research that revealed how dogmatism elbows its way into personal relationships and public institutions. After many years of observing its consequences, which I wove into the content of university courses on personality theory, and with no forthcoming theory on its nature, I decided to originate a theory of plausible causation. As readers explore the nature of dogmatism presented here, they are asked to stretch their thinking as far as humanly possible about the manner in which their own core beliefs are developed, held, and conveyed.

It is much easier to demolish someone else's ideas than to suspend judgment and carefully examine our own. Such analysis requires moving beyond *what* we believe to *why* and *how* we hold beliefs of central importance. Many people do not analyze their beliefs much beyond the *what* stage. Certainly not dogmatists. They have little difficulty explaining the content of their beliefs, and their arrogant pronouncements clearly reveal *how* they believe. Less visible are the psychological reasons why they close their minds to anything that contradicts what they know to be true—absolutely true. In describing fanaticism (a variant of dogmatism), Winston Churchill said, "A fanatic is someone who can't change his mind and won't change the topic."

Psychologists can only infer from observable emotions and behaviors the invisible forces that drive people to close their minds to reason and act in self-defeating ways. The theory of dogmatism proposed here is such an inferential model—a systematized compilation of ideas about plausible causes that account for dogmatism's unique characteristics. For some, it may seem odd to propose a theory that has not been empirically validated, but that is the core of psychology. In a similar vein, "to believe something while knowing it cannot be proved (yet) is the essence of physics."[3] Theory is thus a convenient model that can turn useful fictions into testable predictions.

All of us have encountered dogmatists and dogmatism. We recognize that personal and worldly decisions are made by dogmatists whose default systems include instant, premature judgment and dismissal of opposing or novel ideas. Tenaciously, they cling to their steadfast beliefs when common sense and countervailing evidence suggests they should reexamine their faulty assumptions. With little reflection or humility, they are driven to defend themselves against facts, comments, or questions that they interpret as direct threats to their intellectual integrity and personal dignity. As a result, we cannot get through to them.

Yet, as with all problems, closing our eyes and hoping for the best is surely naive. It is therefore urgent that we study the organization of thoughts, emotions, and behaviors that shape doctrinaire belief systems. We need to know what we're up against *before* zealous movements gain emotional momentum and convert fear to dangerous, self-righteous anger, and *before* the free spirit of democracy is derailed by closed-minded decisions. It behooves our familial, educational, and political systems to counter these dangers with reason, vigilance, and the liberty of open-minded dialogue, all of which strike fear in the hearts of dogmatists, whose social, political, moral, and spiritual values are frozen in time.

§§

Personal views have played no small part in motivating this book. I am perturbed by closed-minded leaders who unilaterally declare unjust or preemptive war or inflict crimes against humanity with impunity. I am bothered too by the discrimination and poverty that disadvantage more than half the human race, particularly women and children. The failure to eliminate systemic racism and gender discrimination is also troublesome, as is environmental degradation and the flagrant examples of corporate dogmatism that infiltrate and unduly influence government decisions. What are we to do about political, economic, and cultural dogmatism that sabotages safety and dignity in the pursuit of imperialistic power, corporate profits, and social entitlement?

Religious fundamentalists who violently attack pro-choice movements or try to enforce their beliefs through government legislation and educational policies also rankle me, as do strident dogmatic atheists who arbitrarily dismiss all believers as naive. They, too, display a level of intolerance that tests my own. Narrow-minded leaders of political, religious, and social movements; dogmatic messianic saviors; and intolerant citizens who threaten civil liberties—these are the people who motivate the rest of us to defend democratic rights and freedoms through writing campaigns or public demonstrations that expose those who clearly threaten the democratic values enshrined in the Declaration of Human Rights. As the novelist Arundhati Roy notes, "The trouble is that once you see it, you can't unsee it, and once you've seen it, keeping quiet and saying nothing becomes as political an act as speaking out. There's no innocence. Either way you are accountable."[4]

But this book is not a platform for my views about social, moral, political, or religious matters. I am unabashedly using this preface to let off a little steam about issues I find disquieting—biases that I think are worth declaring up front should readers want to know where the author stands on issues that are today's playground for dogmatism.

More important than any litany of beliefs, beefs, and biases is an understanding of the deep psychological underpinnings and functional nature behind dogmatism's destructive impact. The issue here is closed minds versus open minds; dogmatism versus reason. It is not about the superiority of one political or religious system over another or the effectiveness of one leader versus another. Neither is it about change versus stasis, for people can dogmatically defend either position.

During formalized debates or panel discussions that present polarized views about contentious issues, people seldom comment on the emotional states that accompany strong beliefs and values. Yet because emotions are an important psychological component of core beliefs, they are as meaningful as the actual beliefs and we are therefore required to study the affective components of belief systems.

§§

The theory of dogmatism presented in this book delves into some rich contributions in the specialized field of personality development. It is not pop psychology, nor is it a how-to or self-help book. While its tone is professional, the content is easily accessible to readers who do not have a background in academic psychology. Curiosity alone will do. To pique that curiosity, chapter 15 offers practical suggestions for dealing with dogmatists in everyday life. The overall objective of *What's So Wrong with Being Absolutely Right* is to create a much-needed dialogue about the elephant under the table, a familiar cliché that, in this case, is better described as the barking dog *at* the table. How many of us know how to effectively confront dogmatic intrusions, injunctions, or dismissals? Isn't it easier to just ignore such rants and hope for the best? Easier, perhaps, but not better, for as former vice president Al Gore writes, "We need to start paying more attention to new discoveries about the way fear affects the thinking process. . . . The implications for progressive democracy are profound."[5]

To advance a theory on how the thirteen disreputable features of dogmatism evolve and what we might do about them, this book will revisit and expand Rokeach's original theory and characteristics of dogmatism and present plausible, causal roots of dogmatism that draw from traditional and modern personality theories and research. The task ahead is fascinating and complex. There are many predisposing and interacting agents that influence dogmatism's course, and attempts to pin down its exact nature and causes are tantamount to pinning down wet watermelon seeds.

Yet failure to investigate the psychological properties of dogmatism leaves us vulnerable to manipulation by dogmatists who knowingly intensify our fears in such a way that we close our minds to reasonable alternatives. In stressful times, people are especially vulnerable to charismatic dogmatists who galvanize the fearful and insidiously infect them with a narrow-minded dogma until, eventually, a critical mass becomes powerful enough to lead governments and civilians in dangerous directions.

A sophisticated knowledge of dogmatism would alert us to its presence so that we can significantly reduce or eliminate its impact on future terrorists, genocide, political extremism, gender discrimination, religious cults, and gang warfare. This ambitious goal requires us to investigate and integrate time-honored psychological theories that are relevant to dogmatism and consolidate their assumptions into a reasonable, compelling theory of causation. First come hypotheses that generate theory, followed by research that presents sufficient data to lend support to the theory. Those theories that tender the prospect of scientific validation are more robust, which is why scientists and readers in general are not interested in theoretical equivocation that leads to meaningless research. Thus, the ideas in this book are explicitly presented with the hope that future research will either validate, modify, or reject them. From there, plausible solutions to the problem of dogmatism may emerge.

Because the characteristics and causes of dogmatism are theoretical, not scientific, the model presented here lacks empirical support. Yet no theory presents incontrovertible evidence, nor is any theory totally free of inconsistencies. All have a few ragged edges, as Steven Pinker notes. Nonetheless, "intuitive psychology is still the most useful and complete science of behavior there is."[6]

To start that intuitive adventure and prepare readers for what lies ahead, chapters 1 and 2 lay the groundwork for a theory of dogmatism by defining the concept within a historical setting and differentiating it from related terms. Rokeach's original assumptions launched the first two of four influential factors outlined in chapter 3. Chapter 4 prepares us for the difficulties psychologists face when they try to explain the multilayered complexities of personality traits such as dogmatism. Chapter 5, the first of three chapters that present the characteristics of dogmatism, delineates distinct thought patterns common to dogmatists. Chapter 6 complements the cognitive errors with three emotional characteristics, and chapter 7 presents the five behavioral characteristics that put the finishing touch on a prototypical dogmatist. Together, these three descriptive chapters organize an otherwise random mixture of unique characteristics into a composite profile of dogmatism—one that scars the face of reason.

Chapter 8 introduces us to Jonah, whose psychological predispositions interacted with a host of environmental events to portray a dynamic system that ultimately degraded his potential for open-minded reason. Throughout the book, major psychological ideas and concepts will be applied to this case study in order to bring to life the unfolding dynamics of dogmatism. Yet, clearly, we do not know all that we might about the developmental pathways to dogmatism, for the antecedents are complex, interdependent systems that are incapable of simplification.

In chapters 9, 10, and 11, we explore three modern perspectives in personality theory that shed light on intransigent personality traits such as dogmatism: evolutionary adaptation, biological vulnerability, and universal traits. Chapter 12 examines early childhood events that, in tandem with baby's budding first tooth, sow the seeds for latent dogmatism. Traditional and contemporary theories of personality development expand our understanding of influential factors that shape this personality trait (chapters 12–15), as does the ancient philosophy of Buddhism (chapter 16). The book ends with several suggestions to prevent dogmatism, or at least keep it on a shorter leash.

This enterprise will untie some tricky Gordian knots, and, in the process, it dare not portray the irony of being dogmatic about dogmatism. Author biases will inevitably appear, but I hope to keep my own mind as open as humanly possible while probing the psychological depths of rigid, closed-minded thinking. The subject matter is provocative and its terrain relatively unexplored, yet ongoing dialogue and research that is rich in imagination will further demystify dogmatism's nature, expose its problems, and implement effective, preventive strategies.

The challenge is to open our minds about dogmatic thought—particularly our own. Humility and humanity are largely at stake, for, as Voltaire said, "Doubt is not a pleasant condition, but certainty is absurd."[7] Doubt requires humbleness, and if more of us were comfortable with less certainty, we would be better equipped to confront the ideological extremism of totalitarian regimes, zealous religious fundamentalism, terrorism, and fanaticism in general.

New insights will help us clear much of the psychological debris that clutters the road to peace and democratic progress. While I dislike prophecies of doom, I fervently believe that without a clear understanding of the nature of dogmatism we are vulnerable to those who would exploit our complacency and manipulate fear such that we constrict our thinking and become oblivious of dogmatic agendas—the dangerous undercurrents that drift us closer to the ravenous maw of Charybdis.

This book invites us to encounter the darker sides of ourselves, and thus disturb predispositions toward a fortress mentality to which we are all vulnerable. The journey is intricate but rewarding, for personal inclinations become institutional manifestations, while an understanding of the psychological, from which the social is derived, offers the promise of greater open-minded clarity about our thoughts, feelings, and deeds, both individually and collectively.

NOTES

1. An exhaustive search of the Internet failed to reveal the author of this excellent metaphor.

2. M. Rokeach, *The Open and Closed Mind* (New York: Basic Books, 1960).

3. I. McEwan, introduction to *What We Believe but Cannot Prove: Today's Leading Thinkers on Science in the Age of Certainty*, ed. John Brockman (New York: HarperCollins, 2006), p. xvi.

4. A. Roy, "The Ladies Have Feelings, So . . . Shall We Leave It to the Experts?" in *Writing the World: On Globalization*, ed. D. Rothenberg and W. J. Pryor (Cambridge, MA: MIT Press, 2005), pp. 7–22.

5. A. Gore, *The Assault on Reason* (New York: Penguin Press, 2007), p. 26.

6. S. Pinker, *How the Mind Works* (New York: Norton, 1997), p. 63.

7. Voltaire, http://www.brainyquote.com (accessed September 5, 2000).

Chapter 1

THE "ABSOLUTE TRUTH" ABOUT DOGMATISM

Historical Background

Changing your mind is the only sure proof that you've got one.[1]

Like pesky wasps buzzing circles around us, people who act as if they are the sole experts on a subject put us on edge. In halls of learning (where we least expect to find it), in governments, in religious temples, in businesses, or in marriages and families, dogmatism is the arrogant voice of certainty that closes one's mind, damages relationships, and threatens peaceful coexistence on this planet.

Why is it that some people obstinately refuse to open their minds to new ideas, even when persuasive, contradictory evidence should give them reason to pause? They simply refuse to see things any other way. Not only do they cling to beliefs with rigid certainty, their lack of interpersonal skills makes them oblivious to the effect their proclamations have on others. From ordinary people to priests, presidents, and professors, dogmatists feel protected by *what* they believe and fail to see that *how* they believe limits their opportunities for success and erodes their credibility. Like the bed in their guestroom, their minds are always made up, but seldom used.[2]

But these are only some of the problems created by the need to be absolutely right. Around the dinner table, dogmatism is there to constrain thought. At social gatherings, dogmatism interrupts free-spirited conversation. During office meetings and government sittings, dogmatism derails progress. The dictatorial bark of dogmatism has interrupted peace and progress ever since humans began articulating beliefs about the world and their place in it. In its mildest form, dogmatism is the voice that asserts: "I am right; you are wrong." Moderate dogmatism presents a stronger variation: "I am right; you are stupid." In Wole Soyinka's words, extreme dogmatism (or zealotry) is vicious and violent: "I am right; you are dead."[3] Understood from a psychological perspective, individual dogmatism is the practice that assures one: "I am right; therefore safe."

Since ancient times, great thinkers have espoused the philosophical importance of being open-minded and cautioned against the perils of doctrinaire thinking. But little was written about dogmatism as a distinct personality disposition until the end of the Weimar Republic in Germany, when Erich Fromm and Wilhelm Reich sought to understand why Germans were drawn to Hitler. Their model of the authoritarian character structure was the academic Cape Canaveral for a group of social scientists in California.[4] These scholars, along with Milton Rokeach and others, wanted to determine what, in the psychology of being human, allowed reasonably civilized, well-educated people to perpetrate the horrors against humanity that plagued the first half of the last century. How could the very societies that sought to ensure the benefits of democratic freedom unleash such atrocities?

Still reeling from the aftermath of two world wars, the Nazi Holocaust, and the bombings of Hiroshima and Nagasaki, Theodor Adorno and colleagues (the Berkeley Group, as it came to be known), developed a questionnaire to measure authoritarian personalities and the belief systems that underlie anti-Semitic prejudice, antidemocratic attitudes, and fascist tendencies. Their Fascism Scale (F Scale) was published in their 1950 book, *The Authoritarian Personality*.[5] However, the F Scale failed to consider authoritarianism among the political right, although extreme socialists, communists, and liberals can also be authoritarian. Consequently, research on the F Scale failed to substantiate any underlying theory, and within a couple of decades, many social psychology textbooks paid little attention to authoritarianism as a personality trait.[6]

Despite empirical shortcomings, the Berkeley Group's efforts generated ideas about a highly related but broader personality trait—that of dogmatism. It is worth noting here that psychologists use the term *personality trait* to refer to aspects of personality that motivate us to think, feel, and act in fairly consistent ways across time and different situations. In that sense, traits allow us to make reasonable predictions about people's behavior, because we observe the same person express his or her unique traits (in this case, dogmatism) in many different situations. Traits are therefore more widespread and enduring than specific habits or behavioral tendencies.[7] We will have more to say about personality traits in chapter 11.

§§

In an attempt to correct the problems inherent in the F Scale, Milton Rokeach outlined the theory and assessment of dogmatism in his book, *The Open and Closed Mind* (1960).[8] In that book he presented revised forms and research findings that applied his Dogmatism Scale (known simply as the D Scale) to various groups and settings. This questionnaire was assumed to accurately measure dogmatism *independent of ideological content*.[9] In other words, believing that authoritarianism and fascism are nested within the broader construct of dogmatism, Rokeach shifted the emphasis from fascist authoritarianism on the political right to dogmatism in general. This redirected focus inspired another flurry of research that lasted approximately twenty-five years. However, as with authoritarianism, interest in dogmatism significantly dwindled. Why?

With the fall of the Berlin Wall and the end of the Cold War, scholars did less research on authoritarianism and dogmatism, perhaps because they optimistically concluded that the triumph of liberal democracy was well within reach. One exception to this was Altemeyer's extensive research into right-wing authoritarianism and, to a lesser extent, dogmatism.[10] Like Rokeach, Altemeyer was dismayed by the twentieth century's legacy of human carnage. People lamented the gross violations of human rights and dignity perpetrated by regimes in Rwanda, Kenya, Sri Lanka, Chechnya, Afghanistan, Bosnia, El Salvador, Guatemala, and Israel. Then came September 11, 2001, a sobering testament that the "rise of exclusionary ideologies . . . the quest for ethnic, linguistic or religious purity, pursued by growing numbers, lies behind much of today's bloodshed. By closing the community to diversity and stripping outsiders of essential rights, these dangerous visions of enforced conformity nourish a climate of often brutal intolerance."[11]

Dogmatism is behind such brutality, and the 9/11 events made us acutely aware of our vulnerability to its force. Dogmatism—not religious fundamentalism, terrorism, or fanaticism in general—is the greatest threat to social, political, and scientific progress.

§§

At a time when major historical, political, and religious developments threaten global peace, a second generation of theory and research on dogmatism is urgently needed to revive the largely abandoned efforts of the 1950s and 1960s. Recent books have been published that describe various aspects of ideological extremism, but there is still no comprehensive theory of the psychological roots of dogmatism and its corresponding features. The time has come for a second generation to reignite dialogue and research on closed-minded, doctrinaire thinking so that we might understand the psychological origins of the problem. Without that, solutions will be short term, at best.

Rokeach is credited with the first attempt to piece together the complex psychology of dogmatism, but his approach was largely limited to the description and measurement of the trait. He did not elaborate on the causal influences that shape doctrinaire thinking. More recently, scholars have made important contributions to our understanding of terrorism (a unique expression of dogmatism), but no comprehensive theory weaves underlying causes—such as biological predispositions, evolutionary predispositions, early childhood development, parenting, social learning, and cultural institutions—into a tapestry of causation.[12]

Though rarely acknowledged as such, the power of dogmatism incites all forms of ideological extremism, including terrorism, cults, certain types of gang warfare, and extreme fundamentalism, whether political or religious. Fundamentalists are those who are "ready to do battle royal for the Fundamentals . . . [yet] in no tradition does one find a complete consensus, even among conservatives, about what the 'fundamentals' of the faith really are."[13] For our purposes, such agreement is secondary. Our primary concern is understanding how people hold and practice the fundamentals of their belief systems so that we can counter the rigid, doctrinaire thinking that does battle in the name of ideology.

To that end, this book provides a model that views dogmatism as an ineffective coping style that compromises one's cognitive, emotional, and social intelligence. While most dogmatic people do not have the power to influence many lives, which makes their dogmatism less visible and tragic, dogmatic authoritarian leaders surely threaten the social order. But first, let us focus our attention on an individual profile of dogmatism. Meet Winnie, who epitomizes the trait's unpleasant nature.

WINNIE

Imagine yourself in a beautiful yard where the warm fragrant air of summer welcomes guests for an evening barbecue. As people mingle, their chatter is light, friendly, and punctuated with laughter. Suddenly, Winnie, an accountant for a local manufacturing firm, pierces the air with her beliefs about a local, protracted strike. With each arrogant proclamation, her fist hammers the table as if to pound truth into people's heads: "Meat packers are typical union guys. They're like little children who run for their Mommy every time something goes wrong. Anyone with half a brain knows you can negotiate with them 'til you're blue in the face, but the only thing they really understand are clear ultimatums. It's time management ordered them back to work, and if they refuse to go, lock them out! Everybody's losing patience—and money! They're lucky union busters didn't put them out on the street long ago."

Mel, a thoughtful man, notices that a couple of people at the table look incredulous. Others let their attention drift. Quietly sipping his beer, Mel contemplates Winnie's haughty assumptions and concludes that engaging her in a give-and-take conversation would be as difficult as deciphering hieroglyphics. He makes three observations about Winnie's personality. First, she is emotionally attached to her viewpoint. Second, she needs to be right about matters over which reasonable folks disagree. And third, she announces her views with brash, absolute certainty.

To everyone's relief, Ted finally gets a word in: "Winnie, it seems to me you're pretty dogmatic about a very complicated issue. In my experience, people who give ultimatums usually get the results they least want. Sure, management could order them back to work, but I don't think that would solve the main problem because . . ." Reflective pauses not being one of her strengths, Winnie interrupts and resumes her monologue: "Oh c'mon Ted. You're like all those bleeding-heart liberals who hate management. . . ." Winnie's dismissal of Ted conveys her belief that people who disagree with her mantle of "truth" are not worth listening to; they are, she feels, probably stupid, ignorant, or in need of therapy. A few moments later, Ted and Mel saunter over to the beer cooler. Mel ponders Ted's exchange with Winnie. "Dogmatic . . . hmm. Good word, Ted. I'd have called her pigheaded—hog-tied to her ideas."

Why does Winnie tenaciously cling to her beliefs like a dog to a bone—a chiseled, meatless bone? She holds court, she obstinately closes her mind to alternative views, she is condescending toward those who disagree with her, and she is seemingly unaware of or unconcerned about how her communication style affects others. What confluence of past experiences shaped her narrow-minded thinking and arrogant attitude? Have you ever met anyone like Winnie?

Those of us who have dealt with the Winnies of this world soon realize that efforts to expand their views or derail their pet topics are generally futile. To question the reasoning behind their beliefs only turns up the volume of their defensiveness. Since Dogmatism 101 is not part of our formal education, our tendency is to simply avoid them if possible—an option less available to people who regularly contend with dogmatic co-workers or relatives.

Worse yet, when people like Winnie get promoted to positions of authority, they stomp around in our institutions of education, religion, politics, justice, the media, and international affairs, leaving Bigfoot imprints of dogmatism. In extreme cases, their thinking so narrows ethical reason and rational thought that they end up taking naive followers on unplanned trips to perilous destinations. These are the dogmatic authoritarian aggressors—the real brutes of dogmatism who have inflicted untold misery on countless innocent people for too many centuries across too many continents.

As the American abolitionist Wendell Phillips advised in 1852, "Eternal vigilance is the price of liberty." The vigilance I have in mind puts dogmatism under the microscope of intense psychological scrutiny. In so doing, we will better understand its causes and effects, and we might then lessen its pernicious influence on social, political, educational, and economic decisions. But before we consider dogmatism from a psychological perspective, we will examine the historical roots that helped generate the model developed here.

DOGMATISM: ANCIENT AND MODERN MEANINGS

Throughout history, believers of various ideologies have clamored to dominate religious and political movements. In this regard, dogmatic beliefs that justify power and dominion over others know no boundaries. Psychologically, belief systems consist of perceptions, cognitions, and emotions that the brain considers to be accurate if not true. While perceptions are interpretations we make about the world based on our sensory systems, cognitions refer to abstract mental processes that continually organize and process these perceptions in unique, meaningful ways. Thus, the terms *cognitive* and *cognition* refer to our brain's abstract organization and interpretation of sensory experiences—what we see, hear, touch, taste, and smell.

Dogmatism presumably emerged with the development of language, through which people began crafting myths and folklore about their experiences, abilities, identities, social roles, and various cultural values. When strong emotions became attached to tales and myths, belief systems ensued, some of which were consolidated in dogma that later became institutionalized. Such dogma was stamped with official authority that had the potential for the rigid trappings of dogmatism. But the first definition of dogma is relatively neutral. *The Oxford English Dictionary* defines dogma as:

> 1. that which is held as an opinion; a belief, principle tenet; *esp.* a tenet or doctrine laid down by a particular church, sect, or school of thought; *sometimes*, [my emphasis], depreciatingly, an imperious or arrogant declaration of opinion. 2. The body of opinion formulated or authoritatively stated; systematized belief; tenets or principles collectively; doctrinal system.

Thus, dogma need not always enact the practice of dogmatism; it may merely reflect the content of institutionalized belief systems that may or may not be practiced dogmatically. According to *Webster's* to be dogmatic is to be "positive; magisterial; asserting or disposed to assert with authority or with overbearing and arrogance; applied to persons; as a dogmatic schoolman or philosopher." Tenets differ in that they do not carry such stamps of authority. *Webster's* again notes: "A *tenet* rests on its own intrinsic merits or demerits; a *dogma* rests on authority regarded as competent to decide and determine."

§§

Conflicts about various belief systems that were formerly settled among families, small bands, tribes, and larger groups (known as chiefdoms) later became settled by the resolute decisions of appointed rulers who had a monopoly on information, which allowed them to exercise arbitrary power. Such muscular control meant they could apply force to indoctrinate people with "official religious and patriotic fervor [and] make their troops willing to fight suicidally."[14] Ruling elites converted supernatural beliefs into religious dogma that institutionalized and justified the chief's authority. Moreover, shared ideology expanded the bonds of kinship that held groups together and motivated people to cooperate, thus enabling large groups of strangers to live together in peace.[15] To further consolidate and legitimize their power, rulers built temples and monuments as visible reminders of their supremacy. Throughout the Middle Ages, the Renaissance, and the Industrial Revolution, European empires used state religions to give kings, queens, and monarchs divine status that legitimized war and the colonization of the Western world.[16]

As recently as three centuries ago there was no question but to automatically accept dogma as pure, even divine, doctrine. Humans have always sought meaningful explanations for existence and effective guidelines for living, and, linguistically, *religion* refers to anything to which one is strongly devoted. Through stories and religious rituals, beliefs and behaviors become transformed. Long before the scientific method became the best practice for developing a body of reliable knowledge, scriptures were routinely endorsed as indisputable truths, and they were adopted and held with absolute conviction, but without much reflection on their accuracy or feasibility. Beliefs were assumed to be divinely inspired, and it is therefore understandable that the terms *dogma* and *dogmatism* were first associated with religion. Given the brutal history of torture and killings that religious dogma inspired, it is also understandable how the term *dogma* acquired a pejorative meaning. Yet religious dogma may be simply perceived as devout teachings based on divine revelation—teachings that promote communal associations that are sustained through ritual.

Agents of ideological dogma proselytize its content in churches, schools, governments, and the media, thereby both shaping and maintaining prevailing belief systems. But the dogma of these social institutions takes on a life of its own, and over time the intentions of its originator become distorted. Just as dogmatic individuals cling to belief systems to maintain a sense of identity, institutions that are threatened with extinction cling to ideology that preserves their raison d'être and managerial privileges. Seen from the psychological perspective of dogmatism, political and religious ideologies are not the key problem in social unrest; their corresponding dogmas simply consist of articulated or written words. The purpose of any dogma "lies in its ability to point beyond itself to a deeper reality which cannot be readily articulated in a simple formula or expression."[17] But when dogma is elevated to absolute truth, it is often accompanied by deeply embedded emotions that compel people to unquestioningly adopt it as a demonstration of loyalty or piety—an act that assuages fear and offers psychological protection. Emotions, not reason, propel allegiance and obedience, and the dogma of yesterday kindles the dogmatism of today, which can be anything but benign.

History records how the ruthless practice of communist dogma made a mockery of its founding ideological principles. We have only to consider Stalin's and Mao's gross distortions of Karl Marx's theory that led to the institutionalized murder of thousands of dissenters and the deaths of numerous others who could not survive the unbearably harsh conditions of labor camps. Throughout the Middle Ages, gross misinterpretations of Jesus Christ's teachings were applied during the Crusades, the Inquisition, and the Catholic Church's witch hunts. These hypocritical misrepresentations of dogma and fantasies chewed up bits of undigested ideology and spit it out as dogmatism. These examples of rigid, individual dogmatism are beleaguered by pervasive, enduring psychological problems that lurk deep beneath the dogma of one's stated beliefs. As we shall see in later chapters, within these murky domains, negative emotions of anxiety and anger contaminate and obscure reason, which ultimately compromises personal and intellectual freedom.

Religious beliefs held sway during the Middle Ages, when uncritical acceptance of dogma was the norm—especially given people's lack of education, their socialization to honor authority figures, and their fear of questioning religious authorities. This culture of religion stifled efforts toward rational inquiry up until the seventeenth and eighteenth centuries, when scientists and philosophers inspired a new Age of Reason. Eminent philosophers and scientists such as Rousseau, Kant, Voltaire, Diderot, Galileo, Newton, Wollstonecraft, Franklin, and Jefferson advocated superstition be replaced by the voice of authoritative reason. They stressed the importance of subordinating religious belief to the power of reason, empirical observation, and critical thinking, and in their struggle to facilitate open-minded inquiry, they began to formulate a scientific approach to knowledge that would gradually replace the Church's dominion over political and religious orthodoxy.

Yet today, as they did centuries ago, dogmatic people continue to assert their beliefs as if they were scientific axioms that do not require proof. It is axiomatic that the earth rotates on its axis and that squares have four equal, perpendicular sides, but is it axiomatic that Jesus rose from the dead or was conceived by the Virgin Mary? When such beliefs are presumed to be self-evident rather than based on evidence, they exonerate the believer from any burden of proof. People who are more flexible in their thinking often reject such faulty reasoning and dislike the proselytizing manner of fervent believers. Many are offended by claims of "truth"—of a "gospel truth" that obliges believers to judge and convert the ignorant. At a funeral service I attended, an evangelical minister proclaimed that people who do not accept Jesus Christ as their savior are "dirty rags." If that is the case, the human species has a mighty big load of soiled laundry needing to be cleansed. Similarly, dogmatists in other religions sanctimoniously condemn the unconverted with a closed-mindedness that commandeers reason. Yet to condemn, control, or rule others from one's own self-doubt and emotional apprehension risks violating people's inalienable rights.

DOGMATISM, COMMON SYNONYMS, AND RELATED TERMS

Psychologists generally agree that *dogma, ideology, opinions, attitudes, values,* and *belief systems* have distinct meanings but three overlapping properties. First, these terms connote individual beliefs about what is true or false, good or bad, desirable or undesirable, right or wrong. Second, all are accompanied by emotions that vary in intensity and duration from mild, transient emotions to passionate, sustained arousal. Such emotions create physiological responses that a person may or may not be aware of. Third, because our attitudes and values consist of several related beliefs that motivate behavior, entire belief systems are more potent than single beliefs.[18]

However, whether a particular belief stands alone or in relation to other beliefs, "beliefs are *principles of action*: whatever they may be at the level of the brain, they are processes by which our understanding (and *mis*understanding) of this world is represented and made available to guide our behavior."[19] And "as long as a person maintains that his beliefs represent an actual state of the world (visible or invisible; spiritual or mundane), he must believe that his beliefs are a *consequence* of the way the world is. This, by definition, leaves him vulnerable to new evidence."[20] Whether one's beliefs are based on facts that attempt to reveal truths or are value judgments that imply behavioral proscriptions, beliefs about either domain reflect attempts to understand ourselves and the surrounding world in a way that enhances the quality of life. Finally, behaviors reveal underlying beliefs much more than verbal pronouncements alone, for, as the adage notes, "Love is as love does." On a broader scale, democracy is as democracy does, and dogmatism is as dogmatism does.

While attitudes and values are typically prominent and enduring, single beliefs and opinions are less persistent and more narrowly circumscribed in their emotional, cognitive, and behavioral parameters. People whose attitudes and values are held dogmatically may be described as opinionated, and although the terms *dogmatic* and *opinionated* imply closed-mindedness, opinions refer more to specific issues that are often of shorter duration and less penetrating. There is nothing inherently destructive about being opinionated, but dogmatism is another matter, especially given its degree of intolerance, its excessive and prolonged emotional baggage, and its harmful behavioral consequences.

Joe's accusation, "The president is lying," reflects an opinion. If he goes on to say "All candidates who run for political office will lie, just to get elected," we now have more than an opinion. We have an indication of Joe's established beliefs about the institution of politics, the nature of politicians, and the political process, and we note that his central political attitudes and values go beyond mere opinion.

While we recognize dogmatism by its visceral reaction in both the dogmatist and nondogmatic listeners, unlike Ted, who described Winnie as "pretty dogmatic about a very complicated issue," few people describe others as dogmatic. More commonly, they refer to closed-minded people as hidebound, redneck, bull-headed, or, as Mel preferred, pigheaded. Others might simply describe people like Winnie as having an inflexible or rigid mind-set—one that will not change the tune or tone.

When Rokeach wrote about dogma and ideological belief systems, he had in mind a "more or less institutionalized set of beliefs"[21] about broader social, cultural, and global issues, as well as highly personalized interpretations of such beliefs systems. In Joe's case, had he gone on to say that "the free market always makes better economic decisions than government" (another single belief), he would have conveyed his associated beliefs about economic policies about, for example, taxation, public health and education, welfare, and the protection of basic human rights.[22] His beliefs about free-market capitalism have personal meaning that directs his thoughts, stirs his emotions, and prompts his behaviors.

Throughout this book the terms *dogma* and *ideology* are used interchangeably, but both are intended to convey closed-minded, rigid convictions about belief systems that have damaging consequences for individuals and groups. Whereas some belief systems reflect cultural attitudes and values that are based on informal, commonsense notions about, for example, marriage and parenting, others are institutionalized policies that are derivative of formal, academic theories. But regardless of how dogma or ideology is derived, ideologues who adopt dogma as inerrant truth bathe reason in excessive emotion. This is not to say that emotions do not or should not accompany reason, for as Nietzsche cautioned, "To eliminate the will altogether, to suspend each and every affect, supposing we were capable of this—what would that mean but to *castrate* the intellect."[23]

§§

Philosophers have long given serious thought to dogma, dogmatists, and dogmatism.[24] More than two thousand years ago, the skeptics first applied the term *dogmatics* to people who believed that absolute truth was attainable through the activity of reason. If one reasoned hard enough and long enough, universal truths would emerge. Such claims did not sit well with two preeminent skeptics—Pyrrho (ca. 360–270 BCE) and Sextus Empiricus (ca. 160–210 CE). These philosophers and their followers believed that reasoning could never distill logical theory into a single truth. Their objective was to examine arguments to determine if equally reasonable counterarguments could be mounted. Any sound opposing argument would show that a declarative statement cannot be considered correct with absolute certainty, and, therefore, any claims of discovering truth are invalid (this is especially so with statements pertaining to abstract concepts, which most psychological constructs are, including dogmatism). By acting on their belief that nothing can ever be proven, only falsified, these and other skeptics dismissed all theories of objective truth as delusions of certainty.[25]

While the skeptics argued that beliefs and ideas are never true, they nonetheless believed that we could become knowledgeable, provided our ideas are supported by solid premises and sound reasoning, and as long as no strong argument provides a better alternative explanation. Even when these conditions are met, we can still go no further than to state that "this is how it seems to me." Once people understand that no one can ever know for certain that any proposition is true, they will cease to strive for absolute truth and, consequently, acquire peace of mind and tranquility (this is the state of ataraxia, as described by ancient philosophers).

In our pursuit of knowledge, we must also guard against the erroneous view of radical skeptics who are lost in a quagmire of doubt, denial, and disbelief.[26] These skeptics refuse to believe any assertion or apparent fact, preferring instead to habitually doubt everything. While the radical or absolute skeptic arbitrarily denies anything without grounds for rejection, the dogmatist arbitrarily asserts truth without grounds for acceptance. The absolute skeptic and the dogmatist are therefore similar in that neither values open-minded inquiry and evidence-based knowledge. We can assume that the absolute skeptic and the dogmatist would occupy extreme ends on a linear scale that measures closed-minded thinking, because both have a rigid approach to ideas and information and both are unable to expand or substantiate views that they arbitrarily reject or cling to with unwarranted certainty.

In contrast, the scientific skeptic has a more broad-minded approach to knowledge. According to Peter Suber, he or she "questions the validity of a particular claim *by calling for evidence to prove or disprove it* [my italics]."[27] Evidence emerges only from a scrupulous, deliberate process of original inquiry, critical thinking, and constructive criticism that validates new knowledge against previous benchmarks of understanding. Suber adds the following ethical and psychological considerations: the task of modern-day skeptics is "to purge our inquiries and beliefs of bias, hasty alliances, and accidental inheritances, to overcome prejudice (literally, pre-judgment, judgment before inquiry), to examine all possibilities with sympathetic interest and critical attention, and to love truth loyally so that we may be spared the embrace of falsehood in the darkness."[28]

A final philosophic distinction that is pertinent to dogmatism requires brief mention. The relativist believes in constructivism, whereby learners derive their understanding from current and past knowledge and experiences.[29] What is true for one individual or society may not be true for another, and we are therefore obliged to tolerate different ethical standards and refrain from interfering with the moral affairs of others. Such relativism has created much controversy, and it is useful here to ponder Simon Blackburn's appeal to remind ourselves of:

> alternative ways of thinking, alternative practices and ways of life, from which we can learn and which we have no reason to condemn. . . . Relativism has often been associated with the expansion of literature and history to include alternatives that went unnoticed in previous times. That is excellent. But sometimes we need reminding that there is time to draw a line and take a stand, and that alternative ways of looking at things can be corrupt, ignorant, superstitious, wishful, out of touch or plain evil. It is a moral issue whether we tolerate and learn, or regret and oppose.[30]

From this we conclude that a life of rational, open-minded cognitive balance is indeed a lifelong challenge.

§§

Individual belief systems are adopted through a complicated process. It is not always clear whether personal statements are components of an overarching, systematized ideology or whether they evolve from personal meaning extracted from organized, institutional ideologies derived from dogma.[31] What is clear—and clearly disconcerting—is the manner in which dogmatists adopt, adhere to, and impose their beliefs on others. Consider the following example.

Sue says, "I'm divorcing Stu because we have nothing in common. He's conservative, I'm liberal. He's Catholic, I'm agnostic. He's authoritarian with our children, I'm more permissive." Is Sue dogmatic? Maybe—then again, maybe not. If she is intolerant of Stu's "stupid beliefs" and insists (without evidence) that her political, religious, and parenting beliefs are inviolate truths that any reasonable person would adopt, then we would consider Sue dogmatic, but *only if she has several other characteristics of dogmatism* (these characteristics are presented in chapters 5, 6, and 7). If Sue concludes that she and Stu simply have too many incompatible beliefs, her decision to divorce Stu would, in itself, not indicate the personality trait of dogmatism, even though the couple have numerous heated disagreements.

At the individual level, gradients of dogmatism all have in common rigid, ideological beliefs, and while political and religious belief systems are assumed to be the most common targets of dogmatism, quite possibly some social science researcher might prove me wrong by discovering that significantly more people are dogmatic about parenting styles and sexual morality. (Why should the Freudians have all the fun?) But regardless of the issues involved, dogmatic minds are closed to new ideas and evidence that refutes their established beliefs. Displays of intolerance and discrimination toward others are justified by uncorroborated or unverifiable dogma that removes the dogmatist from the rational world of history, philosophy, and science. In the extreme, dogmatism plays out the psychological fantasies of fanatics who are devout followers of fundamentalist ideology, such as that seen in suicide missions and terrorist attacks. Among these dogmatists, there is a powerful temptation to join groups that appeal to the weakest link in the chain of their psychological being.

WORKING TOWARD A PSYCHOLOGICAL DEFINITION OF DOGMATISM

A comprehensive psychological definition of dogmatism needs to capture the essence of its entire suite of cognitive, emotional, and behavioral complexity, and it needs to do so with enough precision to render it capable of empirical validation. We will keep in mind that beneath the definition of each characteristic is a network of deep-rooted causes that have serious psychological and psychosocial consequences. What are the patterns of thoughts, emotions, motivations, and behaviors that motivate and sustain dogmatic belief systems? Why do some people transfer their personal autonomy to external agents whose reasoning ability they glorify? What enables some leaders to command followers to surrender their own moral standards and commit atrocities that violate international laws or disregard universal codes of ethics? Why do some people declare that killing is wrong but rationalize its legitimacy when carried out in the name of God, democracy, or freedom? How do individuals develop polarized beliefs that legitimize casting groups of people into "us versus them" dichotomies that justify blame and retaliation against members of an out-group who then become scapegoats for dogmatists' own unacknowledged weaknesses and failed identities?[32] Why do some government leaders declare war and then simplify the complex with categorical rationalizations—win or lose, live or die, honorable or traitorous? Situating the conflict in a political or biblical context of righteous indignation makes their war noble and moral—a simple solution that prevents guilt, strips war of its horror, and turns flesh and blood into mere statistics. It is important to note the catalytic link between emotional vulnerability and dogmatism, especially during uncertain, fearful, or oppressive times, when vulnerable individuals abandon their moral and ethical principles. A compelling theory of dogmatism needs to address these questions as fully and open-mindedly as possible.

Though reference will be made to dogmatism's impact within organizations and institutions, its practice originates within individuals, who ultimately shape all social and cultural institutions. For this reason, the psychological features and proposed causes of individual dogmatism are the heart of this book. But first, a working definition of what dogmatism's basic elements look like is helpful.

The following psychological definition of dogmatism provides the framework for the theory proposed in this book: *Dogmatism is a personality trait that combines cognitive, emotional, and behavioral characteristics to personify prejudicial, closed-minded belief systems that are pronounced with rigid certainty.*[33] As such, it reflects a style of thinking that is derivative of emotions, particularly anxiety, that narrow thought and energize behavior.

This is a psychological definition, but we cannot overlook certain social conditions that interact with psychological predispositions to unleash unconscionable, dogmatic authoritarian aggression (one of five behavioral characteristic of dogmatism that are presented in chapter 7). Although this book focuses on dogmatism as a psychological trait, its development does not independently originate in the psyche; it is clearly influenced by social phenomena. Particularly vulnerable are individuals whose personal risk factors combine with stressful social and cultural environments that suppress independent, rational thought.

§§

Throughout the 1960s and 1970s, social psychologists conducted several experiments to examine situational conformity, obedience, and the influential power of social roles on individual and group behavior. Readers may be familiar with the time-honored studies of Professor Stanley Milgram, who tested ordinary citizens' willingness to obey commands from prestigious authority figures, and Philip Zimbardo, who studied the power of situations to exact role-playing behaviors from prison guards and inmates. Using different methods, these researchers studied people's willingness to inflict pain on individuals who posed no threat (Milgram's studies),[34] and research subjects' abuse of power and status in strong situations where they felt entitled to humiliate others (Zimbardo's prison study).[35] These researchers revealed that, to a shocking degree, people in strong situations will follow the dictates of authority figures and conform to role expectations. If ordinary citizens are vulnerable to aggress against others when confronted with strong situational pressures, we would expect dogmatists to acquiesce with greater intensity and frequency, especially those who endorse extremism "in order to commit acts of violence, and their special logic, which is grounded in their psychology and reflected in their rhetoric, becomes the justification for their violent act."[36]

Yet all of us internalize role expectations that define our place within social situations and institutional structures. Among the numerous possible roles that shape self-identities—parent, teacher, friend, artist, or spouse, for example—each contains social norms of behavior that are defined within social networks, some of which overlap. These social networks elicit evaluations that figure prominently in children's and adolescents' self-esteem and search for identity. Young adults who lack a sense of belonging and dignity may seek acceptance through allegiance to a cause. During this normal socialization process, what eventually differentiates dogmatic adults is their desperate need to achieve identity, respect, self-esteem, and dignity. A group that not only welcomes but honors those whose sense of self is inconsistent or fragmented with privileged status and instant dignity becomes powerfully appealing to brittle identities, especially those who seek revenge against people deemed responsible for their psychological alienation and economic disenfranchisement.

§§

If we are to understand the mass psychology of group behavior, a thorough knowledge of the culture's history is necessary to contextualize group goals. Whether the group is predominantly motivated to gain freedom, pursue a particular religious or political ideology, redress social injustice, or seek revenge, its manner of addressing complex issues requires an assessment of the players' motives within broad historical, cultural, and political contexts—a daunting but obligatory task. Dogmatism inevitably reflects an interaction of inextricably linked individual and institutional forces. And while a detailed examination of dogmatism within specific ideological movements is outside the scope of this book, future comparative investigations of group dogmatism in the context of institutional and psychological pressures would provide additional insight into its nature and causes.[37]

Behaviors that reflect the closed-mindedness of dogmatism were present long before the conservative right clashed with the liberal left. Similarly, religious fundamentalists locked horns with secularists on battlegrounds that significantly predate the current conflict between creationists and evolutionary theorists, who seem unable to reconcile their differences.[38] In addition, the demands of environmentalists collide with corporate game plans, feminists struggle against patriarchal power, and academics defend their turf in the very manner that advanced education warns against—a manner that betrays an open-minded pursuit of knowledge.

Failure to recognize and understand the hidden psychological forces of modern-day dogmatism insidiously magnifies its risk such that, by the end of this century, dogmatism might well leave further legacies of homicidal hubris and genocide.[39] Despite philosophic and scientific advances made before, during, and after the Age of Reason, and despite scholarly contributions that emphasize the importance of open-minded inquiry, daunting social and political problems in the early years of this millennium are exacerbated by emotional excesses that gird dogmatism. The result is short-term quick fixes that, more often than not, work against the long-term interests of humanity. As we examine dogmatism's unpleasant characteristics and harmful consequences to one's self and associates (microdogmatism) and to social and cultural institutions (macrodogmatism), quite likely someone you know or have known will breathe vivid life into the black words on these white pages. If you have not encountered dogmatists in the past, chapters 5, 6, and 7 will acquaint you with a few and reacquaint you with those you might have known but perhaps did not think of as dogmatic.

After surveying the characteristics of dogmatism, we will examine proposed forces that conspire to disrupt optimum personality development and incline people to adopt dogmatism as a strategy for coping with life's difficulties. Once we understand some of the predisposing factors that shape dogmatism, we are less likely to react with anger or frustration to its annoying intrusiveness. Chapter 15 suggests how we might effectively challenge the content and style of closed-minded thought. Failing that (and here I speak of dogmatism between family and friends), we may not be able to change dogmatic thinking, although we can change our attitude toward it. Like those pesky wasps, intransigent dogmatic coworkers or relatives are often quite harmless, even though their bloated bravado may suggest otherwise. On a broader scale, however, and despite the philosopher J. L. Austin's view that "history indeed suggests that it may sometimes be better to let sleeping dogmatists lie,"[40] we had best learn how to preempt the threat of dogmatism, for the real danger occurs when the lone sleeping dogmatist is aroused by a group of politically or religiously motivated dogmatic Rottweilers.

§§

The task undertaken here is to review the work of two theorists who have written extensively on dogmatism and authoritarianism (a sub-trait of dogmatism) and incorporate their ideas with traditional and contemporary personality theories to frame a modernized, compre-hensive, psychological model of dogmatism. An equally important goal is to enhance awareness of our own proclivities for narrow-minded thinking. The question is, how objectively can we—you and I—assess psychological impediments that constrict our willingness to open-mindedly consider alternate views?

If, for example, you are a staunch conservative, can you listen to the reasons why someone supports a liberal candidate? Can you *really* listen and fully hear the arguments without being tempted and dis-tracted by a plan to counter your opponent's views? Alternatively, if your belief system about abortion joins the ranks of the pro-choice camp, can you distance yourself enough from your own convictions to understand the beliefs of a pro-life advocate? How accurately can you summarize countervailing ideas before contradicting them with your own? This does not mean that once you have fully considered opposing views you cannot arrive at a comfortable position and choose not to engage, at length, someone whose views significantly differ from your own. You may simply agree to disagree. But first, do you understand that with which you disagree? Genuine understanding requires active listening and hearing.

It is consoling to know that we are all capable of being somewhat rigid, even closed-minded about some of our ideas some of the time. We are inclined to adopt beliefs that accompany the circumstances of our birth and habitually defend them in the absence of thoughtful examination. Beliefs maintained by a combination of complacency and habit are not necessarily dogmatic, nor do they lead to incontrovertible, implacable belief systems that hallmark dogmatism. Dogmatic believers, however, are proud of their unwavering belief systems, even though they would not want to be thought of as dogmatic or pig-headed. Their desire to keep such uncomplimentary awareness and judgment hidden is not any different from the rest of us who want to conceal our own unacceptable thoughts and emotions.

Indeed, the idea that we might be dogmatic would provide as unsettling a self-image as Freud's view that we are all animals driven by unconscious, repressed drives of sex and aggression. All of this is made more complicated by dogmatists' burial of Freudian drives alongside the casket of open-mindedness, and by their conviction that they are moral, intelligent people whose views should be honored. Yet flexible open-mindedness about value-laden belief systems concerning politics, religion, and sex—the three big adrenaline movers—is an ongoing conscientious struggle. Close encounters of our own closed minds are often too close for comfort.

As Korzybski noted back in 1958, the common tendency is for people to make hasty generalizations that lead to misevaluations and self-deception.[41] We arrive at our beliefs for "non-rational reasons and we justify them after."[42] Those with the personality trait of dogmatism have a habit of doing this and generally lack awareness of the doctrinaire manner in which they hold their beliefs. Such insight would shatter their self-image—an image that needs to be continually propped up and preserved by agreement from others. To see themselves as dogmatic would be too chilling to reconcile. When challenged to open their minds about alternative ideas, their inclination is to quickly judge and dismiss (especially ideas that conflict with their own). In doing so, they preserve the illusion that they are rational and open-minded.

§§

What about dogmatism within the realm of academia? I think we can safely assume that while most professors investigate areas and publish papers that are consistent with their own interests and viewpoints, they do so only after intensive prior investigation of competing theories, which they acknowledge. What is more, their scientific explorations are typically vetted by peer reviews to ensure that their theoretical explanations are grounded in reason and not based on dogmatic interpretations of data that are grounded in emotion and superficial judgment.

However, it is interesting to note that research suggests that once people adopt particular beliefs, they are less open to reexamining the validity of those beliefs from different perspectives.[43] Reviewers of scientific research papers are far less likely to publish articles that do not support their own theoretical biases.[44] They are not intellectually disabled, but they can be emotionally rigid and single-minded about beliefs and ideas, especially their own. Intelligent people who are capable of thinking through complex issues but choose instead to cling to traditional paradigms exhibit what Jay Stuart Snelson calls an "ideological immune system."[45] They are the academics who desperately seek to preserve a body of knowledge by immunizing themselves against foreign, cognitive intruders. After all, new ideas might germinate seeds of controversy that would threaten and destabilize their aura of intellectual integrity. Mathematical geniuses, acclaimed musicians and writers, and other highly intelligent people are not resistant to the errors of dogmatic protectionism.

To illustrate: economic professors who dogmatically defend free trade are less likely to present their students with a balanced view that fully examines the public risk in free trade agreements. Similarly, psychology professors who are ideologically bound to the superiority of cognitive therapy might lambaste all Freudian ideas without acknowledging that personal perceptions prejudice their decisions. Numerous other examples reveal that higher education is not an immunization program against academic dogmatism.

This state of affairs is the opposite of what our intuition tells us it should be, yet "educated, intelligent, and successful adults rarely change their most fundamental presuppositions."[46] As Michael Shermer notes, psychologist David Perkins discovered that the connection between ideological rigidity and intelligence quotients unveiled surprising results: the higher the IQ, the greater the person's inability to consider other viewpoints.[47] Social psychology research indicates that very intelligent people and those with high self-esteem are more resistant to changing their views.[48] However, other studies reveal modest correlations in the other direction: "The ability to overcome the effects of belief bias (or knowledge bias) was significantly related to cognitive ability in a formal reasoning task."[49] The results are therefore mixed, and more studies of belief inflexibility around values and formal reasoning are needed. It is possible that people with both types of cognitive rigidity invest time and energy bolstering their own convictions or trying to recruit and convince others because, as Cohen notes, "new and revolutionary systems of science tend to be resisted rather than welcomed with open arms, because every successful scientist has a vested intellectual, social, and even financial interest in maintaining the status quo. If every revolutionary new idea were welcomed with open arms, utter chaos would be the result."[50] The charismatically skilled who succeed at this mission leave important lessons for the rest of us.

Describing someone as an intelligent dogmatist may sound oxymoronic, but we would be naive to assume that all dogmatists are uneducated or of low intelligence. While dogmatism clearly indicates a defective style of rational thinking, it is not, strictly speaking, the product of intellectual deficiency. Something else is brewing beneath the surface. Dogmatic beliefs are driven by psychological needs and emotions that end up giving the appearance of intellectual limitation. As we shall see, beneath the surface there is a host of biological predispositions that interact with various other individual and environmental conditions to shape closed-minded, inflexible thinking.

WHAT DOGMATISM IS NOT

Dogmatism is not the opposite of critical thinking. Although much has been written about how to promote critical thinking skills such as inductive and deductive reasoning, abstract analysis, synthesis, and evaluation of conceptual models, less attention has been given to the deeper psychological conditions that seriously impair one's ability to think critically. People who are prone to dogmatism can learn all the theory available on critical thinking, but if unmet psychological needs are pushing them in dogmatic directions, their minds will not be sufficiently open to turn theory into practice.

Dogmatism should also not be confused with the open-minded, passionate, social activism that creates popular movements for social change. What distinguishes dogmatic activists from their nondogmatic counterparts is the former's arrogant unwillingness to examine an issue from different perspectives and their unjustified rejection of those with opposing beliefs (even though their personal rejection may not be apparent). Open-minded people speak out; they do not lash out. They inspire reflection because they neither oblige agreement nor disdain disagreement. In sharp contrast to self-righteous dogmatic rants that deny opposing views, open-minded, inclusive, passionate reason stirs action. This idea is captured by the anthropologist Margaret Mead (1901–1978), who said, "Never doubt that a small group of thoughtful, committed people can change the world. Indeed, it is the only thing that ever has." I would like to emphasize the word *thoughtful* because without full, open-minded thought, social activism will not necessarily achieve beneficial goals. Overall, people who shape social change are passionate about their beliefs, and although some undoubtedly have characteristics of dogmatism, my guess is that only a small minority have enough specific characteristics to personify dogmatism as defined in this book.

Zealous dogmatists, however, can move society in extraordinary directions. When individual dogmatism ignites group dogmatism, little remains that is thoughtful or useful in social activism. In a study of university students that was then repeated with their parents, "the more zealous people were about their most important outlook (whatever it was), the higher they also tended to score on the DOG [Dogmatism] Scale. . . . Persons championing religious beliefs had the highest zealot and highest DOG scores in both samples."[51] These are the people who feel the urge to assert their beliefs every chance they get and fail to recognize that passion without reason is puerile, reason without passion is sterile, and reason with passion is fertile.

You might be wondering how dogmatists differ from fanatics. According to research, dogmatists, fanatics, and zealots are soul mates, with some distinctions.[52] Linked by their emotional intensity, all are capable of unleashing spiteful, self-righteous vengeance. While not all of them wield sledgehammers to drive their beliefs into the thick skulls of nonbelievers, dogmatists, fanatics, and zealots are all rigidly and emotionally attached to views they adopt as inviolate truth, and they readily dismiss opposing ideas and the people who hold them. Fanatics and zealots, however, show excessive, frenzied enthusiasm for beliefs that have an absurd or bizarre quality. For example, religious fanatics and zealots fiercely believe in the coming apocalypse and rapture, whereupon Jesus Christ will descend to earth and transport all Christian believers to heavenly salvation and reunion with their Lord. While some dogmatists likely share these beliefs, most do not have the emotional extremes of the fanatic or zealot. Nonetheless, overlapping qualities among dogmatists, fanatics, and zealots often blur the distinctions. In general, fanatics occupy what has commonly been referred to as the "lunatic fringe," while dogmatists appear relatively more rational—both in the beliefs they hold and in their less dramatic manner of presenting them. Characteristics of dogmatism are also differentiated from personality disorders that have secured special recognition in the Diagnostic and Statistical Manual of Mental Disorders. These disorders, which have overlapping behavioral characteristics of dogmatism, include the antisocial personality disorder, which exhibits dogmatic, authoritarian aggression; the histrionic personality disorder, which exhibits a preoccupation with power and status; and the narcissistic personality disorder, with its vilification of the out-group and self-aggrandizement. These are all features or subtraits of dogmatism.[53]

THE TRAIT OF OPEN-MINDEDNESS

Why do some people become dogmatic while others do not? Psychologists are currently unable to answer this question, but we can conclude that the personality trait of open-mindedness is an antidote to dogmatism, and people who are cognitively flexible plainly differ from those who are easily threatened, emotionally defensive, and dismissive of anyone who disagrees with them or even proffers opposing beliefs. Open-minded, cognitive elasticity is seen among those who are awestruck by the miraculous beauty of life; they do not need to confine its complexities to explicit, doctrinaire categories of presumed truth. In their personal lives, they are open to considering and accepting different views and have little if any need to change the beliefs and values of people who differ, unless opposing beliefs directly threaten their own or others' freedom. Those with open cognitive systems can comfortably explore a topic as widely and deeply as the conversation takes them. They confront the issue, not the person, and rarely infer motives for an opponent's stated beliefs or jump to conclusions when someone changes the topic. Condescending frowns, sarcasm, and patronizing voices are rare. In their presence, we are relaxed yet poised to respond to whatever topic emerges, be it serious or silly. Able to laugh at themselves and the absurdities of life, open-minded people generally prefer a philosophic sense of humor that is without hostile, pretentious condemnation.[54]

Such individuals are valued partners, family members, friends, and colleagues. Curious and open-minded, they resemble the Athenians of yore who so valued the pursuit of knowledge that they invented the first alphabet, philosophy, logic, principles of political democracy, poetry, plays, and the idea of schools. Open-minded people today are no exception. They recognize "the fallibility of one's own opinions, the probability of bias in those opinions, and the danger of differentially weighting evidence according to personal preferences."[55] Willing to suspend judgment as far as humanly possible, they explore multiple views and are not subservient to the beliefs that underlie social conventions. Because their beliefs are autonomously determined, these people are not easily convinced that certain ideas are absolutely true, nor are they readily manipulated by propaganda. Similarly, because their acceptance, rejection, or reservations regarding social values are authentic, they are less vulnerable to external reinforcements of flattery or bribery. They can detect inherent biases and premature assumptions, accurately process new or challenging viewpoints about complex or controversial issues, and are capable of admitting errors in their own thinking, whereupon they revise their beliefs accordingly. In the words of William James, "To perceive the world differently, we must be willing to change our belief system, let the past slip away, expand our sense of now, and dissolve the fear in our minds."[56]

Open-minded people understand that a demolition act on opposing beliefs is relatively easy; the more difficult task is to distance themselves from personal convictions, to put their egos aside and let them rest awhile. Flexible of mind, they can tolerate ambiguity and uncertainty. They examine ideas that are based on stereotypical reasoning or incomplete information, and they recognize when personal needs shape, control, or distort information. At their best, they are invulnerable to manipulation. Their reasoning emanates from an open-minded appraisal of reality and they accept that eternal, universal truths are elusive. Truths are reasoned, conditional, and probable, not final and absolute. Many would agree with Seth Lloyd: "Unlike mathematical theorems, scientific results can't be proved. They can only be tested again and again until only a fool would refuse to believe them."[57]

Such a provisional stance is not to be confused with wishy-washy, ideological free fall. Open-minded people deliberate as long as necessary about important ethical and scientific principles that are derived from reason. And reason consistently triumphs over emotion, especially in matters concerning ethics and morality. To become better informed about their belief and disbelief systems, they examine the source of controversial facts and opinions and recognize that to rely only on information that substantiates their own beliefs reinforces their biases and stifles objective inquiry. They demonstrate cognitive permeability by openly modifying their previous views and assumptions as necessary.[58] Able to suspend judgment and reflect on opposing ideas, they enjoy sharpening their ideas on the fine, abrasive steel of dissenting voices, agreeing that "minds are like parachutes; they only function when open."[59] They are humble seekers, trudging along a path that echoes Socrates' dictum: "I know nothing except the fact of my ignorance." Socrates surrendered his life to the supremacy of such open-minded reasoning.

Finally, recognizing that the best use of one's intelligence is to first understand oneself, open-minded people are able to examine their own psyches by peering into their genuine thoughts, feelings, and motives as objectively as humanly possible. This self-scrutiny can then be applied to psychological analyses of group motives to determine, for example, if a government is open-minded enough to willingly admit error and make the necessary readjustments.

§§

What conditions shape such a grand approach to thought (perhaps too grand)? Psychologists agree that an intricate combination of evolutionary, psychological, and social influences shape an individual's reasoning capacity, including genes and biology, which interact with the home, school, cultural, and political environment. Cognitively flexible adults are more likely to have been raised by parents who enabled them to feel securely attached, a psychological by-product of unconditional love, respect, and nurturance that was extended throughout their childhood development.[60] Under these conditions, children are encouraged to think for themselves, are rewarded for doing so, and are exposed to a variety of people with diverse beliefs. Supportive home environments are enriched by well-funded preschool, daycare, and educational programs that facilitate an open-minded understanding of themselves, others, and the world of ideas. Such optimum intellectual and social development is shaped by many aspects of a culture, not the least of which is a collective understanding of early childhood influences that are prerequisite for open-mindedness and respect for cultural differences. "For social change to occur, those revised personal constructs must then be institutionalized."[61] While educational institutions clearly emphasize open-minded approaches to knowledge, they have not asked good questions about the broad psychological forces that underlie both cognitive elasticity and closure. Suggestions for protecting individuals and our social institutions against the forces of dogmatism are outlined in chapter 17.

Because individual dogmatism arbitrarily endorses dogma that shapes social institutions, if we do not learn how to monitor and change dogmatic tendencies within ourselves, our children, and our institutions (especially the political socialization and militarization of youth), dogmatism will persist, past injustices will be reignited, and future conflicts will escalate. Peaceful tomorrows cannot be fashioned by dogmatists who enact closed-minded ideologies today.

With this chapter behind us and those challenges ahead, chapter 2 lays the foundation for a theory of dogmatism that builds on Milton Rokeach's 1960 model, which offered the only causal theory of dogmatism until now.

NOTES

1. This quote has been attributed to Richard P. Feynman and Albert Einstein.

2. An Internet search failed to provide the source for the quote that is modified here.

3. W. Soyinka, *Climate of Fear: The Quest for Dignity in a Dehumanized World* (New York: Random House, 2005), p. 118. Soyinka states that the discourse of zealots is more extreme than the dogmatic monologue of "I am right, you are wrong." Zealots believe "I am right; you are dead." Since zealots are an extreme variant of dogmatists, I have adapted this quote to illustrate the range and forms of dogmatic belief.

4. The Berkeley Group conducted research on the authoritarian personality at the University of California at Berkeley. The group included T. W. Adorno, E. Frenkel-Brunswik, D. J. Levinson, and R. N. Sanford.

5. T. W. Adorno et al., *The Authoritarian Personality* (New York: Harper and Brothers, 1950).

6. The F Scale was criticized for focusing exclusively on the measurement of authoritarianism in the political right. The theory of dogmatism and its corresponding D Scale attempted to measure extreme styles of thought in people on *both* the political left and right.

7. G. W. Allport, "What Is a Trait of Personality?" *Journal of Abnormal and Social Psychology* 25 (1931): 368–72. D. C. Funder and D. J. Ozer, *Pieces of the Personality Puzzle: Readings in Theory and Research*, 3rd ed. (New York: W. W. Norton, 2004), state that Gordon Allport is still recognized as providing "one of the earliest—and still one of the best—psychological definitions of a personality trait" (p. 56).

8. M. Rokeach, *The Open and Closed Mind* (New York: Basic Books, 1960).

9. Ibid.

10. B. Altemeyer, *Enemies of Freedom: Understanding Right-Wing Authoritarianism* (San Francisco: Jossey-Bass, 1988), and R. Altemeyer, *The Authoritarian Specter* (Cambridge, MA: Harvard University Press, 1996). (Robert Altemeyer has also published under the name Bob Altemeyer). Altemeyer's earlier work reports results of his Right-Wing Authoritarian Scale, while *The Authoritarian Specter* presents his Dogmatism Scale (also known as the DOG Scale) and various findings from research on its validity and application.

11. J. Isaac, "A New Guarantee on Earth: Hannah Arendt on Human Dignity and the Politics of Human Rights," *American Political Science Review* 90, no. 1 (1996): 70. In this article, Isaac cites the 1992 Human Rights Watch World Report, presented in *The State of the World's Refugees: The Challenge of Protection* (New York: Penguin Books, 1993).

12. When terrorism is understood within the broad historical context in which it occurs, it will reflect vastly different strands and motives for its tactics. Throughout this book, the word *terrorism* is used as it is defined by the *Canadian Oxford Dictionary*, 2nd ed.: "the systematic employment of violence and intimidation to coerce a government or community, esp. into acceding to specific political demands."

13. M. Ruthven, *A Fury of God: The Islamic Attack on America* (London: Granta Books, 2004). These two quotes are on pages 12 and 14, respectively.

14. J. Diamond, *Guns, Germs, and Steel: The Fates of Human Societies* (New York: Norton, 1999).

15. Ibid.

16. Ibid.

17. S. Batchelor, *Alone with Others: An Existential Approach to Buddhism* (New York: Grove, 1983), p. 41.

18. M. Rokeach, *Beliefs, Attitudes, and Values* (San Francisco: Jossey-Bass, 1968). Rokeach states that the different components of attitude are not consistently defined. More than twenty-five years later, Aronson, Wilson, and Akert, in *Social Psychology: The Heart and the Mind* (New York: Harper-Collins College Publishers, 1994), agreed that while social psychologists still have not reached complete agreement on the definition of an attitude, there appears to be some consensus on these three components.

19. S. Harris, *The End of Faith: Religion, Terror, and the Future of Reason* (New York: Norton, 2005), p. 52.

20. Ibid., p. 63.

21. Rokeach, *Open and Closed Mind*, p. 35.

22. I have provided a more detailed explanation and application of this theory than Rokeach outlined in his inaugural theory of dogmatism, as described in *Open and Closed Mind*.

23. F. Nietzsche, *The Genealogy of Morals*, in S. Blackburn, *The Oxford Dictionary of Philosophy* (Oxford: Oxford University Press, 1996), p. 86.

24. D. C. Baltzly, "Who Are the Mysterious Dogmatists of 'Adversus

Mathematicus' Ix 352? (Sextus Empiricus)," *Ancient Philosophy* 18 (1998): 145–71. Baltzly notes that Sextus Empiricus "discusses the views of some unnamed dogmatists" who, Baltzly suggests, "may have referred to Stoics" (p. 145).

25. Sextus Empiricus was a Greek physician and philosopher who defined three schools of philosophy: the Dogmatic, the Academic, and the Skeptic. His three surviving works are *Outlines of Pyrrhonism* (three books on the practical and ethical skepticism of Pyrrho of Elis, ca. 360–275 BCE), *Against the Dogmatists* (five books dealing with the Logicians, the Physicists, and the Ethicists), and *Against the Professors* (six books: Grammarians, Rhetors, Geometers, Arithmeticians, Astrologers, and Musicians). The last two volumes critique the role of professors in the faculties of arts and science.

26. P. Suber, "Classical Skepticism: Issues and Problems," http://www.earlham.edu/~peters/writing/skept.htm (accessed September 23, 2008). This article reviews the rationale and motives of skeptics, academic skepticism, and dogmatism, and illustrates how the philosophic definition of dogmatism differs from the psychological definition. Philosophers claim that people can be dogmatists even if they are not absolutely certain of their beliefs. From a minimalist philosophic definition, "a dogmatist is one who is willing to assert at least one proposition to be true" (p. 10). This contrasts with the broader psychological definition in this book, which incorporates emotional (primarily anxiety) and behavioral characteristics that are highly influential in the personality trait of dogmatism.

27. M. Shermer, *Why People Believe Weird Things: Pseudoscience, Superstition, and Other Confusions of Our Time* (New York: W. H. Freeman, 1997), p. 17. Michael Shermer is the editor of the *Skeptical Inquirer*, which critically examines pseudoscientific claims.

28. P. Suber, "Classical Skepticism," p. 32.

29. J. Bruner, *Acts of Meaning* (Cambridge, MA: Harvard University Press, 1990).

30. S. Blackburn, *Truth: A Guide* (Oxford: Oxford University Press, 2005), p. 66.

31. J. T. Jost, "The End of the End of Ideology," *American Psychologist* 61, no. 7 (2006): 651–70. Jost presents a good historical review of ideology and its various definitions. He notes that the term *ideology* "originated in the late 18th century when it was used mainly to refer to the science of ideas, a discipline that is now known as the sociology of knowledge" (p. 651).

32. J. M. Post, "Terrorist Psycho-Logic: Terrorist Behavior as a Product of Psychological Forces," in *Origins of Terrorism: Psychologies, Ideologies, Theologies, States of Mind*, ed. Walter Reich (Baltimore: Johns Hopkins University Press, 1998).

33. This definition of dogmatism is derived from the work of Milton Rokeach, Robert Altemeyer, and myself, Judy J. Johnson.

34. S. Milgram, *Obedience to Authority: An Experimental View* (New York: Harper and Row, 1974).

35. P. Zimbardo, "On the Ethics of Intervention in Human Psychological Research: With Special Reference to the Stanford Prison Experiment," *Cognition* 2 (1973): 243–56.

36. Post, "Terrorist Psycho-Logic." A summary of Milgram's and Zimbardo's methods and results is presented in chapter 11 notes.

37. Readers interested in studying how political institutions shape psychological functioning are referred to the interdisciplinary journal *Political Psychology*, which is dedicated to the analysis of interrelationships between psychological and political processes. See also F. M. Moghaddam and A. J. Marsella, eds., *Understanding Terrorism: Psychosocial Roots, Consequences, and Interventions* (Westport, CT: Praeger, 2004), and Reich, *Origins of Terrorism*.

38. P. Berman, *Terror and Liberalism* (New York: Norton, 2003), p. 159. Berman notes that terrorism has been with us for more than eighty years: "The revolt against liberalism that got under way after 1914 has never run out of energy, and the impulse for murder and suicide continues to rocket around the globe, and nothing from the twentieth century has come to an end, nothing at all, except the numerals at the top of the calendar and the script in which the revolutionary manifestos are published—this script . . . spells out the same apocalyptic explanation for why, in this hour of Armageddon, masses of people should be killed" (pp. 159–60).

39. Soyinka, *Climate of Fear*. Wole Soyinka suggests that whereas the major source of conflict in the twentieth century was racism, religious fanaticism will incite the most serious clashes of this century.

40. J. L. Austin, *Philosophical Papers*, ed. James O. Urmson and G. J. Warnock (Oxford: Oxford University Press, 1979), p. 75.

41. A. Korzybski, *Science and Sanity*, 4th ed. (Lakeville, CT: International Non-Aristotelian Publishing, 1958), p. xxxvi.

42. M. Shermer, "The Question of God: C.S. Lewis and Freud," panel discussion, *Nova,* PBS, DVD, 2004.

43. G. Abell, and B. Singer, eds., *Science and the Paranormal* (New York: Scribner's, 1981), quoted in Shermer, *Why People Believe Weird Things*, p. 59.

44. J. J. Mahoney, "Publication Prejudices: An Experimental Study of Confirmatory Bias in the Peer Review System," *Cognitive Therapy and Research* 1 (1977): 161–75.

45. J. S. Snelson, "The Ideological Immune System," *Skeptic* 4 (1993): 44–55, quoted in Shermer, *Why People Believe Weird Things*, p. 59.

46. Shermer, *Why People Believe Weird Things*, p. 60.

47. Ibid.

48. N. Rhodes and W. Wood, "Self-Esteem and Intelligence Affect Influenceability: The Mediating Role of Message Reception," *Psychological Bulletin* 111 (1992): 156–71.

49. R. Macpherson, and K. E. Stanovich, "Cognitive Ability, Thinking Dispositions, and Instructional Set as Predictors of Critical Thinking," *Learning and Individual Differences* 17 (2007): 123.

50. I. B. Cohen, *Revolution in Science* (Cambridge, MA: Harvard University Press, 1985), p. 35.

51. B. E. Hunsberger, and B. Altemeyer, *Atheists: A Groundbreaking Study of America's Nonbelievers* (Amherst, NY: Prometheus Books, 2006), p. 64.

52. B. Altemeyer, *The Authoritarian Specter*, pp. 212–13. Altemeyer presents solid intercorrelations among tests he designed to measure dogmatism, right-wing authoritarianism, religious fundamentalism, and religious zealotry. These correlational statistics increase the validity of Altemeyer's DOG Scale.

53. American Psychiatric Association, *Diagnostic and Statistical Manual of Mental Disorders*, 4th ed. (Washington, DC: American Psychiatric Association, 1994).

54. A. Maslow, *The Farther Reaches of Human Nature* (New York: Viking, 1971). A philosophical, unhostile sense of humor is listed as a feature of Being-cognition—an open-minded style of thought that characterizes self-actualizers.

55. K. E. Stanovich, "Reasoning Independently of Prior Belief and Individual Differences in Actively Open-Minded Thinking," *Journal of Educational Psychology* 89 (1997): 342–58. Stanovich cites researchers who, in the tradition of cognitive science, have "examined the influence of prior beliefs

on argument evaluation and demonstrated how prior belief does bias human reasoning" (p. 342). Myside bias effects (failure to view both sides of an issue) are not associated with cognitive ability (Toplak and Stanovich 2003). Baron (2000) also found that a lack of "actively open-minded thinking" is related to myside bias effects. However, Sá et al. (2005) found that the tendency to use unsophisticated forms of nonevidence was associated with lower cognitive ability and lower "actively open-minded thinking."

56. G. G. Jampolsky, *Love Is Letting Go of Fear* (Berkeley, CA: Celestial Arts, 1979), p. 19.

57. S. Lloyd, "Seth Lloyd," in *What We Believe but Cannot Prove: Today's Leading Thinkers on Science in the Age of Certainty*, ed. John Brockman (New York: HarperCollins, 2006), p. 55.

58. G. Kelly, *The Psychology of Personal Constructs*, vol. 1. (New York: Norton, 1955). Kelly's core constructs are similar to Rokeach's central dimension of beliefs in that they are important elements of one's personal identity, which renders such beliefs resistant to change. These core, central constructs have a range of convenience that determines whether new information or constructs will be included or excluded within one's existing framework (p. 59).

59. Quote attributed to T. R. Dewar, http://www.brainyquote.com (accessed October 5, 2005).

60. D. R. Shaffer, *Social and Personality Development*, 4th ed. (Scarborough, ON: Nelson/Thomson Learning, 2000). Secure attachment is defined as "an infant/caregiver bond in which the child welcomes contact with a close companion [parent or caregiver] and uses this person as a secure base from which to explore the environment" (p. 137).

61. W. M. Fox, "Changing Human Behavior and Institutions toward 21st Century Paradigms: A Theoretical Construct," *ETC.: A Review of General Semantics* 56, no. 2 (1999): 147–55. Personal constructs refer to one's unique way of perceiving and interpreting events. We assume such constructs are accurate perceptions that can predict reality with reasonable accuracy. A personal construct may explain, for example, success as either due to hard work or the result of chance.

Chapter 2

OLD PATHS, NEW SHOES

Rokeach's Model and Modern Adaptations

*When men are the most sure and arrogant, they commonly are
the most mistaken.*

David Hume (1711–1776)

Though commonly understood as narrow- or closed-minded, dogmatism is a personality trait that is dark and intricate. Like all personality traits, it is not a singular psychological attribute. On the surface, the archetypal dogmatist reveals a black-and-white portrait that appears deceptively simple, yet when we combine all of dogmatism's cognitive, emotional, and behavior characteristics, that stark portrait takes on vivid color. Given its multifaceted nature, the best we can do in understanding the mystery of any personality trait is make inferences based on observations that are then subjected to scientific analyses that hopefully yield some explanatory power.

This chapter provides the framework for a groundbreaking theory of dogmatism within which its characteristics unfold. We begin by reviewing Rokeach's theory on dogmatism, which made its inaugural appearance in the middle of the twentieth century. His ideas were the springboard for this revised theory, which outlines plausible origins for calcified, black-and-white belief systems that are impermeable to reason.

MILTON ROKEACH'S THEORY

In the 1950s, when Rokeach was developing his theory of dogmatism, Freudian ideas dominated the field of personality theory. The psychoanalytic model viewed all abnormal behavior as a consequence of conflicting conscious and unconscious drives, particularly sex and aggression. It is often easier to gloss over our unpleasant, unacceptable thoughts and feelings with a fresh, heavy coat of psychological paint that conceals our dark side—from both ourselves and others.[1]

Given the pervasiveness of Freudian theory during the last half of the twentieth century, it was not surprising that Rokeach incorporated Freud's view of repressed anxiety in his causal theory of dogmatism. Since the publication of his book in 1960, newer personality theories have chipped away at the pillar of Freudian orthodoxy, and these contemporary models allow for broader perspectives on causation that go beyond unconscious conflict and anxiety as central forces of personality development.

Rokeach's essential contribution was the idea that dogmatism is not merely a cognitive deficit, and that its study should therefore include the influential role of emotions on closed-minded thinking. His approach was prescient, for not until twenty years later did studies begin to seriously examine the dynamic interaction of thoughts and emotions, particularly the effects of anxiety and depression on perceptions and cognitive processing. Prior to this broader analysis, the general practice was to divide the psychological trilogy of thoughts, feelings, and behaviors into discrete, independent units of analysis. Today, despite the inherent difficulties of integrative research on the interactive flow of emotions and thoughts, psychologists accept that holistic approaches make the most robust contribution to understanding psychological functioning. I am reminded here of Heraclitus's famous line, "You cannot step twice into the same river." To extend that metaphor, we cannot step twice into the same psyche, but that should not curtail intelligent inquiry into the stream of consciousness that silently grooves unique personalities.

A CLOSER LOOK AT THE NATURE OF BELIEF SYSTEMS

Two Systems—The Belief and Disbelief Systems

Rokeach defined belief systems as "all the beliefs, sets, expectancies, or hypotheses, conscious and unconscious, that a person at a given time accepts as true of the world he lives in."[2] They represent psychological systems that organize one's entire framework for understanding the world of people and ideas—beliefs that embody institutionalized values and behavior expectations. These belief systems:

1. encompass any set of organized beliefs set forth in institutionalized dogma, or capable of being organized and institutionalized as such. The list is very long, including systems of religion, politics, science, economics, marriage and the family, or any other constellation of related beliefs that individuals and groups adopt.
2. consist of cognitive systems, emotions, motivations, and behaviors that are interdependent constituents of all belief systems.

Although the extent to which beliefs are resistant to change is debatable, studies indicate that there are meaningful, identifiable differences that can be quantified and measured along ideological dimensions, particularly those involving left-right, conservative-liberal, or atheist-believer ideologies. Major political systems of the twentieth century have polarized these distinctions: communism, fascism, socialism, and capitalism all "differ most fundamentally from one another in the distinctive positions they take with respect to two political values, *equality* and *freedom*."[3] We will have more to say about these value differences in later chapters that examine a spectrum of dogmatism's unique characteristics.

Our belief and disbelief systems consist of subsystems that exist on a continuum stretching from acceptance through rejection.[4] Beliefs we consider to be largely true exist within a range of acceptance; those we consider largely false fall within a range of rejection. "In logical systems, the parts are interrelated or in communication with each other according to the rules of logic,"[5] but psychological systems are not always logically or predictable. A person may say he or she believes in universal human rights but emotionally and behaviorally reject a designated out-group, whereupon we would conclude that, at best, he or she is hypocritical. Thus, the word *system*, as applied to beliefs, denotes an entire suite of psychological properties, and parsing personality traits into their constitutive parts is a very challenging task.

The major difference between dogmatists and their more open-minded counterparts is that dogmatists do not hold their beliefs tentatively. They categorically separate absolute belief acceptance from absolute belief rejection, neither of which is open to analysis and reasoned defense. The wider the gap between what people believe and what they reject (absolute belief in capitalism and unqualified rejection of socialism, for example), the more difficult it is for them to rationally examine and integrate opposing beliefs.

In the extreme, dogmatists even reject related beliefs. When dogmatic religious fundamentalists are away from home, they are not likely to attend services in the only Christian church available if that church is of a different denomination. Dogmatic evangelists would not attend Anglican services, for example. Moreover, should questions arise about an entirely different religion, dogmatic believers would prefer to consult their own parishioners rather than read and discuss dissimilar tenets with authoritative sources of that religion. To consult directly with a Muslim, Hindu, Jew, or Christian about their religious tenets, or to read original scriptures from the Koran, Veda, Talmud, or

Bible, would plunge them into the swamp of their disbelief zone. Because religious dogmatists believe theirs is the only religion that offers true salvation, exploring other tenets would be viewed as a mockery of their own chosen dogma—a deviation deserving of condemnation and punishment. Their deeper, unacknowledged fear is that if they questioned the psychological reasons for their steadfast beliefs, their sense of identity and meaning of life would crumble. This raises questions about the relationship between dogmatism and identity, which is outlined in chapter 3 and briefly noted here: dogmatism can be understood as a tool to mend fragmented identities.

The cognitively rigid have difficulty accepting that reasonable people differ. Zealous dogmatists not only denigrate different faiths, they cannot respectfully coexist with people whose beliefs they reject. They may claim they believe in freedom and democracy, yet their visceral rejection of those with different belief systems is obvious. Ironically, they do not recognize that other religious dogmatists of entirely different persuasions are their emotional and cognitive relatives— close relatives. Even though each group of ideological fundamentalists views the other as their bitter rival, psychologically, the commonalities among these groups far outweigh their differences. In reality, their more powerful opponents are those who hold their beliefs with an open mind—people who are more likely to succeed at countering dogmatic religious ideologues because they can openly listen to each other and plan effective strategies that are not based on fear.

Yet even among open-minded believers, many have not seriously studied the original works of their adopted belief systems. Most simply believe what their circumstances of birth taught them and do not proclaim the superiority of their beliefs over all others. Flexible thinking allows them to accept religion as a phenomenon of human construction that inevitably results in multiple belief systems. They are capable of considering several viewpoints in order to arrive, through their own effort, at an informed position about religious beliefs. Willing to do the serious, hard work of thinking, they understand that listening only to views that bolster family and personal biases will prevent them from engaging in a process of open-minded inquiry. Though they may not articulate it as such, their pursuit and integration of contrasting ideas is psychologically rewarding even when, and perhaps because, these ideas challenge their own. Broad-minded people recognize "the fallibility of one's own opinions, the probability of bias in those opinions, and the danger of differentially weighting evidence according to personal preferences."[6] Thus, the function of an open-minded belief system serves a very different purpose from that of one that is closed, which brings us to the next dimension.

THE FORMAL AND FUNCTIONAL ROLES OF BELIEF SYSTEMS

The Formal Role

All belief and disbelief systems fulfill two roles.[7] The formal role of each system is merely the content, or *what* one believes to be valid or invalid. This formal component is easily established by simply examining what people say they believe. It does not incorporate the emotions, intentions, symbolic meaning, and behaviors that sustain people's beliefs. In this sense, the formal content represents only one, rather superficial, dimension of a multilayered system.

The Functional Role

All belief systems serve a purpose. They gratify underlying psychological needs that explain the *why* and *how* of one's belief and disbelief systems. These functional or purposive objectives drive and sustain dogmatism. People with closed systems need to pronounce their convictions in a manner that dismisses other views, preempts reason, and derails intelligent discourse. *Why* dogmatic people adopt and maintain their particular beliefs and *how* they hold and communicate them determines the intensity of their underlying emotions and belief-related behaviors, and both aspects have a protective function. Built into dogmatism is a false pride that functions as a rational defense of the system and practice. There is a vociferous intent to silence the critics and, at the same time, intensify support from the righteous and like-minded. The nature of these protections explains dogmatism's adaptive utility as well as its detrimental consequences, both personal and interpersonal.

Illustrative Example: Alice

While filling out an attitude survey, Alice checks "Strongly Agree" next to the statement, "Most depressed people are weak-willed." Her strong agreement simply defines the formal content, or the *what*, of her belief. If Alice believes she is superior to others, she provides important information about the *why* of her belief, which this statement fails to tap. Assume that Alice believes she has the right to judge others and treat them with patronizing condescension because they are beneath her: they lack her self-discipline, grit, intelligence, and sophistication. Her need to impress, intimidate, and belittle others explain *why* she holds such beliefs, and her haughty manner reveals *how* she conveys her beliefs about people in general, particularly those who are depressed. Alice's self-importance and dismissal of those she considers weak explain the functional *why* and *how* of her beliefs. We could hypothesize that these functional components guide her entire belief system about people with mental illness.

Alice's underlying problem is that she copes with the anxiety that stems from feeling inadequate by portraying herself as superior to others, with a posturing of self-love that is characteristic of the narcissist.[8] Dogmatism is just another means of doing the same thing, only its goals and interpersonal style serve different motives.

In their attempt to convince others of their superiority, narcissists effect an image of perfection; alternatively, dogmatists need to convince others they are right—absolutely right. Both the narcissist and the dogmatist exhibit poor listening and conversation skills, and both demand attention, but the narcissist is less likely to reveal several of the cognitive errors typical of dogmatism. Impostors of confidence,

neither type understands the deep-seated needs their posturing gratifies.[9] Same train, different boxcars.

Why and *how* people hold their beliefs are instrumental to dogmatism's architecture and enduring nature. On an ideological spectrum,
whether one's political beliefs are on the right, middle, or left is irrelevant. Similarly, whether one's religious beliefs are fundamentalist,
agnostic, or atheistic is inconsequential to dogmatism's functional
role. A person who passionately adopts pro-life beliefs because "abortion is sinful, immoral, or criminal" and another person who is
ardently pro-choice because he or she values freedom of choice on the
matter can both be dogmatic about their belief systems if (1) they arrogantly proselytize their own views, (2) their minds are closed to alternative views, or (3) they dismiss or discriminate against others whose
belief systems conflict with their own.

§§

When the narrow- or closed-mindedness of personal dogmatism takes
root in a charismatic leader, dogmatism becomes institutionalized and
degrades the group's collective potential for intelligent thought. Yet
individually and collectively, dogmatism continues to serve its purpose: it assuages individual and group fears of being exposed as inadequate, insignificant, wrong, ignorant, or stupid. Dogmatism keeps
fear alive—fear that is largely manufactured in the psyche.

It bears repeating that *what* people believe is only one indicator of
dogmatism. Incongruities may exist between what people say, how
they say it, and what they do, which requires us to focus less on content and more on the psychological needs that govern the underlying
structure of their belief systems. When dogmatists adamantly try to
convince us of their absolute truth, the purpose of their arrogant proselytizing is to reduce their anxiety and enhance their diminished psychological and social stature, even if that involves summarily rejecting
other views and defensively restating their own unyielding position.
Such spontaneous rejection is more centered in emotions that prevent

a reasonable assessment of contradictory, evidence-based facts. From the dogmatist's perspective, much is at stake. From a psychological perspective, much is lost.

To understand if a person's beliefs come under the black-and-white umbrella of dogmatism, we need to ask a fundamental question. Does the individual's belief system offer psychological protection from anxiety about his or her ignorance or dread of errors? Does the person demand respect for the unassailable truth of his or her cherished beliefs? Is the person unwilling to listen to different views, change his or her mind, or admit mistaken judgment? If so, we would expect that most of the person's important beliefs would be held and pronounced dogmatically because deep, complex psychological needs are the driving force behind such cognitive rigidity.

Strong beliefs are generally thought of only in cognitive terms, yet when accompanied by strong emotions and corresponding behaviors that embody the subtraits of dogmatism, closed-mindedness expands to *self-righteousness*—the type that builds weapons of mass destruction. Emotions transport these weapons to designated targets, and dogmatic, authoritarian aggression unleashes them. Dogmatism assassinates more than the mind. Whether dogmatists blow up a bus, a place of worship, an abortion clinic, or the World Trade Center, their unique psychological characteristics function as protective mechanisms. In subsequent chapters, we will get the flavor of these unsavory characteristics that illustrate how unbridled dogmatism is not only a menace to personal success but violates human rights and derails democracy.

In contrast, people who engage in respectful, reciprocal exchanges of ideas as they vigorously debate the intricacies of complex issues epitomize cognitive flexibility. They value the entire process of questioning and genuinely accept open-minded consideration of alternate views as a necessary, dynamic process that enriches everyone.

BELIEF DOMAINS

In addition to the belief and disbelief systems and the three roles of beliefs (the what, why, and how), Rokeach posited three domains of beliefs. Regardless of how one's belief systems are formed, held, and conveyed, these domains—the central, intermediate, and peripheral—provide important reference points for dogmatism.

The Central Domain of Belief Systems

Imagine three concentric rings expanding from the impact of a heavy rock hitting the still waters of a lake. These rings represent the three domains of belief systems. The first, deep impact symbolizes the central domain of beliefs that have a ripple effect on our core identity and define who we are.

Central beliefs begin in childhood as bipolar generalizations about the external world, others, and oneself: the world is either friendly or hostile, people are trustworthy or untrustworthy, my family is caring or rejecting, God does or does not exist, I am a good person or I am bad. All beliefs begin with what Stanovich refers to as "intentional analysis" or thinking dispositions that are based on one's goals, desires, and beliefs, as well as one's cognitive ability to process information through perceptual analysis, coding mechanisms, and short-term and long-term memory systems.[10] The complexity of these skills varies with educational opportunity, but regardless of opportunity, perceived realities about a host of topics, events, and ethical issues take root in childhood and flourish throughout adolescence and adulthood. Central beliefs thus shape identity, which evolves and consolidates with age.

Central beliefs also reflect worldviews that are initially derived from parents and expanded or modified by teachers, religious and spiritual leaders, peer groups, cultural and political institutions, social myths, and cultural rituals. They include beliefs about marriage and the family, gender, politics and foreign affairs, economics, religion, environmental issues, and so on. Our central beliefs have an impact on people in close proximity, including family members and relatives, friends, co-workers, committee members, colleagues, and neighbors. Parents and other authority figures play such a key role that they occupy a separate domain. While some individuals effortlessly absorb core beliefs of their cultural environment, others take time to assess the validity of culturally established beliefs through a process of soul searching—a process that, for some, creates a great deal of inner conflict.

Illustrative Example: Melody

Melody illustrates her central beliefs when she says, "My husband and I enjoy going to church. The words of the Bible have always been a source of real comfort and I find peace when I'm in the company of people who love Jesus. We must teach our children that prayer and worship are noble values." Melody's central beliefs determine her identity as a devout believer and affirm her important ideas, sentiments, and values, which she likely adopted in childhood. She also discloses her central beliefs about parental and religious responsibilities.

§§

Finally, central beliefs reflect one's perceptions of time.[11] In particular, dogmatists may have a distorted view of past, present, or future events. They may cling to antiquated ideologies, obsess about past injustices, or long for the return of some golden age.[12] A preoccupation with traditional past belief systems that overlooks present-day contexts does not indicate a balanced, integrated time perspective. Implicit in this focus is a sentimental longing for the certainty of what is known; such knowledge assuages anxiety about a disconcerting present and unknowable future. One can live in the past with certainty, but to live in the present and ponder an unknowable future is to live with ambiguity, which strikes fear in the heart of dogmatic people.

Those preoccupied with the future differ from those obsessed with the past. A future-oriented time perspective is seen in those who fixate on some utopia and view the present as merely "a vestibule to the future, unimportant in its own right, full of injustice and suffering."[13] If present beliefs and deeds are diligently practiced according to an authoritative code of ethics and morality, anxiety and ambiguity will dissolve. Present behaviors will earn special privileges later, or protect against future misfortune and condemnation. Dogmatists who rigidly conform to codes of belief and behavior reduce their anxiety of the unknown, prevent future calamity, and feel in control of their lives. However, in both cases—whether one clings to the certainty of the past or holds onto the promise of an ideal future—there is insufficient harmony and balance between past, present, and future time perspectives. And because these temporal perspectives are a small part of their larger problem, the anxiety expressed in their uncertainty and judgment persists in various other subtraits of dogmatism.

The Intermediate Domain of Belief Systems

Returning to our metaphoric lake, the second expanding ring encircles the intermediate domain, which is reserved for beliefs about authority figures.[14] Here, Rokeach did not describe the actual beliefs or behaviors of authority figures themselves; rather, he outlined how dogmatic people perceive those who occupy positions of authority. His Dogmatism Scale was designed to assess thoughts that shape an entire belief system and orientation toward authority figures such as parents, the police, teachers, medical doctors, successful athletes, entertainers, and group leaders, among others. These authority figures exercise a range of power that begins with the direct decision-making power that is experienced early in children's lives when parents (who share their power with nannies, childcare workers, and teachers) exercise direct control over their behaviors. Throughout childhood, adolescence, and young adulthood, individuals broaden their exposure to other authority figures who have enough influential power to shape or modify their beliefs and behaviors. Finally, the intermediate domain also reflects beliefs about the authoritarian use of raw, coercive power that is wielded in more unusual circumstances of war, coup d'états, and correctional institutions and state penitentiaries.

Regardless of which type of authoritative power an individual possesses or is influenced by, early childhood beliefs are shaped by powerful role models who are seen as knowledgeable and whose behaviors are accepted as justifiable. Whether these models enact beliefs that are authoritative and democratic, or authoritarian, dictatorial, and punitive, children's orientation toward them becomes deeply rooted in the neural structures of their brains. In the presence of authority figures, beliefs and the emotions that surround them may not be clearly articulated, but children develop implicit understandings of what authority represents, and later in life they frequently project feelings that were once associated with those who had power over them as children onto other influential authority figures. A woman who was mistreated by her father when she was a little girl may project her original fear toward him onto other males in positions of authority (albeit her feelings may attenuate in adulthood, especially if she is insightful about this tendency). Consider, too, the inclination to change one's attitude and behavior toward an associate whose recent promotion legitimizes influential power. Sudden changes in status can alter the beliefs, feelings, and behaviors toward those with newfound, elevated authority, especially if those left behind have unresolved issues of control related to key authority figures in their early life.

Illustrative Example: Mack

The intermediate domain of beliefs is illustrated by Mack's comment: "My Dad was totally right—power corrupts and it corrupts absolutely! Once bigwig politicians or CEOs gain power, it goes to their heads and they can't be trusted." Mack's intermediate beliefs clearly illustrate his thoughts and feelings about a wide range of authority figures, beginning with his father. If Mack has several characteristics of dogmatism, he will likely have rigid beliefs about the legitimate exercise of authority and the use of punishment to enforce social conformity. He will support the parental use of authoritarian aggression and expect children to show deferential respect through authoritarian submission—prominent features of dogmatism that are presented in chapter 7.[15]

§§

Unlike dogmatists, open-minded people accept the legitimacy of authoritative, socially constructed roles, which are viewed as necessary for society to function. Flexible thinkers question and monitor authoritative mandates, which are not tainted by preconceived notions about the role of authority figures or cluttered with stereotypical beliefs and ascribed personality characteristics. The more open people's minds are toward authority figures, the less inclined they are to fall in step with a leader, especially an authoritarian leader whose ego needs polishing by sycophantic, dogmatic submitters.

Given that people's central and intermediate beliefs are the substance of dogmatism, the belief systems referred to in this book are derivative of these two domains. However, one final domain deserves mention.

The Peripheral Domain of Belief Systems

The third, peripheral ring of beliefs on our metaphoric lake includes ideas or opinions that are independent of or tangential to the first two categories. In the peripheral domain, information is temporarily considered before its content is incorporated with other beliefs in the central domain (core beliefs about self-identity, worldly ideas, close relationships other than authority figures, and time, for example), or the intermediate domain (beliefs about authority figures and the legitimacy of their roles). After brief consideration, new information is either relegated to belief or disbelief domains or simply ignored. Peripheral beliefs either fade or merge with established central or intermediate belief systems.[16]

Illustrative Examples: Daphne and Delbert

Daphne is reading an article to Delbert that claims male brains are more adept at spatial organization than female brains. If neither of them has preconceived opinions about differences in male and female spatial abilities, or clear beliefs about gender differences in overall intelligence, this research finding is registered as a peripheral belief that may or may not become integrated with later beliefs. However, because Daphne has a core belief that females are intellectually superior to males, she promptly rejects "such a ridiculous claim." This peripheral information now becomes lodged in her disbelief system. In contrast, Delbert vigorously nods his head as Daphne reports the findings and readily assimilates its premises with his preexisting central belief that males are superior to females, especially in spatial skills. With little reflection, he consolidates this material with similar beliefs firmly ensconced in his central domain. "Uh-huh, there's the proof, Daphne! Men can pack those winter tires in the trunk of the car faster than women can plead for help. How about another cup of coffee?"

For the most part, peripheral beliefs are so transient and unexplored they might best be thought of as opinions rather than beliefs. To be fully adopted, they must transition out of the peripheral and into the intermediate or central domain. When novel information or ideas support established beliefs or emanate from a respected source, they tend to be accepted and incorporated within central and intermediate domains of established systems.

§§

The three domains of belief systems—central, intermediate, and peripheral—all have functional aspects. *How* the content of these beliefs are held can signal dogmatism, as seen in those who are unable to "receive, evaluate, and act on relevant information received from the outside on its own intrinsic merits, unencumbered by irrelevant factors in the situation arising from within the person or from the outside."[17] In other words, logical analysis can be impaired by psychological factors that lead to a blind adoption of rigid, narrow-minded belief systems that are sustained by psychological necessities—necessities that are extraneous to the actual belief content.

RECENT CONTRIBUTIONS FROM COGNITIVE PSYCHOLOGY

Cognitive psychology has gained considerable prominence since Rokeach presented his theory in 1960.[18] Researchers in the field study observational and vicarious learning and the effects of reward and punishment on learning;[19] they also probe the substance of intellectual thought and higher-order thinking skills that govern the perceptual registration and coding, storing, retrieving, applying, and synthesizing information. They suggest that one's intelligence quotient (IQ), as measured by standardized psychology tests, does not accurately reflect one's capacity for rational or logical thought. If I interpret Stanovich and others correctly, Rokeach's "need to know" approximates the intentional level of analysis that describes an individual's goals or "*what* the system is attempting to compute and *why*."[20] Critical thinking demonstrates an ability to decouple prior beliefs and biases in order to evaluate new evidence and opposing arguments as objectively as possible.

For example, strong myside bias (personal opinions that fail to consider both sides of an issue or argument) and belief biases about factual knowledge that is accepted or rejected according to its believability, rather than logical validity, reflect differences in people's ability to accurately evaluate information.[21] One study found that "the ability to overcome myside bias in informal reasoning tasks was independent of cognitive ability."[22] Yet a broad survey of cognitive psychology research showed little acknowledgement of how individual differences in emotional states (e.g., prior anxiety, frustration, anger, or emotional composure) interact with and influence one's cognitive biases.[23] Cognitive scientists have, as Damasio notes, neglected the impact emotions have on reason, yet emotions affect the ability to express one's full complement of cognitive ability. Indeed, neuroscience research suggests that much cognitive activity occurs at an unconscious or semiconscious level, which is influenced by emotions, and while rational thought may appear as purely rational, it is never completely independent of an emotional context that includes memories and symbolisms that are recorded deep within brain structures.[24]

Since all thoughts are accompanied by some degree of emotion ranging from imperceptible to dominant or interfering, research on the impact of emotions on rational thought is vital. When strong emotions prevail, they diminish "accurate belief formation, belief consistency assessment, and behavioral regulation."[25] Each of us possesses an intellectual capacity that combines with emotional dispositions to determine our quality of analysis and comprehension of information. These skills range from higher-order, algorithmic-level reasoning to lower-level analyses that are governed more by emotions. In particular, strong emotional interference causes smart people to reveal irrational beliefs and dim-witted behaviors.

Because people are prone to behaviors that are consonant with their emotions, strong feelings of disgust about homosexuality, for example, would prevent a homophobic person from voting for a homosexual political candidate or short-listing a well-qualified lesbian for an executive position in the company, even if the homophobe publicly states that homosexuality is a nonissue. Similarly, a computer scientist might have superior analytic skills, but if he harbors prejudicial feelings against women and needs to collaborate with a female colleague, his ability to demonstrate higher-order algorithmic intelligence is compromised. If confronted about his biases, it is unlikely that he would admit, perhaps even to himself, that he is prejudiced against women, but his higher-order reasoning will be contaminated by lower-order emotional interference. Yet it is important to keep in mind that although dogmatists hold illogical beliefs and act in unreasonable ways, they might well have a healthy quotient of intellectual capacity. This modern view complements Rokeach's original thesis that dogmatism is fundamentally a consequence of persistent anxiety.

I am reminded here of Jason Lisle, a PhD (University of Colorado) astrophysicist with the young-earth, creation-science organization called Answers in Genesis. During a presentation at the Creation Museum, Lisle told his audience that he did not admit to being a creationist in graduate school because "some professors will just stop you from getting your PhD if you're a creationist."[26] Christopher Sharp, a published researcher (in the *Journal of Astrophysics*), asked Lisle to explain how it is that if God created the universe some 6,000 years ago, the Sun (also being approximately 6,000 years old) has an abundance of helium in the center—a finding consistent with about 4.5 billion years of nuclear burning. Lisle's answer was that God created the Sun to *appear* that way.[27] The mental gymnastics of dogmatism need no safety net.

Just as an individual's incessant background anxiety makes him or her more vulnerable to arrogant, dogmatic dismissal of those who differ, powerful leaders of institutions who feel their mandates are threatened are not above using dogmatic control to diminish their own anxiety, appear composed, and maintain power. History records examples too numerous to mention where emotion has hijacked reason in dogmatic leaders who then ordered death squads and unspeakable acts of torture to obliterate political dissidents, save the masses, or purify religious infidels.

A CAUTIONARY WORD

In this book, the terms *dogmatic* and *dogmatist* refer only to individuals who clearly and frequently demonstrate a minimum of six out of the thirteen proposed characteristics of dogmatism. These adults have a persistent pattern of defensive, closed-minded belief systems that are held with rigid, arrogant certainty in most situations, much of the time. While researchers should be able to predict aspects of their behavior with a modest degree of accuracy, like all traits, dogmatism is an abstract concept, or a conceptual tool that enables psychological understanding of a person's organizational system of thoughts, feelings, and behaviors. The measurement of its presence and the prediction of its occurrence is somewhat problematic; unlike measuring discrete properties of blood, for example, we cannot pour dogmatism into a vial and quantitatively measure its constituent parts. Like other personality traits, dogmatism resists precise scientific measurement. Thankfully, this imprecision preserves some of the mystery that makes our personality differences so fascinating.

Dogmatism is thus a complex assortment of characteristics, as seen in the prototypical examples portrayed in subsequent chapters. However, two people with identical high scores on a valid dogmatism scale would not likely present the same profile of its characteristics. One might score high on the first three cognitive dimensions, high on one emotional characteristic, and moderately high on the last three behavioral characteristics. The other might score high on the last four cognitive characteristics, moderately high on one emotional feature, and high on three different behavioral characteristics. Yet wherever they go, all who score within the predetermined dogmatism range leave identifiable footprints of dogmatism.

Finally, some people are described as dogmatic even if their behavior reflects only a few, less frequent and intense characteristics of doctrinaire thinking. Those who chronically occupy the margins of dogmatism demonstrate less prominent characteristics that nonetheless insidiously drain their lives of success and enjoyment. And while it is not always easy to decide whether someone is opinionated or dogmatic, opinionated people do not display the full suite of characteristics indicative of dogmatism. They may be on their third marriage and they may have lost friends who described them as too opinionated or overbearing, but they do not persistently reveal the characteristic subtraits of dogmatism. More accurately, they have the shadow syndrome of dogmatism—a cluster of characteristics that represent a less distinct form of a personality trait or psychological disorder.[28] Thus, opinionated people have the shadow syndrome of dogmatism, which silhouettes its unyielding nature.

This book examines and illustrates full-fledged, overt dogmatism, and adults who practice it unequivocally and consistently exhibit strong thoughts, feelings, and behaviors that impair reasoning, disrupt social relationships, and damage careers. Parenthetically, it would be premature to describe any adolescent as dogmatic, since MRI studies of the developing adolescent brain reveal that physical maturation of the prefrontal cortex, which governs abstract thought and mature judgment, does not occur until the midtwenties.[29] It is also necessary to keep in mind that dogmatic people, obnoxious though they may be, are more than the sum of their dogmatic parts. Just as all open-minded individuals are not paragons of open-mindedness and psychological virtue, all dogmatists are not narrow-minded bigots longing for the return of public lynching. If your car broke down and you were stranded on the roadside, there is nothing to suggest that the approaching dogmatic driver would not stop to lend a helping hand.

Now that we have examined the components of belief systems and surveyed distinctions between dogmatism, skepticism, and open-mindedness, we can explore an intriguing example of dogmatism's most dangerous qualities—features that are more often seen in malevolent, dogmatic minority groups than in your closed-minded neighbor, coworker, or ex-partner.

NOTES

1. Carl Jung (1875–1961) developed his theory of Analytical Psychology around five archetypes, one of which is the *shadow*, the inferior part of the personal and collective unconscious. Jung's shadow is similar to Freud's conception of unconscious instincts in that dark, sinister aspects of human nature seek expression and, in the process, create conflict, anxiety, and guilt—which, in Jung's terms, can result in a disintegrated self.

2. M. Rokeach, *The Open and Closed Mind* (New York: Basic Books, 1960), p. 33.

3. Rokeach, *Understanding Human Values: Individual and Societal* (New York: Free Press, 1979), p. 5.

4. Rokeach, *The Open and Closed Mind*.

5. Ibid., p. 54.

6. R. Nickerson, "Why Teach Thinking?" in *Teaching Thinking Skills: Theory and Practice*, ed. Joan Baron and R. Sternberg (New York: Freeman, 1987), p. 30.

7. Rokeach, *The Open and Closed Mind*. The formal and functional roles are Rokeach's terms of division.

8. H. Kohut, *The Restoration of the Self* (New York: International Universities Press, 1977).

9. The borderline personality disorder (BPD), outlined in the *Diagnostic and Statistical Manual of Mental Disorders–IV*, exhibits cognitive splitting in which the person splits abstract concepts into dichotomous, polarized compartments and mentally swings back and forth between the two. For example, people with BPD alternate between seeing themselves and others as all good or all bad, absolutely right or totally wrong. This is similar to compartmentalization, a characteristic of dogmatism that is explained in chapter 5. However, people with BPD also have other symptoms that differentiate them from dogmatists (see American Psychiatric Association, *Diagnostic and Statistical Manual of Mental Disorders*, 4th ed. [Washington, DC: American Psychiatric Association, 1994]).

10. K. Stanovich, *The Robot's Rebellion: Finding Meaning in the Age of Darwin* (Chicago: University of Chicago Press, 2004), p. 151. Stanovich views cognitive thinking styles or dispositional styles as intentional-level psychological constructs, whereas cognitive ability is considered an algorithmic-level construct. See J. V. Kokis, R. Macpherson, M. E. Toplak, R. F. West, and K. E. Stanovich, "Heuristic and Analytic Processing: Age Trends and Associations with Cognitive Ability and Cognitive Styles," *Journal of Experimental Child Psychology* 83 (2002): 26–52.

11. Rokeach, *The Open and Closed Mind*.

12. Rokeach, *Understanding Human Values*.

13. Rokeach, *The Open and Closed Mind*, p. 52.

14. Ibid.

15. R. Altemeyer, *The Authoritarian Specter* (Cambridge, MA: Harvard University Press, 1996), p. 41. Authoritarian aggression and authoritarian submission are part of Altemeyer's Right-Wing Authoritarian Scale. I have incorporated both traits as important behavior characteristics of dogmatism, which are presented in chapter 7.

16. Rokeach, *The Open and Closed Mind.*

17. Ibid., p. 57.

18. Stanovich, *The Robot's Rebellion.* Stanovich provides a comprehensive summary of views from various cognitive psychologists who study intellectual capacities of higher- and lower-order thinking skills. In *The Robot's Rebellion*, Stanovich presents a thorough analysis of different conceptualizations of intelligence, beginning with TASS (The Autonomous Set of Systems that have evolutionary significance) and lower-order, intentional or dispositional systems that can override our evolved, higher-order algorithmic systems used in cognitive processing.

19. R. L. Solso, *Cognitive Psychology*, 6th ed. (Needham Heights, MA: Allyn and Bacon, 2001).

20. Kovis et al., "Heuristic and Analytic Processing," p. 31.

21. R. Macpherson and K. E. Stanovich, "Cognitive Ability, Thinking Dispositions, and Instructional Set as Predictors of Critical Thinking," *Learning and Individual Differences* 17 (2007): 115–27.

22. Ibid., p. 123.

23. Cognitive psychologists who have expanded on traditional approaches to the assessment of conceptual and computational skills include R. J. Sternberg, *Thinking Styles* (Cambridge: Cambridge University Press, 1997); C. M. Kardash and R. J. Scholes, "Effects of Pre-existing Beliefs, Epistemological Beliefs, and Need for Cognition on Interpretation of Controversial Issues," *Journal of Educational Psychology* 88 (1996): 260–71; P. A. Klaczynski, D. H. Gordon, and J. Fauth, "Goal-Oriented Critical Reasoning and Individual Differences in Critical Reasoning Biases," *Journal of Educational Psychology* 89 (1997): 470–85; and R. F. West and K. E. Stanovich, "Is Probability Matching Smart? Associations between Probabilistic Choices and Cognitive Ability," *Memory and Cognition* 31 (1997): 243–51.

24. A. Damasio, *Descartes' Error: Emotion, Reason, and the Human Brain* (New York: Putnam, 1994).

25. Stanovich, *The Robot's Rebellion*, p. 165.

26. C. Hedges, *American Fascists: The Christian Right and the War on America* (New York: Free Press, 2006), p. 127.

27. M. Sharp, "Jason Lisle's Visit to Tucson," http://www.csharp.com/lisle.html (accessed March 26, 2006).

28. J. J. Ratey and C. Johnson, *Shadow Syndromes: The Mild Forms of*

Major Mental Disorders That Sabotage Us (New York: Bantam Books, 1998), p. 11.

29. J. N. Giedd, "Structural Magnetic Resonance Imaging of the Adolescent Brain," in *Adolescent Brain Development: Vulnerabilities and Opportunities*, ed. R. E. Dahl and L. P. Spear (New York: New York Academy of Sciences, 2004), pp. 77–85.

Chapter 3

THE PERSONALITY PUZZLE

Assembling the Pieces

If something exists, it exists in some quantity, and if it exists in some quantity, it can be measured.

E. L. Thorndike, 1905[1]

In 2007 the television program *Frontline* aired a joint PBS/CBC special titled "Canada: The Cell Next Door," a documentary that went inside an Islamic terrorist cell to expose plans to blow up political targets in Canada.[2] When the host, Linden MacIntyre, asked the Muslim infiltrator what causes a group of eighteen Muslims to plot acts of terror, the infiltrator answered, "The wrong kind of influence at the wrong time in a young man's life." MacIntyre responded, "Is it that fragile? Is that all it takes is the wrong kind of information at the wrong time in a young man's life?" The Muslim replied, "I would have to say yes."

To that response I would add: young men who have not been encouraged to think for themselves, who have been criticized or humiliated for doing so, and who have been rewarded for blindly adopting the belief systems of important authority figures are also at risk. Add a mixture of the following and we have the ingredients for intoxicating dogmatism:

1. Innate, evolutionary adaptations for dominance that linger in modern brains.
2. Genetic vulnerabilities, particularly an emotional vulnerability for chronic anxiety.
3. Authoritarian parents who control their children's behavior with rigid rules and the threat of punishment.
4. Early indoctrination of beliefs that discourage natural curiosity and open-minded questioning and reasoning throughout childhood and adolescence.
5. Parental or institutional punishment for independent thought in childhood and adolescence.
6. Authority figures who model an intolerance of ambiguity.
7. Parental inability to facilitate emotional regulation during infancy and childhood.
8. Prolonged exposure to role models who seek revenge for past injustices or promote their ideology as a legitimate entitlement to power.
9. Cognitive impoverishment during childhood and adolescence as a consequence of inadequate government funding for educational infrastructure and programs.
10. Political and economic marginalization of youth.
11. Social instability and the radicalization of youth.
12. Politicized groups with the financial means to ideologically seduce and indoctrinate the disenfranchised and psychologically vulnerable.
13. Membership in a narrow- or closed-minded group that offers the promise of social acceptance, individual recognition, dignity, and honor.
14. Zealous pursuit of a group's rigid, ideological goals.

These fourteen convergent sparks of evolutionary, biological, psychological, social, and political impediments ignite dogmatism. Beginning in infancy and early childhood, individuals predisposed to anxiety and influenced by social learning that insidiously closes their minds habitually obey external demands to unquestioningly internalize dogma that constricts rational thought. In the extreme, this process culminates in monstrous crimes against humanity. The crucial point is that revolutionary or reactionary dogmatists will not open their minds and think for themselves, nor will they evaluate their flawed cognitive processing. Consequently, they cannot logically assess the merit of an ideological movement.

Yet surely all of us are prone to negligent or careless thinking. Our brains lapse into lazy stereotypes, sometimes without a sensible modicum of analysis.[3] A review of research on the natural tendency to prejudge others confirms that we see what we are primed to see through social conditioning that teaches us to make unwarranted judgments, and "however egalitarian we may be (or think we are), our brains are stuffed with stereotypes."[4] Compounding this natural tendency is the psychological need to prejudge and diminish others in order to prop up and shield our own fragile egos.

The self-serving bias is one such shield.[5] We regularly overestimate our strengths and downplay our weaknesses—a convenient strategy that convinces us we are above average in such qualities as intelligence, ethics, social skills, and business or career competence. We are all psychological residents of Lake Wobegon, where "the women are strong, the men are good looking, and all the children are above average."[6] According to the theory of self-serving biases, Lake Wobegoners who survey the characteristics of dogmatism in chapters 5, 6, and 7 would feel immune to its thirteen psychological deficiencies—flaws that thankfully reside in others, not themselves. Yet, in reality, we can all be at least a little vain, judgmental, immoral, deluded, pigheaded, domineering, and irresponsible.[7] Dogmatism is just one more guest at the party.

This chapter prepares us for contemporary, developmental, and traditional views that provide the academic foundation from which all personality traits emerge. In chapter 8 we will note how emotional distress disrupts cognitive processing and intellectual performance, jeopardizing the young child's ability to achieve and express his or her intellectual potential. Similarly, social relationships in infancy and childhood are affected by parents' psychological stability and parenting skills, which interact with the child's biological temperament. Beyond the developmental forces of biology, attachment, and emotion regulation, evolutionary traits that were once adaptive impact current social and cultural experiences and expectations, which have a cumulative, synergistic effect on the child's emerging personality.

PERSONALITY THEORY GAINS PROMINENCE

The underlying causal forces of personality were first addressed near the end of the nineteenth century and the beginning of the twentieth by Wilhelm Wundt, a philosopher and experimental psychologist who studied the nature of introspection, and William James, a physiological psychologist who focused on sensation and perception. At the beginning of the twentieth century, Freud, Jung, and Adler also began articulating their assumptions about human nature, from which their theories of personality were derived. But the field of study that became widely known as *personality theory* did not emerge until the 1930s, when Gordon Allport and Henry Murray's research on observed personality traits inspired this specialized branch of psychology.

The first *Journal of Personality* (formerly *Character and Personality*) appeared in 1932. Since then, theorists have generated more than twenty-five different models that address fundamental questions about the nature and properties of personality. Indeed, psychologists are still expanding the field of study by conducting research on the role of genetics and biology and the influence of evolutionary processes on human personality.

Yet despite remarkable advances in theory and research, psychologists cannot agree on one comprehensive, compelling definition of personality, nor can they provide definitive explanations for any one personality trait and its host of characteristics. At this time, all that is known about any personality trait—dogmatism included—is that traits are extremely complex. The origins of dogmatism are as diverse as the dogmatists who practice it. However, given the inherent difficulties of teasing apart the multifaceted dimensions of personality, theorists and researchers continue to make enormous progress in the scientific study of human behavior, and their efforts have significantly expanded our commonsense notions about personality.

DEFINING PERSONALITY

What do psychologists mean when they speculate about personality, and how accurately can they measure its properties? What accounts for unique differences, even between monozygotic twins who are genetically identical? Do you know of any two people whose personalities are the same? Me neither. It is our very uniqueness that makes the study of personality so fascinating. As we might expect, the subject is so multidimensional that no grand theory has yet integrated all the contributing elements of personality.

In an attempt to establish consensus on a definition of personality, psychologists are studying cognitive, motivational, emotional, social, and behavioral patterns to determine if our subjective notion of personality can be precisely defined. Just as friends, family, co-workers, and colleagues differ widely in their understanding of personality, so too do psychologists differ in their definitions of personality, but the latter employ more rigorous parameters to their analysis. For example, Nora has had two brief encounters with Chris, someone she informally describes as "a man who can charm the sap out of maples in mid-winter." Her perception diverges significantly from that of her co-workers. Might Chris's interactions with Nora vary considerably from his contacts with others such that Nora views his personality traits differently? In other words, how much does the situation influence perceived personality traits? The answers to these questions are not decisive, which makes condensing the dynamic nature of personality into a compelling, concise definition problematic indeed.[8]

While psychologists do not agree on one universal definition, they generally accept that personality is "a complex abstraction that includes the person's unique genetic background (except in the case of identical twins) and learning history, and the ways in which these organized and integrated complexes of events influence his or her responses to certain stimuli in the environment."[9] For Gordon Allport, personality was "something *real* within an individual that leads to characteristic behavior and thought." For Carl Rogers, another personality theorist, the personality, or self, was as "an organized perception of the 'I' or 'me' that lies at the heart of an individual's experiences."[10] In this sense, personality is an enduring, integrated composite of temperaments and behaviors. There are others, notably the behaviorists, who claim that because personality is a complex mixture of elusive, internal dynamics, we cannot conclude that it has stable psychological features. But regardless of the variations in approach and definition, psychologists remain intrigued by behavioral differences, especially those that occur among people in the same situation.[11]

Different theories "direct the attention of the investigator to important questions and provide a standard against which progress in the field can be measured. Without such guidance, explicit or implicit, empirical research is indeed empty and trivial."[12] The academic guidelines that framed the theory of dogmatism in this book are presented with the following caveat in mind: no theory is restricted to statements based only on empirical facts that can be objectively measured. Theoretical assumptions are derived from intuitive reasoning and analyses that emanate from a combination of theories, research, and observation. This theory of dogmatism evolved from two graduate theses in psychology and twenty years of teaching Personality Theory and Abnormal Behavior to university students. Various sources of information and experience became the springboard for an eclectic theory of dogmatism that hopefully will generate new ideas, concepts, and empirical research that further expand our understanding of dogmatism as a personality trait.

Since the origins and causes of dogmatism have not yet been

examined from the lens of personality theory, an appropriate place to start is the acknowledgement of relevant ideas and concepts from these established theories, supported where possible with scientific evidence. Chapter 4 will present the four underlying, influential factors of dogmatism, which postulate that if a child repeatedly experiences several influential factors, then his or her risk for dogmatism significantly increases. That is the best we can do for now.

The usefulness of ideas is never fully confirmed by one theory presented in one book. Readers are encouraged to consider other models that might add to our understanding of dogmatism and present counterarguments to the ideas presented here, or that outline alternative theories that may work better than the one this book delineates.

MEASURING PERSONALITY TRAITS

Psychology tests of personality traits are valid only if they reach statistically significant levels of validity and reliability (often determined by first- and second-order factor analyses and other statistical measures).[13] We infer the existence of a trait such as dogmatism from a number of clearly related traits, known as subtraits, that contribute to its overall essence. On a valid test that measures dogmatism, for example, the trait is assumed to exist if its measurement falls within the extreme range of a trait's scope, since "only behaviors falling at the extremes of dimensions have much meaning for personality; degrees near the middle of dimensions are too ambiguous to allow inferences in which one can be confident."[14]

In the context of trait extremes, let us hypothetically illustrate this by assuming that the personality trait of dogmatism is determined by a score of 80 or greater on a valid dogmatism questionnaire, where scores are within the range of 1–100 and the mean is 50. All people who score between 80 and 100, the designated trait zone, would portray several characteristics of dogmatism. Within that twenty-point zone, we could further categorize people's scores as indicative of moderate, high, or extreme dogmatism. Dogmatists who score on the lowest end of the dogmatism range, from 80 to 86, would reveal moderate degrees of dogmatism, which might not rule out a second dinner invitation. We could also assume that high levels of dogmatism would fall in the midrange (87 to 93), while classic, florid dogmatists would score within the extreme range (94 to 100). These high-scoring dogmatists would have a unique combination of characteristics that broadcast dogmatism, without a megaphone. We could predict that all of our theoretical subjects with moderate, high, and extreme levels of dogmatism would be significantly more closed-minded, rigid, and arrogantly certain of their cherished belief systems than subjects who scored lower than 80 on our hypothetical dogmatism scale.

We now turn our attention to those questionnaires that assess the various components of dogmatism in the general population. Two North American psychologists—Milton Rokeach, an American, and Bob Altemeyer, a Canadian—have designed and researched personality tests that measure the properties of dogmatism.

ASSESSING DOGMATISM

Rokeach's Dogmatism Scale

Form E of Rokeach's Dogmatism Scale (commonly referred to as the D Scale) emerged after several iterations that increasingly refined and more accurately measured the properties of dogmatism.[15] The degree to which people's scale position, or score, differs on a continuum that is anchored by the extremes of dogmatism on the one end (indicated by high scores), and open-minded flexibility on the other (indicated by low scores), is presumed to reflect differences in subtraits of dogmatism. Such was the intent of Rokeach's D Scale—to assess the *how* (functional aspects) of belief systems. But did it?

To establish the questionnaire's statistical reliability and validity, Rokeach administered his D Scale, Form E, to hundreds of subjects throughout the 1950s. At that time, the questionnaire was believed to be an adequate measure of dogmatism, but thirty years of subsequent statistical analyses of statement content and scale design exposed its serious flaws.[16] A comprehensive review of research studies that applied the D Scale to test numerous hypotheses about dogmatism concluded that the scale does not measure closed-minded belief systems in general, and that it is not a valid, internally consistent measure of dogmatism.[17] Why not?

The adequacy of any questionnaire rests on its validity and reliability. Hundreds of studies applied the D Scale to link dogmatism to a diverse range of belief systems about, for example, models of therapy, educational values, attitudes toward women, concerns about the rise of information technology, religious and political beliefs, managerial styles, and even musical preferences. However, findings from these studies are invalid because other researchers have since discovered that the scale does not measure what it purports to measure. In short, the D Scale lacks content validity. Moreover, the D scale "had almost minimal levels of internal consistency, and then shot itself in the foot (heart and head) by failing to control for yea-saying. Thus the primary measure had virtually no construct validity, and the die was cast."[18]

The wording of the D Scale presents another serious problem. Not only are several statements gender biased, but they also do not measure Rokeach's most salient feature of dogmatism—the function, or *how*, of beliefs that explains the purpose dogmatic systems serve.[19] The functions of dogmatic belief systems are the reduction of anxiety, the illusion of knowledge, and false pride in being absolutely right. Yet what the D Scale ends up measuring is, at best, belief content, the more superficial feature of dogmatic belief systems.[20]

However, because Rokeach's D Scale did not accurately tap the construct does not invalidate his ideas about the nature of dogmatism. When psychologists speak of *constructs*, they refer to an idea or abstraction that is of a dichotomous nature, such as dogmatic versus open-minded, introverted versus extroverted, or conscientious versus irresponsible. Rokeach's construct of dogmatism spawned hundreds of studies by graduate students and others who used his D Scale for a good thirty years to test hypotheses, the results of which were reported in credible, peer-reviewed psychology journals. Yet there was little academic criticism that would have alerted researchers to the scale's inherent psychometric problems, at least not until Bob Altemeyer and a few others exposed its poor reliability and validity. Today, few studies use Rokeach's D Scale to validate research hypotheses on dogmatism.

Altemeyer's Dogmatism Scale

Thirty-six years after the publication of Rokeach's D Scale, Robert Altemeyer developed a more reliable, valid measure of dogmatism that he initially called the Doggone Old Gnu Scale (DOG Scale). This scale is reproduced in his 1996 book, *The Authoritarian Specter*.[21] His questionnaire includes a total of twenty statements, ten of which are protrait statements (agreement indicates dogmatism), and ten of which are contrait statements (agreement indicates cognitive flexibility). In contrast with Rokeach's D scale, which contains only protrait items, Altemeyer's scale is a more balanced measure of dogmatism and is formulated on his definition of dogmatism as "relatively unchangeable, unjustified certainty."[22] Although Rokeach's construct of dogmatism implies an unchangeable mind, Altemeyer's definition of dogmatism calls it an "unchangeable, *unjustified* certainty." The difficulty here, as Altemeyer notes, is that "we often cannot say, in all fairness, whether someone's certainty is unjustified. . . . Do you see everything with perfect clarity, with everything fitting perfectly into place?"[23] For this reason, I considered, but rejected, Altemeyer's term "unjustified," and chose instead to simply describe this cognitive characteristic as *rigid certainty*.

Drawing from a subject pool of first-year introductory psychology students and some of their parents, Altemeyer's DOG Scale, though not yet widely researched, appears to be the most valid recent measure of dogmatism out there.[24] The theoretical decisions behind its construction make it an acceptably reliable assessment tool, especially since all of its statements are significantly related to items on Altemeyer's other questionnaires that are pertinent to dogmatism: the Right-Wing Authoritarian Scale, the Left-Wing Authoritarian Scale, the Religious Fundamentalism Scale, the Attitudes Toward Homosexuals Scale, the Posse Against Radicals Scale, and the Zealot Scale.[25]

Statements on a dogmatism questionnaire should ideally tap into as many of the properties of the construct as possible by devising categories that delineate all of its psychological dimensions. Each statement should be designed to clearly assess one, and only one, belief at a time. A double-barreled statement that has two or more ideas embedded in its content presents a serious problem that shows up in four of Rokeach's D Scale statements and in one DOG Scale item. For example, Rokeach states, "In the long run the best way to live is to pick friends and associates whose tastes and beliefs are the same as one's own."[26] This statement is double-barreled in that tastes and beliefs are independent units of assessment. The statement should address only the belief component and omit tastes, which are more indicative of preferences. An example of a double-barreled statement from the DOG Scale is: "People who disagree with me are just plain wrong, and often evil as well."[27] How would people who believe those who disagree with them are "just plain wrong," but not evil, respond to this statement?[28]

Despite my criticisms of the double-barreled problem on one DOG Scale item, the questionnaire "has pleasing levels of internal consistency [and] appears to be a step in the right direction."[29] Its focus is on the relatively unchangeable, unjustified certainty that is consistent with Altemeyer's definition of dogmatism. However, this scale does not tap the emotional and behavioral characteristics of dogmatism. Had Altemeyer included statements that assess these components of dogmatism, his scale would have been a more robust measure of dogmatism as a personality trait, rather than just a measure of cognitive style. Including statements such as, "When someone says something that supports gay marriage, I cannot hide my disgust," would assess the emotional and behavioral elements of dogmatism. Based on the theory of dogmatism presented here, a scale that would improve the current state of assessment would present a balanced questionnaire that includes both protrait and contrait items, presents only single-bar-reled statements, and constructs items that assess the entire suite of emotional, cognitive, and behavioral elements that capture the thirteen characteristics of dogmatism.

Tests that Measure Traits Related to Dogmatism

While some researchers were applying the D Scale to studies of dogmatism, others were investigating properties of related traits. Several psychology journals have reported research on the reliability, validity, and application of the following questionnaires: Intolerance of Ambiguity,[30] Need for Closure,[31] Personal Need for Sructure,[32] various measures of rigidity,[33] the Religious Fundamentalism Scale,[34] the Attitudes Toward Homosexuals Scale,[35] and the Zealot Scale.[36] All of these scales assess characteristics that overlap with dogmatism. A summary of research on the assessment of these related traits, along with the difficulties in drawing conclusions about their relatedness, is provided in the chapter notes.

NO SINGLE TRUTH

With the exception of radical behaviorism, which views the environment as the central force in personality development, psychologists try to understand personality in the context of their assumptions about human nature. Having laid that theoretical foundation, they then propose influential factors that shape personality, including evolutionary processes, genetic and biological predispositions, brain structure and function, and early childhood experiences that involve parenting and social learning. A complex interaction of multiple causes underlies personality traits that differ in qualitative dimensions of intensity, frequency, and duration. As you can see, personality is multidimensional; the inner space of the psyche is as difficult to conquer as the outer space of the cosmos. Putting it all together is mind boggling, which is why specialists in the field tend to limit their studies to what they consider the essential elements of personality. As such, there is no unified theory of personality, much less dogmatism. This is not unusual. After all, there is no unified theory of the amoeba either, and its organization is much simpler than the complexity of human personality.

Theorists who assume that personality is largely controlled by genetic predispositions focus on the biological roots of personality. Known as biopsychologists, they examine the effects of genetic predispositions on brain structure, brain chemistry, experience, and personality. In contrast, psychodynamic theorists view social institutions, particularly the family, as playing the major role in personality; they therefore examine its development in the context of environmental influences. From another angle, humanistic and existential psychologists believe that because we are free to choose how we interpret and respond to events, our personalities are self-authored over the course of a lifetime, and that each of us must take responsibility for the personality we script. A different emphasis is provided by cognitive-behavioral psychologists and social learning theorists, who view cognitive processing as the dominant player in personality development. From this perspective, the structure of personality traits depends on one's quality of thinking (e.g., rational or dysfunctional). Since humans are capable of applying reason to make sense of the social, physical, and abstract world, faulty interpretations of reality are at the core of all maladaptive traits, including dogmatism.

Buddhism has more recently captured the attention of personality theorists. For this reason, we will reflect on Buddhism's philosophic tenets of suffering, dissatisfaction and craving, the troublesome ego, and enlightenment. This philosophy has endured for more than two thousand years and provides a rich guide for understanding our inner selves. As such, Buddhism offers thought-provoking insights that have direct relevance for the study of dogmatism.

Modern psychology acknowledges that some personality traits are shaped by forces of human evolution that primed us for adaptive behaviors that enhanced survival and procreation on the savannahs. Some of these behaviors are less adaptive in today's society, but they linger in old brain structures, occasionally jockeying for position when they should be dormant. Finally, psychologists who study personality traits—the trait theorists—focus mainly on the biological substrates of universal behaviors, such as friendliness, extraversion, openness to experience, conscientiousness, and emotional instability. Their approach to the study of personality offers invaluable insight to our study of dogmatism.

Despite the different approaches and emphases, all of these theoretical perspectives assume that a constellation of personality traits profile degrees of psychological hardiness and vulnerability— enduring styles of idiosyncratic coping that are predominantly adaptive or maladaptive. Each of the models mentioned in this chapter presents significant theoretical departures that merit separate attention. Taken together, chapters 10 through 16 outline plausible contributing influences that shape dogmatism—a personality trait whose seeds are sown in infancy, watered throughout childhood and adolescence, and reach full bloom by adulthood.

The closing of this chapter prepares us for the study of dogmatism's four broad psychological needs and deficiencies that presumably shape its thirteen characteristics, all of which profile dogmatism as an enduring, unattractive personality trait that takes its toll on individuals and society. Chapter 4, to which we now turn, presents the causal influences that build the scaffolding on which the sure-footed characteristics of dogmatism stomp about.

NOTES

1. E. L. Thorndike, cited in D. C. Funder, *The Personality Puzzle*, 4th ed. (New York: Norton, 2007), p. 122.

2. The title of this documentary was part of a PBS series called *World: Stories from a Small Planet*, aired January 30, 2007. CBC correspondent Linden MacIntyre interviewed the informant, Mubin Shaikh, shortly after the arrests of eighteen Muslim men, most of whom were under thirty. All are currently standing trial in Canada.

3. C. Fine, *A Mind of Its Own* (New York: Norton, 2006), pp. 79–104.

4. Ibid., p. 179.

5. L. Babcock, and G. Loewenstein, "Explaining Bargaining Impasse: The Role of Self-Serving Biases," *Journal of Economic Perspectives* 11, no. 1 (1975): 119–37. These authors provide a summary of research on the self-serving bias.

6. "Minnesota Public Radio," in *Wikipedia*, http://en.wikipedia.org/wiki/Minnesota_Public_Radio (accessed January 31, 2007). Lake Wobegon is a fictitious town in the US state of Minnesota, the boyhood home of Garrison Keillor, who reports the "News from Lake Wobegon" on the radio show *A Prairie Home Companion*, broadcast live over Minnesota Public Radio and other radio stations throughout the United States.

7. Fine, *A Mind of Its Own*. Throughout this book, Cordelia Fine presents recent psychology research that reveals the many ways in which our brains trick us into thinking we are autonomous free agents, capable of conscious choice.

8. Every text on personality theory I have examined stresses that different theorists approach the definition of personality differently, and all agree that there is no one definition of personality that psychologists accept as definitive.

9. R. M. Ryckman, *Theories of Personality*, 8th ed. (Belmont, CA: Wadsworth/Thomson Learning, 2004), p. 4.

10. B. Engler, *Personality Theories: An Introduction*, 6th ed. (Boston: Houghton Mifflin Co., 2003), p. 2.

11. J. M. Berger, *Personality*, 6th ed. (Belmont, CA: Wadsworth/Thomson Learning, 2004). For a cogent discussion of the stability of traits in different situations, see pp. 183–92.

12. R. R. McCrae and P. T. Costa, "Toward a New Generation of Personality Theories: Theoretical Contexts for the Five-Factor Model," in *The Five-Factor Model of Personality: Theoretical Perspectives*, ed. Jerry S. Wiggins (New York: Guilford, 1996), p. 55.

13. R. M. Ryckman, *Theories of Personality*, 7th ed. (Belmont, CA: Wadsworth, 2000), pp. 305–308.

14. C. R. Potkay and B. P. Allen, *Personality: Theory, Research, and Applications* (Monterey, CA: Brooks/Cole Publishing, 1986), p. 7.

15. M. Rokeach, *The Open and Closed Mind* (New York: Basic Books, 1960), pp. 413–15. The final version of Rokeach's Dogmatism Scale (known

as the D Scale), Form E is presented in full in *The Open and Closed Mind*. Each statement is a protrait item, meaning it only measures dogmatism; there are no contrait items such as, for example, "I try to guard against jumping to conclusions about new ideas." The forty statements are rated on a six-option, Likert-type scale, which ranges through "I agree a little," "I agree on the whole," "I agree very much," "I disagree a little," "I disagree on the whole," and "I disagree very much."

16. I was among the many graduate students who used the D Scale in my master's thesis, and I obtained results statistically significant in the opposite direction to that which I hypothesized. My conclusions, like Altemeyer's, were that serious problems in the design of the D Scale rendered research findings meaningless. That humbling experience caused me to refocus on the validity of the scale and improve upon its design in my doctoral dissertation. Increasing awareness of problems inherent in the D Scale undoubtedly accounts for the earlier tide of more than one thousand research studies being reduced to a comparative dribble of publications over the last twenty years or so.

17. R. Altemeyer, *The Authoritarian Specter* (Cambridge, MA: Harvard University Press, 1996), p. 214.

18. Ibid., p. 214. *Yea-saying* refers to the respondent's tendency to detect unidirectional wording that reveals what the scale measures and then consistently slant his or her answers in the most socially desirable direction. Tests that include bipolar items (protrait and contrait statements) and fillers (statements unrelated to the construct being measured) increase the scale's validity and reliability.

19. J. Johnson, "The Johnson Dogmatism Scale: Rokeach Revisited and Revised," unpublished dissertation, Walden University, Minneapolis, MN, 1987.

20. Altemeyer, *The Authoritarian Specter*, pp. 192–201.

21. Ibid., pp. 201–208. In these pages, Altemeyer presents his Dogmatism Scale under the heading "An Alternate Conceptualization of Dogmatism." Interestingly, in a more recent book by B. E. Hunsberger and B. Altemeyer, *Atheists: A Groundbreaking Study of America's Nonbelievers* (Amherst, NY: Prometheus Books, 2006), there is no reference to Altemeyer's earlier DOG Scale (Doggone Old Gnu Scale); here, it is referred to simply as the DOG Scale.

22. Altemeyer, *The Authoritarian Specter*, p. 201.

23. Hunsberger and Altemeyer, *Atheists*, p. 59.

24. J. J. Ray, an Australian psychologist, developed a "Short, Balanced F Scale" that has its own problems with validity, and Glenn D. Wilson, from

the United Kingdom, developed a C Scale in 1968 to measure conservative beliefs of Londoners—a scale that, according to Altemeyer, also lacks internal consistency. For a good review of scales designed to assess authoritarianism and rigidity prior to 1983, see J. J. Ray, "The Behavioral Validity of Some Recent Measures of Authoritarianism," *Journal of Social Psychology* 120 (1983): 91–99.

25. Altemeyer, *The Authoritarian Specter*, p. 205. All of Altemeyer's surveys and questionnaires are published in *The Authoritarian Specter*.

26. Rokeach, *The Open and Closed Mind*, p. 79.

27. Altemeyer, *The Authoritarian Specter*, p. 205.

28. Johnson, "The Johnson Dogmatism Scale." The numerous problems of the D Scale are addressed in my unpublished doctoral dissertation, "The Johnson Dogmatism Scale." Robert MacIntyre, my dissertation supervisor at the University of Toronto, provided helpful suggestions for this revised scale.

29. Altemeyer, *The Authoritarian Specter*, p. 215.

30. P. Schultz and A. Searleman, "Rigidity of Thought and Behavior: 100 Years of Research," *Genetic, Social and General Psychology Monographs* 128, no. 2 (2002): 165–209. A summary of research on intolerance of ambiguity concludes that "the research literature on rigidity and intolerance of ambiguity are so closely related that, quite often, the two constructs are treated as synonymous" (p. 170). The emergent properties of an intolerance of ambiguity are elaborated in chapter 5.

31. A. W. Kruglanski, D. M. Webster, and A. Klem, "Motivated Resistance and Openness to Persuasion in the Presence or Absence of Prior Information," *Journal of Personality and Social Psychology* 65, no. 5 (1993): 861–76. The personality trait, need for closure, and corresponding Need for Closure Scale assesses "individual differences in preferences for order and structure and the abhorrence of disorder and chaos" (in Schultz and Searleman, "Rigidity of Thought and Behavior," p. 170). The scale purportedly measures five correlated subsets, two of which appear to be synonymous with one characteristic of dogmatism—intolerance of ambiguity and closed-mindedness (the other three characteristics are decisiveness, preference for structure, and predictability).

32. S. L. Neuberg and J. T. Newsom, "Personal Need for Structure: Individual Differences in the Desire for Simple Structure," *Journal of Personality and Social Psychology* 65, no. 1 (1993): 113–31. The authors suggest that "people meaningfully differ in the extent to which they are disposition-

ally motivated to structure their worlds in simple and unambiguous ways" (p. 114). High scores on this personality disposition are correlated with several psychological tendencies outlined in a summary of research that supports the discriminant validity of the Personal Need for Structure Scale (p. 21). Schaller, Yohannes, and O'Brien note that "people high in PNS tended to engage in simplistic reasoning strategies and formed erroneous stereotypes" ("The Prejudiced Personality Revisited: Personal Need for Structure and Formation of Erroneous Group Stereotypes," *Journal of Personality and Social Psychology* 68, no. 3 [1995]: 552).

33. Schultz and Searleman, "Rigidity of Thought and Behavior." These authors state that "no universally acknowledged and accepted ways to measure [rigidity] exist," despite the existence of over forty-seven measures of rigidity.

34. Altemeyer, *The Authoritarian Specter*, pp. 158–59. This scale consists of twenty-eight items; half are protrait (measuring the religious trait) and half are contrait, such as, "No single book of religious writings contains all the important truths about life" (p. 158). In *Atheists*, Bruce Hunsberger and Bob Altemeyer defines *fundamentalism* as "the belief that there is one set of religious teachings that clearly contains the fundamental, basic, intrinsic, essential, inerrant truth about humanity and deity; that this essential truth is fundamentally opposed by forces of evil which must be vigorously fought; that this truth must be followed today according to the fundamental, unchangeable practices of the past; and that those who believe and follow these fundamental teachings have a special relationship with the deity" (p. 157).

35. Ibid., p. 206. Altemeyer found that of the twenty-nine university students who scored high on the Attitude Toward Homosexuals scale (ATH), all ranked in the top quartile of his DOG Scale after receiving a lecture on the fetal androgenization theory of homosexuality. As Altemeyer notes, "People who believe homosexuals have chosen by free will to be sexually attracted to their own gender have, it seems to me, a lot of findings to explain away. If they cannot do so but still insist they are right, that smacks of dogmatism to me" (p. 207).

36. Ibid., pp. 209–10. In an attempt to measure zealousness, Altemeyer asked how fired up people were about whatever they believed in most. "How enthused were they about their beliefs; their causes? Were they consumed by them? Did disagreement anger them? Did they have the solution to all our problems? Did they proselytize? In short, were they zealots?" (p. 209). Altemeyer's research on the Zealot Scale provides further validity for his DOG Scale.

Chapter 4

SCARRING THE FACE OF REASON

Influential Factors That Shape Adult Dogmatism

The deepest principle in human nature is the craving to be appreciated.

William James (1842–1910)

If the human potential for intellectual growth, creative expression, and personal challenge is universal, why is it that some of us are motivated to climb mountains while others find it difficult to climb out of bed in the morning? Various theories present the underlying mechanisms of human motivation, including the defense and expansion of the self,[1] the fear of failure and need for achievement,[2] survival in the face of death,[3] and psychological needs for belonging, competence and autonomy.[4] These motivations vary considerably among individuals, but each is intrinsic to psychological functioning. If anxiety, which accompanies all of these motivations to some extent, is excessive and prolonged, it promotes defensive strategies that inhibit psychological growth.[5] "People so often stop growing and even actively resist change because they cling to the conceptions of the world and themselves that provided them maximum safety and security. . . . This conflict between the human potentials for creativity and fear lies at the heart of what many refer to as the human dilemma: immense capacity for growth and change that is often thwarted by our slavish dependence on the existing psychological structures that protect us from our fears."[6]

One such structure is dogmatism, which, in the extreme, disfigures the face of humanity. At the individual level, an arrogant swipe of its dogmatic claw scars the face of reason. With changing circumstances and the possibility of insight, these scars may fade with time, but they rarely disappear completely.

This chapter explores the unfortunate combination of early psychological events that culminate in a persistent, closed-minded approach to the world of ideas. We will examine four psychological conditions that occur as a consequence of complex biological, psychological, social, and cultural circumstances that write the program for the psychological software of dogmatism.

FOUR PSYCHOLOGICAL PILLARS OF DOGMATISM

We might speculate that, against a backdrop of biological and sociocultural conditions, four pivotal experiences shape the foundation of dogmatism and subsequently scaffold thirteen of its unique characteristics. We will first familiarize ourselves with these underlying psychological conditions, then examine the characteristics that sustain it in chapters 5, 6, and 7.

The Need to Know

Rokeach used the term *need to know* to describe an innate human striving.[7] Dogmatism is incubated when this first of four psychological necessities becomes frustrated throughout infancy, childhood, and adolescence. Humans have an inherent desire to fully engage in self-determined interests and expand their knowledge about themselves, others, and the surrounding environment. Before our first birthday, fulfillment of this need depended on our ability to apply our hardwired curiosity and language skills in order to understand and successfully adjust to the newness of our existence.[8] This adaptive, autonomous adjustment and personal growth is so crucial to our well-being that, in adulthood, intimate relationships often dissolve when one partner interferes with or tries to control the other partner's need for intellectual growth and self-expansion.

Unlike adults, infants are dependent on others to help them organize and interpret events so that they can formulate an integrated picture of their personal and social world. As such, their early beliefs quite literally reflect the views of their main caregivers, who are responsible for satisfying their quest for knowledge and understanding. Throughout infancy and childhood, curiosity and the pursuit of knowledge are optimized if individuals are encouraged and rewarded for asking questions and solving problems.

Others are not so lucky. "When one's emotional security is highly dependent on the approval of others or when one lacks emotional security because one's self-esteem or worldview is undermined in some way, one is unable to integrate new information in an open and unbiased manner. Rather, the integrative processing is biased toward either pleasing those on whom one is dependent or maintaining the existing organization on which one has been relying for protection."[9]

Uninformed or inadequate parenting, however, is not the only disruptive agent of early cognitive development. Independent thinking is also discouraged in homogeneous, isolated cultures that prevent open discussions of ideas. One recent example is the Mormon arch-polygamist Warren Jeffs, who used methods of indoctrination and punishment to bend vulnerable minds. Similarly, children of the Taliban are raised with narrowly circumscribed ideas and limited social exposure that prevents open-minded considerations of alternative views. Finally, peer pressure is a powerful motivator of human behavior, and children whose parents restrict their socialization to "the right kind" guarantee that peer pressure will further consolidate their own parental beliefs. Under these conditions, curiosity is prematurely hijacked and constricted by anxiety, rigid indoctrination, and limited social and cognitive exposure.

Conversely, youngsters who feel they can safely investigate multiple viewpoints (as much as age-appropriate skills allow) will learn to gradually integrate differences of opinion. These skills are in sharp contrast with those who habitually dismiss ideas as wrongheaded or threatening simply because they have learned to reject ideas that conflict with their own narrow-minded certainty.

The Need to Defend against Anxiety

The single most damaging impediment to innate curiosity and the need to know is the need to defend against unremitting anxiety. Research in child development demonstrates that persistent anxiety, which stems from childhood neglect, abuse, oppression, and poverty, obstructs creative, open-minded thought and jeopardizes emotional and social resilience.[10] This is especially the case with children who are genetically predisposed to higher-than-average levels of anxiety at birth, who then encounter unsupportive or hostile environments. Emotionally vulnerable children raised by punitive or negligent parents redirect energy that otherwise would have been available for healthier pursuits to the control of persistent anxiety.

Anxiety and fear are primal reactions to unpredictable, threatening environments. Originally, anxiety is felt as a subjective experience that can be triggered by repetitive, ruminative thoughts, such as the belief that danger is always lurking about. This belief and response need not be catastrophic: "the degree of intensity is not the issue; it is a *qualitative* experience."[11] Children who experience prolonged, uncontrollable, unpleasant or aversive events respond with anxiety that fosters expectations of helplessness and hopelessness—symptoms that also increase their vulnerability for clinical depression.[12] Childhood experiences, arousal levels, and appraisal processes create feedback mechanisms that groove patterns of cognition and emotion, and while optimum emotional arousal enhances learning, emotional distress clearly disrupts it.

§§

Anxiety inevitably parallels the child's need to know, and even the most optimal care is insufficient to protect against normal childhood feelings of doubt and insecurity. At optimum levels, anxiety motivates children to defend themselves against the distress of being physically small, helpless, and dependent on others in a bewildering world.[13] When we add to inevitable anxiety children's language deficits and rudimentary attempts at problem solving, even psychologically healthy youngsters raised in loving, encouraging environments discover that their fledgling lives are often stressful. Because infants and young children cannot understand and articulate distress that arises from perceptions of immanent danger, it is easy for adults to overlook mild anxiety that nonetheless triggers physiological responses in the child's autonomic nervous system. Fortunately, many youngsters have the psychological resilience to manage their stress without detrimental consequences.

Less fortunate are children plagued with persistent anxiety, fear, and self-doubt. They experience increased heart rate, perspiration, and muscle tension that can cause sleep and gastrointestinal disturbances. Youngsters who live in threatening, incomprehensible environments cannot independently cope with their frightening feelings, which play a prominent role in the configuration of their emotional, cognitive, and personality development. For them, learning to bury their anxiety and fear becomes adaptive. They "typically control anxiety by clinging to their conceptions of self, others, and their world. Such clinging is, of course, antithetical to the integrative processing of new information and experiences through which growth occurs."[14] Children who anticipate criticism when they open their minds to question beliefs soon stifle their innate motivation to expand curiosity, knowledge, and social contacts. Thus, their biological need to know becomes insidiously crippled by the competing need to control excess anxiety, and this effort eventually impairs cognitive performance. In school-age children, anxiety that is amplified to intense fear causes severe heart palpitations, dizziness, feelings of unreality, choking, and trembling; for some, going to school triggers symptoms that accompany panic attacks and specific phobias.

Compounding the problem is a biological predisposition for heightened levels of anxiety. There is an obvious nature-nurture interaction here, and psychologists do not yet know the extent to which a biological predisposition for anxiety, early experiences, and social learning independently contribute to a lifetime of anxious temperament. Nor do they know the specific causes of anticipatory anxiety and pessimistic thoughts that block one's potential for open-minded reasoning. What psychologists do know is that individuals who allow their minds to freely and creatively take flight are generally unencumbered by excess anxiety.[15]

Studies on the impact of social and emotional learning on cognitive development substantiate the claim that youngsters who are deprived of adequate nurturing do not flourish socially and intellectually. Inadequate social learning further intensifies anxiety, impairs children's need to know, and increases their need to defend against anxiety. "The vast majority of childhood anxiety and fear is learned,"[16] and the corrosive effects of these socially learned emotions undermine children's first necessity—the need to know. Children raised in frightening, unstable social environments fly solo in their navigation of social relationships, a flight so fraught with anxiety that it stunts confidence in emotional, social, and academic learning. These children become less willing to take risks; more impatient with (and therefore less discerning of) their small, incremental achievements; less able to understand their feelings; and less capable of thinking clearly in order to solve problems and successfully relate to others.

A vicious cycle is thus set in motion. The more children lose confidence in their ability to understand the world and their place in it, the more anxious they become, which further undermines their information processing and self-reliance. By the time they reach adolescence, cognitive narrowing prevents their integration of knowledge such that new information is largely processed and primarily understood at basic, concrete levels. As a result, they are unable or unwilling to search for inconsistencies among various concepts and ideas, and they do not engage in deeper analyses that might shatter self-protective truths, which they anxiously and blindly adopt. Unquestioning endorsement of external belief systems now impedes an open-minded search for understanding, even in safe learning environments where testing out new experiences is fully encouraged and supported.

Children of domineering parents who impose arbitrary rules, who criticize, ridicule, threaten, and inflict ruthless discipline and physical abuse, leave the child feeling shameful and unwanted.[17] These control tactics cause anxiety that short-circuits a child's inquisitiveness, imagination, and sense of autonomy. A developing brain that continuously divests more energy in neutralizing emotions is a compromised brain that abandons curiosity and independent reasoning. Consequently, the child learns that it is safer to rely on hand-me-down beliefs from authority figures—a problem that we will address in greater detail in subsequent chapters.

§§

Beyond stunted cognitive, emotional, and social growth, childhood anxiety shoulders another, equally damaging fate. When children learn that it is unsafe to think for themselves, their emerging self-doubt suffocates the potential for a healthy, autonomous identity—a consistent self-description that is based on the knowledge of who one is. This type of self-knowledge differs from self-esteem, which answers the question, "Am I a worthy person?" Youngsters can become so psychologically fragmented that, by adolescence, the core of their existence is hollowed out and their personal agency is severely undermined. Not knowing who they are or what they are in the process of becoming, they are frozen in a place they do not want to be, and being in this insecure place robs them of creative thought and the capacity to create a genuine, identifiable self.

When one's identity becomes externally authored by someone

who has been given the power to define one's self, then self-reliance is also shattered and one becomes vulnerable to adopting, without question, externally imposed beliefs. Having abandoned the power of reason, such people cannot explain how they derived their beliefs and developed their worldviews. Without an internalized, trustworthy identity that makes independent decisions, they feel self-estranged, incongruent, and vulnerable. They may cope by desperately effecting an image they hope will define them—a dramatized, inauthentic self whose rigid beliefs are a smokescreen for personal inadequacies. When things go wrong, those who act according to external agendas tend to blame others. Why should they take responsibility for beliefs and behaviors that are other-motivated?

§§

Unlike anxiety and fear, which dampen the intrinsic motivation to expand one's curiosity and knowledge, positive emotions stimulate interest and facilitate integrative learning. Constructive emotions allow full absorption in challenging activities that one feels competent to master, and this successful, *self-directed* exploration reinforces the motivation to expand one's repertoire of experience. This process of engagement stimulates further interest in synthesizing new information. But "anxiety must be effectively managed in order for intrinsically motivated, integrative activities to be pursued."[18] Such anxiety management facilitates the development of authentic identity, and while these individuals would likely agree that "our identity is never as fixed as we think it should be,"[19] their self-acceptance allows them to be more consistent, genuine, open, honest, and spontaneous. Resting on an authentic bedrock of autonomy that stems from intrinsically motivated thoughts and behaviors, they are not controlled by the whims of external fads, fashions, and ideologies. They tend to be more discerning and confident in their choice of relationships, ideological alignments, careers, and hobbies, even if their choices are not mainstream. Because open-mindedness is always at risk for narrowing—a shift that is as imperceptible as sprinting that slips back to walking—the clearer one's authenticity, the less likely such slippage will occur. We will revisit the psychology of authenticity in chapter 14.

Rokeach's assumptions about the psychological causes of dogmatism were consonant with the prevailing Freudian orthodoxy that viewed all psychological disturbance as a consequence of excess anxiety. Post-Freudians and psychologists across diverse fields of specialization also acknowledge the centrality of anxiety in psychological problems. In particular, cognitive-behavioral psychologists consider faulty thinking to be the major source of anxiety, while humanistic and existential psychologists view anxiety as the inevitable consequence of freedom and responsibility.

According to Freud, the neo-Freudians, and Rokeach, many people who lack personal insight believe that if they ignore objectionable, anxiety-provoking aspects of themselves, those aspects will miraculously disappear. Such individuals are referred to as *neurotic*. Although the term *neurotic* is infrequently used by contemporary psychologists, most are still inclined to the view that unwanted thoughts, feelings, and actions that are repeatedly ignored will not go away but will instead grow—within oneself and within clear view of others. Perhaps this explains the course of dogmatism: Don't worry; be dogmatic.

§§

"Anxiety is the dizziness of freedom," wrote Soren Kierkegaard in the mid-1800s.[20] A century later, Erich Fromm stated that freedom comes with a burdensome price tag: it requires us to make decisions for which we are obliged to take responsibility. This yoking of freedom and choice to responsibility tempts us to grant authority figures too much unconditional power. "It is the existence within our own personal attitudes and within our own institutions of conditions which have given a victory to external authority. The battlefield is also accordingly here—within ourselves and our institutions."[21] And when that inner battlefield is dominated by fear and anxiety, freedom loses its value. "Better authority with security than freedom with fear."[22]

Those of us who lack the ability or courage to confront the source of our anguish rely on defense mechanisms—strategies that deny or distort reality so that we do not have to confront unacceptable aspects of ourselves or threats from the external world. Attempts to control anxiety by blocking our awareness of it and rechanneling its energy into compensatory thoughts and behaviors helps us avoid such unpleasant conflict, anxiety, and dread.[23] To illustrate, the defense mechanism known as *projection* allows us to see our own objectionable thoughts, feelings, and behaviors in others while effectively hiding them from ourselves. It is simply easier to project aggressive feelings onto someone else, who we label ill-tempered and hostile, and preserve our self-image of being kind, considerate, and even-tempered. Or, rather than feel anxious about our unacceptable behavior, we make plausible excuses and rationalize that what we did is now justifiable. A student who does poorly on an exam because she spent the weekend partying instead of studying does not want to acknowledge her irresponsible behavior, so she blames the teacher for giving an unfair test.

Regression, another defense mechanism, is seen in the return to childlike behavior, as evidenced by a woman who feels anxious because she fears her partner's attention to an attractive party guest means he will soon reject her. Instead of acknowledging the source of her anxiety, she converts it to hostile indignation and a tirade of verbal assaults that ends with her labeling him "an insensitive moron!" *Reaction formation*, another shield for anxiety, is seen in a politician who converts his unconscious urges for sexual exploitation into a campaign of sanctimonious acrimony against anyone who engages in behavior that reflects his own repressed desires. In all of these situations, anxiety is smothered with thoughts, feelings, and behaviors that camouflage its source. Rather than acknowledge and responsibly confront the anxiety that underlies these inappropriate reactions, we think and act in ways that counteract our genuine thoughts and feelings.

For the dogmatist, these defense mechanisms are legion, as

Rokeach noted in his brief section on the causes of dogmatism: "The more closed the belief-disbelief system, the more do we conceive it to represent, in its totality, a tightly woven network of cognitive defenses against anxiety. . . . Indeed, we suggest that, in the extreme, the closed system is nothing more than the total network of psychoanalytic defense mechanisms organized together to form a cognitive system and designed to shield a vulnerable mind."[24] In this sense, dogmatism is a personality trait that reflects a protective pattern of defenses that are anything but fleeting.

But when does the use of defense mechanisms become problematic or abnormal? We all have blind spots about our genuine motives, and the occasional use of defense mechanisms might provide necessary shelter against full awareness of undesirable thoughts and wishes—awareness that would make us feel anxious or guilty. Psychologists maintain that these defenses become problematic when used *habitually* as a means of coping with persistent anxiety, for if they become patterns of avoidance, they diminish an individual's capacity to know what is real within oneself and within one's immediate world.

Those of us who have not lived with persistent anxiety about who we are, where we are going, or why we feel insignificant in the eyes of others, cannot fully grasp the depth of such suffering. It is understandable that people who feel unable to break free of relentless anxiety caused by self-doubt, worthlessness, shame, or social marginalization may rely excessively on defense mechanisms. Some may choose alcohol or drugs as a convenient escape; others become depressed, paranoid, or hostile. Still others become dogmatic—a strategy that, from the dogmatist's perspective, is the solution to mental anguish. For dogmatists, anxiety becomes barricaded behind walls of truth that give the illusion of absolute knowledge, safety from ignorance, and the promise of social acceptance, respect, and dignity. Yet, in their search for protection against anxiety, they create the very monster that ends up intensifying it. People hardly feel safe when, at some level of awareness, they sense that their cognitive rigidity has deprived them of integrity and meaningful social connection.

§§

These are the dogmatists who surrender their autonomy and freedom to authoritarian rule that structures their lives. It is easy to see how an authoritarian leader's clever manipulation of words could subdue anxiety and instill new beliefs and loyalties in vulnerable minds— necessary conditions that give fanatical movements their momentum. And if anxious adults are vulnerable to submission, then anxious, confused adolescents are even more vulnerable. Prolonged, excessive anxiety and the inexperience of youth increase the need for someone or something to assuage self-doubt and insecurity. By the time these youngsters reach adulthood, some have been so indoctrinated and rewarded for blind allegiance to externally imposed beliefs that dogmatism has emerged as a fixed solution to unfulfilled psychological needs.

Interference with children's need to know and persistent anxiety are Rokeach's two proposed causes of dogmatism, and while these are key contributing factors, they do not go far enough. Research documents the connection between impaired social relationships and cognitive disorganization, and there is good reason to assume that a lack of nurturing social relationships in childhood significantly contributes to the latent development of adult dogmatism. Ideological loyalty symbolizes safety that is rewarded with social recognition and dignity. To challenge cherished ideological principles would show disgraceful disloyalty, a compounding belief that subordinates cognitive processing to the saving grace of dogma. Loyalty to such provides not only a cognitive fix that relieves anxiety, but also a social fix that relieves alienation. Like drugs to an addict, one's acceptance of unadulterated truth injects a steady high of serene confidence and belonging. But the cost of this psychological dependency is a compromised mind, the damage to which we investigate in chapter 5. We now explore the third psychological deficiency that predisposes one to latent dogmatism.

The Need for Social Connection

The fulfillment of children's need to know and their successful defense against anxiety are necessary preconditions for this third innate need, which, if unfulfilled, increases one's vulnerability to adult dogmatism.

Psychologists agree that the gratification of social needs is a prerequisite for optimum psychological growth. "There is no question that we are programmed to seek out the company of peers."[25] Studies in the emerging field of neuroscience conclude that our brains are designed to engage others and forge relationships that satisfy this biological predisposition. Social relationships are not only necessary for early survival, they help us gauge whether we are acceptable to others and whether we are worthy of assistance in our own time of need. They provide reference points for establishing personal and collective identity, and our human capacity for conscious reflection about the quality of these relationships enables us to gratify inherent social needs. Comparisons of our unique characteristics with those of our reference groups are central to the development of self-esteem, identity, and our sense of worth.[26] Throughout this comparative process, we construct our life stories: "To know a person really well is to know a person's story—that self-defining narrative of the reconstructed past, perceived present, and anticipated future. This sense of identity is, or should be, at the heart of personality."[27] Our social connections sculpt a big chunk of that identity, which shapes our personality and all of its attendant traits. Healthy relationships also activate T-cells that kill invading bacteria, "while toxic ones can act like slow poison in our bodies."[28]

"The development of cognition is grounded in social relationships."[29] Social anxiety interferes with optimum cognitive processing and hinders the development of nuanced social tuning. Anxious individuals tend to lack this social skill that, among other things, enables us to tune into people's thoughts and emotions.[30] "Attunement is attention that goes beyond momentary empathy to a full, sustained presence that facilitates rapport. We offer a person our total attention and listen fully."[31] This communicates a genuine desire to fully understand and resonate with another—a desire that cannot be fulfilled when we are anxiously self-focused or too self-conscious to effectively initiate and maintain social contact. People who lack healthy social connections experience a host of unwelcome, confusing thoughts and emotions that impair their identity formation, their ongoing social interactions, and their sense of dignity. You may have noticed that chronically anxious people find it difficult to approach others and maintain a quality of contact that allows them to explore a topic without worrying how others are evaluating them. In close relationships, this inability to wholly attune and connect is a major impediment to intimacy.

To illustrate the universal need for social relationships, imagine yourself recording every thought you have from the time you wake up until bedtime, when you drift into the arms of Morpheus. Most of your mental meanderings would involve "a sea of social thoughts."[32] Echoing Gazzaniga's sentiments, the biologist Humberto Maturana stated that we only have the world we socially create. As social animals, "the world everyone sees is not *the* world but a world which we bring forth with others. . . . Without love, without acceptance of others, there is no social phenomenon."[33] Children who are deprived of loving social relationships lack an inner, psychological harbor that enables them to confidently open their minds as they explore the larger social world.

Emotionally and socially impoverished youngsters who also live in high-risk neighborhoods that provide little in the way of community services to assist them in their struggles are dealt a second painful blow. Governments that inadequately fund agencies that could intervene in family abuse and violence, or that fail to provide support for stressed, poverty-ridden parents, perpetuate a cycle of destabilized psychological functioning in children and their parents. Alienated from nurturing social relationships, these youngsters become fearful and distrusting of authority figures—fears that generalize to a range of other adults and situations.[34] When these psychosocial circumstances combine with a child's biological predisposition for anxiety, they cause biochemical imbalances in brain structures. The neurochemistry of anxiety and fear damages brain structures that have not reached full maturity and further impede the child's ability to cognitively process events.[35] Chapter 10 investigates these claims more fully, but for now we will simply note that biological and environmental circumstances that intensify anxiety narrow the channels of adaptive reasoning in childhood and adolescence. As such, they are seriously implicated in latent dogmatism. Indeed, we might consider anxiety that stems from prolonged stress as the preeminent contributor to latent dogmatism.

§§

So profound is our need to socially connect that the founder of psychology, William James, considered prolonged social isolation and rejection worse than torture.[36] The suffering from social disconnection was well portrayed in the movie *Castaway*, in which Chuck Noland (played by Tom Hanks) becomes stranded on an uninhabited island, literally cast adrift from others. Viewers can empathize with his psychosocial loss of human contact and understand why he befriends Wilson, an anthropomorphized soccer ball that assuages his desperate need for human contact.

Our sense of social identity keeps us sane and gives us what Erich Fromm called a "frame of orientation" that gives life meaning.[37] This need for social connection, recognition, status, and approval is largely fulfilled by social evaluations that begin during infancy and extend throughout the life span. Without social ties, we are vulnerable to symptoms of mental illness that are seen in anxiety disorders, unipolar and bipolar disorders, drug and alcohol dependence, and personality disorders.

Each of the reference groups that family, social institutions, and society in general provide holds the promise of identity and status within the group. Personal identity—your sense of who you are—is primarily rooted in social relationships. It runs deep. How readily would you change your religion, your political affiliation, or your national identity?

Dogmatists may compensate for unfulfilled social connections and fragmented identities by searching for something or someone to gratify their unfulfilled needs. Especially in times of psychosocial instability, anxious, alienated individuals are drawn to groups that offer personal identity and social opportunity—reinforcements that are powerful enough to elicit unquestioning loyalty.[38] Their devotion is not based on a careful assessment of group ideology; rather, it fulfills innate social needs. Even when group objectives are not in one's best interests, if membership assuages suffering that originated in early social disconnection, belonging becomes the palliative glue that mends social alienation, promotes personal identity, and proffers hope for respect and dignity. Dogmatic allegiance may be seen as a solution to such angst and social alienation (though dogmatic people do not acknowledge it as such).

This brings us to our fourth psychological need that, if unfulfilled, increases one's risk for dogmatism, especially if it is accompanied by deficits in any of the three preceding needs.

The Need for Common Dignity

Personal dignity is a core psychological need, the lack of which figures prominently in dogmatism. The *Concise Oxford English Dictionary* defines dignity, a noun, as "the state or quality of being worthy of honor or respect." Wole Soyinka, the winner of the 1986 Nobel Prize in literature, states that dignity is "most meaningfully sought, not within the self as some mystic endowment, but as a product of social interaction."[39] Just as family and close relationships shape individual identity and self-esteem, social community shapes our sense of dignity, without which we feel insignificant and alienated.

"People in all cultures, whether they fully realize it or not, want to wow their neighbors, to rise in local esteem."[40] This desire to create a good impression is matched by an equal desire to avoid ridicule, indifference, or disdain. Throughout the formative years, if alienation and feelings of insignificance are relentless, individuals may be drawn to a group that ends their search for what was needed long ago. To them, group acceptance is a powerful reward that increases loyalty and conformist behavior; submission shelters their loss and grants dignity.

Research on identity and self-esteem supports the view that social relationships primarily determine our identity, whether that identity reflects a consistently integrated self or one that is somewhat fragmented.[41] As social animals, we initially allow others to evaluate and determine our sense of identity and dignity; parents and siblings act as our first social barometers for self-esteem and self-respect. Without close social ties, we fail to fulfill these psychological needs, and what follows is a decrease of social consciousness and an increase in anxiety, which are proportionate to the conviction of one's own impotence.[42] It all begins with parents who provide our earliest social experiences. They strongly influence our emerging sense of identity through gestures and comments that communicate we are loveable, smart, cute, friendly, considerate, and so on. This ongoing discourse serves a social purpose, and when social connections are damaged or severed, when we have no receptive audience for our thoughts and emotions, we have no purpose. We feel alienated not only from those around us but from our inner selves.[43] Dignity denied leaves us devoid of our basic humanity.

Feelings of estrangement can be devastating in adulthood, and their impact on youngsters is unimaginable. When infants and children are deprived of healthy social connections, they become psychologically disorganized; they fail to learn how to regulate their intense emotions and cannot effectively relate to others.[44] Sensing the shame they see in the eyes of those who criticize and dismiss them, they come to believe that "I—all of me—am a mistake." This is a profound shame that differs from the guilt children feel when they make a mistake or violate some moral code of behavior. Shamed children are unable to authentically develop broad social and cultural values that foster social acceptance, friendship, and a sense of community. In contrast, social dignity promotes confidence on the social stage, which enhances feelings of belonging and sustains the belief that one is implicitly respected by a social group or community. Such dignity provides a sturdy emotional backdrop that enhances resilience in the face of failure.

§§

If ever there were a testing ground for dignity and social status, family gatherings and high school reunions are it. They affirm our social worth and dignity. At her twenty-year high school reunion, Eileen is delighted to see that Joe, the basketball star who jilted her, is now wrinkled and bald, with the same crude sense of humor. And much to Walter's satisfaction, the popular tenth-grade cheerleader Sue, who wouldn't deign to talk to him, is now overweight and uninteresting. Chances are Joe and Sue are doing their own status survey of Eileen and Walter, and it is a safe bet that many guests are similarly comparing their own success with others, although most effectively conceal their status anxiety that stems from self-doubt about one's level of acceptable social standing.[45] Not the dogmatist. Reunions are ideal settings for proclamations of dogmatism because they symbolize ruptured social connections, lack of respect, and lost dignity.

As early as adolescence, one means to cope with the anxiety of feeling disconnected and undignified is to try to impress peers with unassailable beliefs. Because society places a high premium on intelligence and interpersonal success, the child who feels insecure at home and is socially shunned at school may seize upon facts and ideas as a means to interest and connect with others—an understandable solution for inexperienced, alienated youngsters who are left to discover for themselves how to safely learn about their world and comfortably feel part of it. But peers generally reject such bold attempts from a "know-it-all," which only intensifies the budding dogmatist's need to further perfect truths that he believes will serve as protection against anxiety and social rejection. Some become so anxiously preoccupied with rejection that age-appropriate development of autonomous ideas and an ability to understand themselves and others become seriously compromised. Many are developmentally arrested at an earlier age of longing. Vulnerable to peer pressure, those who readily acquiesce may mistakenly believe that submission and conformity will yield the connection, acceptance, and dignity they desperately seek.[46] We are not referring here to normal childhood and adolescent conformity, but to extreme conformity that stems from serious psychological deficits in any or all of the four basic needs. By the time these deprived adolescents reach adulthood, their central beliefs have become calcified certainties under which layers of emotional and social debris are buried.

Rokeach maintained that people "will be open to information *insofar as possible,* and reject it, screen it out, or alter it *insofar as necessary.* In other words, no matter how much a person's system closes up to ward off threat and anxiety, it can still serve as a cognitive framework for satisfying one's need to know. . . . One can distort the world and narrow it down to whatever extent necessary, but at the same time preserve the illusion of understanding it."[47] As the need to defend against anxiety increases, the need to know diminishes, and one's mind becomes incrementally closed to different views—all in the unarticulated hope that rigid adherence to beliefs or a cause will secure connection, respect, and dignity.

The danger is that these individuals can be seduced by venal leaders who reach deep into the channels of their psychological vulnerability. A group that offers newfound belonging, identity, and integrity provides welcome relief to those who feel socially adrift, aimless, incompetent, and marginalized,[48] yet the ideology and goals of dogmatic, charismatic leaders are antithetical to their conscientious choice and authentic psychological growth. Their quest for dignity becomes "one of the most propulsive elements for wars, civil strife, and willing sacrifice."[49] Dignity deprivation and its associated anxiety can be so painful, some people optimistically conclude that if they cannot secure social connection and recognition in this world, they will do whatever it takes to secure it in the next—a single-minded pursuit that fuels at least one variant of religious dogmatism. The variant that comes to mind is the one responsible for the terrorism of September 11, 2001—the type that Osama Bin Laden is believed to possess.

Inadequate access to jobs and social services, particularly healthcare and education, deny people a share in the wealth of society, which leaves them disenfranchised and marginalized, both economically and socially.[50] Governments that claim to be democratic yet do not seriously address systemic poverty promote a spectrum of cognitive, emotional, behavioral, and interpersonal difficulties.[51] Thoughts of worthlessness generate anxiety and anger, which fuels revenge and empowers social, political, and military groups. As the gulf between the socially marginalized and the wealthy increases, the situation becomes ripe for a dogmatic authoritarian leader to offer simplistic solutions that further deepen the gulf on both sides and fan the smoldering psychological deficiencies that ignite dogmatism.

When the Reverend Sun Myung Moon of the Unification Church matched and declared engaged 1,410 "Moonies," whom he later married in a mass wedding at Madison Square Garden on June 13, 1998, the brides and grooms complied with his bizarre control—a testament to the strong need for social connection and dignity. Were the marrying Moonies so socially and emotionally deprived that they abdicated their reasoning and responsibility to a supreme, all-knowing father figure whose fanciful beliefs they honored without question? Not knowing individual motivations, it is risky to make sweeping generalizations, but quite possibly members unreflectively adopted the Unification Church's orthodoxy and rituals because they felt guaranteed of permanent social connection and dignity that compensated for early deprivations.

LUCY AND JEROME: NARRATIVES OF DEPRIVED NEEDS

Lucy's early childhood experiences illustrate the consequences of anxiety, failed social connection, and lost dignity, all of which arrested her intellectual potential and made her vulnerable to latent dogmatism. As a bright four-year-old, Lucy exuded curiosity. Her mother exuded impatience. When Lucy asked questions to resolve confusion or doubt, her mother interrupted her lively inquisitiveness: "Give it a rest, Lucy. I already answered you. Don't argue! Why do you have to ask so many questions?" When Lucy became frustrated with such inadequate answers, she was warned, "Watch your mouth when you're talking to me!"

Lucy did not articulate it as such, but she soon learned that to question was to risk. At home, it was safer to keep her thoughts private. Yet all the while Lucy observed her mother seemingly get what she wanted by dominating others. On that bit of home schooling, Lucy got an A+. Mistakenly, she believed that her mother's intimidation tactics would give her a measure of control, power, and dignity in the eyes of her classmates. She would use these tactics to prove she was the brightest student in the class—one who deserved respect. In pursuit of that goal, Lucy became skilled at wearing down her opponents. In the many arguments she initiated, she mimicked her mother's condescending, dismissive tone of authority that insinuated superiority, though this behavior imitation only intensified her feelings of alienation. Little did Lucy know that with repeated practice at being superior, her beliefs, emotions, and behaviors would become strongly entrenched in brain circuits that defined her reality and shaped her personality—including the embryonic trait of dogmatism.[52] By adulthood, her protective childhood narratives had become crystallized in dogmatic belief.

§§

Consider too, the case of Jerome, an eight-year-old who has mild dyslexia. He reads with great difficulty and senses his parents' impatience with his slow progress. Jerome gets anxious and physically withdraws when his parents insinuate that he is lazy. For him, reading has become associated with criticism, and his chronic anxiety around school work now limits his expression of (not potential for) intelligent thought. Subconsciously, Jerome has developed an array of protective strategies that "form a cognitive system designed to shield a vulnerable mind."[53]

This cognitive system, based on an unequal interplay of a need to know and a need to defend against anxiety, frequently and inescapably steers Jerome toward a closed-minded approach to learning. Lacking corrective experiences that would counter his habitual thoughts and feelings, Jerome's capacity for open-minded, psychological insight becomes locked out, allowing closed-minded, dogmatic belief systems to move in. His beliefs become implicitly valued and habitually ingrained because they cushion anxiety and provide an illusory sense of control in a threatening environment.

It is quite possible that by the time Jerome reaches adulthood, his curiosity and interest in acquiring knowledge will have long since faded. Early anxiety and coping strategies that restricted his range of openness to new ideas have prevented him from reaching more sophisticated levels of cognitive processing in adulthood, thus increasing his vulnerability to dogmatism. Equally transparent will be Jerome's difficult emotional adjustment. Many of his co-workers will notice how his psychological insecurities are flagged by emotions that not only constrain his thinking but also deaden spontaneity and undermine his relationships.

§§

Very young children who are handicapped by harsh parental treatment may seek peers who provide some measure of compensation for their loss. Yet it is difficult for the emotionally disabled child to establish comfortable connections if earlier social relationships failed to provide a secure platform on which to build respectful, cooperative, friendships. Like Lucy and Jerome, these children develop a style of thinking that is an adaptive response to an unfriendly, critical, or hostile environment. "For all practical purposes, cognitive style is usually described as a personality dimension influencing attitudes, values and social interaction."[54] A cognitive style borne out of pressing psychological needs to keep anxiety at bay and preserve one's illusion of knowledge and safety consistently distorts one's view of self and others. These distortions crack the foundation of reason, and without skillful intervention, the unwelcome weeds of dogmatism move in to choke flexible, open-minded pursuits of knowledge.

From their perspective, these children are doing the best they can to resolve their psychological difficulties. Unfortunately, those who close their minds and shelter their experiences behind airtight belief systems resort to coping strategies that may later become consolidated in the trait of dogmatism. And traits are not temporary conditions, as we will see in chapter 11.

At this theoretical juncture, the model of vulnerability proposed here assumes that dogmatism is linked to the unsuccessful gratification of four basic psychological needs. When these needs are unfulfilled for prolonged periods of time, children and adolescents become predisposed to latent, adult dogmatism. Through trial and error, they attempt to resolve persistent anxiety with strategies that are detrimental to (1) acquiring and integrating ideas and information, (2) developing effective interpersonal relationships, and (3) gaining personal confidence that promotes socially conferred dignity. These are the strategies that gradually nourish the subtraits of adult dogmatism—psychological consequences that end up wagging the tail of the dogma.

Childhood anxiety is the mortar that eventually seals absolute truth behind heavily barricaded cognitive compartments. Insight into the developmental sequences that predispose individuals to close their minds would help them understand how their personality development was constrained by several characteristics that insidiously short-circuited reason. As adults, if they could explore how their absolute truths provide absolute certainty that guarantees absolute safety and shields them from absolute ignorance and humiliation, they might understand how black-and-white thinking, such as that reflected in this sentence, serves a necessary psychological function. Unshakable dogmatic truths camouflage the deep psychological goals in which they are embedded—goals that render their truths more delusional than factual.

I wish to dispose of the misconception that dogmatism is about ideology. Bolder still, I assume that dogmatism is primarily about identity. Externally authored identity. Fragile, brittle identity. As such, dogmatism should not be confused with greed or revenge that inspires brute force to seize power. Even though people's intentions are framed as an ideological mission to redress ethnic rivalry, poverty, or political conflict, unless their driving motive is a need to be right at all costs, dogmatism is not likely the major player. Of course, there are those who have some combination of dogmatic zeal and unabashed greed, but the dogmatists referred to in this book are primarily people whose core identity has been hollowed out, allowing the rigid, ideological structure of dogmatism to rush in to fill the vacuum. Anxiety started it, and anxiety is the intravenous feed that keeps it alive.

Chapter 1 provided a broad psychological definition of dogmatism, which bears repeating here: *Dogmatism is a personality trait that combines cognitive, emotional, and behavioral characteristics to personify prejudicial, closed-minded belief systems that are pronounced with rigid certainty.*[55] There are thirteen psychological characteristics (five cognitive, three emotional, and five behavioral) that make up this trait. You may be thinking, "Thirteen characteristics! I'm doomed!" But wait. Some of these features are in most of us some of the time, particularly in stressful situations, but few if any of us reveal the entire suite of dogmatic subtraits across many situations—the grand slam of dogmatism. Like ambiverts who have mixtures of extroversion and introversion, the majority of us have some features of open- and closed-mindedness. But even among individuals who have enough features to meet the criteria for dogmatism (six characteristics are the suggested minimum), most do not hold all of their beliefs dogmatically, all of the time. However, those who proselytize absolute truth—even if, for example, their belief system is confined to the worship (or dismissal) of an omnipotent God—are dogmatic if they meet the psychological definition of dogmatism and demonstrate a combination of six or more characteristics. Recall that a belief system is a network of related beliefs, and just as someone who has the personality trait of friendliness is friendly toward most people (including strangers), a person with the personality trait of dogmatism is closed-minded about most beliefs within or among belief systems.

We would hesitate to say that people have the personality trait of dogmatism if their rigid certainty applies to only one belief within a system, even though they clearly exhibit enough features of dogmatism to render that belief closed to question and revision. But it seems reasonable to predict psychological contagion within that system (and among others). A conservative who refuses to consider a single-payer, government-managed health insurance plan would probably hold equally firm to the idea that any other type of government-regulated administration and delivery of public services is untenable, even if evidence-based research were to demonstrate that such practices yield more effective, efficient outcomes. Likewise, dogmatic defenders of a single-payer, government-regulated healthcare insurance plan would presumably dismiss, without consideration, all proposals to privatize any segment of healthcare or other social services. This tenacity of political dogmatism is assumed to extend to religious beliefs as well as other beliefs within different systems that involve values around gender, animal rights, homosexuality, alcohol, marriage and parenting, and so on. People who cling to dogmatic beliefs in one domain likely spread their dogmatism to other domains, because doctrinaire thinking provides them relief from a variety of psychological deficiencies.

Those who lack a minimum of six characteristics around which dogmatism theoretically coheres would not fit the psychological profile for the trait. For example, someone who showed little interest in religion for fifty years but now attends a fundamentalist church and enjoys passionate, opinionated discussions about biblical scripture is not necessarily dogmatic. We will develop a clearer understanding of the essence of dogmatism in subsequent chapters, where we explore its thirteen characteristics in illustrative case studies.

EMPIRICAL IMPLICATIONS

We must be careful not to confuse *causation* (one thing directly causes another) with *correlation* (two or more things are related because they occur together). As far as we know, dogmatism is not the effect of a specific cause, so even if we suggest that dogmatism follows from a biological predisposition for anxiety, fragmented or diminished social connections, lost dignity, a combination of these factors, or other indeterminate influences, nothing yet substantiates the view that these or any other factors directly cause dogmatism. And while recent advances in behavior genetics, neuropsychology, and trait theory have enhanced our understanding of personality, little is known about the exact role of genetics and biology with regard to specific personality traits like dogmatism. Therefore we cannot make any causal statements about biological or environmental factors, which surely interact.

Evidentiary theory requires us to examine all propositions and look for consistencies among them. In all likelihood, the cause of dogmatism is multifaceted, and while we can isolate and empirically analyze what we think are clear contributing factors, our efforts are currently limited to discovering those influences that merely correlate with dogmatism's unique characteristics. To support the thesis that dogmatism is a distinct personality trait, it is necessary to empirically determine the degree to which each of dogmatism's thirteen characteristics are constitutive, interrelated parts of its overall essence.

As credible as the four causal propositions may seem (the need to know, the need to defend against anxiety, the need to socially connect, and the need for dignity), these claims must be empirically tested if they are to be considered scientifically robust. Psychologists are also obliged to examine the information-processing strategies that children adopt to cope with their deficient psychological needs and determine which, if any, are clearly linked to the emergence of adult dogmatism. Future research might well demonstrate that one or more of the four proposed causes are only tangentially, if at all, related to dogmatism.

Although it is inconceivable that the same psychosocial factors that lead some people to become dogmatic would turn others into open-minded paragons of rational thought, we nonetheless need scientific studies that test the impact of multiple contributing factors in order to determine the roots of dogmatism. It may be that I have missed the mark on singling out this network of four intricate influences, in which case I will need to open-mindedly revise or discard my assumptions.

Finally, I do not mean to imply that dogmatism is shaped by a linear progression of the four childhood deficiencies proposed here. All of them interact with one's innate biology and sociocultural influences, which are the subjects of later chapters. For example, a biological predisposition for anxiety surely influences how one interacts with his or her social environment and responds to cultural customs, and any combination of experiences may prevent strong social ties. Similarly, parental ignorance and abuse, systemic poverty, inadequate education, and institutional oppression all contribute to and compound the childhood stress that precipitates premature intellectual closure in a vulnerable mind. But regardless of their source, anxiety and fear constrict flexible cognitive processing.

It is therefore not surprising that the soil in which dogmatism takes root can cultivate ideological extremism and martyrdom—belief systems and behaviors that are presumed to assure dignity for deeply alienated, humiliated, desperate individuals. I am concerned that if we do not subject dogmatism to scientific scrutiny, the legacy of rigid, closed-minded thinking might well be more toxic in the next generation, especially with the help of virtual networks that allow a handful of fanatics to command acts of monstrous evil in the name of God, political revenge, or some other fanciful delusion.

NOTES

1. T. Pyszczynski, J. Greenberg, and J. L. Goldenberg, "Freedom versus Fear: On the Defense, Growth, and Expansion of the Self," in *Hand-*

book of Self and Identity, ed. Mark R. Leary and J. P. Tangney (New York: Guilford Press, 2003), p. 315.

2. J. W. Atkinson, *An Introduction to Motivation* (Princeton, NJ: Van Nostrand, 1964).

3. Pyszczynski, Greenberg, and Goldenberg, "Freedom versus Fear."

4. E. L. Deci and R. M. Ryan, "The 'What' and 'Why' of Goal Pursuits: Human Needs and the Self-Determination of Behavior," *Psychological Inquiry* 11 (2000): 227–68.

5. A. J. Elliot, K. M. Sheldon, and M. A. Church, "Avoidance Personal Goals and Subjective Well-Being," *Personality and Social Psychology Bulletin* 23 (1997): 915–27.

6. Pyszczynski, Greenberg, and Goldenberg, "Freedom versus Fear."

7. The wording and conceptualization of the first and second needs are Milton Rokeach's. See *The Open and Closed Mind* (New York: Basic Books, 1960).

8. N. Chomsky, *Knowledge of Language: Its Nature, Origin, and Use* (Westport, CT: Praeger, 1986).

9. Pyszczynski, Greenberg, and Goldenberg, "Freedom versus Fear," p. 327.

10. P. J. LaFreniere, *Emotional Development: A Biosocial Perspective* (Scarborough, ON: Nelson/Thomson Learning, 2000). Peter LaFreniere's textbook addresses emotional development in infancy and childhood, and shows how biological, cognitive, and social processes are interrelated aspects of nature and nurture in human development.

11. R. May, *The Meaning of Anxiety* (New York: Norton, 1977), p. 58.

12. L. B. Alloy, K. A. Kelly, S. Mineka, and C. M. Clements, "Comorbidity of Anxiety and Depressive Disorders: A Helplessness/Hopelessness Perspective," in *Comorbidity in Anxiety and Mood Disorders*, ed. Jack D. Maser and C. R. Cloninger (Washington, DC: American Psychiatric Press, 1990), pp. 499–543. These authors developed the Learned Hopelessness theory of depression, which is an expansion of Seligman's Learned Helplessness model developed in 1974. When an individual expects he or she will be helpless to control aversive events, a phenomenon known as "depressive predictive certainty" develops, in which anxiety and depression accompany thoughts of hopelessness.

13. A. Adler, *Understanding Human Nature* (New York: Fawcett, 1954).

14. Pyszczynski, Greenberg, and Goldenberg, "Freedom versus Fear," p. 328.

15. M. Csikszentmihalyi, *Flow: The Psychology of Optimal Experiences* (New York: Harper and Row, 1990). Csikszentmihalyi's concept of flow and Abraham Maslow's concept of self-actualization expand on this idea.

16. J. W. Kalat and M. N. Shiota, *Emotion* (Belmont, CA: Thomson Wadsworth, 2007), p. 101.

17. T. Adorno et al., *The Authoritarian Personality* (New York: Harper and Brothers, 1950). Similarly, Hoffman-Plotkin and Twentyman's 1984 research, "A Multimodal Assessment of Behavioral and Cognitive Deficits in Abused and Neglected Preschoolers," *Child Development* 55 (1984): 794–802, found that preschoolers who had been physically abused displayed significant cognitive and social deficits when tested on standardized tests of cognitive ability and observed for specific social skills.

18. Pyszczynski, Greenberg, and Goldenberg, "Freedom versus Fear," p. 326.

19. M. Epstein, *Thoughts without a Thinker* (New York: Basic Books, 1995), p. 47.

20. S. Kierkegaard, cited in R. May, *Freedom and Destiny* (New York: Dell Publishing, 1981), p. 185.

21. E. Fromm, *Escape from Freedom* (New York: Holt, Rinehart, and Winston, 1941), p. 49.

22. P. Tillich, *The Protestant Era* (Chicago: University of Chicago Press, 1947), p. 245.

23. S. Freud, "Analysis Terminable and Interminable," in *Standard Edition of the Complete Psychological Works of Sigmund Freud*, ed. James Strachey (London: Hogarth Press, 1937), p. 237.

24. Rokeach, *The Open and Closed Mind*, p. 70.

25. Csikszentmihalyi, *Flow*, p. 166. Csikszentmihalyi states that eventually science will isolate the chromosomes that are instructed, through biochemistry, to create anxiety when humans are forced to spend time alone. From evolutionary psychology's perspective, this makes sense, given its assumptions that social bonding and cooperation increase a species' chances for survival and reproduction.

26. D. M. Taylor and W. Louis, "Terrorism and the Quest for Identity," in *Understanding Terrorism: Psychosocial Roots, Consequences, and Inter-*

ventions, ed. Fathali M. Moghaddam and A. J. Marsella (Washington, DC: American Psychological Association, 2004); M. R. Leary and D. L. Downs, "Interpersonal Functions of the Self-Esteem Motive: The Self-Esteem System as a Sociometer," in *Efficacy, Agency, and Self-Esteem*, ed. Michael H. Kernis (New York: Plenum, 1995), pp. 123–44.

27. D. P. McAdams, "A Psychology of the Stranger," *Psychological Inquiry* 5, no. 2 (1994): 147.

28. D. Goleman, *Social Intelligence: The New Science of Human Relationships* (New York: Bantam, 2006), p. 5.

29. K. Durkin, "A Lifespan Developmental Perspective," in *Blackwell Handbook of Social Psychology: Intraindividual Processes*, ed. A. Tesser and N. Schwartz (Malden, MA: Blackwell, 2003), p. 56.

30. Goleman, *Social Intelligence*.

31. Ibid., p. 86.

32. M. Gazzaniga, personal e-mail communication, April 23, 2006. Gazzaniga, a renowned cognitive neuroscientist, confirmed his belief that in this century, there will be an emphasis on research that examines the brain mechanisms involved in social processes.

33. H. Maturana and F. Varela, *The Tree of Knowledge: The Biological Roots of Human Understanding* (Boston: Shambhala, 1992), p. 246.

34. Ibid. See also Rokeach, *The Open and Closed Mind*, and W. Grolnick, *The Psychology of Parental Control: How Well-Meant Parenting Backfires* (Mahwah, NJ: Erlbaum, 2003).

35. B. Perry, "Childhood Experience and the Expression of Genetic Potential: What Childhood Neglect Tells Us about Nature and Nurture," *Brain and Mind* 3 (2002): 79–100.

36. W. James, *The Principles of Psychology* (Boston: Holt, 1890).

37. Fromm, *Escape from Freedom*.

38. J. Post, "Terrorist Psycho-Logic: Terrorist Behavior as a Product of Psychological Forces," in *Origins of Terrorism: Psychologies, Ideologies, Theologies, States of Mind*, ed. Walter Reich (Baltimore: Johns Hopkins University Press, 1998), p. 31.

39. W. Soyinka, *Climate of Fear: The Quest for Dignity in a Dehumanized World* (New York: Random House, 2005), p. 97.

40. R. Wright, *The Moral Animal: Why We Are the Way We Are* (New York: Vintage, 1994), p. 265.

41. The concepts of *self* and *identity* are not unitary. They represent an

aggregate of concepts, all of which are determined by one's personal reflections and insight. Concepts such as self-awareness, self-consciousness, self-verification, self-concept, self-knowledge, self-evaluation, self-discrepancy, and self-monitoring all fall within the broad domains of self and identity research. The important point here is that dogmatists lack the ability or willingness to engage in personal reflection that facilitates psychological insight. While they have a self-concept, their psychological identity, like their beliefs, becomes narrow and rigidly formed.

42. R. May, *Psychology and the Human Dilemma* (New York: Norton, 1979), p. 32.

43. S. Blackburn, *Truth: A Guide* (Oxford: Oxford University Press, 2005), p. 156.

44. LaFreniere, *Emotional Development.*

45. A. de Botton, *Status Anxiety* (Toronto: Viking, 2004).

46. S. Pinker, *The Blank Slate: The Modern Denial of Human Nature* (New York: Penguin Putnam, 2002). While Pinker notes that peers play a prominent role in children's personality development and their adoption of beliefs and behaviors, researchers seem generally undecided as to whether parents or peers are the major determinants of adult personality.

47. Rokeach, *The Open and Closed Mind*, p. 68.

48. M. Galanter, "Psychological Induction into the Large Group: Findings from a Modern Religious Sect," *American Journal of Psychiatry* 136 (1980): 1574–79.

49. Soyinka, *Climate of Fear*, p. 91.

50. W. B. Michaels, "Diversity's False Solace," *New York Times*, April 11, 2004, p. 14.

51. Although assumptions about personality and the major psychological concepts used to explain its development differ, traditional and modern personality theories advanced by Alfred Adler's theory of individual psychology, Karen Horney's theory of psychoanalytic social psychology, Carl Rogers's and Abraham Maslow's humanistic psychology, Rollo May's existential psychoanalysis, Albert Bandura and Albert Ellis's cognitive-behavioral theories, and evolutionary psychology all emphasize that without gratification of basic needs for social connection and dignity, healthy personality development is seriously undermined.

52. A. Newberg and M. R. Waldman, *Why We Believe What We Believe* (New York: Free Press, 2007).

53. Rokeach, *The Open and Closed Mind*, p. 70.

54. H. A. Witkin and D. R. Goodenough, *Cognitive Styles: Essence and Origins* (New York: International Universities Press, 1981).

55. This definition of dogmatism is derived from the works of Milton Rokeach, Robert Altemeyer, and the author.

Chapter 5

BLACK-AND-WHITE THINKING

Cognitive Characteristics of Dogmatism

What luck for rulers that men do not think.

Adolf Hitler (1889–1945)

With a hawk's eye we now peer into the thought patterns behind rigid, closed-minded belief systems. The dogmatic thinking under scrutiny is reflected in five cognitive characteristics outlined in this chapter, but these features only describe one broad psychological category of dogmatism—the way dogmatists habitually think about issues relating to their belief systems. Yet within the enduring personality trait of dogmatism, the covariation of thirteen characteristics also includes emotional and behavioral features—two additional categories of subtraits that are presented in the next two chapters.

Dogmatists may appear comfortably settled in their convictions, but are they? More likely, they have learned to suppress their anxious feelings behind rigid proclamations of absolute truth, and their lack of personal and interpersonal insight prevents them from understanding the impact their closed-mindedness has on their cognitive development and social relationships. Before we explore each of the five characteristics in detail, table 5.1 provides an overview of dogmatism's thirteen characteristics.

TABLE 5.1
THE THIRTEEN CHARACTERISTICS OF DOGMATISM

Cognitive Characteristics	Emotional Characteristics	Behavioral Characteristics
1. An Intolerance of Ambiguity	1. Belief-associated Anxiety or Fear	1. Preoccupation with Power and Status (as evidenced by behaviors)
2. Defensive, Cognitive Closure	2. Belief-associated Anger	2. Glorification of the In-group; Vilification of the Out-group
3. Rigid Certainty	3. Existential Despair	3. Dogmatic Authoritarian Aggression
4. Compartmentalization		4. Dogmatic Authoritarian Submission
5. Lack of Personal Insight		5. Arrogant, Dismissive Communication Style

Note: It is assumed that six of these thirteen characteristics are sufficient to determine the personality trait of dogmatism. Of these six characteristics, there is a minimum of three cognitive characteristics, two behavioral characteristics, and one belief-associated emotion.

As we examine fictional, illustrative scenarios that portray the cognitive characteristics, keep in mind that prototypical dogmatists would score on the upper end of a continuous measure of dogmatism. The main characters will surely remind you of people portrayed in novels, movies, and television, and many will resemble, to varying degrees, people you know or have known. But equally important, can we determine how our own cognitive elasticity stacks up against our scrutiny of those we would describe as dogmatic?

People who consistently demonstrate all thirteen characteristics of dogmatism are probably as rare as sleep-deprived cats. However, among dogmatic political, religious, and academic authorities, those with more than six characteristics who gain power in order to impose their beliefs on others would likely use their position of authority to hoodwink vulnerable recruits. They are the dogmatists who justify acts of dogmatic aggression in the name of some lofty ideological pursuit, and their disruptive behavior goes well beyond dominating meetings or dinner conversations. But that is the content of the chapter 7, which examines the behavioral characteristics of dogmatism.

THE FIVE COGNITIVE CHARACTERISTICS OF DOGMATISM

Each of the five cognitive features represents dogmatists' habitual failure to thoroughly acknowledge and investigate complicated issues, whether they are practical, abstract, or ethical in nature. To confront complex issues would intensify dogmatists' anxiety and self-doubt, yet despite this avoidance, they feel an urgency to pronounce truths as if they were miraculous solutions to problems.

The tendency to simplify thought is the grand-daddy of dogmatism that accompanies all five cognitive characteristics. Dogmatists habitually use the brain's approximately 100 billion neurons, which are connected by approximately 160 trillion synapses, to keep things simple. To expand their ideas or beliefs increases their anxiety of not knowing and their fear of being judged as stupid or uninformed. Casting their beliefs in black-and-white terms reduces the anxiety that complex issues invoke and, at the same time, gratifies their rudimentary need to know. After all, when one has a firm handle on truth, why bother investigating the facts? For them, complete certainty rewards them with personal composure. A simplistic categorization of ideas that either support or contradict their core beliefs provides them the illusion of an authentic, intrinsic identity that they believe will enhance social connections and ultimately confer personal dignity. "What seems to be most appealing about militant religious groups— whatever combination of reasons an individual may cite for joining— is the way life is simplified."[1] Yet over-simplification of the complex (for example, all lawyers are crooks) inevitably simplifies the dogmatist's most valuable asset—his or her mind.

To complicate matters, as anxiety builds, intelligent understanding and curiosity crumble. Strategies now emerge as a means to cope with chronic anxiety yet gratify one's narrowed need to know—to "ward off contradiction and thus, maintain intact one's own system."[2] The narrower one's mind becomes, the harder it is to reopen it. A person who needs to feel in complete cognitive control of beliefs, ideas, and information has an obsessive need for truth, the demonstration of which becomes compulsive.

The opposite of dogmatic cognitive simplicity is conceptual complexity—the degree to which one can consider several dimensions of a problem or argument (differentiation) and the degree to which one can recognize connections among components within those dimensions (integration).[3] Conceptual and integrative complexity are particularly necessary for educators and institutional leaders. Indeed, "the outbreak of war is reliably preceded by decreased integrative complexity of national leaders and diplomats."[4] A study of the Gulf War crisis replicated findings of earlier studies, revealing that leaders with low levels of information processing provide early warnings of their intentions to use military force. The situation interacts with such cognitive traits as conceptual simplicity and integrative complexity to yield important predictive indicators for critical decisions that lead to war. American congressional hawks exhibited significantly lower levels of cognitive complexity than congressional doves.[5] On a measure of right-wing authoritarianism (RWA), a component of dogmatism, "no correlation appeared between authoritarianism and cognitive complexity. Some High RWAs had very simple stands [against abortion] but so did some Lows."[6]

During crisis, political leaders who were more collaborative and open to considering a range of options were more likely to negotiate nonviolent resolutions and showed greater resilience when disruptive stress ended.[7] But we should not equate open-minded integrative complexity with morality or the correctness of a final decision, since history reveals that "under certain circumstances, abandoning negotiations and embarking upon armed conflict may be the morally superior, or pragmatically successful move—or both moral *and* successful."[8] For example, American abolitionists of the 1850s made simple demands to end slavery regardless of the costs and consequences, yet integrative complexity among moderate Democrats and Republicans foresaw the dangers—civil war and bloodshed.[9] Would protracted, integrative complexity have been a hindrance or advantage in ending slavery?

At this time it is difficult to disentangle the psychological and environmental factors that impact cognitive complexity, since the trait, situation, and social circumstances combine to influence cognitive capability, especially in stressful situations. Other aspects of daily life that interact with one's cognitive style and hamper cognitive processing include fatigue, boredom, depression, illness (mental or physical), and imminent death. Further research that tests the relation between characteristics of dogmatism and cognitive complexity in a variety of stressful and nonstressful situations would contribute much to our understanding of cognitive processing in those with dogmatic tendencies.

Clearly, individuals who lack conceptual complexity and also have other characteristics of dogmatism will consistently make cognitive errors that ultimately earn them that which they least desire—being seen as uninformed or ignorant. For the dogmatist, not knowing is an embarrassment to be concealed. As an antidote to fear, ignorance, and powerlessness, dogmatism calms the mind and conquers the nameless dread of uncertainty. But it comes at the expense of reasoned judgment and social dignity. As John Kenneth Galbraith warned, "When people are the least sure, they are often the most dogmatic."[10] This includes people who are not deficient in conceptual complexity, which raises the barnyard question: Which comes first: dogmatism that degrades conceptual complexity, or deficient conceptual complexity that invites dogmatism? Or something else?

§§

Psychologists assume that personality traits, of which dogmatism is but one, are enduring.[11] For this reason, people with several characteristics of dogmatism are referred to as dogmatists throughout this book, much like people who demonstrate characteristics of extroversion are described as extroverts. The problem with single trait descriptions is that they reduce one's personality to unitary descriptions that do not capture the totality of one's essence. Because closed-minded believers are more than the sum of their dogmatic parts, they would be more accurately described as people with the personality trait of dogmatism, people who have a consistent pattern of closed-minded thinking, or people who are predisposed to dogmatism. These are all more accurate but cumbersome descriptors that would belabor the prose of this book. I have therefore chosen to use the word *dogmatist*, and in this regard I am guilty of simplifying the complex. But my elimination of tedious qualifiers is intended to simplify language, not people.

Wide awake, think about some of your core belief systems. Do you have strong beliefs about issues regarding marriage and the family, sexuality, parenting, death and dying, business management styles, technology, healthcare, the environment, immigration, religion, or politics, among others? Which beliefs guide your philosophy of life, shape your identity, and inform others about where you stand on matters important to you? Do any provide comfort?

Because the strength of beliefs, emotions, and behaviors differentiate dogmatists from people who are more open-minded and accepting of differences, it is worth exploring *how* we hold some of our own principal beliefs. Select one or two of your strong beliefs. With those beliefs percolating, grab a coffee—a Beliefs Latte—and consider the following questions:

- In times of solitude, do you ever question the validity of your important beliefs?
- How certain are you that your core beliefs are correct?
- How much evidence would it take to convince you that an important belief of yours is invalid?
- Do you welcome opportunities to discuss your beliefs?
- How firmly do you hold your core beliefs?

- If you were to change a central belief, how would that change occur?
- Have you ever been called stubborn or inflexible?
- If someone said "You sound very adamant (or dead certain) about this," what thoughts and feelings would this comment provoke?
- Can you identify the emotional tagalongs of your belief systems, especially when others differ with you? Do you feel energized, tense, annoyed, defensive?
- What feelings arise when introduced to someone whose political or religious beliefs are quite contrary to your own?
- How would you feel if your daughter told you she is seriously dating someone whose political beliefs are to the extreme right (or left) of your own?
- How would you feel if your son told you he has reconsidered his religious beliefs, that they are now 180 degrees from those you taught him?

You might want to keep your answers to these questions in mind as we explore the following cognitive characteristics of dogmatism. We begin with the dogmatist's first stumbling block to reason—an intolerance of ambiguity.

Intolerance of Ambiguity[12,R]

Illustrative statements:

- "I admire people who firmly stick to their guns."[R]
- "A group that tolerates too much difference of opinion cannot exist for long."[R]
- "I get impatient with people who change their minds about important issues."[J]
- "Either you are with us, or you are with the terrorists."[13,J]
- "Once I make up my mind about something, there's no turning back."[J]

- "Negotiating with the enemy sends a clear message of appeasement."[J]

Daily encounters with ambiguity and indecision are universal. In the face of uncertainty, we feel somewhat insecure and restless, especially when we have limited freedom of choice or when we feel pressured to finalize decisions. Ambiguity obscures our options and we paddle about in a swamp of confusion until we find our bearings.

During major life transitions, we worry (the cognitive component of anxiety), fret about the unknown, and overlook the reality that our most important decisions are generally based on insufficient information.[14] In confusing circumstances, anxiety is not only understandable, it is normal. Normal too, is the nostalgia for familiarity.

§§

The more open-minded among us recognize that uncertainty surrounds our most complex, abstract quandaries of existence, particularly the meaning of life and death. For centuries, philosophers, poets and writers have grappled "with the inscrutable mystery of creation."[15] From their struggles emerged myths, dogmas, and belief systems designed to provide personal identity, moral codes, and a sense of community. These doctrines offer clear guidelines that provide comfort and safety, and it matters not whether they are religious tenets, political ideologies, scientific paradigms and explanations, or models of psychotherapy, to name a few. The power of institutional, academic, and cultural dogma lies in its ability to alleviate ambiguity and doubt.

While the human desire for clarity, certitude, and safety during times of change and stress is normal, dogmatists transform these natural desires to dire necessities. They, like all of us, adopt strategies to reduce anxiety and fear that arise from the unknown or from having to understand and cope with new challenges. Lacking open-minded confidence to confront the unknown, dogmatists emphasize the threat in change. Persistent anxiety that is sequestered in the background of daily functioning impairs their ability to investigate, accept, and adjust to ambiguous ideas and situations. The discomfort of that ambiguity stokes the smoldering embers of anxiety until, bellowed by fear, it flares into rigid, closed-minded dogmatism. Its reinforcing properties —certainty and safety—are powerful remedies for anxiety and self-doubt.

Illustrative Example: Arlene and Her Grandparents

Arlene's grandparents help us sense the discomfort of those who cannot tolerate ambiguity. Over Sunday dinner with her grandparents, Arlene raised a personal problem that she hoped an open-minded discussion would help her resolve: "I love Walt, but I'm beginning to worry about how often we argue over where we should get married, what kind of service to have, and who should officiate. He wants a small civil ceremony, but I want the church to sanctify our marriage. I need to talk about this and get some ideas that will help us make the best decision."

Grandma's position was as clear and piercing as a midnight train whistle. "How could you possibly think of marriage outside the family church? That would be a disgrace—to God and your family!" Grandfather's tone was a little more conciliatory. "Well, honey, do we need to discuss this now? I mean, really. Surely you wouldn't flaunt family tradition and have some stranger, some ordinary Justice of the Peace, marry you. That would be blasphemy."

Arlene has ambivalent, mixed feelings about whether she and Walt should have a religious or civil ceremony. What she finds ambiguous is how she will comfortably reconcile Walt's different beliefs about civil marriage with her own belief that a religious ceremony provides the most acceptable legitimacy. The worrisome thought that Walt might end their engagement crosses Arlene's mind when she and Walt argue about this issue, and she wants to find a compromise that would strengthen their love. She had hoped that discussing this problem with her grandparents would help her weigh the relative merit of each preference and reduce her ambiguity, which she can tolerate. She could have given Walt an ultimatum to either accept a church ceremony or end their engagement, but, instead, she is open to discussing this conflict and broadening her options.

Arlene's grandparents lack such flexibility. The content of their religious belief system is so deeply embedded they will not allow any process that facilitates the suspension, reconsideration, or revision of their beliefs. To seriously consider Arlene's problem would crack their ideological edifice of truth. It would require them to transgress the black-and-white boundaries of their religious beliefs, hurling them into an unknowable void—a zone of murky, ambiguous grey that would sever their safety, here and in the heavenly hereafter.

Grandma and Grandpa probably believed they were helping Arlene solve her problem, yet Arlene was so discouraged by their closed-minded intolerance of ambiguity that she decided not to include them in future discussions of religious matters. From Arlene's perspective, their fears aborted what could have been a helpful exchange of ideas within an atmosphere of mutual respect. Thoughtful exploration would have left her feeling supported, not "dissed," as she later described it to Walt.

Arlene's grandparents exhibited hasty judgment and facile reasoning about religion and morality, which minimized their discomfort and banished clouds of ambiguity. Like other dogmatists, they reindoctrinate themselves with perceived truths that gratify their psychological demands for certainty. Questioning is perceived as wavering, and wavering is weak-willed and wishy-washy; such deliberation is the first step toward apostasy. "To the extent that we believe, we renounce our autonomy and willingly depend on the judgment of others."[16] In a dogmatic mind, the abdication of autonomy is absolute.

An intolerance of ambiguity is especially obvious when strong beliefs become outdated. Because such beliefs are inextricably tied to identity, suspending them would impose strange feelings of self-alienation. Adrift from their ideological anchor, dogmatists fill in the missing gaps with ready-made substitutes. Old beliefs are replaced with the sudden, unquestioning embrace of new ones, illustrating what Rokeach called the Silver-Platter Syndrome.[17] In such cases, former beliefs are arbitrarily replaced with an entire set of nicely polished new ones that are presented on a silver platter, preferably by a dazzling, prestigious authority figure. Much like people who are dependent on a partner to define them, dogmatists need a self-defining (versus self-guiding), self-sustaining (versus meaningful) belief system. Closed persons work more efficiently with silver-platter handouts because new beliefs need not be reconciled with old ones through a process of analysis and synthesis.

Dogmatists who yield to the pressure of change do so swiftly, for uncertainty weighs heavy on their shoulders. When faced with doubt, they are vulnerable to seeking the camaraderie and revivalist spirit of a powerful new ideological movement that offers a chance for a fresh beginning.[18] Just as before, their new loyalties and behaviors follow authoritative dictates. Old truths are dismissed as a failure of the belief system, not a failure of their own thinking. It is never oneself who fails to open-mindedly assess the logic and personal meaning of the rejected belief system; the difficulty lies elsewhere. In more extreme cases, the sudden belief transplant of dogmatists is buoyed by complete denial that they ever believed or behaved differently, as the following scenario demonstrates.

Illustrative Example: Orson and the Silver-Platter Syndrome

While resting from a strenuous workout at the gym, Damon's long-term friendship with Orson was suddenly tested when Damon reminisced: "Orson, remember what a staunch communist you were in university days? Your political views today are a hundred and eighty degrees from what they were then." With an air of condescending disbelief, Orson replied, "What on earth are you talking about! I've never been a communist! How could anyone in his right mind believe in communism! Take the examples of . . . (Orson presents a litany of 'unbelievable failures'). I've always been a staunch conservative."

Assuming that Damon's memory was accurate, there are a couple of explanations for Orson's adamant denial of his former beliefs.

The dogmatism hypothesis is that, years ago, Orson used the primitive defense mechanism of denial to shield himself from the internal conflict he experienced when he questioned important issues. In adulthood, if entrenched beliefs become stale or outdated, or if an admired person of status pressures Orson to "get over it" or "get on with the times," he will feel quite threatened by the ambiguity that accompanies change. Moreover, if Orson needs self-assurance and recognition for an absolute grasp of important issues, a sudden, complete change will preserve this need. For dogmatists, an entire belief transplant is an expedient solution.

Of course, it is entirely possible that Orson is not a defensive dogmatist at all. He might have denied his former beliefs because he was simply embarrassed to admit he was once a communist. If that were the case, we would not expect him to go on a tirade about the evils of communism—a more likely defense if other characteristics of dogmatism took up space on Orson's silver platter.

§§

Arlene's grandparents' resistance to change and Orson's denial of it wrap the three of them in black-and-white security blankets that provide illusions of safety and infallibility. Confronting the grey of uncertainty threatens their identity and certainty, both of which are easily disturbed by an unknowable, ever-changing world. The greater the external ambiguity, the greater the likelihood that anxiety and intolerance will dig in and deepen their rigid, dogmatic ruts.

In contrast, before deciding whether to ignore, assimilate, or dismiss information, open-minded people need adequate time to process the content, regardless of how prestigious an authority figure is or how accurate the conveyed, new information may seem. Flexible thinkers resist having new beliefs rammed down their throats without first examining them for themselves.[19] Because their mental performance is not hampered by anxiety, they are able to contemplate novel information in ways that permit a gradual, integrated synthesis of the old with the new. Ambiguity is a signal to carefully question, not anxiously reject. They accept its inevitable occurrence and realize that uncertainty helps one to clarify beliefs "and understand the limitations of our commitment to them."[20]

Defensive Cognitive Closure[R,Jmod]

Illustrative statements:

- "In this country there is only one political party worth listening to."[R]
- "It is only natural that a person would have a much better acquaintance with ideas he believes in than ideas he opposes."[R]
- "Of all the different philosophies in the world, there is probably only one that conveys the real truth."[R,Jmod]
- "I can't bear to listen to conservative propaganda."[J]
- "When it comes to managing social programs like healthcare, private enterprise is the only viable option."[J]
- "The Holy Bible is the only true word of God."[J]

Working in sequence with an intolerance of ambiguity, which is assuaged by rigidly adopting a belief system that provides clear answers, defensive cognitive closure is a specific strategy to reduce the threat from opposing or alternate ideas. When anxiety builds as a consequence of perceived threats to existing beliefs, dogmatists manage the discomfort by immediately judging and dismissing ideas that conflict with what they already know. In this sense, dogmatism is not naiveté. A dogmatist's default reaction to ideas outside his or her existing belief systems is to arbitrarily rebuff them as patently wrong or ridiculous, even though they may not openly declare them as such.

From their perspective, preemptive closure of the mind is a protective maneuver that banishes self-doubt yet preserves the illusion of intelligence. The only questions deemed important are those that dogmatists can answer; those they cannot answer are instantly judged as irrelevant. In their minds, humble admissions of ignorance are signs of stupidity that make them vulnerable to painful judgment and accusation. Therefore, defensive cognitive closure follows quickly on the heels of an intolerance of ambiguity, as dogmatists ardently defend their fixed beliefs—sometimes with arrogant hyperbole. To preserve their identity and self-respect, they spend excessive energy guarding their beliefs against the perceived threat of having to spend even more energy—anxious energy—investigating opposing beliefs. That effort would surely cast doubt on their established views, and similar doubt on their intellect. Open-minded questioning of core beliefs would be seen as equivalent to dismantling them," a process they subconsciously believe would destroy their very identity. Better to reconstruct and strengthen their original beliefs than deconstruct and weaken them with new ones. While this gratifies fundamental needs to allay anxiety and feel safe, their pseudo-safety comes at the expense of their cognitive growth.

Agile thinking is especially necessary when mounting evidence exposes new ways of understanding oneself, others, and worldly ideas. Open-minded thinkers can more readily examine information, and although they may eventually reject it, their thoughtful decision to do so is very different from the dogmatist's outright refusal to even consider it.

These errors of reasoning occur even in the halls of academia, where we least expect to find it. Academics who are prone to dogmatism attack new ideas or theories with such comments as, "You haven't presented anything new here," or, "Philosophers said the same thing years ago." Ideological immune systems have inoculated their minds against intelligent, open-minded discourse. Animated by their own dogma, they use clever, subtle means to intimidate colleagues who are unfamiliar with or challenging of their ideas. "You haven't heard of . . ." (subtext: "you feebleminded philistine"), which brings us to pomposity, another sign of academic dogmatism. Dogmatic professors may obscure their lack of knowledge and rigidity with a veneer of high seriousness that mocks rational argument. Ironically, those who try to create a knowledgeable impression by using polysyllabic words (like polysyllabic) in casual conversation, or by altering simple words to appear as unintelligible code, risk exactly what they dread—appearing ignorant and uneducated. These strategies stifle inquiry and keep new ideas from breaking through a protective, impenetrable barricade. Defensive cognitive closure and a lack of personal insight (discussed later in this chapter) block the unpleasant reality that the integrity of dogmatists is as strained as their interpersonal relationships. Their social disengagement is especially apparent with lower-ranking colleagues who are overly cautious about challenging their ideas.

The problem with all dogmatists, including those in academia, is the fear that changing their minds would unmask and undermine their autonomy, their rank, and their dignity. Among the very people who are educated to be open-minded about ideas and beliefs, those whose insecurities prevent them from being cognitively flexible have underlying emotions that block access to higher levels of abstract reasoning and comparative analysis. They have difficulty progressing through the cumulative stages of knowledge whereby one first learns to remember, and then to understand, apply, analyze, evaluate, and create.[21] Each successive, more complicated level of analysis requires expanded thinking, but people cannot assess new information and blend it with the old if their fears prevent them from opening their minds enough to mull it over in the first place. Dogmatic academics would surely advocate free and critical thinking, but they themselves lack such skills and, consequently, cannot foster it in their students.

An uneasy insecurity haunts faculty who are uninterested in remaining current in their field, or who come from a generation for which the expectation of scholarly publication was less obligatory. Some of these people teach the same material in the same style for years. They may be simply lazy or unmotivated for various reasons, but some are also fearful of change, which prompts them to defend themselves with preemptive, cognitive closure. Among this group are the dogmatists who have always been fearful of change. Failing to acknowledge how far they have fallen behind, they mask their anxiety with cynicism about new theories, research methods, or teaching techniques. What a disservice they do their students, their institution, and themselves.

Perhaps some academics defensively close their minds because they have spent years having to defend their ideas in order to obtain a degree that ensures a career, security, and recognition—for which they all strive. Having written many exams and presented oral and written defenses of their ideas, it is understandable that some continue to act as if every topic of conversation is yet another demand to defend their thesis or dissertation. Join a conversation in a coffee lounge at an academic institution and notice the emotions behind the discussion. Those with passionate enthusiasm clearly differ from dogmatists, who become emotionally distraught and defensive when their ideas are questioned. As Altemeyer notes, they are seldom, if ever, open to the possibility they might be wrong.[22]

Dogmatic academics who are fearful that collaboration will fertilize a cross-section of new ideas dry the well of creativity and smother intellectual inquiry. Theirs is the academic counterpart of cutthroat competition in the corporate world. While many educators and scientists openly collaborate with their peers (especially in the field of cancer research),[23] dogmatic academics swim against the currents of new theories and research. "There is a saying that the discipline of economics makes progress one funeral at a time."[24] With great relief to some, death breathes new life into the halls of learning when people who were overinvested in their intellectual property and unwilling to work collaboratively die. And while academic evangelism is the great irony in higher education, the more tragic loss is stalled scientific progress—both individual and collective.

More commonly, defensive cognitive closure is seen among those with whom we live, work, and associate, as illustrated by Yolanda and Billy-Bob.

Illustrative Examples: Yolanda and Billy-Bob

When her psychology professor introduced a lecture on sexual orientation with research that supports a biological basis for homosexuality, Yolanda rolled her eyes, audibly huffed, and gazed out the window. During a short coffee break with classmates, she announced: "Homosexuality is a matter of choice. Gays and lesbians can decide whether to be normal or not. End of story." One student challenged her assumptions, to which Yolanda replied, "The Bible says homosexuality is a sin. I don't care what the prof says." The following week she failed exam questions on brain differentiation and behavior. She rationalized her poor mark by telling a classmate, "Why waste time studying all that stuff on the brain and behavior when there's no real proof for any of it?"

The functional role of Yolanda's defensive cognitive closure is to shield her mind from new information that conflicts with her cemented convictions about sexuality. She cannot open her mind to make room for a different idea. Instead, she categorically dismisses as irrelevant anything outside her narrow-minded belief system, which reduces anxiety and excuses her from having to weigh the relative merit of different ideas. In the process, she deprives herself of more spacious conversations that would allow for an integration of old ideas with the new. Entrenched beliefs provide safe, simplistic clarity in anxious minds.

§§

Billy-Bob applies defensive cognitive closure differently. Particularly during political discussions, he dominates the conversation and makes feisty comments to the inattentive or unconvinced. When people challenge his views or raise more tangential points, Billy-Bob's frustration shows, "Why can't you just stick to the main issue here? That is not the point!" Billy-Bob cannot comfortably open his mind to fully hear and consider another person's ideas. Even when people seem unreasonable in their thinking, we would do well to consider Galileo's claim, "I have never met a man so ignorant that I couldn't learn something from him."[25] Billy-Bob would disagree with the renowned physicist, preferring instead to polarize, antagonize, and win. His arbitrary rejection of others' conflicting ideas saves him from confronting the shallowness of his own.

Before we conclude that Billy-Bob is dogmatic, we first need to consider whether his comments merely indicate an impatient, boorish lack of social grace. We also accept that some people do monopolize the conversation with mental meanderings that are so far adrift from the topic of conversation that we may stop indulging them. As for Billy-Bob, if he is *frequently* intolerant of people's views, whether their contributions to the conversation are dull, ponderous, or brilliant, his use of defensive cognitive closure suggests that he is not willing to open his mind to new ideas. To do so would expose his ignorance and intensify his anxiety about not knowing. This inability to brook dissent and engage in discussions that present multiple viewpoints distinguishes Billy-Bob's defensive cognitive closure from the next characteristic—rigid certainty.

Rigid Certainty[J]

Illustrative statements:

- "Nothing will convince me otherwise."[J]
- "You have to understand that to stay in power, leaders must be absolutely unwavering in their stance."[J]
- "The things I believe in are so completely true I could never doubt them."[A]
- "I may be wrong about some of the little things in life, but I am quite certain I am right about all the BIG issues."[A]
- "Knowing is enough."[J]
- "My political beliefs are absolutely nonnegotiable."[J]

Cognitive rigidity is seen in views that are held tenaciously, even in the face of discrediting evidence. Rigidity is defined as "the tendency to form and perseverate in the use of mental and behavioral sets."[26] This style of thought makes it difficult for dogmatists to change their minds now or in the future. Dogmatists "will seldom if ever accept that [they] are wrong. . . . It is conviction beyond the reach of evidence to the contrary. It is, as Rokeach said, closed-mindedness."[27] Psychologically, anxiety lingers beneath dogmatists' rigid certainty, ensuring that their blinkered vision stays intact and that open-minded pursuits of knowledge are sacrificed to dogmatic rhetoric. We simply cannot get through to them.

Our brains do not care whether beliefs are based on reality—only the beholders of specific beliefs have such concerns (or not). Therefore, if you really need to believe in something—anything—believe it wholeheartedly and dismiss all evidence to the contrary as patently false, heretic, foolish, or some diabolical attempt to dissuade you from truth. With brains that are obedient servants in this task, dogmatists preserve their beliefs and maintain self-deception. Rigid truth, with a capital T, now triumphs over heresy, with a capital H. The matter is closed to debate. And in between the letters T and H of truth, we find a mighty deep rut of narrow-mindedness.

The credulity of rigid people is puzzling until we realize that dogmatism certainty helps them cope with underlying anxiety while simultaneously proving their intelligence—a struggle that becomes apparent when others question their beliefs or present contradictory evidence. Rigid certainty is designed to demolish contradictions, preserve existing views, and buttress fragile, insatiable egos. Once again, we see how dogmatic belief systems serve two powerful but conflicting motives: the need to know and the need to ward off threatening aspects of reality.

We would expect dogmatists to strongly agree with the illustrative statements introduced at the beginning of this segment on rigid certainty, and we would also expect them to answer these questions honestly and unabashedly, because unwavering resolve is a trait they admire in themselves and others. The tone of dogmatism becomes apparent in the next chapter, but it is useful to note here that dogmatism is often, though not always, angry, evangelical (in the broad interpretation), and unjustified. Dogmatic belief systems are generally not evidence-based, and arrogant claims of truth are therefore unwarranted. But belief systems that are conveyed with passionate, justifiable, evidence-based facts can also be dogmatic, *if such systems are closed to reexamination now or in the future.* Enduring, unalterable belief systems, whether backed by evidence or not, whether highly emotional or not, become dogmatic when people refuse to engage in an open-minded exploration of alternative facts or ideas. Such intransigence flags and flanks dogmatism.

§§

Karl Popper, a preeminent philosopher of the arts and sciences, explains what constitutes scientific evidence. In contrast with arbitrary beliefs that are based more on emotion than reason, evidentiary theory has the following qualities:

- It must be able to generate predictions (hypotheses) that are open to scientific investigation that supports or fails to support hypothetical premises.
- It must be capable of being tested and falsified (this is why horoscopes are a hoax: they cannot make clear predictions that can be tested, then supported or refuted—they are not falsifiable, and therefore not scientific).
- It must survive attempts at refutations. Theories are robust if they survive despite refutations of their various components, keeping in mind that no single observation can refute an entire theory.[28]

In the spirit of open-minded inquiry, these are important guidelines for scholarly researchers who want to challenge or advance existing theory, for the enthusiasm of ideas and beliefs is never a substitute for good hard evidence. Outside the realm of academia, people tend to rely on information that they presume is credible. In trying to make sense of the world, our conceptual system devotes just enough energy to provide a comfortable degree of confidence about what we know, even if the conclusions we draw are not based on sound premises. One of our greatest weaknesses is the strong impulse for wishful thinking, to which reason is surrendered.

Religion, for example, gives the believer permission to abandon rational thought, as do other ideological movements that attempt to keep followers tied to unverifiable dogma. For the dogmatic believer, scientific analysis is an abomination of their wishful, comforting fantasies. Is it rational to dogmatically decree that legends, myths, rumors, crystal balls, and Ouija boards are acceptable bases for truth? As Dennett notes, "We wouldn't for one moment pay respectful attention to any scientist who retreated to 'If you don't understand my theory, it's because you don't have *faith* in it'. . . . Any such declaration would be an intolerable abdication of responsibility as a scientific investigator, a confession of intellectual bankruptcy."[29]

Yet most of us have neither the time nor inclination to scientifically investigate the facts or premises of our beliefs. And we recognize that social conversation would be pedantic and tedious if people felt compelled to substantiate every view with credible references, countervailing arguments, or scientific evidence. In the casual flow of conversation, we find it neither necessary nor desirable to offer a crash course on what we know. Because scrupulous analysis of the facts demands conscious effort and skill, we tend to believe information from sources we deem trustworthy. We accept what seems right, and we may choose not to seriously reflect on the issue or seek further information because we are too busy, too tired, or simply unmotivated. We settle for less and take our chances. In other words a mind half open helps us get by, and saves a lot of time.

§§

Consider Herb and Helen. Herb's political beliefs are largely based on lecture notes and readings from his political science courses—a reasonable foundation on which to formulate his beliefs. He prefers dialogue to debate and enjoys discussing his views with classmates. Like Herb, Helen prefers to formulate important ideas on the basis of sound principles that can be corroborated; she uses measured, tentative language when talking about her beliefs and ideas. Neither Herb's nor Helen's belief systems are rigid or unjustifiable.

Rigid certainty, however, comprises an unyielding emotional intensity, a refusal to see things differently, and a failure to admit error. The taste of humble pie is too bitter for these dogmatists who assume infallibility. All this is made more complicated by the fact that "we often cannot say whether other people's certainty is justified. But we can measure how open they are to the possibility they might be wrong. And we can see how they react to disconfirming evidence."[30] Time and further scientific investigations may—or may not—add proof to the pudding. History documents how every age has held beliefs and facts that subsequent ages have demonstrated to be erroneous, if not absurd. Consider, for example, that prior to 1530, and for more than a millennium after that, people preferred Ptolemy's view that our planetary home, not the Sun, was the center of the universe. Science later confirmed Copernicus's theory that the Earth constantly rotates on its axis as it circles the Sun—a belief that was considered sheer lunacy in the middle of the sixteenth century. Science eventually proved that Copernicus did not derive a fanciful theory; it was true. His discovery required people to revise their belief that humans are omniscient—a revision that most people, especially religious dogmatists, found hard to accept. In the sixteenth century, popular opinion did not tolerate epistemological challenges to church dogma, particularly from scientists set on perturbing the foundation, scope, and validity of people's existing beliefs. Three centuries later, Darwin's theory of evolution presented an even greater threat to established, religious belief.

Copernicus's and Darwin's beliefs were based on observation and conjecture, but their beliefs were scientifically analyzed—a rigorous enterprise that few people meticulously practice. Yet science is a rigorous *approach* to knowledge that gives its findings significant credibility by revising fundamental assumptions and inferential knowledge in a manner that validates or rejects propositions. Its merit stems from the belief that one might be wrong, and acceptance of that guiding principle makes one less likely to impose one's beliefs on others. As Bertrand Russell said, "Science is at no moment quite right, but it is seldom quite wrong, and has, as a rule, a better chance of being right than the theories of the unscientific. It is, therefore, rational to accept it hypothetically."[31]

Dogmatists short-circuit that approach, even when their ideas emanate from the substance of genius. Preferring to skip the demanding rigor of the scientific approach, they go directly to desired conclusions that, at best, leave them with half-truths. In higher education, dogmatic scientists are inclined to use fraudulent statistical manipulations that gratify their psychological need for truth and dignity. As statisticians in the social sciences acknowledge, statistics can be "tools for fools,"[32] and there are many such abuses in the annals of academic research. It seems odd that intelligent people are so afflicted—their very brilliance lies in the ability to think so far outside the box that they are not even in the warehouse. Yet people can be highly intelligent, creative, *and* dogmatic. As such, they are unable to emotionally distance themselves from their own ideas to objectively reconsider and, if necessary, alter the anemic reasoning behind their stance. But, as discussed earlier, among the small percentage of the gifted population there is no privileged protection from dogmatism. When dogmatic intellectuals' claims are discredited with solid verifiable evidence, they defensively refuse revision and inadvertently disclose a serious error: excess emotional attachment has corked their ability for flexible, comparative analyses.

People may be dogmatic about ethical or moral principles that are of philosophic concern. For example, female circumcision is a practice within a broad belief system that ought not occur because it clearly violates human rights that are enshrined in international law. Legal experts from disparate interest groups and cultures have developed such laws (e.g., the Universal Declaration of Human Rights) to protect against such violations. Someone recently asked, "Are these people dogmatic? Is there ever room for certainty?" When an individual or group approaches difficult issues with a process of open-minded, thoughtful deliberation that precedes conclusions, there is room for *qualified* certainty. There is, however, little, if any, room for unqualified, dogmatic conviction about an entire belief system. Granted, in the realm of values, ethics, and morals, there are many grey areas that philosophers help bring into sharper focus. Without expanding on the ethics of philosophy, it seems the best we can do for now is draw from the expertise of tribunals made up of international, multicultural professionals. These individuals can determine the merit and dangers of value-laden practices, and then institute universal laws that protect all civilians from the harmful consequences of dogmatically enshrined beliefs and values.

Illustrative Example: Clara

Clara makes her living as an astrologer. She is ever so willing to pronounce her starry ideas to anyone within earshot. Because she is adamantly certain that the position of celestial bodies determines one's personality and influences worldly affairs, her mind is hermeneutically sealed to any scientific explanations that would discredit her conviction. Unlike those with defensive cognitive closure, who will not engage in discussion, she welcomes every opportunity to proselytize her beliefs, which are as rigid as any this side of the Twilight Zone.

Clara prefers to pillory conflicting views rather than explore and expand her own. Were she to submit her beliefs to closer scrutiny she would have to confront doubt, uncertainty, and the likelihood that her emotions govern her reasoning—a humiliating acknowledgement that would require her to alter or reject her beliefs. Fortifying them is therefore more appealing. Clara does this by recruiting and indoctrinating new followers, who reinforce her convictions and allay her anxiety. Each recruitment consolidates her beliefs, confirms her persuasive powers, strengthens her sense of autonomous identity, and creates a community of like-minded believers that promote social connection and dignity. Assume that Clara has several other characteristics of dogmatism and we can imagine that, until her last breath is taken, she will consult the stars. If Clara were to loosen her grip on these implacable beliefs she would lose her footing and, like Dorothy, feel she was no longer in Kansas.

§§

Refreshingly different are people whose open-minded confidence is such that criticism—even accusations that they have taken leave of their senses—neither diminishes nor deters them. Flexible thinkers understand that as long as their reasoning is sound and verifiable, they can at least defend their right to state what they believe. They "tend to be more conscious of the abstract process; more aware of the distortions in their verbal maps; more flexible in altering their symbolic maps to fit the world."[33] They hold their beliefs with tentative assurance until presented with credible information that disconfirms their views, at which point they discard or amend them—and soften their voice.

"Truth consists in accurate representation of the intrinsic nature of reality."[34] When searching for answers to difficult questions, those whose minds are open accept that knowledge derives from various ways of knowing that represent reality as best as possible, without demanding confirmation of their views or intelligence. This stance is also seen in people who are passionate about their beliefs but open to the idea they might be wrong. In accordance with John Stuart Mill's philosophy of liberalism, these people have every right to act on beliefs they assume are accurate, as long as such beliefs have not been clearly and accurately refuted. But there is no justification for assuming truth for the purpose of denying its refutation, regardless of how correct or true one's beliefs or ideological system may appear to be. All systems must be fearlessly revisited and, if necessary, revised, or they will become as dead as Ptolemy and his geocentric dogma. We need people to vigorously challenge existing dogmas, both emotionally and cognitively, in order for believers to broaden their understanding of the existing tenets and assess whether they are robust enough to thrive.

§§

Because rigid certainty is somewhat yoked to the first two cognitive characteristics—intolerance of ambiguity and defensive cognitive closure—a final example helps review and clarify the nuances and distinctions among all three.

Clarifying Distinctions: Doug

Moe reminded Doug, his co-worker at the manufacturing plant, that their annual performance review was scheduled for next month. Moe said, "I'll bet Chris [their supervisor] will ask us the standard question: 'How do you think your coworkers would describe the manner in which you deal with problems?' I'm never sure how to answer that question." Doug knows how to answer it, without reservation. His response differentiates the first three cognitive characteristics of dogmatism.

"Well Moe," said Doug, "if Chris asks that same old question one more time, I'll repeat exactly what I said last year. I'm the sort of guy who likes clear rules that everyone plays by. Chris needs to be exact about specific targets. (Intolerance of ambiguity) I don't see why we can't just stick with what works and stop wasting time discussing highfalutin' ideas that haven't been put to the test." (Defensive cognitive closure) Moe then asked Doug, "Is that why you missed so many company workshops? You don't want to hear new ideas and discuss whether they'll work or not?" Defensively, Doug declared, "Frankly, if attendance were optional, I wouldn't go to any of them, especially those New Age, touchy-feely workshops on communication skills. (Defensive cognitive closure) The sessions are totally phony. They're absolutely useless as far as helping people get along with each other, and they certainly don't help the people who need an attitude adjustment." (Rigid certainty) I've been around long enough to know what works and what doesn't. There's only one sure way to improve performance around here—increase salaries. As for improving social skills so we can all be one happy family, that will never work. (Rigid certainty) I don't want to waste time discussing the matter." (Defensive cognitive closure)

Over supper that night, Moe told his wife, "Small wonder Doug never gets promoted. He's so defensive. And he's arrogant. He has no idea that behind his back, we call him Doggone Dogmatic Doug. If everyone had his attitude, our company would go down the tubes."

To summarize, new information makes Doug anxious because he might have to acknowledge his ignorance. By tenaciously clinging to staunch old beliefs, he reconfirms their absolute truth and his own inerrancy. Doug's dogmatism may march ahead of reason, but psychologically, his cognitive errors and interpersonal bravado make sense to him. They assuage his anxiety and trick him into believing he is worthy of respect and dignity. Dogmatic delusions are simplistic but deceptively protective (what dogmatists see confirms what they believe, and what they believe selects what they see).

If your co-workers are generally open to attending professional development sessions that help them stay current or gain insight, and if they value meeting to discuss ideas that might improve performance and working conditions, you may think the foregoing scenario is an exaggerated, rare occurrence. Yet many of us have worked with people like Doug, whose behavior persistently reflects a closed-minded unwillingness to exchange and implement new ideas. Such individuals fail to recognize that lasting, productive change is the product of open-minded creativity, collaboration, and the awareness that important transformations advance through patient, incremental improvements.

We have all met people with some of Doug's characteristics, yet many business and institutional departments hire and retain employees like him. Progressive administrators and CEOs would be reluctant to keep people like Doug on the payroll, especially if they occupy managerial positions. As for governments, that might require another chapter—or book.

Rigid certainty can dominate groups whose decisions seriously threaten the social order. When someone within the group questions its rigid dogma, dogmatic members defend its ideology with rhetorical, lengthy justifications that masquerade as rational, intelligent analyses. The collective need to stay the course suspends logical, analytic thinking; the verisimilitude of dogmatic belief is enough. Yet a society that substitutes open-mindedness and scientific evidence with sacrosanct ideology can go dangerously awry. This is especially true among citizens who feel socially, politically, or economically marginalized, who lack autonomy, who are young and inexperienced, or who believe the group will patch up their fragmented identities and give their lives meaning.

Compartmentalization[R]

Illustrative statements:

- "Even though freedom of speech for all groups is a worthwhile goal, it is unfortunately necessary to restrict the freedom of certain political and religious groups."[R]
- "People who try to prevent others from exercising freedom of speech should themselves be censored."[J]
- "The highest form of government is a democracy, and the highest form of democracy is a government run by those who are most intelligent."[R]
- "God loves all his children—except gays and lesbians."[J]

Compartmentalized thinking is quite the nefarious talent in the dogmatist's cognitive bag of tricks. Partitioning and sealing contradictory beliefs in separate, isolated chambers protects dogmatists from the anxiety and conflict that would ensue were they to acknowledge that they simultaneously hold logically incompatible views.

Conflicting choices and decisions are part of daily life. We procrastinate in the face of pressing obligations; we crave unhealthy food and drink; we buy things we know we don't need. Inconsistencies are common among our beliefs, emotions, and behaviors. Many supporters of the environmental movement drive gas-guzzlers short distances when they could easily walk or hop a commuter train; others toss various recyclables in the trash even though they are committed to recycling bottles, cans, and magazines. Rational people who are concerned about global warming try to reconcile their conflicting thoughts and behaviors in a manner that allows for reasonable reflection, compromise, and change. Conversely, dogmatists fail to acknowledge such contradictions—to themselves and others.

A facile solution to resolve the paradox of conflicting beliefs is to box in one's thinking and construct compartments that house dogmatic, internal contradictions. Safely bolted behind separate closed doors, isolated beliefs allow their host to perpetuate a make-believe world of illogical certainty. The dogmatic practice of communism provides a striking example of compartmentalized beliefs and behaviors, in that the extreme partitioning of ideological practice from theory means dogmatic despots can commit crimes against humanity and all the while proclaim that they value communal sharing as the supreme economic goal of socialism. Evil in the name of good.

Similarly, compartmentalization is active in a democracy that condemns undemocratic nations for invading other countries, even though under the guise of spreading world peace, democracy, and human rights, that same nation hypocritically justifies preemptive strikes and the militarization of space. A government that supports despots of oppressive regimes elsewhere, or that thumbs its nose at the International Criminal Court while singing the praises of democracy, is either guilty of dogmatic compartmentalization or it has "a lot of splainin' to do." Under the guise of protection, the compartmentalization of political dogmatism paradoxically frees citizens from tyranny while, at the same time, shortens many lives with bombs that "deliver" democracy. Similarly, economic dogmatism protects the "haves" who declare their disingenuous commitment to ending the poverty of the "have-nots."

§§

Examples of compartmentalization are often embedded in the language of religious dogmatism, where posturing about moral values is abundantly evident. Wrapped in the rhetoric of antiatheism, antihomosexuality, antiabortion, anti–gun legislation, and anti–abolition of capital punishment, their self-righteous agendas expose the illogic of compartmentalized thinking. They closet the Christian tenet to love thy neighbor as thyself in one compartment and seal off contradictory beliefs to reject (or even murder) those with opposing belief systems. They support war and the extralegal use of torture, yet refuse to acknowledge that these practices contradict their support for universal human rights. The more their illogic is challenged, the more they feel threatened and the harder they try to fortify inconsistent beliefs and behaviors in bunkers of segregated content.

Terrorist "psycho-logic" is quintessential compartmentalization. "Polarizing and absolutist, it is a rhetoric of 'us versus them' whereby we must fight against the evil-doers."[35] Moreover, "If the basic premise is that they are evil and we are good, then it logically follows that the moral imperative is to destroy them."[36] Consumed by judgmental rage, terrorists readily adopt this reptilian reasoning, which makes a spectacle of their emotions and behaviors.

Compartmentalization is also lodged in our social institutions; it pervades our daily lives and obscures rational thought. Politicians and leaders worldwide, along with ordinary citizens, are skilled at this type of cognitive carpentry. We see it in people like Marjorie, who believes that abortion should be outlawed yet supports the death penalty and the right to bear arms. She also believes in human rights but thinks homosexuals and lesbians should not be entitled to common law unions, let alone marriage. It is not that Marjorie is incapable of rational thought, but the anxiety that underlies her dogmatism narrows her access to reason. By sealing her contradictory beliefs in separate compartments she can avoid confronting the inherent contradictions in her flawed reasoning.

Those who claim it is wrong to kill innocent civilians yet make exceptions for infidels, apostates, or the protection of democracy vividly illustrate widespread examples of compartmentalization. In the name of peace, God, and democracy, their political and religious beliefs have been compartmentalized to permit incarceration, torture, and murder—all of which seal their contradictory beliefs in cognitive cubicles that countenance and justify their behavior. Social psychologists use the term *cognitive dissonance* to describe "a state of tension that occurs whenever a person holds two cognitions (ideas, attitudes, beliefs, opinions) that are psychologically inconsistent, such as "Smoking is a dumb thing to do because it could kill me" and "I smoke two packs a day."[37] To reduce the tension arising from such dissonance and restore consonance, the person either quits smoking or rationalizes that smoking is not all that harmful. Dogmatism and its feature of compartmentalization is similar to cognitive dissonance theory in that dogmatism is also a strategy that maintains cognitive consonance, but dogmatic belief systems are presumed to originate in early psychological deficiencies that are more complex, serious, and pervasive than those that underlie cognitive dissonance. Furthermore, because dogmatic people tend to lack personal insight, they are less likely to be aware of, much less confront, dissonance caused by cognitive or behavioral misalignments, and they are therefore more likely to resort to the simplicity of compartmentalization.

§§

People inclined toward open-minded complexity of thought can grapple with the larger picture and, without breaking into an existential sweat, recognize the contradictions among their beliefs. Prepared to tackle their cognitive inconsistencies and gain new insight, they stand in stark contrast to dogmatists who deny, rationalize, or defend their contradictory beliefs and blithely carry on.

We need not assume that anxiety is always the culprit of compartmentalization. Some people are quite aware of contradictions they might try to reconcile. What differentiates them from dogmatists is the cavalier manner in which dogmatists dismiss any need to recognize and readjust their incompatible beliefs. Urgent psychological needs, not beliefs per se, account for their compartmentalized contradictions that oversimplify the complex.

To summarize these first four cognitive characteristics, because dogmatists cannot tolerate a lack of clarity (intolerance of ambiguity), they preserve their belief systems in various ways. Some refuse to even discuss opposing views (defensive cognitive closure), some hammer home their beliefs because they are convinced they are right and need others to agree with them (rigid certainty), and some keep their conflicting views isolated in separate cognitive chambers (compartmentalization). They all simplify the complex. Yet the tendency to oversimplify things and look for information that confirms our established beliefs is common. We believe what we do because we knowingly want to, especially when evidence is lacking or tedious to access. In contrast, dogmatists believe what they do because they *need* to, in spite of compelling evidence that is readily available and with which they are familiar. Moreover, to a certain degree, they lack psychological insight, the last cognitive characteristic to which we now turn our attention.

Lack of Personal Insight[R]

Illustrative comments:

- "If people don't want to hear my point of view, that's their problem."[J]
- "People often oppose me just to provoke me and start an argument."[J]
- "I can't understand why people consistently avoid me."[J]
- "I have a hard time convincing others that my views are correct."[J]
- "When I talk about my religious beliefs, most people either ignore me or change the topic."[J]

- "What's the point in mulling over regrets—what's done is done."[J]
- "The neighborhood pub offers better, cheaper therapy than any shrink."[J]

Accurate, personal awareness of feelings and motivations varies from person to person. Many people are unwilling to closely examine the real reasons for feeling or behaving as they do, and this lack of personal insight is dogmatists' greatest wound, for it prevents them from recognizing their own closed-mindedness. The very prerequisite for change is unavailable in those who dismiss or trivialize the importance of introspection. And while nondogmatic people are also unreflective, they are less anxious about psychological introspection and more receptive to its benefits.

In order to gain insight about their reliance on external authority and move toward autonomous self-sufficiency, dogmatic people would first need the motivation to seek greater psychological understanding. The problem is, they rarely reflect on their genuine emotions and motives, preferring instead to stiffen their upper lip, clench their jaw, and maintain a high opinion of their certainties and cognitive capacities. Ask a dogmatist what self-knowledge he or she fears most, and the likely response would be "nothing." Instead, their anxiety aborts, revealing psychological probes, which would be demoralizing. But dogmatism disguised is Socrates denied, for his maxim to "know thyself" rings hollow in closed minds.

The rigidly dogmatic differ from those who knowingly deceive others while trying to convince them they are right. Dogmatists deceive *themselves*. They are not only right, they are righteous. They are not only knowledgeable, they are wise. In this sense, dogmatism runs deeper than self-deception, self-justification, and self-righteousness. It is self-denial that, above all, keeps one safe. We would hardly expect dogmatic people to ask themselves *why* they are thinking what they are thinking, for even if they sought such insight, I suspect few explanations would come to mind. It is hard to imagine them saying something like, "Come to think of it, I really am rigid and narrow-minded. One of these days I'll have to ask myself what I'm so afraid of. If I could let go of my anxiety and fear I might stop trying to convince everyone that I'm right. Why do I get so annoyed with people who won't admit I'm right, and downright angry with people won't admit they're wrong? Perhaps the fault lies with my own demands and expectations. Could it be that sometimes I am wrong about important matters? If so, what's so wrong about being absolutely wrong? And what's so right about being absolutely right? It won't be easy, but I need to probe these questions. If I could find a way to lighten up and be easier on myself, maybe I would be easier on others? Surely it's not too late to teach an old dogmatist new tricks?"

Illustrative Examples: Leroy, Dr. Smart, and Marion

A lack of personal insight is evident in Leroy, whose other cognitive features keep this last one company. He spends most of his weekends at a local bar, ranting about the ineptitude of the current government. When people with opposing views make casual political comments, Leroy thinks he is "graciously tolerating" them by deigning to listen, even though he dismisses them as ignorant. This is an important point, because although he could reasonably, even passionately, reject a particular view, Leroy attacks the person rather than the argument. He insults others: "People who think like you are a threat to democracy!" Leroy knows he has difficulty making friends, but because he fails to examine his own role in social rejection, his regrets are, as Sinatra crooned, "too few to mention." Until recently Leroy defined himself as a politician, but his resounding defeat in the last election cost him his seat in government. Magnifying his misery, his wife Betty recently said, "For twenty years I've tried to understand and support you, to talk through our problems. All I get from you is stonewalling and accusations. Why do you think marriage counseling is a waste of time and money when we haven't even tried it? If you won't agree to counseling, I'm leaving."

Leroy still cares for Betty and does not want their marriage to end in divorce, but when he tries to understand their marital problems he drifts into a dazed zone, as if he is overcome by some mysterious, cognitive vertigo. His emotions become numb, his thinking narrows, and his behavior becomes bar-bound. Long ago, Leroy barricaded his inner self behind a protective wall that blocked his emotions and his potential for personal insight. Though he finds temporary solace in alcohol, drinking only reinforces these barriers, intensifies his anger, and compounds his deeper problems. He is oblivious to the impact his adamant views have on others and does not recognize how his emotions jaundice his thinking, damage his interpersonal relationships, and rob his marriage of intimacy. The thought of what he might discover if he came to know himself is frightening. From Leroy's perspective, insight about the source of his interpersonal difficulties and excessive drinking would only increase his despair. If he cannot find the courage to open his mind, he will have to find the courage to live with it closed.

Dr. Smart also lacks personal insight, but she expresses it differently. She thinks that being a scientist automatically merits power and status, seizing every opportunity to lecture colleagues about the importance of including scientific research in all university courses. Professors recognize her views as legitimate, but they steer clear of her angry, defensive sermons. We could hypothesize that Dr. Smart's rigid belief system rewards her with a strong sense of identity, but her dogmatism blocks personal insight. She is unaware that her self-constructed, glorified identity causes bouts of anxiety and depression, the source of which she will not explore. To cope with social ostracism and loneliness, she immerses herself in academic research and rationalizes that colleagues who refuse to meet with her are simply ignorant—or ignorant and simple.

§§

While few people never avoid self-scrutiny, *consistent* failure to acknowledge and understand the source of unpleasant feelings prevents one from acquiring useful insight. Contrast Leroy and Dr. Smart's psychological difficulties with people who seek professional help to convert psychological problems into personal growth. They acknowledge their lack of understanding about self-defeating behaviors and genuinely want to replace their cognitive deficiency with insight. Unlike dogmatic believers, people with more open-minded belief systems can reflect about the personal meaning of their core beliefs and consequent emotions and behaviors. This is not to suggest that we should try to understand every underlying motive for all of our beliefs and behaviors; such endless searching for explanations would drag us down. But people capable of introspection are able to spend time quietly examining their thoughts, emotions, motives, and behaviors, particularly when they recognize the importance of doing so, as our next example illustrates.

Marion made an appointment with a psychologist because she was depressed about her inability to meet deadlines. As a result, on several occasions she has been passed over for promotions at work. Marion's apology for arriving late to her first therapy session was revealing: "My only serious problem is that I'm the world's worst procrastinator. I can't manage my time. I never seem to complete work assignments on schedule and I'm known for keeping friends waiting. I'm late for everything, even crucial deadlines. It's a wonder I don't procrastinate with my next breath!" In therapy, Marion gained insight about her lingering anger over her father's overbearing control: "Dad would never try to understand what I wanted. He just issued orders as if I were some kind of private in his personal army. If I didn't obey, I was punished—not physically, but emotionally. Dad would glare at me, issue threats, put me down, and refuse to talk to me." Now, at the age of thirty-three, Marion is gaining insight about her rebellious need to do everything on her own terms and in her own time. This is Marion's way to retaliate and secure personal freedom. Perhaps she makes everyone wait for her as a means to regain control and get even with her father. As Marion examined her problem from different angles, she began to understand possible motives for dragging her feet. In the process, conscious choices gradually replaced the unconscious re-actions that were sustaining her habitual procrastination.

Similarly, the more dogmatists recognize that their underlying anxiety prevents them from acquiring an open-minded approach to knowledge, the more they gain insight about their motives for needing to be seen as purveyors of truth. They then no longer need others to confirm their wisdom and bend to their way of thinking. With an awareness of the protective strategies they cultivated to keep their minds rigidly closed, they can choose to open their minds to new ideas and change their self-defeating, protective maneuvers. Therapy can be a difficult but rewarding journey, but first one's mind must be suffi-ciently open to its possibilities.

Beyond therapy, artistic expression provides another avenue for personal insight. As vanguards of the collective human psyche, artists communicate their deepest doubts and fears through a variety of mediums that provide access to human emotions and insecurities. Through the canvas, screen, stage, books, poems, song, and sculpture, artistic works speak to us in a manner that allows the artist and the receiver to connect at a deep level, and this connection can rejuvenate the spirit and give meaning to life. Emily Dickinson's poem "I Measure Every Grief," Leonardo DaVinci's painting *Mona Lisa*, and Edvard Munch's art noir *The Scream* all depict the profound human need to know and connect with others through mutual suffering, loss, loneliness, and insight. They reveal that self-knowledge is never an end in itself but "a means of liberating the forces of spontaneous growth."[38] The vulnerable self-exposure of artistic communication is an invitation to open our minds, explore, and share in the complexities of life that are nested within the collective psyche of human existence.

Dogmatists tend to decline such invitations. For them, denigrating art is easier than emptying their minds of preconceptions. Easier because they cannot become fully immersed in the moment and absorb the ambiguity of artistic communication. Easier because they are not cognitively adventuresome and imaginative enough to open their senses in order to fully see and hear or touch and taste. Those who say, "I could never understand why people spend hours sitting and staring at paintings in art museums," or "What's there to see in weird designs and blank faces?" shed light on their closed-minded lack of any artistic expression of humanity's universal experiences. We observe their visibly visceral reaction to novel modes of expression, particularly those of the avant-garde that frustrate the dogmatist's preference for simple, linear creations with uncomplicated, unambiguous messages.

To claim that all dogmatists are incapable of appreciating artistic expression would be to engage in careless hyperbole. Similarly, it would be irrational to assume that all flexible, open-minded people want to become engrossed in art so that they can contemplate the deeper psychological meaning of their existence. But those who are less anxious and more cognitively supple can open their minds to artistic expression in all realms of creativity, should they choose to do so. With emotional calm and heightened awareness, open minds are better able to appreciate, understand, and resonate with the unifying power and existential depth of artistic expression.

SUMMARIZING THIS CHAPTER AND PREPARING FOR THE NEXT

The preceding five characteristics are the alchemy of dogmatic, cognitive conviction. We will explore the deeper reasons for the dogmatist's use of these cognitive strategies in chapters 9 through 16, ending here with the recognition that people who lose their ability to think with a clear, open mind also lose their freedom.

Recall that the criteria outlined at the beginning of this chapter are necessary to determine the trait of dogmatism—a trait that has a minimum of six characteristics, three of which come from the cognitive domain. These cognitive characteristics include:

- Intolerance of ambiguity
- Defensive cognitive closure

- Rigid certainty
- Compartmentalization
- Lack of personal insight

If we keep these qualifiers in mind, we will be less inclined to label ourselves or our friends, family, former partners, colleagues, and bosses as dogmatic. Parenthetically, I considered including preoccupation with morality (of which sexual behavior would figure prominently) as a distinct characteristic of dogmatic thinking, because preoccupation with sex is one of the nine traits of the authoritarian personality, assessed by the Fascism Scale (1950).[39] Despite current polarized views on sexuality, especially as it relates to homosexuality, AIDS, abstinence, and abortion, and despite people's increased exposure to explicit sexual scenes on the Internet, movie screens, and television, I vetoed the idea because I think beliefs about morality are embedded in the five cognitive characteristics, which cover a wide spectrum of specific belief systems.

Finally, while these cognitive features of dogmatism are critical for its designation, the emotional and behavioral characteristics presented in the next two chapters are equally important. The definitions and illustrations of these remaining eight characteristics, in combination with the five cognitive characteristics presented here, will complete our portrait of a prototypical dogmatist.

Having familiarized ourselves with the cognitive characteristics of dogmatism, we can conclude that all five features are destructive for individuals, groups, and societies. And it only gets worse.

NOTES

1. J. Stern, *Terror in the Name of God: Why Religious Militants Kill* (New York: HarperCollins, 2003), pp. 5–6.

2. M. Rokeach, *The Open and Closed Mind* (New York: Basic Books, 1960), p. 37.

3. P. Suedfeld, K. Guttieri, and P. E. Tetlock, "Assessing Integrative

Complexity at a Distance: Archival Analyses of Thinking and Decision Making," in *The Psychological Assessment of Political Leaders*, ed. J. M. Post (Ann Arbor: University of Michigan Press, 2003), pp. 246–70. Complexity theory is a successor to George Kelly's theory of personal constructs (*The Psychology of Personal Constructs*, vol. 1 [New York: Norton, 1955]). The authors distinguish between *integrative complexity*, which refers to differences in differentiation and integration from situation to situation, and *conceptual complexity*, which refers to customary levels of cognitive functioning indicative of a personality trait (also known as *trait complexity*). These researchers note that moderate correlations exist between conceptual complexity and personality characteristics such as extroversion, social adeptness, nonconformity, and narcissism that "may be a factor in leadership success" (p. 250). In addition, a study that used the integrative complexity coding system to analyze confidential interviews with eighty-nine members of the British House of Commons found that moderate socialists interpreted policy issues in more integratively complex or multidimensional terms than did moderate conservatives who, in turn, interpreted issues in more complex terms than extreme conservatives and extreme socialists (p. 365).

4. P. Suedfeld and D. C. Leighton, "Early Communications in the War against Terrorism: An Integrative Complexity Analysis," *Political Psychology* 23, no. 3 (2002): 585–99. These authors refer to P. E. Tetlock, D. Armor, and R. Peterson, the authors of "The Slavery Debate in Antebellum America: Cognitive Style, Value Conflict, and the Limits of Compromise," *Journal of Personality and Social Psychology* 66 (1994): 115–26, who state that although simple strategies are "more economical and may lead to crisp, neat, rapid solutions," they are also risky in that simple strategies not only tend to ignore important information about one's allies and opponents, they may result in "rigid adherence to a failing plan" (p. 587). The cognitive characteristics of dogmatism reflect these errors in mental processing.

5. M. D. Wallace, P. Suedfeld, and K. Thachuk, "Political Rhetoric of Leaders under Stress in the Gulf Crisis," *Journal of Conflict Resolution* 37, no. 1 (1993): 94–107.

6. R. Altemeyer, *The Authoritarian Specter* (Cambridge, MA: Harvard University Press, 1996), p. 277.

7. Suedfeld, Guttieri, and Tetlock, "Assessing Integrative Complexity," pp. 255–56.

8. Ibid., p. 257.

9. Ibid.

10. http://www.answers.com/topic/dogmatic (accessed Jan. 16, 2008).

11. R. R. McRae and P. T. Costa Jr., "The Stability of Personality: Observations and Evaluations," in *Current Directions in Personality Psychology*, ed. Carolyn C. Morf and O. Ayduk (Upper Saddle River, NJ: Pearson Education, 2005), pp. 3–8.

12. Items followed by a superscripted *R* denote an original statement on Rokeach's Dogmatism Scale, published in *The Open and Closed Mind*. Bob Altemeyer's DOG questionnaire, which is published in *The Authoritarian Specter*, contains twenty statements: ten that measure dogmatism and ten that measure open-mindedness. The superscript *A* designates an Altemeyer original. The Johnson Dogmatism Scale (JDS), Form D (my scale), consists of forty statements: thirty items tap dogmatism, ten are Rokeach originals, five are Rokeach items modified by myself, and fifteen are Johnson originals. The remaining ten items are fillers that are unrelated to the construct *dogmatism*. Original or revised items from the JDS are designated with the superscript *J*. My modifications of Rokeach's and Altemeyer's statements are superscripted with *R, Jmod* and *A, Jmod*, respectively.

13. This is a direct quote from President George W. Bush's televised "Address to a Joint Session of Congress and the American People," Washington, DC, September 20, 2001.

14. S. Kopp, *If You Meet the Buddha on the Road, Kill Him!* (New York: Bantam, 1979), p. 234.

15. R. May, *The Cry for Myth* (New York: Norton, 1991).

16. A. Dulles, in D. Dennett, *Breaking the Spell: Religion as a Natural Phenomenon* (New York: Penguin, 2006), p. 364.

17. Rokeach, *The Open and Closed Mind*, p. 234.

18. E. Hoffer, *The True Believer* (New York: Harper and Row, 1951).

19. Rokeach, *The Open and Closed Mind*, p. 242.

20. T. Gover, *A Delicate Balance: What Philosophy Can Tell Us about Terrorism* (Boulder, CO: Westview Press, 2002), p. 135.

21. L. W. Anderson and D. R. Krathwohl, eds., *A Taxonomy for Learning, Teaching, and Assessing: A Revision of Bloom's Taxonomy of Educational Objectives* (Boston: Allyn & Bacon, 2000). Krathwohl has revised B. S. Bloom's taxonomy (*Taxonomy of Educational Objectives: The Classification of Educational Goals* [New York: Longmans, Green, 1956]), which represented a sequential, cumulative hierarchy whereby mastery of each cat-

WHAT'S SO WRONG WITH BEING ABSOLUTELY RIGHT

egory depends on the successful mastery of the previous one. Bloom's categories begin with knowledge and progress through comprehension, application, analysis, synthesis, and evaluation. In Krathwohl's modernized revision, the original number of categories has been retained with important changes: remember, understand, apply, analyze, evaluate, and create. This new guide enables teachers to adapt curriculum planning and delivery of instruction to specific learning objectives.

22. Altemeyer, *The Authoritarian Specter*.

23. In a PBS television interview, medical experts agreed that cancer researchers are highly collaborative. Paul Nurse, the president of Rockefeller University; Harold Varmus, the president of Memorial Sloan-Kettering Cancer Center; David Nathan, president emeritus of Dana-Farber Cancer Institute; and Deb Schrag of Memorial Sloan-Kettering Cancer Center were interviewed by Charlie Rose in the *Charlie Rose Science Series*, Episode Four: "The Latest in Cancer Research," April 19, 2007.

24. F. Fukuyama, *Our Posthuman Future* (New York: Farrar, Strauss and Giroux, 2002), p. 66.

25. http://www.history.mcs.standrews.ac.uk/Quotations/Galileo.html (accessed June 18, 2006).

26. P. W. Schultz and A. Searleman, "Rigidity of Thought and Behavior; 100 Years of Research," *Genetic, Social and General Psychology Monographs* 128, no. 2 (2002): 165.

27. Altemeyer, *The Authoritarian Specter*, p. 201.

28. K. Popper, *Conjectures and Refutations* (New York: Basic Books, 1963).

29. Dennett, *Breaking the Spell*, p. 363.

30. Altemeyer, *The Authoritarian Specter*, p. 202.

31. F. Wheen, *How Mumbo Jumbo Conquered the World: A Short History of Modern Delusions* (New York: Perseus, 2004), p. 98.

32. B. Martin, "Scientific Fraud and the Power Structure of Science," *Prometheus* 10 (1992): 83–98. For an excellent analysis of how statistics can be manipulated to fit the researcher's biases, see Joel Best's book, *More Damned Lies and Statistics* (Berkeley: University of California Press, 2004).

33. N. Postman, *Conscientious Objections: Stirring up Trouble about Language, Technology, and Education* (New York: Vintage, 1988), p. 142.

34. S. Blackburn, *Truth: A Guide* (Oxford: Oxford University Press, 2005), p. 165.

35. W. Reich, *Origins of Terrorism: Psychologies, Ideologies, Theologies, States of Mind* (Baltimore: Johns Hopkins University Press, 1998), p. 25.

36. M. Crenshaw, "An Organizational Approach to the Analysis of Political Terrorism," *Orbis*, no. 29 (1985): 465–89.

37. C. Tavris and E. Aronson, *Mistakes Were Made (But Not by Me)* (Orlando, FL: Houghton Mifflin Harcourt, 2007), p. 13.

38. K. Horney, *Neurosis and Human Growth: The Struggle toward Self-Realization* (New York: Norton, 1950), p. 15.

39. T. W. Adorno et al., *The Authoritarian Personality* (New York: Harper and Brothers, 1950).

Chapter 6

STIR IN COLOR

Emotional Characteristics of Dogmatism

Understanding "the other" will pose the 21st century's greatest social challenge.

Charles Taylor

When the five cognitive features outlined in the previous chapter combine with the three emotional characteristics presented here, our black-and-white portrait of dogmatism takes on vivid color. This chapter is considerably shorter than those that present the cognitive and behavioral components of dogmatism, primarily because anxiety—a central feature of dogmatism—is a theme that runs through several theories in upcoming chapters. The brevity of this one does not, therefore, diminish the important role emotions play in the development of dogmatism.

Humming in the background of all cognitive deliberations are emotions, which have been called "the energy for thought."[1] Unlike feelings, which are transient, emotions are more enduring. They dramatically influence thoughts and behaviors, which compels us to expand our definition of narrow-mindedness beyond simple cognitive rigidity. The evocative memory of Winnie, who was as unpopular as wasps at a barbecue, reminds us that black-and-white thinking is not her only annoying trait. Strong emotions and observable behaviors embellish that which is uppermost in her mind. And Winnie is not alone.

Like your dogmatic next-door neighbor who drops in to borrow your power saw and launches into a monologue on the upcoming election, or like the uninvited, preachy relative who shows up for Thanksgiving dinner and all you can do is hope against disaster, the emotions of such individuals animate dogmatism (and the content of this chapter).

Along with their frustrating, sometimes dangerous presence, each emotional characteristic must have at least three cognitive features and two of the behavioral characteristics before we can reasonably assume that someone has the personality trait of dogmatism. As previously noted, six out of thirteen characteristics are sufficient to determine the trait's presence, and although most features grab our attention, the emotional characteristics are so obvious they trumpet dogmatism, even without the rest of the band.

EMOTIONAL CHARACTERISTICS

Belief-Associated Anxiety and Fear[2,J]

Illustrative statements (As you read each example, think about the emotion that accompanies it):

- "Once I get wound up in a heated discussion, I just can't stop."[R]
- "During important meetings, I need to know where everyone stands."[J]
- "My blood boils whenever a person stubbornly refuses to admit he's wrong."[R]
- "When people question my core beliefs, I sometimes get so rattled my heart pounds."[J]
- "People who want to change my thinking about politics or religion had better think twice."[J]
- "In this house we don't talk politics or religion."[J]

Many emotions accompany beliefs, especially core beliefs. The four that are most implicated in dogmatic belief are anxiety, fear (which falls on the same physiological continuum as anxiety), anger, and existential despair. Anxiety and anger have the same etymological origin in the Indo-Germanic language—*angh*, which means "constriction." As we shall see in the chapter on evolution, these emotions continue to have adaptive value if they occur in response to threatening environments. However, when they float feely in the background of daily living, they constrict thought, which has implications for dogmatism.

Like oxygen, anxiety is key to our survival. It focuses our attention and releases the necessary adrenaline to escape a burning building, break an athletic record (instead of a leg), or write passionate prose. At optimum levels, anxiety improves performance across a wide range of skills,[3] but beyond a higher-than-optimum range, it impairs attention, memory, problem solving, and reasoning ability.[4] Perhaps you have noticed that anxious people seem unable to clearly process events; in particular, they do not fully hear what others say. Compounding matters, they underestimate their ability to cope with life's demands, and they interpret innocuous or mildly unpleasant events as dangerous.[5] Anxiety signals a loss of control, and because one cannot feel simultaneously anxious and in control, people with persistent anxiety try to conceal it from themselves and others. They also present an edited version of their real selves—one that they hope gives the appearance of self-assurance and competence. To some degree this is understandable and natural, but like any emotional extreme, intense, prolonged anxiety creates a host of problems, one of which is dogmatism. The energy used to bury anxiety impedes access to open-minded reason and distorts perceptions of reality. Strong emotions pressure the rational mind to come up with defensible reasons, and many characteristics of dogmatism are ushered in and uttered within unpleasant emotional states that dogmatists find hard to recognize, interpret, and reconcile.

The five cognitive characteristics of dogmatism that were presented in the last chapter protect against the anxiety and fear of not knowing, and because anxiety is assumed to underlie all of dogmatism's cognitive and behavior characteristics, its presence is a prerequisite for the trait. All this suggests that political or religious leaders who want to manipulate the minds of their minions first need to inculcate fear that narrows reason. With impunity, such leaders can then impose their ideological agendas on an anxious, obedient following—some of whom will even glorify the leader as a benevolent savior.

Illustrative Example: Molly

Molly provides a good example of someone who is blind to the emotional characteristics that underlie dogmatic belief. An administrator at a local bank, Molly has closed, fossilized beliefs about business management and the manner in which meetings should be organized and chaired. Add five parts cognitive and behavioral drama to her rigid proselytizing, and few combinations would more seriously damage her credibility and social relationships. During meetings, Molly nervously drums her fingers and in a gawking manner shifts her penetrating gaze from face to face as if she were searching the playground for her lost child. She interrupts others, finishes their sentences, dominates the conversation, and ends most of her sentences with one word—a high-pitched "yes?" Colleagues are attuned to her obvious distress and urgent need for agreement, but Molly is less attuned to her underlying feelings that communicate more than she intends. Her silent message, one that she distances even from herself, is, "I feel insignificant unless my views are heard ahead of and above all others. My views and ideas *must* be endorsed; if they aren't, people will think I'm stupid." The clues to Molly's dogmatism are her anxious need to drown people's thoughts in a monologue of her own and her inability to quietly absorb the moment without needing to control it. She is unaware of the deep feelings that cloud her thinking and impair her ability to communicate effectively.

Excess anxiety is Molly's silent, unwanted instigator of dogmatic, outdated beliefs. Although she thinks she interprets matters accurately, persistent anxiety that idles in the background constricts her thinking and distorts her interpretations. Chronic anxiety creates unremitting, ineffective worry—the habitual worry that is outside the boundary of voluntary control.[6] This unmanageable quality gives pervasive anxiety its abnormality, in the sense that its uncontrollable presence is relatively infrequent in the general population (intense, time-limited anxiety is more accurately described as fear, which may be seen in phobic reactions to specific objects or situations). Persistent anxiety that hovers beneath the surface causes distortions that are anchored more in the host's imagination than external reality. Simple questions spark unnecessary apprehension that prompts lengthy explanations, all of which further obstruct rational thought and reasonable decisions. All of these factors keep rigid, traditional beliefs entrenched.

§§

Consider the psychological underpinnings of the following strident pronouncement that Geoffrey, a sales executive who is embarrassed by low profit margins, makes to his staff: "Look. It's patently obvious that your plan will not work . . ." Hearing this comment, listeners might not make a direct link between Geoffrey's words, emotions, and reasoning, but his visceral emotions are palpable. Geoffrey's communication style suggests that his rigid beliefs have been marinating in an anxiety that soaks up certainty and premature judgment—antidotes that assuage his self-doubt. Unaware that his urgent pronouncements stem from an emotional undertow that sequesters belief in closed-minded compartments, he cannot separate the emotional chaff from the cognitive wheat. Strong, emotional attachment to his beliefs renders Geoffrey unwilling to logically assess information that conflicts with what he already knows, for that would intensify his anxiety, threaten his certainty, and shatter his identity. Like water on the Wicked Witch of the West, questioning any one belief would cause a meltdown of the entire system, taking with it Geoffrey's brittle identity, as well as the flexible splendor of an open mind.

Anxious hypervigilance not only prevents people like Geoffrey from living fully and freely in the moment, it also constricts their sense of humor. They miss the witty one-liner and the punch line of jokes, and they become easily embarrassed and annoyed by impromptu frivolity. Unable to step back and laugh at life's absurdities and their own frailties, they rarely let loose with spontaneous, unrestrained laughter. Their sense of humor is more inclined toward blatant sarcasm and hostility that betrays a racial, ethnic, or gender bias—which brings us to the next emotional characteristic of dogmatism.

Belief-Associated Anger

When orthodox dogma merges with anger, reason is annihilated by folly and incivility. People who are emotionally attached to their beliefs often exhibit *habitual* defensiveness and aggression that accompanies dogmatism. Like masks donned to conceal anxiety, anger also masks self-doubt, providing a safe place to hide. Anger asserts, "I am right; you are wrong." To the onlooker, such hostility gives apathy an appealing glow. But aggressive antagonism functions to obscure the very anxiety that generates it. By effecting a bold facade, arrogant, authoritarian dogmatists blind themselves to the anxiety that launches a tirade of judgment designed to keep their true feelings hidden.

Illustrative Example: Chuck

You may recall a time when you questioned the cherished beliefs of a dogmatic person and felt as if you had detonated a psychological cluster bomb. Marc has. He tried to engage Chuck, his business colleague, in a discussion about their company's financial support for postsecondary education. "Given current profits, I think the company should reconsider the amount of money we donate to the university. We could certainly make a sizeable increase to our scholarship fund." Chuck's abrasive, opinionated reaction was a machine-gun volley of invective against all university students. "Students should pay their own way in this world! Their biggest problem is that they refuse to work at menial jobs and earn their degree. They'd rather loaf about and let their parents foot the bill. We'd be better off funding community programs, not immature students!" Marc refused to indulge Chuck's hostile, argumentative position. As he left Chuck's office, he calmly said, "You seem to have very strong feelings here. I'd like all of us to discuss this idea at our next planning meeting."

Chronically on edge, people like Chuck lack awareness of the deeper anxiety that fuels their irritation and anger. When others question their beliefs or try to influence them toward greater open-mindedness that might alter their thinking, they smother their anxiety with belligerent, closed-minded dogmatism. Because dogmatists fear people whose views differ, those with opposing beliefs are considered enemies. Emotional flash points cloud reason and protect a fragile identity against anyone who "dares insult my intelligence." Add shrewd charisma to the mix, and dogmatism discharges dogmatic authoritarian aggression, a unique characteristic that has somber, far-reaching consequences that are examined in the next chapter.

Existential Despair[R]

Illustrative statements:

- "In the long run, nothing I do will make a difference."[J]
- "Most people just don't give a damn for others."[R]
- "Fundamentally, the world we live in is a pretty lonesome place."[R]
- "The apocalypse is near."[J]
- "Life is nothing but a game of Russian roulette."[J]

Borrowing from existential philosophy, specialists in existential psychology study "the individual's confrontation with the givens of existence."[7] They muse about inexorable anxiety, isolation, and emptiness—all of which we encounter as we struggle to find meaning in the face of imminent death.

This is our human dilemma. Our beliefs about these inescapable human conditions evolve, quite naturally, from early childhood experiences.[8] The key point here is that childhood nurturance and encouragement shape authenticity—a personality trait that reflects a consistent, internalized, and integrated self that acts autonomously. This self-perception is largely determined first by external social evaluations, and second by internal self-evaluations.

The intricate fabric of social roles in modern society requires us to adapt to different settings and enact different roles. As such, our genuine selves are seldom completely meshed with our circumstantial selves; these identities are never completely unified. Psychologists have investigated this chameleon-like enactment of roles, and while some propose that our identities adjust to the roles we play,[9] research indicates that, whatever the degree of complexity in our social selves, it is the relative autonomy and integration of our inner sense of identity interacting with social roles that determines authenticity and psychological well-being.[10] When one's autonomy is largely replaced with extrinsic definitions and determinations, authenticity or genuineness is compromised. And because authenticity has been linked to a host of positive traits—such as friendliness, extraversion, and openness to new experiences—without authenticity, psychological well-being is jeopardized.[11]

§§

Even in supportive environments, children's encounters with the world are frequently stressful. Chronic anxiety (such as that seen in the generalized anxiety disorder) creates unremitting, ineffective worry—the habitual worry that is outside the boundary of voluntary control.[12] If anxiety persists into adolescence, they become increasingly inauthentic, are attracted to cults of celebrity and personality, and adopt identities that are fashioned by others. The reliance on external agents constricts their development of cognitive systems that would otherwise enhance an intrinsic sense of identity and enrich interpersonal relationships. Indeed, the entire process of therapy is undertaken to reveal the source of anxiety, conflict, and despair that often begins in childhood.

There is a saying, "Never do for a child what the child can do for him or herself." When children are encouraged and rewarded for independent thought and action, they develop the courage to make authentic choices. More importantly, their later beliefs and behaviors are largely derived from autonomous decisions for which they assume responsibility, even though none of their choices proffer guarantees of success.[13]

In contrast, dogmatic people's personal identities are extrinsically defined and governed; as such, they readily lose their balance, especially when their external world of people and ideas falters. They despair about their inability to control events that would keep their lives ordered and stable, and their lack of personal insight prevents acceptance of human imperfection and the inevitability of change. Such people have a slender grasp on the commonalities of human experience—the vulnerabilities they and the rest of us face as we try to manage our lives, find meaning in existence, and make sense of a complicated, sometimes bewildering world. If, as some existentialists believe (notably Camus), life is absurd, then cynicism and despair seem rational reactions to an irrational world. And if we add to the prolonged anxiety that underlies dogmatism several other characteristics that shape it, then it is easy to see how one's belief systems can calcify in despair and pessimism.

Illustrative Example: Edna

Consider Edna, now in her fifties. She constantly grumbles about the terrible state of the world to anyone who will listen to her laments about "scandalous politicians, the male patriarchy, humanity's hopeless greed, and the wretched state of the world." A homebody, Edna has few interests and limited social contacts. She rarely listens to her husband's views with an open mind and complains when he turns on the television to hear the evening news: "We don't need to be reminded of all the madness and corruption in this world! Surely there's something better to watch." Edna despairs about the "trap of traditional holidays that have utterly no meaning beyond a corporate agenda to get people to buy things they don't need," complaining that "mass consumption is destroying the planet." She has some interesting, valid views, but the manner in which she relates them is rigid and closed-minded and distances her from others. The last time she did something special for someone was ten years ago, when she gave her husband a shirt for his fortieth birthday.

Edna's decision to opt out of buying presents or doing something special for people is, in itself, certainly not a sign of dogmatism. Her choice reflects but one of many beliefs that deny the importance of ritual celebrations that strengthen social ties and give meaning to life. She seems unaware that, as difficult as these connections sometimes are, the *we* of our existence expands our views and inoculates us against existential isolation and despair. Edna's anxiety and intolerance of ambiguity combine with her defensive cognitive closure and lack of personal insight to restrict her cognitive growth and fracture her relationships. Dogmatic rigidity, despair, and cynicism dampen hope, and it is hard to envisage Edna enjoying solitude and quiet content in her later years. Recall from the first chapter that one characteristic of Rokeach's dogmatism is a narrow time perspective that causes people to obsess about the past or dwell on some future utopia. Edna seems stuck in the past, unable to enjoy the present or anticipate the future. Alone in a zone of dogmatism, she lives a life of despair that seems destined to end like Tolstoy's Ivan Ilyich, who was unaware that he was "dying badly because he lived badly."[14]

§§

In the context of dogmatism, existential despair has another serious consequence. Dejected about their hapless, hopeless lives, people who crave a new life of purpose and pride are attracted to groups whose efforts and achievements they can proudly proclaim as their own. Groups that seek to establish a new world order mold fresh identities in closed minds, and it is not enough for dogmatic converts to moderately embrace a movement, for "moderation cannot supplant and efface the self they want to forget."[15] Instead, they zealously embrace an ideological cause—and in that zeal, a surrogate self is reborn. Not only does an extreme identification with "the cause" help conceal lost faith in themselves, the ideological dogmatism of a group allows members to escape the burden of freedom and autonomy. Liberty weighs heavy on dogmatic minds. Preferring instead to be controlled by the tenets and commands of dogma, they are comfortable being a thread in a tightly knit cloak of unity and security. The ideological group gives them identity and dignity while simultaneously offering refuge from anxiety, failure, ignorance, despair, and disconnection. They retreat into a cocoon of certainty.

An exaggerated, pseudo-self-confidence ensues, ignited by a nationalistic or revivalist spirit of omnipotence. Existential despair is now replaced with single-minded, unrestrained determination to change society for the good of the nation, the love of God, or some other ideological mission. Neodogmatists now draw strength from the group's slogans and shibboleths, which drench them with dogma and quench their thirst for absolute truth and dignity. This medley of dogma, existential meaning, and dignity are potent remedies for personal alienation and existential despair.

Dogmatic, religious extremists who merge with political zealots can forge a social revolution of fervent, religious nationalism. This is the goal of the American Christian warriors whose fundamentalist movement, Battle Cry, produced Christian rock shows across America in the summer of 2007. The evangelist Franklin Graham called on youths to engage in a "battle for the souls of men," declaring, "No souls can be saved without the shedding of blood. Blood must be shed!"[16] Similarly, Ron Luce's Teen Mania movement blends the sword, the cross, and the American flag to symbolize a merger of politics and religion that does battle with nonbelievers and those of different faiths. Luce is himself the product of a broken home and teenage drug addiction, and his comment near the end of CNN's six-hour documentary *God's Warriors* is telling: "As long as there are hurting, broken young people, then I have got a job."[17] As he sees it, his job provides teens with a sense of social connection, meaning, and dignity amid despair. These qualities are achieved by projecting his own unresolved psychological conflicts on impressionable youngsters, whose emotions he hijacks and whose minds he closes.

§§

Open-minded, rational thinkers often ignore or shy away from the revolutionary fervor of zealotry. Yet the very people who might restrain radicalized, dogmatic movements often fail to act because they sense the depth of psychological need that propels doctrinaire followers. This is a grave error on the part of intelligent citizens who are uninformed about the nature of dogmatism, particularly in times of uncertainty and social upheaval. When the wrath and hope of despairing dreamers runs loose in the streets, do we join them, bolt the doors, run for our lives, or try to engage them in dialogue? Whatever the choice, there are some ways in which informed individuals can prevent, or at least interrupt, the force of dogmatism in its early stages (various suggestions are outlined in chapters 15 and 17).

The next chapter further animates our portrait of dogmatism with the five behavioral characteristics. As we shall see, the cognitive and emotional features of dogmatism widen the gulf between open- and closed-minded reason. Collectively, all three categories deepen the trenches of what might be called "dogmasochism." Chapter 7 completes the thirteen characteristics of dogmatism by examining its last constellation of features—the five behavioral characteristics—to which we now turn our attention.

NOTES

1. P. J. LaFreniere, *Emotional Development: A Biosocial Perspective* (Scarborough, ON: Nelson Thomson Learning, 2000), p. xi.

2. As with the previous chapter, the superscripted letters indicate whether Rokeach, Altemeyer, or myself authored each specific characteristic. Cases where I have modified Rokeach or Altemeyer's original titles will be superscripted with *R, Jmod*, or *A, Jmod*.

3. H. J. Eysenck and M. W. Eysenck, *Personality and Individual Differences: A Natural Science Approach* (New York: Plenum, 1985). Research results presented by these authors reveal that worry (the cognitive component of anxiety) interferes with performance. The adverse effects of anxiety on students' exam performance results in lower grade point averages. According to the Yerkes-Dodson principle, performance peaks when anxiety is at moderate levels, while too much or too little impairs performance.

4. B. Alansari, "The Relationship between Anxiety and Cognitive Style Measured on the Stroop Test," *Social Behavior and Personality* 32, no. 3 (2004): 285.

5. G. C. Davison et al., *Abnormal Psychology: Canadian Edition* (Etobicoke, ON: Wiley, 2002). People who battle major depression make similar cognitive errors.

6. American Psychiatric Association, *Diagnostic and Statistical Manual of Mental Disorders*, 4th ed. (Washington, DC: American Psychiatric Association, 1994).

7. I. Yalom, *Existential Psychotherapy* (New York: Basic Books, 1980), p. 8.

8. M. Rokeach, *The Open and Closed Mind* (New York: Basic Books, 1960). Although developmental and personality theorists now accept the validity of this statement, it is important to emphasize that it was fundamental to Rokeach's overall theory.

9. K. J. Gergen, *The Saturated Self: Dilemmas of Identity in Contemporary Life* (New York: Basic Books, 1991).

10. R. M. Ryan and E. I. Deci, "On Assimilating Identities to the Self: A Self-Determination Theory Perspective on Internalization and Integrity within Cultures," in *Handbook of Self and Identity*, ed. Mark R. Leary and J. P. Tangney (New York: Guilford, 2003), p. 268; R. W. Robins, J. K.

Norem, and J. M. Cheek, "Naturalizing the Self," in *Handbook of Personality: Theory and Research*, ed. Lawrence A. Pervin and O. P. John (New York: Guilford Press, 2003), p. 449.

11. K. M. Sheldon et al., "Trait Self and True Self: Cross-Role Variation in the Big Five Traits and Its Relations with Authenticity and Subjective Well-Being," *Journal of Personality and Social Psychology* 73 (1997): 1380–93.

12. American Psychiatric Association, *Diagnostic and Statistical Manual*, pp. 432–39. Stress is linked to attachment disorders, including childhood phobias (especially school phobia) and conduct disorder (diagnosed in adolescents).

13. E. Fromm, *Escape from Freedom* (New York: Holt, Rinehart, and Winston, 1941).

14. Yalom, *Existential Psychotherapy*, p. 33.

15. E. Hoffer, *The True Believer* (New York: Harper and Row, 1951), p. 16.

16. S. Taylor, *Battle Cry: Ron Luce's Holy War*, http://www.truthdig .com/report/item/20060523_battlecry_ron_luce/ (accessed August 26, 2007).

17. Christiane Amanpour, Chief International Correspondent for CNN, hosted a six-hour series titled *God's Warriors* that provided examples of dogmatic, militant extremists among Jewish, Islamic, and Christian sects. CNN, August 21–23, 2007.

Chapter 7

ADD A LITTLE ACTION

Behavioral Characteristics of Dogmatism

Anyone who conducts an argument by appealing to authority is
not using his intelligence; he is just using his memory.
Leonardo da Vinci (1452–1519)

Vividly imagine the following scenarios. After reading each one, pause and give yourself time to reflect on your thoughts and emotions. Notice the feelings that spontaneously emerge as you read each vignette.

1. You suddenly notice the flashing lights of a police car that is directly behind you. You pull over to the side of the road and stop. The officer stops just ahead of you, gets out, and is now walking toward your car.
2. You are seated at a fund-raising dinner. People around the table begin introducing themselves and the person beside you says, "Hello, I'm Dr. Wright, head of the Physics Department at [a local university]."
3. You arrive at a party in very casual clothes. You had assumed it would be an informal gathering, but people are quite formally dressed.

4. While driving your car on a warm sunny day, you approach a red light. Slowing to a stop beside you is the driver of a Porsche convertible, top down, whose sustained look at you has no discernible facial expression.

5. Your physician says, "Do you mind if we relate to each other on a first-name basis? I'm not big on titles."

As you fully envisioned each scenario, which particular thoughts and emotions escorted you through the hypothetical encounters? Did any of the people automatically acquire power and status? What feelings did the police officer, physics professor, party guests, driver of the Porsche, and your physician engender? Did you imagine them male or female? What were their approximate ages, races, and ethnicities? Were any of them from a racial minority group?

Uncensored answers to these questions might be telling. Since people think, feel, and act according to their deeply held belief systems, it may be worthwhile to monitor our psychological reactions when we encounter people and circumstances that symbolize power and status. But beliefs do not always translate to specific behaviors, and even when they do, there may be another belief lingering in the background that is inconsistent with what we observe. In public, people may behave respectfully toward a minority group but be negatively biased against them. This incompatibility occurs because attitudes become habitual and implicit; many have strong emotional elements that originated in childhood, the source of which people are often unaware.[1] Because early attitudes are more resistant to change, they are more likely to become manifest in behaviors (known as *explicit attitudes*).

We now examine the first of five such behaviors that accompany dogmatic belief systems.

BEHAVIORAL CHARACTERISTICS

Preoccupation with Power and Status[R]

Illustrative statements:

- "If I won the lottery I would really impress people with my new-found wealth."[J]
- "In this complicated world of ours the only way we can really know what's going on is to rely on leaders or experts we can trust."[R]
- "I have a hard time viewing police officers as people who are simply doing their job."[J]
- "I'm impressed by people who look like a million bucks."[J]
- "It's hard to be my relaxed, fun-loving self when I'm around important people."[J]
- "Priests (depending on your religious beliefs, substitute Imams, Rabbis, Shamans, etc.) are holy men of God who deserve to be treated with reverence."[J]
- "I would feel less anxious if approached by a female police officer than a male officer."[J]

A preoccupation with power and status is the first of five behavioral characteristics of dogmatism—one that may lead to prejudicial, discriminatory actions, both verbal and physical. In the psychological sense, *status* refers to an individual's personal evaluation of his or her abilities, successes, and worth in the eyes of others. From a social perspective, status is determined by one's position within a social or economic hierarchy and is conferred by others who estimate one's value within the group. Without a sense of worth, people feel socially disconnected, devalued, and lacking in dignity.[2]

Like our primate cousins, we arrange ourselves in dominance hierarchies, and while physical dominance has been somewhat subdued by evolutionary adaptations and educational progress, the tendency to organize ourselves along culturally defined hierarchies of status remains. "If one looks around at a society, one quickly discovers that many of these hierarchies are age-graded. Sixth graders feel themselves superior to fifth graders and dominate the playground if both have recess together; tenured professors lord it over untenured ones and carefully control entry into their august circle."[3] Many psychologists today accept the view that humans are first and foremost social animals who, similar to other primates, arrange themselves in hierarchies that determine social connections, status, and dignity.

From an evolutionary perspective, natural selection rewarded social learners who observed and copied the most successful individuals. "The hunger for status, like all appetites, can have its uses; spurring us to do justice to our talents, encouraging excellence, restraining us from harmful eccentricities and cementing members of a society around a common value system. But like all appetites, its excesses can also kill."[4] All too often, people with status are granted automatic, unqualified prestige. And while societies and relationships function more smoothly when respect is the default mode, there are no sacred cows. Presidents are not above the law, and clergymen have chosen their careers just like everyone else. Should they be imbued with reverence just because they and their followers believe God has called them? Many others are unconvinced and prefer to dismantle human deification. Political correctness must have sensible boundaries, controversial as those boundaries might be.

§§

Prior to the ideology of meritocracy, social mobility largely depended on one's social class at birth—a tradition that reflected an unjust distribution of rewards. Then and today, low-paid employees who work in menial jobs are demoralized by their paltry remuneration and general invisibility in the eyes of strangers. No matter how objectionable or unfair it may seem, those with eminent status who wear expensive brand-name clothes, own multimillion-dollar homes and yachts, drive prestigious cars, and adorn themselves with costly jewels are noticed

—usually ahead of others. The personal pride and dignity they feel is fed by a culture that distinguishes the wealthy as morally good and assumes they are happier than those lacking such wealth.[5] Beyond the object itself, the more powerful reward of the Porsche convertible is the perceived attention and status it affords. Some owners would reject this analysis and claim they purchase high-end luxury items for their quality, not for status. While this sometimes may be the case, more than a few buy the Porsche because their next-door neighbor has a loaded BMW. But no one is "born to shop," though many are insidiously brainwashed by peers and the media to reward corporate Goliaths who manipulate people's insecurities (especially adolescents). In the malls, in the classrooms, and elsewhere, we observe the prepackaged identities that equate style and material possessions with overall success, attractiveness, and happiness. Conspicuous consumption compensates for inconspicuous insecurities.

The universal tendency for people to notice power and status in others and desire the same for themselves gratifies childhood longings that unrestrained capitalism bolsters—material possessions ensure recognition and safety. Linda McQuaig states that today's *Homo economicus*, a mutant of the new capitalist, is driven by unrestrained, insatiable greed for material possessions. The need to acquire things has reached the point "where elaborate international legal systems have been put in place to ensure not only that greed and the pursuit of material gain are given legal protection, but that they are given *supremacy* [italics in the original]."[6] While no single cause sustains a culture's dominant ideology, economic values are shaped and fortified by social institutions and the media, who promote the acquisition of expensive goods that become symbols of success and status. Wealth is equated with virtue and worthiness, while humble possessions are equated with moral deficiencies.[7] Industrialized nations are so influenced by these symbols that the Pavlovian drool over the rich and powerful has become, for some, a preoccupation with power and status—a core behavioral characteristic of dogmatism that must be accompanied by a minimum of five other features.

If modern humans strive for social ties that reward us with respect, and if respect is granted by a society that admires ostentatious wealth, then the failure to acquire these goods promotes feelings of social inadequacy. The dogmatic idolatry of the marketplace is a presumed solution to this discomfort, and as long as Western cultures glorify mass consumption and assume that markets can best dispense social services like healthcare and education, wealth will symbolize psychological safety. The marketplace drapes closed-minded consumers with a visible cloak of status that perpetuates global poverty, political conflict, and environmental degradation. Economic dogmatism is the major source of planetary destruction and social cleavages that result in 40,000 children dying daily from poverty and contaminated water.[8] While children die and the earth is plundered, the dogmatic ideologue goes on yet another shopping spree that pays homage to the god of the marketplace. At the corporate level, economic ideology and material idolatry are monstrosities of dogmatic delusion.

Feeling inadequate, dogmatists are hypervigilant for status symbols. On being introduced to someone, they immediately want to know the person's line of work, type of residence, race, and ethnicity. Individuals with low status are deemed less deserving of time and respect, while people of stature leave dogmatists awestruck, ingratiating, deferential, and easily intimidated. The idea of "bosses" captivates them.[9] And although they have conflicting views of power relations, admiring it in some and fearing it in others, they covet power for themselves because they see it as automatically conferring respect and dignity. More importantly, symbols of power psychologically camouflage their incomplete and insecure sense of identity.

Dogmatists who are preoccupied with power and status assume they will become recognized, even admired, for careers that confer nobility of character. They are drawn to professions that reward them with visible displays of status, believing that uniforms and badges grant instant authority and respect. By limiting their associations to those with status or vicariously observing the rich and famous, they may try to effect a prestigious image. They become Vance Packard's "status seekers"[10] and Francis Fukuyama's "status-conscious animals."[11] As Rokeach noted, by overidentifying with symbols of high standing, "an attempt is made to defend against feelings of aloneness and isolation, of self-hate and misanthropy."[12] Those who defend against personal inadequacy by achieving status are prone to "closed belief-disbelief systems [that] provide a systematic cognitive framework for rationalizing and justifying egocentric self-righteousness and the moral condemnation of others."[13] With the single, closed-minded pursuit of money and status, cooperation and sharing are devalued, while people who are neither a threat or a benefit hardly exist.

Central or core beliefs about human nature, though not always clearly articulated, guide our opinions of others, and people prone to dogmatism form rigid, exaggerated impressions. They often displace the harsh judgment of their childhood on others—especially those of the designated out-group. As Rokeach emphasized, "It is assumed that the more closed the system, the more closed will be the content of such beliefs to the effect that we live alone, isolated and helpless in a friendless world; that we live in a world wherein the future is uncertain; that the self is fundamentally unworthy and inadequate to cope alone with this friendless world; and that the way to overcome such feelings is by a self-aggrandizing and self-righteous identification with a cause, a concern with power and status, and by a compulsive self-proselytization about the justness of such a cause."[14]

To capture the sentiment embedded in this quotation, one of Rokeach's D Scale items asks respondents to rate the intensity of their agreement with the following: "It's all too true that people just won't practice what they preach."[15] On a scale that ranges from strongly agree to strongly disagree, how would a self-righteous dogmatist who views others as inferior and untrustworthy respond to this statement?

Dogmatists not only need to convince people of their truths about God, politics, business management, or some other ideological treasure—they also need to convince others of their righteousness. To plant themselves firmly in the camp of saints, they try to impress others with their goodness, their loyalty, and their conscientious work ethic, feats that they presume self-aggrandizement will enhance. No less remarkable is their ability to convince themselves that their status is elevated if they can undermine the accomplishments of others. But those who toot their own horn with the hope of muting those of others simultaneously broadcast their self-doubt and deep-seated insecurity, at least to those who listen carefully. Perceptive listeners find it odd that self-aggrandizers seem so insensitive to the negative impact their self-promotion has on others. Less transparent are the underlying causes and perceived rewards that drive such behavior. Because self-aggrandizement compensates for dogmatists' feelings of inadequacy, it is easy to see why they use it as a tool that will presumably secure status and dignity, at least in their distorted judgment.

Overt bragging, which is common in children, persists in dogmatic adults who create pompous, pretentious images, especially around matters of cultural importance—money, power, morality, success, philanthropy, and the real show-stopper, intelligence. Hoisting themselves on their own petard of self-righteous superiority, they lack the personal insight to observe others' reactions, and they rationalize the personal consequences of rejection because they will not fully contemplate the social impact that their underlying motives produce.

To summarize, dogmatists who are preoccupied with power and status are riddled with anxiety and self-doubt. Highly motivated to join the ranks, even if only vicariously, of those with power and status, they bolster their self-image by promoting infallible knowledge, status symbols, and nobility of character.

Glorification of the In-Group and Vilification of the Out-Group[R]

Illustrative statements:

- "There are two kinds of people in the world: those who are for the truth and those who are against the truth."[R]
- "People who work hard to make their fortune should be honored with special status and privileges."[J]

- "Most neoconservatives have antisocial motives."[J]
- "Bleeding-heart liberals know only one thing—how to squander the public purse."[J]
- "Gays and lesbians are abominations of God's creation."[J]
- "Immigrants must honor the truism, 'When in Rome, do as the Romans do.'"[J]
- "More often than not, the poor are irresponsible and indolent."[J]
- "Those who misinterpret or try to change the word of God do the devil's work."[A,16]

Differences inspire thought along a rational-irrational continuum, and those preoccupied with power and status tend to peremptorily assign others to an in-group (us) or an out-group (them). Such categorizations are determined by superficial personal qualities and ideological allegiances. People with power and status are granted privileged access to the in-group while outsiders are disdained or dismissed because of their race, ethnicity, age, economic standing, gender, or any other prominent feature that distinguishes them from members of the in-group. Dogmatic people irrationally judge those in the out-group as infidels, social irritants, or misfits, and they do not see that their harsh, categorical judgment reduces their own dignity more than it diminishes those they stereotype. In addition, their hasty prejudgment of ideas and beliefs accounts for their glorified acceptance of people whose beliefs they accept, and for the vilified rejection of people whose ideas they reject. Prejudice is a "hostile or negative attitude toward people in a distinguishable group, based solely on their membership in that group."[17] Beyond preconceived notions about what people *are* like, prejudice also includes prescriptions of what people in certain groups *should* be like. It therefore has both descriptive and prescriptive components.

Stereotypes emerge when people prejudge individuals and groups by inferring a broad "generalization about a group of people in which identical characteristics are assigned to virtually all members of the group, regardless of actual variation among the members. Once formed, stereotypes are resistant to change on the basis of new information."[18] And while all of us develop stereotypes because "our brain is calibrated to trust anyone who happens to be a 'member' of the group or any authority figure,"[19] dogmatists are especially good at this. They rigidly embrace certain beliefs. They may believe, for example, that the wealthy, the patron saints of capitalism, should be glorified as industrious and intelligent, while the poor should be vilified as lazy, corrupt, and unintelligent. This type of moral justification distances them from the out-group and fortifies bonds to the in-group, which further justifies their arrogant superiority and dismissal of those judged inferior. Equally precarious, they displace all moral responsibility onto a leader and just follow orders. Particularly in times of war, they are more concerned with authorities' behavior than their own, and therefore they take no responsibility for civilian casualties, for whom they feel little if any remorse.[20] Once this is accomplished, they can dehumanize their victims.

A dogmatic person would likely agree with several of the following statements:

- Islam is the only true religion (or Christianity, Judaism, Hinduism, etc.).
- Women are more emotional than rational.
- The elderly are useless drains on society (or the unemployed, immigrants, etc.).
- Homosexuals are sinners (the category of "sinners" is seemingly endless).
- Christianity must be spread throughout the world (or Islam, Judaism, Buddhism, etc.).

All of these beliefs reflect a closed-minded cognitive style typical of polarized, compartmentalized thinking that is derived from an image of people not grounded in reality—an obsessive image that sustains prejudice. For example, dogmatists enjoy being in the actual or vicarious presence of people they view as idols, and they are unable to recognize that the characteristics they attribute to such heroes are merely fabrications of their own closed minds. Identification with the powerful in-group gratifies their need for membership and belonging. Social acceptance and respect are huge payoffs that reinforce uncritical allegiance to in-group ideology, its leader, and group members. Such sycophantic, glowing admiration could light a small Christmas tree. Radiant adoration of the in-group compels them to dismiss people whose ideological allegiances differ from their own; they even reject family and friends. Contempt for those who disagree gives arrogant dismissal its marching orders. As for people who represent neither a direct threat nor a clear benefit, they do not exist. Yet some dogmatists who want to be seen as politically correct cleverly disguise their prejudices, contempt, and bigotry.

All of us look for guidance in our lives, but dogmatists look for answers that only heroes can provide. Nondogmatic people are perplexed by the dogmatist whose blind reverence fails to recognize that "if you have a hero, look again: you have diminished yourself in some way."[21] In contrast, open-minded people are less impressed with the hyped glory of saints, saviors, and instant television idols—a mockery to human achievement. But even those with supple minds may have psychological barriers that narrow their thinking about heroes and idols. It therefore seems fitting to remind ourselves of Francis Bacon's philosophic position that "idols are the profoundest fallacies of the mind of man."[22]

§§

On what basis do dogmatists determine in- and out-group membership? Those who believe that there is justice in the world and that everything happens for a reason are more likely to conclude that the poor, the nonbelievers, the mentally ill, the homosexuals, and the parents of troubled children are failures who single-handedly brought about their own misery and therefore deserve to suffer. These are the dogmatists who convince themselves that they are superior to such irresponsible, immoral people. They may not articulate their beliefs as clearly, but their smug sense of superiority reigns supreme in a world that dishes out just deserts. The stronger the fantasies of personal righteousness, the greater the intolerance and indifference to others' loss and suffering. To Hobbes's dictum that the life of man is "solitary, poor, nasty, brutish, and short," self-righteous dogmatists would add "and justifiably so for the ignorant, lazy, and undeserving."

The more narrow and bigoted the dogmatic belief, the more simplified and polarized the social judgment. Dogmatic people overlook human complexity as they venerate and defer to in-group elites and demean and discriminate against out-group miscreants.[23] Once the boundaries of the in-group are rigidly set, privileged members have the exclusive right to establish membership criteria for others—a presumed right that accounts for the ease with which they dismiss the out-group's different beliefs, ideas, and customs. Yet if the in-group were able to understand the source of their deep, divisive dislikes, they could create a safe place for the discussion of differences *with* outsiders. "Them" and "us" could blend into a unity that accepts different realities and realizes more hopes and dreams. For dogmatists, this is exceedingly difficult, because the insight necessary to remove such barriers would threaten the very identity that in-group membership secures.

The in-group's wagons become so tightly circled that their philosophy and allegiances arrest critical analysis and revision of current dogma. "This phenomenon is known as *groupthink*, defined as a kind of thinking in which maintaining group cohesiveness and solidarity is more important than considering the facts in an objective manner."[24] The symptoms of groupthink include: (1) an illusion of invulnerability; (2) belief in the moral correctness of the group; (3) stereotyped, simplistic views of those designated members of an inferior out-group; (4) self-censorship of concerns or questions that would "rock the boat"; (5) direct pressure on dissenters to conform; (6) an illusion of unanimity; and (7) "mind-guards," whereby group members protect the leader from contrary views.[25]

In these settings, decisions are made exclusive of outside information that proffers alternative views and strategies. Moreover, because groupthink fails to consider the risks inherent in closed-minded decisions, the group does not develop contingency plans in the event of failure.[26] Invulnerable to influence, it denounces those who challenge its ideological dogma, which further radicalizes its stance. Consider groupthink in the context of dogmatism. Leaders who preside over cohesive, insular groups that face an external threat generally make very poor decisions,[27] and the judgment of strong dogmatic leaders is even more injudicious. Drowning in a swamp of ideology, they desperately try to convince the group that dissenters are deserving of dogmatic authoritarian aggression (discussed later in the chapter).

Prejudiced beliefs that are bolstered by black-and-white dogmatic thinking strengthen the dogmatist's resolve to unquestioningly obey orders, especially those issued by charismatic leaders. When unwarranted, reverential truths unite a group of like-minded believers who have considerable power, they generate a momentum that far exceeds the damage one dogmatist can inflict on others—a momentum that closes the minds of its members and threatens cultural stability.

Another consequence of dogmatic glorification and vilification is the inability to objectively evaluate the quality of message content separately from the qualities of the messenger. Dogmatists quickly and superficially judge the messenger, which impairs their ability to hear the message in its entirety. If the messenger is seen as a valued in-group member, the dogmatist positively biases the message, but if the messenger is seen as an outsider, dogmatic eyes deafen dogmatic ears and intelligent thought narrows. A simple difference of opinion becomes a personalized attack, and anyone who disagrees with them, even if only about one issue, is written off. As Rokeach stated, "The more closed the belief system, the more difficult should it be to distinguish information received about the world and information received about the source."[28]

To support this claim, research demonstrates that efforts to change people's beliefs or persuade them to adopt new ones depends more on the personal qualities of the messenger than what the messenger says.[29] Attractive speakers with obvious expertise exude convincing credibility, even if the message is clearly based on faulty reasoning. We are generally reluctant to criticize people in positions of power—whether they be presidents, scientists in lab coats (yes, even those with pen protectors), physicians, or accomplished airline pilots. Copilots have gone down with the plane rather than insist the pilot is making a deadly decision.[30] If the general public tends to agree with messages delivered by attractive, prestigious people, dogmatists are even more gullible. Their inability to fully hear and thoughtfully consider the legitimacy of message content is overshadowed by image and co-existing emotions, leaving dogmatists to glorify authority figures as absolute experts whose messages deserve uncritical endorsement.

Thus, rather than examining the evidence, dogmatists examine appearances. The biased image takes both the message and the dog-matist's mind hostage. Although solid research on the interaction between dogmatism, message credibility, and source impressions is lacking, we would expect dogmatic individuals to be difficult to dis-suade unless exposed to highly credible sources—sources who appear to support at least some beliefs that are compatible with the dogma-tist's. Research on persuasion suggests that trustworthy, believable, prestigious, and attractive communicators are effective communica-tors[31] and we could expect that, to dogmatists, these features would be especially appealing. Future research that relates dogmatism to var-ious attributes of the messenger would complement current theories on social persuasion.

Finally, and against their best interests, right-wing dogmatists tend to support government policies that grant the wealthy, whom they ven-erate, special privileges, such as tax breaks and munificent expense accounts. They excuse the affluent for their failure to help relieve the suffering of the marginalized and dispossessed. This only preserves the posturing of wealthy, socioeconomic dogmatists, who may appear sympathetic to the needs of the poor. However, when the surface of their humanitarian posturing is scratched, they bleed callous indiffer-ence to the misfortune and suffering of the poor. Equally problematic are the dogmatists who, in the name of left-wing ideology, venerate the poor and vilify the wealthy. When their rhetorical, high-minded socialist posturing is questioned, they too reveal a callous indifference to human rights and freedoms.

Dogmatic Authoritarian Aggression[A,JMod]

Illustrative statements:

- "Crush the enemy before the enemy crushes you."[J]
- "Social activists are all left-wing nuts who deserve to be silenced."[J]
- "Most people just don't know what's good for them."[R]
- "Infidels deserve to suffer eternal hell and damnation."[J]
- "Some kids just need a good whuppin'."[J]
- "A revolutionary movement is justified in using violence to defeat the forces of rampant capitalism."[J]
- "Increased crime and drug use is caused by parents and educators who are too soft on discipline."[J]
- "Prisons give inmates so many luxuries that they end up being more rewarded than punished."[J]
- "They [Canadians] better hope the United States doesn't roll over one night and crush them. They are lucky we allow them to exist on the same continent.[J,32]

The sweeping, harmful consequences of this third behavior component evolves from the preceding two features of dogmatism: preoccupation with power and status, and glorification of the in-group and vilification of the out-group.

As defined by *Encyclopaedia Britannica*, *authoritarianism* is the "principle of blind submission to authority, as opposed to individual freedom of thought and action. In government, authoritarianism denotes any political system that concentrates power in the hands of a leader or a small elite that is not constitutionally responsible to the body of the people." While most people in positions of authority are assumed to have specialized, authoritative knowledge, only a minority of them practice authoritarianism. Those who do so can be both aggressive and submissive in their behavior.[33]

The unspeakable brutality that was perpetrated by Hitler, Stalin, and Mussolini, and the American bombings of Hiroshima and Nagasaki in 1945, prompted social psychologists of the last century to investigate the psychology of fascism, authoritarianism, and dogmatism.[34] What, in human nature, caused the leaders of these civilized, reasonably well-educated nations to unleash such atrocities?

In their study of authoritarianism, the Berkeley Group of social scientists (referred to in chapter 1) concluded that people with authoritarian personalities are condescending, punitive, and hostile toward those they consider socially inferior.[35] Moreover, their world view is one of habitual suspicion and threat, which intensifies their own mistrust and suspicion.[36] To cope with that threat, they rely on authority figures who provide order and safety, and who demand that those who do not conform to conventional codes of conduct be punished.[37] We could assume that they arbitrarily adopt the belief systems of authority figures because such beliefs reduce anxiety and assure safety. We might also assume that because these belief systems anchor their sense of identity, they will directly aggress against those who threaten their beliefs, and that they will follow authoritarian directives to commit crimes against humanity. These behaviors reduce dogmatists' anxiety and intolerance of ambiguity and secure their personal identity and safety. For these reasons, authoritarianism is considered a behavioral subtrait of dogmatism.

More than three decades after *The Authoritarian Personality* and its subsequent F Scale were published, Robert Altemeyer used his Right-Wing Authoritarian (RWA) Scale to test the psychological properties of authoritarianism. His 1996 book, *The Authoritarian Specter*, documents the findings from numerous studies that assessed authoritarian aggression, authoritarian submission, and conventionalism.[38] In 1992 Altemeyer also devised the DOG Scale, which he designed to tap what he considered dogmatism's salient feature—unchangeable, unjustified certainty (research results from administrations of that scale are reported in *The Authoritarian Personality*).[39] For the past twenty years, Altemeyer has established himself as an authoritative voice on right-wing authoritarianism, and, more recently, he is doing the same with his measure of dogmatism.

Altemeyer defines *authoritarianism* as "the covariation of three kinds of attitudes: authoritarian submission (to established authorities), authoritarian aggression (against anyone the authorities target), and conventionalism (adhering to the social conventions thought to be endorsed by society and the established authorities)."[40] Since authoritarians are found among both right- and left-wing ideological extremists, the construct does not refer only to right-wing conservatives, neo-conservatives, or fascists. Both right- and left-wing ideologues reflect two core psychological components of authoritarianism: (1) pervasive fear that incites authoritarian aggression, and (2) a self-righteous morality that justifies authoritarian aggression and authoritarian submission.[41] The word *aggression*, as applied to both leaders and followers, refers to "intentionally causing harm to someone," and any such act is "accompanied by the belief that proper authority approves it or that it will help preserve such authority."[42] Generally speaking, when revolutionary leaders and followers oppose the existing order, they are left-wing authoritarians; those who impose or follow strict orders that entrench the existing order, or that restore a more traditional one, are right-wing authoritarians.[43]

In his book, *The Authoritarian Specter*, Altemeyer summarizes the personality characteristics of people who scored high on his RWA Scale. Like the Berkeley Group before him, Altemeyer found that high scorers view the world as a dangerous, fearful place, quite possibly because their parents repeatedly warned them that such is the case. Combine these teachings with the experience of having authoritarian parents, and the child's "feelings of vulnerability could produce an 'aggressive defense' against a hostile, dangerous world."[44] They endorse abuses of power by leaders who are implicitly trusted, and they demonstrate prejudicial attitudes and discriminatory behaviors against racial, ethnic, nationalistic, and linguistic minorities. High scorers also tend to be sexist and support gay bashing. Authoritarian personalities are yea-sayers who uncritically accept, without sufficient evidence, ideological dogma as truth.[45] Self-righteous and twisted by prejudice, they take pleasure in administering punishment to those who shun or violate traditional roles and rules. Any breach of their own moral standards for acceptable behavior will be absolved through prayer and religious piety. These people may instigate conflict within and between groups, and then draw attention to their heroic efforts to resolve the very tension they created.

Research on the personality trait of authoritarianism inspired Rokeach to investigate the nature of dogmatism. Throughout the 1960s he incorporated several subtraits of authoritarianism in his inaugural theory and measurement of dogmatism. He claimed that our beliefs about legitimate roles of authority figures and our psychological orientation toward them reflect our degree of open- versus closed-mindedness. So important was the underlying idea of authoritarianism that when Rokeach parsed dogmatic belief systems into central, intermediate, and peripheral domains, he reserved the entire intermediate domain for beliefs about authority figures.

Rokeach's intermediate domain of dogmatism did, however, contain a glaring omission. In his book *The Open and Closed Mind*, Rokeach frequently referred to authoritarianism but did not define what he meant by the construct. Given that nine out of forty items on his Dogmatism Scale were considered subtraits of authoritarianism, it seems odd that Rokeach dismissed the importance of first defining the trait under scrutiny. He simply noted, "we will focus a good deal of attention on the formulation rather than the explanation of concepts."[46] However, the concept of authoritarianism represents almost 25 percent of Rokeach's D Scale, and a concise definition of the trait would have been helpful. Which definition of authoritarianism did he have in mind when he constructed his test for dogmatism: the Berkeley Group's, his own, a dictionary's, or some hybrid definition? What is clear is that Rokeach viewed authoritarianism as a subtrait of dogmatism. He stated, for example, "the more closed the belief-disbelief system, the more will authority be seen as absolute and the more will people be accepted or rejected because they agree or disagree with one's belief-disbelief system."[47]

§§

Normally, all societies accept the structure and enforcement of moral and legal codes of conduct, and authority figures are necessary to enforce the rules and laws inherent in these regulations. Such policies and procedures protect individual rights and provide ethical guidelines that humanize a well-functioning, civic society. Much of our psychological safety and cultural stability depends not only on how these purveyors of authority exercise their power, but also on how children and adults interpret and respond to authoritative laws and their corresponding enforcement. Of necessity, we accept societal regulations and seldom question the legitimacy of rules that govern our daily lives—at least those of us who live in democratic societies.

We comply with rules and laws because, as children, we learned to obey our parents, as well as daycare workers, teachers, and law officers, among others. Teachers were wise, and police officers commanded respect. Authority figures were symbols of knowledge and power whose legitimacy warranted respect that extended into adulthood. In most circumstances, and in the long run, people generally comply with regulations because they believe not only that it is the right thing to do, but also that it is simply easier to obey than defy social mores and laws. Such obedience affords protection and rewards. Even so, there is considerable variation in the degree to which adults perceive and react to authority figures in general, particularly among those who are more open-minded than closed-minded.

Dogmatists have an arbitrary, absolute reliance on authority figures to enforce rules and regulations that presumably will preserve conventional behavior and reduce ambiguity. Their need for clear directives, their obedience of conventional rules, and their deference to authority figures who enforce those rules complies with their excessive need for order and control, without which they feel uprooted. As such, many prefer to live in homogeneous groups or societies where everyone obeys the same rules of conduct. These rules ground the community and its citizens in similar, complementary behaviors and identities. When traditional beliefs and customs need to accommodate change, dogmatists' rigid ideas about ethics and morality are shaken. For example, increasing multiculturalism and flexible expansion of laws that incorporate respect for diversity destabilizes their identity and challenges their ability to independently assess the legitimacy of new rules in a changing social order. Dogmatists are forced to fall back on themselves, and in the process they no longer feel protected and safe— they lose their psychological balance. How can they rely on a self that is externally governed when external governance is in transition?

Dogmatic authoritarian aggression is seen in closed-minded, fearful leaders who issue orders to aggress against civilians—orders that closed-minded, fearful followers willingly obey.[48] To distinguish this characteristic from belief-associated anger subsumed under the emotional characteristics of dogmatism (chapter 6), dogmatic authoritarian aggression pertains *only to dogmatists who give and/or follow orders to aggress against others.*[49] The submission of dogmatic leaders and followers is in direct service to a higher authority or ideology, and both use aggression to dominate, control, intimidate, or eliminate others—an egregious abuse of power that violates human rights. Thus, depending on one's rank and circumstance, dogmatic authoritarian aggression and dogmatic authoritarian submission can alternate within the same person. In effect, many dogmatists would reveal both subtraits (dogmatic leaders, parents, and educators, for example, who give orders also follow them, and both types punish violators). The important point here is that the more prolonged and pervasive the dogmatist's fear of ambiguous, uncontrollable events, the more his or her fear masquerades as dogmatic authoritarian aggression or pious, dogmatic authoritarian submission. In either case, as Al Gore notes, fear and anxiety assault reason, and "demagogues have always promised security in return for the surrender of freedom."[50]

Lakoff notes that, from a political and economic perspective, authoritarians are more concerned about a functioning economy, social security, and the acquisition of personal property.[51] Regardless of whether they give or follow orders, their behavior reflects extreme, narrow views about the nature of authority. They believe authoritarian aggressors have the right to be mean-spirited, cruel, and vicious. Lacking self-esteem, authoritarian people admire role models who give simple orders that, if obeyed, will strengthen their own sense of identity and dignity.[52] In a dogmatic mind, these beliefs are legitimate because they derive from absolute truth about moral superiority, and this truth justifies self-righteous abuses of power.[53]

Hannah Arendt has also written extensively about the kind of authoritarian aggression that goes beyond personal ambition—aggression that is willing to "sacrifice everybody's vital immediate interests to the execution of what it assumes to be the Law of History or the Law of Nature."[54] To those laws, I would add the Law of God. Dogmatic people in positions of authority wield power that is arbitrary, illegitimate, and unjust, as opposed to collaborative, legitimate, and democratically constrained by constitutional law. In the upper ranks of power, the most dangerous dogmatists are those who dehumanize members of the out-group by denigrating them with labels (e.g., "animals," "scum"), and administering punishment that is much more severe than that given to in-group violators. The latter at least remain humanized.[55]

To understand why dogmatists are more likely to aggress against or submit to others, we must first ask what purpose both behavior patterns serve. Dogmatists obey authority figures because they regulate and simplify the complexities of everyday life by imposing unambiguous moral values and behavior regulations that reward conformists with respect, dignity, and honor. Authoritarian authority figures offer external structure to those lacking internal, autonomous control of their lives—a structure that simultaneously compensates for deficits in children's need to know (about themselves, others, and the surrounding world) and their simultaneous need to defend against excess, persistent anxiety. Clear lines of authority assuage such anxiety, especially when circumstances require adjustment to ambiguous situations or rapid change. Correspondingly, these rules also strengthen the sense of personal identity that satisfies the dogmatist's need for safety. While conformity is a necessary component of civilized society that allows groups to become cohesive and work toward common goals, a reverence for conformity and excessive, blind obedience promotes the exclusion and punishment of nonconformists. Authoritarian parents who use punishment to control behavior shape authoritarian personalities in their children.

Summarizing the assumptions of James Dobson, an American evangelist and the author of *Dare to Discipline*, Lakoff states that Dobson and his followers believe in the strict father model, in which

> there is an absolute right and an absolute wrong. Children are born bad, in the sense that they just want to do what feels good, not what is right. . . . What is required of the child is obedience, because the father is a moral authority who knows right from wrong. . . . The only way to teach kids obedience is through punishment, painful punishment when they do wrong. This includes hitting them, and some authors on conservative child rearing recommend sticks, belts, and wooden paddles. . . . The same discipline you need to be moral is what allows you to prosper.[56]

From this system of beliefs about parenting, it follows that leniency at home, in the courts, in prisons, and other government institutions is viewed as a dangerous license for corruption and lawlessness. To combat such vice, children need to gain self-discipline through the threat of punishment. Then, when they become adults, they will not dare loaf about and benefit from wasteful government handouts that encourage immoral, immature dependency on social programs.

Lakoff writes, "Dobson is very clear about the connection between the strict father worldview and free market capitalism." The moral people are those who prosper, and moral people believe in and follow the word of God. For Dobson, money not only talks, but those who don't have it are persecuted. His book *Dare to Discipline* has sold more than 3.5 million copies, and he is heard on the radio in 116 countries, with an estimated listening audience of more than 200 million; he also appears daily on eighty American television stations.[57]

In the hands of dogmatic authoritarian aggressors, anger ratchets up dogmatism to an extreme hatred and bigotry that justifies, in their minds, sadistic attacks on others. Of dogmatism's thirteen characteristics, dogmatic authoritarian aggression moves dogmatism's influence beyond the personal and into the public domain, where, as Albert Camus warns, "To insure the adoration of a theorem for any length of time, faith is not enough, a police force is needed as well."[58] Attempting to institutionalize and enforce their beliefs, dogmatic authoritarian aggressors believe they "have the inherent right to decide for themselves what they may do, including breaking the laws they make for the rest of us."[59] Yet, "*something* else is at work here, for authoritarian aggression is done in the name of some higher authority. This authority gives the attack legitimacy in the minds of the aggressors, and they will often say they are proud of what they did . . . [but] what they did was almost always extraordinarily cowardly."[60] Whether their brutality was rationalized as necessary to preserve the state, defend their religious beliefs, protect democratic values, or safeguard a way of life, a muscular interpretation is that their cowardice and brutality was single-handedly sponsored by dogmatism, through which, in the end, they destroy themselves to save themselves.

Beneath this dogmatism, the "something else" that is at work here is deep-seated anxiety, fear, and alienation—the foundation upon which dogmatism is built to house prejudice, discrimination, and dogmatic authoritarian aggression. When underlying anxiety is converted to self-protective anger that is partnered with other characteristics of dogmatism, aggression rears its ugly head. By whatever means necessary, dogmatic authoritarian aggressors are driven to impose their truths on others—especially God-given truths that consecrate violence. And members of the Dog Squad either wield power or submit to commanding authority figures who aggress against scapegoats in order to fortify their own fragile identities and safely ensconce themselves in a cradle of sanctimonious moralism.

In times of political rebellion or all-out war, the most dangerous dogmatists are those whose fears lie in ambush until their viciousness is unleashed against random, innocent civilians. While enemies may modulate their aggression through fear of punishment, rarely do such fears fully constrain the deeper psychological needs that motivate their behavior. Victims are murdered, kept in detention centers, subjected to stress techniques, or held without charge and fair trial because they serve as scapegoats for deep wellsprings of fear and dogmatic, self-righteous indignation—the psychological brew that foments dogmatic authoritarian aggression.

As has often been the case, dogmatic authoritarian leaders have deftly manipulated impressionable people whose obsession with power and status has prepared them to glorify the in-group and follow the leader's orders to aggress against outsiders. This is the mark of success for political or religious leaders who cling to past injustices and demand unwavering commitment to their narrow-minded, vengeful cause. Needing the respect that their high-ranking political status generates, such leaders are not above staging contagious anger that elicits the very emotions necessary to parasitize closed minds—minds that will obediently follow orders to inflict unconscionable atrocities against humanity. This extreme dogmatism is also seen in leaders who skillfully ignite zealotry, fanaticism, and in-group reverence among the fearful, the vengeful, and those who believe they are privileged followers destined for greatness. Desperate for recognition, power, and status, leaders and followers alike fail to see that their perceived status is superficial and hollow.

Dogmatic authoritarians project their fears, anger, and insecurity on those they judge inferior. With a smug sense of superiority that absolves themselves of any blame for their discriminatory, dehumanizing behaviors, they judge others as animals or believe that a woman is worth only a quarter of a man, and they unflinchingly torture, rape, and murder in the irrational belief that their brutality is justified because it supports ideological ideals.

Historically, dogmatic rationalizations have radicalized people to join vigilante movements, fight wars, and commit genocide. Dogmatic and arrogant leaders are legion, and the sycophants who do their bidding are hardened ideologues who endorse killing and exonerate other authoritarians of the same behavior. This type of murder is legitimized because it is, after all, against those who are "not like any of us." As Voltaire said, "Those who can make you believe absurdities can make you commit atrocities." And those dogs will not greet you at the door, much less bring your slippers.

Many atrocities have been perpetrated in the name of deities, demons, and despots. Fire and brimstone, fear and torture, witch-hunts, sexual assault, and purges have all been driven by dogmatic, authoritarian aggression. These movements ignore philosophic principles of human rights—principles that aggressors simplify and compartmentalize as irrelevant impediments to their ideological mission. Their style of thinking is so obscured by perverted fear that the first act of violence they commit is against their own mind. Once that demolition of reason is accomplished, empathy is lost and others are easily converted from friend to foe, saint to sinner, or neighbor to foreigner. Such simplistic judgments disallow an open-minded acceptance of all humanity. As Reinhold Niebuhr reminds us, "groups are more immoral than individuals."[61] There is a convenient dispersion of responsibility when someone else calls the shots or when individual behaviors are obscured by the group.

Institutions that aggressively work to the advantage of special interest groups create self-serving mythologies that disadvantage others. Their mandates cleverly sway public opinion to endorse values that favor the powerful until the disadvantaged become blind to the reality that their complacency has been manipulated to implicitly legitimize policies of the governing elite—policies that work against the public's best interest. Complacency amidst political dogmatism is complicit dogmatism, the mutuality of which piles more bricks on the wall that barricades intelligent discourse. Still, as Neil Postman reminds us, "It is certainly true that he who holds the power to define is our master, but it is also true that he who holds in mind an alternative definition can never quite be his slave."[62]

Dogmatic authoritarian aggressors are the slaves of dogma, radicalized by those who challenge their beliefs and insult their dignity. Yet individuals who seek revenge for past injustices perpetuate an endless cycle of protracted warfare. Indeed, as William Faulkner wrote, "the past is never dead. It's not even past."[63] Such is the downward spiral of dogmatic authoritarian aggression. Belief systems and behaviors that are reinforced by powerful authoritarians can become weapons of such mass destruction that when the opportunity arises, the dogmatic authoritarian aggression of Mount Dogmatism erupts, wiping out innocent victims in its flow of ideological lava.

§§

Independent of the interpersonal and social costs, dogmatists' scathing judgment and authoritarian aggression takes a personal toll. Self-righteous anger is always twinned with physiological arousal of the sympathetic nervous system that responds with gradients of intensity to help us fight or flee stress (known as the fight-or-flight response).[64] But all of us "face more than simple fight or flight options, which compounds our natural bodily response to stress [and] there are huge individual differences in how people respond to stress. Genetic, developmental, and experiential differences help to produce varying responses to similar conditions."[65] Whether we respond to the stress of a realistic or imagined threat, prolonged anxiety and anger keep the fight-or-flight response in the active phase, which keeps adrenaline coursing through our veins.

In the case of dogmatic authoritarian aggression, the fight response is primed for anger that ranges from mild attacks—such as those seen in put-downs, sarcasm, racial slurs, and crude jokes—to extreme physical assault. Research on the physiological reactions of aggression, especially prolonged hostility, reveals that chronically elevated stress hormones not only strain the coronary and gastrointestinal systems, they also impair immunological functioning.[66] Thus, emotions disrupt brain function and physiological systems.

What accounts for and maintains this psychological predisposition for anger? We will delve into the details in later chapters when we investigate causal influences of dogmatism, simply noting here that deep-seated anxiety and fear combined with intolerance and prejudicial judgment are the agents of diffuse anger. In their dogmatic hearts of darkness, fear is the invisible escort of blustering dogmatic rhetoric, bloated hubris, and anger that is displaced on safer targets. Common bullying behaviors of childhood later become attached to belief systems that move playground aggression to homes, boardrooms, prisons, political platforms, and religious pulpits.

Dogmatic Authoritarian Aggression and Psychopathy

Having defined dogmatic authoritarian aggression, an important comparison with the antisocial personality disorder (psychopathy) is necessary. Although these disorders have points of convergence that may make them appear indistinguishable, the underlying pathways that shape each disorder have different psychological motivations and functions that yield distinct features, and justify their distinct categories. Psychopaths are aggressive in that their behavior is, at the very least, predatory, but all psychopaths are not dogmatic. They are charming, remorseless manipulators who intimidate others and, if necessary, use cold-blooded violence to achieve their self-serving goals.[67] However, unlike dogmatists, psychopaths do not typically conform to rigid ideological belief systems that they unquestioningly adopt. Psychopaths use aggression for personal gains, not for ideological goals or the psychological protection such goals provide. Conversely, while dogmatists with the trait of dogmatic authoritarian aggression may be sarcastic and condescending, most of them are not evil psychopaths. Moreover, the cold, calculating nature of psychopathy reveals a lack of anxiety, which is the prominent emotional characteristic of dogmatism. Catch a psychopath in a bold-faced lie, and chances are good he or she won't even flinch.

Dogmatists differ from psychopaths in that their dogmatism

attempts to compensate for (1) persistent anxiety, (2) a fragile or inauthentic identity, and (3) a perceived lack of social connection and dignity. While some dogmatists may develop the manipulative skills of a charming psychopath, they do not recruit their minions in order to swindle them. Rather, they proselytize and recruit members for some ideological cause that compensates for their own psychological deficits.

Dogmatic Authoritarian Submission[A,JMod]

Illustrative statements:

- "The worst crime a person could commit is to publicly attack the people who believe in the same thing he does."[R]
- "Obedience and respect for authority are the most important virtues children should learn."[A,68]
- "People who criticize their heads of state or military personnel are traitors who threaten national security."[J]
- "Government leaders have the right to disregard national and international laws."[J]
- "Important decisions should only be made by experts."[J]
- "It's high time young people learned to respect their elders."[J]
- "What our country needs is a strong, determined leader who will crush evil and put us back on a path to salvation."[A,69]
- "If people would talk less and work more, the world would be better off."[J,70]

History is replete with examples of political, military, and religious leaders who brainwashed the vulnerable into mindless obedience. These include Hitler, Stalin, Mao Ze-dong, Pol Pot, Idi Amin, Papa Doc and Baby Doc Duvalier, Mullah Mohammed Omar, Kim Jong-il, Osama bin Laden, Saddam Hussein, Reverend Jim Jones, and other tyrannical dictators from royal families, military juntas, and ruling party elites. Motives for civilian obedience have varied; some obeyed out of fear, while others willingly submitted to those perceived as messianic redeemers or liberators. Regardless of motive, leaders who adorn themselves with titles, uniforms, badges, or robes use the media and other means to seduce the emotionally and cognitively vulnerable into authoritarian submission.

Religious zealotry vividly illustrates dogmatic authoritarian submission, "and its temper—one that, ironically, is grounded in the doctrine of submission—has grown increasingly contemptuous of humanity, being characterized by arrogance, intolerance, and violence."[71] Adults who, *without question*, acquiesce to the demands of religious authority figures, do so out of narrowly focused, emotionally driven needs. Burdened by anxiety and an intolerance of ambiguity, they long for certainty and the assurance of safe passage. As children, they were taught that blind acceptance of religious dogma is a virtue. Many religious dogmatists are unable to go beyond the childhood indoctrination that squelched their eager curiosity when their parents identified them as a Muslim, Christian, or Jew, for example. Yet Richard Dawkins notes that a child is "not a Muslim child but a child of Muslim parents. That child is too young to know whether it is a Muslim or not. There is no such thing as a Muslim child."[72] I think Dawkins would agree that there is also no such thing as an atheist child.

In contrast, children who are educated in a respectful, open-minded family and cultural environment learn *how* to think—*what* they think is secondary. This enables them to independently determine, without guilt and psychological flogging, their religious, political, and other belief systems. Above all, their minds are not shackled by pseudoscience.

Yet most of us depend, to some extent, on authoritative sources for information. The difference between dogmatic people and those who are cognitively flexible is that the latter have a *rational* reliance on authority. Authoritarian submitters represent extremes of ingratiating loyalty, for they imbue authority figures with heroic motives and attributes. Their "curiosity succumbs to fear, often masquerading as pious submission."[73] Exemplary models of conventional behavior, they fear being conspicuous—within or outside the group. Because they are exceptionally status conscious, they respect influential authority figures with whom they identify, and they believe that such identification enhances their own significance and dignity.

These features are among the many characteristics of dogmatists who overidentify with a leader and a cause. In a confusing world, an anxious, insecure person is attracted to the bold certainty of authoritarians who may symbolize the yearning for protective parents. Dogmatists imitate such certainty and accept the leader's principles and methods as legitimate and true. They are the lapdogs of acquiescence. Blind to the manipulative motives of dogmatic authoritarians, they focus on superficial qualities and symbols and magnanimously exaggerate the importance of presidents, priests, prophets, and others who they imbue with unqualified honor. Dogmatic leaders with a history of brutality are the benefactors who are highly motivated to isolate the segments of their ideology that can be uniquely interpreted and then used to justify retributive violence and bloodshed.

Such dogmatic authoritarian aggressors are heads of state that govern millions, religious leaders who preside over large congregations, CEOs of big corporations, or parents who control their children—even their adult children. Yet these people, who are fewer in number than their followers, would be powerless if dogmatic authoritarian submitters did not acquiesce out of fear or idolatry driven by their own psychological deficiencies. As long as submitters fail to understand and address their impoverished needs, they will prop up the equally impoverished psychological needs of predacious demagogues. Whether a leader's motives for achieving group objectives are ethical or unprincipled, logical or irrational, or legal or illegal is of little concern to dogmatic submitters. Those who arbitrarily assume the underlying dogma is infallible adopt group motives, missions, and means because they guarantee psychological comfort. Self-assured, single-minded leadership inspires confidence in dogmatic followers, who psychologically merge with those who have the answers and will assure them respect and reward their loyalty with dignity.

Strict Adherence to Conventional Conduct

Rigid conventionalism is a component of dogmatic authoritarian submission that is seen in unwavering, conformist beliefs such as "people
must always be loyal, respectable members of society."[74] As a sub-
category of dogmatic authoritarian submission, strict adherence to
conventional codes of conduct is common in those preoccupied with
power and status, who glorify an in-group, and who focus on the messenger's qualities rather than message content. Obsequious obedience
reflects this excessive submission to mainstream values and customary
codes of behavior.[75] By overidentifying with absolute authority and a
cause, by accepting reinforcements that arise from this identification,
"an attempt is made to defend the self against feelings of aloneness
and isolation, self-hate, and misanthropy."[76]

Behavior conformity provides certainty in an unpredictable world,
and dogmatists' strict adherence to explicit rules and regulations
secures identity and safety, which is why they oppose violations of
established codes of conduct. Pervasive anxiety from infancy and
early childhood continues to fuel anxiety, which becomes masked with
the bold certitude that convention, rules, and conformity are absolutely necessary. The only right and proper behavior is that which
complies with traditional social conventions that support established
belief systems.

Dogmatic people are obedient conformists not because they lack
intelligence, but because anxiety has weakened their reasoning. As
adults, they default to obedience because they learned early on that to
submit was safer than to question or challenge. They mistakenly
assign power to leaders based on presumed, admirable personality
characteristics and ignore or underestimate the broad impact of complex social and situational influences that impact tradition in a
changing world.[77] As such, their conformity is governed by emotion
and superficial factors rather than reasoned compliance. Psycho-
sclerosis of the mind has prevented an independent evaluation and
reexamination of their habitual judgment of unconventional behav-

iors: "You're wearing that? Going where? With who? Reading what? Doing that!" Dogmatic, rigid conviction about behavior conventions gives them an aura of self-righteousness, but confidence built from an excessive need to conform and the gratuitous judgment of others is a sham. (Some would add an *e* to that last word.)

For reasons of safety and social connection, dogmatists agree that responsible, respectable adults *should always* eat and drink in moderation, exercise and attend church regularly, view cleanliness as next to godliness, follow a daily routine, and go to bed at a decent hour. If you think that these comments do not reflect dogmatism, I would ask you to reconsider the italicized words *should* and *always*, which have an urgent, demanding tone. Are any of these people Joe Cool on the beach with a beer in hand, laughing uproariously to the punchline of a joke about life's absurdities?

Dogmatists are similarly constrained at work, in many cases by the occupations they choose. Comfortable in careers that explicitly outline and enforce regulations, they gravitate to traditional institutions that hierarchically arrange levels of employment within work environments that provide a clear structure. Those who hold positions of authority are rule-bound and punitive. One strike and you're out! Their externally defined identity undermines their ability to independently determine in which circumstances they will conform and with which rules they will comply.

A distortion of moderate, traditional nationalism is seen in dogmatic patriotism—a unique example of strict adherence to convention in which dogmatic, self-evident imperatives reinforce the sacrosanct codes of conventional morals and social behavior. Their extremely patriotic, myopic obedience divests energy in honoring and preserving the nation-state, the flag, national leaders, common ethnic rituals, and conventional behaviors that adhere to traditional custom and reduce one's motivation to understand race and ethnic differences. "Nationalism is a distorting mirror in which believers see their simple ethnic, religious, or territorial attributes transformed into glorious attributes and qualities. The source of homicidal hubris, systematic overvaluation of the self results in systematic devaluation of strangers and out-siders."[78] According to Daniel Dennett, the great danger of symbols is that "they can become *too* 'sacred.' An important task for religious people of all faiths in the twenty-first century will be spreading the con-viction that there are no acts more *dis*honorable than harming 'infidels' of one stripe or another for 'disrespecting' a flag, a cross, a holy text."[79]

Dogmatists are seduced by the glamour of national heroism, and the next best thing for those not grounded in their own identity is to secure a national one that is fervently patriotic—one that has a self-righteous, pompous tone that demands obedience and loyalty. And just as dogmatic individuals need ideology for identity, dogmatic nations need enemies to conquer, for ideology and imperialism are the life blood that sustains both individual and national dogmatism.

In contrast, people who are open-minded are less reliant on author-ities to structure their world. They are not compelled to comply with regulations, especially those they consider unjust or illegal. As such, they are angered by dogmatic authoritarian aggression and thoughtless submission that leads to violations of human rights. Open-minded people may turn to authority figures for guidance, but they do not need them to provide the absolute answers that their dogmatic counterparts seek. Chauvinistic judgment and exclusion is unacceptable to flexible thinkers who ponder abstract concepts of nationhood and nationality beyond the context of rigid, concrete borders. They recognize the importance of nationalism in moderation, and they would agree with Charles Taylor that "we have no choice but to be cosmopolitans and patriots; which means to fight for the kind of patriotism which is open to universal solidarities against other, more closed kinds."[80] Said dif-ferently, "cosmopolitanism embraces the cosmos, patriotism the parish—it is parochial."[81]

Broad-minded people are also less apt to grant authority figures unilateral power. They recognize when group leaders and followers manipulate information to propagandize their audience, which is the preliminary step for dogmatic leaders who want to execute unpopular reform. They distinguish obedience to a just authority from legitimate disobedience to unjust authority. Open-minded patriots engage their nation in dialogue with others and expose the dangers of dogmatic, narrow-minded patriotism. If this fails, civil disobedience is justified. As Henry David Thoreau wrote, "All men recognize the right of revolution; that is, the right to refuse allegiance to, and to resist, the government, when its tyranny or inefficiency are great and unendurable."[82]

When democratic rights and freedoms are abused, courageous, open-minded thinkers protest—even if they suffer at the hands of authorities they deem illegitimate. In their determination to redress injustice, they do not abuse the rights of others. What injustice? Whose injustice? How do we determine if protest is open-minded and legitimate? These are the slippery fish that philosophers have tried to grasp for centuries, but whatever the debate, dogmatists sully it with their inability to open-mindedly collaborate to solve difficult problems and entertain new ideas.

Arrogant, Dismissive Communication Style[J]

Illustrative statements (attach adamant, emotional emphasis to the following statements):

- "You're in no position to talk!" (The speaker proceeds to expose a personal flaw or recall some past mistake of his or her rival.)[J]
- "Since when did you become an expert on . . . ?"[J]
- "Just one more thing you need to know before I finish—and this is absolutely important. . . ."[J] (The speaker continues his or her monologue)
- "I doubt you've even considered that . . ."[J]
- "I need you to understand that . . ."[J]

Striking isn't it, how many ways there are to preface arrogant, dogmatic statements? Equally striking are the number of inferences one can make about such prefaces. The foregoing illustrative comments signal, at best, gauche attempts to communicate. We identify the underlying emotion as defensive anger, and while that is a reasonable reading, the deeper feeling is likely anxiety or fear, masked by anger. As Susan Blackmore put it, their "thunder and conviction betray an anxiety."[83] Those who are low self-monitors are often unaware of the gestures and facial expressions that transcend their words to provide additional, often unintended, psychological meaning.[84] Because dogmatists lack personal insight, they are largely oblivious to their visible displays of anxious certainty.

A good conversation about value-laden topics requires social skills that even the open-minded may lack. At times, any one of us can lapse into an arrogant, dismissive style of communication that is hardly an invitation for thoughtful discussion and social connection. And even though arrogant people may consistently present their views with more certainty than the rest of us are comfortable with, their manner of speech, in itself, is not enough to personify dogmatism. But combined with other characteristics, arrogant, dismissive communication is a useful indicator of a closed mind. When dogmatists feel threatened, they interpret differences of opinion as attacks on their most vulnerable attribute—their intelligence. We soon learn that when we challenge their ideas we also challenge the image they need to effect, project, and protect. Innocuous questions become red alerts to their adrenal glands, simple inquiries are twisted into accusations, and answers become needless justifications.

Communication—verbal and nonverbal—is derivative of thought, and anxiety impairs its quality. When dichotomous belief systems are conveyed with arrogant, dismissive communication, we witness something beyond closed-minded thinking. Intentional or not, dogmatists invite conflict rather than collaboration, and they fail to recognize that most interpersonal exchanges provide opportunities to invite people in or show them the door. Have you ever experienced the following?

At the beginning of what you thought would be a pleasant, interesting discussion, the topic was suddenly derailed by a dogmatic monologue that was emotionally prefaced with: "Look! You're not telling me anything new here. . . ." What is the subtext of this conversation stopper? Individuals who begin their statements with this arro-gant certainty convey palpable self-importance—at least on the sur-face. Even though the person may be unaware of the dismissive quality behind such a statement, to the listener there is an unwelcome meta-message that goes beyond literal meanings. Other prefaces that dogmatists mistakenly hope will empower their statements include:

- "Any person with half a brain knows that . . ."
- "Make no mistake about it, . . ."
- "Listen! The truth of the matter is . . ."
- "Look, . . . !"
- "Oh c'mon, . . . !"

With an understanding of dogmatism, complete the above sen-tences with this postscript: ". . . although I'm not totally convinced I'm right about this, which makes me feel anxious and insecure." This is the unspoken, meta-message of dogmatic arrogance that is intended to obscure anxiety. On their own, these statements do not flag dogma-tism, but, at the very least, they are socially awkward preambles. If used to intimidate and quarantine others' ideas, a very different picture emerges, one that is unlike the fleeting acts of social clumsiness. As we shall see in subsequent chapters, this conversational picture is composed of longstanding, underlying emotional and imaginal com-ponents of which the speaker and listener are unaware. Similarly, single words can flag dogmatism. Indiscriminate use of strong adjec-tives that describe opposing ideas as crazy, idiotic, or insane may indi-cate rigid, polarized thinking and underlying emotions that close the mind and mangle the message.

The twin of dogmatic arrogance is dogmatic pomposity, the deluded belief that pretentious language will impress or intimidate others. Preferring to indoctrinate rather than discuss, to preach rather than propose, dogmatic people may use uncommon words and jargon —the meaning of which is obscure—that end up offending the very audience they hope to impress. Compounding their problem, a gullible audience that offers them unstinting praise strengthens their dogmatic conviction that their implacable truths deserve recognition and praise. Such is the absolute truth of dogmatism, and it's hard to iron the wrinkles out of that irony.

If social insensitivities are the spark of disengagement, then *dogmarrhea* is the fire alarm that has everyone running for the exit. A variation of logorrhea (excessive wordiness), dogmarrhea is another unpleasant feature of dogmatic communication that, depending on the audience, is the dogmatist's strong suit. Though it often leaves people feeling ambushed, frustrated, and manipulated, dogmatists use these monologues to hopefully impress others. You have likely noticed that those who adamantly believe they have captured truth have difficulty following and incorporating aspects of a discussion; they are seldom attuned to others and cannot allow a spontaneous, mutual flow of conversation to run its course. With a shoot-and-reload style of communication, they talk *at* others, not *with* them, and they lack the ability to fully hear different opinions because they are too eager to make their next point. While they appear to be listening, something quite different is going on behind their attentive façade: they are reloading to take another shot at converting ignorance. Agreement is their bounty. Have you ever heard a dogmatist paraphrase what you just said? The likelihood of that is as remote as a traffic light in the Sahara.

Similarly, after patiently listening to a dogmatic rant, have you then tried to change the topic—to no avail? Attempts are usually futile, for the psychological function of arrogant monologues is to convince you that they are right and you are wrong. Patient listeners may delude dogmatists into believing that they are infallible, reputable, intelligent, and safe. Yet without inviting others to exchange views, there is little development of dogmatists' own ideas. Eventually, their persuasive tactics backfire, for they cannot expect to convince people whose ideas they refuse to consider, nor can they expect others to support ideas and policies that were designed without encouraging and seriously considering their thoughtful contributions.

Beyond the verbal, messages meet more than the ear. We also

"hear" with our eyes, and we notice when nonverbal cues contradict the verbal. The rich inner texture of the message is conveyed through body language that may be dripping with emotional and physical add-ons that dogmatic people are generally unaware of. Research demonstrates that, universally, humans are very good at recognizing underlying emotional states in facial expressions. While different cultures use different words to describe these expressions, there is significant agreement about the feeling state behind strong facial messages, particularly disgust, joy, fear, anger, and sadness.[85] We may think we are in complete control of our facial expressions, but "our faces are also governed by a separate, involuntary system that makes expressions that we have no conscious control over."[86]

Closely study the silent body language of a dogmatist whose beliefs you question. Disagreement elicits sighs, frowns, and rolling eyes, especially in reaction to statements from those the dogmatist judges to be inferior. Other emotional adjuncts include visible muscle tension and rigid body posture, a strident voice, and a stern facial expression that is stuck in an unattractive resting position. In other words, body language heralds their edginess.

Imagine that you are practicing your lines for a play in which you play the role of a narrow-minded aspiring writer. As the lead actor who shines the spotlight on dogmatism, you say, "What you need to understand here is that the masses are massively stupid." Try changing your tone of voice, emphasizing different words, altering your facial expression, and gesticulating with that distracting physical counterpart of shoot and reload—the finger jab. Like a traffic cop, thrust your palm outward to convey another equally obnoxious display of body language. Each alteration of tone and body language provides a rich source of information about the impersonated, intended message—one that is loaded with combustible verbal and nonverbal language.

We would also expect dogmatists to use ad hominem arguments in their rejection of alternative views. Personal attacks on people the dogmatist categorizes as ignorant or of low status are used to discredit everything an individual says and does. The purpose of this fallacious strategy is to shore up one's own unassailability while undermining the intelligence and credibility of others. Such ad hominem reasoning is twofold: it dismisses both the idea and the person conveying it, and even though egregious arrogance may bolster one's closed-minded belief system, it also damages the dogmatist's own credibility and integrity.

Arrogant, dismissive communication is injudicious on several other counts: (1) it rarely convince others that one is right, (2) it seldom persuades people to change their minds, (3) it alienates others rather than impresses them, and (4) it ultimately fails to reduce the dogmatist's chronic anxiety and insecurity. Dogmatic proclamations are not really for the captive audience, they are for the captive mind that utters them, and what appears as an external show is driven by an internal need.

In contrast, open-minded people are more likely to use tentative words like *valid*, *useful*, *indicates*, or *suggests*, which hold one's attention more than strong declarative statements that distract and antagonize. Faced with dogmatic speech, listeners disengage, change the topic, become the devil's advocate, or make a hasty retreat. Contrast the previous examples of arrogant, dismissive communication with these open-minded, respectful comments that invite dialogue:

- "Given what you just said, I'll reconsider my position."
- "I'm interested in what led you to believe/think/say/do . . ."
- "Perhaps I need to readjust my thinking here."
- "Have I understood you to mean that . . ."
- "Is there some way we can reach a compromise?"
- "Are there common interests we might be overlooking?"
- "I differ with you on that." (To differ with someone encourages dialogue, whereas the comment, "I disagree with you," has an adversarial tone).
- "Perhaps we should more closely examine . . ."
- "Have we left anything out?"[87]
- "What questions should we ask that would help us better understand this?"

Politicians who change their original positions are accused of flip-flopping, and while it may be true that some do so to garner votes, those who succinctly explain their new views as a consequence of open-minded exploration of new facts should garner respect, not ridicule. Does the following statement sound wishy-washy and weak, or convincing and intelligent?

"In determining whether to vote for increased military funding for our troops, I have examined all sides of the issue. Given the changes in circumstances and based on recent evidence, I have altered my views. Pundits, pollsters, and my political opponents may accuse me of flip-flopping, but on all complex issues I intend to keep my mind open as I examine the facts, and to change my position if necessary. The following, recent information now leads me to vote against further military expenditures. . . ."

Is this politician's credibility barometer rising or falling? How would dogmatic military personnel view this explanation?

§§

In business, dogmatists in management or executive positions prefer organizations that are hierarchically arranged, and they generally favor formal presentations over informal dialogue. Alfred Korzybski, a specialist in general semantics, recommends adding the phrase "to me" to the verb "to be," which does not give people and ideas what appear to be permanent characteristics. He suggests, for example, prefacing statements like "The CEO is a genius" with "To me, the CEO is a genius." How many of us agree with this general principle yet fail to practice it? Adding one more practice in humility, Korzybski also recommends that we habitually end our statements with an unspoken "et cetera" to caution that our beliefs merely reflect current, limited perceptions that do not warrant proclamations of truth.[88] As I see it, it doesn't take a particularly tall forehead to see that we could all benefit from such practice . . . et cetera.

Many books have been written on effective interpersonal communication, but the language of dogmatism is rarely identified as such. Yet, because most communication provides an opportunity to connect or distance us from others, our conversational style continually enhances or diminishes the quality of our social relationships. Tentative qualifiers—such as "In my opinion . . . ," "As I see it . . . ," "Based on my information . . . ," and "What I would like to emphasize is . . ."—convey a willingness to engage others in respectful, open-minded dialogue. It cannot be overstated that our communication style teaches others how to treat us, sometimes before we open our mouths. Broad-minded people can respect the right of others to differ without necessarily respecting the behavioral consequences of their opposing beliefs. They may never respect abortion, for instance, but they can respect (in the sense of *understand*) the cultural tradition or circumstances that fostered different attitudes about abortion.

Dogmatic leaders of ideological movements are easily recognized by a communication style that condenses complex issues into brief, simplistic phrases that are readily adopted.[89] Phrases like "bourgeois mentality" were used in Communist China to prevent freedom of speech that could challenge the status quo. Similar examples of jargon—such as "axis of evil," "war on terror," or "tools of Satan"—reflect categorical, compartmentalized beliefs that promote anxiety and constrict thought in those predisposed to dogmatism. The intent of simple-minded proclamations is to manipulate the audience by using repetitive, fear-inducing rhetoric that foments anxiety and squelches complex thought and controversy.

As we conclude this segment on dogmatic communication, it is worth acknowledging that informal conversation often includes flip comments that are simply maladroit. Some people habitually interrupt others or launch a monologue of ideas they think deserves attention, but they do not have an urgent need to convince others that their closed-minded, rigid beliefs are infallible, nor do they pressure others for agreement. To assume the presence of dogmatism as a personality trait, arrogant, dismissive communication must be accompanied by at least five other distinguishing characteristics.

§§

The preceding five characteristics unveil the behavioral characteristics of an archetypal dogmatist. In summary, they are:

1. Preoccupation with power and status
   (includes self-aggrandizement)
2. Glorification of the in-group; vilification of the out-group
   (includes difficulty distinguishing message content from the personal qualities of the messenger)
3. Dogmatic authoritarian aggression
4. Dogmatic authoritarian submission
   (includes strict adherence to conventional conduct)
5. Arrogant, dismissive communication style

Until now, the characteristics of dogmatism have been loosely organized. With thirteen clearly defined subtraits and corollaries, we can now organize patterns of behavior that were previously random mixtures of bewildering, self-defeating behaviors into a coherent personality trait. When we add these five behavioral characteristics to the five cognitive characteristics presented in chapter 5 and the three emotional characteristics presented in chapter 6, we see that the psychological variability of dogmatism provides a unique spectrum of thoughts, feelings, and behaviors. Taken together, these characteristics clearly differentiate dogmatists from open-minded, flexible thinkers who hold their beliefs more tentatively.

Although various features of dogmatism come close to describing all of us some of the time, dogmatic people are set apart by the number of traits they possess and the rigid manner in which they reveal them over time and across different situations. All adults, including the well educated, make the same common errors of reasoning found in dogmatists, but they make these errors less frequently and for different reasons. They may be unmotivated, even unable, to critically analyze the depth or validity of their analyses and arguments, but, unlike dogmatists, they do not close their minds to the possibility they might be wrong, nor do they arrogantly confront and dismiss those who differ. They are aware of their limitations and are capable of monitoring and reflecting on the quality of their own thought.[90]

Regardless of the different sources and degrees of intensity that distinguish dogmatists from their more open-minded counterparts, the unique characteristics of dogmatism drape themselves over anxiety and heavily cloak the rigid belief systems beneath it—systems that are anchored in distorted perceptions of safety, knowledge, identity, and dignity. In order to satisfy an ever-growing appetite for truth, the archetypal dogmatist becomes insidiously more closed-minded, more certain, more authoritarian, more arrogant—and sometimes more dangerous. Just think of Adolf Hitler.

WHAT LIES AHEAD?

Chapters 9 through 16 present plausible psychological explanations of the forces that contour the thirteen characteristics of dogmatism. While numerous influential factors are examined, none defends dogmatism as a solution to unresolved childhood issues or excuses dogmatists who blame society for the manner in which they hold their rigid beliefs. The burden of responsibility for adult dogmatism rests solely with dogmatists, even though their adult belief systems may have emerged from unfortunate childhood experiences that pressured them to adopt the belief systems that their family, culture, or some other social group cherish. In childhood, the psychological need to know, the need to allay anxiety, and the need to establish strong social ties and acquire dignity all impact personality, but readers would likely agree that how adults go about fulfilling these needs is a matter of choice and responsibility.

While ideological fanatics manifest several of dogmatism's thirteen characteristics, many dogmatic believers present fewer characteristics in less obvious ways. Their unique constellation of characteristics may nonetheless narrow their minds and test their friendships, but, overall, they have a minimal impact on the cultural landscape. We can assume that, at least in the industrialized world, there are fewer extreme dogmatists at the helm of power (though I would not make that claim with rigid certainty). Yet this is of little consolation when careful scrutiny of historical records—dusty and new—teaches us that dogmatic ideologues still occupy positions of influential power and impose their belief systems with dangerous consequences.

Now that we have familiarized ourselves with the characteristics and presumed causes of dogmatism, it is logical to investigate the deeper, underlying biological and environmental catalysts for dogmatism. What components, complexities, and surprises might we find if the conceptual nut of dogmatism were cracked open? How manifest and enduring is this trait? If someone has several dogmatic characteristics at the age of twenty, will he or she continue to be rigidly closed-minded fifty years later? What causes some people to convert their anxiety to dogmatism while others may simply become chronically worried, overly dramatic, depressed, narcissistic, or drug addicted? These are the difficult psychological questions that subsequent chapters probe, but it is worth noting here that, given the complexity of the human brain, psychologists are like the chained prisoners doing time in Plato's cave, trying to make sense of shadows dancing on stone walls.[91]

In an effort to unchain them, we need to apply our knowledge of auspicious psychological theories that lend credence to our assumptions. What might these theories say about dogmatism and the four proposed influential factors outlined in chapter 4? One such theory examines human behavior that has endured for millennia. I speak here of positioning the study of dogmatism within the broad framework of evolutionary psychology, which reminds us that human traits are always situated within the history of our evolving species. Some behaviors have endured because they were adaptive hundreds of thousands of years ago, and some of those earlier adaptations remain as residual temptations that are dangerous impediments to modern-day survival. Chapter 9 focuses our attention on primeval behaviors that still press for expression—some of which have morphed into present-day dogmatism.

Before we examine proposed causal links to dogmatism, we visit Jonah, whose personal history serves as an illustrative backdrop into which major theoretical threads can be woven, creating a tapestry of dogmatism. That tapestry is anything but black and white.

NOTES

1. A. G. Greenwald, J. E. Pickrell, and S. D. Farnham, "Implicit Partisanship: Taking Sides for No Reason," *Journal of Personality and Social Psychology* 83 (2002): 367–79.

2. A. de Botton, *Status Anxiety* (New York: Pantheon Books, 2004).

3. F. Fukuyama, *Our Posthuman Future* (New York: Farrar, Strauss and Giroux, 2002).

4. De Botton, *Status Anxiety.*

5. Ibid. To maintain status in their own eyes, de Botton presents various narratives of poor people over the last two millennia (see his chapter 3 on meritocracy). For example, those of low status "were the true creators of wealth in society and therefore were deserving of respect," while the rich were "not worth honoring, for they were both unscrupulous and destined to meet a bad end" (p. 54).

6. L. McQuaig, *All You Can Eat: Greed, Lust, and the New Capitalism* (Toronto: Penguin Canada, 2001), p. 7. McQuaig's term *Homo economicus* refers to the major players in modern economics: "the human prototype who is pretty much just a walking set of insatiable material desires. He uses his rational abilities to ensure the satisfaction of all his wants, which are the key to his motivation. And he isn't considered some weirdo; the whole point of him is that he represents traits basic to all of us—*Homo Economicus* 'R' Us, as it were" (p. 12).

7. De Botton, *Status Anxiety*; G. Lakoff, *Don't Think of an Elephant* (White River Junction, VT: Chelsea Green, 2004).

8. According to UNICEF, 26,500–30,000 children die each day from poverty. And they "die quietly in some of the poorest villages on earth, far removed from the scrutiny and the conscience of the world. Being meek and

weak in life makes these dying multitudes even more invisible in death." This statistic is based on children under the age of five. If it included six- and seven-year-olds, the numbers would be significantly higher. http://www.globalissues.org/TradeRelated/Facts.asp (accessed March 21, 2008).

9. R. Altemeyer, *The Authoritarian Specter* (Cambridge, MA: Harvard University Press, 1996).

10. V. Packard, *The Status Seekers* (New York: William Petersen, 1959).

11. Fukuyama, *Our Posthuman Future*.

12. M. Rokeach, *The Open and Closed Mind* (New York: Basic Books, 1960), p. 69.

13. Ibid.

14. Ibid., p. 75.

15. Ibid., p. 76. This statement is #29 on one of Rokeach's earlier versions of his Dogmatism Scale.

16. B. E. Hunsberger and B. Altemeyer, *Atheists: A Groundbreaking Study of America's Nonbelievers* (Amherst, NY: Prometheus Books, 2006). This statement paraphrases one of Altemeyer's items in his Religious Emphasis Scale, p. 43.

17. E. Aronson, T. D. Wilson, and R. M. Akert, *Social Psychology: The Heart and the Mind* (New York: HarperCollins College Publishers, 1994), p. 498.

18. Ibid., p. 499.

19. A. Newberg and M. R. Waldman, *Why We Believe What We Believe* (New York: Free Press, 2007), p. 258.

20. A. Bandura, "Mechanisms of Moral Disengagement," in *Origins of Terrorism: Psychologies, Ideologies, Theologies, States of Mind*, ed. Walter Reich (Baltimore: Johns Hopkins University Press, 1998), pp. 161–91.

21. S. Kopp, *If You Meet the Buddha on the Road, Kill Him!* (New York: Bantam, 1979), p. 223. This statement is #18 of the 43 items in Kopp's "Partial Register of the 927 (or was it 928?) Eternal Truths," which he titled "An Eschatological Laundry List" (p. 223).

22. S. J. Gould, "Bacon, Brought Home," *Natural History* 108, no. 5 (1999): 29.

23. Rokeach, *The Open and Closed Mind*, p. 63.

24. I. L. Janis, quoted in Aronson, Wilson, and Akert, *Social Psychology*, p. 348.

25. Aronson, Wilson, and Akert, *Social Psychology*, p. 349. Adapted from Janis, *Group Think*.

26. I. L. Janis, *Group Think*, 2nd ed. (Boston: Houghton Mifflin, 1972).

27. For a good summary of group decision making and related research, see L. A. Lefton, L. Brannon, M. C. Boyes, and N. A. Ogden, *Psychology* (Toronto: Pearson, Allyn and Bacon, 2008), pp. 519–24.

28. Rokeach, *The Open and Closed Mind,* pp. 57–58.

29. Aronson, Wilson, and Akert, *Social Psychology*, p. 292.

30. E. Tarnow, "Self-Destructive Obedience in the Airline Cockpit and the Concept of Obedience Optimization," in *Obedience to Authority: Current Perspectives on the Milgrarn Paradigm*, ed. T. Blass (Mahwah, NJ: Erlbaum, 2000), pp. 111–23.

31. R. E. Petty and D. T. Wegener, "Attitude Change: Multiple Roles for Persuasion Variables," in *The Handbook of Social Psychology*, ed. S. T. Fiske, D. T. Gilbert, and G. Lindzey (Boston: McGraw-Hill, 1998), pp. 323–71.

32. Ann Coulter, commenting on Canada's failure to join American forces against Iraq. Fox News, *Hannity & Colmes*, November 30, 2004.

33. Altemeyer, *The Authoritarian Specter*. Altemeyer presents a compelling compilation of research that suggests that if we fail to understand the forces that shape authoritarian personalities, we do so at our peril. Authoritarian aggression and authoritarian submission were first investigated by Adorno et al. (1950), who devised the Fascism Scale (F Scale) to assess the authoritarian personality. The serious problems of that scale with validity and reliability have been reviewed by Rokeach, Altemeyer, and myself in the development of our own scales—all of which tap aspects of authoritarianism as conceived by the Adorno model. Altemeyer's three characteristics of the Right-Wing Authoritarian (RWA) Scale are the first three identified by the F Scale, which assesses nine facets of authoritarianism. Altemeyer deleted the other six components of the F Scale because "they were not supported by F Scale research" (p. 46). Although the titles of the characteristics are identical, Altemeyer more thoroughly defines all three and provides a rationale for his own conceptualization of terms. Also, unlike the Adorno group and Rokeach, Altemeyer does not assume that unconscious Freudian conflicts underlie right-wing authoritarianism or dogmatism.

34. T. W. Adorno, E. Frenkel-Brunswik, D. J. Levinson, and R. N. Sanford, *The Authoritarian Personality* (New York: Harper and Brothers, 1950); Rokeach, *The Open and Closed Mind.*

35. P. G. Zimbardo and F. L. Ruch, *Psychology and Life* (Glenview, IL: Scott-Foresman, 1975).

36. Adorno et al., *The Authoritarian Personality*.

37. Ibid.

38. Altemeyer, *The Authoritarian Specter*.

39. Ibid.

40. Altemeyer and Hunsberger, *Atheists,* p. 97.

41. Altemeyer, *The Authoritarian Specter*.

42. Ibid., p. 10.

43. Ibid.

44. B. Altemeyer, *Enemies of Freedom: Understanding Right-Wing Authoritarianism* (San Francisco: Jossey-Bass, 1988), p. 147.

45. Altemeyer and Hunsberger, *Atheists,* p. 110.

46. Rokeach, *The Open and Closed Mind,* p. 11.

47. Ibid., p. 77.

48. Altemeyer, *The Authoritarian Specter,* p. 10. In his endnotes to chapter 1, Altemeyer states, "Both leaders and followers can be authoritarian. Hitler, a notorious example of authoritarian leadership, believed his authority to do what he wanted superseded all human rights, laws, and treaties. The millions of Germans who readily accepted his authority exhibited authoritarian submission" (pp. 309–10).

49. Ibid.

50. A. Gore, *The Assault on Reason* (New York: Penguin Books, 2007), p. 24.

51. Lakoff, *Don't Think of an Elephant*.

52. A. Bandura, *Self-Efficacy: The Exercise of Control* (New York: Freeman, 1997).

53. B. Altemeyer, "The Other 'Authoritarian Personality,'" *Advances in Experimental Social Psychology* 30 (1998): 47–92; Rokeach, *The Open and Closed Mind*.

54. H. Arendt, *The Origins of Totalitarianism* (New York: Harcourt, 1968), pp. 461–62.

55. A. Bandura, B. Underwood, and M. E. Fromson, "Disinhibition of Aggression through Diffusion of Responsibility and Dehumanization of Victims," *Journal of Research in Personality* 9 (1975): 253–69.

56. Lakoff, *Don't Think of an Elephant,* pp. 7–8. Here, Lakoff summarizes the set of assumptions behind the strict father model.

57. C. Hedges, *American Fascists: The Christian Right and the War on America* (New York: Free Press, 2006), p. 82.

58. A. Camus, *The Rebel: An Essay on Man in Revolt* (New York: Vintage Books, 1956), p. 122.

59. Altemeyer, *The Authoritarian Specter,* p. 9. Strictly speaking, this quote refers only to authoritarian aggression, but since I have subsumed authoritarianism under dogmatism, I think the quote aptly applies to dogmatic people who also have the trait of authoritarian aggression. Thus, the quote is also relevant for dogmatic authoritarian aggressors.

60. Ibid., p. 310.

61. M. L. King Jr., "Letter from Birmingham City Jail," in *Civil Disobedience: Theory and Practice*, ed. Hugo A. Bedau (New York: Pegasus, 1969), p. 76.

62. N. Postman, *Conscientious Objections: Stirring Up Trouble about Language, Technology, and Education* (New York: Vintage, 1988), p. 25.

63. W. Faulkner, *Requiem for a Nun*, http://en.wikiquote.org/wiki/William_Faulkner (accessed February 18, 2008).

64. The fight-or-flight stress response was originally delineated in the General Adaptation Syndrome, developed by Hans Selye, in 1946.

65. M. S. Gazzaniga, R. B. Ivry, and G. R. Mangun, *Cognitive Neuroscience: The Biology of the Mind* (New York: Norton, 1998), p. 514.

66. B. S. McEwan, "Protective and Damaging Effects of Stress Mediators," *New England Journal of Medicine* 338 (1998): 171–79.

67. R. D. Hare, S. D. Hart, and T. J. Harpur, "Psychopathy and the *DSM-IV* Criteria for Antisocial Personality Disorder," *Journal of Abnormal Psychology* 100 (1991): 391–98.

68. This item on Altemeyer's RWA Scale is identical to item #1 of the F Scale.

69. Altemeyer, *The Authoritarian Specter*, item #21 of his RWA Scale (reprinted here with permission).

70. This item is taken from the California F Scale, Adorno et al., *The Authoritarian Personality*.

71. W. Soyinka, *Climate of Fear: The Quest for Dignity in a Dehumanized World* (New York: Random House, 2005), p. 125.

72. Ibid., p. 3.

73. Ibid., p. 127.

74. Altemeyer, *The Authoritarian Specter*, p. 11.

75. Ibid., pp. 11–12. Although Altemeyer defines conventionalism as "adherence to social conventions" as revealed in right-wing authoritarian

beliefs about religion, the family, women, sex, and the nation, the same ideas can be applied to dogmatists who strictly adhere to traditional codes of behavior. Both dogmatists and authoritarians believe "people should strive to be well-behaved, properly dressed, respectable, and in general to stick to the straight and narrow" (p. 11).

76. Rokeach, *The Open and Closed Mind*, p. 69.

77. S. Presley, "Positive Steps to Becoming Less Vulnerable to Influence and Authority," *Free Inquiry* 15, no. 1 (1994): 29. Social psychologists call this error "the fundamental attribution error" that explains the tendency for people to overestimate the extent to which human behavior is due to the person's personality or dispositional characteristics, and to underestimate the role of the situation.

78. M. Ignatieff, *The Warrior's Honour* (Harmondsworth, UK: Penguin Books, 1999), p. 51.

79. D. Dennett, *Breaking the Spell: Religion as a Natural Phenomenon* (New York: Penguin, 2006), p. 257.

80. C. Taylor, "Why Democracy Needs Patriotism," *Boston Review* 19, no. 5 (October–November 1994). Taylor's essay is in response to Martha Nussbaum, "Patriotism and Cosmopolitanism," *Boston Review* 19, no. 5 (October–November 1994).

81. T. Gitlin, "Varieties of Patriotic Experience," in *The Fight Is for Democracy*, ed. George Packer (New York: HarperCollins, 2003), p. 115.

82. H. D. Thoreau, *Walden—Essay on Civil Disobedience* (New York: Airmont Publishing, 1965), pp. 237–38.

83. S. Blackmore, *The Meme Machine* (Oxford: Oxford University Press, 1999), p. xiii.

84. R. B. Adler and N. Towne, *Looking Out/Looking In* (Fort Worth, TX: Harcourt Brace Jovanovich, 1993), pp. 66–67. These authors describe high self-monitors as those who are "more aware of their impression management behavior than others. . . . They have the ability to adjust their communication to create the desired impression. By contrast, low self-monitors express what they are thinking and feeling without much attention to the social reaction their behavior creates.

85. M. Gladwell, *Blink: The Power of Thinking without Thinking* (New York: Little, Brown, 2005), pp. 201–14. Gladwell presents Paul Ekman's development of a taxonomy of facial expressions.

86. Ibid., p. 209.

87. David Marshall, president of Mount Royal College, Calgary, AB, ends many of his talks and summaries of group reports with "Have we [or I] left anything out?" This question communicates interpersonal values of inclusive, respectful, open-minded dialogue.

88. Postman, *Conscientious Objections*. Lamenting the fact that Korzybski is largely unheard of today, Neil Postman devoted a chapter in this book to Korzybski's ideas about how semantics, the study of the meaning of words, provides us with the illusion that through language we construct the meaning of the world. In reality, words about anything merely describe our unique abstractions about things that are continually changing.

89. R. J. Lifton, *Thought Reform and the Psychology of Totalism: A Study of "Brainwashing" in China* (New York: Norton, 1961).

90. R. L. Solso, *Cognitive Psychology*, 6th ed. (Needham Heights, MA: Allyn and Bacon, 2001). Awareness of one's own thought processes has been termed *metacognition*, which "refers to the ability to monitor, control, and organize mental activity" (p. 266).

91. Plato's famous allegory of the cave, in simplistic terms, is symbolic of our difficulty to accurately interpret reality. He questioned the very nature of reality by imagining the human species as chained prisoners in a cave, where they see only the shadows cast on the cave's wall and mistakenly accept these shadows as reality. Outside the cave, the sun represents the Form of the Good, or the world of reason, to which Plato assumed few people have access.

Chapter 8

MEET JONAH

A Developmental Narrative of Dogmatism

What follows is a fictional narrative of Jonah and the life events that incrementally degraded his cognitive potential and simultaneously molded a brittle personality trait of dogmatism. His story provides an illustrative portrait that gives meaning to the theoretical models outlined in subsequent chapters.

MEET JONAH

From the time baby Jonah took his first breath, he seemed more sensitive than most newborns to light, noise, temperature, and touch. With every cry of protest, his little limbs would stiffen, provoking anxiety in his mother, Louise, who was baffled as to how she could calm her baby's edgy disposition. She became especially upset when her husband, Harold, ordered her to "do something with that fussy baby," yet when she consoled Jonah, Harold criticized her "mollycoddling." For Louise, motherhood was increasingly burdened by self-doubt and anxiety that paralleled her newborn son's uneasy temperament. Their shared emotional distress robbed both mother and baby of pleasurable, happy moments together.

Marching to his own dogmatic drum, Harold operated from an inflexible belief that today's parents are far too permissive. Although he cared for his son, he seemed to take little pleasure in father-son interactions, many of which were brief. Harold believed that babies must learn, at a very early age, how to "tough it out," which meant that tiny Jonah was frequently left to his own devices—and tears. He often cried as if his little heart were broken.

Jonah was unknowingly shaping his relationship with his parents—an anxious, insecure mother and an overcontrolling, distant father. Jonah's biological predisposition for anxiety only increased the strain on his parents' marriage, which, for the most part, was burdened with tension and drained of intimacy, mutual caring, and respect. Louise and Harold rarely discussed childhood concerns, much less their beliefs about raising children. Their lack of parenting skills and preoccupation with personal problems prevented them from giving Jonah the nurturing and reassurance that all babies, particularly anxious ones, require. Had Jonah's temperament been bundled in calm, cheerful smiles and coos, his parents might have responded to him with less anxiety and frustration, but that was not to be.

Jonah clearly sensed, but could not understand, the emotional stress that enveloped his home environment. His father often spoke to his mother from a superior plane that conveyed his unspoken belief that women should conform to traditional, subservient roles. Louise considered marriage and parenting the two most important measures of success for a woman, yet felt she was rapidly losing confidence in her ability to demonstrate either. Her interactions with Jonah became erratic—one moment she would smother him with love, the next she was anxious and complaining.

During Jonah's first two years, negligent parenting and frustrating social interactions accompanied critical periods of brain growth that left Jonah with persistent, vague feelings of apprehension. Although he could not articulate it as such, Jonah felt that he had entered a frightening, sometimes chaotic world. His mother's moodiness, his father's emotional distance, and his inability to understand the surrounding environment intensified Jonah's diffuse anxiety, which further compromised smooth transitions and maturation of his developing nervous system.

BEYOND INFANCY

During childhood and adolescence, Jonah's relationship with his parents fluctuated from occasional displays of affection (particularly from his mother), to frosty if not hostile rejection from his father. Harold was the strict disciplinarian in the family who often criticized his son's questions, which he interpreted as impertinent, ridiculous intrusions that tested the edge of his tolerance. His father unfavorably compared Jonah to his older sister Ruth—a name that he boasted was short for Truth. Ruth was the "obedient, intelligent" child in the family, and her questions rarely met the ridiculing jabs her father reserved for his only son. When Jonah asserted his ideas or opinions, his dad frequently mocked or ignored them: "What on earth makes you think that?" Jonah soon learned that thinking for himself and questioning parental views would leave him feeling dismissed or humiliated. He thought his father looked for excuses to deride him. Because his parents believed strict discipline made children responsible, independent adults, they imposed strict rules and threats of punishment that were weapons of thought and behavior control that intensified Jonah's chronic, free-floating anxiety.

Belittled for expressing his feelings, Jonah became an expert at controlling his emotions, particularly his frustration and anger. Without understanding why, he converted his anger to guilt and anxiety. Jonah's implicit reasoning went something like this: "Since Dad treats me badly, I must be bad." This conclusion was the result of flawed reasoning that intensified his insecurity and anxiety. Rather than express his frustration and anger, he internalized it. Yet out of anger that he could not understand came self-blame and guilt. Jonah's only protection against such emotional distress was to block it out, and he soon became very skilled at emotional numbing. Given the circumstances, this was adaptive, but prolonged repression eventually alienated him from his real feelings. At times he was genuinely puzzled by his lack of emotion. Events that stirred positive and negative feelings in others had an anesthetizing effect on Jonah. At the age of twelve, during his grandfather's memorial service, Jonah felt strangely removed from the ceremony, as if he were an uninvited voyeur.

Jonah's parents were stern role models of tradition that valued obedience, respect for elders, self-discipline, hard work, financial independence, and religious devotion. They believed that children who adopt these values early in life are assured success, status, and honor in adulthood. Conformity and deference to authority figures were drilled into their children. Louise and Harold openly criticized people who followed different religious paths or voted for the "wrong" political party. They restricted their children's social contacts to "the right kind—our kind—of people." Beneath the surface of the prejudicial drama being played out at home, Jonah's young mind was developing a hardwired picture of an unpredictable world, one that was filled with two categories of people—the righteous and the rest.

School only added to Jonah's misfortune. His teachers could not provide him with the necessary attention and support that may have compensated for his negative home environment. Government cutbacks to education meant classes were overcrowded and individual teacher-student contact was minimal. The classroom was a benign extension of Jonah's home environment, in that teachers who could have consistently encouraged him, reinforced his curiosity, and validated his questions were generally unavailable. The only time Jonah felt relaxed and secure was in the church that he and his parents regularly attended.

Unable to feel comfortable at home and school, Jonah became insidiously closed-minded to ideas that differed from family values. When classroom discussions centered on current events, he adhered to his parents' inflexible, correct, and unalterable views. The adage "seeing is believing" was replaced with "believing is seeing." By the time Jonah reached adolescence, he preferred science courses that did not require him to ponder ethical and value-laden issues. When questioned about his personal beliefs, Jonah became argumentative and defensive. In the cafeteria over lunch one day, he belligerently told a self-professed atheist that "anyone who denies the existence of God will suffer eternal damnation." That encounter resulted in his being labeled a "crazy fundamentalist."

Throughout his teens, Jonah never questioned his beliefs and values. Autonomous thoughts and decisions about belief systems were something he never even considered, and discussions that veered outside his beliefs threatened his security. With confident, pat answers, he could intimidate others and further convince himself that his views were irrefutable. By mid-adolescence, Jonah's internalized values and his *unquestioning obedience* to authority figures had become as natural as wearing matched socks. Yet, at some level of awareness, he knew that his home environment was oppressive, particularly the extreme parental monitoring of television viewing. Except for finding solace in biblical scriptures, Jonah did not enjoy reading, nor did he take an interest in television news reports.

While Jonah admired his father's unwavering confidence, he also resented Harold's emotional detachment, especially around adolescent issues of personal concern. Gradually, Jonah became oblivious of the extent to which his home, school, and social experiences became as narrow as his belief systems and as distant as his emotions. In his senior years, classmates described him as a lone wolf. His aloof, self-righteous moralism gave him an air of superiority—or so he thought. To Jonah, snap judgments came easily; people were either strong or weak, leaders or followers, saints or sinners, intelligent or stupid.

Throughout adolescence, Jonah enjoyed teaching the gospel to small groups of children in weekly Bible lessons. Inspired by the experience, he finally felt knowledgeable, respected, and self-assured. After graduating from high school, Jonah majored in education at the city university and was hired as a first-grade teacher, and he believed that he was "chosen" to educate young minds about that which he deemed most important—traditional religious values. Children needed to respect their elders, something Jonah felt was dangerously lacking in modern society. Strict enforcement of rules would reward children who obeyed and punish those who did not. With naive optimism he tried to reinstate prayer at the beginning of each school day, which would save children from becoming lost souls.

ADULTHOOD

At twenty-five, Jonah met and married Eleanor, a school secretary who was also devoutly religious. She believed committed Christians were moral, responsible, hard-working citizens who studied the Bible. She was a meek, undemonstrative woman who took pride in her work. When she and Jonah had their first and only son, Matthew, Eleanor was filled with love but felt anxious about the responsibilities involved in parenting. She told her sister that Jonah thought she was an unfit mother and, worse yet, he seemed to be "just going through the motions of a married man." He rarely confided in her and seemed emotionally cold and aloof. She wished she could do something to add some spontaneity, intimacy, and vitality to their lifeless relationship, but, not knowing where to start, she gradually withdrew into complacent resignation.

As a father and teacher, Jonah was a strict disciplinarian. His students disliked him, as did his colleagues, who were irritated by his gratuitous religious and political intrusions. They criticized his pedagogical assumption that students are like sausages who need to be stuffed with facts. Jonah's personality also clashed with administrators; he often disagreed with their refusal to enforce school rules and policies. At age thirty-five, he felt alienated and disillusioned with his teaching career. His hopes to effect change in the curriculum had soured and he seriously questioned his role in the education process. Most evenings were spent staring blankly at televised sporting events, home-repair programs, and right-wing talk shows. He was uninterested in works of art, except for simple photography or symmetrical, traditionalist paintings that were representational. The only poetry that made sense was that which rhymed, and he liked the words and tunes of good-old, Bible-thumping gospel music.

Eleanor indulged her husband's sermons and found shrewd ways to escape his vanity. Perhaps because Jonah felt more tolerated than loved, he had two casual sexual affairs, and while each encounter relieved his chronic feelings of emptiness, the reprieve was only temporary. It wasn't long before Jonah's disillusionment about who he was and where he was going left him feeling like a calving glacier—large chunks of who he thought he was were breaking off and dissolving into a cold, turbulent sea of confusion.

Then came an offer that infused Jonah's life with new meaning. Hired as the superintendent of his church, he resigned from teaching and devoted himself to increasing the church's profile. He worked with a Web site designer to create a cyberspace church that would attract people with strong, like-minded values. Here, committed parishioners could blog about fundamentalist religious values. Church sermons and the Web site stressed the importance of restoring prayer in schools, denouncing sex education, and electing school board officials and government legislators who would oppose abortion, gay marriage, and the teaching of evolutionary theory in schools. Brethren were encouraged to reach out to politicians and assure them that those who supported their religious values would win votes.

To Jonah and fellow parishioners, freedom of speech and religion meant God-given rights to legislate biblical truths—truths that should be incorporated in public school curricula. Jonah firmly believed that freedom of speech and religion meant that the religious views of his church had a legitimate place in public schools.

At forty-one, Jonah attended a political forum at which the party incumbent, a polished platform speaker, denounced stem cell research. He was moved by the politician's claim that "all types of stem cell research interfere with God's plan." During the question period, Jonah went to the microphone and made an impassioned plea to vote against any legislation that destroyed life or sanctified gay marriage. He was inspired by what he considered encouraging applause from like-minded people in the audience. A divine spark ignited a new passion—Jonah became politically active. He glorified the party leader, whom he secretly thought was divinely inspired, and worked tirelessly on his reelection campaign. At public forums and door-knocking campaigns, he learned to skillfully weave his religious values into political rhetoric.

His dedication paid off. Party officials recognized Jonah's devotion and chose him as an electoral candidate in an upcoming election. He surrounded himself with party advisors and spent weekends strategizing how to cleverly promote traditional values in a manner that would resonate with voters. To Jonah's delight, he was elected for two successive terms in office. Within six years, he was elected as party leader and subsequently led the party to victory in the next election—an astonishing feat. Jonah was a major player in the ruling elite, and while his party did not have overwhelming support in the electorate, it did have a mandate to govern. At the personal level, Jonah felt vindicated. He believed he was a man of destiny who had won his father's respect; indeed, he was triumphant.

With Jonah as party leader, caucus meetings took on an officious, ominous tone. Policy discussions made it implicitly clear that for continued success and reelection, party members had best not challenge the leader. Party cohesion and solidarity began to outweigh careful consideration of political, economic, and social circumstances. Basic democratic principles slowly eroded, along with freedom of speech and civil rights, which were sacrificed to dogma and groupthink.

As party leader, Jonah became adept at avoiding questions from the media or responding with flip, shallow answers. Policy manuals from previous government programs were dismissed as "dusty old books" and party officials proposed initiatives with a tone of adversarial bravado that made a mockery of intelligent inquiry. Media personnel or party insiders who questioned the party line put Jonah on the defensive. Disrespectful of differences, he labeled those with progressive ideas as "left-wing nuts" and openly derided university professors as "academic hacks who are out of touch with the real world."

To Jonah's delight, ownership of the media became concentrated in a few outlets, two of which financially supported Jonah's party—loyalty that did not go unnoticed or unrewarded. Eventually, reporters became annoyed with party officials' indifference to the press and unwillingness to answer questions about important issues in a timely, accountable manner. People began to suspect hidden agendas when Jonah and elected officials arrogantly refused to attend public forums and engage in public debate. Party minions unabashedly turned a deaf ear to such criticism—a decision that proved costly in the following election, which gave the opposition party a clear majority. That outcome had little humbling effect on Jonah and the reelected incumbents who secretly believed they would win back their "God-given right" to rule.

The same party tactics that were used to bowdlerize the opposition and the media were naively applied to internal factions jockeying for power, which led to a leadership convention. By the narrowest of margins, Jonah was reinstated, but his fear of losing power tightened his vise grip on party loyalty. At a press conference, a news reporter said, "Sir, the general public and some of your own party officials have accused you of being undemocratic." The insightful reporter paused and continued, "What are you so afraid of?" Jonah was blunt. "I'm afraid of nothing. Next question." Shortly after, a senior party member told the press that she was resigning because the party had become "dangerously dogmatic."

Jonah subconsciously sensed a loss of respect from his associates. He regretted that his relationship with his wife and son were seriously strained and he suffered prolonged bouts of insomnia. He worried that his political career was coming to an abrupt end, and he feared he would leave a legacy of failure and dishonor.

At the age of fifty-six, Jonah now battles depression; in the middle of long, dark nights he worries about a future in which doubt, cynicism, and emptiness will be his only close companions. He has no one to share his deep concerns with, and his only source of solace is his unwavering religious devotion that convinces him he is safe—in need of no one but the Lord. Yet this is not enough to shake his chronic melancholy and lethargy. How do you envisage Jonah's future?

§§

In preparation for the remaining chapters, three basic questions are worth pondering. People may not clearly articulate and answer them, but their lives are governed as if they have at least implicitly considered them. Where do you stand on these issues?

(1) Is personality, with all its various traits, *largely* determined by one's genetic blueprint, and if so, are we born good but gradually corrupted by society? Or are we little savages at birth whose social relationships and cultural institutions shape into civilized beings?

(2) Is it the case that we come into this world more closely resembling blank slates upon which social and cultural events mould our unique personality traits? If this is your assumption, which types of environmental experiences promote optimum versus unhealthy personality development?

(3) To what extent does human consciousness and free will determine how we express our biological natures as we interact with our social and cultural environment? In other words, are humans active agents who resourcefully plan and direct their ongoing experiences despite genetic predispositions and environmental circumstances? If so, as authors of their unique personalities, must they take responsibility for the personalities they creatively construct?

(4) In our current state of evolutionary development, is it possible for humans to entirely rid themselves of behaviors that had adaptive value eons ago?

Which critical forces, both internal and external, shape a pattern of brittle dogmatism in adulthood? Jonah's case study helps us apply ideas and concepts from several theoretical models to understand some of the fascinating dynamics that likely contributed to his eventual dogmatism. Chapter 9 presents the first of these models—a psychological perspective that examines personality development in the context of deep time.

Chapter 9

IS HUMANITY HARDWIRED
TO SHORT-CIRCUIT REASON?

Theories of Evolution

Our modern skulls house a stone age mind.

Cosmides and Tooby[1]

Imagine a group of scholars from the social sciences who have been invited to join a taped, roundtable forum to be televised later (I have PBS's *Charlie Rose* show in mind here). As the program begins, the host asks the panelists to discuss the recent discovery of seventy-three members of a cult, mostly women and children, who submitted to a cult leader's messianic, authoritarian control over their lives. What accounts for these adults' surrender of their identity, autonomy, morality, and dignity such that, as parents, they knowingly allowed their children to be physically and sexually abused by elder members of the compound? In the psyche of messianic egomaniacs, what enables them to force young teens to marry and bear their children? One panelist prefaces her answer with the following:

> May I begin by saying that delving into the psyche of such men requires a mighty big shovel, one that digs into the evolutionary backwaters of deep time. It may be useful to consider sexual conquest, territorial aggression, and the struggle for dominance as

having their origins in evolutionary processes that primed humans for emotions and behaviors that were adaptive millennia ago. Our ancient ancestors, themselves benefactors of evolved survival strategies, endured by making quick, arbitrary decisions that were adaptive on the African savannah eons ago. Remnants of those behavior traits remain in old structures of modern brains. We have not evolved long enough to banish ancient whisperings that nudge us toward maladaptive, anachronistic behaviors, and we might now be in serious trouble, given that enormous advances in modern technology combine with biological prods for dominance and aggression that threaten human survival. If we're lucky, evolution will bestow us with the hard-wired capacity for moral and ethical behaviors that currently exist in only a few megabytes of psychological software.

Until such time as cooperation and compassion overwrite human aggression, power, and rivalry, we will use outdated behavior programming to solve modern-day problems. Fortunately, our evolved intelligence has crafted laws that limit destructive, deadly forces of human behavior—a useful adaptation—but without an understanding of our psychological heritage, default modes will continue to apply short-term solutions to long-term problems, and this short-sightedness could ultimately plant us in the graveyard of extinction.

With this broader, evolutionary landscape in focus, I'd like to suggest that ever since we came down from the trees, variants of human evolution have combined with genetic predispositions and social learning to shape the type of cult worship we will address tonight. I don't think we can explain cult behavior by blaming parents or social institutions (of which the family is but one). That was the traditional approach of psychologists in the twentieth century. Increasingly, psychologists acknowledge that ancient predispositions for sex, dominance, and aggression are vestigial stirrings in baby's personality repertoire long before parental genes and social influences deal their hand at shaping his or her personality traits—in this case, dogmatism. These traits have no international borders.

The host and TV viewers might wish for a little seamless editing here, since only within the last few decades has evolutionary psychology gained prominence as a specialized division of psychology, linking ideas from evolutionary biology (notably, Darwin, and later, E. O. Wilson and others), to modern-day behaviors. When is the last time you heard someone suggest that certain behaviors are hard to extinguish because they are part of our evolutionary heritage? Yet, "slowly but unmistakably, a new worldview is emerging."[2] Attempts to unravel threads in the mysterious tapestry of personality, with all its attendant traits, typically begin with close examinations of personality theories that were developed during the last century. These models derived from research during the industrial and postindustrial era, without serious consideration of constraints from evolutionary biology. Thus, before we begin any individual analysis of personality traits like dogmatism, it is useful to place our assumptions within the broad framework of human evolution, which now has a rich body of literature in the fields of evolutionary biology and evolutionary psychology.

§§

In the late 1980s, the field of evolutionary psychology (EP) emerged to redefine the nature-nurture debate. Applying the knowledge of evolutionary biology to the long, slow march of the evolving human psyche, EP has since become an exciting, rapidly growing discipline. David Buss, a leading proponent of EP, commented in his 1,028-page *Handbook of Evolutionary Psychology*, "A decade ago, a handbook of this scope would have been impossible. . . . Now the body of work has mushroomed at such a rapid rate that I had to make difficult decisions about what to include for this volume to keep it a reasonable length."[3]

EP adopts an interdisciplinary approach: it "is not an area of study, like vision, reasoning, or social behavior. It is a *way of thinking* about psychology that can be applied to any topic within it."[4] Viewing the mind as crafted by natural selection, which favored traits that led to reproductive success, EP goes beyond traditional avenues of psychological inquiry to investigate the psychological development of the hominid lineage. It probes the deepest layers of our universal psyches for clues about traits that have been honed by thousands of years of natural selection and a process of functional differentiation that, overall, is adaptive for species survival. Why have so many species become extinct over time, and how might we apply what we know about them to prevent the extinction of our own?

Human traits of interest to evolutionary theorists include language acquisition, mate selection, jealousy, dominance, parenting, sexuality, and aggression (to name a few). In the language of EP, these traits are known as *adaptations*—traits that have shaped human nature since the beginning of our primate evolution and linger on in modern-day behaviors. But before we examine human traits, we first need to review some key developments charted by evolutionary biology, since these developments laid the foundation for evolutionary psychology.

EVOLUTIONARY BIOLOGY

Evidence for the biological evolution of all planetary life has been well documented in many scholarly books and journals particularly in the areas of biology (particularly ecology and biological anthropology), paleontology, zoology, archaeology, geology, chemistry, botany, and psychology. These academic disciplines provide a comprehensive view of deep time that, combined with geologic records, unequivocally confirm that humans evolved from a common ancestor—a theory that "is way beyond reasonable doubt, creationists notwithstanding."[5]

What enabled *Homo sapiens* to biologically enhance their reproductive success as they evolved from cave-dwelling hominids (ca. 4 million years ago), to *Homo habilis* (ca. 2.5 million years ago), to *Homo erectus* (ca. 1.5 million years ago), to *Homo sapiens* (ca. 195,000 years ago)? Social scientists have speculated that survival and biological reproduction was enhanced by evolving social skills that allowed *Homo sapiens* to succeed where other hominoids failed. However, from our prehistoric Lower Paleolithic environment to modern times, our evolving social skills have not kept pace with astounding advances in science that, ironically, outpace our ability to prevent war, infanticide, sexual exploitation, economic collapse, corporate cheating, and countless other impediments to human progress. "*Homo dogmaticus*" is one such maladaptive obstacle that has evolved in conjunction with emergent traditional dogmas of literate societies.

Charles Darwin's theory of evolution, outlined in his 1859 seminal work, *On the Origin of Species by Means of Natural Selection*, explained species survival as a process of natural selection:

> As many more individuals of each species are born than can possibly survive; and as, consequently, there is a frequently recurring struggle for existence, it follows that any being, if it vary however slightly in any manner profitable to itself, under the complex and sometimes varying conditions of life, will have a better chance of surviving, and thus be *naturally selected*. (Italics in original)[6]

Darwin assumed that the whole of nature selects offspring best fit to survive, and those who have a competitive advantage over other members of the population or species are those best equipped to acquire limited resources such as food, water, shelter, and other necessities of life. These individuals survive long enough to reproduce and leave healthy offspring that, in turn, are capable of reproduction. As Dennett notes, "We always need to remember Orgel's Second Rule: Evolution is cleverer than you are."[7] Could devolution be our ultimate fate?

Equally important was this Darwinian idea: species that best adapt to their environment are more successful at attracting mates and reproducing. This demonstrates "fitness," which, in the strict parlance of evolutionary biology, refers only to a species' competence at reproducing offspring. Fitness was originally measured by simply counting the number of progeny, but the concept of fitness has since expanded to include *any* means by which organisms can increase the probability of their genes being copied and represented in future generations. *Inclusive fitness* describes an organism that successfully perpetuate "copies of his or her genes into subsequent generations either by producing offspring himself or herself, or by helping relatives survive and reproduce, or both."[8]

§§

Modern humans are biologically similar to the great apes, particularly chimpanzees, whose genetic code is more than 98 percent identical to humans.[9] It is worth noting that this value of similarity is only for the regions of human and chimpanzee DNA that have been sequenced. What is often reported is based on a fraction of the genome and, with further sequencing, the value may increase or decrease. But chimpanzees and humans certainly share the same sense organs and react similarly to facial expressions; both have circadian rhythms of activity, need sleep, stretch their curious minds, and share comparable dental patterns and shoulder structure. We also have certain types of broad-based dispositions in common—chimpanzees, for example, are the only other mammals who, like humans, kill members of their own species. Since we are part of their lineage, this suggests that our own proclivity for murderous, authoritarian aggression is deeply rooted in our primate history.[10]

DEOXYRIBONUCLEIC ACID OR DNA: DISTINCTLY NEW ADAPTATION

In 1962, James Watson, Francis Crick, and Maurice Wilkins were awarded the Nobel Prize for their discovery of deoxyribonucleic acid (DNA) and four smaller molecules, called nucleotide bases, which are linked in a double helix that contains complex genetic instructions coded for all living organisms. "The real scientific issues concern the design, nature, and number of these evolved mechanisms."[11] How have these molecules instructed the human genome such that we evolved complex emotions and behaviors throughout our evolutionary history?[12] A common misunderstanding about genes and molecules is that they are designed primarily to serve species propagation. But, as Pinker notes, this is fallacious reasoning:

No human being (or animal) strives to spread his or her genes. Genes selfishly spread themselves. They do it by the way they build our brains. By making us enjoy life, health, sex, friends, and children. . . . Our goals are subgoals of the ultimate goal of the genes, replicating themselves. As far as *we* are concerned our goals, conscious or unconscious, are not about genes at all, but about health and lovers and children and friends.[13]

Or about being right, at all costs.

Yet genes merely provide a behavioral potential; they are incapable of strict biological determinism. Genes furnish the potential for language in general (not English), for the care of children (not for authoritarian parenting), and for body adornment (not the low-rise jeans of today or some other fashion fad of tomorrow). For this reason, EP cautions us to avoid the "nothing-butism fallacy—a fallacy that assumes our behaviors are nothing but products of our genes or nothing but products of our environment."[14] EP also reminds us that adaptive vestiges from the past are a fundamental, not incidental, part of the evolving human brain that can push some of us toward inappropriate behaviors. The pushiness of dogmatism may be derivative of dominance-seeking tendencies that were on the scene long before the intervention of complex language that produced myths, scientific methods, and social institutions.

§§

The following seven traits have enabled primates to adapt and procreate during Paleolithic evolution and beyond:[15]

1. *Activity*: The total energy output that is expressed in vigorous, energized behavior.
2. *Fearfulness*: Cowering, escape, and wariness, which activate physiological arousal of the autonomic nervous system.
3. *Impulsivity*: Acting on the spur of the moment without pause, planning, or reflection.

4. *Sociability*: Preferring to be with others rather than live a solitary existence.
5. *Nurturance*: Helping others, which includes altruism.[16]
6. *Aggressiveness*: Verbally or physically threatening or attacking others.
7. *Dominance:* Seeking and maintaining superior status over others.

Each of these traits evolved alongside adaptive, higher-order thinking skills that used increasingly complex, abstract reasoning to solve problems. Similarly, with increased emotional understanding and regulation, the richness of social connections became easier and longer lasting, enabling humans to fulfill their social needs and achieve a sense of status and dignity.[17]

EVOLUTIONARY PSYCHOLOGY—AN ACADEMIC ADAPTATION

In studies of human behavior, psychologists have consistently overlooked destructive inclinations that are remnants of our evolutionary past—a shortcoming that is evident in many theories of personality and academic texts in the field. With the exception of William James, who wrote about instincts in his 1890 book, *Principles of Psychology*, and Freud, who viewed humans as animals with instincts of sex and aggression, most personality theorists have not considered our evolutionary history as an integral component of human nature. EP redresses that oversight by expanding our thinking about ancient psychological urges that hang out in modern brains, some partying a little later than they should.

Personality theorists who fail to acknowledge the role of evolution do not situate their analysis in a broad enough context to fully illuminate current human behavior traits. Yet traditional perspectives have consistently overlooked the millennia of biological and cultural influences, which left footprints that cannot be ignored. Recently, it has become increasingly apparent that to omit the role of evolution in personality development is short-sighted, if not theoretically remiss.

In the realm of academia, psychologists who include evolutionary considerations in their theories, research, and lectures are themselves adaptive educators who emphasize the painstaking, incremental stages of change. As such, they have adapted their evolved intelligence to an understanding of ancient adaptations that impact the cognitions, emotions, and behaviors of modern humans, who still possess a suite of relict genes from our distant past. These prehistoric elements continue to ride the coattails of modern adaptive traits such as cooperation, civility, conscientiousness, and open-mindedness. Dominance-seeking, aggressive, self-serving behaviors are selective pressures that remain as evolutionary leftovers in a world drastically altered by science.[18] Primitive old-brain adaptations viscerally intrude upon modern brain structures, and it is wise to consider these infringements in the context of modern culture and present-day institutions.

Social dominance is one such carryover that was adaptive several millennia ago. Within nomadic groups, the dominant members survived because they seized a disproportionate share of food and other scarce, life-preserving resources. Survival was a full day's work for hunter-gatherers, who were constantly vigilant for eating and mating opportunities. Their daily task was to have lunch, not be lunch—and procreate for dessert. Survival depended on an efficient fight-flight sympathetic nervous system that responded to threats and opportunities with hasty judgments that were "on average, better than those of an individual's competitors, given the costs and benefits involved."[19]

Snap judgments that were adaptive during the Stone Age (2.5 million years ago to approximately 5,000 years ago), linger today in evolutionary backwaters that urge us to reenact maladaptive behaviors.[20] It is humbling, if not enlightening, to think of ourselves as harboring behavioral tendencies of anxious primates that inhabited the African savannahs and snowy Arctic plains.[21] Even though modern strategies to establish hierarchies of dominance, power, and status differ from those of our ancestors, biological residuals account for what is commonly referred to as the "elephant under the table." Evolved primates of the modern variety pound the table, stiffen their backs, scowl, and sharpen their verbal weaponry to impress or defeat others. Dogmatism is merely symbolic of primate chest thumping that occurs during business meetings and government sessions.

Sophisticated modern humans "practice dominance most effectively not by bullying people, but by doing favors, sharing attention, seeking allies, and using tactics of diplomatic negotiation."[22] Whatever the method and style, dominance is the invisible guest at every social occasion where people assess their place in the established hierarchy of power and status. Have you ever observed a group of males when an attractive woman enters the room? Eye contact, mannerisms, tone of voice, and body language all signal the unspoken rules of enduring, elaborate social codes of dominance. The struggle for dominance is seen today in maladaptive aggression that exploits the poor and ravages the planet, that threatens and eliminates entire species and ecosystems, that declares war on nations who pose no immediate or foreseeable threat, and that leads to the blind, rigid pursuit of a course of action.

Research indicates that in problem-solving situations, once people choose a course of action, their willingness to change is reduced. They are inclined to cling to their first choice[23] and initially resist information that does not conform to their original hypothesis, especially when more complex information is introduced.[24] We would expect dogmatic people to replicate these findings in spades. Such rigidity may reflect a larger evolutionary tendency that the scientific philosopher Thomas Kuhn appealed to in his explanation of scientific progress. He argued that the history of science is "punctuated by violent intellectual revolutions that overturn long periods of conservative puzzle-solving."[25] This is Kuhn's notion of paradigms and paradigmatic shifts, one example being radical behaviorism, which seriously challenged Freudian orthodoxy. Major shifts of thought are followed by periods of relative stagnation in which scientific exploration strengthens the current paradigm, *often without seriously questioning it*, until a new, more compelling model emerges. At the level of the individual, this process may partially explain the reluctance to reject one's original position. Narrowing it down to the dogmatic level, this same process weighs in to explain caricatured, rigid certainty.

MODERN-DAY HOMINIDS—DOGMATISM CREEPS IN

In the genetic lottery for brains, hominids won the jackpot. While *Homo sapiens* (Latin for "wise man") possess the cognitive capaciousness that enables us to walk on the moon, ancient behaviors for which we were previously primed can now drastically impede human progress. Although these throwbacks to earlier adaptations are not all beneficial for species survival, in the overall cost-benefit analysis it appears that evolution has primarily been our ally, not our foe.[26] Beneficial adaptations that linger in our evolutionary repertoire of behaviors include nurturing our young, reflex behaviors, perceptual preferences, intuitive mathematics, spatial cognition, mimicry, language acquisition, and social intelligence that involves the complexities of cooperation, status, and morality—all valuable species-specific behaviors that have endured for good reason.[27] From early childhood acceptance of parental beliefs and values, we expand our willingness to accept established enclaves of knowledge that we assume, through an act of faith, are largely accurate. Our ability and readiness to learn certain beliefs and behaviors increases our chance of survival, not to mention finding a mate and procreating. Such adaptive learning was first made possible by evolutionary forces acting on genes that structured our brains, and this was supplemented by environmental reinforcement, punishment, and social learning that modified beliefs and behaviors, one of which was to nurture our young. "Nurture—learning in all its various forms—doesn't happen by magic. . . . It occurs when evolved learning adaptations are exposed to the environment."[28]

Another example of evolutionary programming is seen in infant-caregiver attachment, which assures babies protection and enhances their survival. Offspring whose parents demand strict obedience provide them an adaptive tool in the human survival kit: they are more likely to survive. Inattentive, disobedient, or rebellious Paleolithic toddlers suffered premature death shortly after learning to enjoy their evolved bipedal status. They ambled into alligator swamps or leopard lairs—the modern-day equivalent is straying into traffic or tumbling into backyard swimming pools. Fortunately, most tiny tots avoid such disasters because evolution has primed them to obey adult rules and regulations across a wide spectrum of behaviors, all of which promote survival and transmit social and cultural standards for adaptive behavior. Young children, who are entirely dependent on their parents for protection from anxiety, lack the cognitive resources for seriously questioning what they are told. They accept myths, theories, and worldviews passed on by authority figures, with little integrative processing or consideration of alternatives. With increased maturity, exposure to different views, and quality education, older children learn to differentiate, analyze, and organize new information, then integrate it with the new or reject it, *depending on the extent to which, as children, they were encouraged to think for themselves.* Thus, the evolution of obedience has adaptive value as long as youngsters are not duped and pressured by adults to endorse fanciful stories as absolute fact.

From primitive to modern-day societies, children have gradually evolved a set of social learning competencies that reflect complex cognitive, emotional, and interpersonal skills. Through successive transmissions of morally binding customs—which were passed down from one generation to the next as small clans expanded to tribes, societies, cultures, and entire nations—children learned to adopt the cultural beliefs and practices of the group and avoid social taboos. These biological needs and the tendency to develop the necessary skills for their gratification sought resolution throughout our past experiences—all of which gradually consolidated, over time, as part of our evolving social history. Personal, historical experiences have incrementally and collectively nudged us to where we, as a species, are today:

> Over evolutionary time, humans developed a "need to belong," a drive to form and maintain at least a minimum number of lasting, positive, and significant interpersonal relationships.... People in virtually every known society typically belong to small, primary groups that involve face-to-face interactions [and] universally appear to respond with distress and protest to the end of a relation-

ship. . . . Interpersonal concerns and relational structures strongly influence cognitive processing.[29]

As mentioned in previous chapters, if the innate need for positive social connection is unfulfilled, cognitive processing and interpersonal learning may crystallize in dogmatic belief systems and dogmatic styles of interpersonal judgment and communication.

Social connection, yes. Crowd connection, no. EP notes that, historically, humans prefer mingling with small groups—an innate evolutionary preference that makes us vulnerable to social and simple phobias. A phobia is a self-acknowledged, uncontrollable, irrational fear,[30] and simple phobias of insects and animals are more common than phobias of electrical outlets or cars because, in our ancient past, avoiding life-threatening critters, creatures, and circumstances conferred survival advantages.[31] Some modern phobias are therefore considered to be misplaced evolutionary adaptations that remain in the crevices of our old-brain neural structures and prepare us to fear dangerous things and situations. Persistent symptoms of self-acknowledged irrational fears that occur in the presence of the phobic object or situation create intense physiological symptoms that may well be throwbacks to adaptive fears that protected humans from immediate danger.[32] The environment in which such learning occurred has changed, but the predisposition for such learning remains, waiting to attach itself to harmless objects or situations that have not even been encountered. People who seek therapy for an irrational fear of cats, for example, have simply brought forward too much of a good thing: an outdated overreaction that was formerly adaptive.

§§

To include EP as part of our theory of dogmatism, we must address the survival value of rigidly clinging to beliefs and defending them with certainty—in many cases, arrogant certainty. This tendency is attributable, in part, to ancient adaptations that were passed on and remain today, even though their adaptive value is obsolete in the modern world. Which evolutionary forces favored brain circuitry that preserved the capacity for characteristics of dogmatism during the course of human evolution? Are characteristics of dogmatism merely remnants of adaptive behaviors from hunter-gatherer societies that no longer have value in modern civilizations?

To answer these questions, EP casts a wide net that examines human nature over vast time periods. But first, consider these situations:

1. In an impatient voice, your manager pressures you to submit your overdue report.
2. During a class lecture, your professor scowls and belittles your comment.
3. Your mother criticizes your career choice.

EP inquires about the extent to which ordinary behaviors trigger instant, defensive reactions, as if your boss, professor, and mother were symbolic predators waiting to pounce from tall grasses on the savannah. How far can we go with this idea? Is it also possible that, at some level, even close friends and lovers who question your beliefs symbolize ancient aggressive competition for scarce goods, particularly food and sex? Maybe.

Many components of the characteristics of dogmatism reviewed in earlier chapters are untimely behavior twists that were historically adaptive in primitive environments, by which is meant more than just a physical location.[33] They remain because they define the essence of humanity—deep unities of "such bedrock elements of life as gratitude, shame, remorse, pride, honor, retribution, empathy, love, and so on."[34] As EP notes, the existence and variability of these traits is obvious, but the causes are not. Why do universal personality traits that are detrimental to our reproductive success remain part of our evolutionary heritage? What made us vulnerable to wrapping belief systems in tightly bound garments of closed-minded, absolute truth?

Historically, our belief systems come to us secondhand—passed down from generations of myths and storytelling that transmit knowledge. In times of stress, when understanding complex issues is all the more challenging and time consuming, this deferential posturing can be adaptive. Because attempts at "figuring out which combinations of ideas, beliefs, and behaviors make someone successful is costly and difficult, selection favored a general copying bias, which tends to make prestigious individuals generally influential,"[35] and because social learning is more generalized than specific, prestigious people model traits that are often imitated.[36] In the realm of human behavior, these traits may diverge from optimum adaptation, and the degree and quality of divergence determines the survival or extinction of a species.

The evolutionary and biological predispositions for anxiety (the emotional component of dogmatic thinking), are exacerbated by cultural memes—a term first coined in 1976 by Richard Dawkins. *Memes* are units of cultural expectations for beliefs and behaviors that have been transmitted over generations of learning. They invade cultural institutions of government, family, education, religion, art, the media, and so on, acting like viruses that replicate cultural values in the minds of citizens and insidiously shaping fads, fashions, catchy words, phrases, and beliefs.[37] Thus, memes are to cultural evolution what genes are to species evolution. There is a difference, however:

> Though memetic and genetic evolution are subjected to the same basic principles of blind variation and natural selection, memetic evolution is much more flexible. Genes can only be transmitted from parents to offspring (or parent as is the case of asexual reproduction), but memes can, in principle, be transmitted between any two individuals (though it will become more difficult the larger the differences in cognitive mechanisms and language are).[38]

When bundled together, complex memes are the basis of religion, ethics, and numerous other "isms"[39] that consolidate in beliefs about such things as education and health care, government and military spending, global warming, and sexual practices (the list is long). Memes are agents of culture; some are grounded in logic, some in faith, some in narratives, and some in unreflective habit. They survive because they are compatible with universal, genetic endowments.[40] Yet while genes shape memes, memes are not part of our common genetic heritage. Consider suicide bombers: these young men (they are rarely, if ever, old) willingly die in order to increase the probability that the meme will live on in the narratives of believers who transmit religious ideology and honor martyrs with the highest praise. This "memetic evolution will be several orders of magnitude faster and more efficient than genetic evolution. It should not surprise us then that during the last ten thousand years, humans have remained essentially unchanged on the genetic level, whereas their culture (i.e., the total set of memes) has undergone the most radical developments."[41]

Memes long preceded formal education. For hundreds of thousands of years, people were not taught how to intelligently evaluate cultural myths and narratives; they did not possess the necessary cognitive skills to assess the merit of transmitted beliefs, including religious memes that were institutionalized in order to replicate religious dogma. Religions are "self-serving and self-perpetuating ideational complexes that hoodwink us into spreading their message."[42] Today's children and adolescents absorb and replicate these culturally transmitted memes via their parents, educators, peers, the media, and influential role models, and they perpetuate them in adulthood, often with inadequate assessment of their merit or functional value. Adults who do not stop to evaluate parental and cultural indoctrinations of their own childhood languish in mimetic mindlessness. Their brains have become insidiously programmed by what Balkin calls "cultural software," which programs a host of unexamined beliefs that may or may not be in their own or humanity's best interests.[43] Some files should be dragged to the trash folder.

Before society developed civil laws that kept our animal behaviors on a short leash, religious memes used the threat of God's punishment or the promise of salvation to keep people from violating the edicts of holy dogma. Fear of God's wrath restrained base instincts long before secular laws stepped in to replace supernatural ordinance. One way to think about the adaptive significance of religious dogma is to consider the human infant's need to rely on, indeed love, his or her biological parents—an inherent, adaptive tendency that promotes survival. Since humans are preprogrammed for parental love, a clever strategy of behavior control would be to extend that predisposing need by constructing myths about an all-powerful, supernatural father who bestows heavenly rewards or metes out punishments of hellfire and eternal damnation. This meme has largely kept individuals from killing each other, stealing from their neighbors, and violating such established cultural norms as public displays of full nudity or sex in the park. This is all well and good, but there is no limit to humanity's imagination in pressuring others to conform and obey, and ancient myths that governed behaviors eons ago wander through modern brains and remind us that breaking God's laws is as punishable as breaking modern, secular laws.

One could reasonably argue that religious communities provide social visibility that keeps moral transgressions in check and counterbalance the impersonal technological communities that isolate people in virtual space and time. Given the strength of our evolutionary whispers, perhaps two sets of laws—one religious and one secular—are necessary to keep outdated behaviors in check and maintain order in a rapidly changing society.

§§

Zealous dogmatists replicate memes that are narrow-minded and discriminatory; they remain fervently loyal to in-group supporters who pay blind allegiance to the dogma of cults, and they consign themselves to powerful political or religious organizations that are designed to disable open-minded, rational thought. Dogmatic loyalists disdain out-group social activists and do what is necessary to keep people in line, thereby strengthening the power of their cultivated memes. It is no surprise that children whose parents model a rigid, closed-minded acceptance or rejection of beliefs become more suitable hosts for rigid, cultural memes.

The dogma that underlies certain ideological memes is successful over time and across cultures because the information it transmits fulfills basic psychological needs. Beliefs are by-products of culture, and these "viruses of the mind" invade our social institutions and shape the values and behaviors of our youth, including members of inner-city gangs who adopt the memes of their specific subculture. Such memes that thrive when cultural conditions facilitate their penetration.[44] Some facilitate individual growth in the cultural organism; others promote anxiety and guilt. Parasitic memes are found in businesses that arrange their rewards on the pyramid plan; in governments whose taxation policies clearly favor the wealthy; in some religious institutions that insidiously and excessively instill guilt for normal human imperfections; in advertisements that promote high-calorie, nonnutritional foods; and in all other institutions whose memes infect cultural progress.[45] These are the mean meme machines that are maintained by dogmatism, and they demand scrutiny and exposure if we are to live in a healthy, just society.

Because cultural memes control us more than we recognize, students should learn about them as part of their basic education. Long before registration in postsecondary courses, students can grasp the essence of meme power and its potential to close people's minds. With broad awareness of how they insidiously obscure our thinking, students can learn to recognize memes that surreptitiously infuse vulnerable minds through deliberate, repetitive persuasion. Future research could examine the extent to which the content of memes influence minds that are more vulnerable to colonization. Are some types of memes more likely to disable open-minded, rational thought? Would educational awareness about the power of memes reduce adolescent vulnerability to their unquestioning adoption, or would peer and media pressure override such learning? Memes survive because people are more drawn to narratives than numbers. When it comes to statistics, "the mere word can cause otherwise intelligent people's eyes to glaze over. At our core, we are storytellers, not statisticians."[46] Yet factual, scientific statements derive from fictitious narratives, the content of which becomes reformulated as precise statements that are subjected to scientific analysis.

§§

During social unrest, dogmatic followers need dogmatic leaders. Even when social and political conditions stabilize, the entrenched anxiety and constricted thought processes that pattern dogmatic authoritarian submission perpetuate an indiscriminate dependence on external authorities for guidance and leadership. What is so adaptive about that?

Our prehistoric ancestors needed protection from countless unknown and uncontrollable forces, including being attacked by predatory animals and marauding humans. For millions of years, social dominance would ensure that the strong and powerful would govern and defend the group. Since modern humanity represents but a grain in the salt timer of evolutionary progress, it makes sense that those ancient adaptations remain. Thus, the dogmatist's fascination with power and authority might well reflect an ongoing evolutionary struggle for social dominance, as seen in the behavior characteristics outlined in chapter 5.

In today's complex society, we still seek protection from unmanageable, threatening forces, just as we did eons ago. Technological access to a world of information threatens people who are easily intimidated by a proliferation of ideas and information that, in their minds, creates confusion, exposes their ignorance, and further exacerbates anxiety. Dogmatism may thus be seen as a cognitive fight-or-flight survival tactic, through which dogmatists struggle to preserve unyielding truth and flee what Al Gore calls "inconvenient truth." The closed-minded can now visit hundreds of Web sites that provide easy access to one-sided, extreme views that tighten the bolts on prejudiced cognitive chambers and ignite incendiary discriminatory behaviors— behaviors that depth psychology sees as manifestations of our inner "shadow."[47] The *shadow* is an abstract term analogous to evolutionary psychology's concept of *whisperings*, and while both the shadow and ancient whisperings use aggressive means to counteract threat, the evolutionary perspective examines our dark side with a more penetrating lens that exposes the aggressive aspects of dogmatism as modernized expressions of evolutionary adaptations.

A cognitive error that was more adaptive when life was extremely Hobbesian is the "tendency to analyze everything as an immediate, personal phenomenon: what does this mean to me? Whatever gets close to us, in space or time, is immediately overemphasized."[48] This modern error of judgment may be a throwback to prehistoric times, when people were less inclined to consider the lasting consequences of behavior, especially given the ubiquitous, exigent dangers that threatened to curtail a comparatively short lifespan. Planning five moves ahead was hardly adaptive when predators were lurking in the bushes or over the hill. Brute force and verbal dominance yielded immediate, protective gains, and these prehistoric adaptations continue to take up valuable space in modern cognitive and emotional mainframes. And while the social and cultural conditions of today keep formerly adaptive, aggressive behaviors on a shorter leash than when humans roamed the grasslands eons ago, that leash remains dangerously long. "The basic social responses of hunter-gatherers have metamorphosed from relatively modest environmental adaptation into unexpectedly elaborate, even monstrous forms in more advanced societies."[49]

§§

All of the primate-shared traits presented earlier have adaptive and maladaptive poles of behavior that determine survival and reproductive capacity. Each of the seven traits is presumed to have a genetic component, although there are different degrees and types of expression. This suggests that primates—including humans, who are active but not emotionally overreactive—are more likely to attract a mate. People who are more fearful, aggressive, or impulsive than usual are, on average, less likely to reproduce, which means that, over time, maladaptive extremes will be culled by natural selection. "Such nonadaptive features could arise simply by chance; or they could be incidental side-effects of other traits that are adaptations."[50] In this sense, dogmatism may be an incidental offshoot of primate traits that include heightened fearfulness, dominance, and aggressiveness. We are already familiar with the idea that a biological predisposition for anxiety may shape dogmatism. Similarly, sudden, intense anxiety that was adaptive thousands of years ago may be a maladaptive tagalong that shows up on playgrounds, in classrooms and offices, and at social gatherings. "Destructive emotions remain in the repertoire of the human heart as a trade-off in the evolutionary quest for survival."[51]

Dominance, the second trait that is shared by primates and humans, is common to all social animals; it is a key component of dogmatic authoritarianism aggression and its corollary, dogmatic authoritarian submission. It therefore seems feasible, from an evolutionary perspective, to view both types of authoritarianism as originally adaptive. While many mammals establish dominance by brute force alone, within the behavior domains of apes and humans, "dominance hierarchies serve to support the establishment and maintenance of social structures that are critical to the efficient distribution of limited resources, division of labor, and minimization of social conflict."[52] Nature documentaries describe forceful play in young animals as necessary preparation for hunting prey in adulthood. What about the rough and tumble play of young boys? At play, boys strive for group dominance and leadership, and they use more aggressive techniques than girls to maintain group status, especially when competing for valuable or limited resources.[53] Once dominance hierarchies are established, prosocial cooperation tends to replace aggression—an adaptive strategy that increases resource sharing between both dominant and submissive group members and decreases the likelihood that weaker members will (1) steal from others, or (2) form a coalition to overthrow the dominant players.[54]

"An individual's position in a social group affects whom he or she interacts with and how, and children must learn not only their own position in such hierarchies but also those of other children."[55]

Beginning in early childhood, dominant children are those who are sociable and helpful, yet also aggressive enough "not only to acquire resources for themselves but also to protect their friends and display prosocial behaviors to those who affiliate with them."[56] Youngsters with social status optimally balance aggression and dominance with prosocial behavior, a recent view that counteracts the tendency to judge all childhood aggression as a sign of emotional immaturity. Socially popular children strategically use appropriate levels of dominance, aggression, and sociability to get more toys (as long as they later share them), and have more friends (as long as they are not too bossy). Adaptive dominance? Perhaps.

Boys and men "use more verbal and physical aggression than females of all ages," and while some girls use social exclusion and tactics like gossip to damage other girls' reputations, the overall degree of relational aggression is considerably less in females than in males.[57] Research across the lives of both men and women reveals that "men place greater importance on coming out ahead and women are more focused on maintaining social harmony."[58] Yet both genders are biologically social; they have "innate needs to be accepted as members of a group and to enhance their status within their groups."[59] Determinants of social success seem to require a hierarchy within which some members are dominant as a means of gaining status and power, while others submit to the dominant players to ensure protection. Do you know of anyone who starts his or her day with the reminder, "Today, I'll reign in all of my evolutionary whisperings?" Even if such were the case (albeit worded differently), by nightfall, chances are good that dominance, submission, anxiety, or anger would find expression somewhere along the way, which is somewhat disquieting. But, as with all personality traits, they only become problematic if they are excessive, frequent, and prolonged.

The ever-present dominance of animal behavior has reproductive advantages, but it is hard to see how modern-day dominance—the linchpin of dogmatic authoritarian aggression—is adaptive. Its usefulness, gauged by reproductive success, has limited value. While some females are attracted to dominant males because they are dependent on men who will define them and make most of their decisions, the domineering, arrogant posturing of dogmatic males does not have survival value for the species, especially given modern technology and weaponry. Neither does the dominance of authoritarian parents whose closed-minded modeling and use of strict rules and punishment to control behavior create tense family environments that linger in the memories of CEOs, professors, and official heads of government. The emotional residue of authoritarian parenting and imitative learning derails conversations among friends, colleagues, co-workers, family members, and marital partners when its presence collides with common civility.

From an evolutionary perspective, one could argue that corporate dogmatism stems from the fear of losing individual financial power, which would deprive the wealthy of social status, for which humans have been primed by evolution. Dogmatic, right-wing authoritarians are alpha males who have the privilege of deciding whether to share their resources, and since the possibility exists that sharing may result in someone getting more than oneself, any economic socialism is risky business, at least from an evolutionary standpoint. Opening one's mind to the possibility that equitable distribution of essential goods would benefit all frays the black-and-white fabric of economic dogmatism that is designed to secure material gains and social status.

If I may, I'd like to use an example of Canadian politics that, from an evolutionary perspective, perhaps explains why Alberta's right-wing dynasty has ruled Canada's wealthiest province for seventy-three successive years. Since the discovery of oil in 1947, Alberta has become second only to Saudi Arabia in proven reserves of oil deposits. Prior and subsequent to these discoveries, right-wing parties have maintained their grip on political power in Alberta, and on March 3, 2008, the electorate once again gave the ruling party a massive majority—72 out of 83 seats in the legislature. Economic dogmatism may be the driver here, since many Albertans gain psychological and economic rewards—directly and indirectly—from oil and gas. When it comes to entertaining policy alternatives that would slow growth in the oil industry, cap greenhouse gas emissions, and share the wealth, voting Conservatives support the status quo and refuse to see things any other way. The fact that such gains come at the expense of future generations and the environment is secondary to corporate and political dogmatism that favors short-term, immediate prosperity and status over long-term social planning and sustainable development. Could archaic evolutionary whisperings for dominance offer some explanation for this power monopoly?

§§

Evolutionary psychologists claim that because certain traits are universal features of personality, evolution must have preserved their adaptive dimensions to enhance human survival and fitness. In chapter 11, we explore the history and content of what has come to be known as the Big Five traits of personality and we will then link those traits to the seven evolutionary traits examined in this chapter.

While EP addresses ancient behavioral tendencies that arrest general progress, psychologists will need to go sufficiently beyond an understanding of built-in evolutionary predispositions if they are to provide lasting solutions for recalcitrant human problems. A comprehensive analysis of dogmatism that bridges EP perspectives with biological and trait perspectives as well as clinical psychology (the study and treatment of abnormal behavior) is needed if we are to better understand the causes and characteristics of dogmatism.

JONAH'S DOGMATISM FROM AN EVOLUTIONARY PERSPECTIVE

In the beginning, Jonah is a product of random selection and genetic mutations from earlier, primitive life forms. The framework within which evolutionary psychologists understand his dogmatism would place his dominance-seeking, aggressive behaviors within the historical context of primate evolution. Jonah's deep-rooted anxiety, intolerance of ambiguity, defensive cognitive closure, lack of personal insight, dogmatic authoritarian aggression, dogmatic authoritarian submission, and arrogant dismissive communication are all psychological anachronisms that leave him stuck in the wrong place at the wrong time. He mistakenly believes that by rigidly adhering to black-and-white belief systems he will secure rewarding social ties, status, and dignity. Yet like other dogmatists, Jonah is not someone who has simply failed to evolve. Despite the various evolutionary, biological, psychological, social, and environmental factors that conspired to curtail his open-minded thought, Jonah's intellectual *potential* for open-minded reasoning remains. Evolutionary psychology would view Jonah's dogmatic submission to religious and political dogma as a remnant of evolved hierarchies for dominance and submission, both of which are often expressed as deference to a supreme, dominant figure, namely, God. As E. O. Wilson notes, "Behavioral scientists from another planet would notice immediately the semiotic resemblance between animal submissive behavior on the one hand and human obeisance to religious and civil authority on the other. They would point out that the most elaborate rites of obeisance are directed at the gods, the hyper-dominant if invisible members of the human group."[60]

With this chapter behind us, our personality puzzle of dogmatism is taking shape, but many intricate pieces still need assembly. In chapter 10 we survey modern contributions to personality theory from the specialized field of biopsychology, which studies the role of genes and biology on developing personality traits.

Biopsychologists would agree that Marxists who believe they can reshape human nature through social engineering, Nazis who believe eugenics is the best option for reshaping humanity, and Islamafascists who believe a globally enforced sect of Islam will reconstruct human nature overlook the importance of evolution and genes. This extreme myopia exists despite psychologists' caution that, at this juncture, research on human nature is still more exploratory than explanatory, which we would expect given the vast complexity of the human genome and the structure and biochemical functioning of the brain.

Still, scientific explorations into the intricacies of the human brain allow for measured assumptions that are surely preferable to ideological assumptions based on emotion and prejudicial judgment. What do psychologists and neuroscientists know about the biological nature of personality traits? Chapter 10 attempts to provide plausible answers.

NOTES

1. L. Cosmides and J. Tooby, "Evolutionary Psychology: A Primer," *Center for Evolutionary Psychology*, http://www.sscnet.ucla.edu/comm/steen/cogweb/ep/EP-primer.html (accessed January 9, 2007).

2. R. Wright, *The Moral Animal: Why We Are the Way We Are* (New York: Vintage, 1994), p. 4.

3. D. M. Buss, "Introduction: The Emergence of Evolutionary Psychology," in *The Handbook of Evolutionary Psychology*, ed. David M. Buss (Hoboken, NJ: Wiley, 2005), p. xxiii.

4. Ibid.

5. S. Pinker, *How the Mind Works* (New York: Norton, 1997), p. 162.

6. C. R. Darwin, *On the Origin of Species by Means of Natural Selection, or The Preservation of Favoured Races in the Struggle for Life* (London: John Murray, 1859), p. 5.

7. D. Dennett, *Breaking the Spell: Religion as a Natural Phenomenon* (New York: Penguin, 2006), p. 187.

8. B. R. Hergenhahn, *An Introduction to Theories of Personality* (Englewood Cliffs, NJ: Simon and Schuster, 1994), p. 442.

9. J. H. Relethford, *The Human Species: An Introduction to Biological Anthropology* (New York: McGraw-Hill, 2003), p. 251.

10. D. F. Bjorklund and A. D. Pellegrini, *The Origins of Human Nature: Evolutionary Developmental Psychology* (Washington, DC: American Psychological Association, 2002), p. 25.

11. L. Cosmides and J. Tooby, "Evolutionary Psychology: A Primer."

12. Ibid.

13. Pinker, *How the Mind Works*, p. 44.

14. D. P. Barash, *The Whisperings Within: Evolution and the Origin of Human Nature* (New York: Penguin, 1979), p. 45.

15. D. M. Buss, *Personality: Evolutionary Heritage and Human Distinctiveness* (Hillsdale, NJ: Erlbaum, 1988), p. 10.

16. Barash, *Whisperings Within*. From an EP perspective, Barash maintains that the existence of "real, honest-to-God altruism simply doesn't occur in nature" (p. 135). People help others for reasons that are ultimately selfish—they favor their relatives because relatives share our genes, and they help their neighbors because they hope that at some time in the future, their neighbors will help them.

17. I. Eibl-Eibesfeldt, *Human Ethology* (New York: Aldine de Gruyter, 1989).

18. R. Ornstein and P. Ehrlich, *New World New Mind: Moving Towards Conscious Evolution* (New York: Touchstone, 1990).

19. P. M. Todd, R. Hertwig, and U. Hoffrage, "Evolutionary Cognitive Psychology," in *The Handbook of Evolutionary Psychology*, ed. David M. Buss (Hoboken, NJ: Wiley, 2005), p. 778.

20. Barash, *Whisperings Within*. Barash chose the term *whisperings* to emphasize that these biological pulls are just that, whispers. They are not shouts that would have a more deterministic nature.

21. K. N. Laland and G. R. Brown, *Sense and Nonsense: Evolutionary Perspectives on Human Behavior* (Oxford: Oxford University Press, 2002), p. 178. Stone Age people lived not only on the African savannahs, they also lived in "deserts, next to rivers, by oceans, in forests, and in the Arctic."

22. R. Conniff, "I Want to Be Boss: The Psychology of Dominance," *Discover* 21, no. 5 (2000): 79.

23. G. Abell and B. Singer, eds., *Science and the Paranormal* (New York: Scribner's, 1981), quoted in M. Shermer, *Why People Believe Weird Things: Pseudoscience, Superstition, and Other Confusions of Our Time* (New York: W. H. Freeman, 1997), p. 59. During a problem-solving task, subjects were told that their first choice of a solution was either right or wrong. Findings revealed that the subjects' first guess had the effect of narrowing their thinking such that they rejected alternative solutions. They were slow to consider information that did not confirm their original hypothesis, especially when new, complex information was presented. Even more interesting, despite there being no obvious solution to the problem, subjects found one by focusing on coincidental relationships. These findings are also supported by earlier studies that concluded dogmatic persons do not learn well when operating in novel situations or when the solution is novel (M.

Rokeach, T. S. Swanson, and M. R. Denny 1960; B. Mikol 1960; S. V. Zagona and L. A. Zurcher 1965; and J. Jacoby 1967). These studies are reported in S. Maddi, *Personality Theories: A Comparative Analysis* (Georgetown, ON: Irwin-Dorsey, 1980).

24. K. E. Stanovich, *The Robot's Rebellion: Finding Meaning in the Age of Darwin* (Chicago: University of Chicago Press, 2004), pp. 97–98. The tendency for what we believe to bias contradictory evidence is also addressed by R. S. Nickerson, "On Improving Thinking through Instruction," in *Review of Research in Education*, ed. Ernst Z. Rothkopf (Washington, DC, 1998), pp. 3–57, and J. Evans and M. Ridley, *Mendel's Demon: Gene Justice and the Complexity of Life* (London: Weidenfield and Nicolson, 2000).

25. P. Stokes, *Philosophy: One Hundred Essential Thinkers* (Toronto: Indigo Books, 2003), p. 203.

26. S. Pinker, *The Blank Slate: The Modern Denial of Human Nature* (New York: Penguin Putnam, 2002).

27. Bjorklund and Pellegrini, *Origins of Human Nature.*

28. E. H. Hagen, "Controversial Issues in Evolutionary Psychology," in *The Handbook of Evolutionary Psychology*, ed. David M. Buss (Hoboken, NJ: Wiley, 2005), p. 159.

29. H. T. Reis, W. A. Collins, and E. Berscheid, "The Relationship Context of Human Behavior and Development," *Psychological Bulletin* 126, no. 6 (2000): 847.

30. American Psychiatric Association, *Diagnostic and Statistical Manual of Mental Disorders*, 4th ed. (Washington, DC: American Psychiatric Association, 1994).

31. Barash, *Whisperings Within.*

32. American Psychiatric Association, *Diagnostic and Statistical Manual.*

33. In evolutionary psychology, "evolutionary" has been referred to as the Environment of Evolutionary Adaptedness (EEA), which reconstructs common problems that our ancestors had to face and solve, independent of geographic location (see Cosmides and Tooby, "From Evolution to Behavior: Evolutionary Psychology as the Missing Link," in *The Latest on the Best: Essays on Evolution and Optimality*, ed. John Dupre [Cambridge, MA: MIT Press, 1987]).

34. Wright, *The Moral Animal*, p. 8.

35. J. Heinrich and F. J. Gil-White, "The Evolution of Prestige: Freely Conferred Deference as a Mechanism for Enhancing the Benefits of Cultural Transmission," *Evolution and Human Behavior* 22, no. 3 (2001): 184.

36. Ibid., p. 176.

37. R. Dawkins, "Viruses of the Mind," *Free Inquiry* 13 (1993): 34–38.

38. F. Heylighen, "Selfish Memes and the Evolution of Cooperation," *Journal of Ideas* 2, no. 4 (1992): 77.

39. R. G. Grimes, "General Semantics and Memetics: A Tentative Relationship?" *ETC.: A Review of General Semantics* 55 (1998): 31.

40. D. E. Over, *Evolution and the Psychology of Thinking: The Debate* (New York: Psychology Press, 2003).

41. Heylighen, "Selfish Memes and the Evolution of Cooperation," p. 77.

42. K. N. Laland and G. R. Brown, *Sense and Nonsense: Evolutionary Perspectives on Human Behavior* (Oxford: Oxford University Press, 2002), p. 216.

43. J. M. Balkin, *Cultural Software: A Theory of Ideology* (New Haven, CT: Yale University Press, 1998).

44. Dawkins, "Viruses of the Mind."

45. Stanovich, *The Robot's Rebellion.*

46. T. Kida, *Don't Believe Everything You Think: The 6 Basic Mistakes We Make in Thinking* (Amherst, NY: Prometheus Books, 2006), p. 17.

47. The *shadow* is one of Jung's five archetypes or primordial images that represent universal predispositions to respond to the world in characteristic ways. Unconscious thoughts, feelings, and actions that are unacceptable to one's self-image and in conflict with social standards are an inevitable part of our human baseness and animalistic impulses. Denial of our shadow causes inauthenticity, hypocrisy, and deceit.

48. Ornstein and Ehrlich, *New World New Mind*, p. 92.

49. E. O. Wilson, *On Human Nature* (Cambridge, MA: Harvard University Press, 1978), p. 89.

50. S. J. C. Gaulin and D. H. McBurney, *Evolutionary Psychology* (Upper Saddle River, NJ: Pearson Education, 2004), p. 36.

51. D. Goleman and the Dalai Lama, *Destructive Emotions: How Can We Overcome Them?* (New York: Bantam Books, 2003), p. xx.

52. D. F. Bjorklund and C. H. Blasi, "Evolutionary Developmental Psychology," in *A Handbook of Evolutionary Psychology*, ed. David H. Buss (Hoboken, NJ: Wiley, 2005), p. 838.

53. Bjorklund and Pellegrini, *Origins of Human Nature.*

54. Ibid.

55. Bjorklund and Blasi, "Evolutionary Developmental Psychology," p. 838.

56. Ibid., p. 839. These authors provide a comprehensive summary of developmental research on the effects of childhood aggression and prosocial behavior on dominance hierarchies, popularity, and status.

57. E. E. Maccoby, *The Two Sexes: Growing Up Apart, Coming Together* (Cambridge, MA: Harvard University Press, 1998), p. 89.

58. J. D. Duntley, "Adaptations to Dangers from Humans," in *The Handbook of Evolutionary Psychology,* ed. David M. Buss (Hoboken, NJ: Wiley 2005), p. 228.

59. R. D. Smither, "Authoritarianism, Dominance, and Social Behavior: A Perspective from Evolutionary Personality Psychology," *Human Relations* 46, no. 1 (1993): 37.

60. E. O. Wilson, *Consilience: The Unity of Knowledge* (New York: Knopf, 1998), p. 289.

Chapter 10

BIOLOGICAL BEGINNINGS

Our Neuronal Hardware

More may have been learned about the brain and the mind in the 1990s—the so-called decade of the brain—than during the entire previous history of psychology and neuroscience.[1]

A. R. Damasio

Our incisive probe into the depths of dogmatism will now examine the underlying biological predispositions that shape characteristic adaptations to change—namely, personal and environmental factors.[2] These elements are "*characteristic* because they reflect the enduring psychological core of the individual, and they are *adaptations* because they help the individual fit into the ever-changing social environment."[3] As such, they are not haphazard. For example, if a person is energized by the presence of others, socializing becomes a characteristic adaptation because it fulfills biologically based emotional and behavioral predispositions that conform to social extroversion. Similarly, if biologically predisposed anxiety is reduced because one feels respected for promulgating truth, dogmatic pronouncements may become habitual, characteristic adaptations. Although the trait of dogmatism is not biologically based, higher-than-average levels of anxiety do have a biological basis, and since anxiety is presumed to figure prominently in dogmatism, then dogmatism might well be genetically based, at least indirectly. Genetic predispositions push us in trait-specific directions.

Traits like extroversion and dogmatism have typical thoughts, emotions, and behaviors that become generalized across many situations. As we shall see, personality traits also have significant biological roots that determine their stability and hardiness. Still in its infancy, biopsychology (a biological approach to the study of the brain and behavior) cannot yet provide us with a convincing body of evidence that links specific genes to brain structure, function, and traits like dogmatism.[4] More likely, personality traits are governed by multiple interacting genes that influence the release of various brain chemicals in response to internal and external events. The field does, however, introduce exciting discoveries that allow us to make cautious extrapolations about the biological underpinnings of personality traits. Eventually, biopsychologists may determine which genes have an impact on structural systems in the brain that, in combinatioin with other functions, exhibit a vulnerability to persistent disruptions in thoughts, feelings, and behavior.

THE GENETIC AND BIOLOGICAL FOUNDATION OF PERSONALITY

An increased understanding of the human brain and the impact that cultural institutions and learning have on brain structure and function will enable us to grasp the nature of personality traits, especially traits like dogmatism, which have beleaguered progress on this planet for millennia. Unlike evolutionary psychology, which studies universal behaviors that have endured throughout our evolutionary history, behavior genetics examines the role of genes on contemporary behaviors.

An explosion of research has recently identified brain chemicals that are implicated in all aspects of psychology, and these molecules of the mind have become the focus of scientific research that will permanently alter the way we see ourselves.[5] Specialists in the fields of neuroscience and biopsychology are gathering information from brain imaging techniques and the human genome to unravel the secrets behind human thought processes (a branch of neuroscience called *cognitive neuroscience*, which studies higher-order brain function), and the neural mechanisms of emotions (another division of neuroscience called *affective neuroscience*).

Even more astonishing is the recent theory that the epigenome, which adds another level of complexity to the genome, turns the expression of genes on or off as a result of one's interaction with the environment. Gene activation or suppression is what accounts for progressive, evolutionary adaptations in multicellular plants, animals, and humans. Although neuroscientists cannot yet explain exact functions of the biological systems involved in the regulatory mechanism that turns genes on and off, genes normally in the off position are regulated by DNA-binding proteins that turn them on, while genes normally in the on position are regulated by proteins that turn them up, down, or off. "Many of the DNA-binding proteins that control operator genes are influenced by signals received by the cell from its environment."[6] Unless some genes are present but nonfunctional (and therefore considered off) as we engage our brains in such tasks as reminiscing about a pleasant event, responding to a crying baby, or reacting to criticism, each experience acts as a light switch that affects gene sequences. Since genes are coded for the production of certain chemicals, a person without the specific gene sequence that manufactures a particular chemical will react to an environmental circumstance differently from someone whose gene sequence is coded for an overabundance of that chemical. Excesses or deficits of these chemical neurotransmitters and hormones activate inappropriate emotional responses such as extreme anxiety, anger, or depression. Though the data are equivocal at this stage, excessive anxiety is linked to defects in the GABA system (gamma-aminobutyric acid, which is an inhibitory neurotransmitter), and when people with such impairments encounter stressful environments, their anxiety is magnified beyond normal levels.[7]

In this sense, genes are not destiny; environmental influences such as maternal behavior (pre- and postnatal) and environmental stressors shape the genetic expressions of emotions and personality traits. There is even evidence that, in some cases, the effects of famine on one's grandparents can influence one's life expectancy—effects that are transgenerational.[8] Today, genetic technology uses preimplantation genetic diagnosis (PGD) to test the embryo for a host of disease-associated genes.[9] Understanding the epigenome and PGD are two profound scientific advances, and their magnitude of discovery is as grand and controversial as the discovery of DNA and its implications for cloning. Will these startling scientific advances incrementally render our nature less than natural and our humanness less than human?

BIOPSYCHOLOGY

Biopsychology and neuroscience are broadening the twentieth-century view that family, cultural institutions, and social learning are the only major players in personality development—normal and abnormal. Along with genes, which are the blueprint for life, neuroscience studies the chemical molecules that make up the central nervous system (the brain and spinal cord). These molecules create electrical charges, a component of the physiology of life that is key to survival. For example, when we sense danger, multiple electrochemical firings activate our sympathetic nervous system and prepare our body for a fight-or-flight reaction to a perceived threat. Physiological reactions include increased heart rate, blood pressure, perspiration, and a host of other responses. When the threat subsides, electrochemical reactions in the parasympathetic nervous system calm this flurry of activity and our body returns to normal functioning.

Genes program brain structures and neurotransmitters (chemical messengers) to process psychological mechanisms such as thoughts and emotions. For example, an excitable amygdala, which is a midbrain structure, is linked to increased brain activity in the right prefrontal cortex—part of the neocortex that is implicated in persistent anxiety and social inhibition.[10] The long-term stability of emotions such as anxiety and behaviors such as social inhibition is now questioned, since research suggests that some neuroplasticity occurs, which is to say that the structure and function of neurons is much more flexible and nonlocalized than previously believed. The nervous system is capable of rewiring itself by changing the neuron's cell type, location, and interconnections.[11] This plasticity, the hallmark of the gestation and prenatal period, unfortunately becomes less malleable beyond critical postnatal periods. Even so, research indicates that when the aging brain is challenged to learn new tasks, dopamine increases and establishes new networks of cells that enhance cognitive performance, particularly memory.[12]

§§

Let us return to the beginning. From the moment of conception, something in our biological make-up predisposes us for personality traits like extroversion and dogmatism, and it may be that biology gets on the dogmatist's nerves as much as anything people might say or do. To date, neuroscientists do not know the extent to which dogmatism is genetically based, nor can they say anything about its degree of heritability, but heritability (h^2) can be quantified, and future measures of h^2 for dogmatism are feasible, even if those measures reveal a quantity that is very small.

To clarify what this means, heritability is a statistically derived percentage that suggests how much gene accounts for observable differences in personality traits, where difference represents the range of variance.[13] We can determine the aggregate, net effect of a combination of factors by examining trait similarities among identical twins, for example, and then statistically correlate their scores with scores of their nontwin siblings. This helps us determine their relative similarity. However, "because behavior is multiply determined, it is unlikely that any *single factor* [my emphasis] can explain more than 10 percent of the variance."[14] Nonetheless, studies of trait similarity among twins consistently demonstrate that universal personality traits have clear genetic underpinnings. "It is difficult to ignore or paper over the evidence that many traits, including the Big Five dimensions of Extraversion and Neuroticism, are at least moderately heritable and that genetic influences work to promote trait stability over time."[15]

When genetic predispositions for certain emotional traits are repeatedly activated by environmental factors, the combined impact of such repetition physically alters brain structures and these structural differences account for discrepancies in "habitual levels of arousal and thresholds for emotional responses."[16] Thus, "the physical properties are not sufficient, just as the physical properties of bricks are not sufficient to explain architecture. . . . Something in the *patterning* of neural tissue is crucial."[17]

Neuroscientists have found that "the concepts we think with are physically instantiated in the synapses and neural circuitry of our brains. Thought is physical. And neural circuits, once established, do not change quickly or easily."[18] Because molecular structures consolidate early childhood thoughts and emotions in circuits of long-term memory, these circuits continue to influence ongoing experience. In particular, prolonged distress or trauma seriously impacts neural circuitry.[19]

Abusive or negligent parents limit a child's "ability to regulate the length, intensity, or frequency of distressing emotions like anger, terror, or shame."[20] This emotional dysregulation is further exacerbated if, in infancy, a baby does not experience pleasurable releases of oxytocin and other brain chemicals that are secreted during positive social connections. Known as the hormone of love, oxytocin evokes an inner sense of emotional calm and balance. "The systems that secrete these chemicals of nurturing love include familiar parts of the social brain."[21] Children who experience secure attachment have been provided with solid chemical and social foundations that assist growth and connections of neural sites in specific brain areas. In turn, these connections enhance emotional development. Nurturing parent-child relationships thus cause chemical releases that enhance self-esteem, confidence, and resilience in the face of inevitable mistakes and misfortune.

When children's pleasure-inducing chemicals are reduced or absent because of repeated strong emotions, their brain activity fires and wires differently. Without loving, nurturing parents who activate the chemicals that scaffold children's positive self-image, children are less resilient to stress and lose confidence in their ability to control their emotions, establish social ties, and perform cognitive tasks. Consequently, they may become clingy and dependent.[22] This desperate need to be accepted by peers in childhood and adolescence stems from the absence of a solid platform of love and self-acceptance. At the very least, these socially deprived children and adolescents require training in assertive communication, which may inoculate them against manipulative peer pressure. Without such skills, they are at risk for arbitrarily adopting group values and succumbing to peer pressure with little or no awareness that their compliance compensates for early social and emotional deprivation. In a vulnerable mind, if biological beginnings load the dice for anxiety, one's adaptive emotions, rational thought, and defense against peer pressure are seriously undermined. Anxious children whose social relationships are impoverished are vulnerable to dysfunctional relationships in adulthood—notably, anxious or avoidant styles of intimacy.[23]

Yet brain structures, neurochemistry, and the neural activity involved in emotion are enormously complex, and neuroscientists cannot yet explain the cause or function of neurochemical imbalances that influence emotions. While there is clearly substantial variation in emotional expression among people, we have not yet been able to determine how much of that variation or difference is due to genetics alone. Thus, we tend to blame genes for our annoying traits, though genes are not singularly culpable. Research also indicates that good nutrition, along with nurturing parents, impinges on the child's genetic expression of traits—findings that deliver a harsh "blow against the naive view of genetic determinism: that our experiences don't matter —that genes are all."[24] Thus, experience plays an important role in neuronal patterning. It changes the brain's plasticity or malleability— quantitatively and qualitatively—by increasing or decreasing the number of functioning neurons and their synaptic connections. With each experience, genes orchestrate a molecular response. "If you are raised in a nurturing environment, there are actually demonstrable, objective changes in gene expression."[25] This means that even though some of us are more genetically predisposed to anxiety than others, the level and expression of anxiety varies considerably depending on the quality of our experiences. Environmental influences and one's response to stress impact decision making, and all three interact to determine gene expression. Assumptions that someone is poor or in jail because he or she is lazy or makes bad choices are clearly over-simplifications. While our genetic blueprint starts the music, the environment interacts with specific genes to determine the quality and enjoyment of the dance. And when flawed genes combine with harsh environments, we can't feel the rhythm and our steps falter.

This intricate, interactional view of biological, psychological, and social forces challenges the traditional view of the environment as a separate, external force that acts upon the individual. In the world according to psychology, the consensus is that genes form an inter-esting reciprocal relationship with the environment—the ultimate teamwork of personality development. Genes activate traits that select environments compatible with those genes, but it can also work the other way around, in that environments activate genes, which together select complementary environments. In this sense, our physical and social environs reflect the composition of our DNA; that is, genetically influenced emotions affect how people "select, construct, or perceive their environments."[26] Although the environment may have condi-tioned us to perceive things in a certain way, genes sway our percep-tions about what goes on in and around us. They mediate how we con-struct our identities and social roles within different settings.

Because we tend to choose environments compatible with our biology, in that selection process we create a kind of psychological-cultural law of supply and demand. Situational preferences may influ-ence our chance encounters, but our genes indirectly manipulate our decisions about such things as career choice, political and religious affiliation, and preferences in friends, spouse, entertainment, sports, hobbies, and fashion. In turn, all choices that accommodate personal desires also impact the environment. For example, if a majority of university students prefer psychology to math courses, administrative planning would factor in those preferences. Similarly, if a significant proportion of the population were dogmatic, we would expect to find authoritarian administrators governing the country, and cultural institutions would personify the various characteristics of dogmatism. Popular themes of movies and novels would be those in which the main characters oversimplify complex issues; heroes, for example, would enact traits of dogmatic authoritarian aggression and arrogant, dismissive communication. They would be prejudicially motivated by power and status and short on personal insight. Do any Hollywood blockbusters come to mind?

§§

Steven Pinker suggests that the quality of parental nurturing accounts for approximately 5 percent of our personality. Genes, meanwhile, contribute roughly 50 percent, and the other 45 percent comes from observing and imitating peer groups outside the family.[27] This view is not without controversy, especially the idea that parents are only responsible for about 5 percent of their progeny's personality development (that is largely independent from what their parents contribute through genetic transmission of emotional and behavioral predispositions).

Psychologists of different persuasions claim that parents play a much more prominent role in shaping their children's personalities and belief systems, and they are not alone. Parents also believe they have a significant and positive influence on the development of their child's personality. Recent research presents a compromise: "parents typically play initial leading roles in the inculcation of basic values, but peers seem to have greater influence in lifestyle issues such as appearance, social activities, and dating."[28] University students who scored high on Altemeyer's Right-Wing Authoritarian Scale (RWA) were "significantly more likely to attribute their opinions to the influence of their parents and their religion," while students with low RWA scores cited the source of their attitudes as "own experience" and "peer influence."[29]

AFFECTIVE NEUROSCIENCE: THE MYSTERY, MARVEL, AND MISERY OF EMOTION

Beginning in the 1980s as an outgrowth of cognitive neuroscience, affective neuroscience became an enterprising field that examines the "intricate web of neural connections linking thoughts and feelings, cognition and emotion."[30] Affective neuroscientists focus on the impact of emotions on cognition and investigate the biological basis of emotional competencies. Why are some people more competent than others at regulating and synchronizing their emotional states? Research in affective neuroscience sheds light on the biological origins of anxiety, the prime emotional suspect for dogmatism.

Like cognitive neuroscience, affective neuroscience continues to break new ground, even though scientific studies of emotion are extremely challenging. It is easier to understand the specific function of the brain's sensory and motor areas than to grasp the complexity of emotions, especially since emotions vary widely within and among individuals and across experiences. Using modern technological tools such as positron emission tomography (PET scans), functional magnetic resonance imaging (fMRI), and diffusion tensor imaging, affective neuroscience studies the impact of emotions on neuronal activity in the limbic system (the amygdala, hippocampus, hypothalamus, and other structures) and the higher-order reasoning cortex.

Researchers have found that when the amygdala, a midbrain structure, detects anything that signals danger, it activates an electrochemical fear response.[31] This gut feeling, or low-road reaction, does not initially involve conscious processing by the neocortex—the new brain, or high road, that processes information and engages in abstract reasoning. Low-road reactions are instant, reflexive, and protective adaptations that are part of our evolutionary history. Rather than waiting for the high-road cortex to determine that the bee falling from the car visor is dead, our amygdala signals danger and we reflexively pull back.[32] Even an angry look is alarming enough to activate the amygdala, which "can influence the entire working of the cortex,"[33] making it difficult for high-road analysis to take control of low-road emotions. When the experience subsides, we may use high-road reason to reduce anger, anxiety, or sadness, but rarely can we entirely banish strong emotions at will. Such emotions take the brain hostage, whether they arise from sudden fright, bad news, caustic insults, or perceptions of long-standing injustice.

The protracted Palestinian-Israeli conflict provides a useful example of what is going on here. As long as both sides feel they need to defend themselves against injustice and use aggressive means to do so, Israelis and Palestinians will live in fear and anger. These ongoing emotions short-circuit the transmission of incoming information to the higher-order, reasoning skills of the cerebral cortex. Persistent, strong emotions narrow thought and perpetuate problems such that, as Michael Ignatieff wrote, "the bodies of the past were never safely dead and buried; they were always roaming through the sleep of the living in search of retribution."[34] In Israel today, they roam the *streets* of the living.

Among other functions, the prefrontal cortex, or executive center, of the brain modulates emotions and plans behaviors. It regulates or dysregulates the fear response from the amygdala, which the hippocampus (another midbrain structure) records and consolidates in memory, storing both the emotion and the context in which the emotion occurred. The amygdala, the prefrontal cortex, and the hippocampus are so closely interconnected that if the hippocampus malfunctions we may experience moods that are inappropriate to the situation. When children are repeatedly teased or ridiculed, for example, the felt anxiety may resurface in neutral or congenial social settings, biasing their interpersonal perceptions and interpretations.[35] Such children may become angry and defensive in response to innocuous questions, or they may feel extremely embarrassed or ashamed when they make simple mistakes.

These emotional reactions are linked to previous stress-related responses that linger about, impairing cognitive function. An emotionally activated amygdala releases cortisol, a powerful hormone "that binds to receptors in the hippocampus, the net effect of which is to disrupt hippocampal activity, weakening the ability of the temporal lobe memory system to form explicit memories."[36] Under prolonged stress, cortisol levels accumulate and alter brain function such that unique perceptual representations of oneself, others, and the surrounding world may become distorted.[37] The switch that turns on the memory of events long ago "involves turning on the genes in brain cells that lead to the production of new proteins."[38] These proteins grow new synaptic connections that further alter brain circuits, some of which "become *static and closed, and invested in defensive structures to guard against anticipated assaults* (my emphasis) that potentially trigger disorganizing and emotionally painful psychobiological states."[39] Genes that program extra connections in one area or decreased quantities of neurotransmitters in another influence a person's emotional and cognitive functioning, which impact personality development, and these genetic and biochemical processes could figure prominently in the development of dogmatism.

When the brain is moderately aroused, its focus allows working memory to function without undue interruption from the more primitive centers. However, if concentration is interrupted by anxiety and self-doubt about one's performance, "systems involving emotional processing such as the amygdala have detected a threatening situation, and are influencing what working memory attends to and processes."[40] In a hypervigilant state, thoughts become negatively biased, cognitive focus is narrowed, and the person has trouble putting things together. Such disruption impacts the emotional and cognitive regions of the brain, jeopardizing both the structure and function of brain circuitry.

§§

Perhaps, as Andrew Newberg and M. R. Waldman claim, there is a biological need for truth.[41] Through meditation or prayer (we might include indoctrination here), the simple process of focusing on the positive feelings of connection to a greater power or meaning in life releases dopamine, which increases one's sense of well-being and sparks a clearer vision of reality. Repetition of this focused state of frontal lobe activity reinforces the strength of one's original belief and stimulates related positive thoughts and feelings that enhance one's psychological security about possessing truth. Truth feels good, and the repetition of positive thoughts grooves neural circuits of emotion and memory.

Alternatively, if, through prayer or indoctrination, one focuses on anxious thoughts about a punishing God or the idea that the world is a threatening, fearful place, one's cognitive interpretations create emotional states that stimulate limbic activity, which the hippocampus records in long-term memory. Because the brain (in this case, the hippocampus), is sensitive to our survival, it is more efficient at storing negative experiences than positive ones. People who focus on pessimistic, fearful, or depressive thoughts release hormones and neurotransmitters that reinforce these negative beliefs, creating a pattern of pessimistic perceptions that seem as real as the words on this page. The end result might well be a dogmatic perception of reality in which beliefs become embedded in neural circuitry, and "contradictory evidence often cannot break through the existing connections in the brain."[42]

In a groundbreaking study that used neuroimaging to test the neural responses of partisan political subjects when presented with threatening information about their chosen candidate, findings revealed that the subjects' higher-order reasoning centers were relatively inactive, compared to the neural activity in their emotional circuits. Subjects became motivated to positively bias the news in order to maintain their political views and minimize the negative emotional states caused by the dissonant information. By altering the information, they reduced their emotional distress, strengthened their original, preferred beliefs, and restored harmony among brain systems.[43] This reinforcement process of restoring cognitive consonance in the face of unpleasant information that causes cognitive dissonance supports a biological explanation for fixed belief systems.

Any ideology that one perceives as either threatening or rewarding stirs emotions that may permanently alter brain circuits. If children who are biologically predisposed to anxiety are brainwashed to believe that God will save and protect true believers but will punish atheists, apostates, and infidels, the positive emotions engendered through prayer and belonging are mixed with negative, even hateful, emotions toward nonbelievers or any religious out-group. These emotions take on a reality of their own—a reality that is especially good at continually reinforcing negative emotions and beliefs about outsiders.[44] An emotionally stimulated mind that is chronically perturbed by negative judgments is less receptive and less able to absorb contradictory information.

§§

Chronic arousal also hampers the ability to effectively interact with others, disrupting what Daniel Goleman calls *social intelligence*—"a shorthand term for being intelligent not just *about* our relationships but also *in* them."[45] Here is how the process presumably unfolds.

Increased social opportunities alter and enrich the quality and quantity of neuronal connections that forge the growth of new pathways in the neocortex. These socially mediated learning experiences interact with biological structures that are primed to "switch on" during critical time periods, during which repeated experience and social learning strengthen hundreds of thousands of brain circuits.[46] Within this forest of neuronal branches is a newly discovered class of brain cells called *mirror neurons* that groom social intelligence. Along with our biological programming for language and imitation, these mirror neurons fire in brain areas that code the feelings and actions of the people we observe, all of which suggests there are neural substrates for complex social behaviors, social organization, and perhaps even empathy.[47]

Imagine what this does to infants and young children who have a biological predisposition for anxiety, who repeatedly observe their parent's facial expressions of frustration or anger while being criticized or threatened. They develop circuits of fear that damage their full range of intellectual, emotional, and social functioning. This simultaneously impacts their developing personality traits, especially the Big Five universal traits, which we survey in the next chapter. We will simply note here that scientific evidence supports a biological basis for Openness to Experience—one of these Big Five traits. Being open to new ideas and experiences may be influenced by individual differences in the dopaminergic system, which regulates the release of dopamine, a powerful neurotransmitter that affects brain function in the prefrontal cortex.[48] Since the polar opposite of Openness to Experience is Closedness (the trait most relevant to dogmatism), the closed-minded manner in which dogmatic people process information may be due to some failed mechanism in the transmission of dopamine. More-over, given that "there is substantial heritability for traits related to Openness,"[49] of which authoritarianism is but one, and given that authoritarianism is a facet of Closedness, then quite possibly there is a genetic basis for dogmatism's behavioral characteristics (dogmatic authoritarian aggression, dogmatic authoritarian submission, glorifica-tion of the in-group, vilification of the out-group, and preoccupation with power and status). Further support is obtained from research on right-wing authoritarianism, which found that scores on a measure of authoritarianism were significantly similar among biological parents and their children, and among siblings.[50]

Biological pathways are present at birth, and babies who exhibit high anxiety shortly after delivery reveal how a genetic predisposition for disruptive anxiety in infancy contributes to childhood fears or aggression, even when the child is raised in a warm, supportive family. Many people, especially parents and relatives of angry, unmanageable children, believe that difficult children are just born that way, and while there is likely some truth to that claim, various avenues of research suggest that although the role of genes is substantial, genes and biology are mediated by factors not yet fully understood.[51] Psy-chologists remind us that while the environment influences the *expres-sion* of genes,[52] both are important actors on the stage of personality development.

Whether experience involves a new challenge, a direct threat, a pleasant or unpleasant memory, or learning a different skill, experience changes the brain "through fresh connections between neurons or through the generation of utterly new neurons."[53] New neurons? Could the very idea be such good news that the last sentence produced neuronal growth and new connections in readers' minds? Perhaps, at least according to recent research that claims an *active* brain generates new neurons.[54] Such is the powerful potential of the brain's neurochemistry that impinges on memory, learning, and personality development.

§§

Finally, the biological basis of psychological function influences the outcome of psychotherapy, the success of which depends on the client's range of adaptive capacity. Unbeknownst to the client (and sometimes even the therapist), the work of both therapist and client alters circuits in the client's brain. For example, in therapy, clients learn that their disruptive emotions from years of repeated abuse in infancy and childhood need no longer obscure their ability to see things differently.[55] Although cognitive reframing and restructuring is not straightforward and simple, it appears that early, hardwired views of the world may be modified if clients are motivated to work on altering their perceptions. Such insight and adaptive change are somewhat shaped by biological influences. In considering the outcome of therapy goals, the therapist would ideally assess the client's levels of cortisol, immunological functioning, baseline activation levels of the amygdala, and functioning of the left prefrontal cortex, which governs positive emotions such as optimism and enthusiasm.[56] These biological substrates interact with thoughts, emotions, and behaviors that alter the process of therapy such that old patterns are weakened and new ones strengthened. Thus, dogmatic people who have some insight that their rigidity is causing problems, who are not closed-minded about the potential benefits of therapy, have good prospects for successful treatment.

TWIN STUDIES: FURTHER SUPPORT FOR THE GENETIC BASIS OF TRAITS

Research that compares trait similarities among identical, or monozygotic (MZ), and fraternal, or dizygotic (DZ), twins with other first-degree relatives provides important information about the contributing roles of genes and the environment on personality traits. The assumption is that since traits have significantly higher degrees of expressive similarity among twins, especially MZ twins, they presumably have a genetic basis.

In time, sophisticated modern techniques will help geneticists and neuroscientists identify genetic markers associated with specific personality traits such as anxiety—the assumed emotional precursor to dogmatism. Recent twin studies revealed that MZ twins raised in shared environments scored consistently and significantly more alike on measures of anxiety than did fraternal twins. Once again, we can speculate that, since anxiety is an aspect of the Big Five personality trait known as Neuroticism (which, along with Openness to Experience, is related to dogmatism), there may be a heritable component to dogmatism. One problem with gathering information, however, is that parental ratings of twin similarity are subject to biases, in that parents tend to inflate the degree of similarity they report in MZ twins, and thus overestimate the degree of genetic similarity.[57]

The EAS Temperament Survey[58] has been used to compare twins reared together on levels of emotionality, which is defined as "the tendency to become (autonomically) aroused easily and intensely."[59] Twins' degree of similarity, as measured by correlating their scores, was significantly higher than chance expectations. Since magnitudes of correlation can range from −1.00 to +1.00, and since a correlation of +.61 is "quite strong" and a correlation of .29 is "rather weak,"[60] findings that MZ twins had correlations as high as +.61 on emotionality while DZ correlations dropped to +.29 suggest that genes account for as much as 50 percent of a particular personality trait. Note that although MZ twins have identical genes, they do not produce identical scores on personality trait measures (assuming the questionnaire for the trait is a valid measure). If their scored relationships were a perfect +1.00, we would conclude that the measured trait was 100 percent heritable, or completely genetically based, but data show this to never be the case.[61] Joseph LeDoux provides an important caveat here: "Genes account at most for half of a given trait, *not* that half of all personality is accounted for by genes."[62]

Researchers have also compared differences in the degree of similarity between MZ twins (reared together and apart), DZ twins, siblings, and other first- and second-degree relatives. They found that, in the case of anxiety, although trait and genetic similarity are positively correlated, "at best, research suggests that the heritability of many behaviors is in the range of 30 to 50 percent. So overall, these studies yield strong evidence for the genetic heritability of anxiety, meaning that only about 1/3 to 1/2 of behavior variation is due to genetics; the majority of the variance is due to environment."[63]

At this time, enough evidence exists to conclude that the degree of twin similarity on all of the Big Five personality traits strongly implicates genes as active players in personality development, even though behavioral geneticists have yet to determine the exact genetic contributions for trait similarity.[64] Despite this imprecision, twin similarity is compelling enough to lead some proponents of the biogenetic perspective to suggest that personality "trait *structure* [my emphasis] can be attributed almost entirely to genetic influences."[65]

This suggests that individuals who respond to genetic predispositions for chronic anxiety by developing several characteristics of dogmatism have learned that their unquestioning acceptance of dogma is an adaptive way to manage biologically structured predispositions for emotions. Closing their minds helps reduce relentless anxiety and self-doubt. Thus, these people are reinforced for cognitive rigidity, and behavior that is reinforced is likely to continue until dogmatism becomes an ingrained personality trait. We might conclude that although there is no gene for dogmatism per se, "there likely is a genetic influence on relative responsiveness," in that genes influence enzymes that incline the body to react to environmental stimuli in specific ways.[66]

If, as proposed by Rokeach and myself, anxiety lays the foundation upon which dogmatism is built, and if anxiety is genetically based, then dogmatism has a genetic, structural component that surely interacts with other predisposing factors.

The preceding arguments enable us to conclude that there is no specific heritable gene for dogmatism, except to the extent that genes are the building blocks of brain structures that predispose their host to a range of emotions—anxiety and fear being those most implicated in this personality trait. "There is almost certainly considerable heritability in measures of dogmatism, although one presumes that what is inherited is the tendency to think dogmatically, not the particular articles of faith that typify dogmatic people in particular times and places."[67] And the tendency to think dogmatically is a consequence of a biological predisposition for anxiety. It bears repeating that although we are drawn to environments that are compatible with our inborn predispositions, "such gene-environment interaction does not detract from the significance of parenting, education, and other interventions."[68] In learning environments that intensify anxiety, one may develop an anxiety disorder such as a specific phobia, a social phobia, the generalized anxiety disorder, or obsessive-compulsive disorder (as presented in the Diagnostic and Statistical Manual, fourth revision). Or dogmatism. And all of these psychological problems have multiple interacting influences, including genes, in utero and postnatal chance occurrences, and social influences that impact the wiring of the brain in indeterminate ways.

It is reasonable to suggest that genes initially create an emotional predisposition for anxiety that structurally facilitates a dogmatic style of thinking, especially in authoritarian environments. It may also be the case that genes indirectly contribute to all four of the proposed causes of dogmatism outlined in chapter 4. Genetically based, chronic anxiety corrupts the integrity of cognitive, emotional, and social functioning such that Rokeach's second psychological need, the need to control anxiety, frustrates the need to know and socially connect. To complete the progression, these three disruptions have unfortunate consequences for the fourth need, the need for dignity. Thus, we can think of genes as the predisposing matches that, when struck by certain environmental circumstances, ignite and fan the flames of dogmatism.

JONAH'S BIOLOGICAL PREDISPOSITION FOR DOGMATISM

We can now understand how, at an early age, Jonah was biologically and environmentally primed for dogmatism. His biologically based anxiety and fretfulness, which were evident at birth, might well have been the necessary conditions that put him on a trajectory of latent, adult dogmatism. Functional at birth, Jonah's amygdala registered his emotional experiences in unconscious neuronal pathways. During infancy and early childhood, every time his parents responded to his anxiety with indifference and frustration, stress hormones activated Jonah's amygdala, which built another fear circuit. As with all children, Jonah's hippocampus, which stores conscious memories in the contexts in which emotions occur, was not fully mature until about age three.[69] This means that his early neglect created unconscious memories for strong emotions, the context and source of which Jonah might never access. "Unconscious emotional memories can therefore have widespread, long-lasting effects without our having any understanding of what is triggering certain responses or feelings."[70] During the first three years of his life, Jonah's hippocampus was particularly adept at embedding negative experiences into long-term emotional memory, and although the details of those memories were as yet not capable of being recorded, his amygdala was doing an excellent job of signaling threat and building corresponding neuronal pathways throughout his developing brain.

Later, when Jonah's father criticized him for asking questions, neuronal firings in his amygdala once again switched on specific genes programmed to release additional cortisol and other anxiety-specific proteins that exacerbated his genetic vulnerability for anxiety. While these unpleasant experiences did not structurally alter Jonah's DNA, they did create patterns of electrochemical circuits that uniquely wired his brain. As he tried to make sense of his environment, chronic apprehension continuously grooved these circuits, which ultimately impoverished and boxed in his thinking. Jonah's genetic programming for a sensitivity to threat might well have shaped a political orientation (though not party preference per se) toward conservative thinking, which seeks to preserve the status quo. A recent study found a significant positive correlation between sensitivity to threat and a preference for military spending, arbitrary search warrants, school prayer, and civilian freedom to bear arms.[71]

Early, chronic anxiety gradually led Jonah's high-road cortex to conclude that it was unwise to question externally imposed beliefs. His neuronal circuits biased the decisions he made, two of which were to conceal his anxiety as best as possible and close his mind to any ideas that conflicted with those that ensured safety. Years of criticism had laid heavy memory cables throughout his limbic system, the center of the brain that is largely responsible for emotions.

By adolescence, Jonah had discovered that when his core beliefs were questioned, dogmatic conviction camouflaged the anxiety that would otherwise have been front and center. Yet Jonah was unaware of the extent to which he inappropriately projected remnants of his early psychological history onto others—distortions that socially distanced him from others. Over the years, this and other defenses also distanced him from his emotions such that now, in midlife, Jonah is left with persistent, vague feelings of restless emptiness.

Jonah's past experiences are alive and well, living in present patterns of thought. And while his limbic system does not differentiate old emotions from those that are ongoing, its sensitivity to past emotions lingers and becomes activated by present triggers. In particular, when Jonah's important beliefs are challenged, a cascade of emotions are released that resemble those activated in childhood when his father chastised or ridiculed him.

But early wirings of Jonah's neural circuits, particularly those having to do with his emotions, can be rechanneled. With hard work, Jonah can create new circuits, but this would depend on his motivation to acknowledge and meet the challenge of change head on. Now in his late fifties, my guess is that we would not find Jonah browsing through the psychology section of his local bookstore. As mentioned in chapter 4, dogmatists not only lack personal insight, they fear it. It is also unlikely that we would find him in a therapist's office. Like most dogmatists, Jonah would view therapy as a psychological crutch for those who cannot get beyond their diapers.

The next chapter situates what we've learned about dogmatism's intersecting evolutionary, genetic, and biological factors within the broad context of personality traits. What are some adjectives people use to describe your personality? Do you think your traits are chameleon-like, or are they fairly resistant to permanent change? You may find that when we examine the nature of personality traits, interesting surprises will stimulate your thinking about the hardiness and resilience of your own characteristic emotions and behavioral dispositions.

NOTES

1. A. R. Damasio, "How the Brain Creates the Mind," *Scientific American* 12, no. 1 (2002): 4–9.

2. R. R. McCrae, "Human Nature and Culture: A Trait Perspective," *Journal of Personality Research* 38, no. 1 (2004): 3–14.

3. R. R. McCrae and P. T. Costa, "A Five-Factor Theory of Personality," in *Handbook of Personality: Theory and Research*, ed. L. A. Pervin and O. P. John (New York: Guilford, 1999), p. 144.

4. J. P. J. Pinel, *Biopsychology* (Boston: Allyn and Bacon, 2006). Pinel outlines the anatomy and function of the nervous system; sensory and motor systems; brain plasticity; motivational factors of hunger, sex, sleep, and drug addiction; and psychiatric disorders of thought and emotion.

5. R. J. Davidson, D. C. Jackson, and N. Kalin. "Emotion, Plasticity, Context, and Regulation: Perspectives from Affective Neuroscience," *Psychological Bulletin* 126, no. 6 (2000): 890–909. The authors provide a comprehensive review of advances in biopsychology prior to the beginning of this millennium.

6. J. Pinel, *Biopsychology*, p. 38.

7. G. C. Davison, J. M. Neale, K. R. Blankstein, and G. L. Flettlett, *Abnormal Psychology: Canadian Edition* (Etobicoke, ON: Wiley, 2002), p. 184.

8. Nova Teachers (Ghost in Your Genes), http://www.pbs.org/wgbh/nova/teachers/programs/3413_genes.html (accessed October 18, 2007). This PBS documentary on *Nova* aired October 16, 2007. It explored "how the epigenome—the body's complex chemical network that controls gene expression—plays a role in human biological destiny."

9. ReproMed, the Toronto Institute for Reproductive Medicine, *Preimplantation Genetic Diagnosis,* http://www.repromed.ca/pgd_toronto.html (accessed October 20, 2007).

10. J. Kagan, "Born to Be Shy," in *States of Mind*, ed. Roberta Conlan (New York: Wiley, 1999), pp. 29–51.

11. M. S. Gazzaniga, R. B. Ivry, and G. R. Mangun, *Cognitive Neuroscience: The Biology of the Mind* (New York: Norton, 1998), p. 484. These authors note that while the development and neural plasticity of the brain is enormously complex, it is most pronounced during gestation and early development.

12. N. Doidge, *The Brain That Changes Itself: Stories of Personal Triumph from the Frontiers of Brain Science* (New York: Viking, 2007).

13. S. Freeman and J. C. Herron, *Evolutionary Analysis* (Upper Saddle River, NJ: Prentice Hall, 1998). The total variance consists of V_A (the additive effects of genes), V_I (the interaction of genes at different loci), V_D (dominance effects), and V_E (environmental effects).

14. R. Plomin and A. Caspi, "Behavioral Genetics and Personality," in *Handbook of Personality: Theory and Research*, ed. Lawrence A. Pervin and O. P. John (New York: Guilford, 1999), p. 252. These authors stress that explanations for 50 percent of the variance in identical twins "is an astounding achievement in personality research, which has been pushing against a glass ceiling of explaining more than 10 percent of the variance, as indexed by correlations of .30."

15. D. P. McAdams, *The Person: An Introduction to Personality Psychology* (New York: Harcourt Brace, 1994), p. 12.

16. B. Engler, *Personality Theories: An Introduction* (Boston: Houghton Mifflin Co., 2003), p. 342.

17. S. Pinker, *How the Mind Works* (New York: Norton, 1997), p. 65.

18. G. Lakoff, *Whose Freedom? The Battle over America's Most Important Idea* (New York: Farrar, Straus, and Giroux, 2006), p. 10.

19. B. Perry, "Childhood Experience and the Expression of Genetic

Potential: What Childhood Neglect Tells Us about Nature and Nurture," *Brain and Mind* 3 (2002): 79–100.

20. A. Schore, *Affect Dysregulation and the Origin of the Self: The Neurobiology of Emotional Development* (New York: Norton, 2003). Schore documents how repeated stress causes emotional malfunction in the orbitofrontal cortex, the growth of which depends on the quality of parent-child interactions.

21. D. Goleman, *Social Intelligence: The New Science of Human Relationships* (New York: Bantam, 2006), p. 164.

22. Ibid., p. 165.

23. Ibid.

24. Ibid., p. 151. Here, Goleman cites a comment from John Crabbe in a conversation about Crabbe's research on epigenetics that studies the ways in which change affects how genes operate.

25. D. Goleman and the Dalai Lama, *Destructive Emotions: How Can We Overcome Them?* (New York: Bantam Books, 2003), p. 189.

26. K. J. Saudino, "Moving beyond the Heritability Question: New Directions in Behavioral Genetic Studies of Personality," in *Current Directions in Personality Psychology*, ed. Carolyn C. Morf and A. Ozlem (Upper Saddle River, NJ: Pearson, 2005), p. 61.

27. S. Pinker, *The Blank Slate: The Modern Denial of Human Nature* (New York: Penguin Putnam, 2002).

28. H. Sebald, cited in *New Society: Sociology for the 21st Century*, ed. R. J. Brym (Toronto: Harcourt, 2001), p. 59.

29. R. Altemeyer, *The Authoritarian Specter* (Cambridge, MA: Harvard University Press, 1996), p. 63. A total of 1,022 students formed the subject pool that responded to the same questionnaire in two separate studies, one conducted in 1979 and one in 1981.

30. Goleman, *Destructive Emotions*, p. 184.

31. Ibid. Richard Davidson is the director of the Laboratory for Affective Neuroscience at the University of Wisconsin.

32. J. LeDoux, "The Power of Emotions," in *States of Mind: New Discoveries about How Our Brains Make Us Who We Are*, ed. Roberta Conlan (New York: Wiley, 1999), p. 135.

33. J. LeDoux, *Synaptic Self: How Our Brains Become Who We Are* (Middlesex, UK: Penguin, 2002), p. 223.

34. M. Ignatieff, *The Warrior's Honour* (Harmondsworth, UK: Penguin Books, 1999), p. 186.

35. Goleman, *Destructive Emotions*, pp. 202–203.

36. LeDoux, "The Power of Emotions," p. 223. For a review of studies on these findings, see chapter 9, pp. 235–59.

37. LeDoux, *Synaptic Self*.

38. E. Kandel, "Of Learning, Memory, and Genetic Switches," in *States of Mind: New Discoveries about How Our Brains Make Us Who We Are*, ed. Roberta Conlan (New York: Wiley, 1999), p. 152.

39. Schore, *Affect Dysregulation*, p. 127.

40. LeDoux, *Synaptic Self,* p. 288. LeDoux cites Michael Davis, who writes, "Anxiety might be a function of the bed nucleus of the stria terminalis, a brain region that is considered an extension of the amygdala. . . . Because the inputs to the two structures [amygdala and bed nucleus] are different, they might be activated under different conditions—the amygdala in response to immediately present threats, the bed nucleus to anticipated ones" (p. 290).

41. A. Newberg and M. R. Waldman, *Why We Believe What We Believe* (New York: Free Press, 2007). The subtitle of their book is *Uncovering Our Biological Need for Meaning, Spirituality, and Truth*. See chapter 7, pp. 167–90.

42. Ibid., p. 254.

43. D. Westen, P. S. Blagnov, K. Harenski, C. Kilts, and S. Hamann, "The Neural Basis of Motivated Reasoning: An fMRI Study of Emotional Constraints on Political Judgment during the U.S. Presidential Election of 2004," *Journal of Cognitive Neuroscience* 18, no. 11 (2006): 1947–58.

44. Newberg and Waldman, *Why We Believe What We Believe*.

45. Goleman, *Social Intelligence*, p. 11.

46. Ibid., p. 161.

47. G. Rizzolatti and L. Craighero, "The Mirror-Neuron System," *Annual Review of Neuroscience* (2004): 169–92.

48. C. G. Deyoung, J. B. Peterson, and D. M. Higgins, "Sources of Openness/Intellect: Cognitive and Neuropsychological Correlates of the Fifth Factor of Personality," *Journal of Personality* 73, no. 4 (2005): 825–58. The authors of this study point out that "in both concrete and abstract domains, the exploratory tendency is likely to be regulated, at least in part, by the neuro-modulator dopamine. The dopaminergic system is particularly responsive to novelty, and its activation triggers exploratory behavior" (p. 828).

49. R. R. McCrae, "Social Consequences of Experiential Openness, *Psychological Bulletin* 120 (1996): 332.

50. S. Scarr, *Race, Social Class, and Individual Differences in I.Q.* (Hillsdale, NJ: Erlbaum, 1981). The author reports that a correlation of authoritarian scores between parents and their biological children was as high as .40, while siblings scores correlated at .36. Correlations of adoptive parents, adoptive children, and siblings were significantly lower than those of adoptees and their first-degree relatives.

51. D. C. Rowe and E. Van Den Oord, "Genetic and Environmental Influences," in *Personality: Contemporary Theory and Research*, ed. Valerian J. Derlega, B. A. Winstead, and W. H. Jones (Belmont, CA: Thomson Wadsworth, 2005), p. 78. This heritability correlation is based on monozygotic or identical twins raised apart. The same authors conclude that "the effect of family environments on most traits is a very weak one." Still, if the average heritability is 50 percent, that leaves a lot of room for speculation as to what accounts for the other 50 percent.

52. B. Engler, *Personality Theories: An Introduction* (Boston: Houghton Mifflin Co., 2003).

53. Goleman, *Destructive Emotions,* p. 21. In this segment, Goleman notes that in 1998, "neuroscientists discovered that new neurons are continually being generated in the adult brain"—a finding that rendered obsolete the previous belief that we are born with a fixed number of neurons that change only in their number of synaptic connections (p. 23).

54. P. S. Eriksson, E. Perfilieva, T. Bjork-Eriksson, A. M. Alborn, C. Nordberg, D. A. Peterson, and F. H. Gage, "Neurogenesis in the Adult Human Hippocampus," *Nature Medicine* 4, no. 11 (1998): 1313–17; Goleman, *Destructive Emotions.* Goleman quotes Richard Davidson on stem cells: "Neurogenesis is the brain's ability to continually build new neurons right on into old age, though the rate of growth slows—perhaps as a function of monotony" (p. 239).

55. LeDoux, *Synaptic Self.*

56. Goleman, *Destructive Emotions*, pp. 197–98.

57. Saudino, "Moving beyond the Heritability Question," p. 58.

58. A. H. Buss and R. Plomin, *Temperament: Early Developing Personality Traits* (Hillsdale, NJ: Wiley-Interscience, 1984).

59. A. H. Buss, *Personality: Temperament, Social Behavior* (Needham Heights, MA: Allyn and Bacon, 1995), p. 50. Emotion, as measured by the EAS Temperament Survey, does not include the low arousal state of depression. For a summary of findings on twin studies, see pp. 50–51.

60. D. C. Funder, *The Personality Puzzle* (New York: Norton, 2007).

61. A. Tellegen, D. T. Lykken, T. J. Bouchard, K. J. Wilcox, N. L. Segal, and S. Rich, "Personality Similarity in Twins Reared Apart and Together," *Journal of Personality and Social Psychology* 54 (1988): 1031–39.

62. LeDoux, *Synaptic Self,* pp. 29–30.

63. Engler, *Personality Theories*, p. 317.

64. Plomin and Caspi, "Behavioral Genetics and Personality," p. 253. When results of self-report ratings were compared to ratings of two other peers, these authors found that the degree of similarity between twins and their peers' ratings is significantly more alike than different, and such similarity is greater than what we would expect to find by chance, thus bolstering the case for a sizable genetic contribution to personality traits. Genetic research that includes self-reports; interviews; objective laboratory measurements (where possible); family, educational, and occupational records; marital histories; and mental health agencies, schools, hospitals, police, and other observers would provide substantial evidence for genetic and environmental influences on specific traits. While comprehensive measures are very difficult to obtain, the greatest range possible for data collection about people's observable traits would enhance the accuracy of causal statements, particularly when the subjects are identical twins.

65. R. R. McRae, "Personality Structure," in *Personality: Contemporary Theory and Research*, ed. Valerian A. Derlega, B. A. Winstead, and W. H. Jones (Belmont, CA: Wadsworth, 2005), p. 204. Nathan Brody, in "Heritability of Traits," also supports the conclusion that "the structure of the trait is in part derivable from genetic relations among the trait components [and that] changes in the phenotypic measure were partially controlled by genotypes" (pp. 117–18).

66. H. S. Friedman and M. W. Schustack, *Readings in Personality: Classic Theories and Modern Research* (New York: Allyn and Bacon, 2003), p. 174.

67. Personal e-mail communication from Robert R. McCrae, October 30, 2006.

68. Engler, *Personality Theories,* p. 317.

69. Conlan, *States of Mind.*

70. Ibid., p. 143.

71. P. Jackman, "Biology and the Ballot Box." Jackman reviewed John Alford's research in the *Globe and Mail*, September 19, 2008, p. A2. http://www.globeandmail.com (accessed September 23, 2008).

Chapter 11

PERMANENT SCARS OR TEMPORARY WOUNDS?

Dogmatism from the Trait Perspective

*However much people might vary, they have certain things in
common by virtue of their common human nature.*

Steven Pinker[1]

In 1936, Gordon Allport, the original trait theorist, began his inquiry
into the number and nature of personality traits by extracting 17,953
dictionary words that describe people in their daily social interactions.[2] Over the past seventy years, Allport's extensive lexical approach has been considerably condensed, and the specific language of
traits now offers a fine-tuned, useful taxonomy of terms that provides
the basis for theory and research on personality traits (also referred to
as *dispositions*). Dogmatism is one such trait, and this book parses its
essence into thirteen characteristics or subtraits. Trait theorists in the
first half of the last century naturally overlooked the contributing role
of evolution and neuroscience on trait development, since these specialized fields only emerged as distinct disciplines in the latter half of
the twentieth century. The content of this chapter expands on traditional trait theory by examining dogmatism within the context of
modern trait theory, which includes evolutionary psychology and

biopsychology. Those readers who are interested in a more thorough review of the early history of trait theory may refer to the references listed in the chapter notes.[3]

THE NATURE OF TRAITS

Using computer analyses, psychologists study personality traits to determine the general dimensions of thoughts, feelings, and behaviors.[4] Referred to as *temperaments* in infants and children, personality traits are "stable individual differences in emotional reactivity,"[5] and they are influenced by psychological, biological, and environmental events. Yet the very concept of personality traits is not without controversy. There is a great deal of indecision as to whether the abstract terms associated with traits simply describe them, or whether they imply biological and environmental causes that underlie their structure. Some psychologists consider traits a collection of learned habits; others view them as having a genetic basis that shapes observable, characteristic adaptations to one's environment.[6]

Psychological definitions aside, all of us observe others and assign descriptive labels to their behavior. Inherent to human nature is our ability to rapidly assess strangers in everyday life and extraordinary situations—a handy little skill when we find ourselves in dangerous situations or search for a mate. If a stranger were to approach you at night and ask for spare change, you are not likely to engage him in a conversation about the movie you just saw. You instantly and intuitively assess his prominent physical and psychological features before reacting. When you later describe the encounter to a friend, you draw a select few descriptors from thousands of trait adjectives to depict the stranger's appearance and personality. Do we really need a trait bank with that many words to accurately describe people?

Apparently the answer is yes, and for good, evolutionary reasons.[7] People are first and foremost social animals, born with innate predispositions to use symbols—words, letters, and numbers—that provide us with a basic template for language, which helps us describe and predict human behaviors.[8] Eskimos have many words for snow because they are surrounded by it, travel on it, and once made their homes from it. By contrast, southerners describe snow in simpler terms: cold and white. Because we are all social animals, there is a universal tendency to invent many words to describe that which is central to human existence: other people.[9] It is as if we have to objectify people before they become fully visible to us.

Adolescents are helpful in this regard, perhaps because they are more preoccupied with rating, dating, and mating than the rest of us. They create new words that locate personality descriptors within historical time frames, giving us modern words like *cool*, *awesome*, and *geek*. Fifty years ago, *hip*, *hood*, and *bimbo* were popular trait terms. "All aspects of human personality which are or have been of importance, interest, or utility have already become recorded in the substance of language. For throughout history, the most fascinating subject of general discourse, which has also been vitally necessary to survival, is language that accurately describes human behavior."[10] These thousands of words have evolved because we continue to accept them as reasonably accurate descriptors of personality characteristics, and accurate descriptions facilitate accurate predictions.

When we think of friends and family, we not only draw from our stored word bank, we also recall a wealth of perceptual experiences—a cluster of organized impressions, interpretations, and memories that allow us to grasp someone's unique essence. Our impressions are more stable and organized than haphazard because, over time and on average, personality traits are more consistent and predictable than inconsistent and capricious.[11] In general, people's personalities reflect enduring traits that "are among the strongest predictors of happiness, distress, career success, marital satisfaction, and even longevity, among other important life outcomes."[12] The consensus among trait theorists is that traits have stable properties; different situations do not buffet our personality traits about like autumn leaves in gusts of wind. On the whole, we can trust our perceptions, intuitions, and expectations about people's personalities, especially those we have observed in different settings over a number of years.[13]

Take Jake. Well liked by family, friends, and co-workers, his wife describes him as a happily married, loving father of three. Jake's co-workers see him as a considerate, responsible, and likeable employee who has a dry wit. By economic standards, Jake is middle class. Given what we know about him, if Jake's company declared bankruptcy and he lost his job, or if his wife died suddenly, would his personality deviate such that others might then see Jake as short-tempered, cynical, introverted, or paranoid? And what about Jonah, the feature character in this book? Are his personality traits fixed or flexible? Is he destined to spend a lifetime in the doghouse of dogmatism? Personality trait theorists who investigate the stability of traits over the lifespan of individuals try to determine the extent to which genes and the environment influence stability and change.[14]

Current research indicates that sudden fortune or misfortune will not significantly alter Jake's, Jonah's, yours, or anyone else's personality traits (keeping in mind that psychologists view traits as strong, persistent emotions and behaviors).[15] This does not mean that people's personality traits will not vary. For example, those who experience or witness a life-threatening event may develop post-traumatic stress disorder. The psychological impact of trauma can cause prolonged suffering—recurrent flashbacks, nightmares, feelings of emotional detachment, impaired concentration, and sleep disturbances—all of which can alter one's personality.[16] This is particularly so if, prior to the trauma, the person did not have a social support network, had been previously traumatized, had a preexisting psychological disorder (especially an anxiety disorder), or had a family history of mental illness (a parent with bipolar disorder, for example).[17] The symptoms of post-traumatic stress disorder occur in response to events outside the realm of normal human suffering, such as natural disasters, combat fatigue, and terrorist attacks. And while many of us have suffered from a serious accident or illness, job loss, or death of a loved one, most of us are resilient enough to return to former levels of personality functioning within a reasonable time frame.[18] This is because "individual differences in personality traits are extremely stable in adults, with retest correlations in the .60 to .80 range over periods of up to 30 years."[19] So, overall, our perceptions of others are more accurate than not, and, generally speaking, the language we use to describe people we know is representative of them much of the time, as are the trait descriptors others use to describe us.[20] Would you rather have someone describe you as mysterious and ethereal or as aloof and detached? These trait descriptors all share a common essence, although the second two traits are less flattering than the first.

§§

Psychologists use traits to refer to prominent, enduring characteristics —an understanding that may differ from that of the layperson who assumes that someone has a trait if its outstanding feature is present, even though that feature may vary considerably across time and situation. However, from a psychological point of view, traits must meet specific criteria. They must, for example, fall outside the average range of distribution on a trait measure. Thus, trait scores on a valid personality test are anchored within the upper or lower range on a continuum of scores. A dogmatism questionnaire provides one such assessment. Within a given population, trait researchers compare the thinking styles, emotions, and behaviors of people who score within the high, middle, and low range on the trait's measure to statistically delimit trait characteristics within certain boundaries. People who have the trait would score within its criterion range, whereas the rest of us would score outside it. Some of us might, for example, occasionally dominate a conversation or present a viewpoint with adamant certainty, but if such behaviors are transitory, they do not characterize the trait of dogmatism.[21] Thus, while many people occasionally act in trait-specific ways, their emotions and behaviors are less predictable than people who have a personality trait, as evidenced by behavior that is enduring and consistent across many situations. But however we determine the existence of dogmatism, a person assumed to have the trait is dogmatic relative to the majority of people in a given population.

Recently, a major television news report ended with a human interest segment on the personality traits of introversion and extroversion. Viewers were asked, "Are you an introvert or an extrovert?" The reporter neglected to mention that while all of us lean more in one direction than the other, those of us who score within the midrange would not qualify as extroverts or introverts in the strict psychological sense. While this dichotomous framing of the question is misleading, the reporter was simply following a common practice that fulfills the human need to categorize ourselves and others, erroneous as that may be.

We organize and classify things, people, and events in distinct groups, often without much consideration for the potential consequences. Readers of this book are now familiar with the rationale for applying the term *trait* only to people who would anchor the upper or lower range on a continuum of scores for a valid scale—in this case, dogmatism. While the majority of people would fall outside the designated trait zone, those who do not—those who are dogmatic—have several subtraits of dogmatism that are enduring and widespread enough to impair social relationships and arrest progress across many domains.

Finally, distinct, observable traits such as table manners, gesticulations, style of dress, or handwriting (the list is long), are considered *expressive* traits that stand alone; they do not constitute personality traits, which are the substance of this book.

THE TROUBLE WITH TRAITS

When psychologists talk about traits, they refer to relative degrees of difference that fall on a continuum of points distributed between two polar opposites. The general population, especially dogmatic people, typically think of traits as falling in dichotomous, either-or categories: someone is selfish or generous, successful or unsuccessful, attractive or unattractive (all stereotypes of modern culture). Problems arise when people describe others according to their most dominant trait, which is then seen as an absolute description of their total personality. This biased view may camouflage nuanced, idiosyncratic discrepancies in personality—a closer look reveals that a person described as friendly, for example, has a number of subtraits or components of friendliness that fall along a continuum of measurement. He or she also has a variety of other personality traits, some more adaptive than others.

Consider this scenario: On your return from a summer holiday, a colleague whose opinions you value describes Kelly, a new employee, as "so charismatic she can charm the sap out of maples in midwinter." If, after meeting her, your early impressions turn out to be very similar to your colleague's, might you then want to know if Kelly's charming personality extends beyond the work situation. When is she not so charming?

Psychologists ask such questions. Because a comprehensive analysis provides the best evidence for personality traits, researchers like to investigate the role of genetics, brain chemistry, life experiences, social learning, personal choices, and the various beliefs people like Kelly have about themselves and others. Understandably, most of us are not so thorough in our personality assessments. We simply apply the adjective that most closely describes people we encounter and assume, sometimes erroneously, that the descriptive label we assign today predicts similar behaviors tomorrow and into the future. However, these spontaneous, superficial descriptions are used to categorize and then stigmatize and discriminate against individuals and entire groups. Simple descriptions used to define people often go too far.

At the same time, "one realizes how awkward it would be to refer to everything in its most precise and pedantic form every time one refers to it."[22] You would not describe your friend Rose as "predisposed to procrastinating with most tasks," any more than you would say, "Rose appears to have the personality trait of procrastination." Such language, though accurate, would sound odd. "Rose procrastinates" is sufficient. And just as Rose does not procrastinate all the time, in all situations, neither does Jonah, the main character in this book, act dogmatically in every social exchange. He does not cling to and pronounce all of his beliefs with equivalent degrees of dogmatic tenacity, but he persistently exhibits enough subtraits of dogmatism for us to assume that he has the personality trait of dogmatism.

This brings us to the central problem. Until we can fully understand the multidimensional aspects of personality, we cannot predict their occurrence with consistent, precise accuracy; neither can we presume to fully know the characteristics and causes of personality traits like dogmatism. Deep within all trait structures are complex psychological organizations that sustain individuality, and psychologists who study one's unique personality puzzle may never assemble all the pieces in a complete, firmly interlocking picture, even when their approach to that task is systematic and scientific. That is why psychology is sometimes criticized for having a wishy-washy, touchy-feely approach that fails to conclusively explain human behavior. But these criticisms overlook the complexity of the subject matter and the relative newness of personality as a specialized field of psychology. We have to accept incremental gains here, and recognize that much of the time we are trying to lasso the clouds.

THE POWER OF THE SITUATION

Beginning in the 1960s and throughout the 1970s, situation theorists challenged trait theory assumptions about the nature and stability of traits. The situationists argued that, since we cannot predict people's behavior with any substantial degree of accuracy, situations that people find themselves in play a more prominent role in determining behavior than do personality traits. Proponents of the situationist approach were highly critical of trait theorists' static view of personality, claiming instead that personality is neither consistent nor predictable, because behaviors change as a consequence of the situations in which people find themselves.[23] Trait theorists, they claimed, were not only misguided, their ideas about traits such as friendliness or dogmatism were "mainly stereotypes in the minds of observers rather than dynamic forces in the lives of actors."[24] Situationists thus shifted the investigative focus of personality from internal dispositions like anxiety, introversion, and dogmatism to external situations that were assumed to be key mediators of trait expression. This shift began a decade of controversy that has often been referred to as the trait-situation debate.

Do you think that strong situations could significantly alter your personality, and if so, how quickly would you return to your natural self when back in familiar surroundings? Might you be noticeably extroverted in some situations but introverted in others; closed-minded some of the time (especially in the presence of closed-minded people) and open-minded in other circumstances?

Several famous social psychology experiments undertaken in the 1960s and 1970s sought to determine the degree of influence of the situation on two personality traits—obedience and social conformity. Stanley Milgram tested the extent to which people, acting as teachers, would violate their code of ethics and obey orders from authority figures to inflict pain on learners (confederates of the experimenter).[25] Another prominent social psychologist, Philip Zimbardo, investigated the role situations play on the expression of social conformity. He wanted to determine how quickly people would assume their respective roles when placed in a mock prison environment where they role-played either an inmate or prison guard.[26] Findings from these experimental studies are documented in many social science books and peer-reviewed psychology journals. Overall, the results of the Milgram and Zimbardo studies, as well as a recent BBC prison study on perceived individual and group autonomy,[27] indicate that in unusually strong settings the situation mediates people's existing traits in surprising, uncharacteristic ways. (See the chapter notes for a summary of these experiments).

Unfortunately, these studies lacked baseline data on preexisting trait levels in the subjects (teachers, prison guards, and inmates), none of whom were tested for relevant personality traits prior to the experiments. What were their levels of authoritarianism, compliance, self-esteem, anxiety, and dogmatism *before* they agreed to participate in the experiment? Despite this lack of information, researchers concluded that because exceptional situations clearly alter one's characteristic ways of behaving, trait theorists need to take greater account of the situational circumstances when they talk about traits as if they were stable, enduring personality characteristics.

Contemporary trait theorists are doing just that. They agree that situations alter behavior, but they do not agree that they significantly alter the underlying *structure* of individual traits, much of which is genetic in nature.[28] Like a kaleidoscope with complex shapes and gradations of hue, simple environmental twists can display colorful new configurations of personality, but the brighter, dominant colors continue to attract our attention. Similarly, prominent and persistent demonstrations of behavior capture the interest of trait psychologists who research the stability of individual differences.[29]

After more than thirty years of the trait-situation debate, the *interactional* view moved in to help settle the dispute. The interactionist perspective views personality traits as a product of biological, psychological, environmental, and social influences.[30] Your parents, your education system, your friends, your genes, your decision to watch reruns of Archie Bunker, or your regular viewing of *The Colbert Report* (which parodies what *All In the Family* vividly portrayed) will not single-handedly make you dogmatic. Personality is a continuous interaction "of traits, motives, and situational pressures. There is no justification for an 'either-or' position in this area."[31] Past emphases on personality traits as consistent aspects of personality or inconsistent reactions to different situations are, according to the interactionists, both stale. Proponents of both sides are right in the following sense: traits can describe, influence, and predict trends in behaviors with a degree of accuracy that exceeds chance expectations. This is especially so throughout adulthood, when traits stabilize. On average and over time, some people will consistently be "more sociable, or nervous, or talkative, or active than others. And when the situation changes, those differences will still be there."[32] Shoring up the situation side of the debate, psychologists also agree that "with respect to *momentary* [my italics] behaviors, the situation side is right: Traits do not predict, describe, or influence behaviors very strongly."[33]

Walter Mischel, a staunch advocate of the situationist view in 1968, has extensively modified and expanded his earlier position. He now sees personality as a multidimensional system in which thoughts and emotions temporarily alter behavior. Mischel's cognitive-affective personality system (CAPS) assumes that personality is a relatively stable network that includes the individual's

> goals, expectations, beliefs and affects, as well as self-regulatory standards, competencies, plans, and strategies. Each individual is characterized by a relatively stable activation network among the units within the system, reflecting the culture and subculture, as well as the individual's social learning history, genetic endowment, and biological history (e.g., temperament).[34]

Mischel, the main proponent of the situation theory some forty years ago, has turned the debate he started on its head—an excellent example of open-minded, cognitive elasticity.

We can safely conclude that dogmatism is not an isolated part of one's personality system. It is organized within the whole of one's genes and biology, which interact with environmental conditions, institutions, social relationships, and learning. As an adult, if you were placed in a life-threatening situation that demanded obedience to some dogma, you might *pragmatically* acquiesce and pose as an ardent supporter of the group—a posturing that outsiders might view as dogmatic. Yet once the pressure of the situation lifted, you would return to your original, more flexible approach to ideas and situations—unless you already had the trait of dogmatism or were strongly leaning in that direction.

In short, our personality traits are characteristic ways of responding that each of us assumes, accurately or inaccurately, will maintain our psychological equilibrium. They remain relatively fixed—we are not going to be open-minded on Wednesday but dogmatic on Monday and Tuesday.[35] But how are we to think about the many people who seem rigidly opinionated about a particular belief system but change their minds and conclude, in a thunderbolt of awareness, "I'm seriously mistaken"? According to the psychological definition and research on traits, and given the psychological definition of dogmatism, it seems safe to presume that either these individuals are open-minded and do not have the enduring trait of dogmatism, or that they will quickly kick sand in the face of their old belief system and replace it with the unquestioning adoption and dogmatic certainty of a new one (the Silver-Platter Syndrome referred to in chapter 5).

In some cases, persistent social pressure from those we care about may motivate us to alter seemingly intransigent beliefs and behaviors. But it bears repeating that because personality change occurs at the speed of glacial retreat, especially in older adults, and because deep psychological needs and motives underlie behaviors such as dogmatism, enduring change about important, core beliefs are relatively rare.[36] Traits endure throughout the lifespan, and for this reason, "personality psychologists should use traits without apology."[37] As you have gathered, the analysis of dogmatism presented in this book does just that, but it also incorporates an interactional view that considers biology, learning, and the environment as important factors in the development of dogmatism.

THE BIG FIVE: TRAIT THEORY FRESHLY GROUND

For many years now, trait researchers have been collecting data on personality traits. Self, peer, and professional ratings of traits like extroversion and conscientiousness have been subjected to mathematical manipulations in order to identify their common properties. These statistical analyses have yielded five descriptive clusters of universal traits that have since become widely known as the Big Five.[38] Of special interest here, dogmatism is subsumed under the negative pole of Openness to Experience.

While much of the research literature supports the utility of the

Big Five, considerable controversy remains about the underlying structure of each factor, as well as the trait titles (especially the trait of Openness to Experience, which has been previously referred to as Intellect and Culture).[39] Moreover, evidence to support the claim that each trait is an independent measure is lacking.[40] Indeed, a major criticism of distilling personality traits into five factors is that it inevitably reduces the rich complexity of human personality. Yet critics who think five factors are too few[41] are countered by those who think the inclusive criteria of each factor is too broad.[42] Despite these criticisms, trait psychologists continue refining and increasing the predictive value of each Big Five trait construct.[43] Although the model has established empirical links with a variety of personality inventories and has been endorsed by personality researchers from various theoretical orientations, the Big Five (also referred to as the Five-Factor Model) is not a theory per se. It does, however, organize phenomena that can be used as a launching pad for explanatory theory. As such, the Big Five "cannot be easily dismissed and deserves serious theoretical attention."[44] Because dogmatism is subsumed under one of the five poles, it is necessary to summarize this branch of trait theory.

In an effort to interpret the Big Five dimensions of personality, Paul Costa and Robert McCrae organized and integrated more than forty years of empirical studies on personality traits, the findings of which were used to develop their Five-Factor Theory (FFT) of personality.[45] The FFT assumes that personality scores on the Big Five supertraits, each of which consists of six facets, or subtraits, describe personality structures that are universal, stable over time, and heritable. The key (and controversial) assumption of the FFT is that "the basis of traits is solely biological."[46] These biological underpinnings of personality traits influence how individuals adapt to their environment, but "genetics are only one part of the biological influence intended by the FFT. Brain diseases, environmental toxins (e.g., lead), intrauterine hormonal influences, and so on are also potential biological bases of traits."[47] Thus, biology determines traits, which then adapt to the cultural environment. McCrae uses the term *characteristic adaptations* to describe these secondary psychological adaptations, which include "knowledge, skills, attitudes, goals, roles, relationships, schemas, scripts, habits, even the self-concept."[48] According to FFT, these adaptations are expressions of psychological features; they are secondary to personality traits, which are primary, biologically based structures.

§§

To test their hypothesis that traits are biologically based, Costa and McCrae constructed the NEO-PI scale,[49] and a later, revised scale, the NEO-PI-R,[50] to measure each of the Big Five constructs. Additionally, they hoped to eliminate much of the redundancy in existing personality questionnaires that measure overlapping properties of similar traits. After compiling the data from various studies, McCrae and Costa concluded that the Big Five crop up consistently throughout many cultures, whereas other traits occur less frequently. Thus, these five personality factors are not only universal, they are central to personality.[51] Because the NEO-PI-R has also established sound empirical associations with other widely used personality tests, its usefulness is now broadly accepted among personality theorists from various orientations. After more than twenty years of research on the Big Five, the consensus among psychologists who study personality today is that five major universal traits do indeed capture the essence of personality "motives, schemas, plans, and presumably other variables that must be invoked to account for human individuality."[52] This Five-Factor Model is therefore considered a useful taxonomy of human behavior and can provide a foundation on which to build causal theories of personality.

Perhaps the greatest contribution of the Big Five and the Five-Factor Theory is that they illustrate the relatedness of personality constructs. The case could be made for categorizing traditional personality constructs in later chapters—Erikson's *basic mistrust,* Horney's *moving against,* Roger's *incongruence,* Adler's *striving for personal superiority*, and Maslow's *D-love*—as subtraits of a positive or negative pole of one of the Big Five traits. For example, Adler's striving for superiority could be subsumed under the negative pole of Agree-ableness. Dogmatism, as defined in this book, is considered an aspect of Closedness—the opposite pole of Openness to Experience, as defined in the next section.

THE BIG FIVE PERSONALITY TRAITS AS MEASURED BY THE FIVE-FACTOR THEORY[53]

Factor 1: Openness to Experience (referred to as *O*, this trait has formerly been referred to as *Intellect and Culture*)

Openness to Experience consists of one's desire to seek and appreciate new experiences for their own sake. This trait also reflects one's degree of tolerance for and exploration of the unfamiliar.

Characteristics of High O Scorers

Characteristics of this trait include being artistic, curious, imaginative, insightful, open to new ideas and values, and original. High scorers have wide interests, vivid fantasies, artistic sensitivity, depth of feeling, behavioral flexibility, intellectual curiosity, and unconventional attitudes.[54] Openness to Experience is "a dimension of personality, not intellectual ability, and many people score high in O without having a corresponding high IQ."[55] Taken together, the subtraits of O suggest tolerance, liberalism, adaptability, flexibility, and a searching, inquiring intellect.[56] People with these attributes are well placed in academia, the media, and business. Related traits are nonauthoritarianism and freedom from dogmatism.[57]

Characteristics of Low O Scorers (referred to as Closedness *or* Closed*)*

Low O scorers are marked by conventional behavior, an unadventurous spirit, an unanalytical mind, narrowness of interests, boorish-ness, and a lack of artistic appreciation. Those who score within the Closed range favor conservative values and repress anxiety.[58] People who are closed to experience are not necessarily defensive or narrow-minded in the sense of being intolerant and judgmental. Rather, they are characterized by a preference for the familiar, practical, and concrete. They also show a lack of interest in experience for its own sake.[59] They may, however, be authoritarian and dogmatic.[60] Just as O does not reflect intelligence per se, neither does Closed necessarily reflect a lack of intelligence.

Factor 2: Neuroticism (referred to as *N*; also known as *Negative Emotionality*, or simply *Emotionality*)

This trait reflects emotional instability rather than emotional stability and adjustment. It identifies individuals who are prone to psychological distress, unrealistic ideas, excessive cravings or urges, and inadequate coping responses.

Characteristics of High N Scorers

High N scorers are worrisome, anxious, angry, hostile, self-conscious, impulsive, insecure, inadequate, depressed, hypochrondiacal, and nervous in general.

Characteristics of Low N Scorers (also described as Emotionally Stable)

Low scorers are described as having a calm, relaxed, even disposition. Their composure indicates psychological stability.

Factor 3: Extroversion (referred to as *E*, is also known as *Surgency*)

The trait of extroversion is determined by the quantity and intensity of interpersonal interactions, activity level, need for stimulation, and capacity for joy.

Characteristics of High E Scorers

Individuals with high E scords are person-oriented, sociable, active, talkative, optimistic, fun-loving, affectionate, assertive, and excitement seeking.

Characteristics of Low E Scorers (labeled Introversion)

Low E scorers are reserved, quiet, aloof, task-oriented, retiring, and timid. They are also described as shy and inhibited.[61]

Factor 4: Conscientiousness (referred to as C)

This trait reveals an individual's degree of organization, persistence, and motivation in goal-directed behavior.

Characteristics of High C Scorers

These individuals are organized, reliable, hard working, persevering, self-disciplined, punctual, scrupulous, neat, ambitious, careful, self-reliant, dutiful, and ambitious.

Characteristics of Low C Scorers

Low C scorers tend to be aimless, unreliable, lazy, careless, lax, negligent, weak-willed, and hedonistic.

Factor 5: Agreeableness (referred to as A)

Agreeableness pertains to the quality of one's interpersonal orientation along a continuum that ranges from friendly and compassionate to oppositional and antagonistic.

Characteristics of High A Scorers

Individuals with this traits are generally soft-hearted, good-natured, trusting, helpful, altruistic, friendly, compliant, modest, tender minded, forgiving, gullible, and straightforward.

Characteristics of Low A Scorers

Low A scorers are characterized as cynical, rude, superstitious, uncooperative, vengeful, ruthless, irritable, manipulative, hostile, and noncompliant.

HOW STABLE ARE THE BIG FIVE TRAITS?

While a range of these five traits exists among people, most adults keep their basic personality traits pretty much intact, despite natural disasters, unstable marriages, loss of jobs, bankruptcy, or serious illness.[62] Studies indicate that some traits are more stable than others, depending on (1) how they are measured, and (2) an individual's life history.[63]

A comprehensive survey on trait stability research drew the following conclusions: (1) with age, traits become increasingly consistent, (2) trait consistency peaks between the ages of 50 to 70, and (3) "the peak after age 50 is high enough to support the conclusion that personality traits are essentially fixed at this age."[64] Early childhood experiences influence the transition from childhood temperaments to adult personality traits,[65] and the consistency of traits is comparatively low in childhood, increasingly more stable during the college years through to age 30, and highly stable between the ages of 50 and 70.[66]

An intermittent reassessment of traits in adults over twenty- to thirty-year periods (known as *longitudinal studies*) suggest that the net effect "of life experiences on personality traits is apparently—nothing!"[67] This claim has stirred considerable controversy. Opponents who challenge the biological basis of traits view trait development as more dynamic and open to change in childhood than in adulthood.[68] The point here is that although there are not modifications in one's genetic blueprint, genetic *expression* can vary over time. Thus, dogmatists can learn to modulate their voices and be less domineering in social settings (a social modification), but proponents of trait stability who assume genetics plays a vital role in behavior predispositions would claim that dogmatic minds are predisposed to be consistently more closed than open. If anxiety is the major precursor to dogmatism, then a biological predisposition for anxiety is a predictor variable for latent dogmatism. Of course, this does not mean that all people who struggle with chronic anxiety become irrevocably dogmatic, but a biological predisposition for anxiety puts them at risk for narrowing their interpretations of childhood experiences, which, along with other factors, predisposes them to dogmatism.

Future research will hopefully stabilize the research pendulum that swings from supporting trait stability to emphasizing trait variation. For now, it seems safe to conclude that stereotypes that, for example, depict all older people as doomed to become "withdrawn, depressed, or rigid are just as unfounded as the naive assumption that with old age comes wisdom."[69] And while the bad news is that people who are dogmatic at thirty are highly unlikely to jump out of their rigid cognitive ruts at fifty, the good news is that those of us who are curious and open-minded in our thirties will not likely become insufferably dogmatic in our older years.

Findings on the stability of the other Big Five factors reveal that Conscientiousness tends to increase with age, with the strongest increase occurring in the second decade. Of the other factors, agreeableness increased during the 30s; Neuroticism declined with age for women but showed little change in men; Openness to Experience showed small declines with age; and Extraversion declined with age in women, but not in men.[70]

As we close this general discussion of the Big Five universal traits, it is important to emphasize that psychologists view all personality traits as multiply determined. Keeping this in mind, we next apply the two traits pertinent to the causes and characteristics of dogmatism.

DOGMATISM AND THE BIG FIVE PERSONALITY TRAITS

Of the Big Five personality traits, two are directly related to dogmatism: Closedness (Closed, or C), which is the opposite of Openness to Experience (O), and Neuroticism (N). We can assume that the negative pole of O and the positive pole of N reflect the essence of dogmatism.

Though I do not assume that dogmatism is itself the polar opposite of O, especially given the lack of consensus as to what O comprises, the descriptive facets of Closed do incorporate several of dogmatism's core characteristics. Closed describes one's cognitive and emotional approach to the surrounding world of people and ideas. It represents a failure to expand one's "breadth, depth, and permeability of consciousness."[71] The extent to which we choose to become absorbed in our world surely reflects both a capacity and willingness to open or close our minds to a variety of ideas and interests, and this tendency is not limited to culture or intelligence.[72]

Closed, as McCrae defines it, acknowledges the work of Rokeach. Quoting McCrae, "There is a very real sense in which this review can be seen as a contemporary elaboration of his [Rokeach's] basic ideas."[73] You will recognize many of the subtraits of dogmatism in McCrae's description of Closed, which

> is manifested in a preference for familiarity, simplicity, and closure. . . . Closed individuals will tend to draw sharp lines between in-group and out-group and prefer the former to the latter—tendencies that will lead to fervent patriotism. They will follow the rules they were taught, including obedience to authority. They will expect that others also follow the rules; if they do not, they will advocate strict punishment, not because they are vindictive but because punishment is the simplest way to enforce conformity. They will have little use for intellectuals or scholars—practitioners of the aptly named "liberal arts"—whose work is of questionable utility. They will regard sex with suspicion, as a dangerously powerful stimulus that must be tabooed to maintain psychic equilibrium and social order.[74]

From this description, we see how McCrae's definition of Closed incorporates the following five characteristics or subtraits of dogmatism: intolerance of ambiguity, defensive cognitive closure, glorification of the in-group and vilification of the out-group, dogmatic authoritarian submission (and its corollary, strict adherence to conventional conduct), and dogmatic authoritarian aggression as it applies to punishment of nonconformists. Those who value conformity favor punishment as a necessary consequence for wrongdoing. However, punishment as seen in the brutal behaviors of dogmatic authoritarian aggression is carried out for complex psychological reasons, as discussed at length in previous chapters.

It is interesting to note that the facets of O are also significantly related (with a negative correlation) to Altemeyer's concept of Right-Wing Authoritarianism (RWA). As expected, people who scored high on the RWA Scale scored significantly lower on all dimensions of O as assessed by the NEO-PI-R.[75] If the RWA is linked to O, and dogmatism is linked to the RWA, then, axiomatically, dogmatism and O are also inversely related traits. If this is the case, the question becomes: Should O's polar opposite of Closed include dogmatism as a facet of that pole?

As it stands, the definition of the negative pole of Closed does not clearly address people who: (1) are threatened by ambiguous information, (2) defensively close their minds to beliefs that differ or conflict with their own, (3) hold their beliefs with rigid certainty, (4) compartmentalize their own conflicting beliefs, or (5) lack personal insight (and its corollary, intolerant rejection of the artistic). Obviously, these people are closed in the FFT sense, and it would therefore seem reasonable to include these characteristics of dogmatism as facets of the Closed dimension of FFT. While this may seem straightforward, incorporating the remaining, equally important characteristics of dogmatism complicates matters in that they would need to be integrated with the other four Big Five traits.

In particular, dogmatism's subtraits of belief-associated anxiety and fear, belief-associated anger, and existential despair are characteristic, emotional extremes that could be subsumed under Neuroticism, while the characteristics of dogmatic authoritarian aggression and arrogant dismissive communication would fit within the negative facets of Agreeableness. The Extraversion Scale has relevance for zealous, dogmatic group messiahs who would anchor the high end of that scale, since this is an auspicious trait for dogmatic leaders needing to advance their cause. In such exceptional cases, we could predict that zealous dogmatists would score low on O and A and high on N, with a very good sprinkling of E. Parenthetically, we could hypothesize that the Big Five trait of Conscientiousness would not be significantly related to any of dogmatism's thirteen characteristics.

A recurrent theme in this book is that anxiety impairs open-minded cognitive processing and is therefore the hallmark of dogmatism. However, high scorers on Neuroticism would experience chronic anxiety, yet they obviously are not all closed-minded as variously described by McCrae, Altemeyer, and myself. But high N's and low O's would certainly be vulnerable to dogmatism. The FFT notes that high scorers on N experience chronic negative moods, and "the recurrent nervous tension, depression, frustration, guilt, and self-consciousness that such individuals feel is often associated with irrational thinking, low self-esteem, poor control of impulses and cravings, somatic complaints, and ineffective coping."[76]

Given this description, I suggest that the facets of Closed and Neuroticism (as measured by the NEO-PI-R) and dogmatism (as measured by Altemeyer's Dogmatism Scale), would correlate nicely. However, significant correlations among these measures could still dodge the essence of dogmatism. People who cling to their beliefs with rigid certainty and fail to see things any other way, even in the face of compelling, contradictory evidence, are not clearly represented in the FFT. At this stage, it seems prudent to leave it to the psychometricians, who measure traits, to empirically decide whether and how to incorporate dogmatism and its various characteristics in the Big Five and its FFT measures.

§§

We could predict that ideological dogmatists—as determined by their scores on the Altemeyer Right-Wing Authoritarian Scale, Zealot Scale, Ethnocentrism Scale, Attitude Toward Homosexuality Scale, Posse-Radicals Scale, and Dogmatism Scale[77]—would also score moderate to significantly high on the following NEO-PI-R scales: the Closed pole of Openness to Experience, the Unfriendliness pole of Agreeableness, Neuroticism (particularly anxiety), and Extroversion. Combined with subscales of the NEO-PI-R, Altemeyer's scales would provide an inclusive battery of tests that could be used to assess dogmatism, individually and collectively, in social institutions, including marriage and the family, politics, education, religion, business management, and the military. Levels of dogmatism could also be examined in social movements that address issues about the environment, abortion, gun control, the death penalty, gay marriage, and any other belief systems about which dogmatists proselytize. High scorers on all of the foregoing measures of dogmatism and its components would epitomize the most extreme dogmatists. Let us hope they don't have pups.

EVOLUTIONARY PSYCHOLOGY AND THE BIG FIVE

Evolutionary psychologists have gone beyond outlining the seven traits that enabled primates to survive (as outlined in chapter 9) to ask the following question: Which of the universal Big Five personality traits have qualities that, in combination with the seven primate traits, are well suited to contemporary social environments—qualities that are adaptive in the psyches of all humans, across time, space, gender, and race?

Openness to Experience/Intelligence

Who will be innovative or astute enough to promote human progress? Will liberal, socialist, or conservative dogma best enhance long-term survival, or will some combination of these traditional political and economic perspectives emerge?

Conscientiousness

Who will complete important tasks? Delegating responsibilities to a conscientious person means the assignment will likely get done in an effective, timely manner, which stands to benefit others.

Extroversion

Who is likely to become powerful, high in status, and influential? Human societies are hierarchical to some degree, and a person high in extroversion is more likely to become a leader than a person with the trait of introversion. It is also personally adaptive to know who is dominant—who has power and status, and whose ally we should become—knowledge that is equally adaptive in helping us avoid antagonizing those with status.

Agreeableness

Who will contribute to group goals by cooperating in a friendly, respectful manner? Can our leader be trusted, or does the group need to maneuver around him or her?

Neuroticism

Who can handle stress? Who will persist, even thrive, in difficult situations, and who will succumb to pressure?[78]

We can now combine the Big Five with the seven evolutionary traits to predict which ones will significantly contribute to dogmatism. They are:

1. Closedness (the negative pole of Openness to Experience)
2. Neuroticism
3. Extroversion
4. Agreeableness
5. Fearfulness (a facet of the Big Five's trait of Neuroticism)
6. Dominance (a negative facet of the Big Five's trait of Agreeableness)
7. Aggressiveness (a negative facet of the Big Five's Neuroticism and Agreeableness)

All of these personality traits influence human survival and reproductive success. We gravitate to people who are creative, self-reliant, scrupulous, responsible, extroverted, friendly, good natured, and emotionally secure. Conversely, we tend to avoid those who have narrow interests and are closed minded, irresponsible, lazy, aloof, uncooperative, and anxious. Evolutionary psychology assumes that evolution plays the major role in determining the existence of these traits, which are broadly based in genetic predispositions (keeping in mind that the environment in which evolution and genes interact shapes their final expression). Evolutionary and environmental experiences mold inherited predispositions into various styles of thought, emotions, and behaviors throughout a lifespan of psychological and personality development.

Open-mindedness is one such style of thought that incrementally evolved as part of higher-order thought mechanisms. By virtue of inherited cognitive circuits that are universal, *Homo sapiens* gained a capaciousness of consciousness and conscience that differentiates us from all living organisms.[79] We are primed by evolution to make assumptions about the nature of the world and the nature of our humanness, particularly given our innate ability for language that enables us to probe inherent psychological strengths and weaknesses.

TRAIT THEORISTS AND PERSONALITY THEORISTS

We conclude this chapter with a brief comparison of trait and personality theory. Other than research that makes a case for the biological basis of traits, trait theorists have offered little in the way of causal explanations for trait-specific behaviors. Their theories are predominantly descriptive. Although trait theory is obviously within the realm of personality, the difference between trait and personality theorists is that personality theorists begin by constructing terms, which they then link to their proposed explanatory theories of personality. For example, Adler used his constructs *feelings of inferiority* and *striving for superiority* to explain human motivation—both of which are reflected in one's *lifestyle*. Horney maintained that, as a consequence of unfortunate parenting experiences and cultural *hypercompetitiveness*, people develop *neurotic trends*, one of which is the neurotic's *moving against* others as part of his or her *search for glory*. Although personality theorists often do not refer to their major concepts as traits, it is hard to see how their concepts differ significantly from concepts such as those proposed by the Big Five.

In a very real sense, psychologists who develop process-oriented, explanatory theories of personality devise major concepts, variously called *personality* or *theoretical constructs*, the names of which may not be found in standard dictionaries. Defensive cognitive closure is one such concept. In the case of dogmatism, it is a subtrait that represents facets of the FFT's construct of Closed, and it corresponds to the dictionary meaning of pigheadedness. However, defensive cognitive closure has a comprehensive psychological meaning that is unique to dogmatism, and it therefore warrants its own nomenclature.

Which brings us to an important point. In this book, the thirteen subtraits of dogmatism are characteristic patterns of thoughts, feelings, and behaviors that describe its essence. These subtraits presumably emerge from four plausible, underlying causes. In other words, dogmatism, as presented here, is a descriptive trait that is linked to plausible, explanatory theory. That clarification is necessary, for much of the criticism of trait theory is that proponents fail to make such explanatory links. For example, the Big Five trait of Extroversion is presumed to exist universally, yet trait theory traditionally offered no explanation for why some people become extroverts and others become introverts.

We should also note, however, that personality theories developed by psychologists are all criticized for their lack of explanatory power. Their presumed causes or influences cannot be conclusively validated by empirical research, even if the premises that underlie their scientific investigations are sound. This is to be expected, because in determining the extent to which genes, biology, social environments, and one's unique learning history contribute to trait development, personality theorists are still on the runway, waiting for flight clearance. Such is certainly the case with dogmatism, inasmuch as the conceptual-causal links presented in this book have yet to be supported by scientific evidence. However, our scientific inability to conclusively link descriptive traits to causal theories does not invalidate efforts to understand their nature. A useful taxonomy of human behavior is the necessary starting point from which causal theories and predictions can be tested.[80]

The next chapter introduces us to influential factors that rob children of a healthy start to understanding themselves, others, and the world around them. You have met Jonah, whose infancy and childhood laid the foundation for dogmatism that, throughout his life, insidiously damaged his relationships, his marriage, and his political career. Chapter 12 begins a journey into the multilayered developmental events that interacted to shape Jonah's potential for dogmatism at a very early age. In his case, those influences were the source of the midlife crisis that smothers him in a "slough of despond."[81]

NOTES

1. S. Pinker, "A Biological Understanding of Human Nature: A Talk with Steven Pinker," *Edge,* http://www.edge.org/3rd_culture/pinker_blank/pinker_blank_print.html (accessed June 29, 2007).

2. G. W. Allport, *Personality: A Psychological Interpretation* (New York: Holt, 1937).

3. L. A. Pervin, *The Science of Personality* (New York: Wiley, 1996), p. 43. Pervin acknowledges the excellent summary of the history of trait theory from 1950 to the present in O. P. John, "The 'Big Five' Factor Taxonomy: Dimensions of Personality in Natural Language and in Questionnaires," in *Handbook of Personality: Theory and Research*, ed. L. A. Pervin (New York: Guillford, 1990), pp. 66–100. Robert McCrae and O. P. John also provide a good historical summary of research in their preface to the FFT and its subsequent applications in "An Introduction to the Five-Factor Model and Its Applications," *Journal of Personality* 60, no. 2 (1992): 175–215.

4. S. C. Cloninger, *Theories of Personality: Understanding Persons*, 2nd ed. (Upper Saddle River, NJ: Prentice-Hall, 1996), p. 233.

5. H. S. Friedman and M. W. Schustack, *Readings in Personality: Classic Theories and Modern Research* (New York: Allyn and Bacon, 2003), p. 162.

6. R. R. McCrae and P. T. Costa Jr., "Toward a New Generation of Personality Theories: Theoretical Contexts for the Five-Factor Model," in *The Five-Factor Model of Personality: Theoretical Perspectives*, ed. Jerry S. Wiggins (New York: Guilford, 1996), p. 69.

7. G. Saucier and L. R. Goldberg, "The Language of Personality: Lexical Perspectives on the Five-Factor Model," in *The Five-Factor Model of Personality: Theoretical Perspectives*, ed. Jerry S. Wiggins (New York: Guilford, 1996), pp. 21–50. These authors make the case that the language of behavior description has served an adaptive, evolutionary purpose.

8. N. Chomsky, *Knowledge of Language: Its Nature, Origin, and Use* (Westport, CT: Praeger, 1986).

9. H. H. Clark and E. V. Clark, *Psychology and Language: An Introduction to Psycholinguistics* (New York: Harcourt, 1977).

10. R. B. Cattell, "The Description of Personality: Basic Traits Resolved into Clusters," *Journal of Abnormal and Social Psychology* 38 (1943): 483.

11. Cloninger, *Theories of Personality*, p. 203.

12. W. Fleeson, "Moving Personality beyond the Person-Situation Debate: The Challenge and the Opportunity of Within-Person Variability," in *Current Directions in Personality Psychology*, ed. Carolyn C. Morf and O. Ayduk (Upper Saddle River, NJ: Pearson Education, 2005), p. 21.

13. B. W. Roberts and W. F. DelVecchio, "The Rank-Order Consistency

of Personality Traits from Childhood to Old Age: A Quantitative Review of Longitudinal Studies," *Psychological Bulletin* 126 (2000): 3–25. These authors provide a comprehensive summary of longitudinal research on the stability of personality traits.

14. Pervin, *Science of Personality*, p. 172. Pervin cautions psychologists not to be overly simplistic about personality change and stability. "We want to be able to consider the continuity, consistency, or coherence that can be present in the midst of apparent change while at the same time leaving room for recognition of radical, discontinuous change" (p. 173).

15. R. R. McCrae and P. T. Costa Jr., "The Stability of Personality: Observations and Evaluations," in *Current Directions in Personality Psychology*, ed. Carolyn C. Morf and O. Ayduk (Upper Saddle River, NJ: Pearson Education, 2005), pp. 3–8. There is a simple explanation for stability in the face of change, say McCrae and Costa: "People adapt to their circumstances rapidly, getting used to the bad and taking for granted the good" (p. 5).

16. American Psychiatric Association, *Diagnostic and Statistical Manual of Mental Disorders*, 4th ed. (Washington, DC: American Psychiatric Association, 1994), p. 428.

17. G. C. Davison, J. M. Neale, K. R. Blankstein, and G. L. Flett, *Abnormal Psychology: Canadian Edition* (Etobicoke, ON: Wiley, 2002). These authors reference studies that support this claim (p. 198). They also note that consistent evidence supports the prediction that a healthy dose of intelligence can be protective because it is linked to effective coping skills.

18. The *Diagnostic and Statistical Manual of Mental Disorders* considers a reasonable time frame to be one month. During this time, if stress is disruptive and debilitating, the person is diagnosed with the acute stress disorder. After one month, if symptoms persist, a diagnosis of post-traumatic stress disorder is warranted.

19. McCrae and Costa, "The Stability of Personality," p. 206.

20. J. J. Conley, "The Hierarchy of Consistency: A Review and Model of Longitudinal Findings on Adult Individual Differences in Intelligence, Personality, and Self-Opinion," *Personality and Individual Differences* 5 (1984): 11–26.

21. A. Thorne, "Conditional Patterns, Transference, and the Coherence of Personality across Time," in *Personality Psychology: Recent Trends and Emerging Directions*, ed. David M. Buss and N. Cantor (New York: Springer, 1989), pp. 149–59. Thorne calls these *conditional patterns of personality* that

do not reflect genuine traits, in that they are only expressed in response to certain situations or conditions.

22. L. A. Goldberg, "How Not to Whip a Straw Dog," *Psychological Inquiry* 5, no. 2 (1994): 128.

23. W. Mischel, *Personality and Assessment* (New York: Wiley, 1968).

24. D. P. McAdams and J. L. Pals, "A New Big Five: Fundamental Principles for an Integrative Science of Personality," *American Psychologist* 61, no. 3 (2006): 207.

25. S. Millgram, *Obedience to Authority: An Experimental View* (New York: Harper and Row, 1974). To test people's willingness to obey authority figures, research subjects were duped into believing that they were helping lab-coated researchers examine the effects of punishment on learning and memory. In each study, some of which varied the experimental conditions, teachers (the only true subjects in the experiment) were first required to experience the degree of discomfort that forty-five volts of electricity delivers. The participating teachers were then instructed to administer increasingly intense electric shocks to a mock learner who pretended to make frequent mistakes. The learner was the researcher's confederate, an out-of-view accomplice who play-acted being shocked. In front of the teacher were labels on switches that ranged from "Slight Shock" through several gradations, the last of which was labeled "Danger: Severe Shock, XXXX, 450 volts" (presumably a near-death jolt). Reading a list of word pairs to the confederate learner, who frequently faked mistakes, a distinguished authority figure instructed the naive teacher to "Please continue" administering the shocks when the learner erred. One hundred percent of the subjects pulled the lever labeled "Strong Shock," and zapped the learner with at least 135 volts of punishment. An astounding 62.5 percent of teachers delivered an equally astounding 450-volt "XXXX-rated" shock, despite earlier warnings that the learner had a heart condition. Even though the learner heaved a convincing, painful gasp of "Ugh" over the intercom, the teacher still continued to deliver shocks that ultimately reached the maximum 450 volts. When the accomplice learner screamed, "Let me out of here! My heart's bothering me!" the teacher obeyed the command: "Please go on. The experiment requires that you continue. It is absolutely essential that you continue." Subsequent variations of design placed the teacher between two confederate members of the Teaching Team. When the confederates continued to shock the learner up to the maximum 450 volts, 92 percent of the subjects also obeyed. However, when con-

federates refused to continue shocking the learner after pleas to quit, only 10 percent of the teachers went on to shock the learner at the full 450 volts. Obedience in these altered conditions was influenced more by their peers (Team Teachers' disobedience) than the authority figure. We could assume that the 10 percent who continued following orders even after two members of the Teaching Team stopped obeying would ceiling out on a valid dogmatism scale, especially on those statements designed to assess one's degree of dogmatic authoritarian aggression and dogmatic authoritarian submission. The Milgram and Zimbardo studies can no longer be replicated because the American Psychological Association proposed new ethical standards for the treatment of research subjects shortly after both studies were completed. However, Reicher and Haslam's recent study of group dynamics and the psychology of tyranny (dogmatic, authoritarian aggression) was the first to use permissible ethical procedures to design a mock prison and test the effects of shared identity and values on collective behavior. (See note below.)

26. P. Zimbardo, "On the Ethics of Intervention in Human Psychological Research: With Special Reference to the Stanford Prison Experiment," *Cognition* 2 (1973): 243–56. This article not only gives a synopsis of the prison experiment, it also addresses the arguments levied against "ethically based decisions about interventions in human experimentation" (p. 244). Social psychologists designed a mock prison—the "Stanford County Jail"—in the basement of Stanford University to test the influence of strong situations on common role behaviors of prison guards and inmates. One group of subjects was assigned to positions of prison guard, while the other group became the designated prisoners. Both groups of research subjects were play-acted by university students. Guards were costumed in uniforms and carried handcuffs and billy clubs. The uniformed prisoners were secluded behind metal bars in rooms with bucket toilets and simple cots. The experiment was scheduled to run for two weeks, but guards so fervently adopted their roles they became abusive toward inmates, and within a week the study was abandoned. Equally surprising, inmates became submissive. Twenty-one well-educated, middle-class young men rapidly became sadistic bullies or demoralized victims when they assumed clear roles in these exceptional, strong situations.

27. S. D. Reicher and S. A. Haslam, "Rethinking the Psychology of Tyranny: The BBC Prison Study," *British Journal of Social Psychology* 45 (2006): 1–40. These researchers conducted what came to be known as "The BBC Prison Study," which demonstrated that in times of political instability,

as long as the group perceives it can effect change, members will identify with each other and work together in cooperative, collaborative ways. Whether for moral or immoral goals, the empowering dynamics of group membership can psychologically sway its members to cooperate when they believe they can defend themselves against tyranny. The size of group membership alone gives the group legitimacy in the minds of anxious people. The same researchers suggest that when a social system disintegrates to the extent that citizens lose their group identity and shared values, they become anxious and vulnerable to joining clearly structured groups that are hierarchically ordered. This seems to be the case even if they suspect that by joining the group they will abdicate personal responsibility for assessing the logic of group objectives. These are the circumstances in which the most heinous deeds occur. Historical records provide many examples of this human folly; a notorious example being the collapse of the German Weimar Republic, which paved the way for Hitler and the Third Reich.

28. D. C. Rowe and E. J. Van Den Oord, "Genetic and Environmental Influences," in *Personality: Contemporary Theory and Research*, ed. Valerian J. Derlega, B. A. Winstead, and W. H. Jones (Belmont, CA: Thomson Wadsworth, 2005).

29. Cloninger, *Theories of Personality*. Over the past forty-five years, researchers have applied statistical manipulations (typically, factor analysis) to distill more than 17,000 adjectives in *Webster's New International Dictionary* that describe personality traits into a smaller group that best represents the most common traits. During the 1940s, Raymond Cattell used factor analysis to narrow the field of descriptive adjectives to sixteen source traits (meaning an individual's prominent, central traits) that were presumed to represent the building blocks of personality.

30. Called the *biopsychosocial model*, this model encapsulates the current view that personality is a rich combination of biological, psychological, and social influences that continually interact to shape unique personalities. As a model of illness—physical and psychological—the biopsychosocial view was first proposed in 1977 by Dr. George Engle, a psychiatrist who stated that all clinicians must inquire about the patient's feelings, beliefs, and social relationships to get a complete (or holistic) understanding of the source of their physical illness and psychological (mental) problems.

31. R. Stagner, "Traits and Theoreticians," *Psychological Inquiry* 5, no. 2 (1994): 167.

32. D. Funder, *The Personality Puzzle* (New York: Norton, 2001), p. 86. In chapter 4 of his book, Funder summarizes research from proponents who emphasize the importance of internal traits and proponents who stress the important role of external situations on personality development (this debate has been referred to as the trait-situation debate, the state-trait debate, and the trait-state debate).

33. Fleeson, "Moving Personality beyond the Person-Situation Debate," p. 15.

34. W. Mischel, Y. Shoda, and R. Mendoza-Denton, "Situation-Behavior Profiles as a Locus of Consistency in Personality," in *Current Directions in Personality Psychology*, ed. Carolyn C. Morf and A. Ozlem (Upper Saddle River, NJ: Pearson Education, 2005), p. 12.

35. R. R. McCrae, "Personality Structure," in *Personality: Contemporary Theory and Research*, ed. V. A. Derlega, B. A. Winstead, and W. H. Jones (Belmont, CA: Wadsworth, 2005), pp. 192–216.

36. J. A. Krosnick and D. F. Alwin, "Aging and Susceptibility to Attitude Change," *Journal of Personality and Social Psychology* 57 (1989): 416–25. Change at the individual level is slow; change at the scientific level, slower still. In science, corroboration over years of accumulated research is necessary before paradigm change occurs, since, as noted earlier, revolutionary theories are often met with resistance and skepticism before they are broadly accepted, at which point they are subjected to yet another round of critical analysis. In this development, known as the Hegelian dialectic, one concept (thesis) inevitably generates its opposite (antithesis), and the interaction of these leads to a new concept (synthesis). This in turn becomes the thesis of a new triad of unfolding events. Similarly, the psychology of *being* is fundamental, but it evokes its antithesis, *not being*, which necessitates a synthesis of *becoming*. If this process is rational, it contributes to individual progress. When people seek change through therapy, old thoughts, feelings, and behaviors are exposed to new ideas that, with persistent motivation and practice, create a synthesis of new, more adaptive thoughts, emotions, and behaviors. This goal of therapy does not intend to replace one's entire personality any more than the goal of science intends to replace an entire scientific theory.

37. Fleeson, "Moving Personality beyond the Person-Situation Debate," p. 21.

38. L. R. Goldberg, "Language and Individual Differences: The Search for Universals in Personality Lexicons," in *Review of Personality and Social Psychology*, ed. Ladd Wheeler (Beverly Hills, CA: Sage, 1981), pp. 149–66.

39. "Openness to Experience" has also been labeled and described as "Culture" (L. R. Goldberg 1990; D. Norman 1963; E. C. Tupes and R. E. Christal 1961; J. M. Digman and N. K. Takemoto-Chock 1981; D. W. Fiske 1949; and P. J. Costa and R. R. McCrae 1985).

40. J. Block, "A Contrarian View of the Five-Factor Approach to Personality Description," *Psychological Bulletin* 117 (1995): 187–215.

41. L. A. Pervin, "Further Reflections on Current Trait Theory," *Psychological Inquiry* 5, no. 2 (1994): 169–78. Here, Pervin summarizes his own and others' criticisms of current trait theory, notably the Five-Factor Model.

42. R. M. Ryckman, *Theories of Personality* (Belmont, CA: Wadsworth/Thomson Learning, 2004), pp. 639–40. Ryckman presents a detailed summary of research and outlines the problems inherent in reducing the complexity of personality to five poles or clusters. However, he concludes that "even with its limitations the current five-factor model is an important breakthrough in the study of personality" (p. 641).

43. Mischel, Shoda, and Mendoza-Denton, "Situation-Behavior Profiles as a Locus of Consistency in Personality." These authors state that "perhaps most remarkable is the discrepancy between the bold claims of predictive utility made for trait constructs like those in the Big Five . . . and the low validity coefficients (mean $r = .22$) . . . when examining the sources cited to support them" (p. 158). (Note: r stands for correlation, or the degree to which one variable can be predicted from information about another variable.)

44. D. M. Buss, "Social Adaptation and Five Major Factors of Personality," in *The Five-Factor Model of Personality: Theoretical Perspectives*, ed. Jerry S. Wiggins (New York: Guilford, 1996), p. 181.

45. P. T. Costa Jr. and R. R. McCrae, "From Catalog to Classification: Murray's Needs and the Five-Factor Model," *Journal of Personality and Social Psychology* 55 (1988): 258–65.

46. R. R. McCrae, "Human Nature and Culture: A Trait Perspective," *Journal of Personality Research* 38, no. 1 (2004): 5.

47. R. R. McCrae, e-mail message to the author, October 23, 2006.

48. McCrae, "Human Nature and Culture," p. 5.

49. Costa and McCrae, "From Catalog to Classification."

50. P. T. Costa and R. R. McCrae, *Revised Neo Personality Inventory (Neo-Pi-R) and Neo Five-Factor Inventory (Neo-FFI) Professional Manual* (Odessa, FL: Psychological Assessment Resources, 1992).

51. R. R. McCrae and P. T. Costa Jr., "Validation of the Five-Factor

Model of Personality across Instruments and Observers," *Journal of Personality and Social Psychology* 52 (1987): 81–90.

52. D. P. McAdams, "A Psychology of the Stranger," *Psychological Inquiry 5* (1994): 145.

53. The titles and description of subtraits are compilations of R. R. McCrae and O. P. John 1992; L. A. Pervin 2006 (table 2.2, p. 44); and R. M. Ryckman 2004. The labels and subtraits differ among researchers who interpret them somewhat differently. For a thorough review of these concerns, see R. R. McRae and O. P. John 1992.

54. R. R. McCrae, "Social Consequences of Experiential Openness," *Psychological Bulletin* 120, no. 3 (2006): 323.

55. McCrae and John, "An Introduction to the Five-Factor Model and Its Applications," p. 198.

56. A. R. Hakstian and S. Farrell, "An Openness Scale for the California Psychological Inventory," *Journal of Personality Assessment* 76, no. 1 (2001): 110.

57. McCrae, "Social Consequences of Experiential Openness." In this article, McCrae cites research findings that suggest effective social change requires people who are high in Openness to Experience and low in dogmatism.

58. McCrae and John, "An Introduction to the Five-Factor Model," p. 198.

59. R. R. McCrae and P. T. Costa Jr., *Personality in Adulthood* (New York: Guilford,1990), pp. 41–42.

60. McCrae, "Social Consequences of Experiential Openness," pp. 323–37.

61. Ryckman, *Theories of Personality*, p. 639.

62. W. Mischel, *Introduction to Personality* (Orlando, FL: Harcourt Brace Jovanovich, 1993). Mischel notes that certain traits have stability that begins with early childhood "chain effects" that accelerate and "trigger long sequences of interconnected events that impact on the person's subsequent opportunities and options, often greatly limiting them" (p. 557). Longitudinal studies reveal that ill-tempered boys become ill-tempered men.

63. Pervin, *Science of Personality*, p. 174.

64. Roberts and DelVecchio, "The Rank-Order Consistency of Personality Traits," pp. 4–5. The authors note other research findings on factors that influence trait stability: (1) consistent environments that contribute to personality stability; (2) on the basis of twin studies, inconclusive estimates are

that up to 80 percent of trait stability is due to genetics; (3) certain psychological characteristics contribute to trait stability, such as cognitive and emotional resilience, self confidence, and competent planning; (4) when there is a "goodness-of-fit" between situational demands and psychological capabilities, people consistently interact with their environments in ways that best fit their personalities; (5) a strong sense of personal identity influences trait stability and role consistency.

65. Roberts and DelVecchio, "The Rank Order Consistency of Personality Traits." The authors state that "temperaments tend to be distinguished from adult personality traits in that they are often linked directly to neurobiological functioning at birth, as well as to the early childhood environment" (p. 5). Temperament has also been defined as stable differences in four aspects of infant and child reactivity: (1) physical activity level, (2) emotional arousal, (3) sociability, and (4) aggression and impulsivity. In Friedman and Schustack, *Readings in Personality*, p. 163.

66. Roberts and DelVecchio, "The Rank Order Consistency of Personality Traits." In their summary of longitudinal research on trait stability, these same authors conclude that "trait consistency increased from .31 in childhood to .54 during the college years, to .64 at age 30, and then reached a plateau around .74 between ages 50 and 70 when time interval was held constant at 6.7 years" (p. 3).

67 R. R. McCrae, "Personality Structure," in Derlega, Winstead, and Jones, eds., *Personality: Contemporary Theory and Research*, p. 206.

68. W. Graziano, "Personality Development in Childhood," in *International Encyclopedia of the Social and Behavioural Sciences*, ed. Neil J. Smelser and P. B. Baltes (Elmsford, NY: Pergamon, 2004), pp. 11295–300.

69. McCrae, "Personality Structure," pp. 192–216. Noting the difficulty of conducting valid longitudinal studies, McCrae summarized findings from a number of longitudinal studies, including some that began in the 1960s, and concluded that "individual differences in personality traits are extremely stable in adults, with retest correlations in the .60 to .80 range over periods of up to 30 years." Subsequent research on the Five Factor Model also confirmed these findings in all five factors, in both male and female adults. McRae cites research by Roberts and DelVecchio, whose research shows that "personality is more fluid in younger adults and adolescents" (p. 206).

70. McCrae and Costa, *Personality in Adulthood.*

71. McCrae, "Social Consequences of Experiential Openness." This is McCrae's recent, broad definition of Openness to Experience.

72. Ibid.

73. Ibid., p. 325.

74. Ibid., p. 326.

75. P. D. Trapnell, "Openness versus Intellect: A Lexical Left Turn," *European Journal of Personality* 8 (1994): 273–90.

76. McCrae and John, "An Introduction to the Five-Factor Model," p. 195. McCrae and John summarize McCrae and Costa 1987.

77. R. Altemeyer, *The Authoritarian Specter* (Cambridge, MA: Harvard University Press, 1996). For interested readers, Altemeyer presents all items from these scales in this book.

78. S. J. C. Gaulin and D. H. McBurney. *Evolutionary Psychology*, 2nd ed. (Upper Saddle River, NJ: Pearson Education, 2004), p. 216. Here, the authors present D. Buss's explanation for the socially adaptive features of the Big Five personality traits.

79. L. Cosmides and J. Tooby, "Evolutionary Psychology: A Primer," *Center for Evolutionary Psychology*, http://www.sscnet.ucla.edu/comm/steen/cogweb/ep/EP-primer.html (accessed January 9, 2007).

80. Assuming the measurement criteria are met, an objective questionnaire measures the trait in question such that a person's score accurately locates him or her on a continuum of that trait—a location that allows us to predict how he or she might react to current events (known as *concurrent validity*) or future events (known as *predictive validity*). Both concurrent and predictive validity are examples of *criterion validity*, or the extent to which a test is linked to specific behaviors it is designed to measure and predict. Personality inventories like the Minnesota Multiphasic Personality Inventory (MMPI) measure many traits at once; it has 550 items grouped into ten different scales that assess abnormality. Similarly, the California Psychological Inventory (CPI) groups 462 items into 20 scales that measure such traits as dominance, empathy, self-control, and tolerance.

81. In John Bunyan's novel *Pilgrim's Progress*, the character Christian is so weighted down with guilt that he sinks into a "slough of despond."

Chapter 12

THE DOGMATIST IN THE CRIB

Critical Milestones of the First Two Years

Emotions eventually serve as the architect of intelligence.[1]

The field of developmental psychology lends a deeper understanding to the four proposed causes of dogmatism outlined in chapter 4, briefly restated as: (1) chronic pervasive anxiety that (2) undermines the need to know, which (3) impairs social connections, and (4) diminishes one's sense of personal dignity.

Like all personality traits, dogmatism evolves from a matrix of biological and socialization processes that begin in infancy. Of particular interest is the impact that early pair-bond attachment patterns and the infant's emotional learning have on biological substrates. These complex events and structures interact to play a vital role in the quality of the neonate's (less than one month), and infant's (less than one year)[2] emerging brain systems, social perceptions, and emotional expression. Such are the early biological, emotional, and social interactions that begin to weave a developmental fabric from which personality traits are cut.

Different theorists describe different developmental threads that may cause the fabric to unravel, thus exposing children to any number of disruptive or maladaptive orientations—one of which coheres in adult dogmatism. We begin by examining biological states that influence emotional, cognitive, and social development, all of which conspire to chronicle eventual dogmatism.

PERSONALITY DEVELOPMENT—BIOLOGICAL BEGINNINGS

With architectural brilliance, our genetic inheritance lays the foundation for personality development. Early circumstances and social experiences interact with genes and biology to construct a frame within which personality becomes patterned, and each design is an intricate masterpiece.

Developmental psychologists and neuroscientists who study the nervous system examine the impact of neurological and biochemical differences on the brain's emerging emotional and cognitive functions. Babies' nervous systems respond to their surroundings in a manner consistent with their biology, and the unique sequencing of events program their brain development throughout infancy and childhood. Biology thus sets the stage for early temperament, which is "a rubric for several noncognitive, dispositional constructs [that] include activity level, fearfulness, irritability, joyfulness, and a variety of other behavioral tendencies,"[3] or, alternatively, "a tendency to experience and express emotions, including their regulatory aspects."[4] Despite definitional variations, the term *temperament* shares four common features: "the constructs are largely, but not exclusively, emotional in nature; they appear in infancy; they are relatively stable for significant periods of development; and they have biological substrates."[5]

The brain is a self-organizing system.[6] All babies progress through various developmental milestones beginning in utero and throughout early development, during which time the brain grows from approximately 400g at birth to over 1000g at 24 months. As infants express emotions and experiment with behaviors, their brain systems adapt to their internal and external environments by organizing, pruning, and then reorganizing various systems that are biologically designed for specific tasks.[7] During the first two years, rapid spurts of brain organization and growth create astonishing cognitive and emotional development, and, within this organization of experience, infants begin to construct a reality that forms the basis for beliefs about themselves, others, and the world. Here is how researchers explain that adaptive process.

Growth of the newborn's brain proceeds in predictable stages, beginning with the more primitive structure known as the hindbrain or brainstem, which regulates reflex activities that are critical for survival (e.g., cardiac, circulatory, muscular, and respiratory reflexes; sleep; and attention). These nonvoluntary behaviors are largely present before birth, having developed during sensitive prenatal periods when brain neurons moved about before clustering and settling in predetermined locations. The successful migration of neurons depends on genetic endowment and different environmental influences that affect prenatal growth, including the mother's diet, drugs, infections, and her general quality of physical and mental health.

Before birth, some neurons begin to settle in the brainstem, others in the midbrain, and some migrate to the cortex (the outer covering of the brain that is also known as the cerebral cortex).[8] This process forms interconnected networks that coordinate specific functions like balance and vision. Specialized neurons "are designed to change in response to external signals,"[9] and their structures mature with experience such that new and repetitive experiences cause neuronal groupings to become streamlined for specific operations.[10]

At birth, the brain is prepared for a flurry of activity that allows neurons to migrate to specific locations and perform their biologically programmed tasks. Coinciding with this rapid brain development are critical periods, or

windows of vulnerability during which the organizing systems are most sensitive to environmental input [and] there are different critical periods for different functions (e.g., regulation of anxiety, mood, abstract thought) because the different systems in the brain develop (or mature) at different times in the life of the child. Optimal development of more complex systems requires healthy development of less complex systems because these brain systems develop in a sequential fashion, from brainstem to cortex.[11]

During the process known as *synaptogenesis*, dramatic alterations in each neuron's axon, dendrites, and synapse help connect adjacent neurons. These neuronal changes occur in different brain areas at different times and account for

> the developing brain having far more synapses than will be present in the adult brain: one part of brain development consists not of growth, but of "pruning" of the number of synaptic connections between neurons, a process which appears to be a variety of "fine tuning" of the brain in response to environmental stimuli, and results in the reduction of the number of synapses to adult levels.[12]

This onset of accelerated development in different brain regions is indicated by sudden increases in metabolic activity, whereby neurons consume more energy as they mature and connect with adjacent neurons. During these stages of rapid growth, new circuits of neurons develop in a self-organizing process so that the brain forms stabilized structures of neurons, as in the limbic system, for example, whose structure plays a significant role in emotions. The maturation of these various structures depends on quality experiences that stimulate neuronal growth and strengthen connecting brain circuits, especially during rapid spurts of development.

§§

The midbrain, which controls states of arousal and emotion, matures later than the primordial brainstem and works in conjunction with the cerebral cortex, the brain's crowning glory. Also referred to as the neocortex, or simply the cortex, it initially helps babies interpret the sights, sounds, smells, touch, and taste of sensory input, among other functions. The task of the forebrain (part of the cortex) is to make sense of emotions and gradually program cognitive skills such as language and problem solving. But baby's most valuable birthday gift is his or her estimated 100 billion neurons, which are responsible for regulating all mental and emotional life. These neuronal cells are the nervous system's basic building blocks; they are designed to receive and transmit electrochemical messages that code all perceptions and emotions. Added to this astounding intricacy are the trillions of synapses that form an unimaginable brain-wide web that connects each neuron to thousands of other neurons.[13]

Aside from the limbic system, which largely governs emotion, the human cortex mediates functions that involve many complex physiological and mental processes, the maturation of which require prolonged stages of development throughout childhood and adolescence. Brain maturation progresses sequentially, which is to say that first we breathe and eat, then we develop language and social skills. With increased function and practice, we become curious about and skilled at such things as music, art, literature, and manipulating numbers. Consider the state of blissful, romantic love. We often replay moments of togetherness several times over, nostalgically revisiting the tiniest detail of what your partner said or did. Each rehearsal creates chemical changes that are stored in systems associated with thought and mood. Unbeknownst to our partner, and often ourselves, if we remember what our sweetheart said on that first date, it is our rehearsal of detail that accounts for our recall fifteen years later, not our superior intelligence or memory. Learning and memory are facilitated by the rehearsal of new information or cognitive practice. Similarly, repetitive behaviors of gymnastics or violin concertos strengthen active connections of neurons.

Researchers at the National Institute of Mental Health and the University of California have recently concluded that some of these higher-order brain functions are not fully developed until young adulthood.[14] And if, during critical growth periods, the mother's mood is frequently depressed or anxious, she downloads her own program of disruptive emotions onto baby's CD-ROM of biology, upsetting his or her stress-sensitive brain systems. Mom's emotional distress increases the release of her baby's stress hormones, and this causes disequilibrium and dysregulation of brain chemistry. When such disruptions become severe and prolonged, the chemical imbalance can be toxic enough to cause cerebral cell death. Some babies react to this insult by withdrawing and resigning themselves "to the inevitability of overwhelming, even psychically deadening, danger,"[15] as we shall see shortly when we examine theories of attachment.

Fortunately, most early development is not so traumatic, but if, during the first two years of biological, emotional, and social development, the infant encounters three psychological stumbling blocks, normal psychological growth is jeopardized. In response to internal and external threat, it is only natural that infants and young children will gradually develop strategies that shield them from nonsupportive, nonnurturing environments, especially if they have a biological predisposition for anxiety.

BIOLOGICAL PREDISPOSITIONS AND LATENT DOGMATISM

While anomalies in brain structure have been linked to cognitive impairment and reduced sensory processing, the function of specific genes on infant brain structures that govern behavior and temperament is largely unknown. Scientists have yet to determine, for example, how much of the variation in babies' inherent anxiety and reactions to stress (other than the stress of birth) is due to genes alone. Research does, however, indicate that there is a wide range of "individual differences in the tendencies to express the primary emotions."[16] Babies' levels of physiological arousal (heart rate, skin temperature, and brain activity in the prefrontal cortex) and frequencies of crying remain fairly constant over several days.[17] One study compared four-year-olds' degree of introversion with their arousal levels in infancy and found that a significant number of introverted babies who had tense posture and increased heart rate during infancy were more likely to be introverted four years later. Interestingly, none became extroverted. In contrast, infants who were physiologically calm in infancy tended to be uninhibited and sociable at age four, and it was rare for any of them to later become inhibited, shy children.[18] Biological beginnings are thus significant indicators of personality traits.

These findings lend support to a biological basis for the Big Five personality traits and their polar opposites—introversion versus extroversion, emotional stability versus emotional instability, open to experience versus incurious and closed, agreeable and friendly versus antagonistic, and conscientious versus unreliable—the five, universally common personality traits that we examined more closely in chapter 11. Such traits are "heritable, with perhaps 40 to 50 percent of the variation in a typical population tied to differences in their genes."[19] Substantial evidence now supports the claim that many behaviors have a biological basis that governs much of the child's developing brain, including its structure, biochemistry, and function.

Steven Pinker notes that "all the potential for thinking, learning, and feeling that distinguishes humans from other animals lies in the information contained in the DNA of the fertilized ovum."[20] As previously noted, despite their having identical genomes, when one identical twin has a trait, the likelihood the other will also have it is usually no more than 50 percent. Other studies indicate that "genetic differences account for between 20 to 50 percent of the variability of personality within a population."[21] If we consider that it takes only a small amount of genetic variation to produce observable differences in same-species offspring, the degree of personality variance dictated by heritability is powerful enough to play a vital role in determining psychological traits. Rather than alterations in one gene resulting in differences, most psychological traits—such as extroversion, anxiety, and dogmatism—are the result of genes and coding sequences interacting at different loci (fixed positions on chromosomes).[22] To further complicate matters, genetic mechanisms also combine with powerful chemicals—hormones and neurotransmitters—to exert detrimental or positive effects on early development.

Ongoing research on the molecular genetics of specific behaviors will enhance our understanding of the processes involved. As it stands, we have to be content with what little we know about biology's impact on psychological development, whether it be emotional, cognitive, motivational, behavioral, or social. We might conclude that as much as 50 percent of biology predisposes one to develop the specific enduring trait of anxiety that sows the seeds for latent adult dogmatism. What factors account for the other 50 to 80 percent of personality development?

Developmental psychologists note that the brain's early self-organization, referred to earlier, unfolds *in the context of relationships*. A baby's unique brain biology and emotional states influence the mother's (or any primary caregiver's) reactions, and, together, they begin a complex, reciprocal relationship that is crucial to the overall quality of the baby's biological, emotional, and social development. During these interactions, varying states of arousal activate different systems in the developing brain. When babies are emotionally calm, they can explore their surroundings, because the cortex is not being interrupted or bombarded by competing emotional signals from lower systems (the brainstem and midbrain). Alternatively, when they are anxious, these lower systems are activated, and when arousal is unduly prolonged, it interferes with optimal functioning in higher cognitive systems. Parents and caregivers who are alert for signals of emotional distress, who calm the baby before his or her emotions escalate, help the baby's budding brain systems progress through a normal process of maturation.

§§

It was originally thought that emotions emanated primarily from structures in the limbic system, which mediate arousal. More recently, differences of opinion have surfaced regarding the structures involved in emotional processing, and neuroscientists today believe that mechanisms in the limbic system wash over many parts of the brain and therefore have "wide-ranging effects on most aspects of brain functioning and mental processes."[23] What this means is that early on, multiple developing brain systems can so impact childhood and adolescent development that, by adulthood, one's emotions and thoughts reflect habitual personality traits, one of which is dogmatism.

Applying this information to our case study of Jonah, when he became emotionally aroused in infancy, many neuronal systems were activated across his brainstem and midbrain (primarily the amygdala), whether in response to signals from the environment, such as parental frustration, noise, and room temperature, or signals from internal bodily systems and states, such as brain chemistry and hormones that respond to hunger, thirst, and fear. When Jonah became emotionally stressed, an excess of hormones (corticosteroids) circulated throughout his brain—hormones that, in some cases, may have been toxic enough to destroy connections in his maturing limbic system. His biologically excitable amygdala and sympathetic nervous system acted in concert with his frontal lobe—a portion of Jonah's brain that sits over the forehead and coordinates judgment, planning, and working memory—to influence his ability to plan and achieve goals.[24] The prefrontal cortex is the executive center of Jonah's brain; it is clearly affected by emotional experiences that alter gene expression and overall functioning. This interplay of genetics, biology, and experience also influenced Jonah's ability to cope with and recover from stress.

A lack of consistent nurturing and environmental stress can cause abnormalities deep within the midbrain's neural connections. During arousal, potent hormones are released—adrenaline to the body and noradrenalin to the brain. Arousal is filtered through and appraised by the amygdala, a midbrain organ that transmits information (anxiety or fear, for example) to parts of the brain for further evaluation, so that many systems become involved in emotional processing and emotional memory. Through experience, the frontal cortex, which governs emotional reasoning, modulates emotional signals from the amygdala and hippocampus before these signals flood the brain with overwhelming emotion. But if the limbic system and prefrontal cortex are aroused by frequent, prolonged emotions, genes activate the noradrenaline system and the child's emotional resilience is compromised.[25] Excess anger, fear, and depression can shrink the hippocampus (antidepressants presumably forestall this shrinkage),[26] and disrupt normal developmental stages of cognitive, emotional, and social growth.

§§

If anxiety were 100 percent genetically based, then the degree of its presence compared with its degree of absence (what psychologists call *variation*) should correspond to the presence or absence of genes or gene structure. We would then expect that the co-twin of an identical twin who suffers from an anxiety disorder would have the same disorder. Because this is never the case, we can assume that anxiety is not exclusively genetic in nature.

As yet, there is no evidence that specific genes shape, much less determine, specific personality traits. Biological predispositions, yes; biological determinism, no. Jonah's brain may have been preprogrammed for an anxious temperament due to both genetic and intrauterine factors, but his biological predisposition for what Jerome Kagan calls a "high-reactive, inhibited temperament"[27] was not a genetic code that programmed Jonah for latent dogmatism. The wide difference in genetic predisposition and the equally wide variation in their expression allow only tentative assumptions about a relationship between personality traits and infant biology, temperament, and the social environment. Current understanding of these processes, relationships, and differences is, like Jonah, in its infancy.[28]

However, from a biological perspective, we can conclude that, at birth, Jonah had higher-than-average levels of certain neurotransmitters and hormones—biochemicals that lowered his threshold of tolerance for external stimulation and stress. Jonah's biology designed a fragile nervous system that needed extra care and responsive soothing during infancy, and although his parents did not intend to neglect or abuse him, they were clearly uninformed about effective parenting skills and unable to provide a supportive environment that would have cushioned their son's biological vulnerability for anxiety. Consequently, Jonah did not receive the critical emotional care so necessary for children who are biologically at risk for anxiety.

While temperaments differ remarkably at birth, when hypersensitive nervous systems like Jonah's collide with stress from inadequate parenting, optimum growth is surely compromised. In the throw of the genetic dice, Jonah's biological game plan hit an unlucky streak of environmental circumstances that further destabilized his critical periods of development.

Readers will agree that no parent is perfect, and the type of parenting referred to in this chapter is that of extreme, *persistent* inadequate nurturing. Parents who are occasionally overdemanding or critical (meaning all parents), will not permanently alter their children's personality development.

THE BIOLOGICAL IMPACT OF NEGLECT OR ABUSE

Young children with a history of neglect or abuse experience chronic hyperarousal that elevates their hormone levels and causes "chaotic biochemical alterations in the infant brain."[29] The imposition of early abuse, negligence, or trauma on supersensitive biological systems seriously impairs children's ability to sort out their emotions. Their worlds become a heavy, unsettling fog of feelings, and boundaries that separate fantasy from reality may break down. In school, such interference causes deficits in cognitive performance, inappropriate classroom behavior, impaired social relationships, and low self-esteem.[30] This aggregate of misfortune also impairs the development of empathy, an important social skill that helps the child understand the depth of another's distress or suffering. Without empathy, one cannot cultivate close friendships in childhood and intimate relationships in adulthood.[31]

Unlike Jonah, infants who are born with healthy biological predispositions have the necessary base materials that enable psychological development to flourish, especially in nurturing environments. Research documents that nurturing, stimulating environments augment brain connections and increase the density of the cells' dendrites and synapses.[32] Enriched environments unequivocally enrich brain development, which in turn facilitates psychological adaptation. Parents who cradle their infants' biological beginnings in the warmth of soothing, reassuring cuddles thicken their babies' cortical connections and jump-start their emotional resilience. This allows for a depth of age-appropriate cognitive and social skills throughout their infancy and childhood.

We next raise the curtain on psychological experiences that parallel the importance of biological brain growth. In preparation, ask yourself the following question: As a child coming home from school, how did you usually *feel* as you approached the entrance to your home?

THE IMPORTANCE OF EARLY ATTACHMENT SYSTEMS

Throughout the 1970s and 1980s, John Bowlby pioneered a model of emotional, cognitive, and behavioral development in infancy.[33] Bowlby speculated on the consequences of infant and early childhood attachment (pair-bonds), separation, and loss. *Attachment* is defined as "a behavioral system designed to provide proximity to attachment figures, who ensure the protection and hence the survival of offspring."[34] It is also defined as "a close emotional relationship between two persons, characterized by mutual affection and a desire to maintain proximity."[35] Current theoretical refinements and new classifications have evolved since Bowlby's original work, but major categories of attachment endure, providing a sufficient base for understanding the possible role of attachment systems on later personality traits like dogmatism.[36]

Deep within the intricate nexus of Jonah's young brain, social capabilities were unfolding. At birth, his biosocial brain was most suited for a rich social environment that orchestrated other brain systems, and the quality of his interpersonal relationships significantly influenced developing circuits and pathways, especially during sensitive periods of growth.[37] Throughout Jonah's infancy, social interactions began an attachment process that, at its core, depended on parental sensitivity and responsiveness to his early distress signals.

Jonah's anxiety at being separated from his primary caregivers inadvertently shaped his interpretation of key social relationships and influenced his emotional and social development. The general consensus among child psychologists is that mother-child relationships lay a solid foundation for children's emerging views about people and the surrounding world. In turn, their beliefs influence their social behavior and future relationships. Clearly, a psychologically handicapped mother seriously impedes all of her child's psychological development, and this is especially true if her baby's natural development is compromised by a biological predisposition for anxiety. When maladjusted, uninformed, indifferent, or malevolent adults fail to gratify their babies' emotional and social needs, resilience to stress hangs by a thread, jeopardizing emergent social development. By the time these children reach adulthood, they have no memory of early psychological stress that occurred during infancy, when they were unable to secure the care they needed.

Studies reveal that caregivers who cannot create close bonds during the first two years of a child's life increase the child's vulnerability to personality disorders, cognitive difficulties, and fractured intimate relationships in adulthood. These "residuals of early relationship experiences affect later functioning in relationships with the same and other partners,"[38] and such problems are difficult to remedy (which makes the case for professional intervention as early as preschool and kindergarten).[39]

SECURE ATTACHMENT

"Under certain conditions, the attachment system is activated strongly, leading the child to seek and to be satisfied with nothing less than close proximity to and contact with the attachment figure. These conditions include the *full range* of internal and external stressors or threats, for example, illness, fatigue, strange environments and persons, being alone, and the attachment figure's absence."[40]

Securely attached infants expect that their primary caregivers will tend to their needs and offer protection in stressful times, and the strong emotional bond that ensues increases their desire to maintain proximity between themselves and their main caregiver.[41] The central feature of attachment is the infant's desire to maintain proximity to his or her mother, especially when frightened. If, as a result of actual or impending loss, that bond is absent or broken, the infant plunges into extreme distress.[42]

Thus, newborns are biologically primed to seek physical closeness to caregivers as a frontline defense against stress. Mothers who are attuned to their baby's emotional signals and respond with appropriate attention help them acquire "secure attachment during and beyond the neonatal period."[43] Throughout the developing mother-child relationship, "the child is always an active partner in the interaction, signaling when the needs for closeness and protection are present and must be satisfied."[44] An attentive mother can accurately read her baby's growing tension and respond in the context of "mutually attuned selective cueing . . . In this interactive matrix both partners match states and then simultaneously adjust their social attention, stimulation, and accelerating arousal to each other's responses."[45]

At approximately two months of age, a wave of social and emotional experiences are caused by one crucial, newly acquired skill— eye contact. What ensues is "by far, the most potent visual stimulus in the infant's environment."[46] The mother-infant gaze becomes so arousing that the baby must temporarily avert his attention to prevent overstimulation. If Mom is emotionally in step with baby, she allows him a moment to pause and calm himself before resuming another round of playful social connection and emotional learning. During such exchanges, infants and mothers are not generally aware that they are engaging in mutual regulatory systems of arousal.[47] What this means is that mothers who respond to their babies in a synchronous manner enable them to maintain optimum levels of positive social arousal. Each cycle rotates from quiet alertness to exciting connection followed by a pause, until the mother reestablishes engagement and repeats the cycle. These reciprocal, harmonious exchanges facilitate deep, abiding trust and feelings of safety.[48] Mother's ongoing emotional states and parenting skills continuously interact with her infant's biological and psychological states, and these complex exchanges shape the ensuing attachment pattern.[49]

Because a mother's responsiveness to her infant's distress determines the quality of attachment, a parent's ability to accurately monitor her or his own emotions is of critical importance.[50] Parents who approach their distraught babies with calm feelings of tenderness provide secure attachment and create a solid emotional base within which infants' psychological growth, resilience, and resourcefulness are anchored throughout child development, adolescence, and adulthood.[51] Strong attachments in early childhood are the foundation for intimacy in adulthood. Thus, the importance of secure attachment cannot be overstated; it is crucial for healthy psychological development throughout the life span.

Primary caregivers who consistently and appropriately respond to an infant's distress facilitate secure attachment. Without being burdened by anxiety and insecurity, these infants are content to explore and play on their own. At the same time, language development allows parents to gradually teach their babies how to recognize and express their emotional needs. When mutually pleasant emotional exchanges are frequent, mother-infant interactions resonate to optimize rapidly accelerating brain growth, which in turn facilitates the infant's emotional and interpersonal learning. Conditions that enhance development of these early systems have an additional benefit—they increase the infant's desire to cooperate with caregivers, which further strengthens the attachment bond.

By their second year, children are capable of self-reflection. In particular, they can assess their ability to obtain the protection they need—an assessment that shapes their developing beliefs about their own competence and the trustworthiness of others. These beliefs are negatively impacted by separation from the primary caregiver, and it is therefore imperative that daycare workers, nannies, and babysitters understand and respond to anxiety with calm, soothing reassurance. In so doing, they establish trust, which enables infants to resume curious engagement with their environment. Babies, toddlers, and children who feel securely attached become more confident, self-sufficient, and resilient when environmental circumstances disrupt their routines. With secure attachment, parents can gradually move from early, continuous responding to intermittent receptivity.[52]

Optimum attachment is impossible when babies fail to solicit the comforting reassurance that comes from soothing, rhythmic rocking and calm vocalizations. Infants who are left alone in their cribs for extended periods, or who fail to get loving care when they are cold, hungry, anxious, or frightened, "may either withdraw or become hyper-excitable, vigilant, and/or disorganized."[53] Chronic apprehension and insecure attachment makes them feel unsafe and insecure.

A few words are needed about the differences between neglect and abuse. Compared with the volumes of literature on the damaging effects of physical and sexual abuse in childhood, research on the short- and long-term consequences of infant and child neglect is minimal.[54] Yet neglect is the most prevalent form of child mistreatment, so it is not surprising that the lack of research on child neglect has been referred to as the "neglect of neglect."[55] While neglectful parents are psychologically detached and fail to provide their children with necessary and sufficient care, they are not abusive, in that they do not inflict physical and mental cruelty on them.[56] In this sense, neglect contrasts sharply with abuse, for the latter occurs when "needed care is generally provided, but is accompanied by excessive anger, harshness or hostility."[57] Abused children (especially the physically abused) are more likely to come to the attention of intervening authorities, which has made research on the psychological consequences of abuse more feasible than studying the effects of chronic neglect.

INSECURE ATTACHMENT

Prolonged separation from the primary caregiver causes emotional, cognitive, and social disorganization. Frightened infants in unsupportive environments are innately programmed to seek attachment, and if their pleas for protection and closeness are ignored or minimally supported, a serious mismatch occurs between their environment and their innate needs. Unable to manage or reduce their discomfort, these infants experience insecure attachment, causing them to spend much of their mental energy trying to reconnect with the main caregiver. When repeated attempts fail, they may react with clinginess or aggressive confrontation; some become "extremely passive, disconnected, and bewildered."[58] As Mary Ainsworth notes: "To the extent that the environment of rearing approximates the environment to which an infant's behaviors are phylogenetically [species] adapted, his social development will follow a normal course. To the extent that the environment of rearing departs from the environment to which his behaviors are adapted, developmental anomalies may occur."[59]

A large body of evidence conclusively links infant biological predispositions for anxiety to specific attachment patterns.[60] Insecure attachment is one such developmental anomaly in which two types— disorganized or dysregulated attachment—may occur.[61] Infants who rarely smile, and who also exhibit disruptive or demanding behaviors, most likely experienced repeated rejection by caregivers who were emotionally and behaviorally unavailable or inconsistent in their responses.[62] As these infants approach early childhood, they begin to view themselves and others quite differently from their securely attached counterparts, and such perceptions shape their expectations (or internal working models) for later social relations.[63] Worse yet, they consider themselves unlovable and incapable. Struggling to maintain psychological equilibrium in the midst of turmoil, these children learn to mistrust themselves and others because they cannot get past the burdensome thoughts and anxiety that erode their self-confidence. Such emotionally laden appraisals leave them frozen in past insecurities that continually haunt and undermine accurate appraisals of ongoing experience. When this happens to children born with a genetic predisposition for anxiety, biological predispositions interact with social maltreatment to further jeopardize all other critical periods of psychological development in the early, formative years.

§§

A mother is both connected to and independent of her child, and her emotions will vary, especially when she is preoccupied with personal problems. Stress interferes with her ability to appraise and respond appropriately to her child's emotions. For example, one mother might assume that, more often than not, her baby's crying is manipulative attention-seeking. Others will sense an infant's need for connection and consistently respond with cuddling. Still others respond with alternating periods of tender loving care, normal distancing, smothering enmeshment, negligence, and even abuse. Mothers also handle baby's food preferences and dislikes differently. A baby's refusal to eat bananas may be viewed by one mother as a food sensitivity; she shows little concern when her baby spits it out, and then offers a preferred alternative. Another might view the same refusal as willful rebellion and take stern measures to convince the child to eat. Yet another mother becomes overanxious because she sees her child's refusal to eat certain foods as a litany of dislikes the child "inherited from Grandma." Despite these varying parental appraisals and reactions, parents who consistently pamper, neglect, punish, or abuse their children fail to facilitate secure attachment and protection.

Feeling alone in a hostile environment, neglected or abused youngsters apply desperate solutions to diminish or deny aspects of their frightening experiences. Given their inexperience and cognitive immaturity, one adaptive strategy is to repress their thoughts and emotions, for they cannot possibly understand or deal with the relentless anxiety that stems from being made to feel unwanted, uncared for, or worthless. Whatever their strategy, neglected children experience assaults on the attachment system, which foster emotional, cognitive, and behavioral breakdown. Alternating episodes of emotional repression, disengagement, or angry outbursts ensue, yet every failed attempt to gain affection and security increases tension, which eventually becomes consolidated in negative attitudes that are fairly resistant to change.[64] In early childhood, insecure attachment damages their self-concept (what one knows or believes about one's self) and their self-esteem (how they feel about themselves), both of which occur in the context of social cognition (how one thinks about his or her self in relation to others and the world in general). These various aspects of the emerging self form a bouquet of self-presentation that projects a rosy, colorful, or wilted self-image.

By adulthood, insecurely attached children have consistent patterns of approaching and relating to others. Dogmatism is one such pattern—flawed attempts that are to social disconnection in adulthood what desperate attempts for social connection are to early childhood. The dogmatic adult assumes (without articulating it as such) that adopting beliefs and holding them with adamant certainty will compensate for childhood insecurities. But bold assertions go beyond superficial declarations of truth. Dogmatic declarations may silently assert the need for a substitute parent who will compensate for early psychological deprivations and remedy past injustices. Anxiety that is derivative of insecure attachment can foster extreme dependence on others, which increases one's vulnerability for dogmatic, authoritarian submission. Insecure attachment and the ensuing anxiety may also be converted to dogmatic, authoritarian aggression, but whatever the expression of insecure attachment, the final result is persistent feelings of disconnection, powerlessness, and insignificance.

Not recognizing that their early emotional distress is taking its toll on current cognitive, emotional, and social expression, dogmatists continue to believe that a confident portrayal of absolute truth, or of piously rigid, moral beliefs and behaviors will impress others. In the end, their closed-mindedness garners that which they least want and prolongs that which they least received—disrespect, disconnection, and lost dignity.

Few people confront dogmatists with the assertive honesty of Ted, who, you will recall from chapter 2, responded to Winnie's rant about unions with, "It seems to me you're pretty dogmatic about a very complicated dispute." Yet Winnie is innately social. She cares about connecting with others more than proselytizing her dogmatic belief systems, and, in this sense, we can think of her dogmatism as a strategy to obtain the love, respect, and dignity she has longed for since infancy and childhood. Winnie's early psychological deprivations are still seeking resolution through dogmatism—a more complicated, enduring coping strategy than that of insecurely attached children whose dramatic pleas for love and security are obvious. We do not know whether, as a child, Winnie was insecurely attached, but her arrogant dismissal of alternate views and her disdain for people whose ideas differ from hers suggests that such was the case. Consequently, dogmatism has become a rigid, stable component of her personality.

THE EFFECTS OF EARLY ATTACHMENT ON COGNITION AND LATENT DOGMATISM

Specific attachment styles are clearly linked to cognitive abilities. Securely attached children "are more able to generate and capitalize on opportunities for interaction and learning."[65] Relevant to dogmatism, infants who experience secure attachment are better able to assess new information, show greater creativity,[66] and are less likely to have thoughts constricted by prolonged anxiety.[67] As previously mentioned, all of us have an innate need to know, yet we also need to defend against anxiety that interferes with our biological needs to connect socially and acquire dignity. All four needs are facilitated by secure attachment that calms a baby and helps the developing child gradually learn how to take an accurate reading of self, others, and the expanding environment. Conversely, the anxiety from insecure attachment suffocates the need to know and impairs social relationships, which prevents dignity. At some level of awareness, dogmatists may recognize that their posturing as experts does not gain them the respect they desperately seek. However, at a deeper, unconscious level, they are not aware of the extent to which past anxiety and alienation govern their current thoughts, emotions, and behaviors that, in turn, reduce their opportunities for social connection and dignity. Lacking insight, they continue to think, feel, and behave in ways that undermine psychological hardiness and resilience. An unfortunate combination of vulnerable biology and insecure attachment are two of three major impediments to confident, open-minded reasoning.

BABY JONAH'S ATTACHMENT PATTERN

Given Jonah's biography, it is clear that his parents fell short of providing him the necessary conditions for secure attachment. His mother suffered from chronic anxiety (much of which was sustained by marital problems). When Jonah signaled distress, her reaction disturbed those parts of Jonah's developing brain that process emotion and social interaction. Frequent, distressing experiences altered his brain structure, and although Jonah was not yet able to articulate his understanding, his feelings were strong enough to produce this psychological reading of the situation: "I'm helpless, unlovable, and all alone in a very scary place." Unable to rely on his parents to respond with sensitivity that assured protection, Jonah and his parents began a disturbing cycle: the more upset he became the more inadequate his parents' responses, further intensifying Jonah's frustration, sadness, and sense of isolation. He could not depend on his parents to shield him from life's bewildering experiences. Insufficient love and inadequate care, comfort, and soothing all combined with Jonah's biological predisposition for anxiety to tightly weave a tapestry whose threads were impossible to tease apart. Further complicating matters, his father believed that children should be seen and not heard, that letting them cry themselves to sleep at night would make them tough. With a clear conscience, his father's badly informed belief system enabled him to detach himself at the very time when his son's critical periods of emotional and social growth needed responsive nourishing. Such paternal detachment only strengthened Jonah's feelings of insecure attachment.

Thus, Jonah's biological temperament met with inadequate social experiences and a tense home environment that collectively put him on a path to insecure attachment. With language acquisition, he began to articulate thoughts about his parents and people in general—thoughts that became stored in brain circuits. Insecure attachment ensured that his thoughts would become increasingly narrow, unreflective, and simple.[68] In Jonah's case, his perceptions and expectations gradually revealed a picture of himself as an unworthy, incompetent child, living with emotionally unavailable parents who were unpredictably rejecting.

Along with Jonah's biological predisposition for anxiety and inadequate parenting, a further damaging consequence emerged. His childhood emotions so bombarded his daily thoughts and constricted his ability to think and reason clearly that he lacked confidence in his ability to elicit the care he needed. Of the first three developmental milestones that are so important to psychological health, Jonah was batting zero on two of them. Things were not about to get better.

EMOTION REGULATION IN INFANCY

Does road rage take root in infancy? Only within the last decade have psychologists believed the answer to this question is quite likely yes. It presumably begins with a failure in emotion regulation, the third critical milestone of infant development that parallels the brain's rapid biological development and social attachment patterns.

Over the last thirty-five years, developmental psychologists have emphasized the importance of emotional awareness and regulation for optimum psychological development. Parents and educators have only recently tuned in. For the better part of the twentieth century, the commonsense notion was to react to fretful babies in a manner similar to that of Jonah's parents, who believed that babies would become expert little manipulators if parents consistently calmed their pleas for attention. Fulfill babies' basic needs, yes, but do not give them too much attention, for that will only spoil them.

Developmental psychologists reject that approach to parenting, emphasizing instead that the smooth coordination of emotions and cognitions optimizes problem solving. Emotions fuel thought; they are the basis for elaborate, adaptive, cognitive patterns in infancy, and they are therefore intimately linked to cognitive processing and development.[69] This unified view of progressive emotional and cognitive growth has recently captured the attention of both cognitive and affective neuroscientists.

Throughout human evolution, and within each individual's psychological development, emotion activates and propels reason such that, together, they achieve new levels of healthy neuronal connections and brain organization. But things don't always go smoothly; these processes can also cause neuronal disruption and brain disorganization.[70]

When babies become emotionally distressed they are too inexperienced and cognitively immature to know how to calm themselves, and they must therefore depend on others to teach them to gradually become aware of and take control of their feelings; that is, as much as humanly possible. Infants are genetically primed for emotional expression and responsiveness, and their ability to send emotional signals is innate and adaptive. Such signals "integrate all of the different roots and branches of the intelligence tree, including social and emotional skills, language skills, and visual-spatial thinking skills, as well as a range of cognitive and academic abilities."[71] In the first two years, if babies receive consistent nurturing from caregivers who model adaptive emotional responses, they become incrementally aware of their own, infant emotions. With increasing emotional awareness and sensitivity, optimum learning ensues. In nurturing environments, infants gradually learn that when they signal distress, their mother's response will provide protective, consoling care. With time and experience, they learn more nuanced facial and vocal expressions, all the while enhancing their language comprehension. As they expand their vocabulary, they are better able to convey their feelings with rudimentary language skills, which in turn facilitates their ability to calm themselves. Parents who help their infants and children put words to their vaguely understood emotional distress increasingly fine-tune the infant's knowledge of emotions—information that becomes biologically mapped on baby's developing brain circuits.

The key point is that babies only learn to recognize and regulate their feelings within the context of social interactions. In the presence of a responsive caregiver, they gradually differentiate their emotional reactions to internal states (hunger or cold) and external conditions (angry voices or overstimulation). They then graduate to the more difficult task of learning how to regulate their emotions, and this "adaptation demands a flexible system that can respond in a nuanced manner to its environment (rather than in a fixed, more global manner)."[72]

To facilitate baby's learning of emotion regulation, it is crucial that parents are capable of monitoring and regulating their own states of arousal.[73] Caregivers who cannot disguise their anxiety or irritation dysregulate, accelerate, and intensify the baby's unpleasant emotions to an all-consuming proportion, at which point the infant cannot put his or her emotions aside long enough to pause and think (albeit in rudimentary ways). As they grow older, their prolonged fear and anger prevents them from understanding and articulating their frightened response to people's frowns and scowls, for they cannot cognitively process others' emotions when their own midbrain's emotional frenzy blocks access to their higher-order thinking skills. Prolonged emotional distress thus interferes with a young child's ability to understand the source of his or her frustration and anger. They only know they are upset. Chronic, destabilized emotions interfere with a wide range of abilities, compromising other areas of psychological development, especially during the brain's critical growth spurts.[74]

Within the context of the mother-child attachment system, mothers who are responsive to infant distress successfully facilitate their babies' learning about unknown, sometimes overwhelming, emotions. For although all infants' emotions are biologically primed, learning how to calm themselves when they feel emotionally distraught comes from experience in an emotionally facilitative environment—one that also teaches them the impact their expressed emotions have on others. Here is how mothers facilitate such learning.

An empathic, calm mother reads her infant's growing distress and responds with comforting words of empathy: "Oh Sweetums, you're upset. There, there, it's okay, Mommie's here." This response helps baby pause, and in that *important brief moment of learning*, baby takes a deep breath, hesitates, and gradually becomes aware that his or her emotions need not be so overwhelming. The brevity of that pause is the first baby step on the learning curve of emotion regulation. In nurturing arms and during crucial emotional pauses, baby gradually learns to transform frustration to tolerable annoyance, sadness to disappointment, fear to concern. As mother and baby coregulate and downplay their emotions, the baby becomes increasingly more confident and assertive rather than insecure and angry or withdrawn. This gradual increase in the baby's ability to pause and regulate emotions enables him or her to focus attention such that learning becomes optimized.[75]

In a supportive, loving environment, daily exposure to complex emotional signals to and from their caregivers slowly teaches infants how to communicate and self-regulate their preverbal emotions through a process called "reciprocal, co-regulated emotional interactions."[76] This refers to a type of preverbal, conversation-like communication of emotions that enables mother and baby to communicate and modulate their moods in response to each other's emotional expression. When mothers respond to emotional distress with soothing words, babies learn the first important lesson about pauses—that pauses help them take a breath, which mitigates strong feelings and promotes emotional learning. Babies soon learn, for example, that if they smile at Mommy, they can make Mommy smile back.

Infants who lack secure attachment and emotion regulation discover that when they have a temper tantrum they upset Mommy and keep her busy with them. During this interaction, they develop a rudimentary understanding of causation, which enhances the growth of neurological pathways upon which childhood imagination and curiosity are built—processes that prepare an infant's brain for later, higher-order cognitive skills. Thus, parents who facilitate secure attachment and early emotional learning and regulation confer an educational advantage that promotes adaptive cognitive and social understanding throughout childhood, adolescence, and adulthood.

Such is not the case when parents fail to respond to their babies' moods with calm reassurance. They developmentally arrest their babies' emotional learning such that children remain "locked into global emotional states (catastrophic emotions) and fixed actions."[77] During such emotional upheaval, infants cannot understand the nuances of emotional expression; rage and frustration, sadness and disappointment, fear, anxiety, and concern are largely undifferentiated. This learning failure serves to intensify their distress until they are overcome by uncontrollable chaotic screeches of desperation.

Have you ever noticed that when a baby and his mother are emotionally engaged the baby giggles with joy until he suddenly stops and diverts his gaze, as if to say "that's enough for now, Mom! Give me a rest." In response, if Mom also diverts her gaze, pauses, and gives him emotional space, he soon initiates another round of playful social and emotional exchanges. Conversely, if mom does not recognize baby's subtle emotional cues and, instead, pushes him to continue, baby's delight suddenly turns to frustration and rage. When Mom ignores his signal to pause, baby's feelings escalate until he suddenly finds the game too intense. Earlier squeals of delight become replaced with frantic screams that communicate "Stop it! Leave me alone!" Mom does not understand that when she ignores her baby's need to tune out, calm down, and regroup, she unintentionally overwhelms him. She also circumvents his important emotional learning.

Even adults need time for emotional solitude, but we can manipulate our environment or request that others give us time to ourselves. We also dislike being bombarded with other people's emotional dysregulation, hence the phrase, "Chill out!" Surely, if adults get upset by strong emotions—theirs and others'—baby's emotion commotion is significantly magnified by inexperience and language deficits.

§§

Intelligent behavior depends on the degree to which individuals and groups can successfully understand, regulate, and openly discuss their emotions when it is appropriate to do so. Such effective emotional management facilitates complex problem solving. Those who learn to regulate their emotions in childhood are better able to cognitively focus and build healthy relationships, which require social sensitivity and empathy. When parents encourage their children to talk openly about their feelings, youngsters learn to disclose their emotions and, in the process, become more skilled at reading other people's emotional states. This begins an important process of empathic learning,[78] which facilitates social relationships.

Research also indicates that emotional and social intelligence is critical for analytical approaches to visual-spatial problems, perceptual motor problems, vocal-verbal problems, and other abstract intellectual problems.[79] Further conceptual and empirical work on attachment theory and emotional regulation in the context of a biological predisposition for anxiety could be undertaken in the context of adult dogmatism. This would provide a rich foundation on which to build successful early attachment patterns and emotion regulation that together enhance self-esteem, social connection, dignity, and open-mindedness. Broadly speaking, these early psychological necessities channel an individual's healthy, growth-promoting thoughts, feelings, and behaviors.[80]

By extension, we can assume that when large groups or entire cultures endure years of prolonged fear, they will more likely respond to a leader who can empathize and reciprocate their feelings in an emotionally regulated, nuanced manner. For those adults who have learned to regulate their emotions during early growth spurts of critical brain development, the consequences of not having an empathic leader are not as damaging as they are to the emotionally and cognitively vulnerable. People unskilled in their own emotion regulation, who later join a reactionary or revolutionary movement that is led by a leader with dysregulated emotions, are more susceptible to dogmatic author-itarian aggression or dogmatic authoritarian submission—both of which may have disastrous consequences.

BABY JONAH'S EMOTIONAL LEARNING

When baby Jonah stretched out his arms and fretfully looked to his mother or father for comfort, he was sending emotional signals that conveyed a clear message: "I need you to pick me up, reassure me, and calm me, because I can't yet do that for myself." Unfortunately for Jonah, his mother often reciprocated with a message that signaled: "What's wrong with you? Why can't you settle down?" His father's response was equally insensitive: "Stop it. There's no need to fuss!" Mom's anxiety and Dad's annoyance puzzled and frightened baby Jonah, who tried another round of engagement, to which his parents responded with even less empathy. Their reactions further aggravated Jonah's biological predisposition for anxiety and jeopardized the growth of several developmental pathways in his brain. An incapacity to understand and regulate his emotions during infancy and early childhood likely contributed to his later inability to show or discuss feelings, which caused marital and other problems in later years.

During Jonah's critical periods of early development, his parents fulfilled his basic needs for food and physical comfort, but they did not adequately respond to his psychological needs for consolation and reas-surance during times of emotional distress. They consistently invali-dated or overreacted to his emotional signals, and without experience in reciprocal emotional expressions that would have enabled him to temper his own anxiety, Jonah's emotional discomfort intensified. Anx-iety and frustration are the only available options for a baby whose inexperience cannot assist him in calming his frightening emotions.

Persistent, unregulated emotions cut a wide swath of damage across Jonah's emotional, social, and cognitive development, and by the time he was four years old, he had learned that it was less stressful and more adaptive to smother his anxious confusion rather than give it full reign. This was a clever adaptation to a stressful environment, yet learning how to repress anxiety and rage is not nearly as adaptive as learning to recognize such emotions, manage them, and let them subside—a skill that Jonah's parents could not help him acquire.

Had Jonah's parents responded to his anxious signals by cuddling, rocking, patting, and consoling him with soft, reassuring words, Jonah would have paused long enough to learn that he could lower the intensity of his anxiety. Each similar experience would have consolidated previous learning until Jonah realized that, for the most part, he could manage his emotions. He needn't be deluged with feelings he cannot understand, moderate, or control. Instead, like other children who cannot safely monitor and control their emotions, Jonah found it difficult to understand his feelings, and that difficulty interfered with his ability to learn social skills.[81] It is not surprising that shortly after getting his driver's license, Jonah could not control his anger toward other drivers. To address the question raised earlier in this chapter, emotional regulation in infancy is a good inoculation program against road rage in adolescence.

§§

Psychological theories on the vital role of emotions, which accompany all learning, provide clues to the genesis of psychological dysfunction, including dogmatism. Caregivers who appropriately reciprocate early emotional signals prepare the infant's brain to assimilate raw, unconscious emotions in the amygdala that, in turn, signals higher brain systems. Feelings then become increasingly coordinated with a wide range of mental functions in the developing neocortex.[82] This learning is crucial during times of specialized development.[83] A mother's voice is more than a pleasurable and educational source of stimulation; her nurturing presence enhances the baby's ability to function across all domains of emotion, cognition, socialization, and other behaviors. Thus, the importance of emotion regulation cannot be overstated; it is crucial to an infant's psychological growth, security, and equilibrium, all of which become platforms for future complex social and emotional skills that facilitate open-minded reasoning and healthy relationships. Disruptions in the growth of any of these critical developmental milestones have long-term consequences that impinge on the brain's normal biological processes, on secure attachment, and on emotion regulation.

EMOTIONAL DYSREGULATION AS A PRECURSOR TO DOGMATISM

At the time Rokeach formulated his theory of dogmatism, modern attachment theories and the importance of emotion regulation had not yet been articulated. Yet, in retrospect, Rokeach's original view that cognitive growth flourishes in the absence of prevailing anxiety was not only prescient, it was also consonant with later theories of attachment and emotion regulation. Young children who are predisposed to healthy biological development, who are securely attached and able to regulate their emotions, have flight clearance for open-minded reasoning. During critical periods, development soars and their entire personality becomes progressively more integrated and resilient, as opposed to disintegrated and rigid. A very different picture emerges when developmental disruptions prevent secure attachment and adaptive emotion regulation, which not only jeopardizes the brain growth and integration that is necessary for open-minded reasoning but also impairs social learning.

SUMMARIZING THE THREE CRITICAL MILESTONES THAT APPLY TO BABY JONAH

Pivotal stages in the interacting trilogy of brain biology, infant attachment, and emotion regulation illuminate how Jonah's predisposition for anxiety and his fretful, unanswered pleas for social connection jeopardized his potential for a range of developmental tasks. Success in the first two years of development was crucial to his later ability to understand emotions that arose from his own thoughts about himself, others, and worldly belief systems. Instead, early emotion dysregulation co-incided with Jonah's history of insecure attachment, and together they further stressed his maturing biological systems that had inherent risk factors.[84] Although his early psychological deprivations were not severe, we can assume that they were damaging enough to discourage him from trusting others to help him understand and cope with distress. Jonah's interpersonal connections were also short-circuited, and he subsequently learned that the harder he tried to engage others, the more likely he would be ignored, misunderstood, or chastised.

Insecure attachment during infancy was also fundamental to Jonah's later dogmatism. Feeling apprehensive and incomplete, Jonah relied on external resources to heal the wounds from psychological deficiencies. Incorporating the religious ideology of a group gave him identity and dignity that was self-fulfilling and rewarding. For Jonah, religious devotion symbolized displaced, secure attachment that was absent long ago. We could assume that his need for parental nurturing was displaced onto a holy figure who could repair the wreckage of insecure attachment in infancy. This attachment was so strong that any religious questions were met with defensive, cognitive closure. In Jonah's case, his predisposition for dogmatism was not extreme, but we can well imagine how some individuals might find ideological movements so personally gratifying that even self-sacrifice for the cause becomes a virtue—noble proof of one's incontrovertible beliefs, ideological loyalty, and undeniable worth. In their minds, denied dignity becomes glorified respect.

We can summarize the importance of optimum biology and learning by drawing from accumulated evidence, which shows that psychological health for Jonah and all other infants requires: (1) brain development that is not undermined by biological predispositions for excesses or deficits in hormones and neurotransmitters, or in structural brain abnormalities; (2) an environment that allows the infant to feel securely attached to a primary caregiver; and (3) optimum parenting that teaches the infant how to gradually understand and regulate his or her emotions. Had Jonah been securely attached, and had he learned to self-regulate his emotions, he likely would have been more self-affirming and able to maintain positive, respectful social relationships. These core strengths would have promoted the psychological balance, resourcefulness, and resilience that were developmentally arrested in early childhood.

Additional research is necessary to determine the exact nature of these impacts, but enough evidence exists to conclude that "while experience may alter the behavior of an adult, experience literally provides the organizing framework for an infant and child. Because the brain is most plastic (receptive to environmental input) in early childhood, the child is most vulnerable to variance of experience during this time."[85]

IMPLICATIONS FOR FUTURE DEVELOPMENTS

For all the Jonahs in the world, what we have learned about their early childhood has important long-term consequences. With so much riding on the detection and prevention of early risk factors, the implications for investing in early childhood development are clear. Inadequate funding of daycare, childhood education, and parenting programs imperil us all. "Ghosts from the nursery" haunt ongoing psychological development and create untold perturbations in psychological functioning.[86] Ultimately, these deficits can lead to fractured relationships with friends and family, inadequate job performance, marital breakdown, and mental health problems. And dogmatism.

Future research needs to address some fundamental questions. First, to what extent do biological predispositions for anxiety interact with early childhood attachment difficulties such that they jeopardize emotion regulation and cognitive development? When and how do deficiencies in these childhood needs begin to foment ideas that later morph into rigid, dogmatic belief systems? Longitudinal studies that tie these early developmental anomalies to adult dogmatism are needed before we can adequately answer these questions.

Having surveyed three major developmental sources that build the foundation of psychological development in infancy, we next examine traditional personality theorists who have made significant contributions to understanding traits like dogmatism. Chapter 13 begins the first of several theories on the fascinating dynamics that shape personality beyond infancy, drawing from important concepts that have relevance for dogmatism. Ideas presented in this chapter are linked throughout chapters 13 to 16, which expose the environmental fault lines that fracture developing minds and predispose them to adult dogmatism.

NOTES

1. S. I. Greenspan and S.G. Shanker, *The First Idea: How Symbols, Language, and Intelligence Evolved from Our Primate Ancestors to Modern Humans* (Cambridge, MA: Da Capo, 2004), p. 50.

2. The actual timelines for defining infancy vary among cultures and professionals, but several sources indicate that infancy lasts up to one year after birth (also known as the babe-in-arms stage, when baby cannot yet walk or talk), followed by early childhood (ages 2 to 5), childhood (ages 6 to 12), and adolescence (ages 13 to 19).

3. H. H. Goldsmith and C. Harman, "Temperament and Attachment; Individuals and Relationships," in *Current Directions in Personality Psychology,* ed. C. C. Morf and O. Ayduk (Upper Saddle River, NJ: Pearson, 2005), p. 118.

4. D. L. Molfese and V. J. Molfese, *Temperament and Personality Development across the Life Span* (Mahwah, NJ: Erlbaum, 2000).

5. Goldsmith and Harman, "Temperament and Attachment," p. 118.

6. A. Schore, *Affect Dysregulation and Disorders of the Self* (New York: Norton, 2003), p. 5.

7. Ibid.

8. Ibid.

9. B. D. Perry, R. A. Pollard, T. L. Blakley, W. L. Baker, and D. Vigilante, "Childhood Trauma, the Neurobiology of Adaptation, and 'Use-Dependent' Development of the Brain: How 'States' Become 'Traits,'" *Infant Mental Health Journal* 16, no. 4 (1995): 273.

10. Schore, *Affect Dysregulation*.

11. B. D. Perry, *Maltreated Children: Experience, Brain Development and the Next Generation* (New York: Norton, 2007).

12. J. Hall, "Neuroscience and Education: A Review of the Contribution of Brain Science to Teaching and Learning," 2005, http://www.scre.ac.uk/resreport/pdf/12 (accessed March 18, 2007).

13. J. P. Pinel, *Biopsychology*, 6th ed. (Boston: Allyn and Bacon, 2006).

14. National Institute of Mental Health, Therapists' Perspectives, "New Imaging Study Reveals Path of Brain Maturation," http://www.4therapy.com (accessed March 20, 2007).

15. J. M. Davies and M. G. Frawley, *Treating the Adult Survivor of Childhood Sexual Abuse: A Psychoanalytic Perspective* (New York: Basic Books, 1994), p. 65.

16. H. H. Goldsmith and J. J. Campos, "Toward a Theory of Infant Temperament," in *The Development of Attachment and Affiliative Systems*, ed. Robert N. Emde and R. J. Harmon (New York: Plenum, 1982), pp. 161–93.

17. A. F. Korner, C. A. Hutchinson, J. A. Koperski, H. C. Kraemer, and P. A. Schneider, "Stability of Individual Differences of Neonatal Motor and Crying Patterns," *Child Development* 52 (1981): 83–90; E. L. Lipton and A. Steinschneider, "Studies on the Psychophysiology of Infancy," *Merrill-Palmer Quarterly* 10 (1964): 102–17.

18. R. Conlan, *States of Mind: New Discoveries about How Our Brains Make Us Who We Are* (New York: Wiley, 1999), p. 41.

19. S. Pinker, *The Blank Slate: The Modern Denial of Human Nature* (New York: Penguin Putnam, 2002), p. 50. These five dimensions of personality traits are known as "The Big Five."

20. Ibid., p. 45.

21. K. J. Saudino, "Moving beyond the Heritability Question: New Directions in Behavioral Genetic Studies of Personality," in *Current Directions in Personality Psychology*, ed. C. C. Morf and A. Ozlem (Upper Saddle River, NJ: Pearson, 2005), p. 57.

22. Pinker, *Blank Slate*.

23. D. J. Siegel, *The Developing Mind* (New York: Guilford, 1999), p. 122; J. LeDoux, *Synaptic Self: How Our Brains Become Who We Are* (Middlesex, UK: Penguin, 2002).

24. Schore, *Affect Dysregulation*.

25. Ibid., p. 115.

26. D. Goleman and the Dalai Lama, *Destructive Emotions: How Can We Overcome Them?* (New York: Bantam Books, 2003), p. 187.

27. J. K. Kagan, "Born to Be Shy," in *States of Mind*, ed. Roberta Conlan (New York: Wiley, 1999), p. 49.

28. A. H. Buss and R. Plomin, *A Temperament Theory of Personality Development* (New York: Wiley-Interscience, 1975). The term *temperament* is generally used to describe biological aspects of personality that are identifiable, characteristic ways of *infant* responding, whereas *personality traits* are relatively consistent, broad patterns of behavior that occur across different situations and remain relatively stable throughout one's lifespan.

29. Schore, *Affect Dysregulation*, p. 119.

30. B. Egeland, "A Longitudinal Study of High-Risk Families: Issues and Findings," in *The Effects of Child Abuse and Neglect: Issues and Research*, ed. Raymond H. Starr and D. A. Wolfe (New York: Guilford, 1991), pp. 33–56.

31. Schore, *Affect Dysregulation*.

32. M. C. Diamond and J. Hopson, *Magic Trees of the Mind: How to Nurture Your Child's Intelligence, Creativity, and Healthy Emotions from Birth through Adolescence* (New York: Dutton/Plume, 1998).

33. J. Bowlby, *Attachment and Loss*, vol. 1, *Attachment* (New York: Basic Books, 1969); *Attachment and Loss*, vol. 3, *Loss, Sadness, and Depression* (New York: Basic Books, 1980).

34. J. Bowlby, *Attachment and Loss*, vol. 2, *Separation*, cited in D. Westin and A. K. Heim, "Disturbances of Self and Identity in Personality Disorders," in *Handbook of Self and Identity*, ed. Mark R. Leary and J. P. Tangney (New York: Guilford, 2003), p. 656.

35. D. R. Shaffer, *Social and Personality Development*, 4th ed. (Scarborough, ON: Nelson/Thomson Learning, 2000), p. 466.

36. K. H. Brisch, *Treating Attachment Disorders* (New York: Guilford, 2002).

37. B. D. Perry, "Childhood Experience and the Expression of Genetic Potential: What Childhood Neglect Tells Us about Nature and Nurture," *Brain and Mind* 3 (2002): 79–100.

38. H. T. Reis, W. A. Collins, and E. Berscheid, "The Relationship Context of Human Behavior and Development," *Psychological Bulletin* 126, no. 6 (2000): 855.

39. S. Goldberg, *Attachment and Development* (New York: Oxford University Press, 2000), p. 124.

40. J. Solomon and C. George, "The Place of Disorganization in Attachment Theory: Linking Classic Observations with Contemporary Findings," in *Attachment Disorganization*, ed. J. Solomon and C. George (New York: Guilford, 1999), p. 392.

41. Goldberg, *Attachment and Development*, p. 135.

42. Perry, "Childhood Experience."

43. Bowlby, *Attachment and Loss.*

44. Brisch, *Treating Attachment Disorders*, p. 15. Brisch discusses the importance of representational and behavioral aspects that interact in the caregiver-child dyadic system. In particular, physically or psychologically handicapped children inevitably influence their caregiver's response, and parental expectations that are dashed or challenged may be "distorted, filtered, ignored, or amplified in such a way so as to prevent sensitive, balanced caregiving responses" (p. 382).

45. Schore, *Affect Dysregulation,* p. 140.

46. Ibid., p. 75.

47. D. N. Stern, *The Interpersonal World of the Infant* (New York: Basic Books, 1985), p. 53.

48. A. Schore, "The Self-Organization of the Right Brain and the Neurobiology of Emotional Development," in *Emotion, Development, and Self-Organization*, ed. Marc D. Lewis and I. Granic (New York: Cambridge University Press, 2000), pp. 155–85.

49. R. C. Pianta, R. S. Marvin, and M. C. Morog, "Resolving the Past and Present: Relations with Attachment Organization," in *Attachment Disorganization*, ed. J. Solomon and C. George (New York: Guilford, 1999), pp. 379–98.

50. Schore, *Affect Dysregulation.*

51. Brisch, *Treating Attachment Disorders.*

52. Greenspan and Shanker, *The First Idea.*

53. Ibid.

54. H. Dubowitz and M. Black, "Child Neglect," in *Child Abuse: Medical Diagnosis and Management*, ed. R. M. Reece (Philadelphia: Lea & Febiger, 1994), p. 161.

55. K.vA. Kendall-Tackett and J. Eckenrode, "The Effects of Neglect on Academic Achievement and Discipline Problems: A Developmental Perspective," *Child Abuse and Neglect* 20 (1996): 161–70.

56. Goldberg, *Attachment and Development*.

57. Ibid., p. 11.

58. Solomon and George, "The Place of Disorganization in Attachment Theory," p. 9.

59. M. D. Ainsworth et al. *Patterns of Attachment: A Psychological Study of the Strange Situation* (Hillsdale, NJ: Lawrence Erlbaum, 1978), p. 9

60. Goldberg, *Attachment and Development*, p. 77.

61. Solomon and George, "The Place of Disorganization in Attachment Theory." Other types of insecure attachment include *avoidant attachment*, where toddlers protest little or not at all when the mother leaves, and then avoid her when she returns. Avoidant children do not appear distressed or upset by the attachment figure's departure. If they become upset, many of them can be comforted by a stranger. When the attachment figure returns, the child does not want a reunion but rather ignores or snubs the attachment figure, and if the child does approach the attachment figure, it is often in a tentative manner. Avoidant attachment applies to approximately 20–25 percent of children. Another type of insecure attachment is that of *anxious-ambivalent attachment*, which is seen in approximately 10–15 percent of children, who anxiously cling to the attachment figure. When she leaves, the child becomes inconsolably upset, and when she returns, the child will first elicit then reject caring contact. For instance, the child may want to be held, but then fight to be released, or the child may cling to the attachment figure while trying to hit her.

62. Ainsworth et al., *Patterns of Attachment*.

63. J. Bowlby, *Separation*, cited in Westin and Heim, "Disturbances of Self and Identity in Personality Disorders," p. 656. An *internal working model* is a mental construct that may be voluntarily or involuntarily evoked. It recalls residual memories of early relationships and potentially affects the quality of later relationships.

64. Solomon and George, "The Place of Disorganization in Attachment Theory."

65. E. Waters, J. Wippman, and L. A. Stroufe, "Attachment, Positive Affect, and Competence in the Peer Group," *Child Development* 50 (1979): p. 828; Goldberg, *Attachment and Development*. Goldberg states that "the most consistent evidence supports the prediction that secure or autonomous individuals will have cognitive advantages over those who are insecure" (p. 167).

66. A. Obholzer, *Security and Creativity at Work* (Philadelphia: Brunner-Routledge, 2001).

67. M. Mikulincer, "Adult Attachment Style and Information Processing: Individual Differences in Curiosity and Cognitive Closure," *Journal of Personality and Social Psychology* 72 (1997): 1217–30.

68. D. J. Siegel, *The Developing Mind* (New York: Guilford, 1999), p. 4.

69. L. A. Stroufe, "Attachment Classification from the Perspective of Infant-Caregiver Relationships and Infant Temperament," *Child Development* 56 (1985): 1–14.

70. Greenspan and Shanker, *The First Idea*.

71. Ibid., p. 247.

72. Ibid., p. 266.

73. Schore, *Affect Dysregulation*, p. 142.

74. C. M. MacLeod, "Anxiety and Cognitive Processes," in *Cognitive Interference: Theories, Methods, and Findings*, ed. I. G. Sarason and G. R. Pierce (New York: Erlbaum, 1996), pp. 47–76.

75. M. Csikszentmihalyi, *Flow: The Psychology of Optimal Experiences* (New York: Harper and Row, 1990).

76. Greenspan and Shanker, *The First Idea*.

77. Ibid., p. 32.

78. D. L. Laible and R. A. Thompson, "Attachment and Emotional Understanding in Preschool Children," *Developmental Psychology* 34 (1998): 1038–45.

79. Greenspan and Shanker, *The First Idea*, p. 248. This developmental description condenses the more comprehensive model of emotion regulation presented by Greenspan and Shanker.

80. J. Hart, P. R. Shaver, and J. L. Goldenberg, "Attachment, Self-Esteem, Worldviews, and Terror Management: Evidence for a Tripartite Security System," *Journal of Personality and Social Psychology* (2005): 999–1013. These authors integrate studies on attachment theory and terror management theory and provide evidence that "much of human behavior is directed toward maintaining a sense of psychological security and minimizing conscious and unconscious apprehension and anxiety about personal vulnerability—including, ultimately, death" (p. 999).

81. P. J. LaFreniere, *Emotional Development: A Biosocial Perspective* (Scarborough, ON: Nelson Thomson Learning, 2000), p. 181.

82. Siegel, *The Developing Mind*.

83. Greenspan and Shanker, *The First Idea*.

84. Schore, *Affect Dysregulation*.

85. Perry, "Childhood Experience," p. 88.

86. R. Karr-Morse and M. S. Wiley, *Ghosts from the Nursery: Tracing the Roots of Violence* (New York: Atlantic Monthly, 1997).

Chapter 13

DIGGING DEEP INTO DOGMATISM

Psychodynamic Perspectives

What you do speaks so loud I cannot hear what you say.
Ralph Waldo Emerson

Chapter 12 familiarized us with three unfortunate developmental handicaps that impact normal development in infancy: a biological vulnerability for anxiety, emotional dysregulation, and insecure attachment to primary caregivers. This chapter introduces the first of three traditional models in the field of personality theory—the psychodynamic view that includes contributions from Alfred Adler, Karen Horney, and Erik Erikson. These theorists provide insight about social forces that begin in early childhood and predispose children like Jonah to incrementally close their minds and develop a patterned view of the world. One such pattern coheres in adult dogmatism.

While it is not my intention to review Freud's theory of personality, it is worth noting his perspective on anxiety, especially since anxiety is considered central to dogmatism. Freud believed that our persistent struggle to curb anxiety causes us to repress thoughts, feelings, and past behaviors. Our major motive is to reduce tension arising from biological and psychological drives—the ideal state that is never achieved due to the constant bombardment of social proscriptions. From the time we acquire language, we learn that it is unacceptable to give full rein to our desires: "If you can't say anything nice, don't say anything at all." "First you work, then you play." Instinctual urges concerning survival, sexuality, and aggression have to adjust themselves to the demands of parents and teachers, whose task is to instill the requirements of social living. An inability to successfully resolve these conflicts leads to neuroticism, by which Freud meant persistent anxiety and guilt.

Much of Freudian theory is dismissed by modern-day psychologists, but most would agree that the personal decisions we make about what to conceal or publicly reveal are often clouded by a hazy if not lazy awareness that blurs and distorts our real motives and emotions.[1] That camouflaged view is reflected in a Buddhist saying: "Just as a finger can't touch itself, the mind can't know itself."[2]

In this chapter, another source of anxiety is considered as important an influence on personality development as the Freudian view of unconscious conflict. When the instinctual desire to know and understand ourselves, others, and the world is contaminated by criticism, sarcasm, scorn, teasing, and punishment, the implied, if not explicit, message is: "You are incapable, unworthy, and unlovable." Children are highly sensitive to such judgments, even if subtly conveyed, because they are physically and emotionally immature and inexperienced. Anxiety floods their stream of consciousness, drowning curiosity and open-minded learning in a sea of emotion. If early corrective intervention is unavailable, their approach to thinking becomes compromised by disruptive emotions. Adults who fail to acknowledge and guard against these profound obstacles to learning unintentionally perpetuate emotions that, if frequent, intense, and prolonged, strip children of their cognitive potential and predispose them to dogmatism in later life.

PSYCHODYNAMIC THEORIES OF PERSONALITY

The psychodynamic theorists (sometimes referred to as post-Freudians or neo-Freudians) challenged Freud's psychoanalytic assumptions about human instincts and unconscious conflict, proposing
instead that cultural institutions and social relationships play a significant role in shaping personality traits such as dogmatism. We now
examine those traditional currents of personality development. As
with all major theorists, we will note their central concepts in italics.

Individual Psychology: Alfred Adler (1870–1937)

"All psychological phenomena are unified within the individual in a
self-consistent manner."[3] This quote, especially the word *self-consistent*, captures the essence of personality from Adler's perspective.
Although aspects of one's personality may appear maladaptive or
fragmented, the whole of one's behavior is unified. From the individual's perspective, this unity makes sense in that his or her
"thoughts, feelings, and actions are all directed toward a single goal
and serve a single purpose. Inconsistent behavior does not exist. If
seen in relation to the final goal of superiority or success, all of a
person's actions are consistent and meaningful."[4]

Adler's individual psychology connects a number of developmental dots to outline a portrait of personality that begins in infancy.
His concepts are highly relevant to a causal theory of any personality
trait, and they shed light on the origins of mistaken goals, one of which
is dogmatism. Different from evolutionary psychology and biopsychology, individual psychology assumes that maladaptive personality
traits are the consequence of predisposing social influences.

Within the first two years of life, infants experience inexorable
feelings of inferiority that stem from conditions of physical smallness,
intellectual immaturity, inexperience, and *organ inferiority* (by which
Adler meant physical handicaps such as poor eyesight or hearing,
health problems, and other physical problems). Obviously, these

youngsters cannot fully process the anxiety that accrues from help-lessness and dependency, but it exists nonetheless. This innate anxiety can work to their advantage or disadvantage, depending on the degree to which adults encourage or discourage their attempts to understand and control events. Successful adjustment depends on how children use their imagination to construct unique narratives about (1) who they are, (2) how trustworthy others are, and (3) the predictability and friendliness of the world around them. This imaginative *creative self* is central to personality development.

Using their creative selves, children author fictions that shape their personal and interpersonal beliefs, their degree of emotional stability, and their behavior goals—all aspects of personality that are well established by the time they begin school. Adler assumed that the con-tent of children's unique narratives determines how they digest and assimilate past, present, and future experiences. Children attach greater importance to those experiences that mesh with their creative narratives of the world. The power of these selective childhood fic-tions lies in children's ability to determine *guiding self-ideals*—goals that they believe will help them master life's challenges and gain a sense of personal significance. Such goals become consolidated in a pattern of behavior that Adler referred to as the *style of life*, or *lifestyle*, which develops as a consequence of inner beliefs and goals as well as environmental influences. "These different lifestyles develop early in childhood. Adler suggested that the lifestyle is pretty clearly estab-lished by the time a child is five years old," at which time we can observe the child's consistent way of thinking, feeling, and acting.[5] In early childhood and beyond, a lifestyle is not clearly articulated, since many of its components and goals are not consciously available to a child. As we shall see momentarily, Jonah did not recognize the under-lying fictions that shaped his inappropriate goal for power over others.

Unlike Freud, who maintained that thoughts, feelings, and behaviors were either conscious or unconscious (a dichotomy that has since fallen out of favor), Adler maintained that unconscious desires could indeed be accessed. "The conscious life becomes unconscious as soon as we fail to understand it—and as soon as we understand an unconscious tendency, it has already become conscious."[6] The key Adlerian point is that personality is shaped by subjective beliefs that may not be accurate representations of external reality because they were formulated during early stages of intellectual immaturity. While children are excellent observers, they are poor interpreters of what they see and experience. They mistakenly interpret the world and their place in it. Moreover, they act as if their perceptions are accurate and unalterable. Some of them remain stuck in faulty conclusions drawn from years of childhood experiences, and they therefore live their lives trying to make reality conform to early childhood perceptions, interpretations, and demands.

Despite a dependence on others for survival, all children are motivated to overcome their dependency on others and achieve unique accomplishments. To compensate for inevitable inadequacies, they begin *striving for superiority*—a biological drive that seeks independence, competence, and mastery. "The striving for perfection is innate in the sense that it is a part of life, a striving, an urge, a something without which life would be unthinkable."[7] This explains the two-year-old's favorite word: "No!" In itself, the Adlerian term *superiority* does not necessarily mean striving to control and dominate others, though one may choose to gain significance in this manner. Rather, it conveys the innate motivation to set goals, aim for perfection, and gain a sense of mastery over our immediate environment.

In adulthood, striving for superiority can reflect unhealthy pursuits that are self-centered, or productive goals that benefit humankind. Regardless of how appropriately or inappropriately we strive to master life's challenges, "The one dynamic force behind people's behavior is the striving for success or superiority."[8] Throughout life, we set goals that promote feelings of significance and determine how we might best contribute to society. In this sense, Adler claimed that we are always moving from *minus* to *plus*—"a striving from incompletion to completion."[9]

Children born into encouraging family, social, and cultural environments develop life-styles that typically reflect productive patterns of *social interest*, which is integral to human nature. This innate need for social contact expands with age and maturity to incorporate the welfare of society.[10] As such, social interest is an important aspect of human evolution that advances the best interests of humanity. However, social interest is only an innate tendency; it must be nurtured in childhood.

Three major life tasks reflect the degree of one's social interest: the ability to contribute to society through productive work; the ability to cooperate, help, and share with others; and the ability to form deeply intimate and satisfying relationships.[11] Problems that occur in any of these three critical areas are always social in nature.[12] "The one factor underlying all types of maladjustment is an underdeveloped social interest. People who lack social interest tend to (1) set their goals too high, (2) have a rigid and dogmatic style of life, and (3) live in their own private world. . . . In short, people become failures in life because they are over concerned with themselves and care little about others."[13]

Children raised in harsh, punitive, or negligent environments create fictions that steer them away from social interest and toward mistaken lifestyles. Of the many types that Adler outlined, the three main mistaken lifestyles are: (1) the *ruling type* who seeks to dominate others, (2) the *getting type* whose goal is to passively depend on others, and (3) the *avoiding type* who sidesteps issues and avoids dealing with them. Unable to understand that problems are best solved by collaborating with and helping others, children employ *safeguarding strategies* that shield persistent anxiety and fears of inadequacy. Moreover, these strategies, or "protective mechanisms such as aggression, withdrawal, and so on maintain exaggerated feelings of superiority."[14] These goals foster social disconnection, which, as outlined in chapter 3, is the third influential factor that shapes dogmatism. They stand in sharp contrast to the lifestyle of the *socially useful type*, who respects and cooperates with others to help build a better community.

From an Adlerian perspective, dogmatic authoritarian aggression and arrogant, dismissive communication are safeguarding tendencies that evolved from early childhood goals of the ruling type, whose goal was to overpower and control others. These childhood goals, which were based on inaccurate perceptions and faulty narratives, also serve to protect a very fragile self-esteem. Unfortunately, such fictions and goals also trick children into believing that if they can dominate and defeat dominating others, they will overcome life's difficulties. While seriously mistaken goals are often modified as a person matures, Adler maintained that mistaken goals are seldom drastically changed. It is impossible to eliminate mistaken goals when you are not conscious of them, or their origins, especially when they have become intricately connected to self-identity. Early strivings that compensated for a child's felt weakness (e.g., believing one is athletically clumsy, unintelligent, or unlikable) persist, now motivating adolescents and adults to behave in ways that help them feel equal or superior to others. The child who felt intellectually incompetent becomes the adult who consistently has to prove that he or she is smarter than everyone else. It is important to note that whether the child was actually less intelligent than other children matters less than how the child felt about his or her perceived incompetence.

When children set inappropriate goals to compensate for relentless *feelings of inferiority*, problems arise. Original, normal feelings of inferiority that become prolonged and exaggerated culminate in an *inferiority complex*—a term first coined by Adler to convey the psychological suffering of children who are unable to overcome perceived inadequacies. Burdened by excessive feelings of inferiority, children create fictions that promote unhealthy *personal strivings for superiority*. Faulty childhood fictions convince children they are weak, incapable losers. Their commensurate goal may be to give up and withdraw, thus avoiding their responsibility to face life's tasks. Other children mistakenly believe that they can overcompensate for their inferiority by trying hard to please everyone. Still others are determined to gain self-worth by bullying younger siblings and classmates, or seeking revenge. These children have all developed what Adler termed a *superiority complex*—the neurotic counterpart of normal striving for superiority and mastery.

Corresponding behaviors accompany all neurotic fictions, creative though they may be. Children then "act-as-if" the stories they tell themselves are the only correct solutions to their problems.[15] Worse yet, because they believe their solutions are unalterable, children rigidly cling to them throughout adolescence and into adulthood, even though their goals are no longer reasonable or appropriate. Their early fictions have become roadblocks to healthy personality, in that they continue to steer them toward mistaken goals, all in the misguided belief that such goals will compensate for perceived weaknesses and, at the very least, gain them social respect and dignity.

Here are some creative fictions that begin in childhood. They are creative in the sense that children construct them in the hope of making sense of their world so that they can solve problems. But fictions are not based on reality.[16]

- "I will feel strong and superior if I dominate and manipulate people to give me what I want."
- "I am only significant if I am noticed, so I will keep others busy with me."
- "If I retreat into the safety of my own world, others won't notice me; they'll never know how stupid I am."
- "If I work hard to please others, I will be liked and cared for."
- "If I get even with others, they will see me as powerful—someone not to mess with."

Do any of the foregoing beliefs reflect social interest? Children cannot design a psychologically healthy lifestyle that incorporates social interest if they are excessively focused on defending themselves. Plagued by inferiority, they are unable to get outside themselves to discover that social interest can be a solution to their problems. Severe childhood inferiority sentences children to prolonged emotional and social immaturity, and Adler's term *inferiority complex* describes the pervasive feelings of anxiety that they struggle to manage.

Any perceived confirmation of their fictitious beliefs gives children a sense of mastery. When parents or peers reward their misguided beliefs and behaviors by, for example, ignoring bullying, reinforcing attention-getting with attention, or praising submissive behaviors, they confirm the child's fictions and goals. And if obedience and narrow-minded beliefs are praised but open-minded thought is discouraged, the theme of the child's creative narrative is often one of deference. People in positions of authority must always be obeyed and respected. When early fictions and goals become strengthened, rigid patterns of thought and behavior become increasingly ingrained.

The Creative Fictions of Dogmatism

With respect to dogmatism, one such adult pattern that emerges from earlier goals is the mistaken belief and goal that "I am safe, respected, and powerful when I get others to agree with me" (a creative fiction that could be modified to include, for example, "people must agree with me and adopt my religious and political beliefs"). Those who feel empowered by dogmatically pressuring others to agree with them may mistakenly confuse coercive acts of agreement with willing compliance and respect.

From an Adlerian perspective, their dogmatism emerges from a misguided but unifying goal that overcompensates for masked feelings of inferiority. In children, a rigid goal to be recognized as right at all costs serves to unite thoughts, emotions, and behaviors in a life-style that, in adulthood, characterizes many of the thirteen characteristics of dogmatism. Goals that drive dogmatism also thwart one's innate predisposition for Adlerian social interest. Future Adlerian research will hopefully correlate creative fictions (today referred to as *narratives*) of childhood and adolescence with various characteristics of adult dogmatism.

To summarize, discouraged children develop unhealthy creative fictions and then act as if their fictions are correct and unalterable. Such rigidity transforms early beliefs into persistent goals that coalesce in lifestyles. Due to a lack of experience and incomplete intellectual development, children's fictions reflect inaccurate appraisals about themselves, others, and worldly beliefs. With anxiety and an inferiority complex hovering in the background, they create narrative themes of imminent danger, failure, or unrealistic power. These rigid fictions continually refuel mistaken goals that preempt personal growth and social interest. From this theoretical view, dogmatism can be understood as a collection of mistaken goals in adulthood that are a reenactment of misguided childhood fictions.

Understanding Jonah's Dogmatism from an Adlerian Perspective

Such was the case with Jonah. According to Adler's philosophy, by the time he was five, Jonah had developed a creative fiction that, though largely unarticulated, went something like this: "It's not safe to question my parents or think for myself because my ideas are always wrong, stupid, or bad. Maybe if I obey my parents and agree with what they say, I will convince them that I am good and loveable." These were the early narratives that guided corresponding goals that Jonah believed would help him master life's early challenges. Instead of overcoming his feelings of inferiority by striving for positive goals (which young children are incapable of determining), Jonah's discouragement pushed him toward a mistaken but understandable goal of submissive compliance. He had discovered that subservience reduced the emotional discomfort of ridicule. In Jonah's uniquely resourceful way, he learned how to overcome a harsh, unpredictable home environment by devoting mental energy to goals that would provide self-protection. By the time he entered first grade, such absorption crowded out curious exploration of new ideas and impaired his ability to socially connect with classmates. A huge "Detour" sign had steered him off the natural path of social interest.

With creative fictions like Jonah's, is it any wonder that he narrowed his thinking and became intolerant of diverse views? Imagine how different things might have been if, during his early years of schooling, Jonah had been exposed to teachers who could effectively edit his childhood fictions about himself, others, worldly events, and ideas. Imagine a teacher skilled in Adlerian techniques who monitors her reactions to Jonah and recognizes how his submissive withdrawal in the early grades makes her feel helpless and discouraged.

Using her emotional reaction as a guide to Jonah's mistaken goals, this teacher could say something along these lines: "Jonah, I notice you are very clever at getting people to leave you alone. That way, they won't expect much from you." In a friendly tone, she added, "In fact you are so good at it you could write a book about it! I think you would like me to ignore you, maybe even give up on you. I am not going to do that. My job this year is to help you enjoy using your good mind to ask questions—and all questions are good ones. Together, we can do some fine schoolwork. What do you think of that idea? Would it be all right with you if I talked to your parents about this? That might sound pretty scary to you, but wouldn't it be cool if you found out that school can be an exciting place to be? School! Cool! Way cool! I am really looking forward to working with you Jonah."[17]

Notice how the teacher used implicit encouragement to give Jonah credit for the goals that made sense to him. In her approach, she effectively modeled the Adlerian concept of social interest that was seriously lacking in Jonah's childhood and adolescence. Even though his fictitious beliefs about people outside the family were somewhat altered during adolescence, they still guided his overriding goal to master life's difficulties and compensate for perceived weaknesses. Jonah adhered to the belief that as long as he never wavered from his parents' convictions—beliefs that would become fixed in his own identity—he could succeed. By volunteering to teach children the gospel, he achieved an important guiding self-ideal that fulfilled his personal strivings for superiority: "I can earn the respect of others by persuading children at church that my religious views are correct and indisputable."

To accommodate his fictitious belief that religious commitment made him superior to others, Jonah adopted a holier-than-thou, smug disdain of nonbelieving classmates. This creative story shaped slightly different goals (what Adler called *guiding self-ideals*) from those derived from earlier childhood fictions ("I'm only safe if I agree with and obey my parents"). Teaching children now enabled him to feel superior—a chosen follower of God's word. He also believed that his prayers would "free those condemned to hell"—further proof of his superiority.[18] Jonah believed that if he regularly prayed for the nonbelievers and sinners in this world, he would be rewarded in heaven. Though he never carefully thought about it, he believed he was on the only true path to eternal salvation. What he failed to observe was the very different effect his religious proselytizing had on others. Unlike Jonah, most parishioners were not deluded by beliefs that made them feel superior to others; church attendance simply rewarded them with social connections that gave meaning and spiritual guidance to their lives.

His choice of a teaching career can be seen as an extension of early beliefs and goals—an ideal opportunity to pressure impressionable children into agreeing with his views and convincing them of his righteousness. Thus, he continued his mistaken goal of the ruling type. Jonah's later career as church superintendent seemed an even better fit for realizing his fictions, but the crowning glory was his political success, which assured him that his creative fictions were absolutely correct—if one has unwavering beliefs in Christ the Savior, prayer, and the power of the church, he or she will be guaranteed respect and dignity, and abundant success and prosperity will follow.

Jonah spent hours imagining how he could help the party enshrine his religious views in political legislation, for that would confirm his creative fictions and goals such that he would finally overcome a lifetime of deep-seated inferiority and accomplish Adlerian completion and perfection. But, as Adler warns, "We must not be confused by the fact that some neurotics seem to be benevolent and wish to reform the whole world. This wish to reform the whole world can be merely a response to a keenly felt minus situation. Where the minus situation is strong, the striving to overcome will also be strong."[19]

Thus we see how, in later years, Jonah's behavior remained consistent with his single childhood goal and sole purpose—striving for personal superiority that he thought would compensate for hidden feelings of inferiority. He took every opportunity to weave religious beliefs into conversations so that he might impress and convert nonbelievers. Not realizing that Jonah needed to subordinate others to his self-righteous morality, others simply saw him as strident and over-bearing. According to the world of Jonah, "in this world, I only count if I can get others to believe what I want them to."

It is unlikely that Jonah was aware of his deepest strivings. It is also unlikely that he recognized how much he operated from the rigid childhood fiction that God, religious doctrine, and prayer would help him master life's difficulties. If he couldn't gain his biological father's love, safety, and respect, the Divine Father would surely bestow such blessings upon him.

Thus, when Jonah listened to the impassioned political speech on stem cell research, he heard it with ears of the obedient child who respected, honored, and obeyed all authority figures. Jonah's mistaken childhood narrative was still striving for superiority and recognition. He was convinced that he could compensate for feelings of inferiority by adopting and obeying religious truths, and this certainty assuaged his anxiety yet satisfied his need to know. These were the fictions that endured, the fictions that eventually inspired Jonah to become politically active with the "only right political party." Unwavering commitment to party views would assure him of social connection and dignity. While the content of his new political fictions differed from earlier ones, the underlying goals remained the same: to achieve superiority over others so that he would win their admiration. In Adlerian terms, Jonah's dogmatism is the result of a number of forces that coalesced in a mistaken lifestyle, which shaped many of dogmatism's thirteen characteristics.

On the surface, it may appear that Jonah had social interest. After all, he was a member of a religious group and a political party whose beliefs and goals were, in Jonah's view, indisputable. However, Adler would view Jonah's type of social connections as hollow. Instead of being motivated by a genuine valuing of close relationships and com-munity ties, Jonah was driven by personal strivings for superiority. Certainly this does not mean that those who attend church regularly do so out of a personal need for superiority. As with all psychological motives, those that are excessively driven are neurotic, a term Adler used frequently. Neurotic churchgoers with *superiority complexes* attend church for appearances, and they feel smugly righteous as they judge parishioners for such things as style of dress, manners, career or academic accomplishments, and social skills. These individuals do not go to church to maximize their social interest, but rather to maximize their psychological survival and minimize self-doubt. We might also note here that Jonah sought personal superiority through extramarital affairs because they presumably confirmed his manhood (Adler called this the *masculine protest* that compensates for deep feelings of inferiority). Whatever the motivating force, his affairs were hardly conducive to Adlerian social interest, nor did they reflect healthy, mature strivings for intimacy and marital cooperation.[20]

Adler helps us understand Jonah's dogmatism as an exaggerated *overcompensation* for persistent feelings of inferiority—all at the expense of social interest. Overcompensation for his inferiority complex is seen in Jonah's mistaken goals that shaped a lifestyle in which he acted as if his truths entitled him to feel superior to others—a posturing that many people found offensive.[21]

Initially, others viewed the adult Jonah as simply determined to convince them of his absolutely correct religious and political views. As is often the case with psychological matters, his audience likely overlooked Jonah's deeper psychological needs. From an Adlerian perspective, his rigid proclamations are much more than attempts to persuade others. Such pronouncements are drastic measures to gain recognition and respect among family and peers, to reduce the anxiety that surfaces from persistent feelings of inferiority that he overcompensated for with creative fictions of overweening pride and superiority. It bears repeating that Jonah was born with the same needs as everyone else, but his early discouragement forced him to fulfill those needs in inappropriate ways. His early fictitious beliefs and mistaken goals arrested reason and logic that would have facilitated decisions beneficial to himself and the social community.

From Jonah's perspective, his thoughts, feelings, and behaviors always had a unitary purpose—to compensate for feelings of inferiority by striving for superiority and setting goals that would master life's difficulties. Unfortunately, Jonah's goals deprived him of social interest and the satisfaction that comes from feeling connected to the larger human community—a connection that is still and deep. Such a connection can only be achieved when one feels grounded in personal security.

What would it take to help Jonah recognize that he needs to change his fictions and goals if he is to replace emptiness with meaning? Adler would have Jonah revisit early childhood fictions that served to determine his past, present, and future. Jonah's goals made sense at the time, but they have since deprived him of the main goal in life that is more gratifying than any other—that of social interest. An Adlerian counselor would help Jonah become aware of his early fictions and mistaken goals by giving him daily assignments that would enhance awareness of how his goals influence his daily thoughts, emotions, and behaviors. This growing awareness would allow him the freedom to change his beliefs and live with social interest and a quiet confidence that would positively affect the lives of those with whom he interacts.

Psychoanalytic Social Psychology: Karen Horney (1885–1952)

Like many psychodynamic personality theorists, Karen Horney believed that the seeds of personality development are sown and watered in early childhood and in full bloom by approximately age five. Her personality theory offers a heuristic variation on the forces and events that shape personality, especially those that concern the role of parenting.

Horney believed that *basic anxiety* that is prolonged and outside the normal range of anxiety has its origins in faulty parenting and societal values that promote unhealthy competition. Addressing the role of parenting, Horney claimed that parents impair their children's psychological development if they are enmeshed in their own problems, are uninformed about parenting skills, or are uncaring, rejecting, or abusive. Certainly these conditions exacerbate the usual anxiety that infants feel as they face a mysterious, new world. The normal development of infant's and young children's minds is disrupted when parents are "dominating, overprotective, intimidating, irritable, overexacting, overindulgent, erratic, partial to other siblings, hypercritical, indifferent, etc. It is never a matter of one independent factor, but always the whole constellation that exerts the untoward influence on a child's growth."[22] Horney called these disruptions and insults to child security and integrity *basic evil*—the most emotionally laden concept in the personality literature. Perhaps it was her own mother's stern, cold parenting that accounted for Horney's choice of words here, for surely overprotective and overindulgent parents are not evil. We would agree, however, with Horney's view that children who are deprived of love and protection develop pervasive feelings of being alone and helpless in a hostile world.

Horney suggested that children initially react to basic evil with *basic hostility*. Because children are biologically and psychologically dependent on their parents yet incapable of understanding their compromised situation, they react to parental ignorance or mistreatment with frustration and anger. Early on, they sense that, in a punitive environment, it is not safe to get angry with individuals on whom you depend for care. Thus, children learn to conceal their basic hostility, but although their anger goes underground, it is never completely or successfully banished. Repressed childhood anger is replaced with feelings of diffuse apprehension or *basic anxiety*—an unwanted consequence of repressed basic hostility. When the source of this anxiety persists, children cannot spontaneously be themselves and successfully relate to others. They begin to construct an artificial, *idealized self* that convinces them they are safe in an unsafe world.

To complicate matters, Horney maintained that children raised in a culture of *hypercompetitiveness*—a society that places a premium on winning—become insidiously driven "to avoid losing at any cost as a means of maintaining or enhancing one's feelings of self-worth."[23] When excessive competition permeates the learning and social environment, it squelches children's natural desires, abilities, and goals, fomenting neurosis, by which Horney meant excessive feelings of anxiety, guilt, and shame. The child becomes neurotic (a term that was frequently used in the middle of the last century) and devotes excessive "energies to the task of molding himself, by a rigid system of inner dictates, into a being of absolute perfection."[24] Note the word *absolute*, which is so common in the dogmatist's lexicon.

Horney wove several other conceptual threads into her psychological theory of personality development—threads that reinforced the black-and-white cloak of dogmatism. To cope with the anxiety of feeling inadequate in a highly competitive, threatening world, children develop various strategies to manage their harsh environmental circumstances. They cleverly craft an *idealized self* that they assume will protect them from the anxiety that criticism and competition triggers. The product of punitive environments that impair effective social learning, these ideal constructions become a caricature of who they really are, and this artificial, protective self eventually obliterates the *real self*—an innate inner source of potential that everyone possesses but is unique to each individual.[25]

The direction the idealized self takes may vary, but it consistently portrays an unhealthy psychological response to a hostile environment that becomes consolidated in one of three exaggerated *neurotic trends,* which stifle healthy personality development. These trends are maladaptive patterns of behavior that neurotics mistakenly believe will solve their basic anxiety. Typically, one option predominates and submerges the other two, but regardless of which neurotic trend takes precedence, all three are designed to resolve deep longings for emotional stability and social safety.

The Three Neurotic Trends and Their Solutions for Safety[26]

Of the three neurotic trends, one that the idealized self may develop is that of excessive *compliance*. Young children, adolescents, and adults who adopt this trend unrealistically and indiscriminately *move toward* other people with obsequious compliance. They have a morbid dependency on others, and in adulthood they seek out partners who are seen as superior and therefore capable of taking care of them. Fragile and helpless, they subordinate their sense of autonomy to others, who define them. Martyrs' self-sacrifice to the manipulative will of others epitomizes this trend. Such self-subordination provides a protective solution to their insufferable anxiety.

In a desperate attempt to prove independence and self-sufficiency, some children begin to abandon their real selves and start *moving away* from others—the second of Horney's neurotic trends. The solution for their basic anxiety is to become detached by psychologically and socially withdrawing from a competitive world that they believe guarantees failure. They find excuses to avoid the pressures of life's challenges, especially those that involve social engagement. While they appear excessively self-sufficient and independent, their excessive need for privacy is considered neurotic, in that it keeps others "outside the magic circle of the self."[27]

Horney's third alternative is the neurotic trend of *moving against*. In this instance, neurotics attempt to dominate others and gain power through hostility, narcissism, and arrogance. They need to be right. They mistakenly believe that their superior competence and mastery will earn recognition and admiration, which will confirm their idealized self-image. Their life motto is, "If I have power, no one can hurt me."[28] This trend redirects the repressed basic hostility they felt toward their parents toward those who are vilified members of an outgroup. They may manipulate and exploit others in order to remove them from the competitive playing field in an attempt to gain personal recognition and power.[29] This neurotic trend has the most relevance for dogmatism, as it reflects deep needs to achieve power, status, and dominance, which are sought through arrogant, dismissive communication and dogmatic, authoritarian aggression.[30]

Horney claimed that those who are markedly stuck in one of the neurotic trends pursue a *search for glory* that also originates in childhood. Children try to perfect specific behaviors with the hope of vali-

dating their fantasized, idealized self. The more fortified their idealized image, the heavier the blockade that obscures aspects of their real,
genuine selves. Basic anxiety prevents them from forming healthy
social relationships such that they subordinate themselves to others,
aggressively dominate them, or become detached and socially aloof.
For such a person, "the degree of blindness and rigidity in his attitudes
is in proportion to the intensity of the basic anxiety lurking within
him."[31] The neurotic becomes driven by a search for glory and preoccupied with a *tyranny of shoulds*—inexorable drives to "endure everything, to understand everything, to like everybody, to always be productive—to mention only a few of these inner dictates."[32]

To this list I would add several characteristics of dogmatism, all of
which are misguided attempts to fulfill an inner search for glory. Each
of dogmatism's thirteen subtraits represents a unique application of
Horney's tyranny of shoulds, as well as *blind spots*—defense mechanisms that block out glaring contradictions in one's thoughts, feelings,
and behaviors.[33] Dogmatists assume that their perfection of each misguided trend, or each characteristic subtrait of dogmatism, will be triumphantly rewarded with social connection, respect, and dignity.

In the process of perfecting one dominant neurotic trend, Horney
claimed that neurotics repress the other two. For example, people with
an excessive need to move toward others repress their normal desire
to achieve success through a natural (versus neurotic) drive to compete and achieve independence. They also have difficulty balancing
this need to please with a normal desire for solitude. In contrast, excessive needs to move away and become detached from others renders the
normal desire for intimacy unfulfilled, because people stuck in the
dominant trend of moving away cannot sustain contact at a deep interpersonal level. Detached from others, they are deprived of the satisfaction that comes with normal strivings for recognition of personal
goals and successes. Finally, the neurotic trend of moving against is
achieved at a psychological price, because the normal need to move
toward and connect with others is repressed. In addition, a neurotic
who moves against others consigns the normal needs for solitude and

independence (normal needs to move away) to the periphery of his or her personality.

In summary, anxious children develop neurotic trends that will preserve their idealized selves and shield them from the discomfort of pervasive, basic anxiety. Unfortunately, their solutions move them in unhealthy trends or directions. Unlike children who can satisfy their curiosity as they safely explore their environment and navigate their social world, children with basic anxiety are hampered in their ability to spontaneously move among the three normal expressions of neurotic trends. Perhaps the most observable feature of any trend is Horney's tyranny of shoulds, which presents clear examples of inappropriate reactions to psychologically unforgiving environments.

In sharp contrast to Horney's neurotics are children who harmoniously blend their desires to autonomously connect and comply with others in such a way that they achieve a measure of recognition that affords healthy independence and self-sufficiency. Generally speaking, most of us do not have histories of parental neglect or abuse, nor have we been raised in hostile environments. Psychologically grounded, we are aware of our different moods and express our desires for interpersonal relatedness by moving fluidly among wanting to approach, confront, or withdraw from others, as appropriate. Because we can successfully balance alternating movements (as opposed to adopting one excessive trend and repressing the other two) we easily move toward, away from, and against others in a style that maintains positive social relationships and personal dignity.

Understanding Jonah From Horney's Perspective

Such was not the case with Jonah. Applying Horney's theory, Jonah's early feelings of basic hostility toward his parents for failing to attend to his needs were soon converted to basic anxiety. At some primitive level, Jonah understood that getting angry with the very people he most depended on would result in punishment. Infants instinctively know they need others, and they initially move toward their parents or caregivers for protection, even when their caregivers are negligent, punitive, or abusive. This need to feel safe is so important that some adults continue to excessively move toward their parents in the enduring hope that they will receive from their parents what they emotionally needed throughout infancy and childhood.

To feel safe in a hostile world and gain affection and approval, young Jonah developed an idealized self that reflected the neurotic trend of excessively moving toward others. Driven by the tyranny of shoulds, his childhood fantasies created a false, idealized image that convinced him that if he complied with authority figures and adopted their beliefs without question, he would be safe in an otherwise unpredictable, unsympathetic world. Unlike children who spontaneously explore their environments and social worlds because they are free from unrelenting anxiety, young Jonah found it difficult to let down his guard and allow his authentic, real self to emerge. While it is normal for children to move excessively towards others in early childhood, by the time they reach adolescence, those who are psychologically adjusted and socially competent—those without basic anxiety—have acquired the ability to reasonably balance all three normal trends of social engagement. Jonah's prolonged basic anxiety in childhood prevented synchronous movement between Horney's three normal trends and an extreme, neurotic fixation on one pattern of social movement.

It is unreasonable and unfair to think of Jonah as a neurotic child, but we can see how his attempts to seek safety gradually became insidiously neurotic in later years, especially in adolescence and adulthood. In Jonah's early childhood, Horney's trend of moving toward fulfilled psychological needs; he responded to conditions in a manner that was normal, not neurotic. He sought comfort and freedom from anxiety by pleasing his parents. However, in a different, adolescent environment, his relationships with classmates were marked by a shift to the neurotic trend of moving against. He was dismissive, even disdainful of those who did not share his religious beliefs, and this rejection of the out-group continued throughout his adulthood. Thus, although Horney would see Jonah as stuck in the moving toward mode in childhood, he subsequently moved against others—his classmates and, later still, his colleagues, political cohorts, the democratic electorate, and the media. Jonah's need to proselytize and dominate conversations were typical of moving against strategies that reflect a need for power, recognition, and admiration—primary modes of relating to others that we commonly see in dogmatic people. His idealized image and search for glory mistakenly assumed that this orientation would earn him respect and dignity.

Given Jonah's personal history, his family's religious group and political affiliation propelled his search for glory and confirmed his idealized image, both of which helped him cope with early childhood deprivation, loss, and buried emotions.

Having applied Horney's theory to the development of Jonah's personality trait of dogmatism, we are left with an important question: To what extent were his religious views and political career driven by a tyranny of shoulds that he assumed would gratify his search for glory, even at the expense of others' civil liberties and democratic freedom?

Ego Psychology: Erik Erikson (1902–1994)

Erik Erikson's psychodynamic theory of personality was derived by developing and organizing eight categories of descriptive traits that unfold in sequential stages from birth to death. Like Adler and Horney, Erikson organized personality traits into constructs (categories with bipolar dimensions) to describe personality development throughout the lifespan. Each of the eight dichotomous poles illustrate children's decisions about themselves and others. At each of the eight stages of psychosocial development, the individual encounters a crisis (by which Erikson meant a turning point in one's life that requires decisions that inadvertently strengthen or weaken one's overall psychological functioning).[34]

Beginning in infancy, the first important decision is whether to basically trust or mistrust others. The choice between *basic trust* and *basic mistrust* is made by approximately the age of two, and it hinges on the quality of care infants receive. Its resolution shapes children's expectations as to whether others will treat them with consistent care, indifference, or hostility. This initial decision is of utmost importance to the success or failure of all subsequent stages.

In a healthy, nurturing family, children who are nurtured and re-affirmed gain basic trust that helps them acquire age-related competencies throughout childhood and beyond. Basic trust provides the necessary platform upon which children gradually mature and build confidence in their abilities to form close friendships; it also gives them confidence to initiate and learn new behaviors. These early friendships are prerequisite to their ability to sustain loving, intimate relationships in adulthood and contribute to the next generation through procreation and work. Two-year-olds who acquire basic trust are more apt to later develop a *sense of autonomy* (versus *shame and doubt*), *initiative* (versus *guilt*), and *industry* (versus *inferiority*) throughout childhood. These first four stages end at adolescence, and although the sequences are invariant, the resolutions or decisions children make along the way remain fairly stable. While there may be some degree of variation, it is limited, since children who are mistrustful do not gain the confidence necessary for Erikson's subsequent stages. For example, they find it difficult to take the initiative and set new, age-related goals that require industrious self-direction and assurance.

During adolescence, four identity conditions emerge. Instead of developing healthy *ego identity,* youngsters who have not resolved earlier crises experience *role diffusion*, whereby they lack a clear identity and firm sense of commitment to goals. In this state, they may feel diffuse boredom, pessimism, irritability, unfocused anger, and feelings of helplessness.[35] While adolescence is a type of moratorium, or waiting period, in which important decisions are entertained, some adolescents prematurely choose *foreclosure*, in which they make strong commitments to specific goals, beliefs, and values without examining whether such uncritical allegiances are in their best interest. Studies show that those who follow the path of foreclosure generally admire their parents and fully endorse their values, without question. If this stage continues well into adulthood, it inclines one toward authoritarianism, rigidity, and prejudice toward others.[36] Dogmatic adults like Jonah would closely approximate this Ericksonian concept. Their personality development reflects a prolonged *identity crisis* in which the adolescent (and later, the adult) "will either have a weak ego and suffer a 'confusion of values' or search for a deviant group to be loyal to."[37]

A very different psychological profile is likely to emerge in adolescents whose environments fostered healthy psychological growth. More inclined to develop a clear sense of *identity* (versus role *confusion*), they feel confident they can achieve *intimacy* (versus *isolation*) as they move from adolescence to young adulthood (ages eighteen to twenty-four). These adults have a relatively consistent, stable sense of self, and they are more likely to successfully master turning points in middle and old age. They choose *generativity* (the ability to contribute to the next generation) over *stagnation*, and *ego integrity* (general satisfaction with one's life despite mistakes and failures) over *despair*. They accept death as part of life and do not cling to resentments or regrets. Erikson claimed that without a solid foundation of basic trust in the first two years of life, children begin to mistrust others and themselves, and they come to doubt their ability to act independently, think independently, and achieve intimacy. They lack dignity as a result of their being uninvolved and noncontributing members of the larger society.

In such cases, trust, autonomy, and identity are impaired. The danger is that the establishment of healthy, autonomous initiatives in later adolescence and adulthood is lost, replaced by an externally defined identity. Those with self-confirmed identities have confidence in their inner continuity—a stable integration and consolidation of earlier stages.[38] Individuals without such clear identities tend to form unhealthy relationships and work in unsatisfying careers. In their senior years, many become bitter and cynical; they stagnate in despair. These are the people whom Erikson assumed were, as children, denied opportunities to develop trusting relationships that would secure autonomous identities, successful relationships, productive careers, and a desire to promote the well-being of the next generation. For Erikson, the breeding ground for all unhealthy personality traits like dogmatism is a paucity of basic trust in the first two years of life—something that was glaringly absent in baby Jonah's early life.

Understanding Jonah from Erikson's Perspective

Jonah's lack of basic trust left him feeling inadequate to the task of determining his own future. Without sufficient parental nurturing, he began to feel diffuse shame and doubt, and he questioned his ability to safely engage his curiosity or make age-appropriate decisions. These first two stages are vital to the subsequent development of autonomy, yet by the time Jonah was three years old he seriously doubted his ability to function competently and independently. Prior to adolescence, Jonah's personality development had formed a pattern of mistrust, shame and doubt, and inferiority—hardly a secure beginning from which to construct a clear sense of identity that would buffer the normal difficulties and disappointments of life. Failing to find a healthy resolution to earlier life stages, Jonah was vulnerable to wholeheartedly adopting his parents' religious beliefs. While it is normal in adolescence to adopt beliefs without seriously questioning their validity, psychologically hardy teens do not interpret all questions about their beliefs as direct blows to their self-esteem and identity. Erikson did not address the trait of dogmatism per se, but I think he would agree that early mistrust in others and, more importantly, mistrust in oneself are the origins of rigid, protective belief systems that can morph into later dogmatism.

Though he did not articulate it as such, Jonah assumed that his religious and political beliefs and efforts would assure a stable identity that would promote generativity and integrity in his later years. Yet because Jonah lacked basic trust, such accomplishments were only marginally within reach. According to Erikson, Jonah's mistrust would have also hindered his ability to form a close, personal bond with his wife—the sixth stage of psychosocial development, in which one moves toward intimacy or isolation. As he approached middle age, he became more cynical and despairing than peaceful and content. Jonah felt that, as Erikson said, "time is too short for the attempt to start another life and to try out alternative roads to integrity."[39]

SUMMARY OF PSYCHODYNAMIC THEORIES

Adler, Horney, and Erikson's theories all stress the importance of parental nurturing and encouragement that provide children a safe environment within which they can optimize their psychological and social development.[40] Psychologists from our next field of personality theory, humanistic and existential psychology, agree that children's views of themselves, others, and the world they inhabit depend on how they are consistently treated throughout childhood and adolescence. Obviously, a few unpleasant experiences in an otherwise supportive home environment, or a few pleasant experiences in an otherwise unsupportive environment, will not put a big dent in the child's conceptual framework of self and others. However, the overall environment, whether it is one of continual support, neglect, or punishment, crafts enduring personality traits, and children who are frequently subjected to inadequate or abusive parenting during their formative years are undoubtedly at risk for impaired psychological functioning. Children whose minds are genetically predisposed to anxiety are surely all the more compromised.

As noted in the previous chapter, the quality of parenting is still considered a critical component of healthy personality growth, even among biopsychologists and recent trait theorists who focus primarily on the genetic determinants of behavior. In his summary of the relative importance of biology and parenting as contributing factors in personality development, David Funder states, "The overwhelming scientific evidence, simply put, is that parents *do* matter."[41] Despite criticisms that the psychoanalytic models presented in this chapter do not lend themselves to scientific analysis, contemporary research continues to investigate unconscious mental processes, the influence of past experiences on current functioning, self-deception, and unconscious conflicts, which lends credence to the ideas put forth by the eminent theorists reviewed in this chapter.[42]

In the next chapter, we shall see that one of the founding fathers of humanistic psychology, Carl Rogers, wholeheartedly agreed that parents play a significant role in their children's personality development. His theory is woven from assumptions that differ from those of the three psychodynamic theorists just surveyed, and readers will find that it has important implications for strengthening their own social relationships at all levels.

We now turn to the ideas of humanistic and existential psychologists, which are relevant to the personality trait of dogmatism.

NOTES

1. V. J. Derlega, B. A. Winstead, and W. H. Jones, eds., *Personality: Contemporary Theory and Research*, 3rd ed. (Belmont, CA: Wadsworth, 2005), p. 13. These authors present the "Two Parents of Personality Psychology" as Sigmund Freud and Wilhelm Wundt, noting that the latter studied physiological phenomena more than broad aspects of personality.

2. S. Batchelor, *Living with the Devil* (New York: Riverhead Books, 2004), p. 99.

3. J. Feist, *Theories of Personality*, 3rd ed. (New York: Holt, Rinehart, and Winston, 1994), p. 125.

4. Ibid. Here, Feist summarizes Adler's idea of psychological unity that fundamentally underlies all goal-directed behavior.

5. B. Engler, *Personality Theories: An Introduction*, 6th ed. (Boston: Houghton Mifflin, 2003), p. 102.

6. A. Adler, *Problems of Neurosis* (New York: Harper Torchbooks, 1964), p. 163. In this explanation, Adler avoids the Freudian dichotomy of the unconscious and the conscious.

7. H. L. Ansbacher and R. R. Ansbacher, eds., *The Individual Psy-*

chology of Alfred Adler: A Systematic Presentation in Selections from His Writings (New York: Basic Books, 1956), p. 104.

8. J. Feist, *Theories of Personality*, 3rd ed. (New York: McGraw-Hill, 1994), p. 125.

9. H. L. Ansbacher and R. R. Ansbacher, *Alfred Adler: Superiority and Social Interest: A Collection of Later Writings* (New York: Norton, 1979), p. 52. This husband and wife team of Adlerian scholars were internationally recognized for their efforts to organize and clarify Adler's ideas. This book is a collection of Adler's later writings.

10. Ibid.

11. Ibid., p. 37.

12. Ibid.

13. Feist, *Theories of Personality*, p. 139.

14. Ibid., p. 737.

15. R. M. Ryckman, *Theories of Personality*, 7th ed. (Belmont, CA: Wadsworth/Thomson Learning, 2004), p. 114. Hans Vaihinger, a philosopher, developed the philosophy of "as-if" in which he maintained that people create imagined ideas that guide their behavior and act as if their ideas are accurate interpretations of events. The central theme is that our goals are based on fictions that may or may not be accurate interpretations of reality, especially since they are developed early in life when experiences and the child's intellect are limited and underdeveloped.

16. D. Dinkmeyer, "The C Group: Integrating Knowledge and Experience to Change Behavior—an Adlerian Approach to Consultation," *Counseling Psychologist* 3 (1971): 63–72. These beliefs that shape childhood goals are adapted from Dinkmeyer. I have included one other goal beyond the four he outlined here: the goal to please others.

17. Dale Johnson is an Adlerian counselor who provided ideas for these Adlerian interventions through an e-mail message to the author, February 5, 2007. In his message, he stressed that the suggested interventions "just scratch the surface of what could be done."

18. Ansbacher and Ansbacher, *Alfred Adler: Superiority and Social Interest*, p. 57.

19. Ibid., p. 90.

20. For Adler's views on marriage, see A. Adler, H. L. Ansbacher, and R. R. Ansbacher, *Cooperation between the Sexes: Writings on Women and Men, Love and Marriage, and Sexuality* (New York: Norton, 1982).

21. A. Adler, *Understanding Human Nature* (New York: Fawcett, 1954). Adler maintained that, to compensate for their deficiencies, children with persistent feelings of inferiority strive for exaggerated feelings of superiority and act as if they were superior to others—a posturing that others dislike.

22. K. Horney, *Neurosis and Human Growth: The Struggle toward Self-Realization* (New York: Norton, 1950), p. 18.

23. Ryckman, *Theories of Personality*, p. 141.

24. Horney, *Neurosis and Human Growth*, p. 13.

25. Ibid., p. 17.

26. The definition and characteristics of these three trends is adapted from Horney, *Neurosis and Human Growth*.

27. S. Cloninger, *Theories of Personality: Understanding Persons*, 2nd ed. (Upper Saddle River, NJ: Prentice-Hall, 1996), p. 165.

28. K. Horney, *The Neurotic Personality of Our Time* (New York: Norton, 1937), p. 98.

29. Engler, *Personality Theories*, p. 131. In Horney's neurotic trend of moving away, she also included the need for perfection and unassailability—the belief that independence and self-sufficiency will guarantee admiration for their perfection. This ensures that others will be unable to find fault or criticize them for their performance.

30. Ibid. Engler cites Horney's books *Self-Analysis*, *Our Inner Conflicts*, and *Neurosis and Human Growth*—all original sources that explain her concept of neurotic trends and corresponding styles of social movement.

31. Horney, *Neurosis and Human Growth*, p. 19.

32. Ibid., p. 65.

33. Ibid., p. 143.

34. E. H. Erikson, *The Life Cycle Completed: A Review* (New York: Norton, 1982, 1997). Erikson's theory is interesting and widely acknowledged, but his eight stages of psychosocial development are more detailed than this book has space to cover. Interested readers can refer to his book *Identity: Youth and Crisis* (New York: Norton, 1968), which outlines each stage and its successful and unsuccessful resolution, which influences all subsequent stages.

35. A. S. Waterman, "Identity in the Context of Adolescent Psychology," in *Identity in Adolescence: Processes and Contents*, ed. A. S. Waterman (San Francisco: Jossey-Bass, 1985), p. 13.

36. A. S. Fulton, "Identity Status, Religious Orientation, and Prejudice," *Journal of Youth and Adolescence* 26 (1997): 9.

37. Engler, *Personality Theories*, p. 165.

38. E. H. Erikson, *Childhood and Society* (New York: Norton, 1950).

39. Ibid., p. 232.

40. Other notable psychologists who examine the role of anxiety on personality development include Carl Jung, Harry Stack Sullivan, and object relations theorists such as Melanie Klein, Margaret Mahler, Otto Kernberg, and Nancy Chodorow. All assume that the development of healthy relationships depends on early child-parent relationships that enhance or hinder psychological and personality development. They propose that an "inborn drive to form and maintain human relationships is the basic need from which other drives derive their meaning" (Engler, *Theories of Personality,* p. 183).

41. D. C. Funder, *The Personality Puzzle* (New York: Norton, 2001), p. 224. For interested readers, Funder cites two other excellent sources of information on research findings that support the claim that skilled parenting is critical in the early years: N. Eisenberg, T. L. Spinrad, and A. Cumberland, "The Socialization of Emotion: Reply to Commentaries," *Psychological Inquiry* 9 (1998): 317–33, and W. A. Collins et al., "Contemporary Research on Parenting: The Case for Nature *and* Nurture," *American Psychologist* 55 (2000): 218–32.

42. D. Westen, "Psychoanalytic Approaches to Personality," in *Handbook of Personality: Theory and Research*, ed. L. Pervin (New York: Guilford, 1990), pp. 21–65.

Chapter 14

THE BARK OF DOGMATISM

Humanistic-Existential Contributions

Freedom and responsibility always imply each other and can never be separated.

Rollo May[1]

Have you ever wondered if your personality would be the same had your parents treated you differently? What if those of you who were raised in loving, supportive families had instead been born to harsh, critical parents? Imagine too, those of you who felt you never quite measured up to others' expectations, that your childhood and adolescence had been filled with unconditional parental love. How might your adult beliefs about yourself, others, and the surrounding world differ as a result of your circumstantial parenting? Who primarily authors your most important decisions? Do you have the courage to set challenges that could enhance and enrich your life, even though you might not succeed? Can you live fully and freely in the moment, unencumbered by thoughts and feelings that are outside the present situation? Against human tragedy, suffering, and your own inevitable death, do you question the meaning of life? These are only some of the issues that humanistic and existential psychologists address in their theories of personality development—and the philosophical assumptions about human nature, from which their theories derived, vary considerably from those of other personality theorists.

Carl Rogers and Abraham Maslow, the leading proponents of humanistic psychology, which gained prominence in the 1950s, were the founders of the Third Force in personality theory. Offering an alternative to the first two forces, psychoanalysis and behaviorism, humanistic theory gave momentum to the human potential movement of the 1960s, in which a group of intellectuals promoted the belief that people in supportive, nonthreatening environments will strive to achieve their full potential. During this time, the Esalen Institute at Big Sur, California, presented seminars by such notable scholars as Carl Rogers, Abraham Maslow, Paul Tillich, Linus Pauling, and Arnold Toynbee, among others.

Existential psychology, also an important branch of this new Third Force, arrived on the scene at approximately the same time. Similarities between the humanistic and existential movements account for the frequent, hyphenated reference to both as the humanistic-existential model. The following are common underlying assumptions of these theories:

1. Both consider the role of human consciousness on unique perceptual interpretations.
2. Both emphasize that, regardless of circumstances, we have the freedom to choose how we will interpret and respond to events.
3. Both agree that, if we have the freedom to choose, then we are responsible for the choices we make. Implicit in this assumption is the idea that we cannot blame others for our misfortune, because we are free to interpret and react to life experiences along a continuum that ranges from reasonable to unreasonable.
4. Both emphasize the important role of individual authenticity in psychological well-being.

These two schools of personality theory differ in that the humanistic theorists are much more optimistic than the existentialists in their assumptions about human nature, the potential for positive psychological growth, self-fulfillment, and resilience. Existentialists challenge humanistic assumptions about innate human goodness and accept that the shortcomings and difficulties inherent in human adaptations to the harsh realities of existence, particularly imminent death, present us with inescapable burdens. To exist is to be vulnerable to losing our psychological balance and making choices that cause suffering to ourselves and others. Despite these theoretical differences, important ideas and concepts from the humanists and the existentialists enable us to broaden our understanding of the psychological conditions that influence personality development and give rise to personality traits such as dogmatism.

HUMANISTIC AND EXISTENTIAL THEORIES OF PERSONALITY

Person-Centered Theory: Carl Rogers (1902–1987)

Carl Rogers proposed that at the core of human nature is the innate motivation to self-actualize, which is

> the urge which is evident in all organic and human life—to expand, extend, become autonomous, develop, mature—the tendency to express and activate all the capacities of the organism. . . . This tendency may become deeply buried under layer after layer of encrusted psychological defenses . . . but it is my belief that it exists in every individual, and awaits only the proper conditions to be released and expressed.[2]

Rogers's somewhat grand assumptions have been criticized by behaviorists and evolutionary psychologists. Are humans innately driven toward maturity, creativity, and productivity that will flourish, provided environmental circumstances and social institutions support individual growth? Because institutions are a product of human nature, opponents of the humanistic model believe it is unreasonable to assume that humanity is even capable of building social structures that will radiate the necessary qualities on which self-actualization thrives— individually and collectively. Critics claim that we are incapable of erecting such structures because human nature is not like that of a rose, which innately blossoms under the right conditions. More likely, they claim, humans are beleaguered by instincts and drives that thwart the very self-actualization needed to build these ideal, Rogerian institutions.

Carl Rogers refuted these criticisms. He spent years developing a theory and research to substantiate his claim that unimpeded growth occurs when the necessary and sufficient external conditions are in place. One such necessity is the *unconditional positive regard* that is seen in parents who always, and without condition, fully accept the whole child, even though they reject and discipline his or her harmful or immoral behaviors. Such parents set reasonable limits on childhood behaviors yet allow their children to freely express their thoughts and feelings. Consistent, unconditional positive regard fosters that which naturally resides in all children: an innate predisposition for *congruence* (also known as *genuineness*). Congruent children are in touch with and can express their genuine feelings, thoughts, and behaviors without fearing harsh, arbitrary reprisals. At the core of these children is the belief that they are always loveable as they are, even though their behavior is sometimes undesirable or unacceptable. Consequently, they tend to be spontaneous and genuine. As adults, they openly and comfortably express their thoughts and true feelings.

According to Rogers, good parenting demands another equally important quality. Supportive parents consistently empathize with their children; they go beyond listening to fully hearing and accurately communicating an understanding of the child's feelings and concerns. Such empathy is the necessary precondition for insight and psychological growth, and parents who provide unwavering, unconditional positive regard and *empathic understanding* help their children recognize and accept their genuine selves. When these conditions are present, children are able to internalize what Rogers calls *positive self-regard*, a state of self-acceptance that is the springboard for *self-actualization*.[3] External positive regard shifts to internal positive self-regard, which promotes self-esteem.

When parents extend these conditions to their children, they not only positively affect their children's view of most authority figures outside the nuclear family—they also enhance their budding self-esteem. Children who view adults as generally trustworthy are more likely to develop the confidence that facilitates open-minded reasoning—both of which protect against latent dogmatism. For Rogers, unconditional positive regard and empathy are the foundation for enduring cognitive curiosity and flexibility, emotional stability, and behavioral competence—a view that resonates with the four needs outlined in chapter 2. If ungratified, these needs are influential factors that shape adult dogmatism.

This does not mean that parents should shower their children with excessive adulation or exhaust themselves by relentlessly finding ways to promote their children's self-esteem. "Family life has become phony, because parents are convinced that children need constant assurances of parental love, so if they don't happen to feel very loving at a particular time or toward a particular child, they fake it. Praise is delivered by the bushel, which devalues its worth. Children have become the masters of the home."[4] While most parents simply try to do what is best for their children, some are anxiously overconcerned and overinvested in them; they model a range of unhealthy beliefs and behaviors, particularly the belief that in a competitive society children will surely fail unless they are pushed to excel.[5] "The threat parents experience translates into increased control" of their child's success and happiness.[6] These are the parents who, because they perceive the world as harsh and demanding, use authoritarian means of discipline and control—punitive, invasive strategies that they mistakenly assume will protect their children from failure. Anxious about being inadequate parents and fearful of raising underachievers, they dogmatically pursue beliefs and practices that, in the end, subvert their best intentions.

428 WHAT'S SO WRONG WITH BEING ABSOLUTELY RIGHT

Conversely, parents who moderately and judiciously praise their children help them move from absolute dependence on their parents to provisional self-dependence and, eventually, autonomous functioning. These children develop beliefs that evolve from the authority of their own voice, and their behaviors are commensurate with their thoughts and emotions. Able to take their place in the world as *fully functioning* members of society, they live openly and honestly in the moment, free from needless defensiveness.[7] As fully functioning adults, they trust their ability to process information and "emerge *from* experience," rather than twist ongoing experiences or design new ones that fit the mold of preconceived views.[8] In short, because they are *congruent*— or true to themselves—others perceive them as genuine.

Research links unconditional positive regard in childhood with adult open-mindedness.[9] Children who feel valued for who they are, and who are listened to regardless of how they feel or what they think, develop positive self-regard. Of central importance to dogmatism, they are not riddled with anxiety that closes their minds, diminishes their curiosity, and builds defensive barriers.

On the contrary, children whose parents create *conditions of worth* teach their children, often unwittingly, that they are only loveable if they meet certain conditions: *if* they excel at school, *if* they are obedient and respectful, *if* they are shining all-stars, *if* they conform to masculine or feminine roles, *if* they wholeheartedly adopt their parents' beliefs, and so on.

This conditional parental love teaches children they must perfect the imperfect, that only parts of them are precious and loveable, while the whole is not. Under such conditions, children must work hard to prove they are worthy of love, but since perfection is impossible to achieve, much less sustain, at any given moment they do not feel fully loved and accepted for who they are. Without a unified, consistent self on whom they can rely, they learn to think, feel, and behave in accordance with definitions and instructions issued by authority figures. Worse yet, they learn not to seriously question the merit of demands that are more authoritarian than authoritative.[10] In adolescence and adulthood, they become what Rogers referred to as *incongruent*—what they feel and what they say and do is discordant. They lack integration and consistency, so that others describe then as phony, hypocritical, deceitful, and manipulative.

§§

Several of the nine characteristics that depict the authoritarian personality trait are found in parenting styles that lack unconditional positive regard and empathy. More focused on evaluating rather than understanding the child's thoughts, feelings, and behaviors, the authoritarian parent attempts to shape, control, and judge the child's behavior and attitudes in accordance with rigid, absolute standards of conduct, which Diana Baumrind described as

> theologically motivated and formulated by a higher authority. She [the parent] values obedience as a virtue and favors punitive, forceful measures to curb self-will at points where the child's actions or beliefs conflict with what she thinks is right conduct. She believes in keeping the child in his place, in restricting his autonomy, and in assigning household responsibilities in order to inculcate respect for work. She regards the preservation of order and traditional structure as a highly valued end in itself. She does not encourage verbal give and take, believing that the child should accept her word for what is right.[11]

This includes telling the child what to feel, even when the child clearly feels something quite different. For example, a young child who tells his mother, "I hate Uncle Joe because he teases me," feels misunderstood if his mother corrects his feelings: "Oh c'mon now, you love your Uncle Joe! Stop saying such nasty things. Uncle Joe is a good man." A more appropriate response would softly acknowledge the child's feeling state: "You don't like being teased by Uncle Joe. Let's see if we can figure out a way to solve this problem." With this empathic response, the child not only feels understood, he feels empowered to resolve difficult interpersonal situations.

Parents who frequently dismiss or contradict their children's feelings engender self-doubt, anxiety, and cognitive distortions. When children's natural feelings are incompatible with an authoritarian parent's conditions of worth, "tension develops and is felt as anxiety or uncertainty."[12] Children cope by disguising or burying their true feelings. Moreover, adults who tell children what they *should* think and feel promote incongruence that closes the door to discussions of different perspectives and behaviors. These conditions of worth instantiate psychological insecurity and incongruence that eventually narrow thinking and constrict possibility.

Conversely, parents who mirror children's thoughts and feelings validate rather than deny their experiences. This does not mean that the parent unconditionally allows children to act on intense emotions such as anger or jealousy. When parents convey a deep understanding of how the child feels and respond compassionately to the child's concerns or distress, the child hears "I notice you, I feel with you, and so I act to help you."[13] By allowing children to at least verbalize how they feel and what they think, parents extend unconditional love that not only helps them become more congruent, it also inclines them to accept the parent's right to set limits on behaviors. These authoritative parents help keep their children's minds open and curious. They guide them with encouragement and verbal give and take, and they provide reasons for their decisions and solicit their children's opinions. Authoritative parenting is "positively associated, though at generally moderate statistical levels, with children's independence and autonomy in both cognitive and social realms, with ability to control aggression, with social responsibility, and with self-esteem."[14] Like authoritarian parents, authoritative parents also establish firm rules and confront misbehavior, but the manner in which authoritative parents use discipline promotes lasting independence and congruence. Authoritative parents also tend to model honest, open communication. Their children do not grow up feeling they have to effect a false image that conforms to external scripts and consequently betrays their natural, genuine selves.

Children raised by authoritarian parents tend to lack social competence, spontaneity, and self-esteem—deficiencies that rob them of the ability to cultivate empathy and friendships.[15] As adults, they generally lack the autonomy that is necessary to set goals and determine their own ethical standards; they are more likely to rely on external authorities for guidance.[16] Their motivation to experiment with new behaviors that would expand their worldview has been undermined.[17] As the adage states, never do for children what they can do for themselves. Relative to dogmatism, never *think* for children who are capable of thinking for themselves, and never *feel* for children in a manner that coerces them to agree with feelings that are incongruent with their own.

Understanding Jonah's Dogmatism from a Rogerian Perspective

Dogmatism begins at home. Rogers would say that Jonah's lack of personal insight—a cognitive characteristic of dogmatism—stems from his childhood inability to integrate feelings, thoughts, and behaviors. His incongruence originated in early deficits of unconditional positive regard and empathy, as evidenced by his father's conditions of worth and authoritarian control, both of which prevented Jonah from blending his true thoughts, feelings, and behaviors into a consistent whole—into a congruent, integrated self. Instead, Jonah learned to distort, deny, and repress his true feelings. By adulthood, he was unaware of the extent to which his early fears toward his parents accounted for his unqualified acceptance of, even reverence for, their religious and political belief systems.

On the surface, the adult Jonah appears congruent—dogmatically congruent. But recall that dogmatism is a response to the anxiety of not knowing, the difficulty of accepting ambiguity, and the apprehension of having to think for oneself in the face of uncertainty. Unfortunately, Jonah's ongoing experiences of youth robbed him of the ability to authentically understand and express his true thoughts and feelings. Conditions of worth prevented his natural movement from parental dependence to congruent self-reliance. For Jonah, dogmatism became his ticket to safety and respect—a journey that veered so far from congruence that he ultimately lost his way to authentic being. Jonah cannot control his anxiety because it is buried, and he cannot alter his belief systems because they are sealed in closed, protective compartments. Options to see himself and his world more openly and objectively have long since been narrowed and obscured by silos of incongruent thoughts, feelings, and behaviors.

§§

Not that the rest of us are always authentic and congruent. None of us are completely aware of, or act in accordance with, what we genuinely think and feel. But neither do most of us become seriously alienated from our true natures. We hang out in the middle zone of awareness and put our time in. But if, as children, we were frequently and repeatedly uncertain and distrusting of our inner experiences, we too would have doubted our true feelings and lost confidence in our ability to think for ourselves. We might well have searched for something that would make us feel good about the subjective "me" inside. Dogmatism provides that ostensibly solid alternative because it relies on external agents to compensate for earlier deprivations. Such is the appeal of charismatic leaders. And preachers. And professors. And partners.

And psychologists. An effective therapist facilitates the client's move toward positive self-regard by extending what the client's parents withheld—unconditional positive regard and empathy. On a safe therapeutic journey, clients can rummage through their closet of buried emotions and learn to accept their feelings and imperfections. They begin to see that it is normal to experience negative feelings and unkind thoughts, for we are all occasional visitors to the sinister basement of dark emotions, confusion, primitive desires, and self doubt. Those who feel stuck in that dungeon might find Rogerian therapy particularly effective at helping them unravel opposing desires and imposing morals that create conflict and incongruence. By providing the unconditional positive regard and empathy that clients could not fully experienced throughout childhood, the therapist facilitates congruence. This enables clients to openly and spontaneously express unacceptable aspects of themselves as they come to realize that they need not be haunted and controlled by repressed or distorted feelings, thoughts, and memories. Their fragmented, incongruent selves gradually become integrated and congruent. Former disabling emotions lose their power, and, in their place, positive self-regard emerges—the necessary foundation for constructive, open-minded thought. What would this do for dogmatic people? Old, impermeable boundaries would crack open; personal insight might flouish; and worldly ideas might broaden.

Such self-awareness provides the scaffolding for genuineness, without which optimal choices are limited. If, somewhere along the way, dogmatic individuals can experience greater self-acceptance, integration, and congruence, through whatever methods available—serendipitous or otherwise—they can open their minds, which have been closed, and experience emotions, which have been denied.

A criticism of Rogerian therapy is that it focuses on feelings at the expense of cognitive understanding. An alternative to this model comes from therapists who believe that for Jonah to overcome his dogmatism, he needs to work at eliminating the demanding, distorted beliefs that lead to inappropriate emotions and habitual behaviors. Rogerian therapy might make Jonah feel better, but, according to cognitive therapists, it won't help him get better.[18]

Human Motivation: Abraham Maslow (1908–1952)

Abraham Maslow was also a prominent advocate of humanistic theory. Like Rogers, he believed that we are born with an innate capacity for creativity, joy, and goodness. Yet this intrinsic nature can easily be damaged by an unhealthy environment that arrests personality development at one or more levels, which Maslow developed and named the Hierarchy of Needs.[19]

Deficiency needs, or *D-needs* (also referred to as *basic needs*), are prerequisite for higher levels of growth, or being needs (*B-needs*, which are also called *meta needs*), which people aspire to when D-needs are largely met. Maslow arranged the D-needs in a hierarchy that assumes basic needs must first be gratified before higher levels of psychological functioning are attainable (though he recognized that exceptions within this hierarchical progression can and do occur).

Applying Maslow's Basic Needs to Dogmatism

Maslow's theoretical premise is that the first four of five basic needs must generally be met before one can fulfill the higher B-needs, which are relative to dogmatism because they include *being-cognition*—a state of open-minded, nondogmatic assessment and enjoyment of all things worldly.[20] Of the four basic D-needs that humans are motivated to fulfill, the first level of needs that must be gratified are primary, *physiological needs*. These include the need for food, water, sex, and sleep, and they must be gratified before we can go about satisfying the second level of needs—*safety needs*. As Maslow said, "It is quite true that man lives by bread alone—when there is no bread."[21] If we are starving, we have no energy or means to move to a safer residential district, or to emigrate to a country that has protective laws, greater economic opportunity, and democratic freedom. Second-level safety needs include physical security, economic stability, and protection from the threat of war, illness, and other forces of instability. Such political and economic stability not only protects against starvation, it provides freedom from daily fear, anxiety, and confusion.

Once physiological and safety needs are largely gratified, people are motivated to fulfill the third level of Maslow's needs—the *need for belonging and love*. Like Rogers, Maslow claimed that individuals have an innate desire to establish social connections that fulfill needs for belonging and love. If this third level of deficiency needs is largely satisfied, people are then capable of *being-love*, which is the capacity to extend nonjudgmental, noninterfering, and nondemanding love to others. Having fulfilled these first three basic needs, "one's self expands, becomes more integrated, and more and more behavior becomes self-determined."[22]

A breakdown in any of these three core needs imperils fulfillment of the fourth need—*the need for esteem.* Esteem needs are of two types: (1) pride in our accomplishments, and (2) recognition from others, which grants us dignity.[23] When fourth-level esteem needs are largely met, psychological growth or being needs emerge. B-needs consist of innate desires to broaden our understanding, explore new ideas and talents, and actualize our potential—needs that are clearly deficient in those who have the personality trait of dogmatism. People who experience moments of *B-cognition* and *B-motivation* are able to perceive events accurately without distorting them to fit rigid preconceptions. B-cognition makes them less inclined to be judgmental of themselves, others, and ideas.[24] These are mature meta needs that transcend self-absorption and concrete perceptions of the world—perceptions that a child or adolescent cannot experience because "he hasn't even grown up in the abstract yet. He is innocent because he is ignorant."[25] But in order to get to that place, core needs must first be gratified.

In support of Maslow's claim that higher needs occur later in personality development, research on higher-order thinking skills (abstract thought, metaphorical thinking and imagery), "suggests that differences between younger and older subjects increase with respect to certain abilities."[26] As children and adolescents intellectually mature, they are increasingly able to synthesize language and mathematical operations into a multilayered system of related concepts. However, few educators address the extent to which underlying anxiety interferes with a student's ability to open-mindedly examine his or her thoughts about belief systems, especially those that are emotionally laden. According to Maslow, without this skilled intervention, these students will have great difficulty gratifying B-cognition and B-motivation, both of which lift one to higher levels of self-actualization.

The cognitive ability to open one's mind about personal emotions and beliefs does not fall within the framework of a general educational curriculum, which primarily assesses intellectual skills and the students' understanding of course content. I do not mean to suggest that all educators dismiss important concerns about personal beliefs. Rather, educators themselves have been taught to emphasize an intellectual grasp of content; they deemphasize teaching about emotions that impact one's flexibility of thought about course content. While many teachers integrate critical thinking skills with course content and facilitate personal expression of feelings about important issues, few consistently encourage students to seriously examine their emotional reactions to beliefs that differ from their own. Enhancing student awareness of how emotions interfere with cognitive functioning would surely facilitate a more open-minded approach to knowledge and problem solving, at all educational levels. This idea is so important that we will revisit it in the final chapter.

§§

Maslow claimed that the ability to think abstractly is necessary for B-cognition—a quality of thought that grasps essential commonalities in human struggles and worldly issues. It requires close examination of beliefs and values, with as much detached objectivity and creativity as humanly possible. B-cognition enables people to view their roles and responsibilities within the larger framework of humanity. Despite the challenges, or because of them, great thinkers, scientists, and artists with B-cognition make profound contributions to science, art, and literature that go well beyond basic survival, safety, belonging, and esteem needs. This important notion is illustrated in Mozart's music, Descartes' mathematics, Renoir's impressionism, Blake's poetry, and Hawking's physics, to name but a few. All have influenced our way of being. They and countless others inspire us to lose ourselves in pursuits that test our highest potential for creative, productive thought. B-cognition breaks the barriers of tradition, physical limitations, and present time. One becomes lost in a new and wonderful world where dormant talents come alive, consciousness expands, and one finds far greater meaning to life than ever imagined possible.

B-cognition also "means forgiving one's self because of under-standing one's self. It means the transcendence of remorse, regret, guilt, shame, embarrassment and the like."[27] Its hallmark is authentic being, which frees one from the bondage of fixed ideas, interpersonal evaluations, mindless cultural conventions, and parental expectations. People with B-cognition demonstrate "the very highest and most inclusive or holistic levels of human consciousness—the final stage of transcendence."[28]

Achievement of such optimum functioning depends on good gover-nance, which Maslow defines as leadership that meets its obligations to adequately fund institutions that enhance *everyone's* personal growth. "It is now quite clear that actualization of the highest human potentials is possible—on a mass basis—only under good conditions."[29] It is also quite clear that the D-cognition of dogmatic believers is more likely to emerge from societies that do not provide the solid foundation on which gratification of Maslow's D- and B-needs depend.

Deficient in their needs for belonging, love, and esteem, dogmatic people cannot transcend their anxiety long enough to let go of ego defenses that prevent them from feeling safely connected to humanity and nature. They are developmentally arrested in D-cognition—the acquisition and judgment modes that keep them busy comparing them-selves to others. D-cognition is also maintained by prejudices and stereotypes that reflect the language of disapproval and condemnation. Interests are narrow, and humor is punctuated with themes of sarcasm and hostility.[30] People who are developmentally arrested in D-cognition have habitual, unarticulated feelings and self-evaluations that convey the following beliefs and feelings: "I do not feel comfortable or safe; I don't seem to belong anywhere; I feel invisible; at the core of me, there is no consistent sense of who I am or where I'm going."

Maslow's parsing of cognitive abilities into D- and B-cognition is consonant with several cognitive, emotional, and behavioral charac-teristics of dogmatism, as outlined in chapters 5, 6, and 7. Yet what seems to be missing in Maslow's self-actualization theory is a deeper analysis of what prevents people from psychologically transcending core D-needs. Psychological growth is surely influenced by one's biology, the surrounding environment, and the quality of past and present social relationships. Unlike Rogers, who outlined a theory of early developmental experiences that promote incongruence and prevent self-actualization, Maslow did not develop a theory of personality that presents plausible causes for arrested B-cognition and self-actualization. His ideas do, however, remind us that civic societies that fail to adequately fund programs to assure provisions for D-needs impair the psychological growth of their citizens. Parents can also be remiss in these provisions, but Maslow did not theorize about the characteristics and consequences of adequate versus inadequate parenting.

Understanding Jonah's Dogmatism as a Consequence of D-Needs

To some extent, Jonah is still thinking with the mind of the child he once was—the child who felt small, unworthy, weak, and unintelligent. Jonah the child, who could think only in concrete terms, became the adolescent who was afraid to question and the adult who would not risk opening his mind to abstract analysis. He was unable to exercise his intellect with equanimity, and equally unable to authentically examine his childlike acceptance of beliefs handed down by authority figures. All that he was capable of back then is all that he dare not go beyond now. To open-mindedly question his beliefs would seriously jeopardize his fulfillment of deficiency needs, and that failure further impairs his potential for growth and being-needs.

Jonah's father was equally trapped in D-needs; his dogmatism reflects what Maslow described as "too much the conqueror demanding unconditional surrender."[31] Although both parents gratified Jonah's basic physiological needs, they nonetheless hampered his further psychological progression up the hierarchy of needs. With such core deficiencies, Jonah fell into a state of psychological stagnation that prevented him from experiencing B-cognition and self-actualization in later life.

Maslow stressed that people capable of functioning in states of B-cognition are not perfect. While they can frequently lose themselves in tasks of intense, awe-inspiring moments of appreciation that may last for hours, such *peak experiences* are interrupted by normal imperfections of "superficial vanity, pride, partiality to their own productions, family, friends, and children."[32] Similarly, open-minded people are not always open-minded in their thinking, and dogmatists are not dogmatic every moment of their waking day. To pigeonhole them into nothing but D-cognition would be to risk a serious error that cuts too close to the bone of dogmatic compartmentalization.

Surely there are times when people like Jonah can be fully absorbed by projects or adventures in which they temporarily abandon anxiety and self-doubt. Conceivably, Jonah would not have earned a degree in education had he not been able to wedge his mind open about some issues contrary to his own, even if he was largely an imposter of cognitive flexibility much of the time. In his subconscious mind, teaching would provide indirect compensation for his early psychological deficiencies, for he would gain respect from his students and colleagues. Similarly, he was motivated to enter politics so that he could enact legislation that fulfilled religious imperatives, and these initiatives would presumably have conferred status and dignity— deficiency needs that were aborted by his students, colleagues, and the electorate. His authoritarian parenting and strict discipline with students were two strong indicators that Jonah was developmentally arrested at D-cognition. All things considered, it would appear that as Jonah approaches his sixth decade, he will still be struggling with D-needs that continue to short-circuit open-minded being-cognition.

We now turn to the existentialists for additional insight into the influential forces that moved Jonah's personality development on a path toward dogmatism.

Existential Psychology: Rollo May (1909–1994)

As we continue excavating major concepts from volumes of theory relevant to dogmatism, it is worth noting that most personality theorists address the universal inevitability of anxiety. Because the lens through which each theorist peers into the nature and causes of existential angst differs, steadying the magnifying glass over existential psychology reveals much.

The existential theory of anxiety is itself somewhat anxiety provoking, drawing as it does from the gloomy writings of existential philosophers who grapple with the essence of human existence. Sartre, Nietzsche, Kierkegaard, Binswanger, Boss, and Frankl are just a few of many notable existential psychologists, all of whom propose quite a different source of anxiety from that of Freud, the neo-Freudians, the cognitive-behavioralists, and humanistic psychologists. Rollo May, a prominent existential psychologist, thought that a principal source of anxiety is our continuous struggle to cope with the inevitability of physical death, which continually hovers in the background of daily consciousness. Invisible, unknowable events create, sustain, and end all life—an awareness that is a source of deep sorrow, joy, and humility. Such awareness motivates some and psychologically overwhelms, disables, and even destroys others.[33]

The immense mystery of life brings forth existential anxiety from which we cannot escape. We realize that death will some day end all that we know and feel, and all that we are in the process of becoming. Perhaps that is why many of us have, as Shakespeare wrote, "immortal longings."[34] Uncertainty, helplessness, and diffuse but vague apprehension that accompany thoughts of death are more debilitating than specific fears because death anxiety has no discernible object to fear. The pervasive, chronic quality of such anxiety has more than the absurdity of life in its grip—we cannot prevent the identity meltdown that death accomplishes when we are no longer a living presence. Even the memories others have of us fade and die with our departure until, eventually, every trace of psychological identity is gone. Within decades, nothing remains of our human essence—zip, zilch, nada, squat.

Adding to our persistent fear of death and ultimate nothingness, we must also cope with the confusion and ambiguity of daily living. In the face of such angst, the quality of our existence is defined by one of two critical choices. We can choose to courageously *find meaning in life* despite being "thrown into the world at a given moment in time and space, with certain inborn capabilities and limitations" that cause periods of inevitable suffering, tragedy, and ultimately death.[35] In this case, we courageously accept the challenge to find meaning in existence. Or, we can *escape our freedom to choose* responsible engagement (a choice in itself) and risk a life of quiet longing and despair. By freedom, May meant "*openness*, a readiness to grow; it means being flexible, ready to change for the sake of greater human values."[36] It is, as May argued, a conscious decision to search for meaning despite impending death.[37]

At the individual level, freedom enables self-determination and authenticity. Those of us who are unable to find value and meaning in daily existence, restrict our freedom, autonomy, and dignity and intensify our *existential anxiety* (the failure to courageously confront life's challenges and develop one's potential).[38] This type of anxiety cannot be circumvented; it is part of our personality, which we cannot willingly abandon (except through drugs or suicide). And our personality, being imperfect, is frequently tempted to choose psychological death—by which May meant a death that differs from physical death. Psychological death occurs when we fail to choose psychological growth and well-being over cynicism, despair, and dread. Anything that threatens our personal identity contributes to this psychological death, which is eventually experienced as a loss of self-esteem, self-respect, and dignity. Such perceived threats prevent us from experimenting with what is perhaps our most undervalued yet important psychological strength—the ability to take risks.

The plot thickens. Unhealthy decisions, which all of us occasionally make, create existential guilt because, at some level of awareness, we know when our decisions evade responsibility. Like existential anxiety, *existential guilt* shadows our daily existence, threatening to degrade our identity and dignity. At a deep, ontological level (the level of our being), normal anxiety and guilt are the engines that propel one's natural tendency to create a unique, meaningful existence. However, there is also a natural tendency to behave irresponsibly, which undermines attempts to live courageously. Perhaps, as Proust claimed, happiness and survival demand existential anxiety, guilt, misery, and suffering. "We suffer, therefore we think, and we do so because thinking helps us to place pain in context. It helps us to understand its origins, plot its dimensions, and reconcile ourselves to its presence."[39]

§§

Because beliefs and values are a significant part of our existence, we become anxious when they are threatened. We are forced to reexamine who we are and what we value—individually and collectively. Such was the case in 2001 after the September 11 attacks on symbols of American values. In the aftermath of crimes against humanity, "every individual experiences greater or lesser threats to his existence and to values he identifies with. . . . But the human being normally confronts these experiences constructively, uses them as 'learning experiences' (in the broad and profound meaning of that term), and moves on in his development."[40]

This is not the likely scenario for dogmatists, who cope with anxiety by repressing and replacing it with "two major bulwarks of denial: belief in personal specialness and belief in an ultimate rescuer."[41] The problem with dogmatism is that those who practice it react to existential anxiety by trying to avoid or control it. Neither works. Existential anxiety cannot be consciously manipulated. For example, rapidly changing political, social, or economic circumstances threaten cherished values that are central to identity. Ensuing confusion and anxiety make us vulnerable to accept arbitrary explanations that satisfy our need to know and temporarily assuage fear and anxiety. In the process, we risk abandoning our freedom to question and our ability to make independent, authentic decisions. This freedom from responsibility reduces the anxiety of having to think and act for ourselves. Instead, some of us cling to beliefs and ideologies that rescue us from the anxiety of nonbeing. The thought of examining and expanding our views creates emotional distress that is continuously nourished by the fear of falling into a meaningless void. To protect against existential death and nonbeing, dogmatists rigidly bind themselves to ideologies and traditional customs that resist the birth of new insights. Yet mindless conformity is merely an alternative mode of nonbeing, and conformists who surrender their identity and deny their potential for growth are haunted by a semiconscious disquiet that stems from their faint awareness that they lack the courage to make difficult choices for growth—choices that confront life. As Rokeach said, "The closed mind, for fear of the new, is a passive mind."[42]

The closed mind also accepts, unconditionally, traditional myths that give life meaning and significance.[43] These stories or narratives shape personal and cultural values around important issues such as birth, death, freedom, and responsibility. They are the substance of universal patterns that dwell in human consciousness and construct compelling myths about, for example, pioneering, self-reliant mavericks like the Lone Ranger, Horatio Alger, Calamity Jane, and Daniel Boone. These American pilgrims symbolized a rebirth of humanity by leaving behind European struggles of injustice, persecution, and poverty. Individualism became the mythic theme of Americans who place a premium on competition, property, and prosperity—myths that gave promise to the American Dream.[44]

May viewed these myths as necessary for survival on the frontier. Before his death in 1994, he lamented that early, adaptive American myths had morphed into exaggerations of grotesque materialism and vile competition, both of which rely on exploitation. Defining personal success in terms of material acquisition destabilizes individuals and community and opens the door to political corruption and scandal. Who are the modern-day equivalents of Tommy Douglas, Eleanor Roosevelt, Martin Luther King Jr., Albert Schweitzer, Mahatma Gandhi, and Nelson Mandela (among others)? A loss of significant role models weakens the social fabric such that people lose the sense of their significance and begin to feel powerless. These feelings create a deeper alienation from oneself, others, and anything of real meaning and value. And people who feel estranged from anything of real value lose their ability to establish intimate relationships. They confuse sex with love and engage in indiscriminate, shallow sexual fusion that, like a narcotic, dulls the senses.[45] While this fusion temporarily assuages the angst of existential loneliness, every superficial sexual connection inevitably leaves them feeling anxious and empty, as if another slice of themselves had been carved from their frozen existence.[46]

Such is the rugged individualism of modern society that increases anxiety, narcissism, and depression. "Failure to engage in the competitive struggle is a threat to the quasi-esteem for one's self—which, quasi though it may be, is all one has in such a situation."[47] We become fractured, alienated individuals; the residue of lost authenticity and lost community.

While every society has groups that struggle to preserve past myths and values, every society also has creative individuals who challenge and expose the values and ethics of tradition. Both groups—those who preserve and those who question—generate healthy conflict that revitalizes society. Without the tension that these opposing beliefs and goals create, social values would either disintegrate into chaos or calcify in rigid conformity.[48]

Anything that hides our fears of ultimate disintegration provides "a protective shield designed to control the potential for terror that results from awareness of the horrifying possibility that we humans are merely transient animals groping to survive in a meaningless universe, destined only to die and decay."[49] Lacking such protection, anxiety and emptiness further alienate us from the beauty and awe of nature. "When a person feels himself inwardly empty, as is the case with so many modern people, he experiences nature around him also as empty, dried up, dead."[50] Changing social and cultural conditions exacerbate an already vulnerable or troubled psyche. Values that were once the sustaining force of one's identity collapse, and the struggle for meaningful existence becomes a tragic psychological legacy of emptiness, social isolation, and insignificance.[51] Gloomy enough?

To prevent this calamity, an adamant defense of traditional beliefs may protect against the breakdown of traditional values. If, as Rokeach said, personal anxiety smothers our need to know, and if, as May claimed, cultural values foster excess competition, confusion, doubt, and alienation, then it follows that as society becomes more complex and competitive, people, on average, will experience heightened anxiety that narrows thought and starves the need to know. One way to cope with chronic anxiety that's driven by the modern myth of success is to close our minds to the complexities of change and the unknown, and instead cling to simple, familiar traditions that mercifully show us the way.

But according to May, there can be no genuine return to and reaffirmation of established values or earlier dogmas, because each one of us has no lasting essence. Humans are always in a *state of becoming*, involved in a process of living that consists of disruption and change. We can only live now; we create the historical situation in which we currently exist. We need to continually rethink our beliefs and values—reaffirming some, discarding others, or creating new ones.[52] The choices are limitless, and it remains our responsibility to work together to establish values that actualize human potential. If we accept our anxiety as a natural consequence of change, we are better able to confront it with a constructive open-mindedness that increases our understanding of the debilitating effect anxiety has on reason.[53] This increased intellectual freedom, which is fundamental to all other freedoms and expands our thinking, which also expands our options.

The state of becoming is something that dogmatists, with their intolerance of ambiguity, dread. Examination of the new represents an indictment of the past, and their contrived defenses against the past have built a seemingly solid foundation of present security and identity. Although they would disagree, they are not paragons of human agency, living an authentic existence. Dogmatism is the protective shield that keeps them from the dreadful awareness that they, along with the rest of us, are trying to survive in a world that appears meaningless—a world in which all physical beings decay into nothingness. Courage, according to the existentialists, is the antidote. Open-minded courage.

Understanding Jonah's Dogmatism from May's Existential Perspective

By the time Jonah graduated from university, his religious and political beliefs were impenetrable. Throughout his teaching career, existential anxiety grew alongside his failure to convince others that traditional religious values needed to be reinstated. He remained oblivious of his inability to open-mindedly question dogma and take responsibility for developing autonomous, authentic values. Given what we know about Jonah's unfortunate childhood, this analysis may sound harsh, but the existentialists would claim that, despite his misfortune, Jonah has the freedom to make independent choices in adulthood. Regardless of his biological predisposition for excess anxiety and the childhood circumstances into which he was thrown at birth, he is responsible for exercising the freedom to question and determine his own beliefs and existence. Evading this responsibility accentuates his existential anxiety. By rigidly holding onto traditional values, which he refused to authentically question, Jonah kept his anxiety at bay until at the age of fifty-six and existential spasms morphed into smoldering disillusionment and cynicism.

Jonah's biography allows us to theoretically bridge May and Rokeach on the roles of anxiety and inauthenticity as precursors to dogmatism. Their views also mesh with Erich Fromm's writings on of the burden of freedom.[54] Like May, Fromm maintained that loneliness and isolation, which symbolize death, are inescapable conditions of being human. The burden of freedom requires us to confront the reality of human existence so that we can free ourselves and take responsibility for the *choices* we make *now*. The deterministic forces of our birth (e.g., innate constitution, intellectual potential, external conditions, and other limitations) and the freedom to choose how we perceive and react to such forces, are the existential challenges that give life meaning in the face of death.[55]

Sartre's poignant phrase "man is condemned to be free"[56] summarizes the difficulty of having to make choices between connection and aloneness, conscientious commitment and evasion of responsibility, courage and cowardice, open-mindedness and dogmatism. Under the stern gaze of his parents and God, Jonah seemed unable to exercise his freedom and make authentic choices throughout most of his life—choices that would have enhanced his sense of self and psychological well-being. Had Jonah been able to freely question his beliefs and perceptions, he still might have willingly adopted his parents' religious and political values, but his choices would have been the result of his own open-minded, authentic reasoning. On such a solid platform of authenticity, free choice would have added zest and meaning to his life.[57] Such authenticity would have given him a strong sense of identity and dignity, which would have further enabled him to sustain intimacy with his wife—extramarital affairs as a solution to alienation and loneliness would have been unnecessary.

Ironically, the very thing he tried to reinvigorate in others—a return to traditional values—was not an authentic aspect of Jonah's being. He had not waged battle with his own psyche, which would have helped him understand his relentless dependence on others for acceptance and respect. This move toward freedom would surely have exacerbated his anxiety, but in the trenches of that battle, integrity and dignity would have been the victors. In the earlier sentiments of Proust, and the words of American president James A. Garfield, "The truth will set you free, but first it will make you miserable."

It was simply easier and safer for Jonah to blindly adopt religious and political truths, rather than cultivate his own paths to knowledge. External truths defined his identity and magically assuaged his anxiety. By clinging to dogmatic beliefs, Jonah would not have to probe his vast psyche, consider the absurdities and disappointments of life on earth, or accept the disquieting possibility that a heavenly hereafter does not exist. An understanding of the psychological consequences of Jonah's early childhood deprivations and biological vulnerabilities allows us to speculate that Jonah freely chose dogmatic religiosity as a means of coping with his burden of existential anxiety and existential guilt.

§§

The manner in which Jonah wielded political power was classic political dogmatism that gratified infantile fantasies of personal omnipotence. The psychiatrist Robert J. Lifton coined the term *revolutionary immortality* to describe how some leaders cope with death anxiety. Driven by fears that death will destroy their self-affirming mission, zealous revolutionaries seek to preserve themselves and their movement by contriving a rebirth of fanaticism (Mao's Cultural Revolution is the prototype of this zealotry). And as long as followers keep the revolution alive, the despot's counterfeit ticket to immortality has no expiry date.[58]

These motives also drive the emotional characteristics of dogmatism—belief-associated anxiety, fear, and anger that culminate in existential despair, dogmatic authoritarian aggression, and dogmatic authoritarian submission. While Jonah was not moved to violence, his outright dismissal of those who disagreed with him and his refusal to govern democratically were driven by protective, deep-seated needs and psychic inundations that prevented what he most desired—social connection, respect, and dignity. Believing that personal and political immortality would compensate for those impoverished needs, he was unable to see that his own dogmatism was his biggest impediment to psychological fulfillment.

Chapter 15 outlines two remaining traditional models that help us further explore entrenched dogmatic belief. Turning the page on this chapter, we next review cognitive-behavioral and social learning theories that put in place a few more pieces of our personality puzzle that, when complete, will portray an interlocking profile of dogmatism.

NOTES

1. R. May, *Psychology and the Human Dilemma* (New York: Norton, 1979), p. 180.

2. C. R. Rogers, *On Becoming a Person: A Therapist's View of Psychotherapy* (Boston: Houghton Mifflin, 1961), p. 63.

3. C. R. Rogers, *Client-Centered Therapy: Its Current Practice, Implications, and Theory* (Boston: Houghton Mifflin, 1951).

4. J. R. Harris, "Zero Parental Influence," in *What Is Your Dangerous Idea?* ed. J. Brockman (New York: HarperCollins, 2007), p. 179.

5. E. M. Pomerantz and M. M. Eaton, "Maternal Intrusive Support in the Academic Context: Transactional Socialization Processes," *Developmental Psychology* 37, no. 2 (2001): 174–86. These researchers found that the more parents worried about children's success at school, the more they applied controlling techniques at home.

6. W. S. Grolnick, *The Psychology of Parental Control* (Mahwah, NJ: Erlbaum, 2003), p. 113.

7. C. R. Rogers, "The Concept of a Fully Functioning Person," *Psychotherapy: Theory, Research, and Practice* 1, no. 17–26 (1963).

8. Rogers, *On Becoming a Person*, pp. 188–89.

9. R. R. McCrae, "Social Consequences of Experiential Openness," *Psychological Bulletin* 120, no. 3 (2006): 323–37.

10. Rogers, *On Becoming a Person*.

11. D. Baumrind, "Effects of Authoritative Parental Control on Child Behavior," *Child Development* 37, no. 4 (1966): 890.

12. B. Engler, *Personality Theories: An Introduction*, 6th ed. (Boston: Houghton Mifflin Co., 2003), p. 373.

13. D. Goleman, *Social Intelligence: The New Science of Human Relationships* (New York: Bantam, 2006), p. 58. Goleman explains the three distinct types of empathy as "*knowing* another persons feelings, *feeling* what that person feels, and *responding compassionately* to another's distress." (Italics in original.)

14. E. E. Macoby and J. A. Martin, "Socialization in the Context of the Family: Parent-Child Interaction," in *Handbook of Child Psychology*, ed. P. H. Mussen (New York: Wiley, 1983), pp. 1–102; cited in D. P. McAdams, *The Person: An Introduction to Personality Psychology* (New York: Harcourt Brace, 1994), p. 356.

15. I am reminded here of George Clooney's comment that actors who do not have the genuine quality of friendliness, for example, cannot convincingly portray that trait in character roles. Interview on *Charlie Rose*, April 13, 2008.

16. D. Baumrind, "Current Patterns of Parental Authority," *Developmental Psychology Monograph* 4 (1971), in McAdams, *The Person*, p. 356.

17. R. Koestner, R. M. Ryan, F. Bernieri, and K. Holt, "Setting Limits on Children's Behavior: The Differential Effects of Controlling versus Informational Styles on Intrinsic Motivation and Creativity," *Journal of Personality* 52 (1984): 244–48.

18. A. Ellis made this comment during my fellowship program at the Ellis Institute, New York, 1999.

19. A. Maslow, *Motivation and Personality*, 2nd ed. (New York: Harper and Row, 1970).

20. Ibid.

21. Ibid., p. 38.

22. T. Pyszcznski, J. Greenberg, and J. L. Goldenberg, "Freedom versus Fear: On the Defense, Growth, and Expansion of the Self," in *Handbook of Self and Identity*, ed. M. R. Leary and J. P. Tangney (New York: Guilford, 2003), p. 323. From the perspective of self-determination theory, "intrinsic motivation instigates optimal self-development and more elaborate and extensive self-organization." Like Maslow's B-cognition, intrinsic motivation allows for the subjective enjoyment felt when one is capable of thorough engagement in a challenging activity.

23. Maslow, *Motivation and Personality*, p. 45.

24. A. H. Maslow, *Toward a Psychology of Being* (New York: Van Nostrand, 1962).

25. A. H. Maslow, *The Farther Reaches of Human Nature* (New York: Viking, 1971), p. 256.

26. R. L. Solso, *Cognitive Psychology*, 6th ed. (Needham Heights, MA: Allyn and Bacon, 2001). The abilities tested are those Jean Piaget, a developmental psychologist, assumed occur in stepwise development of qualitatively different thought. The last stage, formal operations, occurs between the ages of 11 and 15, when the child is able to operate on earlier, concrete dimensions of thought and move beyond physical reality to consolidate isolated thoughts into hypothetical worlds. He can now "evoke systems of thought not immediately given by reality" (p. 388).

27. Maslow, *Farther Reaches of Human Nature*, p. 271. For a complete list of Maslow's thirty-five characteristics of self-actualization (also known as B-cognition and transcendence), see chapter 21, "Various Meanings of Transcendence" (pp. 269–79).

28. Ibid., p. 279.

29. Ibid., p. 7.

30. Ibid.

31. Ibid., p. 144.

32. Ibid., p. 175.

33. Not only does such awareness create individual sensitivities about the meaning of life, this *qualia*, or subjective self-awareness that consciousness enables, is inherently unknowable to others. An ineffable, private quality of consciousness, qualia is what allows you to perceive the color blue or the meaning of a poem in a manner that can never be fully communicated to or known by another.

34. From Shakespeare, *Antony and Cleopatra*, act 5, scene 2.

35. McAdams, *The Person*, p. 425.

36. R. May, *Man's Search for Himself* (New York: Norton, 1953), p. 159.

37. V. Frankl, *Man's Search for Meaning* (New York: Simon and Schuster, 1963). Frankl, an eminent existential psychologist, emphasized that we are all responsible for the choices we make. "Everything can be taken from a man but one thing: the last of the human freedoms—to choose one's attitude in any given set of circumstances, to choose one's own way" (p. 104).

38. R. May, *The Meaning of Anxiety* (New York: Norton, 1977).

39. A. de Botton, *How Proust Can Change Your Life: Not a Novel* (New York: Vintage, 1997).

40. May, *The Meaning of Anxiety*, p. 210.

41. I. Yalom, *Existential Psychotherapy* (New York: Basic Books, 1980), p. 152.

42. M. Rokeach, *The Open and Closed Mind* (New York: Basic Books, 1960), p. 23.

43. R. May, *The Cry for Myth* (New York: Norton, 1991).

44. Ibid.

45. R. May, *Love and Will* (New York: Norton, 1969).

46. Ibid.

47. May, *The Meaning of Anxiety*, p. 196.

48. Ibid.

49. T. Pyszczynski, "Why Do People Need Self-Esteem? A Theoretical and Empirical Review," *Psychological Bulletin* 130 (2004): 438.

50. May, *Man's Search for Himself*, p. 69.

51. R. May, *Freedom and Destiny* (New York: Dell Publishing, 1981).

52. Ibid.

53. May, *Man's Search for Himself*. Rollo May's term for open-minded self-awareness is *consciousness of self*, or the "capacity to see one's self as though from the outside [which is] the distinctive characteristic of man" (p. 84).

54. E. Fromm, *Escape from Freedom* (New York: Holt, Rinehart, and Winston, 1941).

55. Rollo May notes that deterministic forces that accompany our birth may limit our choices, but an awareness that we are forced to make decisions despite these limitations represents the subjective nature of our being that responds to objective givens. This is what May refers to as the "human dilemma," about which he wrote an entire book, *Psychology and the Human Dilemma* (New York: Van Nostrand Reinhold, 1967).

56. J. P. Sartre, *Being and Nothingness* (New York: Simon and Schuster, 1943).

57. May, *Man's Search for Himself*, p. 212.

58. R. J. Lifton, *Thought Reform and the Psychology of Totalism: A Study of "Brainwashing" in China* (New York: Norton, 1961). Lifton's term *totalism* also applies to ideological groups that do not wield political power, and in this sense, totalism differs from the narrower concept of *totalitarianism*.

Chapter 15

NAILING TRUTH TO THE MAT

Cognitive-Behavioral Models and Social Learning Theory

The greatest griefs are those we cause ourselves.
Sophocles (ca. 496–406 BCE)

A friend criticizes your taste in music at a social gathering. What immediate thoughts and feelings are triggered? Someone cuts you off in traffic. Do you get angry? Do people who experience prolonged sadness after their partner leaves them feel depressed because of the rejection? Does extreme anxiety cause students to do poorly on exams? No, according to the cognitive theories of personality development. People get extremely angry, depressed, or anxious as a consequence of their thoughts about an event; the event itself is not the cause of their emotional distress. If Edith tells you she cannot get over Jim, who left her two years ago, it is not Jim who continues to drag her down emotionally, it is Edith's own thoughts.

Readers who are familiar with B. F. Skinner's theory of radical behaviorism, which gained prominence during the middle of the last century, might wonder why I have not drawn from his model to explain dogmatism as originating in reinforcement and punishment from the environment. For Skinner, the behavioral determinist, our environment explains everything about our personalities. If we want to create appropriate behavior, all we have to do is scientifically study and administer the environmental rewards that will modify desired behaviors. Alternatively, if we want to eliminate inappropriate behaviors, we simply need to scientifically study and administer punishment as a consequence of specific behaviors. We can then apply *reinforcement* and/or *punishment* (change the environmental circumstances) to create or eliminate behavior.[1] Thus, dogmatism, as examined from a Skinnerian perspective, is simply inappropriate behavior that is learned; it can be readily unlearned or *extinguished* through punishment. Today, Skinner's theory is considered not only very limited in scope, but also quite controversial, which is why I decided to acknowledge but not include it as an important contribution to this book's theoretical model of dogmatism.

COGNITIVE-BEHAVIORAL THEORY

Cognitive models of personality development draw from the philosophic tradition of rationalism that emerged during the Enlightenment —an eighteenth-century movement that favored empiricism, reason, and the scientific approach to knowledge. Cognitive psychologists hold the view that people have control over the thought processes that shape their emotions and behaviors. The way people think primarily determines their personality traits, and the way they feel about events that happen—either now or in the distant past—is a consequence of their beliefs about various experiences.

Cognitive behavioralists assume that if an individual thinks differently, he or she will feel and behave differently. Since thoughts— functional and dysfunctional—are the foundation of personality, those who want to alter or reinvent aspects of their personality can do so by changing the way they think about themselves, others, and important events in their lives.

THE COGNITIVE-BEHAVIORAL THEORY OF ALBERT ELLIS (1913–2007)

Jean-Paul Sartre's famous dictum that "Hell is other people" strikes a chord in all of us, but so too does the idea that our deepest source of joy comes from social connections. According to Albert Ellis, a leading proponent of cognitive-behavioral therapy and founder of rational emotive behavior therapy, flawed thinking prevents us from finding pleasure in living. Thus, those who fully agree with Sartre have dysfunctional thoughts that deny them healthy psychological adjustment to life's daily challenges. Ironically, the very last thing dogmatists would consider as the source of their problems is their own dysfunctional beliefs. How can absolute truths be dysfunctional? What they continue to overlook is the deeper purpose their belief systems serve.

§§

Ellis maintained that to discover the source of troublesome behavior, psychologists and their clients need not probe unconscious conflicts, past parenting patterns, or environmental dispensations of reward and punishment. The key to impaired functioning is found in people's habitual, *dysfunctional beliefs*, which determine and maintain disruptive emotions and dysfunctional behaviors.

Rational emotive behavior therapy (REBT) is based on the assumption that dysfunctional beliefs, while normal in childhood, are the source of disturbing emotions and behaviors that, if not corrected, may endure throughout adolescence and adulthood. Ellis frequently quoted Epictetus, the Stoic philosopher who lived during the first century of the Common Era: "People are disturbed not by things, but by the view which they take of them."[2] Our anxiety, depression, anger, and other unpleasant emotions are primarily caused by our tendency to dwell on experiences that we repeatedly interpret in dysfunctional ways. We distort ongoing evaluations of experience and reindoctrinate ourselves with these habitual thoughts—distortions that further disrupt ongoing emotions and behaviors in fairly predictable ways.

As with most psychological models, REBT digs beneath the surface to reveal the underlying causes of dysfunctional emotions and behaviors. To understand dogmatism, it is crucial to examine it in the context of the dysfunctional beliefs that shape and maintain it. Though the content of beliefs may be of questionable accuracy or merit, the actual dysfunction does not begin here; it originates in the demanding nature of beliefs, not in their content. Unrealistic demands cause the abnormal feelings and ineffective behaviors that accompany such characteristics as dogmatic authoritarian aggression and arrogant, dismissive communication, among others. Whether unpleasant emotions are repressed or consciously felt, REBT first focuses on the demanding quality of beliefs, which causes inappropriate emotions and behaviors.

To illustrate, if someone insults you and you respond with an angry volley of vitriol, the insult alone does not cause your hostile feelings and behavior. No one can make you angry or depressed, according to Ellis. People can frustrate, annoy, disappoint, and inconvenience us, but they do not have the power to send us into emotional fits of rage, nor can they plunge us into the depths of despair. Not unless we give them permission to do so. Our thoughts alone direct emotional and behavioral idiocy (to use one of Ellis's favorite expressions).

Although Ellis acknowledged that stressful family dynamics can influence one's beliefs, he maintained that troubled adults have pervasive, dysfunctional thought patterns that remain centered in childish demanding. Difficult people are generally unaware of the tapes in their heads that consistently demand retribution, attention, perfection (of self and others), fairness, loyalty, self-control, respect, happiness, and other irrational dictates that stem from unreasonable beliefs. Neurotics (by which Ellis meant emotionally disturbed people) believe they absolutely *should* and *must* live easy, stress-free lives and solve every problem with flawless ease and perfection.[3] They *must* be recognized and respected for their beliefs and behaviors (Ellis called this "musturbating"). In the end, these faulty beliefs ensure a stressful life in which childlike beliefs sustain excessive emotions and dysfunctional behaviors that fracture relationships, jeopardize careers, and prevent happiness. And mistaken beliefs spare no one; they are the major source of the dogmatist's psychological problems.

Ellis's theory underscores the idea that when we feel upset it is because we have habitual thoughts about a multitude of experiences and desires that bear little or no resemblance to reality. Is it reasonable to expect others to conform to our wishes? Believe what we believe? Respect or admire us? It may be nice, preferable, and desirable for people to think and do what we would like them to, but is it absolutely necessary? Are such beliefs rational? Is it logical to tell ourselves that we must succeed at something? That we should always be kind? Articulate? In Control? Responsible? Considerate? And that others should as well? In short, is it rational to demand perfection? The person who declares "I can't stand this!" reveals dictatorial, dysfunctional beliefs that ordain he or she should not have to suffer the inconveniences that life presents all of us on a daily basis. Adherence to such unreasonable beliefs guarantees emotional disruptions that create problematic behaviors, all of which results in unhappiness, unpopularity, disrespect, and a host of psychological disorders, including dogmatism.[4]

Ellis maintained that the potential for both rational and irrational thought is innate. We are predisposed to be happy, helpful, and productive, but we also have tendencies toward intolerance, superstition, procrastination, perfectionism, and any number of self-defeating thoughts and behaviors that prevent psychological well-being.[5]

> Note that you (and others) tend to hold irrational ideas that create neurosis unconsciously rather than consciously. You often consciously know it makes no sense for you to expect almost everyone to love you, to expect to do things well all the time, to refuse to stand any frustration, or to seriously worry about all threatening possibilities. But, underneath, you firmly and deeply believe this nonsense.[6]

Yet philosophically, if we agree that all humans are fallible, it follows that imperfection in ourselves and others is inevitable. Failure to accept such flaws perpetuates self-defeating thoughts, feelings, and behaviors—in that order. We needlessly blame others, ourselves, circumstances, social conditions, and worldly events for our personal misery. But we can all eliminate, or at least reduce, psychological distress if we apply the following analytic steps to unpleasant events in our lives. The key to understanding this is simple, claimed Ellis. It's as easy as A, B, C.

External events and internal triggers (including thoughts that recall experiences or plan for the future) are all *activating events*—which are the (A) that instigates *beliefs* (B). These beliefs are more or less reasonable, appropriate, and logical—or unreasonable, inappropriate, and illogical. The *consequent reactions* (C) are twofold—emotions and behaviors that do not result from the actual event (A). Rather, (C) occurs as a consequence of rational or dysfunctional beliefs (B) about activating events (A). Psychologically disturbed people have many free-floating beliefs and habitual demands of which they are largely oblivious and, therefore, do not articulate. This is why, when someone tells a dogmatist that his intense feelings or inappropriate behavior stem from faulty logic, he is likely to become inordinately defensive.

How many times have you heard someone say, "I'm so angry because he (or she) did. . . ." Ellis would say that the anger does not stem from what the other person did or did not do. (A) does not cause (C)—anger, in this case. That is what the person conveniently, but mistakenly, would like to believe. Similarly, Patty does not procrastinate with an important task because she is lazy, unmotivated, or irresponsible. She procrastinates because she mistakenly believes she absolutely should be able to play first and work later. "I *must* not have demands placed on me!" She might also procrastinate because she believes she must complete a task perfectly—a belief that overwhelms her with anxiety. Perhaps a combination of both beliefs contributes to her problem. Regardless, her extreme emotions and problematic behavior are the consequence of unreasonable beliefs about the task at hand. When those beliefs have a demanding quality, the (C) will be excess emotions that cause troublesome behaviors. Demanding beliefs that are *habitual yet unarticulated* suggest life should always run smoothly, pleasantly, and perfectly. Bad things should not happen! I should not have to put up with this! I deserve respect! I must be perfect! I'll never find anyone to love me! I should continue to upset myself over and over about . . . (some past event that the person resents and continues to dwell on)! These are characteristic dysfunctional beliefs of daily living that, if habitual, are psychologically disruptive and interpersonally damaging.

Dogmatic people have such beliefs. One of their dysfunctional beliefs is that they must always appear knowledgeable. They should have the right answers and solutions to all problems. Have you ever noticed the flash of fear that crosses a dogmatist's face when the conversation is redirected to something he or she knows little or nothing about? The fear is quickly suppressed, but its presence announces the habitual, dysfunctional thought, "I should always sound knowledgeable. It's totally embarrassing if I can't say something intelligent about this issue." Even dogmatists would agree that this is not a reasonable thought, yet beneath the surface, the habitual tape keeps rewinding in their heads, and this alone, according to REBT, determines inappropriate emotions and behaviors, which are significant components of dogmatic belief systems.

Dogmatic people also believe (irrationally) that others *must* agree with their views. Moreover (and this is a critical component), they tell themselves, "It's terrible and I can't stand it when people disagree with me, contradict me, or try to get me to change my mind! They ought to know better! They should respect me."[7] These thoughts routinely hover in the background and lead to emotional upheavals that, in turn, create childlike behaviors. Again, people with such faulty thinking do not articulate their demands so blatantly, to themselves or others. Even raging dogmatists are usually clever enough to temper their words, at least in certain situations. But their pressure of speech, tone of voice, body language, and emotional expressions are the observable consequences of hidden dysfunctional beliefs that become contemptuous confrontations, which imply "How dare you question . . . ," or, "How could you possibly be so stupid!"

These unreasonable thoughts account for the dogmatist's extreme emotions and behaviors that test our patience. Recall from chapter 2 that it is not *what* dogmatists believe but *how* they believe that is problematic. The demanding, emotional quality that accompanies what a dogmatist says is rooted in his or her dysfunctional beliefs. Anger, anxiety, rigidity, and arrogance are not the main problem. The unreasonableness of their self-imposed beliefs and demands is the source of their problem—in this case, their dogmatism.

§§

The seeds of dogmatism are sown in childhood when, for example, a mother anxiously demands, "Don't do that or people won't like you. You'll have no friends!" Children learn to believe that it is disastrous if people don't like them. In reality, throughout life, there will always be someone who does not fancy our company. Even if we were successful at getting everyone to like us, someone would surely dislike us because everyone else likes us! Nor could we get everyone to hate us—even Hitler has sympathizers and admirers. Irrational beliefs are not based on reality.

Children are also indoctrinated with values and belief systems that are emotionally laden or threatening: "If you question this belief you are bad (or stupid, or unlovable)." Early in the development of mental processes, children's minds are inevitably shaped and controlled without their awareness and consent. This only becomes harmful if, as their cognitive development unfolds, they are not encouraged to think for themselves. Lingering at the core of many dogmatic belief systems is the child's initial activating event (A), the parental *admonition* to believe as they do, and the child's fear and compliance (C), which could not be rationally mediated at the belief level (B) because his or her intellectual tools are too underdeveloped. Given that neuroscientists now recognize the destructive impact strong emotions have on the developing brain, it is understandable how indoctrinated children and youth carry their beliefs—indeed, feel trapped by them—into adulthood.[8] In childhood, they may have been admonished. "In this family everyone goes to university. You're nothing unless you've got a degree. No child of mine is going to end up working in a low-paying job that doesn't deserve respect." In their youth, opening their minds to question their parents' beliefs triggers anxious reminders of repeated warnings from early childhood. For many, it is simply easier to keep their minds closed.

When dogmatists are challenged, they needlessly defend themselves, not because they are questioned (activating event), but because their beliefs (B) about people's right to challenge them are dysfunctional. And those beliefs, not (A), always cause (C) their disruptive emotions and behaviors. Once we understand the unreasonable quality of their beliefs, we understand the source of their problem. Mary is not dogmatic because she has an angry disposition or because she is intolerant of others. Mary is dogmatic because her style of thinking is habitual and demanding. As mentioned in chapter 6, when people preface statements with such comments as, "It's perfectly clear to anyone who knows anything about . . . ," we can hear the anxiety or anger and demandingness that accompanies their inappropriate beliefs, and we are inclined to wonder why they are so certain. So adamant. So demanding. Why do they insist that others respect them for having nailed truth to the mat? Because they are thinking in irrational, dysfunctional ways. Ellis maintained that if they were to drop their demands, they would be more rational and less anxious, angry, depressed, defensive, or cynical. In the case of dogmatism, flawed reasoning fails to relieve their anxiety and secure what they believe they *must* have—infallible knowledge, social respect, and dignity. These are the serious, unmet needs that are unfortunately sustained by equally serious faulty reasoning that is dysfunctional yet unobservable.

How to Nondogmatically Challenge Dogmatic Thinking

REBT teaches us how to recognize and deal with dysfunctional beliefs in our personal lives, in our relationships, and in the helping professions. Changing the dysfunctional beliefs in the (A), (B), and (C) process requires (D), (E), and (F), where (D) stands for *disputations*, (E) stands for *effective, rational beliefs*, and (F) stands for appropriate *feelings*.

In the unlikely event that a dogmatist went for therapy, an REBT therapist would uncover and dispute his or her demanding, dysfunctional beliefs. Friends, spouses, coworkers, and colleagues can also consider how they might use the (D), (E), and (F) guidelines to effectively challenge faulty logic. The trick is to identify the dogmatist's dysfunctional beliefs about activating events, which he or she does not articulate clearly. Once the dysfunctional beliefs are established, we can apply the disputations that modify thoughts and reduce maladaptive emotions and behaviors.

Jonah helps us out here. Recognizing the demandingness that lies behind his dysfunctional beliefs, the therapist, a colleague, or a friend would first dispute his beliefs. For example, Jonah might reveal his religious beliefs by saying something along the lines of, "Atheists deserve to suffer the wrath of God." The REBT approach would ask Jonah, "Where is the evidence that God will condemn all nonbelievers?" Jonah might quote the Bible, at which point the disputer could ask, "How does the Bible constitute evidence? Without empirical evidence, I cannot be convinced." The challenger could also dispute Jonah's beliefs that "All children must be educated in basic traditional values. Rules must absolutely enforce those values by rewarding self-discipline and punishing disobedience and disrespect." An REBT intervention could ask, "Where is it written that all children *must* obey your orders or they deserve to be punished?" One might simply draw attention to Jonah's word "all" or ask him, "Is it reasonable to assume that others *should* live their lives according to your plan?" Or, "Are your adamant beliefs getting you what you want in life?" That last question would give him something to ponder in his quieter moments *if* he is at all introspective.

These types of disputations would introduce Jonah to effective, rational beliefs (E) that replace his demands with preferences, thus creating more reasonable views of himself, others, and the world of ideas. Perhaps Jonah would consider the underlying causes of his dogmatism if asked, "How do your beliefs and the way you convey them make you feel safe? Earn you respect? Give you dignity?" These are therapist interventions that would incorporate strategies from other therapy models to apply an eclectic or broad understanding of theory and therapy.

Effective, rational beliefs (E) reduce disruptive emotions like anxiety, anger, and depression. Jonah has been plagued with anxiety since childhood, and although he has managed to largely repress it, when he fails to get people to agree with his beliefs, or when he feels challenged to defend them, the same childhood anxiety, self-doubt, and frustration are triggered—emotions that have been maintained by entrenched, habitual "musts" and "shoulds." If Jonah can replace his demands with preferences and tell himself that "It would be nice if . . . ," "It would be preferable (or convenient, or desirable) if . . . ," he would notice that not only do his feelings become less intense, his actions become more appropriate to the situation.

Thus, REBT would teach Jonah how to listen for his dysfunctional, unreasonable beliefs, notice his exaggerated words that accompany them, and recognize the strong emotions and misguided behaviors that follow. By disputing and replacing his dysfunctional beliefs with rational, effective beliefs (E), Jonah's strong feelings (F) would diminish and his behaviors would become more appropriate. Preferences would then replace demands, and Jonah would stop proselytizing and accept that people have the right to differ, even if he views their differences as wrong or misguided. These rational, effective beliefs would create more appropriate feelings and behaviors.[9]

If dogmatic people can become more philosophical about the reality of human imperfections, they will become less demanding, feel more at ease with others, and gain the respect and dignity they (and all of us) desire. This takes practice, however, and cannot be achieved without persistent, careful monitoring of thoughts—thoughts that have become habitual and ingrained. The dogmatist is unaware that a pattern of dysfunctional thinking has become rigidly established, and it is therefore important that any attempts to challenge dogmatic thinking do not convey tones of demanding expectation that the dogmatist *must* change his or her beliefs. That would only infect the cure with more dogmatism.

Quite likely, the most that friends and family members can do is calmly note the demanding, unreasonable quality of dogmatic thinking, or repeat one word that sounds extreme, and let things go at that. In the privacy of their own thoughts, they might consider their closed-mindedness and its unpleasant effect on themselves and others. In some cases, close acquaintances might want to go one step further and casually suggest, "I can see that you're very passionate about your views, but I think that if you were a little less demanding about your beliefs, you'd feel differently—you wouldn't be so emotionally upset, and you wouldn't be so bothered by this. Our discussions might also be more enjoyable and rewarding." For this comment to be effective, it would have to be calmly repeated (paraphrased differently) a few times. Alas, in some cases, it may be wiser to take J. L. Austin's advice that "it may sometimes be better to let sleeping dogmatists lie."[10]

Unlike other therapists, an REBT therapist would not help dogmatists gain insight about the effects of their early childhood experiences. Such probes are outside the focus of REBT, which assumes that *how* the person currently thinks creates their problems—whether his or her thoughts are about past, present, or future events is inconsequential. Nor would a cognitive therapist explore biological vulnerabilities that might contribute to a person's dogmatism. In particular, anxiety would not be their focus of concern. By practicing the REBT method to dispel dysfunctional beliefs (using imagery and other techniques), dogmatic people could learn to think, feel, and behave more effectively. The overall purpose is to help them relax and take themselves and others less seriously so that they can improve the quality of their lives—especially their relationships and careers.

An REBT Perspective on the Source of Jonah's Dogmatism

From an REBT perspective, Jonah's rigid, doctrinaire beliefs can be seen as a product of childhood beliefs that we would hardly call dysfunctional. In his family, he learned that quiet obedience was in his best interest, since asking questions was risky. In a vulnerable young mind, it is understandable that Jonah would begin to think, "I *must* figure out how to be good or I'll be punished." If we really step outside our own minds for a moment and try to see the world from young Jonah's perspective, we see that he was cleverly adapting to a harsh reality.

We would hardly expect Jonah, the child, to believe the following: "I would certainly prefer that my parents accept me as I am. I'd like them to encourage me to think independently, but that's idle dreaming. I'll just play along with these folks and bide my time until I'm old enough to leave home. Meanwhile, I'll ask my teachers the questions I can't ask at home; I'll surf the Internet on library computers and read books that present different views on important matters—views my parents won't allow me to entertain much less discuss with them."

Children are not capable of such reasoning. In Jonah's case, by the time he reached adolescence, his emotional safety had taken precedence over cognitive curiosity for so long that it would have been impossible for him to step outside his safely constructed boundaries. He had learned to protect himself by acquiescing to those more powerful than himself—his parents, his teachers, the preacher, and God. Early beliefs had crystallized in tapes that silently traversed the neural circuits of his brain, and those tapes created a narrative that continually reinforced his established, dysfunctional beliefs.

The story Jonah told himself—the source of his later dysfunctional beliefs—went something like this: "If I question the beliefs of authority figures I will suffer terrible consequences, so I will obey and respect them. This will confirm that I am good, for they are right and I am wrong. Just as the lyrics in the song say, 'I am weak but thou art strong.' People who don't share my religious beliefs need to be shown the error of their ways—they should change their minds and accept God's truth. I'll help them do this by actively promoting the Word of God that's written in the Holy Bible. That will prove that I am a loyal follower of the church. Failure to fulfill that obligation would be terrible—a cross I simply couldn't bear."

These core beliefs led Jonah to conclude, in adolescence, that issues like abortion, homosexuality, and gay marriage were abominations of the Word—prejudiced beliefs that Jonah thought were moral imperatives. As an adult, Jonah habitually reactivated earlier beliefs that were set in stone. He believed his thoughts were rational, but because they were accompanied by strong emotions that vied for attention, his capacity for reason was diminished.

§§

These are the types of dysfunctional beliefs that, at the collective level, lead to discriminatory practices and violations of human rights. Where is the evidence that any mortal being has such a handle on truth that he or she is entitled to constrict the freedom of others? Where is the evidence?

Groups generally do not verbalize dysfunctional thoughts in the manner portrayed here, but their actions imply that, at the cognitive level, analysis is confined to low-level intellectual processing—processing that may or may not be consonant with reason.

We now leave the development of closed-minded dogmatism as seen from Ellis's variant of cognitive-behavioral theory and examine how the social learning view has much to offer our understanding of personality traits like dogmatism.

SOCIAL LEARNING THEORY

Social learning theory (SLT) is a branch of cognitive-behavioral theory that examines the nature and consequences of thinking styles that develop in the context of social relationships. Its underlying assumption is that all behavior is learned as a product of social interaction. Behavior can therefore be unlearned by reframing perceptions about oneself, others, and the world of ideas. Personality development begins when infants and children observe others and decide whether to imitate what they observe based on their anticipated outcome of reward or punishment. Simple observations and imitations of behavior are inevitable, and children who are offered attractive incentives to imitate a role model's beliefs and behaviors readily learn both.[11] A child who is raised in a family where both parents demonstrate a narrow-minded, bigoted approach to the complexities of life, and who is also praised for doing the same, will more likely than not imitate that behavior. In adulthood, the child's default tendency is to reboot the shallow thought structure learned from his or her parents.

Observations and behavior imitation further influence the assumptions children make about themselves, others, and the world—thoughts that accurately reflect or distort reality. This social learning affects children's cognitive flexibility and the extent to which they later question institutionalized beliefs of the dominant culture. In their early years, it is natural for children to accept parental beliefs without question, but if parents encourage them to think for themselves, their minds more readily entertain alternative viewpoints as they mature. In other words, it is the *quality* of thought behind the assumptions and interpretations children make about themselves, others, and the world of ideas that shapes their personalities and influences how they later develop important personal, interpersonal, social, and cultural belief systems. The *content* of their thoughts is secondary.

Children who grow up perceiving others as generally untrustworthy interpret behaviors and social roles differently from those who learn to basically trust others. Repeated, prolonged exposure to mistreatment by one or two central figures in a child's life will undoubtedly shape his or her beliefs, and children mistakenly generalize their negative experiences from one or two authority figures to all adults, assuming they too will treat them badly. According to the cognitive-behavioralists, this type of loopy logic figures prominently in all problematic emotions and personality traits, including that of dogmatism.

THE SOCIAL LEARNING THEORY OF ALBERT BANDURA (1925–)

In the 1970s, Albert Bandura, the founder of social learning theory (SLT), outlined the principles that govern behavior.[12] Observational learning, memory, beliefs about one's competence, and personal motivation determine one's goals and personality. For example, deciding whether to become a political candidate involves a host of anticipated rewards and punishment, established beliefs about the prevailing cultural and political institutions, and beliefs about one's ability to perform the necessary behaviors to get elected. Whether one becomes a doctor, a drug addict, or a despot, a constellation of belief expectancies determine one's life choices that, in turn, shape enduring personality characteristics, including dogmatism.

Social learning theory would view dogmatism as a process of learning that has its origins in modeling and belief expectancies about what might happen if one were to imitate or enact observed behaviors.[13] Consonant with Skinner's radical behaviorism, social learning theory acknowledges that reward and punishment play an important role in shaping personality, but other factors are considered equally if not more important agents, especially learning as a consequence of early social interactions.

Bandura's major concepts of *modeling* and *observational learning* emphasize the influential power of role models in children's social learning that occurs with or without immediate rewards or punishment from the environment. "Of the many cues that influence behavior, at any point in time, none is more common than the actions of others."[14] Children attend to people's behavior, encode or interpret it, and store it in their memory systems, where it is available for reenactment in chosen circumstances. As children vicariously observe influential role models, they apply four cognitive processes, or *personal determi-*

nants, that help them decide whether or not they will imitate the observed behaviors. This process of learning through observation is central to personality because children (observers) conclude that they will experience similar rewards or punishment if they imitate various role models' behavior (typically parents, peers, authority figures, or prestigious people).[15] Such observation and imitation is indispensable to personality development, for as William James noted, our experiences are based on what we first decide to attend to.[16] Young children attend to and imitate adult behaviors, which may or may not be to their advantage. For example, they may learn to attribute unrealistic, exaggerated qualities to people in positions of power, and therefore conclude that political, religious, or educational leaders have the right to mete out concrete rewards and punishment. This is especially likely if their parents teach them to view these elders as all-knowing, all-powerful protectors who will confer dignity on those who become their loyal supporters.

This ongoing modeling and imitation accounts for one's acquired personal and social competencies, both of which shape personality and its many traits. Social learning theory claims that the power of *self-efficacy*—the belief that one has the capacity to perform certain behaviors—complements observational learning and imitation. Self-efficacy is the individual's belief that he or she can generate and coordinate the necessary thoughts, emotions, social skills, and behaviors required to achieve certain goals. It is not to be confused with self-esteem, which involves one's feelings about one's personal worth. While success inadvertently enhances self-esteem, the belief that one can try new behaviors that might succeed is a crucial component of psychological competence—intellectual, emotional, and social.

Social learning theory would suggest that self-efficacy, modeling, and imitation shape such behaviors as dogmatic authoritarian submission, which is based on the enduring belief that "I am unable to determine my own values and behaviors." People who feel this way lack self-efficacy—a prerequisite for individual autonomy. Although Bandura does not elaborate on the emotional or biological components of self-efficacy, it is reasonable to speculate that anxiety undermines self-efficacy, and since anxiety is a major component of dogmatism, deficits in self-efficacy may explain other characteristics of dogmatism, including an intolerance of ambiguity; defensive, cognitive closure; dogmatic, authoritarian aggression; preoccupation with power and status; glorification of the in-group and vilification of the out-group; and strict adherence to conventional conduct.

It all begins with children who believe they are incapable of thinking for themselves. They lose confidence in their ability to overcome anxiety and self-doubt, which impairs their ability to autonomously and open-mindedly assess the merit of belief systems. Gradually, their minds close and they adopt, without question, the prevailing beliefs of authority figures such as parents, peers, priests, professors, and presidents. Later, when someone challenges their beliefs, they may become defensive, withdrawn, or angry because they cannot rationally explain how they arrived at their conclusions when such conclusions were not independently drawn. Thoughts are influenced by beliefs in one's self-efficacy, and children who are ridiculed for thinking independently suppress their natural curiosity, intelligent inquiry, and readiness to experiment with new ideas. When anxiety replaces curiosity, many choose to calm the storm by adopting someone else's plan—even if, in later life, that plan violates their own moral standards and requires them to aggress against others.

For the dogmatist, the alleviation of anxiety and isolation is highly rewarding, as is the gratification that social connection, identity, and dignity offer. Ideological allegiance is simply a means to a psychological end. When we consider that institutions are designed to get the results they achieve, it is not surprising that when leaders high in self-efficacy lead a narrow-minded *psychological* mission, they know which strategies will evoke beliefs, emotions, and behaviors that promote their aims.

§§

Bandura's theory incorporates three interdependent interactions of psychological components in human development—cognitive abilities (including beliefs), behaviors, and the effects of those interactions on the immediate environment. All three interact in a reciprocal manner to shape personality traits such as dogmatism. Each component or *determinant* affects the other two, which is why Bandura called this entire process of social learning *triadic reciprocal causation*.[17] From this perspective, dogmatism would be conceptualized as an interaction of *personal determinants* (P); actions, known as *behavior determinants* (B); and the *environment* (E). Personal determinants consist of cognitive processes, emotions, and biology that direct one's behavior, such as beliefs that determine who to vote for, which books to buy, which career to pursue, who to become friends with, and who to marry. These two determinants—person and behavior—alter one's immediate environment. For our purposes, we are largely concerned with the thoughts and behaviors that influence the personality trait of dogmatism and its impact on broader, ideological enclaves.

For example, dogmatists who anxiously defend their thoughts (P) that a charismatic political leader will offer psychological security because he is the purveyor of truth, will act (B) to support these leaders and their causes. Dogmatists' cognitive commitment and behavioral attendance at organized events will alter the political environment (E), by publicly confirming its values and goals, recruiting new members, and so on. Such decisions and behaviors reciprocally influence thoughts about the success or failure of actions, which either reinforce (increase) or punish (decrease) future behaviors—all of which further alter the political party's structural and public environment through such behaviors as financial contributions, volunteer committees, and fund-raising activities. In a similar vein, academic institutions open more sections of popular courses, theaters show hit movies, and television programming responds to viewer preferences. Personal determinants affect membership in ideological movements, and therefore the thoughts and behaviors of dogmatic leaders and followers influence and are influenced by triadic reciprocal causation.[18]

This may sound so obvious you are wondering why Bandura developed an entire theory to explain it, but prior to Bandura, psychologists overlooked or downplayed the *interactive* effect of the person, the person's behavior, and the environmental conditions in which the person's thoughts and behaviors operate. According to Bandura's theory, it would be inaccurate to conclude that someone has the personality trait of dogmatism without taking into account the beliefs that shape dogmatic behaviors, since both interact to select specific environmental circumstances that are compatible with those beliefs and behaviors. In turn, the person's dogmatic behavior influences the environment in an ongoing, interactive manner. This means that if we want to understand dogmatism, we must go beyond the person and the family in which he or she was raised. We need to consider the interactive effect of all social relationships and cultural institutions (E) that influence, promote, and maintain dogmatic thoughts (P) and actions (B). This three-way reciprocity sheds light on the successes and failures of, for example, hobbies, careers, and interpersonal relationships, as well as the rise of public institutions, political and religious movements, institutional planning, new trends, and so on.

Although social learning theory does not directly address dogmatism, we can assume that it would support the idea that dogmatic individuals were rewarded in their youth for attending to, imitating, and relying on external authority figures to determine and validate both themselves and their belief systems. Their unique personal determinants shaped belief systems that were largely derivative of other people's ideas, especially external role models who managed to convince these youngsters of their inviolate truth.

Whatever the specific determinants of dogmatism may be, dogmatists inaccurately appraise information. A preoccupation with power and status, for example, accounts for the unrealistic, exaggerated qualities dogmatists attribute to people in positions of power. These personal determinants affect membership in ideological movements, and thus the thoughts and behaviors of dogmatic individuals, their leaders, and other followers influence and are influenced by the social environment.[19] You may have noticed that SLT makes no mention of the interactive role of evolution on personality development. Perhaps a quadratic reciprocal model—in which the person, behavior, environment, and evolved behaviors interact to profile unique personality traits—will be forthcoming.

§§

Those who are co-opted by charismatic, dogmatic leaders fail to recognize that these leaders are also heavily influenced by Bandura's triadic model of causation. People in positions of authority who offer simplistic solutions manage to attract equally dogmatic followers, who likewise oversimplify the complex. And, as we saw in chapter 7, dogmatic authoritarian submitters gladly dedicate their allegiance to the dogma, to the leader, and to the enthusiastic followers of a group that they perceive (but do not articulate) as capable of providing psychological security and identity. Bandura explains this perpetuation of healthy or unhealthy group ideology as *collective efficacy*, which is the members' shared confidence in the group's ability to organize and perform actions that fulfill its mandate.[20]

Research on reciprocal determinism within groups is extremely challenging because the combined effects of personal and collective efficacy on individual and group behaviors in a given situation is immensely complicated. Moreover, if we add a fourth influential dimension of evolutionary psychology to Bandura's model, it becomes all the more daunting to scientifically measure and quantify the entire suite of interacting components that shape personality.

A Social Learning Perspective of Jonah's Dogmatism

Applying Bandura's major concepts to Jonah, we see how modeling, imitation, and perceived self-efficacy all contributed to his dogmatism. His parents were important role models whose religious and political beliefs he observed and imitated at an early age—a normal childhood tendency. However, in Jonah's case, he mistakenly believed not only that his adherence to parental beliefs would assure care that had been lacking, he also believed that unquestioning adoption would protect him from ridicule and scorn. These were the personal determinants that strengthened Jonah's beliefs and facilitated the gradual closing of his mind. In adolescence and early adulthood, his religious beliefs combined with his behaviors to further reinforce his alliance with the church, so that Jonah's beliefs, behaviors, and the environment in which they operated reciprocally determined important aspects of his personality. Personal determinants shaped dogmatic religiosity that benefited the church, which reciprocally rewarded Jonah with employment—a reward that strengthened his commitment and involvement. This mutual interaction of events influenced Jonah's decision to leave the teaching profession and become a politician. In midlife, when electoral support dwindled, self-doubt began to erode his self-efficacy. From a social learning perspective, we see how all three determinants—personal, behavioral, and environmental—conspired to shape and reinforce Jonah's personality trait of dogmatism, a trait that now leaves him feeling cynical and unfulfilled in middle age. While social learning theory assumes early social relationships were the source of Jonah's dogmatism, cognitive-behavioral therapy assumes that Jonah's dogmatism was the result of dysfunctional thoughts, emotions, and behaviors. Both assumptions make valid contributions to our understanding.

§§

As we saw in chapter 10, biological dispositions also figure prominently in the capacity for reasoned objectivity, yet cognitive-behavioral and social learning theories devote little attention to biologically driven, intervening moods that influence thoughts and behaviors. Cognitive-behavioralists suggest that, regardless of one's biological predisposition for disruptive moods, people can still choose to think differently about their biological misfortune, and thereby reduce the disturbing effects their emotional predispositions have on cognitive processing.

These last three chapters have drawn from traditional twentieth-century personality theorists who focused on early childhood influences—all of which have presumed links to dogmatism. Using robust measures, relationships between the following concepts or conditions and dogmatism could be empirically tested. Each of the following statements could be prefaced with, "It is hypothesized that dogmatism is not significantly related to . . ." (Note that this assumption is known as the *null hypothesis*—a statement of no change from the given psychological condition.)

- an inferiority complex that causes one to strive for personal superiority over others.
- narrative constructions that reflect themes of fear and anxiety.
- harsh, authoritarian parenting.
- destructive, overly competitive social values.
- basic mistrust of self, others, and the surrounding world.
- conditions of worth that create anxiety and incongruence.
- inauthentic thoughts, feelings, and behaviors.
- modeling and imitative social learning.
- demanding, habitual, dysfunctional beliefs.

§§

We now turn our attention to an important contribution to personality theory that began more than two thousand years ago. In preparation for an entirely different journey into the psyche, dim the lights, put on some soft music, and prepare your mind for a journey that is as relevant to dogmatism as it is to any other personality trait or ideological practice. Most of all, it has implications for your happiness. I refer here to the philosophy of Buddhism.

NOTES

1. B. F. Skinner, *Science and Human Behavior* (New York: Macmillan, 1953).

2. A. Ellis, *Overcoming Destructive Beliefs, Feelings, and Behaviors* (Amherst, NY: Prometheus Books, 2001), p. 16.

3. A. Ellis, *Reason and Emotion in Psychotherapy*, rev. ed. (New York: Kensington, 1994).

4. A. Ellis, *Reason and Emotion in Psychotherapy* (New York: Lyle Stuart, 1962).

5. A. Ellis and R. A. Harper, *A New Guide for Rational Living* (Hollywood, CA: Wilshire Book Company, 1975).

6. A. Ellis, *How to Live with a Neurotic* (Hollywood, CA: Wilshire Book Company, 1957), pp. 56–57.

7. During my fellowship at the Ellis Institute in New York, in 1999, Ellis frequently reminded us that the most common, unarticulated dysfunctional belief that underlies problematic emotions, behaviors, and maladaptive personality traits like dogmatism is "childlike demandingness."

8. R. Dawkins, *The God Delusion* (New York: Houghton Mifflin, 2006).

9. A. Ellis, *Better, Deeper and More Enduring Brief Therapy: The Rational Emotive Behavior Therapy Approach* (Bristol, PA: Brunner/Mazel, 1996).

10. J. L. Austin, *Philosophical Papers*, ed. J. O. Urmson and G. J. Warnock (Oxford: Oxford University Press, 1979).

11. A. Bandura and W. Mischel, "Modifications of Self-Imposed Delay of Reward through Exposure to Live and Symbolic Models," *Journal of Personality and Social Psychology* 2 (1965): 698–705. In his classic study of observation learning and imitative behavior, Bandura had children observe a film in which adults displayed aggressive behavior toward a Bobo doll (punching, kicking, and yelling at it). The children (subjects) were placed in three groups, each of which observed different consequences for adult aggression. One group observed adults being punished for their aggression; another group observed adults ignoring the aggression, and the third group saw adults being rewarded for their aggression. Children's aggressive behavior was subsequently observed and recorded when they played in the

same room of toys. Those who viewed the adults being rewarded for aggression were significantly more likely to aggress against the Bobo doll when given the opportunity to do so.

12. A. Bandura, *Social Learning Theory* (Englewood Cliffs, NJ: Prentice Hall, 1977).

13. Other major theorists in the field include Julian Rotter, John Dollard, and Neal Miller. I have chosen to present Bandura's theory because, of the three, Bandura emphasizes the social nature of learning, which coincides with my theory that a lack of social connection and dignity figures prominently in dogmatism.

14. The Psi Café, http://www.psy.pdx.edu/PsiCafe/KeyTheorists/Bandura.htm (accessed January 4, 2007).

15. A. Bandura, D. Ross, and S. A. Ross, "Transmission of Aggression through Imitation of Aggressive Models," *Journal of Abnormal and Social Psychology* 63 (1961): 575–82. In this study, Bandura and his colleagues demonstrated three key factors that influence modeling: (1) the characteristics of the model (those most similar to ourselves are more likely to be observed and imitated), (2) observer attributes (those who are low in self-esteem and dependent on others are more prone to imitate the behaviors they observe), (3) modeled behavior that is rewarded increases the likelihood of imitation. This third variable is, according to Bandura, stronger than the other two.

16. R. Goodman, "William James," *The Stanford Encyclopedia of Philosophy* (Spring 2006 edition), http://plato.stanford.edu/archives/spr2006/entries/james/ (accessed June 12, 2007).

17. A. Bandura, *Social Foundations of Thought and Action: A Social Cognitive Theory* (Englewood Cliffs, NJ: Prentice-Hall, 1986).

18. Ibid.

19. Ibid.

20. A. Bandura, *Self-Efficacy: The Exercise of Control* (New York: Freeman, 1997).

Chapter 16

REMOVING THE NAILS

Buddhist Philosophy

The mind is everything.
What you think you become.

Gautama Siddharta (563–483 BCE)

BUDDHIST PHILOSOPHY—LETTING GO

You may be wondering, what does Buddhism have to do with dogmatism? A lot. We will conclude Part III with a section on Buddhist philosophy because many Western psychologists now incorporate Buddhist tradition in their understanding of human existence, particularly its ideas about the roots of suffering. Buddhism's philosophic tenets of *impermanence*, *craving*, *attachment*, *dissatisfaction*, and the *ego* complement our understanding of dogmatism in that all of these concepts cause defective thinking—which, according to Gautama, is a major source of suffering. However, following the *eightfold path* to enlightenment can reduce or eliminate most human frailties and problems.

The philosophic, nontheistic origins of Buddhism date back to the teachings of Siddhartha Gautama, born Prince Gautama about 563

BCE in Lumbini, modern-day Nepal. Legend tells us he was over-protected and surrounded by the palatial luxury of royalty. Married to a beautiful princess, with whom he had a son, Gautama could have lived a life of comfort, safety, and luxury that was fitting for the man who would be king. But Gautama was uneasy about such privileged seclusion; he felt increasingly imprisoned and isolated from reality. Unable to satisfy his curiosity about the world outside his sheltered existence, he became immensely dissatisfied with his life. In his mid-twenties he decided to slip out in the middle of the night and trade his life of royalty for a life of his choosing beyond the palace walls. There, he encountered sickness, old age, and death first-hand—profound experiences that inspired Gautama to reveal the causes of suffering and search for solutions to human misery.

He studied with Yoga teachers in northern India for six years, but Yoga meditation and intense asceticism provided him no satisfactory cures for human suffering.[1] In desperation, he resolved to sit beneath the Bodhi tree until, through prolonged meditation, he devised a practical plan to end suffering. The views he developed and articulated became known as the *Middle Way*—a disciplined approach to life that avoids the extremes of self-indulgence and self-mortification that create human misery.[2] Through his teachings, he became known as the Buddha, a title that means "one who is awake."[3]

Although Gautama was known as the Buddha, near the end of his life he is alleged to have said, "Do not believe anything just because some authority, even me, has said it. Be a light unto yourself."[4] Implicit in this statement is the warning against dogmatism. Later, Gautama's philosophy expanded to form theocratic divisions that included beliefs about reincarnation. These departures went beyond Buddha's original ideas that taught "not a word about God, the Creator, or the soul, not a word about the Buddha or Buddhism."[5] As is often the case, the "ism," or practice of philosophic ideologies, alter the intent of original dogma, particularly after its proponent dies, making room for those consumed by their own egos. Buddhism is as vulnerable to dogmatism as any other philosophy or religion, for, once again, it is not the content of beliefs that is the problem, but rather the psychological needs of the believer. I think it is safe to say, however, that the fundamentalist and evangelical dogma of monotheistic religions is reinvigorated in times of unrest, while Buddhism's philosophic concepts of impermanence and change enable followers to better adapt to change, rather than react to it with closed-minded resistance that clamors for tradition.

More than a thousand years after Gautama's death, his teachings about the path to *enlightenment* aroused the interest of writers in philosophy, psychology, and literature.[6] Like Prince Siddhartha, later philosophers and psychologists tried to shed light on the suffering that stems from avoidance or denial of our inevitable death and decay. While the darkness of death elbows its way into our quieter moments of existence, there is comfort in knowing that our Buddha-nature can put us on a path to mindful awareness and enlightenment. But there is no map that outlines a linear progression from "You are here" to a fixed destiny called enlightenment. Rather, our Buddha-nature sets us on a lifelong journey, a process that helps us extinguish cravings and attachments through the method of mindfulness, through the expression of compassion, and through the essence of wisdom.[7]

We see the idea of *compassion* in the Adlerian concept of social interest, in Erikson's generativity, in Maslow's being values, and in Rogers's unconditional positive regard.

THE FOUR NOBLE TRUTHS

Buddhism fully awakens us to the reality that all things disintegrate. Sentient beings are impermanent; change is inexorable. "Whatever is subject to origination is subject also to destruction."[8] We come to realize that all of us are slowly crumbling as we move closer to death. Though our bodies create new cells to replace those that have died, the process of regeneration slows with age until we become "wasted, full of sickness and frail; this heap of corruption breaks to pieces."[9] To effectively cope with these existential difficulties, the Buddha outlined his Four Noble Truths, which are both the cause and cure for human suffering:

1) All life involves suffering and dissatisfaction.
2) Suffering is caused by craving (longing for things to be other than they are) and attachment (the fear of losing what we think we have).
3) If craving and attachment cease, suffering too will cease.
4) If we follow the Eightfold Path, we can replace craving and attachment with compassion and enlightenment.[10]

DISSATISFACTION, CRAVING, ATTACHMENT, AND THE EIGHTFOLD PATH

From the time we are born until we die, we undergo change. We traverse a life of becoming, change, and termination, and it is the rejection of the fact that all existence is impermanent that creates dissatisfaction.[11] We hunger for permanence and convince ourselves that material possessions, a person's total love and commitment, fame and glory, revolutionary ideas and immutable beliefs will relieve our suffering. Yet the fact is that all we are and all that we do is fleeting, though camouflaged by psychological scaffolding that props up our egos and shields us from the harsh reality of life and death. We clutch at political and religious beliefs, thinking they will satisfy our cravings for truth, and convince ourselves that the dogma behind ideological movements will give us something to hang onto, something solid that will not vanish.

These are ego-related acquisitions that ultimately prove futile because all of them reflect cravings that, like us, will perish. Instead of preventing suffering and sorrow, these "acquisitions" add to unhappiness:

> Ironically, the more we crave to possess and dominate the world and others, the deeper and more unbearable becomes the chasm of our own emptiness. In order to conceal this rapidly widening gulf our

compulsion develops into frenzy. But, however hard we try, we will never succeed in filling an inner emptiness from the outside; it can only be filled from within. A lack of *being* remains unaffected by a plenitude of *having*.[12]

This "having versus being" mode was Buddha's original concern.[13] Quests for more and more and the demand for permanence require us to externalize our autonomy, to transfer it to something else, whether it be an ideology, another person, or material possessions. Yet many of us fail to recognize that the consequence of ignorance and cravings are the source of our suffering. "Anxiety is the mood of ignorance."[14]

We seek inner peace yet overlook the reality and source of our disease. We distract ourselves from emotional distress through work, shopping, and mindless entertainment that allows us to vicariously identify with idols, with the rich and famous, with heroes and heroines, with victims and martyrs. These diversions represent a kind of "*tactical ignorance*, and until an unavoidable big question forces itself upon us, things go more or less all right."[15] Even when psychological discomfort disturbs us, we bury it beneath endless busyness until restlessness, self-alienation, and dissatisfaction become integral to our being. We become strangely numb and disconnected, failing to see that by disregarding our emotional existence we dissect those parts of ourselves that give life joy and meaning.

Such is the case with dogmatists, who have learned to compensate for denied emotions by so fortifying their cognitions that eventually they become caricatures of themselves; they fail to see that what will make them happy lies within. The stronger and louder their beliefs, the weaker and quieter their emotions. "Thinking feels safer because it does not *feel* at all."[16]

Buddhism posits that we must abandon our illusions to counteract our ignorance of existence and see the world for what it is—impermanent, imperfect, and unable to provide us with what we think will make us happy. That is the bold awareness that releases us from suffering. When we accept the world and ourselves for what they truly represent, we stop wanting things to be different and lessen our aversions (anger, resentment, and hate).[17] We let go. Realizing the dynamic process of change inherent in all aspects of life, we accept that everything is knit into a fabric of interconnectedness. Everything is also impermanent, and our awareness and acceptance of this reality enables us to surrender our egos—the unobserved mind, the voice in our head that pretends to be who we desire to be. The ego shelters "unobserved emotions that are the body's reaction to what the voice in the head is saying."[18] We accept our oneness and live in solidarity with others, which is the essence of compassion. In this sense, compassion is not sympathy, nor does it separate people into dichotomous terms and categories—a need that reflects the very essence of dogmatism.

The *non-self* (sometimes referred to as *no self*) is the third characteristic of existence "that sets Buddhism apart from practically all other religions, philosophical and psychological theories and positions."[19] This concept does not reject the self but suggests instead that our sense of self is not as static as our *idea* of our self. Therefore, to affirm one's constancy and worth as if it were a fixed entity is a mistake. This applies to the idea of life after death, which, according to Buddha, is a delusion that reflects craving and attachment—craving for immortality and attachment to an ego. The self or ego "is an imaginary, false belief which has no corresponding reality, and it produces harmful thoughts of 'me' and 'mine,' selfish desire, craving, attachment, hatred, ill-will, conceit, pride, egoism, and other defilements, impurities and problems. It is the source of all troubles in the world, from personal conflicts to wars between nations."[20]

It is also the source of institutionalized religions that are historical outgrowths of suffering, craving, and attachment. Buddhism assumes that orthodox religious doctrines take us further and further away from our inner Buddha-nature—one's God becomes all and we become nothing. "Hence, we feel safe only when we are able to convince ourselves that the concepts and symbols of *our* belief structure are eternally valid and irrefutable. . . . We center our concern on establishing to ourselves and others the unique validity and superiority of our particular beliefs."[21] I am reminded of a friend's childhood experience with a Catholic priest who chastised her for attending a different church that dismissed the notion of Hell. "The priest wagged his finger in my face and said, 'You stay away from it!'" Annoyed and perplexed by the priest's command, she later opined that "God would not have given us brains if he did not want us to use them." Choosing not to accept a religion in which dogmatism appeared integral to membership, she eventually became an apostate. Her reaction is compatible with the view of many readers: a God of the universe would favor open-minded questioning and reason over unquestioning, closed- or narrow-minded dogmatism.

If we can confront and abandon our presumed truths, we become free of entrapments. An individual who seeks to fulfill and live by his Buddha-nature is "characterized by an open, outgoing generosity, tempered by mindfulness and ethical restraint. . . . His mind should be discerning and critical, yet rooted in a deep inner calm."[22] Sincere, open engagement of the new requires sincere disengagement from our egos that cling to old perceptions, needs, and beliefs. Whereas dogmatism glorifies the ego, Buddhism demolishes it.

But biological brains rush in to reveal their cleverness. With billions of neurons for ammunition, our brains are able to trick us into believing we have a solid identity and that by achieving success and acquiring possessions, we will attain continuous happiness. Our innate tendency to compulsively sustain such fixed illusions keeps us rooted in this mindset.[23] Buddhist philosophy maintains that we can never completely possess or eradicate what our minds regard as necessary. The existence of these impermanent essentials, and our perceived need for them, is fashioned by narrow-minded, misguided egos.

A sense of identity and the desire for certain attachments are normal, but a blind pursuit of inadequate solutions for suffering severs us from the totality of existence. That totality is always there; it simply is. Its transitory existence neither starts nor ends, for all things come from "a matrix of conditions and in turn become part of another matrix of conditions from which something else emerges."[24]

In a similar vein, the German philosopher Georg W. F. Hegel (1770–1831) claimed that every idea (thesis) creates an opposing idea (antithesis) that merges with, yet alters, the original idea. This creates a synthesis (provided the synthesis contains within it the original thesis and antithesis, and is able to reconcile both). The synthesis generates a new thesis, and so on. Thus, the Hegelian idea of *being* pertains to all existence and evokes its antithesis—*not being*. The interdependence of these two states produces a synthesis, that *of becoming*.[25] Like life itself, ideas are clouds on a windy day. Some are light, airy companions to the warmth of the sun; others are dark, heavy, and foreboding. But whatever their shape and circumstance, all are ephemeral. I include Hegel's nineteenth-century application of Buddhism here, since his philosophy became an important precursor to various strands of personality theory, especially those of existential psychology and Buddhism.

§§

Buddhism is not a static dogma of truth that frees Buddhist followers from all confusion and doubt. Its teachings offer practical guidelines and methods to those who accept that at the heart of existence is great mystery. Still, there is "freedom present in each moment of experience."[26] We are free to choose whether to focus on or rid ourselves of concerns that distance us from the moment—the *now* that is all there is—the *now* that can quench our thirst for happiness if we only expand our awareness of its complete, awesome presence in the current moment. "You can't get there from here, and besides there's no place else to go."[27]

We can only fully experience *now* if we remove our masks and open our minds to the essence of these first three Noble Truths. These truths help us eliminate suffering by following the Eightfold Path. This path provides a means to purge unhealthy cravings and dissatisfaction from ourselves because it teaches us Right Understanding, Right Thought or Attitude, Right Speech, Right Action, Right Livelihood,

Right Effort, Right Concentration, and Right Mindfulness. As we embark on this journey, we are not expected to abandon all desires, especially those that are self-preserving, but we are required to accept things as they are without becoming attached to the idea that things, people, and events are static and must remain unchanged. This acceptance and lack of attachment places us on the Noble Eightfold Path to enlightenment, which extinguishes much of our craving and suffering.

Closed-minded dogmatism masks one's inherent Buddha-nature and interferes with five of the Eightfold Path objectives, all of which strive for moderation:

1. Right Understanding
2. Right Thought or Attitude
3. Right Speech
4. Right Action
5. Right Mindfulness

While each could be expanded and incorporated with the thirteen characteristics of dogmatism, I will briefly address only those that are central to its practice.

Right Understanding is "the beginning, the middle and the end of the Buddhist path. . . . It is the deepest realization of your own nature, an understanding that is way beyond words or conscious thought."[28] As thoughts and emotions arise in the present, Right Understanding is unencumbered by the ego that evaluates them. Through meditation and contemplation we can discover the extent to which our thoughts color our emotions and energize action. Be cognizant of your thoughts and let them pass, for they are, like everything else, impermanent. Buddhism teaches us to live fully by embracing awareness of the moments that pass by, to let go of habitual thoughts about self, others, and the world. With such awareness, we stop old, routine thoughts from plaguing us with unpleasant, harmful emotions that burden the moment. Right Understanding thus offers a practical solution to thoughts that fuel anxiety, frustration, and anger. Not that we won't have such emotions. But full awareness of them means we will simply notice them as they occur and allow them to pass, rather than escalate into disruptive feelings. Right Understanding frees us because it helps us understand things as they are; it is accomplished by accepting and grappling with the Four Noble Truths, which banish ignorance.

Matthieu Ricard commented that few people spend time trying to understand their minds, which act like spoiled brats running here, there, and everywhere. Yet Ricard suggests that to understand one's mind is more entertaining than going to the movies—an awareness that creates enlightenment, which is the source of happiness, serenity, and psychological freedom.[29] Right Understanding is an adventure dogmatists would rather not take, for it would require them to open locked doors within the psyche, behind which genuine self-knowledge is fearfully sequestered.

When Buddhists talk of *ignorance*, "it has nothing to do with stupidity. In a way, ignorance is very intelligent, but it is an intelligence that works exclusively in one direction. That is, we react exclusively to our own projections instead of seeing what is there."[30] On a daily basis, we spontaneously designate things, people, and ideas as good or bad, desirable or undesirable. We do not see that "the supposed supremacy of rational thought over feelings and emotions turns out to be an illusion."[31] Right Understanding pertains to deep, ongoing emotional awareness about one's illusions.

Such an age-old idea could not be more applicable to dogmatism. "This dependency of views and opinions on the first evaluative impact of feeling is a prominent cause of subsequent dogmatic adherence and clinging [that are] often manifest in heated arguments and disputation."[32] Our problems are caused by attachments and aversions, and to detach ourselves from egotistical demands, we can dispel inappropriate emotional reactions. These are precisely the principles that Albert Ellis applies in his rational emotive behavior therapy approach, which emphasizes the consequences of defective thinking.

Right Understanding will further facilitate Right Speech, for we will be less inclined to speak from uncontrollable anger and anxiety.

This philosophy encourages us to monitor and let go of the thoughts that spur these emotions. People who harshly condemn others and are inconsiderate of their views prevent harmony and unity, while those with Right Speech "speak the truth and use words that are friendly, pleasant, gentle, and useful [and] consider what is appropriate for the time and place."[33]

Equally relevant to dogmatism is Buddha's teaching of Right Mindfulness—an awareness that goes beyond emotions to include our physical body and our thoughts. Negative emotions and actions are the result of thoughts that misperceive reality, and an awareness of thoughts *as they appear* helps us understand their source and accuracy. This process of awareness (or enlightenment) enables us to constructively deal with ongoing thoughts and emotions that influence our actions. Thus, we then see things more clearly, without distortions that are maintained by names and labels; genuine freedom comes from being aware of one's own mind and making good decisions based on that awareness.[34] Since anxiety is linked to dogmatic beliefs, being mindful of our anxiety and closed-mindedness helps us replace them with Right Thought or Attitude—the capacity for selfless detachment, love, compassion, and nonviolence.

Finally, dogmatists are largely unaware of their emotions—especially those consumed by dogmatic authoritarian aggression. Unlike the dogmatist, a bodhisattva is one who "vows to dedicate life to the salvation of all sentient beings, not accepting full liberation until all others are free from suffering."[35] He or she practices Right Action, which consists of "moral, honorable, and peaceful conduct" that is respectful of others.[36] This contrasts sharply with the dogmatist who justifies his destruction of personhood through dogmatic authoritarian aggression. By assigning people to either an in-group or an out-group, and then glorifying or vilifying them, the dogmatist not only negates the other's beliefs, his or her tone of voice implies negation of the other. This is the ultimate failure of Right Action. The dogmatist's need to put others down, denigrate them, and judge the totality of their being shows that he or she has a long way to go and a lot of work to do in this struggle for enlightenment. Mindful of such imperfection in themselves and others, Buddhists strive to extend the warmth of loving-kindness to all sentient beings.

A Buddhist word of caution: Guard against becoming too attached to any of these four Noble Truths themselves, for none provide a panacea for personal, interpersonal, and worldly problems. In the spirit of Buddhism, they are intended as practical guidelines and strategies to alleviate suffering in the world, not ultimate truths that guarantee permanent salvation.

When we open our minds to our inner selves, we can become awakened to an expansive feeling of connection to all sentient beings, a feeling of deep satisfaction that nourishes an enduring love of life. According to Matthieu Ricard, who wrote extensively about happiness, such insight "emerges from a basic approach that allows us gradually to shed our mental blindness and the disturbing emotions it produces and hence the principal causes of our suffering.[37] By happiness, Ricard means "the purging of mental toxins, such as hatred and obsession, that literally poison the mind. It is also about learning how to put things in perspective and reduce the gap between appearances and reality."[38]

Buddhist teachings promote deep, lasting happiness and enlightenment—an inner calm that pervades all that one encounters and an open heart that radiates loving-kindness. This is the Buddha-nature that lies deep within everyone, including the dogmatist. Its presence is like the stillness in the depths of a turbulent ocean. Those of us who are blind to its existence are vulnerable to being buffeted by waves of anxiety, self-doubt, cravings, jealousy, and hatred. Those who adhere to visions of truth, perfection, and happiness as if they were attainable and permanent convince themselves that "by holding on tight to an idea, object, or person, I feel momentarily safe and unafraid."[39] Imperfection and weakness are signs of a lack of confidence; it is a self-pitying, hesitant, timid, and passive sense of self. The Buddhist perspective of imperfections and weakness is very different—such human conditions offer us a stark but realistic view of existence, one that encourages us "to rid ourselves of dependency on the root causes of suffering."[40]

The compulsion to control ideas and ensure their permanence reduces the anxiety of dogmatists' obsession to avoid ambiguity—especially the ambiguity that comes with transition and change. They become trapped in distorted perceptions and frozen convictions. Once dogmatists decide a person is an absolute idiot, villain, or saint, cognitive paralysis robs them of the freedom to live in full awareness of the person's being here *now*, and to accept him or her with loving-kindness. Dogmatists are too attached to their permanent view of things and are therefore not content to live in the here and now. We recognize that the Buddhist concept of "here and now" is difficult to fully grasp, but dogmatists would find the very idea of the "eternal now" incomprehensible. Recall from chapter 6 that, with regard to time perspective, dogmatists are more preoccupied with the past or fixated on some future utopia; they would thus find it difficult to experiment with another way of being that asks them to live more fully in the present.

While Buddhism describes the dangers of an ego addicted to attachments, it does not attempt to explain *why* the unenlightened ego has such imperfections in the first place. That work was left to psychologists and psychiatrists nearly two thousand years later. Nonetheless, Buddhism offers strategies to help us internalize values that lead to a way of thinking that shapes our manner of being. We no longer need a static worldview per se because, as social beings, "every attitude we assume, every word we utter, and every act we undertake *establishes* us in relation to others."[41] A deep recognition and practice of this awareness fosters the kindness and cooperation that emanate from a light spirit, free of attachments. This is enlightenment. This is wisdom. There are no hidden secrets, but there is a lot of work to do.

Dogen, a famous Zen master, once said:

To study Buddhism is to study the self.
To study the self is to forget the self.
To forget the self is to be one with others.[42]

A psychological variation of this emerges from a blend of personality theories:

> To study psychology is to study the self.
> To study the self is to understand the self.
> To understand the whole of one's self means that one is capable of
> being easier on oneself and therefore easier on others,
> being better equipped to make good decisions, and
> being able to live an authentic, productive, happy life.

The pursuit of this uncluttered vision of who we are will take different paths for each of us. The route is not as important as what we find when we get there: that all knowledge is partial, and that truths are, at best, probable. To those of you who have unwavering faith in the truth of beliefs, may you also have unwavering faith in your ability to doubt those beliefs.

A BUDDHIST PERSPECTIVE ON JONAH'S DOGMATISM

From our survey of Buddhist philosophy, it becomes apparent that Jonah's childhood anxiety led to cravings for permanent protection that were later gratified by his fervent adoption of religious ideology. His ego became heavily invested in finding absolute truths—truths that Buddhism rejects because all things are impermanent, including the ego, the soul, and abstract beliefs. Jonah's attachment to a religion that offered permanent salvation and preservation in an afterlife reduced his suffering at the expense of authentic open-mindedness. Detached from his emotions and unaware of his dogmatism, Jonah might benefit from a good map and sturdy compass that could guide him through the Eightfold Path. Perhaps a chance encounter with a Buddhist bodhisattva would, through acts of loving-kindness, introduce Jonah to the Four Noble Truths. The question is: Do you think Jonah would be receptive to Buddhist teachings about the cause of universal suffering?

SUMMING UP

For whatever constellation of possible causes—biological predispositions, an insecure attachment to primary caregivers, an inability to regulate emotions, inadequate social learning, educational discouragement, and other unknown factors—dogmatists' excessive vulnerability
to threat disrupts their psychological functioning. They cope by
building a wall against awareness rather than opening a door to insight.
Unaware that they have repressed the anxiety that emanates from not
being able to fully access knowledge, or confront the inevitability of
death—both physical and psychological—they smother their potential
for open-minded thought with the certainty that what they know will
guarantee them a strong identity, social connections, and dignity. Certainty becomes calcified. Such mistaken posturing, while protective at
one level, increases the probability that others will prove them wrong
or dismiss them, further increasing their anxiety and intensifying their
efforts to defend against such emotional distress and loss.

§§

These last eight chapters have cut a wide swath across the field of personality to address plausible causes of dogmatism—a personality trait
that represents only one dimension of the whole person. The challenge
is to scientifically study all of its attendant thoughts, emotions, and
goal-directed behaviors that function within a dynamic, integrated
whole in an ever-changing environment. The task is daunting. Rigorous research needs to be conducted on all of the complex interacting, often invisible components that shape this personality trait.

While psychologists have made important gains here and offered
various suggestions on how to improve the reliability, validity, and predictive accuracy of trait measures,[43] it remains highly improbable that
they and other social science researchers will ever completely understand
any one personality trait. That can be frustrating to psychology students
who want clear facts that explain, for example, their mother's constant

anxiety, their older brother's narcissism, or their new girlfriend's "hysterical reaction to every little thing." They want personality research to provide clear explanations—something comparable to a binary code that inputs data and exports perfect outcomes, nicely charted like the human nervous system or the periodic table of chemical elements. Given the complexity of the subject matter, however, this is not possible.

But despite the imprecise nature of the discipline, theorists of all persuasions are intrigued by the diverse mixture of personality traits that each of us brings to scenes of daily living. From simple exchanges in polite conversation to the conflict of intimate relationships, from the halls of business and academia to the halls of justice and global institutions, in the scenes of novels and the stanzas of poetry, human behavior and personality traits fascinate and define us. As research avenues apply progressively more robust measures to advance psychological understanding, the theoretical field of personality is evolving alongside our evolutionary traits—expanding its field of inquiry and affirming its adaptive presence.

To contribute to that expanding field, the major influencing factors of dogmatism are summarized and organized in a comprehensive, integrative model of dogmatism (see table 16.1). Originally developed by the psychiatrist George Engel, this biopsychosocial theory was intended as an eclectic model that would improve patient-clinician relationships and patient healing. But the model also offers a useful, integrative approach to understanding the origins of psychological conditions and personality traits. A complete understanding of their origins requires us to consider the complex interaction of biological factors (genes and biology) that influence psychological functioning (thoughts, perceptions, interpretations, narratives, feelings, and behaviors) that respond to environmental stressors that, in turn, influence social relationships. Because all components of this model have a reciprocal impact on all other components, none should be studied in isolation. In trying to understand dogmatism, my premise is that we need to thoroughly investigate each element of the biopsychosocial model, including the impact of evolutionary forces that are at play long before

TABLE 16.1. THE BIOPSYCHOSOCIAL MODEL OF DOGMATISM

Biological	Psychological	Social
Genetics	*Thoughts*	*Parenting*
Genes and heritability	Cognitive development	Attachment theories
	of five specific features	Emotional regulation
		Role modeling
Brain Development	*Emotions*	*Social Learning*
Structure	Anxiety and fear	Observational learning and modeling
Midbrain	Anger	
Frontal lobes	Despair	*Institutions*
Cerebral cortex		Family
Function	*Behaviors*	Education
Neurotransmitters	Dogmatic authoritarian aggression	Media
Hormones	Dogmatic authoritarian submission	Political
	In-group vs. out-group glorification	Religious
	and vilification	
	Stereotyping	*Cultural Memes*
	prejudice and discrimination	
	Arrogant, dismissive communication	

Adapted from G. Engel, "The Need For a New Medical Model: A Challenge For Biomedicine," *Science* 196 (1977): 129–36.

the baby Jonahs of this world take their first breath—and long after they exhale their last.

Our probe into the psychological nature of dogmatism as viewed from modern and traditional theories ends with a clarion call. Scientific investigations into the links between humanity's deeply embedded evolutionary forces and the biological and social factors that influence dogmatism are necessary if we are to fully comprehend and alter its course, for without first understanding the nature of the problem, we cannot seek effective solutions.

We turn now to the final chapter, which offers practical suggestions for preventing the deep roots of dogmatism from taking hold.

NOTES

1. B. Engler, *Personality Theories: An Introduction*, 6th ed. (Boston: Houghton Mifflin, 2003), p. 470.

2. Ibid., p. 471.

3. R. Frager and J. Fadiman, *Personality and Personal Growth*, 6th ed. (Upper Saddle River, NJ: Pearson Education, 2005), p. 404.

4. G. Claxton, *The Heart of Buddhism* (London: Thorsons, 1999), p. 29.

5. H. Nakamura, "The Basic Teachings of Buddhism," in *The Cultural, Political, and Religious Significance of Buddhism in the Modern World*, ed. H. Dumoulin and J. C. Maraldo (New York: Macmillan, 1976), p. 13.

6. A. Maslow, *The Farther Reaches of Human Nature* (New York: Viking, 1971).

Maslow acknowledged that Buddhism, particularly Zen Buddhism, and humanistic psychology both see "the temporal and the eternal simultaneously, the sacred and the profane in the same object" (p. 191).

7. J. Goldstein, *One Dharma: The Emerging Western Buddhism* (San Francisco: HarperCollins, 2002), p. 13.

8. Dhammapada, XI, p. 146. Excerpts from the Dhammapada are taken from Nakamura, "Basic Teachings of Buddhism." Translated as "the path of the Dharma," Dhammapada is a Buddhist scripture that contains 423 verses in 26 categories, most of which address questions of ethics.

9. I. Mahavagga, cited in Nakamura, "Basic Teachings of Buddhism."

10. M. Thompson, *Eastern Philosophy: Hinduism, Buddhism, Taoism, Confucianism, Jainism, Reincarnation, Nirvana, Zen, Vedanta, the Self, Yin/Yang, Ethics* (Chicago: NTC/Contemporary Publishing, 1999), p. 51.

11. T. Nhat Hanh, *The Heart of the Buddha's Teaching* (Berkeley, CA: Parallax, 1998).

12. S. Batchelor, *Alone with Others: An Existential Approach to Buddhism* (New York: Grove, 1983), p. 28.

13. Ibid., p. 31.

14. Ibid., p. 104.

15. Claxton, *The Heart of Buddhism*, p. 65. Italics in original.

16. Ibid., p. 67.

17. Sheng-yen, *Setting in Motion the Dharma Wheel: Talks on the Four Noble Truths of Buddhism* (Elmhurst, NY: Dharma Drum, 2000).

18. E. Tolle, *A New Earth: Awakening to Your Life's Purpose* (New York: Penguin, 2005), p. 134.

19. Engler, *Personality Theories*, p. 474.

20. W. Rahula, *What the Buddha Taught* (New York: Grove, 1974), cited in Engler, *Personality Theories*, p. 474.

21. Batchelor, *Alone with Others*, pp. 122–23.

22. Ibid., p. 114.

23. Ibid., pp. 61–62.

24. Ibid., p. 76.

25. F. Peddle, *Thought and Being: Hegel's Criticism of Kant's System of Cosmological Ideas* (Lanham, MD: University Press of America, 1980).

26. S. Batchelor, *Buddhism without Beliefs: A Contemporary Guide to Awakening* (New York: Berkley Publishing Group, 1997), p. 95.

27. S. B. Kopp, *If You Meet the Buddha on the Road, Kill Him!* (New York: Bantam, 1979), p. 223.

28. Claxton, *The Heart of Buddhism*, p. 125.

29. M. Ricard, guest appearance on *Light at the Edge of the World: Science of the Mind*, History Channel, August 28, 2007.

30. M. Ricard, *Happiness: A Guide to Developing Life's Most Important Skill* (New York: Little, Brown, 2003), p. 27. Here, Ricard quotes Chögyam Trungpa, *Cutting through Spiritual Materialism*, ed. J. Baker and M. Casper (Boston: Shambhala, 1973).

31. Anālayo, *Satipatthana: The Direct Path to Realization* (Birmingham, UK: Windhorse Publications, 2003), p. 162.

32. Ibid., p. 163.

33. Frager and Fadiman, *Personality and Personal Growth*, p. 409.

34. Ibid.

35. Engler, *Theories of Personality*, p. 471.

36. Frager and Fadiman, *Personality and Personal Growth*, p. 409.

37. Ricard, *Happiness*, p. 25.

38. Ibid., p. 23.

39. Batchelor, *Buddhism without Beliefs,* p. 57.

40. Ricard, *Happiness*, p. 162.

41. Batchelor, *Alone with Others*, p. 77.

42. M. Epstein, *Thoughts without a Thinker* (New York: Basic Books, 1995), p. 20.

43. D. C. Funder, *The Personality Puzzle*, 4th ed. (New York: Norton, 2007).

Chapter 17

WHERE TO FROM HERE?

Open-Minded Optimism

The fanatic is never happier or more satisfied in the end; either he is dead or he becomes a joke.[1]

Amos Os

Yes, and in the interim, before the fanatic or the laughter dies, the wreckage left by his or her uncompromising dogmatism is something about which we should be deeply concerned. It seems to me that we are not focusing enough attention on dogmatism's role in human-generated wars; in unjust social, political, and economic policies; and in grave miscarriages of justice that jeopardize freedom and imperil democracy. We do not have a surplus of open-mindedness, especially in the domains of politics and international relations, where the first weapon of mass destruction is bunkered in the mind, safely ensconced behind fear that, in the extreme, creates the type of dogmatism that can morph into manifest evil.

In this book we have probed the major characteristics of dogmatism and examined key influential experiences that purportedly shape its trajectory. Having reached the end of our exploration into the psychology of dogmatism, we conclude that this trait is a complex phenomenon and the conditions that underlie its nature require rigorous scientific analyses. "We need experiments to inform theory, but without theory all is lost. . . . Experiments unguided by an appropriate theoretical framework usually amount to little more than 'watching the pot boil.'"[2] The theory of dogmatism presented here provides such a framework, but, as it stands—and I say this with justified certainty—this theoretical model of dogmatism should be examined with skepticism until scientific research supports or refutes its propositions. That same skepticism should not, however, deter us from creating a fresh dialogue on dogmatism. Indeed, vigorous questioning grounds us in the necessary starting place from which to launch investigations that will ultimately enrich the theory by challenging its assumptions, reevaluating its concepts, researching its various components, and proffering alternative explanations.

Each of the sixteen chapters could be expanded into a book of its own. Although I have highlighted core concepts from various psychological models, I hope that writers with expertise in fields relevant to the study of dogmatism will expand on what I've presented here. Effective, lasting solutions can only emerge from a complete understanding of the problem. On the surface, dogmatism appears as the simplistic pronouncement of crude categories of thought, but having now probed its complex underlying structure, we see that this personality trait is anything but simple. It is driven by habitual, if not largely unconscious, belief systems that are sustained by personal narratives, which, in turn, are propped up by cultural values (or memes) that deeply groove brain circuitry. In some people, these neural patterns become manifestations of rigid thoughts and behaviors.

§§

Throughout this book, my excoriation of dogmatism was intentionally transparent, for I cannot think of one redeeming feature this personality trait has to offer. If you can, perhaps you will enlighten me. Some readers may think dogmatism is necessary in certain situations. Are there not times, you might ask, when attempting to advance a noble cause or rid the world of evil, we should forge ahead even if we do so dogmatically?

Dogmatic, arrogant certainty that pressures others to honor someone's else's handle on truth is never justified. Such posturing masks underlying fear and promotes prejudicial, self-righteous authoritarian aggression, pushing people into polarized camps and relegating reason to the sidelines. Those prone to dogmatism use the very privileges of democracy and freedom to rob others of the same. They are not calm and diplomatic; they do not seek partnership; they are not interested in consensus building—especially in times of social and political unrest. As John F. Kennedy said, "Those who make peaceful evolution impossible make violent revolution inevitable." Behind these movements, dogmatism is a very dangerous advisor.

In some cases, and as a last option, we might need to use force to defend ourselves against dogmatic authoritarian aggressors who attack our liberties and violate our human rights, but this is only acceptable if all attempts to reach conciliation have failed. These attempts begin with open-minded collaboration that ensures the democratic *process* will be applied to resolve clashes between individualism and collectivism, capitalism and socialism, conservatism and liberalism, the secular and the sacred, and so on.

Our understanding of dogmatism should help us be kind, for dogmatic people, like all the rest of us, are struggling with difficulties in their lives. Yet we have to take a stand against the dogmatism of a ruling group, for its leader can triumphantly sway the emotions and behaviors of complacent, uninformed citizens. "It is time for all to recognize that there is no regulating mechanism for the fanatic mind. The sooner this is accepted, the earlier we can move to addressing the phenomenon of fanaticism in its own right."[3] When dogmatic people gain power, it may take years before citizens recognize that their complacency and evasion of social responsibility to become politically involved has serious consequences. And while complacency does not potentiate the same degree of dogmatism as fear, both complacency and fear give license to dogmatic leaders who bear down on humanity with Orwellian impunity. As some people do with frogs, they may gently pick us up and put us in a cool pot of water. You know what happens next. . . .

§§

It is often the case that when serious concerns arise, people gravitate toward those who agree with their own viewpoints. Groups of like-minded souls disperse e-mails to partisan mailing lists with over-lapping contact groups. This is all very comforting. Surrounding ourselves with people who share our values confirms our own convictions, even when the message pitched is in adversarial tones that imply winners and losers. And while those with opposing belief systems may be similarly organizing camps of the converted, surely what is needed is a common forum that allows for frequent exchanges of disparate and opposing ideas. Without open-minded, respectful dialogue, we are without understanding, for there is always a common ground of mutual interest on which to build consensus and partnerships in order to arrive at mutually acceptable solutions that have lasting consequences.

RECOMMENDATIONS

In uncertain times, absolute certainty is dangerous, and I hope to hold your attention a little while longer so that we can examine courses of action that may prevent the forces of dogmatism from digging in. Some ideas have been empirically examined, but much remains to be done. The following list of suggestions attacks dogmatism, root and branch, in an attempt to promote open-minded elasticity and interpersonal civility.

Parenting

Suggested guidelines for parents to facilitate their children's open-minded reasoning and positive psychological growth include the following:

- During discussions with children and adolescents, parents can model open-minded reasoning by asking, "What if I (or you, or we) were wrong? What might that look like? Feel like? How difficult would it be to change our minds?"
- In teaching religious values, Daniel Dennett states, "As long as parents don't teach their children anything that is likely to close their minds through fear or hatred or by disabling them from inquiry (by denying them full access to an education, for instance, or isolating them from the world) then they may teach their children whatever religious doctrines they like. . . . If you have to hoodwink—blindfold—your children to ensure that they confirm their faith when they are adults, your faith *ought* to go extinct."[4]
- Guard against parental ego involvement in a child's success and growth of autonomous thoughts and behaviors. Parents who gloat about their accomplishments promote competition and conditions of worth, which, as noted in chapter 14, foster incongruence and rob children of authenticity.
- Encourage children to take responsibility for their own age-appropriate problem solving and decisions. Comments such as, "I think you can figure out a good solution here" or "We can work together to solve this problem," promote respect, cooperation, and autonomy. When parents tell children how to solve a problem that they are capable of solving, or jump in and solve it for them, they teach them to acquiesce and become dependent on others, or to rebel and oppose them.
- Create conditions in which children can feel good about accomplishments that are self-chosen and self-directed.
- Bribes and the use of rewards and excessive praise to coerce

behaviors that the parent values more than the child are controlling techniques. Be aware of the difference between controlling the child and being in control of behaviors that are unacceptable.[5] Set clear, consistent rules that are respectful of children's views, yet do not involve controlling manipulations.

- Model and encourage curiosity. Deemphasize high achievement and winning. This is difficult to do in a culture that richly rewards competition, which brings us to the next point.

- A culture that overemphasizes and rewards performance with credentials and status can undermine children's enjoyment of exploring their innate curiosity. In hypercompetitive cultures, parents often pressure their children to perform, which impedes their autonomous growth. Because much of society is grounded in competition, it is important that parents facilitate discussions about the dilemma these cultural values create.

- Parents can be effective lobbyists for change. They can, for example, take action against an athletic or educational authority who places too much emphasis on competition and winning. This intensifies anxiety, especially in a vulnerable child, and puts him or her at risk for cognitive closure that may culminate in dogmatism.

- Convey to every child that "just the way you are is good enough for me, to give you all the love that's good enough for you."

Education

Educational institutions are funded to get the results they achieve. In the first decade of this century, approaches to learning that incorporate psychological content throughout the life span would mark a new frontier in education. This is what the geneticist James Watson referred to when he commented, "The past century was the coming together of chemistry and biology. This century will be the coming together of psychology and biology."[6] Education is the major catalyst for this convergence; it can moderate or prevent situations that foment persistent anxiety, which is integral to dogmatism.

The world reflects what we teach. An effective education curriculum stimulates interest in behaviors students were born to gratify; namely, curiosity and social connection. Social constructivism, a theory that explores the ways in which social phenomena help us make sense of our world, emphasizes the role of social agents and social institutions on intellectual development—cognitive, emotional, and social. This holistic approach would shift the educational emphasis from knowledge acquisition to a balanced distribution of cognitive, emotional, and social skills, thus enriching students' entire psychological development. Successful psychological adaptation to a changing world requires educators to encourage children's early fascination with two broad disciplines: psychology and science. This assumption guides the following recommendations.

To enhance the suite of psychological competencies that protect against dogmatism, parents, educators, and students will need to pressure governments to allocate adequate funding and other resources that provision the following.

Early Childhood Education

The psychological environment and skills that I am about to emphasize are important for all children, and they are particularly critical for students who are deprived of empathic understanding and encouragement in their home environments. They require systemic change in the attitudes and behaviors of politicians and educators.

- Children must have equal access to quality daycare and preschool programs in which professionals introduce basic skills to enhance children's early emotional and social development. These objectives require early childhood workers to apply highly specialized training that merits salaries in the range of professors with a PhD. This requires systemic change in cultural values to recognize educational achievement as equal in importance to financial security. Just as effective corporate executives facilitate productivity in employees, teachers should empower students to achieve optimum educational standards. In so doing, educators' salaries should approximate those of top CEOs.

- Especially in the early years, educators need to create safe learning environments that help all students feel comfortable, first and foremost with themselves. Teachers who incorporate psychological skills in the school curriculum will enhance students' personality development, social relationships, and academic progress. You'll notice that the order of this learning trilogy no longer places academic progress first; without emotional balance and social connection, cognitive skills do not flourish. All three competencies are equally important.

- Children with pressing emotional and social problems need easy access to special education teachers throughout their schooling. This includes school psychologists, guidance counselors, education specialists, and other professionals who can assess and provide timely intervention, either in one-on-one sessions, in group settings, or some combination of both.

- As early as daycare, introduce children to the language of feelings so that they can differentiate transitory feelings from more enduring emotional states. This language helps them regulate their emotions, which influences the emotions of surrounding playmates and classmates, and thus contributes to the emotional well-being of their immediate social and learning environment. The language of feelings sets the stage for a critical social skill—the ability to imagine and sense a range of feelings in themselves and others. Language provides the necessary scaffolding for empathy, which is imperative for healthy social relationships.

Beyond Preschool (K–12)

- From preschool throughout senior grades, students could learn empathic listening skills and apply rational thinking to solve personal and interpersonal problems (see chapter 15). The curriculum could incorporate rational-emotive effective education, a course that promotes learning and practice in recognizing dysfunctional beliefs and emotions.[7] A core, applied psychology course, it would teach children how to regulate their emotions and gain interpersonal competence and confidence, which are preludes to open-minded learning. Children as young as ten can learn that psychology, a big word that is fun to spell, is a fascinating subject that helps them learn about themselves and others. Subject content would enable students to understand that even though other people may structure their external world, they alone can learn to control their thoughts, feelings, and behaviors. This learning would promote authenticity, mutual respect, cooperation, and effective interpersonal communication—seminal components of a holistic educational approach that would enhance the psychological hardiness of individuals and communities.

- Teachers who currently address these skills often do so randomly and informally, despite the fact that emotional and social intelligence are fundamental to students' psychological well-being and academic success.[8] By sharpening skills in emotional and relationship management, teachers and students would reap the benefits of a safe learning environment in which open-minded curiosity and understanding thrive. Even though many education systems are designed to achieve a set of well-defined grade-level competencies, emotional and social learning are generally not compulsory components of the school curriculum, yet academic achievement is surely enhanced by these skills.

- A separate subject, effective interpersonal communication, would teach students how to communicate assertively without being overly aggressive or passive. Age-related proficiency in assertive communication and other social skills, such as social manners and effective listening, would enhance self-esteem and facilitate rewarding social connections. These are important preludes to open-minded critical thought that can begin as early as preschool.

Students would learn, for example, that sarcasm and one-upmanship are not socially acceptable. Movies, computer games, television commercials, and other media outlets are saturated with derisive put-downs, many of which are followed by canned laughter that models a lack of empathy. These influential role models promote imitative bullying. Students could discuss the implications of such messages and recognize that, as a conscientious audience, they are potentially powerful lobby groups that could pressure the media to eliminate program and commercial content that models stereotyping and prejudicial attitudes.

- As a component of a basic psychology course (Psychological Savvy 101), youngsters could learn about their commonalities and differences. All children have the same fundamental needs, desires, feelings, and concerns, regardless of their race, nationality, ethnicity, or gender. They need to feel loved, encouraged, and protected, and they want to play with friends, satisfy their curiosity about people and the world in which they live, grow up in safe neighborhoods, and learn in safe environments. Why is it that not all of them are able to do so? As core content, students would discuss these issues and become familiar with psychological concepts like emotional and social intelligence, self-esteem, social roles, prejudice, discrimination, and psychological hardiness. These concepts are essential to a well-rounded general education and should not be reserved for college courses in the social sciences.

- With increasing cognitive development, students could learn the values that a democratic society is designed to protect. Such courses would emphasize that freedom is a privilege against a backdrop of responsibility. At an introductory level, students as young as eight can begin to consider what responsible citizenship looks like in a democratic society. The discussion could gradually broaden from municipal affairs to national and international concerns, emphasizing the value of examining issues from different perspectives. The importance of voting in elections should be stressed and the implications of voter turnout on the electoral process can be discussed.

- Facilitate open-minded discussions about cultural memes. What accounts for the enduring nature and institutionalization of belief systems? Which social and cultural values affect students' lives and how do these values impact their feelings, behaviors, sense of identity, authenticity, and autonomy? Such course content would provide an opportunity for students to explore their own tendencies for indoctrination and closed-mindedness.
- Include educational goals that familiarize senior students with the goals and values of minority groups. Students would learn, for example, that there are many different sects of Islam, including the Shia, Sunni, Jihad, and Wahhabi, and that Christianity has various denominations other than Catholics and Protestants. By situating religious dogma within modern political contexts, students would understand that religious violence is sometimes as much a reaction to political conflict as an expression of extreme loyalty to religious dogma. Such understanding is necessary for nations that view pluralism as a national asset.
- Include course content that helps students recognize and guard against dogmatism. Older students in an advanced psychology course could learn about dogmatism as a personality trait and understand basic links between unfortunate childhood experiences and closed-minded thinking. Given the opportunity, I suggest that they would find the study of dogmatism interesting and personally beneficial for lifelong learning.
- In senior courses, students could identify signs of dogmatism in social and government institutions and assess the extent to which open-minded versus closed-minded approaches determine policies that shape the existing social order and public institutions. For example, students could evaluate leadership styles that reflect inclusive versus exclusive approaches to policy development and problem solving. What belief systems underlie the existing educational and political policies? How

thoroughly do institutional administrators promote discussion and evaluation of policy changes? How can we recognize and reinforce cognitive complexity in our politicians?

- Senior students could study the impact of political and economic dogmatism. For example, which corporations cling to ideologies that justify expanding their reach in the global community without enforcing regulations that protect workers, and without financing practical solutions that redress poverty in the host nation? Neoconservatives make sweeping generalizations that foreign aid is a waste of money—claims that are more ideological than evidence-based. In 1970, wealthy nations agreed that each would meet the United Nations' target of giving 0.7 percent of their gross domestic product (GDP) to tackle global poverty, but to date only Denmark, Norway, Sweden, Luxembourg, and Netherlands have reached 0.7 percent.[9] In a post–September 11 world, what are the consequences of dogmatic, economic ideology in underdeveloped, poverty-ridden countries? People typically vote for policies that directly affect themselves, without exploring the implications of poverty on the quality and security of life for all members of the global community. Informed students could effectively pressure governments to go beyond platitudes to redress social oppression, global inequality, and widespread poverty. Especially in war-torn economies and impoverished environments, early intervention is vitally needed to help children cope with chronic, environmentally induced anxiety and fear that impair higher-order cognitive development. Fearful, fragmented identities cannot learn how to learn. Emotional instability prevents effective information processing, which leaves children vulnerable to increased intolerance of ambiguity that chains them to rigid beliefs—beliefs that further sustain fear and suspicion that cultivate self-righteous, dogmatic revenge.

- Students could learn to recognize that dogmatism drives discriminatory agendas that violate the Declaration of Human Rights. For example, they would learn to identify and expose hate literature. These are ethical issues that are interdisciplinary; they should not be limited to course content in one specific area.

- Introduce students to the power of language, which guides institutional decisions that may serve dogmatic agendas. Familiarize students with language that reinforces the dominant ideology of the ruling elite—those with money, power, and privilege.

- Students can be taught to value the scientific process and differentiate between the quest for rational knowledge and the easy comfort of irrational legend and superstition—the latter of which are impossible to validate. Educational institutions need to apply creative techniques to overcome students' negative attitudes toward science and broaden their enthusiasm for scientific exploration. As a start, they could test the accuracy of presumed truths that are so readily and adamantly pronounced on talk radio, television programs, and other media outlets that emphasize the sensational without providing any scientific validation for such proclamations. Understanding the scientific process would help students contrast competing theories—such as the theory of evolution and intelligent design—and they could then examine reasoned arguments for and against each model of human origin. Teachers who cover evolution theory demonstrate an attitude toward scientific evidence that government officials have scorned; President George W. Bush's "dismissal of evolution is an integral part of this general attitude."[10] The Bush administration's similar dismissal of systematic evidence led to the war in Iraq and their failure to act on scientific evidence that environmental pollution is changing the climate. The process of science also offers the best hope for a sound understanding of psychology that, after all, underlies every human initiative.

- The discipline of science should not favor and groom the intellectual elite any more than poetry courses should privilege auspicious poets. A broad emphasis on open-minded scientific inquiry would allow for new synergies across academic and career spectrums.

- Since many students will become parents, effective parenting should be a mandatory course of study for students in senior grades. Course content would stress the importance of facilitating emotional regulation and secure attachment in infancy. Students would also learn how to encourage and effectively reinforce a child's independent thought and curiosity. As a required course, effective parenting would demonstrate responsible, institutional commitment to the psychological well-being of future generations.

Postsecondary Education

- A mandatory course in the faculty of education would teach educators how to model empathic listening, empathic feeling, and empathic action. Teachers who infuse learning environments with empathy not only enhance their students' self-esteem, they also help students "*see* the other person and open up for him room for existence beside us. This act is called *love*, or, if we prefer a milder expression, the acceptance of the other person beside us in our daily living."[11] Empathy promotes cooperation, the platform for open-minded learning. University courses that taught educators how to structure emotional and social learning skills in the classroom would go beyond lip service to an applied learning that would strengthen emotional health and interpersonal skills.
- Dogmatism is a crossover topic that lends itself to multidisciplinary courses in higher education. As such, graduate students— especially those majoring in the arts—could learn how to recognize its features and predisposing influences across disparate courses and programs.
- Postsecondary institutions and the public could pressure government to establish a science advisory board that would monitor funding and the delivery of resources to strengthen the science component of school curricula.

To summarize, educators need to do more than implement these conditions for change; the inclusion of these recommended courses must be continually nurtured and evaluated as part of ongoing, educational outcomes.

DEMOCRACIES, THEOCRACIES, AND INTERNATIONAL LAW

Three recent major events propelled this theory of dogmatism: the tragedy of September 11, 2001; the Iraq war; and military intervention in Afghanistan. All cause an uneasy awareness that pushes the dogmatically vulnerable into polarized groups that adopt equally polarized, hardened positions: the patriotic and the unpatriotic, the believers and the nonbelievers, the faithful and the infidels, the in-group and the out-group.

The memorial being built at the center of the new lower Manhattan complex not only pays tribute to the innocent victims who lost their lives on 9/11, it also provides a somber reminder that grotesque dogmatism drove those planes into the twin towers of the World Trade Center, the Pentagon, and the Pennsylvania field near Shanksville. While religious piety and political extremism were certainly to blame, the greater culprit was dogmatism—the psychological origins of which began long before that day. As ancient as warfare itself, dogmatism within monotheistic religions has been a source of monstrous evil that embodies abnormal adaptations to one's psychological, social, and cultural exigencies. Ironically, religious dogmatists practice a form of religious Darwinism that preaches, in the parlance of evolutionary theory, successful adaptations as behavior that unquestioningly adopts the saving grace of religious dogma and surrenders to divine guidance that dictates all religious activity. These public, religious practices would be considered adaptive in that they bless believers with survival—here and in the heavenly hereafter. Such is the thinking that builds weapons that, in the end, are detonated not by ideology but by fear, rigid certainty, and self-righteous, dogmatic, authoritarian aggression.

Fortunately, dogmatism is not always as egregious as the deeds of 9/11. Yet ideology, explicit or implicit, can shape social and cultural belief systems that jeopardize the quality of individual thoughts and feelings and erode the quality of cultural life. Values and belief systems determine behaviors that are inextricably tied to historical time frames and cultural contexts. In reference to 9/11, how those attacks are understood "depends entirely on the dictates of one's worldview; although most Americans saw these events as horrific, evil acts of cruelty committed by cowardly madmen, the terrorists and their supporters saw them as heroic acts in the service of a great cause that would ensure them certain death transcendence."[12] These beliefs may be understood as components of a worldview that is designed to buffer anxiety and ensure self-esteem and social connection that guarantees dignity. Belief systems that emerge from a psychological residue of anxiety and resentment among alienated, persecuted, and marginalized people foment and sustain fear, anger, and despair, especially when opportunities that are abundantly available to others are not within reach. Such conditions are the breeding ground for ideological justifications of violence as a means of redress—violence that is propelled more by dogmatism than injustice. To reiterate a point made in chapter 3, dogmatism runs deep—it is more about identity than ideology, and individual identity is best understood within the context of personal, social, political, cultural, and regional histories.

It therefore behooves governments at all levels to take precautionary measures against the fomentation of dogmatism. In the minds of dogmatists, religious ideology is as compelling and powerful as political allegiance, which is why dogmatic ideologues will, if permitted, contaminate the political arena with religious agendas that cross political jurisdictions. "The great strength of religion is that it creates communities, and its great weakness is that it divides communities."[13] Humanity has not managed to curb religious dogmatism and the wars that sustain it. Muslims and Hindus fight against each other in Kashmir, as do Sunni and Shia in the Middle East, Muslims and Jews in Israel, and, to a lesser extent, Christians and atheists in America. Rigid loyalty to religious scripture leads dogmatists to affiliate with political parties that auspiciously conform to their inerrant biblical tenets, and this merging of religion and politics has led to serious perturbations in our postmodern, post–Cold War world. Alongside these troubled boundaries is a dogmatic presence that sullies optimism about the future of democracy, religion, and the species, especially given the historical evidence that religious ideologues have found it difficult to coexist outside the political arena. It has been even more difficult for them to respectfully collaborate inside it.

§§

Democracy matters. A principled democracy enforces regulations to protect against corporate greed and scandals that deplete pension funds or use taxpayers' money for financial bailouts. As long as citizens across the board vote in government officials who believe the private sector is the only efficient manager of key industries, we will continue to witness a failed conservative ideology that enables a few to become rich at the expense of the poor. Governments that are financed by corporate-funded think tanks, which are in cahoots with legislators, promote an extreme ideology that drives a laissez-faire market economy and dilutes the core principles of a fair and just society.

A principled democracy values the importance of citizen participation. Major players recognize that the human mind is hardwired for social connection that assists three other psychological needs: finding meaning, purpose, and dignity in our lives. Strong communities support these needs. Elected officials could assist in the organization of citizen assemblies where people exchange ideas about social and economic policies that impact the environment, the educational system, healthcare, and other shared concerns. Government representatives and agencies would channel these citizen-generated policy proposals to the appropriate government bodies. Overly optimistic? Perhaps. But without healthy communities there is little opportunity for participatory democracy that strengthens relationships and gives life meaning across political, economic, and social domains.

These same conditions would also strengthen ties between business and government, for in a cost-benefit analysis, both agencies would clearly benefit from a collaborative, inclusive, open-minded approach to establishing policies and solving problems.

Given today's abundant wealth and knowledge, inadequate healthcare and education for children is morally, socially, and politically unconscionable. A caring society is a well-educated society that contributes to the physical and psychological health of its citizens. A caring society is a safe society that is not governed by extreme, economic dogmatism that promotes greed or replaces individual freedom with social control. A caring society does not leave people marginalized as strangers in a common land, but continuously strives to remove inequities caused by the narrow-minded pursuit of power and wealth. A GDP of open-mindedness that spans international borders yields a gross national product (GNP) of psychological security, empowerment, and well-being that flourishes today and carefully plans for tomorrow. Any government that claims children are our most important asset, and yet fails to invest in services that optimize the physical, social, emotional, and intellectual growth of its youth, either demonstrates compartmentalized thinking or is hypocritical and shortsighted. World governments have congresses and parliaments that are disproportionately governed by lawyers and former business executives; shouldn't the twenty-first century find ways to encourage more scientists, technologists, educators, and psychologists to run for office? And women?

Local, national, and international governments could better direct international aid that goes beyond short-term military solutions to create the necessary infrastructure for eradicating poverty and educating children. Western nations have the financial resources to successfully redress political, economic, and military fortresses of dogmatism, but without the collective will and without a plan, they will not put in place the long-term provisions necessary to level the playing field.

With these thoughts in mind, politicians who recognize the importance of open-minded, collaborative problem-solving have our ears and possibly our votes, for they would be capable of public statements such as, "Based on the sound arguments I've heard today, I will reexamine my thinking about this important issue." Or, "I apologize for my mistaken judgment regarding this concern." These are the kinds of open-minded statements that strengthen, not weaken, credibility and democracy; they demonstrate leadership that grasps the ambiguity and complexity of problems. Effective democracy stabilizes a nation, and, no matter how wealthy a country's resources or industry, without democracy it doesn't take much to destabilize its leadership and posterity.

Much is at stake when a nation is governed by dogmatic leaders who lack insight and psychological resilience. The obligation of citizenship require us to assess, as best as possible, political candidates' psychological savvy before we elect them. Are those who seek office or reelection available for public debate? Are they composed and thoughtful when facing challenges, conflict, and the unknown, or are they defensive, rhetorical, and curt? Are they inclined to collaborate in times of stress or would they make unilateral decisions? Can they think on their feet and provide answers that go beyond arid rhetoric—answers that convey open-minded, integrative, cognitive complexity?

A good illustration of levels of complexity is illustrated in the following examples taken from US senatorial speeches on abortion.[14] Senators who were low on differentiation, integration, and overall cognitive complexity saw the issue from only one perspective without recognizing other viewpoints, as illustrated in these simple, low-level comments: "Abortion is a basic right that should be available to all women." Or, "To limit a woman's access to abortion is an intolerable infringement on her civil liberties." Notice the following contrasting statement that illustrates higher levels of complex thought, differentiation, and integration of the various issues involved. "Some view abortion as a civil liberties issue; others see abortion as tantamount to murder. One's opinion depends on knowledge of complicated legal, moral, and scientific judgments. What criteria should be used to determine when life begins? Who possesses the authority to resolve these issues?" Here, the speaker acknowledges multiple views and thoughtfully reflects on how to establish criteria that will help deal with tensions that may arise over this issue. These examples illustrate qualitatively different cognitive styles that will help the electorate get a better sense of what to look for in political speeches, especially those concerning value-laden issues like abortion, the death penalty, stem cell research, gun control, and so on. In the domain of politics, social institutions, and business corporations, cognitive styles are only visible when we know what to look for.

Leaders of all groups, especially political bodies, are most credible and trustworthy when they make every attempt to do the hard work of open-minded thinking, for that is prerequisite to inclusive language that promotes collaboration and understanding of multiple identities, ideologies, and historical contexts—all of which shape the soul of a democratic nation. Anything less dilutes the discourse and prevents effective, long-term solutions. As Bertrand Russell said in summing up his lectures about how to save the world, "The first requisite, I should say, is absence of dogmatism, since dogmatism almost inevitably leads to war."[15]

Finally, many modern corporations are merging to become global behemoths that concentrate wealth in the hands of a few without guaranteeing a fair share of profits to the workers who create it. Democracies that fail to implement labor standards that secure basic needs like healthcare and daycare leave workers the victims rather than beneficiaries of shortsighted ideological goals. And while management can make the case that corporations provide jobs and generate wealth that is spread among shareholders, few of its numerous employees can afford to buy shares in the company they work for. To stop this inequitable distribution of wealth, global labor unions and good labor laws are necessary—laws that "don't allow employers to intervene, that don't allow heavy-handed tactics—whether they're the terrible tactics we see in countries like Colombia, or even the tactics we see here in the United States, where we almost start a war at the workplace just because people want to have a chance to change their life."[16]

Educators who nurture students' intelligence by incorporating cognitive, emotional, social, and communication skills that protect against dogmatism need more than government funding. They need to be respected by politicians who encourage participatory democracy in well-connected citizen groups, for "it is precisely in times of difficulty and confusion that the public good needs most to be asserted and imposed by the citizenry and their representatives."[17] Collaborative educators, politicians, and citizen groups provide the necessary checks and balances that offer the best hope for peaceful, productive, and satisfying futures.

THE SACRED AND THE SCIENTIFIC

Certainly mystical, paranormal beliefs are de facto less credible than beliefs derived from rational, empirical scientific investigation. Religious fundamentalists who excuse oppression of others (mostly women) on the basis of scripture, which they prejudicially interpret with rigid certainty, are closed-minded godmatists; there is no empirical basis for their intolerance of ambiguity or dogmatic authoritarian aggression. Religious decrees do not have a legitimate right of practice if they contravene the Declaration of Human Rights. These beliefs are not evidence-based, which surely has greater credibility than beliefs that are only authority-voiced.

"Our scientists are right that religious cruelty has often been the product of our manly inclination to exaggerate our personal importance."[18] From an evolutionary perspective, it would seem that adaptive religions are those that temper this narcissism with humility. In the modern world, there are 2,800 known religions, and an estimated 80 percent of the global population endorses some religious belief system.[19] To suggest that religious believers are all closed-minded and delusional would counter religious fundamentalism with a neo-atheist fundamentalism that overlooks humanity's eternal quest for spiritual gratification.

It seems reasonable to consider religion an outgrowth of evolutionary or epigenetic rules of heredity that bind genes and culture, in which case religion falls within the purview of science, rather than being separate from it:

> *It is the brain that is the common element here.* It is the brain that processes the social signals of others, that initiates and carries out rituals, that believes. It is the brain that is soothed by believing and participating, and a soothed brain is a precondition for a soothed body. It is this soothing, this *need* for it, that gets to the heart of why religions persist.[20]

But the need for science also persists, and the scientific analysis of religious *need* may one day explain what currently eludes us; namely, rational knowledge of the mysterious—of love, evil, suffering, and the source of nature's life force and deep beauty. Scientific logic cannot adequately explain these manifestations. And atheistic scientists should not accuse all religious followers of fear, ignorance, and a longing for salvation that binds and blinds them to dogma. Not all Christians, for example, are biblical literalists. Monotheisms also articulate, in dogma, belief systems about the meaning of life, and they present certain thoughts and behaviors as examples of good sense. Certainly some systems emphasize unquestioning obedience to illegitimate authority, but others highlight religious dogma as a spiritual guide for goodness, morality, and communion that transcends the individual. As E. O. Wilson asks, "Could Holy Writ be just the first literate attempt to explain the universe and make ourselves significant within it? Perhaps science is a continuation on a new and better-tested ground to attain the same end. If so, then in that sense science is religion liberated and writ large."[21] Or perhaps, as the Austrian physicist Anton Zeilinger wrote, "The present battle between science and religion will someday be seen as a battle between two unjustified positions. Science will never be able to prove that God does not exist, and religion will learn that its [own] essence is far deeper than ephemeral questions like whether we were created by evolution or not."[22]

Regardless of assertions from different camps that their unique tradition promotes the greater good, I know of no quantifiable, reliable data that supports the claim that either religion or science wins the award for advancing social connection, humility, compassion, and justice. When we examine the evidence, it is apparent that scientific and religious deeds are both capable of doing more harm than good:

> Did not the narrow focus of science on the evidence and argument of the task at hand allow the production of tens of thousands of nuclear weapons, and are not teams of very able and dedicated scientists today directly involved in constructing plausible scenarios for apocalyptic lunacy? Did not Bertrand Russell argue on the basis of clear and concise thought with full understanding and acknowledgement of opposing views and criticism, that the United States should nuke Soviet Russia before it got the bomb in order to save humankind from a worse evil?[23]

Lively, controversial debates about the benefits and shortcomings of science and religion have gained momentum. In the process, open-minded religious believers, atheists, agnostics, and scientists are mindful of the dangers inherent in dogmatic proselytizing of any strand of belief systems—pro-religious, anti-religious, pro-science, antiscience, or agnostic. Yet science, religion, evolutionary theory, and spirituality are not necessarily incompatible, and if all of us took a psychological journey inside ourselves to understand how our own anxiety, fear, and self-doubt closes our minds, we would open the door to reason and respect across these boundaries. Both scientific theories and religious dogma—string and superstring scientific theories or impersonal and personal theistic theories—are derivative of imagination, regardless of their elaborate articulation that, to some, is interpreted as authoritative truth. However, scientific theory is subjected to more rigorous testing and analysis that, prima facie, gives it more credibility. (You noticed that I tossed in the words "prima facie" to elaborately articulate that last sentence.) The greater risk is ignorance and closed-minded certainty, because "when you are in possession of absolute truth, compromise is not an option."[24] In the end, it is not science or religion that single-handedly prevents the peaceful coexistence of science and religion. Dogmatism in both camps is the culprit.

We are living at a time when religious believers are concerned that the bastion of cultural respect, which religion has enjoyed for centuries, is crumbling. Several books have been written recently by scientists who expose what they consider the psychological delusion and danger of religion, but the number of these books pale in comparison with the tomes of religious writings that line the shelves of bookstores and libraries. Dogmatic religious believers are intolerant of atheists who publicly proclaim their dissatisfaction with religious tradition. Believing religion should be immune from such criticism, religious critics who dismiss atheists often overlook the fact that books on religion far outnumber books on atheism. The magazine *Publishers Weekly* reported in 2008 that the publishing houses of the Evangelical Christian Publishers Association produced 13,400 new titles in 2005 and 2006 alone (not to mention the number of publications from all other religions combined).[25] For the most part, atheists and scientists have simply ignored that fact. Until recently. The combined works of authors such as E. O. Wilson, Richard Dawkins, Sam Harris, Daniel Dennet, Michael Shermer, Christopher Hitchens, and Chris Hedges, to name a few, probe the nature of religion and suggest that the sooner humanity abandons its superstitious beliefs and dependence on a supernatural being, the more rational and better off we will be.

Yet many atheists denounce religion without recognizing its substantial history. Religious belief endures, not because of childlike naiveté and mass ignorance, but because it gratifies an existential need that, at least so far, science cannot demolish. Dogmatic atheists dismiss an important aspect of human existence by downplaying the significance of worldly religions that value peace, brotherly love, and charity, and that comfort the suffering and offer social connection to those who seek communion. Nonetheless, we need to be vigilant regarding religious dogmatists who seek positions of power and use the protection of democratic, secular governments to enact their exclusive religious agendas. As Dennett notes, "In short, the moderates in all religions *are being used* by the fanatics, and should not only resent this, they should take whatever steps they can find to curtail it in their own tradition."[26] The voices of open-minded reason must act to restrain closed-minded dogmatism in religious and political institutions by applying the same principles that govern peaceful coexistence in families, communities, nations, and bodies politic and religious. What is needed is ongoing, open-minded dialogue that recognizes each religion's common values and seeks agreement that world organizations such as the United Nations must enforce separation of church and state. Any religion that believes it has the sacred right to rule by God's laws no longer needs to conform to the laws of democracy or abide by edicts that preserve human rights.

If we are to uphold the secular values of democratic rights and freedoms, then not one single dogmatic atheist and not one single dogmatic religious believer has the right to force his or her dogmatic theology on others. In addition, it is not permissible for special interest groups to pass legislation that violates Article 18 of the Universal Declaration of Human Rights: "Everyone has the right to freedom of thought, conscience and religion; this right includes freedom to change his religion or belief, and freedom, either alone or in community with others and in public or private, to manifest his religion or belief in teaching, practice, worship and observance." But Islamofascists do not have the right to manifest their religious beliefs in the practice of suicide bombings, and Christian fundamentalists do not have the right to physically attack pro-life supporters or agencies. Without a strategy that counters religious zealotry, we may acquiesce to someone else's agenda to promote it. I agree with Karl Popper, who, in 1945, wrote, "If our civilization is to survive, we must break with the habit of deference to great men. Great men may make great mistakes."

§§

Modern communications technology has provided a sounding board for psychologically wounded youth who plot revenge. Internet connections create artificial, permeable boundaries that mobilize and politicize the disenfranchised, the disillusioned, and the fanatically pious. But a strategic use of technology could enable us to reach alienated or disillusioned youth and encourage them to join with the broader community to redress their psychological injury, to piece together their fragmented identities, to promote feelings of social connection and dignity, and to short-circuit dogmatism in the process. If, in this post-9/11 era, moderate groups could find a way to collaborate with alienated youth, they would weaken the appeal of religious and political dogmatism that foments terrorism and war. At the same time, until religious leaders and their followers are willing to "explicitly condemn *by name* the dangerous individuals and congregations within their ranks, they are *all* complicit."[27]

Government advisors need the will and patience to study the political and psychological underpinnings that swell into outrage. Peace *building* precedes peace *keeping*, and a healthy democracy partners policymakers with citizens and social activists, be they atheists, agnostics, or believers. In an open-minded society, governments and social policies are not choked by self-perpetuating, dogmatic ideology. Nor is a healthy democracy constrained by multinational corporations whose shrewd authoritarian executives overrule democratic governments that demand greater transparency and accountability.

INTERNATIONAL LAW

Western democracies have the resources to protect against the dogmatism that inculcates hatred, racism, and state-sponsored terror, or that reduces citizens to state property. The first line of defense is for national and international governing bodies to confront dogmatism as a serious widespread problem.

Cultures differ in their degrees of dogmatism. What most influences those differences is the extent to which citizens, particularly young citizens, live in fear. At the end of World War II, fifty nations met to draw up the United Nations Charter. They realized that universal agreements were needed to protect against genocide, anarchy, imperialist aggression, torture, and other threats to individual, national, and global security. Joint deliberation and binding agreements among all members provide the only legitimate basis for military intervention and rules of warfare. Since its inception in 1945, "the UN, representing many countries, and limited as it is by its procedures, is still in the best position to balance individual state interests and preserve world order. It remains our best hope of avoiding arbitrary force by individual states and the endless cycles of violence we have witnessed. Our environments, economies, and social stability depend fundamentally on an international order grounded in law, as represented by the UN Charter and the Geneva and Hague Conventions."[28]

The United Nation's International Court of Justice has created the legal framework to intervene against human and environmental contraventions. Unfortunately, legislation designed to protect against war and other atrocities has been repeatedly violated with impunity. Recurrent abrogation of the United Nations Security Council rulings continue, as seen in illegal attempts to remove national leaders or change national boundaries. The dogmatism behind such violations is less likely to triumph when national and universal laws are consistently enforced—laws that could inspire confidence through timely interventions that would derail internecine conflict and protect individual rights and freedoms. Every nation needs to actively and transparently commit itself to the UN mission. No nation should be privileged with legal exemption, especially superpowers that have the ability to weaken the UN's mandate to maintain peace.

Benjamin Barber outlines the perils of America's national security strategy—a doctrine that authorizes preemptive strikes against nations or groups capable of launching weapons of mass destruction. He asks us to "imagine an international law that read, 'Nations may only resort to war in cases of self-defense, except the United States, which because it is special can resort to war whenever it wants.'"[29] In effect, this is what the US national security doctrine permits, and the American administration has repeatedly stated that it can implement this plan, even though it would curtail civil liberties at home and elsewhere. An outrageous example of closed-minded compartmentalization, the national security doctrine and its rationale are the war drums of dogmatism. Since when did the moral sanctity of the American government warrant extralegal privileges that the rest of the world would be denied? Ironically, America so values freedom and democracy that it will use whatever means necessary to arbitrarily destroy whosoever threatens its mission to bring peace and democracy to the world. Where is the collective will, nationally and internationally, to vehemently protest this lizard logic? Universal laws drafted by universal bodies have universal agency *only if* they have the power of universal enforcement.

THE MEDIA

The concentration of power in the hands of media moguls who generously donate to political campaigns preserves the dominant ideology and reinforces "other institutions and practices that work together to sustain and legitimize a particular and partial view of social life that defines the roles of specific groups within an overall culture."[30] When the mainstream media is in cahoots with the right, the left, or the dogmatically rigid—political or religious—it becomes the breeding ground for propaganda and spin that cleverly crafts language to favorably position people, power, and policies. Walter Lippmann coined the term *the manufacture of consent*, which, according to former vice president Al Gore, in reference to the Bush administration, "is precisely what happened with the invasion of Iraq."[31] Such manipulation violates the philosophy and ethics of democratic freedom and leaves the public vulnerable to exploitation by those whose dogmatism and greed transcends humanitarian concerns. Knowledgeable, responsible citizens must monitor the media and expose blatant preferential treatment of power relations in the dominant ideology of their culture. As difficult as this is, given today's media conglomerates, a civilization that eliminates conflicts of interest between the media and the state will be a changed civilization.

Responsible media avoids incendiary fear-mongering that narrows the capacity for reason. Through various avenues it exposes the rigid ideological rhetoric of dogmatism's fanatical patriotism that glorifies nationalism and sensationalizes war. To use a common, deceptively innocuous example, the media's reference to murder as "slaughter"—an emotionally laden word—deserves attention. Semantically, animals are slaughtered; people are killed through intentional, criminal acts of violence and murder. To describe murder as slaughter—even if it is of barbaric, genocidal proportion—steers us onto an ambiguous, metaphoric side street. Because the reference group is often blurred, to which group of people does the word *slaughter* refer—the slayers, the slain, or both? Since dogmatists are more likely to view their enemies as animals that deserve to be slaughtered, the media's description of murder as slaughter confirms their narrow-minded beliefs. In so doing, the media promotes misunderstandings that inadvertently goad dogmatic, authoritarian aggression. I therefore recommend that the media use the word *slaughter* only in reference to animals, or as a verb or adverb for bad prose. Applied to people, I suggest, the word is best slaughtered.

Responsible media informs; it does not elevate entertainment above timely information and investigative journalism in order to sell commercials or sensationalize the lives of prominent figures and political candidates. TV programs and "breaking news" often emphasize visceral content while failing to provide objective, background information that is as unbiased as possible.

And finally, while the media has considerable power to shape beliefs, values, and popular culture, the Internet, cell phones, and other technological devices diminish that power by allowing people to go public and become their own press agents. Today, governments use Web sites as agents of virtual spin that enhance, and even supplant, media press releases.

CLOSING THOUGHTS

Given that the spiraling arms race invents ever more powerful weaponry to settle group conflict, it could be argued that our most dangerous predator lurks deep within the minds of genus *Homo*. Without sounding apocalyptic about it, as long as traditions value dogmatic belief systems that reflect an attitude of "me" rather than "we," and of "us" versus "them," we diminish our humanity. Wedged between wealth and poverty is anxiety and fear, which trigger dogmatism turn evolutionary whisperings into screams of revenge.

People who are driven to compete for scarce resources develop negative thoughts, feelings, and behaviors against their competitors until eventually, an entire group of similar people (i.e., racial, gender, political, religious, and sexual groups) are labeled, shunned, attacked, and disadvantaged.[32] Vulnerable individuals seek salvation in organized dogma, and divisive hatreds cast competitors into polarized, adversarial groups, each of which lays claim to lofty morals that are used to justify coercive means to inflict its belief systems on others and punish those who disagree or disobey. What starts out as a narrative for religion often ends up as a platform for politics—a platform that does not recognize that it's better to feed and educate the poor than to jail (or kill) them for acts of revenge.

Yet changing the conditions that foster extreme dogmatism takes commitment, resources, time, and patience. To build a nation of genuinely open-minded educators, parents, and leaders requires a transformational approach that teaches a new way of being. Will the day come when we can be at ease with our differences and unite as a community of respectful traditionalists, liberalists, reformists, atheists, believers, agnostics, artists, and scientists—all working together with open-minded resolve and ethical reasoning to find solutions to current hatreds, injustices, and inequalities?

At this stage in our evolutionary history, a world without dogmatism seems a dream of fanciful optimism, for its roots are deep and personal. Yet I am optimistic that we will use our potential for self-awareness and insight to harness the forces of dogmatism and solve individual and social problems with less ego defensiveness and greater open-mindedness. But we must first change at basic psychological levels that go beyond contemporary agreements for social change. While there is plenty wrong with being absolutely right, there is nothing wrong with opening our minds to the possibility that we might be closed-minded about certain issues. We might even be mistaken.

Mutual respect and peaceful coexistence begin with the inconvenient awareness that, within our own minds, dogmatism competes with open-mindedness on a regular basis. Dennett's term *cerebral celebrity* explains how an inner turmoil of brain systems involving emotion and reason vie for control, and one always triumphs. We must be especially vigilant of fear that energizes dogmatic tendencies, especially during rapid social and economic change or political upheaval, when we are most likely to be unaware of the limits to our own open-mindedness. That is when we close our minds and open ourselves to exploitation. And we need to be vigilant of leaders in governments, social institutions, and corporations who reflect a cognitive simplicity that personifies E. O. Wilson's simile: "Destroying rainforests for economic gain is like burning a Renaissance painting to cook a meal."[33]

Evidence for progress in various areas is reassuring. Much has been written about the urgency to seek common alliance among scientific, political, and religious belief systems, and many people are working to advance open-minded approaches to current problems of climate change, global poverty, and disease. In particular, the environmental movement has gained a groundswell of awareness that is becoming increasingly manifest in corporate action. Planet-friendly groups like the Harapan Rainforest Initiative and citizen-friendly groups like Habitat for Humanity, the World Bank's Millennium Development Project, and the Bill and Melinda Gates Foundation are just a few projects that are healing global wounds. There is also an overall decline in violence, torture, slavery, executions, assassinations, pogroms, and homicide.[34] In a short time span, public inertia about climate change was converted to environmental activism. Thus, the same inertia that allows dogmatism to thrive could be converted to public action that transforms ideological ignorance into open-minded reasoning. Progressive governments, please answer the call.

Dogmatism may be enduring and ubiquitous, but with a focused commitment to the development of rational thinking, we can remedy the dangerous nature of dogmatic belief. For this to happen, we need rigorous, open-minded studies on the conscious and unconscious aspects of personality development that interact with evolutionary forces, biology, and social institutions. Progress on these fronts requires research in which procedures are intricate and their interpretations are elaborate. To that end, I hope the ideas advanced in this book will come alive in constructive dialogue. Inspired analyses will offer infinite promise for a compassionate world that expands open-minded creativity, enhances social relationships and careers, and promotes dignity for all. The theory of dogmatism presented here is a possible start in that direction, for I am all but certain that if we confront the problem of dogmatism from many angles, we will convert its bark into a faint whimper.

NOTES

1. A. Oz, *How to Cure a Fanatic* (Princeton, NJ: Princeton University Press, 2002), p. 63.

2. J. H. Holland, cited in P. A. Corning, *Holistic Darwinism: Synergy, Cybernetics, and the Bioeconomics of Evolution* (Chicago: University of Chicago Press, 2005), p. 46.

3. W. Soyinka, *Climate of Fear: The Quest for Dignity in a Dehumanized World* (New York: Random House, 2005), p. 121.

4. D. Dennett, *Breaking the Spell: Religion as a Natural Phenomenon* (New York: Penguin, 2006), p. 328.

5. W. S. Grolnick, *The Psychology of Parental Control: How Well-Meant Parenting Backfires* (Mahwah, NJ: Erlbaum, 2003). See page 144 for a good summary of suggestions to reduce excessive ego involvement and controlling tactics of parents, which interfere with children's and adolescents' autonomy and psychological well-being.

6. J. Watson, interview by Charlie Rose, *Charlie Rose Show,* PBS, December 14, 2005.

7. A. Vernon has written several books that outline an emotional education curriculum for children and adolescents. These books are published by the Albert Ellis Institute, New York, NY. Order information is available on the Web site: http://www.albertellisinstitute.org (accessed April 23, 2008).

8. D. Goleman, *Emotional Intelligence: Why It Can Matter More Than I.Q.* (New York: Bantam Books, 1995), and *Social Intelligence: The New Science of Human Relationships* (New York: Bantam, 2006). Goleman's books provide excellent resource material for teachers who want to include the teaching of emotional and social skills in early childhood curricula.

9. War on Want, *0.7% Campaign for Greater Aid Spending: Hitting the 0.7% Aid Target,* http://www.waronwant.org/?lid=1664 (accessed June 23, 2007).

10. O. Judson, "Optimism in Evolution," *New York Times*, August 13, 2008.

11. H. Maturana and F. J. Varela, *The Tree of Knowledge: The Biological Roots of Human Understanding* (Boston: Shambhala, 1992), p. 246.

12. T. Pyszczynski, J. Greenberg, and J. L. Goldenberg, "Freedom versus Fear: On the Defense, Growth, and Expansion of the Self," in *Handbook of Self and Identity*, ed. M. R. Leary and J. P. Tangney (New York: Guilford, 2003), p. 316.

13. J. Sacks, *Can We Really Learn to Love People Who Are Not Like Us?* http://www.timesonline.co.uk/tol/comment/faith/article1906580.ece (accessed June 9, 2007). Rabbi Jonathan Sacks is the Chief Rabbi of the United Hebrew Congregations of the Commonwealth.

14. P. Suedfeld and P. E. Tetlock, "Individual Differences in Information Processing," in *Blackwell Handbook of Social Psychology: Intraindividual Processes*, ed. A. Tesser and N. Schwartz (Oxford: Blackwell, 2003), p. 292. These authors provide a thorough analysis of low, moderate, and highly complex cognitions that contrast sophisticated levels of differentiation and integration with cognitive simplicity.

15. B. Russell, *The Autobiography of Bertrand Russell: 1944–1967* (London: George Allen and Unwin, 1970), p. 29.

16. A. Stern, interview by Charlie Rose, *Charlie Rose,* PBS, June 21, 2007. Stern is SEIU (Service Employees International Union) and Wal-Mart Watch president. "Determined to build a truly 21st-century union to ensure

that workers benefit from today's global economy, Stern initiated agreements with multinationals to form effective alliances, started efforts to form global unions, and is collaborating to find new ways for workers to prosper in a growing economy." http://www.seiu.org/about/officers_bios/stern_bio.cfm (accessed February 5, 2008).

17. J. R. Saul, *Reflections of a Siamese Twin: Canada at the End of the Twentieth Century* (New York: Viking, 1997), p. 505.

18. P. A. Lawler, "Manliness, Religion, and Our Manly Scientists," *Social Science and Modern Society* 45, no. 2 (2008): 155–58.

19. Ibid.

20. M. McGuire and L. Tiger, "Close but Not Close Enough," *Social Science and Modern Society* 45 (2008): 159–61.

21. E. O. Wilson, *Consilience: The Unity of Knowledge* (New York: Knopf, 1998), pp. 6–7.

22. A. Zeilinger, "Going beyond Our Darwinian Roots," in *What Are You Optimistic About? Today's Leading Thinkers on Why Things Are Good and Getting Better*, ed. J. Brockman (New York: Harper, 2007), p. 38.

23. S. Atran, "Beyond Belief: Science, Religion, Reason and Survival," Salk Institute, La Jolla, CA, November 5–7, 2006, http://www.edge.org/discourse/bb.html#atran2, (accessed June 15, 2007).

24. R. R. Provine, "This Is All There Is," in *What Is Your Dangerous Idea?* ed. J. Brockman (New York: HarperCollins, 2007), p. 160.

25. A. C. Grayling, *Tome Truths,* 2007, http://www.commentisfree.guardian.co.uk/ac_grayling/2007/06/tome_truths.html (accessed June 16, 2007).

26. D. Dennett, *Breaking the Spell*, p. 300.

27. Ibid., p. 301.

28. D. Swann, "Finding My Voice for Peace," in *Canada and the New American Empire: War and Anti-War*, ed. G. Melnyk (Calgary: University of Calgary Press, 2004), p. 124. David Swann, MD, is a Member of the Legislature, Alberta.

29. B. Barber, *Fear's Empire: War, Terrorism, and Democracy* (New York: Norton, 2003), p. 100.

30. J. T. Wood, *Communication Theories in Action: An Introduction* (Belmont, CA: Wadsworth/Thomson Learning, 2000), p. 292.

31. A. Gore, *The Assault on Reason* (New York: Penguin Books, 2007), p. 96.

32. S. O. Gaines Jr. and E. S. Reed, "Prejudice: From Allport to Dubois," *American Psychologist* 50 (1995): 96–103.

33. This quotation was taken from www.brainyquote.com/quotes/authors/e/e_o_wilson.html (accessed November 24, 2007).

34. S. Pinker, "The Decline of Violence," in *What Are You Optimistic About? Today's Leading Thinkers On Why Things Are Good and Getting Better*, ed. J. Brockman (New York: Harper, 2008), p. 3.

BIBLIOGRAPHY

Abell, George, and B. Singer, eds. *Science and the Paranormal*. New York: Scribner's, 1981.

Adler, Alfred. *Problems of Neurosis*. New York: Harper Torchbooks, 1964.

———. *Understanding Human Nature*. New York: Fawcett, 1954.

Adler, Alfred, H. L. Ansbacher, and R. R. Ansbacher. *Cooperation between the Sexes: Writings on Women and Men, Love and Marriage, and Sexuality*. New York: Norton, 1982.

Adler, R. B., and N. Towne. *Looking Out/Looking In*. Fort Worth, TX: Harcourt Brace Jovanovich, 1993.

Adorno, Theodor W., E. Frenkel-Brunswik, D. J. Levinson, and R. N. Sanford. *The Authoritarian Personality*. New York: Harper and Brothers, 1950.

Ainsworth, M. D. S. "Infant-Mother Attachment." *American Psychologist* 34 (1979): 932–37.

Ainsworth, M. D., M. C. Blehar, S. Wall, and E. Waters. *Patterns of Attachment: A Psychological Study of the Strange Situation*. Hillsdale, NJ: Lawrence Erlbaum, 1978.

Alansari, B. "The Relationship between Anxiety and Cognitive Style Measured on the Stroop Test." *Social Behavior and Personality* 32, no. 3 (2004): 281–94.

Alexander, R. "Evolution of the Human Psyche." In *The Human Revolution*, edited by Paul Mellars and C. Stringer. Edinburgh, UK: University of Edinburgh Press, 1989.

Alloy, L. B., K. A. Kelly, S. Mineka, and C. M. Clements. "Comorbidity of Anxiety and Depressive Disorders: A Helplessness/Hopelessness Perspective." In *Comorbidity in Anxiety and Mood Disorders*, edited by Jack D. Maser and C. R. Cloninger. Washington, DC: American Psychiatric Press, 1990.

Allport, G. W. *Personality: A Psychological Interpretation*. New York: Holt, 1937.

———. "What Is a Trait of Personality?" *Journal of Abnormal and Social Psychology* 25 (1931): 368–72.

Allport, G. W., and H. S. Odbert. "Trait-Names: A Psycholexical Study." *Psychological Monographs* 47 (1936): 1–211.

Altemeyer, B. (*See also* Altemeyer, R.) *Enemies of Freedom: Understanding Right-Wing Authoritarianism*. San Francisco: Jossey-Bass, 1988.

———. "The Other 'Authoritarian Personality.'" *Advances in Experimental Social Psychology* 30 (1998): 47–92.

Altemeyer, R. (*See also* Altemeyer, B.) *The Authoritarian Specter*. Cambridge, MA: Harvard University Press, 1996.

American Psychiatric Association. *Diagnostic and Statistical Manual of Mental Disorders*, 4th ed. Washington, DC: American Psychiatric Association, 1994.

Anālayo. *Satipatthana: The Direct Path to Realization*. Birmingham, UK: Windhorse Publications, 2003.

Anderson, L. W., and D. R. Krathwohl, eds. *A Taxonomy for Learning, Teaching, and Assessing: A Revision of Bloom's Taxonomy of Educational Objectives*. Boston: Allyn & Bacon, 2000.

Ansbacher, Heinz L., and R. R. Ansbacher, eds. *Alfred Adler: Superiority and Social Interest: A Collection of Later Writings*. New York: Norton, 1979.

———, eds. *The Individual Psychology of Alfred Adler: A Systematic Presentation in Selections from His Writings*. New York: Basic Books, 1956.

Arendt, Hannah. *The Origins of Totalitarianism*. New York: Harcourt, 1968.

Aronson, Elliot, T. D. Wilson, and R. M. Akert. *Social Psychology: The Heart and the Mind*. New York: HarperCollins College Publishers, 1994.

Atkinson, John W. *An Introduction to Motivation*. Princeton, NJ: Van Nostrand, 1964.

Austin, John L. *Philosophical Papers*. Edited by James O. Urmson and G. J. Warnock. Oxford: Oxford University Press, 1979.

Babcock, L., and G. Loewenstein. "Explaining Bargaining Impasse: The Role of Self-Serving Biases." *Journal of Economic Perspectives* 11, no. 1 (1975): 119–37.

Balkin, Jack M. *Cultural Software: A Theory of Ideology*. New Haven, CT: Yale University Press, 1998.

Baltzly, D. C. "Who Are the Mysterious Dogmatists of 'Adversus Mathematicus' Ix 352? (Sextus Empiricus)." *Ancient Philosophy* 18 (1998): 145–71.

Bandura, Albert. *Aggression: A Social Learning Analysis*. Englewood Cliffs, NJ: Prentice-Hall, 1973.

———. "Behavior Theory and the Models of Man." *American Psychologist* 29 (1974): 859–69.

———. "Mechanisms of Moral Disengagement." In *Origins of Terrorism: Psychologies, Ideologies, Theologies, States of Mind*, edited by Walter Reich, 161–91, 1998.

———. *Self-Efficacy: The Exercise of Control*. New York: Freeman, 1997.

———. *Social Foundations of Thought and Action: A Social Cognitive Theory*. Englewood Cliffs, NJ: Prentice-Hall, 1986.

———. *Social Learning Theory*. Englewood Cliffs, NJ: Prentice-Hall, 1977.

Bandura, A., and W. Mischel. "Modifications of Self-Imposed Delay of Reward through Exposure to Live and Symbolic Models." *Journal of Personality and Social Psychology* 2 (1965): 698–705.

Bandura, A., D. Ross, and S. A. Ross, "Transmission of Aggression through Imitation of Aggressive Models." *Journal of Abnormal and Social Psychology* 63 (1961): 575–82.

Bandura, A., B. Underwood, and M. E. Fromson. "Disinhibition of Aggression through Diffusion of Responsibility and Dehumanization of Victims." *Journal of Research in Personality*, no. 9 (1975): 253–69.

Barash, David P. *The Whisperings Within: Evolution and the Origin of Human Nature*. New York: Penguin, 1979.

Barber, Benjamin R. *Fear's Empire: War, Terrorism, and Democracy*. New York: Norton, 2003.

Barber, B. K. "Parental Psychological Control." *Child Development* 67, no. 6 (1996): 3296–319.

Baron, Jonathan B. *Thinking and Deciding*. Cambridge: Cambridge University Press, 2000.

Batchelor, Stephen. *Alone with Others: An Existential Approach to Buddhism*. New York: Grove, 1983.

———. *Buddhism without Beliefs: A Contemporary Guide to Awakening*. New York: Berkley Publishing Group, 1997.

———. *Living with the Devil*. New York: Riverhead Books, 2004.

Baumrind, D. "Current Patterns of Parental Authority." *Developmental Psychology Monograph* 4 (1971).

———. "Effects of Authoritative Parental Control on Child Behavior." *Child Development* 37, no. 4 (1966): 887–907.

Beebe, Steven A., S. J. Beebe, and M. V. Redmond. *Interpersonal Communication: Relating to Others*. Needham Heights, MA: Allyn and Bacon, 1996.

Belsky, J., B. Gilstrap, and M. Rovine. "The Pennsylvania Infant and Family Development Project, I: Stability and Change in Mother-Infant and Father-Infant Interaction in a Family Setting." *Child Development* 55 (1984): 692–705.

Benjamin, J., I. Li, C. Patterson, B. D. Greenberg, D. L. Murphy, and D. H. Hamer. "Population and Familial Association between the D4 Dopamine Receptor Gene and Measures of Novelty Seeking." *Nature Genetics* 12 (1996): 81–84.

Berger, Jerry M. *Personality*. 6th ed. Belmont, CA: Wadsworth/Thomson Learning, 2004.

Berlin, Isaiah. *Four Essays on Liberty*. Oxford: Oxford University Press, 1969.

Berman, Paul. *Terror and Liberalism*. New York: Norton, 2003.

Best, Joel. *More Damned Lies and Statistics*. Berkeley: University of California Press, 2004.

Bjorklund, David F., and A. D. Pellegrini. *The Origins of Human Nature: Evolutionary Developmental Psychology*. Washington, DC: American Psychological Association, 2002.

Bjorklund, D. F., and C. H. Blasi. "Evolutionary Developmental Psychology." In *A Handbook of Evolutionary Psychology*, edited by David H. Buss. Hoboken, NJ: Wiley, 2005.

Blackburn, Simon. *The Oxford Dictionary of Philosophy*. Oxford: Oxford University Press, 1996.

———. *Think*. Oxford: Oxford University Press, 1999.

———. *Truth: A Guide*. Oxford: Oxford University Press, 2005.

Blackmore, Susan. *The Meme Machine*. Oxford: Oxford University Press, 1999.

Block, D. "A Contrarian View of the Five-Factor Approach to Personality Description." *Psychological Bulletin* 117 (1995): 187–215.

Bloom, Benjamin S. *Taxonomy of Educational Objectives: The Classification of Educational Goals.* n.p.: Susan Fauer, 1956.

Bowlby, John. *Attachment and Loss.* Vol. 1, *Attachment.* New York: Basic Books, 1969.

———. *Attachment and Loss.* Vol. 2, *Separation.* New York: Basic Books, 1973.

———. *Attachment and Loss.* Vol. 3, *Loss, Sadness, and Depression.* New York: Basic Books, 1980.

Brisch, Karl H. *Treating Attachment Disorders.* New York: Guilford, 1999.

Broad, William, and N. Wade. *Betrayers of the Truth: Fraud and Deceit in the Halls of Science.* New York: Simon and Schuster, 1982.

Brody, N. "Heritability of Traits." *Psychological Inquiry* 5, no. 2 (1994): 117–19.

Bruner, Jerome S. *Acts of Meaning.* Cambridge, MA: Harvard University Press, 1990.

Brym, R. J., ed. *New Society: Sociology for the 21st century.* Toronto: Harcourt Canada, 2001.

Bunge, M. "Absolute Skepticism Equals Dogmatism." *Skeptical Inquirer* (2000): 34–36.

Buss, Arnold H. *Personality: Evolutionary Heritage and Human Distinctiveness.* Hillsdale, NJ: Erlbaum, 1988.

———. *Personality: Temperament, Social Behavior.* Needham Heights, MA: Allyn and Bacon, 1995.

Buss, Arnold H., and R. Plomin. *Temperament: Early Developing Personality Traits.* Hillsdale, NJ: Wiley-Interscience, 1984.

———. *A Temperament Theory of Personality Development.* New York: Wiley-Interscience, 1975.

Buss, David M. "Introduction: The Emergence of Evolutionary Psychology." In *The Handbook of Evolutionary Psychology*, edited by David M. Buss. Hoboken, NJ: Wiley, 2005.

———. "Social Adaptation and Five Major Factors of Personality." In *The Five-Factor Model of Personality: Theoretical Perspectives*, edited by Jerry S. Wiggins. New York: Guilford, 1996.

Camus, Albert. *The Rebel: An Essay on Man in Revolt.* New York: Vintage Books, 1956.

Carpenter, S. "Behavioral Science Gears up to Combat Terrorism." *Monitor on Psychology* 32 (2001): 1–3.

Cattell, R. B. "The Description of Personality: Basic Traits Resolved into Clusters." *Journal of Abnormal and Social Psychology* 38 (1943): 476–506.

Chomsky, Noam. *Knowledge of Language: Its Nature, Origin, and Use.* Westport, CT: Praeger, 1986.

———. *Language and Mind.* New York: Harcourt Brace Jovanovich, 1968.

Christie, R. "Milton Rokeach (1918–1988) [Obituaries]." *American Psychologist* 45, no. 4 (1990): 547–48.

Clark, Herbert H., and E. V. Clark. *Psychology and Language: An Introduction to Psycholinguistics.* New York: Harcourt, 1977.

Claxton, Guy. *The Heart of Buddhism.* London: Thorsons, 1999.

Cloninger, Susan C. *Theories of Personality: Understanding Persons.* 2nd ed. Upper Saddle River, NJ: Prentice-Hall, 1996.

Cohen, I. Bernard. *Revolution in Science.* Cambridge, MA: Harvard University Press, 1985.

Collins, W. A., E. E. Macoby, L. Steinberg, E. M. Hetherington, and M. H. Bornstein, "Contemporary Research on Parenting: The Case for Nature *and* Nurture." *American Psychologist* 55 (2000): 218–32.

Conlan, Roberta. *States of Mind: New Discoveries about How Our Brains Make Us Who We Are.* New York: Wiley, 1999.

Conley, J. J. "The Hierarchy of Consistency: A Review and Model of Longitudinal Findings on Adult Individual Differences in Intelligence, Personality, and Self-Opinion." *Personality and Individual Differences* 5 (1984): 11–26.

Conniff, R., 2000. "I Want to Be Boss: The Psychology of Dominance." *Discover* 21, no. 5 (2000): 72–80.

Corning, P. A. *Holistic Darwinism: Synergy, Cybernetics, and the Bioeconomics of Evolution.* Chicago: University of Chicago Press, 2005.

Cosmides, L., and J. Tooby. "From Evolution to Behavior: Evolutionary Psychology as the Missing Link." In *The Latest on the Best: Essays on Evolution and Optimality,* edited by John Dupre. Cambridge, MA: MIT Press, 1987.

Costa, P. T., Jr., and R. R. McCrae. "From Catalog to Classification: Murray's Needs and the Five-Factor Model." *Journal of Personality and Social Psychology* 55 (1988): 258–65.

———. *The NEO Personality Inventory Manual*. Odessa, FL: Psychological Assessment Resources, 1985.

———. *Revised NEO Personality Inventory (Neo-Pi-R) and Neo Five-Factor Inventory (NEO-FFI) Professional Manual*. Odessa, FL: Psychological Assessment Resources, 1992.

Crenshaw, M. "An Organizational Approach to the Analysis of Political Terrorism." *Orbis*, no. 29 (1985): 465–89.

Csikszentmihalyi, Mihaly. *Flow: The Psychology of Optimal Experiences*. New York: Harper and Row, 1990.

———. "If We Are So Rich, Why Aren't We Happy?" *American Psychologist* 54 (2005): 821–27.

Damasio, Antonio R. *Descartes' Error: Emotion, Reason, and the Human Brain*. New York: Putnam, 1994.

———. "How the Brain Creates the Mind." *Scientific American Special Edition* 12, no. 1 (2002): 4–9.

Darwin, Charles R. *On the Origin of Species by Means of Natural Selection, or the Preservation of Favoured Races in the Struggle for Life*. 1st ed. London: John Murray, 1859.

David, H. P. "Born Unwanted: Long-Term Developmental Effects of Denied Abortion." *Journal of Social Issues* 48 (1992): 163–81.

Davidson, R. J., D. C. Jackson, and N. Kalin. "Emotion, Plasticity, Context, and Regulation: Perspectives from Affective Neuroscience." *Psychological Bulletin* 126, no. 6 (2000): 890–909.

Davidson, R. J., K. M. Putnam, and C. L. Larson. "Dysfunction in the Neural Circuitry of Emotion Regulation: A Possible Prelude to Violence." *Science* 289 (2000): 591–94.

Davies, Jody Messler, and M. G. Frawley. *Treating the Adult Survivor of Childhood Sexual Abuse: A Psychoanalytic Perspective*. New York: Basic Books, 1994.

Davies, M. F. "Dogmatism and Belief Formation: Output Interference in the Processing of Supporting and Contradictory Cognitions." *Journal of Personality and Social Psychology* 75, no. 2 (1998): 456–66.

Davison, Gerald C., J. M. Neale, K. R. Blankstein, and G. L. Flett. *Abnormal Psychology: Canadian Edition*. Etobicoke, ON: Wiley, 2002.

Dawkins, R. *The God Delusion*. New York: Houghton Mifflin, 2006.

———. "Viruses of the Mind." *Free Inquiry* 13 (1993): 34–38.

De Botton, Alain. *How Proust Can Change Your Life: Not a Novel.* New York: Vintage, 1997.

———. *Status Anxiety.* Toronto: Viking, 2004.

Deci, E. L., and R. M. Ryan. "The 'What' and 'Why' of Goal Pursuits: Human Needs and the Self-Determination of Behavior." *Psychological Inquiry* 11 (2000): 227–68.

Dennett, Daniel C. *Breaking the Spell: Religion as a Natural Phenomenon.* New York: Penguin, 2006.

———. *Consciousness Explained.* Boston: Little, Brown, 1991.

Dennis, Wayne. *Children of the Creche.* New York: Appleton-Century Crofts, 1973.

Derlega, Valerian J., B. A. Winstead, and W. H. Jones, eds. *Personality: Contemporary Theory and Research.* 3rd ed. Belmont, CA: Wadsworth, 2005.

Deyoung, C. G., J. B. Peterson, and D. M. Higgins. "Sources of Openness/Intellect: Cognitive and Neuropsychological Correlates of the Fifth Factor of Personality." *Journal of Personality* 73, no. 4 (2005): 825–58.

Diamond, Jared. *Guns, Germs, and Steel: The Fates of Human Societies.* New York: Norton, 1999.

Diamond, Marian C., and J. Hopson. *Magic Trees of the Mind: How to Nurture Your Child's Intelligence, Creativity, and Healthy Emotions from Birth through Adolescence.* New York: Dutton/Plume, 1998.

Digman, J. M., and N. K. Takemoto-Chock. "Factors in the Natural Language of Personality: Re-analysis, Comparison, and Interpretation of Six Major Studies." *Multivariate Behavioral Research* 16 (1981): 149–70.

Dinkmeyer, D. "The C Group: Integrating Knowledge and Experience to Change Behavior—an Adlerian Approach to Consultation." *Counseling Psychologist* 3 (1971): 63–72.

Doidge, Norman. *The Brain That Changes Itself: Stories of Personal Triumph from the Frontiers of Brain Science.* New York: Viking, 2007.

Dolan, R. J. "On the Neurology of Morals." *Nature Neuroscience* 2 (1999): 927–29.

Dreikurs, Rudolf. *Psychology in the Classroom.* New York: Harper, 1957.

Dubowitz, H., and M. Black. "Child Neglect." In *Child Abuse: Medical Diagnosis and Management,* ed. Robert M. Reece, 279–97. Philadelphia: Lea & Febiger, 1994.

Dunbar, Robin I. M. *Grooming, Gossip, and the Evolution of Language.* Cambridge, MA: Harvard University Press, 1996.

Duntley, J. D. "Adaptations to Dangers from Humans." In *The Handbook of Evolutionary Psychology,* edited by David M. Buss. Hoboken, NJ: Wiley 2005.

Dupont, Henry. *Emotional Development, Theory and Applications: A Neo-Piagetian Perspective.* Westport, CT: Praeger, 1994.

Durkin, K. "A Lifespan Developmental Perspective." In *Blackwell Handbook of Social Psychology: Intraindividual Processes,* edited by A. Tesser and N. Schwartz, 44–67. Oxford: Blackwell Publishing, 2003.

Egeland, B. "A Longitudinal Study of High-Risk Families: Issues and Findings." In *The Effects of Child Abuse and Neglect: Issues and Research,* edited by Raymond H. Starr and D. A. Wolfe, 33–56. New York: Guilford, 1991.

Eisenberg, N., T. L. Spinard, and A. Cumberland. "The Socialization of Emotion: Reply to Commentaries." *Psychological Inquiry* 9 (1998): 317–33.

Elliot, A. J., K. M. Sheldon, and M. A. Church. "Avoidance Personal Goals and Subjective Well-Being." *Personality and Social Psychology Bulletin* 23, no. 9 (1997): 915–27.

Ellis, Albert. *Better, Deeper and More Enduring Brief Therapy: The Rational Emotive Behavior Therapy Approach.* Bristol, PA: Brunner/Mazel, 1996.

———. *Growth through Reason: Verbatim Cases of Rational-Emotive Therapy.* Hollywood: Wilshire Books, 1971.

———. *How to Live with a Neurotic.* Hollywood: Wilshire Book Company, 1957.

———. *Overcoming Destructive Beliefs, Feelings, and Behaviors.* Amherst, NY: Prometheus Books, 2001.

———. *Reason and Emotion in Psychotherapy.* New York: Lyle Stuart, 1962.

———. *Reason and Emotion in Psychotherapy Revised.* New York: Kensington, 1994.

———. *Techniques for Disputing Irrational Beliefs (Dib's).* New York: Institute for Rational Living, 1974.

Ellis, Albert, and R. A. Harper. *A New Guide for Rational Living.* Hollywood: Wilshire, 1975.

Engel, G. "The Need for a New Medical Model: A Challenge for Biomedicine." *Science* 196 (1977): 129–36.

Engler, Barbara. *Personality Theories: An Introduction.* 6th ed. Boston: Houghton Mifflin Co., 2003.

Epstein, Mark. *Thoughts without a Thinker.* New York: Basic Books, 1995.

Erikson, E. H. *Childhood and Society.* New York: Norton, 1950.

————. *Identity: Youth and Crisis.* New York: Norton, 1968.

————. *The Life Cycle Completed: A Review.* New York: Norton, 1982, 1997.

Eriksson, P. S., E. Perfilieva, T. Bjork-Eriksson, A. M. Alborn, C. Nordberg, D. A. Peterson, and F. H. Gage. "Neurogenesis in the Adult Human Hippocampus." *Nature Medicine* 4, no. 11 (1998): 1313–17.

Evans, J., J. Barston, and P. Pollard. "On the Conflict between Logic and Belief in Syllogistic Reasoning." *Memory and Cognition* 11 (1983): 295–306.

Eysenck, Hans J. *The Biological Basis of Personality.* Springfield, IL: Charles C. Thomas, 1967.

Eysenck, Hans J., and M. W. Eysenck. *Personality and Individual Differences: A Natural Science Approach.* New York: Plenum, 1985.

Feist, Jess. *Theories of Personality.* 3rd ed. New York: Holt, Rinehart, and Winston, 1994.

Fiedler, Klaus, and J. Forgas. *Affect, Cognition, and Social Behavior.* Toronto: C. J. Hogrefe, 1988.

Field, Tiffany M., P. M. McCabe, and N. Schneiderman. *Stress and Coping across Development.* Mahwah, NJ: Lawrence Erlbaum, 1988.

Fine, Cornelia. *A Mind of Its Own.* New York: Norton, 2006.

Fiske, D. W. "Consistency of the Factorial Structures of Personality Ratings from Different Sources." *Journal of Abnormal and Social Psychology* 44 (1949): 329–44.

Fleeson, W. "Moving Personality beyond the Person-Situation Debate: The Challenge and the Opportunity of Within-Person Variability." In *Current Directions in Personality Psychology,* edited by Carolyn C. Morf and O. Ayduk, 15–22. Upper Saddle River, NJ: Pearson Education, 2005.

Forgas, Joseph P. *Feeling and Thinking: The Role of Affect in Social Cognition.* New York: Cambridge University Press, 2000.

Fox, W. M. "Changing Human Behavior and Institutions toward 21st Century Paradigms: A Theoretical Construct." *ETC.: A Review of General Semantics* 56, no. 2 (1999): 147–55.

Frager, Robert, and J. Fadiman. *Personality and Personal Growth.* 6th ed. Upper Saddle River, NJ: Pearson Education, 2005.

Frankfurt, Harry G. *On Bullshit*. Princeton, NJ: Princeton University Press, 2005.

Frankl, Viktor E. *Man's Search for Meaning*. New York: Simon and Schuster, 1963.

Freeman, S., and J. C. Herron. *Evolutionary Analysis*. Upper Saddle River, NJ: Prentice Hall, 1998.

Freud, S. "Analysis Terminable and Interminable." In *Standard Edition of the Complete Psychological Works of Sigmund Freud*, edited by James Strachey, 216–37. London: Hogarth Press, 1937.

———. *New Introductory Lectures in Psychoanalysis*. New York: Norton, 1974.

Freyhold, M. "Old and New Dimensions of Authoritarianism and Its Opposite." *High School Journal* 68, no. 4 (1985): 241–46.

Friedman, Howard S., and M. W. Schustack. *Readings in Personality: Classic Theories and Modern Research*. 2nd ed. New York: Allyn and Bacon, 2003.

Fromm, Erich. *Escape from Freedom*. New York: Holt, Rinehart, and Winston, 1941.

Fukuyama, F. *Our Posthuman Future*. New York: Farrar, Strauss and Giroux, 2002.

Fulton, A. S. "Identity Status, Religious Orientation, and Prejudice." *Journal of Youth and Adolescence* 26 (1997): 1–11.

Funder, David C. *The Personality Puzzle*. New York: Norton, 2001.

———. *The Personality Puzzle*. 4th ed. New York: Norton, 2007.

Funder, D. C., and D. J. Ozer. *Pieces of the Personality Puzzle: Readings in Theory and Research*. 3rd ed. New York: Norton, 2004.

Gaines, S. O., Jr., and E. S. Reed. "Prejudice: From Allport to Dubois." *American Psychologist* 50 (1995): 96–103.

Galanter, M. "Psychological Induction into the Large Group: Findings from a Modern Religious Sect." *American Journal of Psychiatry* 136 (1980): 1574–79.

Galanter, M., R. Rabkin, J. Rabkin, and A. Deutsch. "The 'Moonies': A Psychological Study of Conversion and Membership in a Contemporary Religious Sect." *American Journal of Psychiatry* 37 (1979): 1574–79.

Gander, Eric M. *On Our Minds: How Evolutionary Psychology Is Reshaping the Nature-versus-Nurture Debate*. Baltimore: Johns Hopkins University Press, 2003.

Gaulin, Steven J. C., and D. H. McBurney. *Evolutionary Psychology*. 2nd ed. Upper Saddle River, NJ: Pearson Education, 2004.

Gazzaniga, Michael S. *Cognitive Neuroscience: A Reader*. Malden, MA: Blackwell, 2000.

Gazzaniga, Michael S., R. B. Ivry, and G. R. Mangun. *Cognitive Neuroscience: The Biology of the Mind*. New York: Norton, 1998.

Gergen, Kenneth J. *The Saturated Self: Dilemmas of Identity in Contemporary Life*. New York: Basic Books, 1991.

Gibson, K. R. "The Biocultural Human Brain, Seasonal Migrations, and the Emergence of the Upper Paleolithic." In *Modeling the Human Mind*, edited by Paul Mellars and K. R. Gibson, 33–36. Cambridge: McDonald Institute for Archeological Research, 1996.

Giedd, J. N. "Structural Magnetic Resonance Imaging of the Adolescent Brain." In *Adolescent Brain Development: Vulnerabilities and Opportunities*, edited by R. E. Dahl and L. P. Spear, 77–85. New York: New York Academy of Sciences, 2004.

Gitlin, T. "Varieties of Patriotic Experience." In *The Fight Is for Democracy*, edited by George Packer. New York: HarperCollins, 2003.

Gladwell, Malcolm. *Blink: The Power of Thinking without Thinking*. New York: Little, Brown, 2005.

Goldberg, L. R. "An Alternative 'Description of Personality': The Big Five Factor Structure." *Journal of Personality and Social Psychology* 59 (1990): 1216–29.

———. "How Not to Whip a Straw Dog." *Psychological Inquiry* 5, no. 2 (1994): 128–30.

———. "Language and Individual Differences: The Search for Universals in Personality Lexicons." In *Review of Personality and Social Psychology*, edited by Ladd Wheeler, 149–66. Beverly Hills, CA: Sage, 1981.

Goldberg, Susan. *Attachment and Development*. New York: Oxford University Press, 2000.

Goldsmith, H. H., and J. J. Campos. "Toward a Theory of Infant Temperament." In *The Development of Attachment and Affiliative Systems*, edited by Robert N. Emde and R. J. Harmon, 161–93. New York: Plenum, 1982.

Goldsmith, H. H., and C. Harman. "Temperament and Attachment; Individuals and Relationships." In *Current Directions in Personality Psychology*, edited by C. C. Morf and O. Ayduk, 115–18. Upper Saddle River, NJ: Pearson, 2005.

Goldstein, Joseph. *One Dharma: The Emerging Western Buddhism.* San Francisco: HarperCollins, 2002.

Goldstein, Kurt. *The Organism: A Holistic Approach to Biology.* New York: American Book Company, 1939.

Goleman, Daniel. *Emotional Intelligence: Why It Can Matter More Than I.Q.* New York: Bantam Books, 1995.

———. *Social Intelligence: The New Science of Human Relationships.* New York: Bantam, 2006.

Goleman, Daniel, and the Dalai Lama. *Destructive Emotions: How Can We Overcome Them?* New York: Bantam Books, 2003.

Gore, Albert. *The Assault on Reason,* New York: Penguin Books, 2007.

Gould, S. J. "Bacon, Brought Home." *Natural History* 108, no. 5 (1999): 28–40.

Gover, Trudy. *A Delicate Balance: What Philosophy Can Tell Us about Terrorism.* Boulder, CO: Westview Press, 2002.

Graziano, W. "Personality Development in Childhood." In *International Encyclopedia of the Social and Behavioral Sciences*, edited by Neil J. Smelser and P. B. Baltes, 11295–300. Elmsford, NY: Pergamon, 2004.

Greenspan, Stanley I., and S. G. Shanker. *The First Idea: How Symbols, Language, and Intelligence Evolved from Our Primate Ancestors to Modern Humans.* Cambridge, MA: Da Capo, 2004.

Greenwald, A. G., J. E. Pickrell, and S. D. Farnham. "Implicit Partisanship: Taking Sides for No Reason." *Journal of Personality and Social Psychology* 83 (2002): 367–79.

Grene, M. "Descartes and Skepticism." *Review of Metaphysics* 52 (1999): 553–72.

Grimes, R. G. "General Semantics and Memetics: A Tentative Relationship?" *ETC.: A Review of General Semantics* 55 (1998): 30–33.

Grolnick, Wendy S. *The Psychology of Parental Control: How Well-Meant Parenting Backfires.* Mahwah, NJ: Erlbaum, 2003.

Hagen, E. H. "Controversial Issues in Evolutionary Psychology." In *The Handbook of Evolutionary Psychology*, edited by D. M. Buss. Hoboken, NJ: Wiley, 2005.

Hakstian, A. R., and S. Farrell. "An Openness Scale for the California Psychological Inventory." *Journal of Personality Assessment* 76, no. 1 (2001): 107–34.

Hamilton, W. D. "The Genetical Evolution of Social Behavior." *Journal of Theoretical Biology* 7 (1964): 1–52.

Hare, R. D., S. D. Hart, and T. J. Harpur. "Psychopathy and the *DSM-IV* Criteria for Antisocial Personality Disorder." *Journal of Abnormal Psychology* 100 (1991): 391–98.

Harrington, Alan. *Psychopaths*. New York: Simon and Shuster, 1972.

Harris, J. R. "Zero Parental Influence." In *What Is Your Dangerous Idea?* edited by John Brockman. New York: HarperCollins, 2007.

Harris, Sam. *The End of Faith: Religion, Terror, and the Future of Reason.* New York: Norton, 2005.

Hart, J., P. R. Shaver, and J. L. Goldenberg. "Attachment, Self-Esteem, Worldviews, and Terror Management: Evidence for a Tripartite Security System." *Journal of Personality and Social Psychology* (2005): 999–1013.

Harter, S. "The Development of Self-Representations During Childhood and Adolescence." In *Handbook of Self and Identity*, edited by Mark Leary and J. P. Tangney, 610–42. New York: Guilford, 2003.

Haught, J. A. *Two Thousand Years of Doubt: Famous People with the Courage to Doubt*. Amherst, NY: Prometheus Books, 1996.

Hedges, Chris. *American Fascists: The Christian Right and the War on America*. New York: Free Press, 2006.

Heinrich, J., and F. J. Gil-White. "The Evolution of Prestige: Freely Conferred Deference as a Mechanism for Enhancing the Benefits of Cultural Transmission." *Evolution and Human Behavior* 22, no. 3 (2001): 165–96.

Hergenhahn, B. R. *An Introduction to Theories of Personality*. Englewood Cliffs, NJ: Prentice Hall, 1994.

Heylighen, F. "Selfish Memes and the Evolution of Cooperation." *Journal of Ideas* 2, no. 4 (1992): 77–84.

Heyman, S. R. "Dogmatism, Hostility, Aggression, and Gender Roles." *Journal of Clinical Psychology* 33, no. 3 (1977): 694–98.

Hjelle, L. A., and D. J. Ziegler. *Personality Theories: Basic Assumptions, Research, and Applications*. 3rd ed. New York: McGraw-Hill, 1992.

Hoffer, Eric. *The True Believer*. New York: Harper and Row, 1951.

Hoffman-Plotkin, D., and C. T. Twentyman. "A Multimodal Assessment of Behavioral and Cognitive Deficits in Abused and Neglected Preschoolers." *Child Development* 55 (1984): 794–802.

Hogan, R. "Personality and Personality Measurement." In *Handbook of Industrial and Organizational Psychology*, edited by Marvin D. Dunnette and L. M. Hough, 873–919. Palo Alto, CA: Consulting Psychologists Press, 1991.

Horney, Karen. *Neurosis and Human Growth: The Struggle toward Self-Realization*. New York: Norton, 1950.

———. *The Neurotic Personality of Our Time*. New York: Norton, 1937.

———. *Our Inner Conflicts*. New York: Norton, 1945.

Humphrey, N. "Bertrand Russell's Dangerous Idea." In *What Is Your Dangerous Idea?* edited by John Brockman. New York: HarperCollins, 2007.

Hunsberger, B. E., and B. Altemeyer. *Atheists: A Groundbreaking Study of America's Nonbelievers*. Amherst, NY: Prometheus Books, 2006.

Ignatieff, Michael. *The Warrior's Honour*. Harmondsworth, UK: Penguin Books, 1999.

Isaac, J. "A New Guarantee on Earth: Hannah Arendt on Human Dignity and the Politics of Human Rights." *American Political Science Review* 90, no. 1 (1996): 61–74.

Jahromi, L. B., S. P. Putnam, and C. A. Stifter. "Maternal Regulation of Infant Reactivity from Two to Six Months." *American Psychological Association* 40, no. 4 (2004): 477–87.

James, William. *The Principles of Psychology*. Boston: Holt, 1890.

Jampolsky, Gerald G. *Love Is Letting Go of Fear*. Berkeley, CA: Celestial Arts, 1979.

Janis, Irving L. *Groupthink*. 2nd ed. Boston: Houghton Mifflin, 1982.

———. *Victims of Groupthink*. Boston: Houghton-Mifflin, 1972.

John, O. P., and S. Srivastava. "The Big Five Trait Taxonomy: History, Measurement, and Theoretical Perspectives." In *Handbook of Personality: Theory and Research*, edited by Lawrence A. Pervin and O. P. John. New York: Guilford, 1999.

Johnson, J. J. "The Johnson Dogmatism Scale: Rokeach Revisited and Revised." Unpublished Dissertation, Walden University, Minneapolis, MN, 1987.

Johnson, J. T., L. M. Gain, T. L. Falke, J. Hayman, and E. Perillo. "The Barnum Effect Revisited: Cognitive and Motivational Factors in the Acceptance of Personality Descriptions." *Journal of Personality and Social Psychology* 49 (1985): 1378–91.

Johnson-Laird, P. N. "Deductive Reasoning." *Annual Review of Psychology* 50 (1999): 109–35.

Jost, J. T. "The End of the End of Ideology." *American Psychologist* 61, no. 7 (2006): 651–70.

Kagan, Jerome. "Born to Be Shy." In *States of Mind*, edited by Roberta Conlan, 29–51. New York: Wiley, 1999.

———. *Galen's Prophecy*. New York: Basic Books, 1994.

———. *Surprise, Uncertainty, and Mental Structures*. Cambridge, MA: Harvard University Press, 2002.

———. *Three Seductive Ideas*. Boston: Harvard University Press, 1998.

Kalat, J. W., and M. N. Shiota. *Emotion*. Belmont, CA: Thomson Wadsworth, 2007

Kandel, E. "Of Learning, Memory, and Genetic Switches." In *States of Mind: New Discoveries about How Our Brains Make Us Who We Are*, edited by Roberta Conlan, 151–78. New York: Wiley, 1999.

Kardash, C. M., and R. J. Scholes. "Effects of Pre-existing Beliefs, Epistemological Beliefs, and Need for Cognition on Interpretation of Controversial Issues." *Journal of Educational Psychology* 88 (1996): 260–71.

Karr-Morse, Robin, and M. S. Wiley. *Ghosts from the Nursery: Tracing the Roots of Violence*. New York: Atlantic Monthly, 1997.

Kelly, George A. *The Psychology of Personal Constructs*. Vol. 1. New York: Norton, 1955.

Kendall-Tackett, K. A., and J. Eckenrode. "The Effects of Neglect on Academic Achievement and Discipline Problems: A Developmental Perspective." *Child Abuse and Neglect* 20 (1996): 161–70.

Kida, T. *Don't Believe Everything You Think: The 6 Basic Mistakes We Make in Thinking*. Amherst, NY: Prometheus Books, 2006.

King, M. L., Jr. "Letter from Birmingham City Jail." In *Civil Disobedience: Theory and Practice*, edited by Hugo A. Bedau. New York: Pegasus, 1969.

Klaczynski, P. A. "Analytic and Heuristic Processing Influences on Adolescent Reasoning and Decision Making." *Child Development* 72 (2001): 844–61.

Klaczynski, P. A., D. H. Gordon, and J. Fauth. "Goal-Oriented Critical Reasoning and Individual Differences in Critical Reasoning Biases." *Journal of Educational Psychology* 89 (1997): 470–85.

Klein, S. B., J. Loftus, and J. F. Kihlstrom. "Self-Knowledge of an Amnesic Patient: Toward a Neuropsychology of Personality and Social Psychology." *Journal of Experimental Psychology* 125 (1996): 250–60.

Koestner, R., R. M. Ryan, F. Bernieri, and K. Holt. "Setting Limits on Children's Behavior: The Differential Effects of Controlling versus Informational Styles on Intrinsic Motivation and Creativity." *Journal of Personality* 52 (1984): 244–48.

Kohut, Heinz. *The Restoration of the Self.* New York: International Universities Press, 1977.

Kokis, J. V., R. Macpherson, M. E. Toplak, R. F. West, and K. E. Stanovich. "Heuristic and Analytic Processing: Age Trends and Associations with Cognitive Ability and Cognitive Styles." *Journal of Experimental Child Psychology* 83 (2002): 26–52.

Kopp, Sheldon B. *If You Meet the Buddha on the Road, Kill Him!* New York: Bantam, 1979.

Korner, A. F., C. A. Hutchinson, J. A. Koperski, H. C. Kraemer, and P. A. Schneider. "Stability of Individual Differences of Neonatal Motor and Crying Patterns." *Child Development* 52 (1981): 83–90.

Korzybski, Alfred. *Science and Sanity: An Introduction to Non-Aristotelian Systems and General Semantics.* 4th ed. Lakeville, CT: International Non-Aristotelian Library Publishing, 1958.

Krosnick, J. A., and D. F. Alwin. "Aging and Susceptibility to Attitude Change." *Journal of Personality and Social Psychology* 57 (1989): 416–25.

Kruglanski, A. W., D. M. Webster, and A. Klem. "Motivated Resistance and Openness to Persuasion in the Presence or Absence of Prior Information." *Journal of Personality and Social Psychology* 65, no. 5 (1993): 861–76.

LaFreniere, Peter J. *Emotional Development: A Biosocial Perspective.* Scarborough, ON: Nelson Thomson Learning, 2000.

Laible, D. L., and R. A. Thompson. "Attachment and Emotional Understanding in Preschool Children." *Developmental Psychology* 34 (1998): 1038–45.

Lakoff, George. *Don't Think of an Elephant.* White River Junction, VT: Chelsea Green, 2004.

———. *Whose Freedom? The Battle over America's Most Important Idea.* New York: Farrar, Straus and Giroux, 2006.

Laland, Kevin N., and G. R. Brown. *Sense and Nonsense: Evolutionary Perspectives on Human Behavior.* Oxford: Oxford University Press, 2002.

Lawler, P. A. "Manliness, Religion, and Our Manly Scientists." *Social Science and Modern Society* 45, no. 2 (2008): 155–58.

Leary, M. R., and D. L. Downs. "Interpersonal Functions of the Self-Esteem Motive: The Self-Esteem System as a Sociometer." In *Efficacy, Agency, and Self-Esteem*, edited by Michael H. Kernis, 123–44. New York: Plenum, 1995.

Leary, M. R., and J. P. Tangney. "The Self as an Organizing Construct in the Behavioral and Social Sciences." In *Handbook of Self and Identity*, edited by Mark R. Leary and J. P. Tangney, 3–14. New York: Guilford, 2003.

LeDoux, Joseph. "The Power of Emotions." In *States of Mind: New Discoveries about How Our Brains Make Us Who We Are*, edited by Roberta Conlan, 123–49. New York: Wiley, 1999.

———. *Synaptic Self: How Our Brains Become Who We Are*. Middlesex, UK: Penguin, 2002.

Lefton, L. A., L. Brannon, M. C. Boyes, and N. A. Ogden. *Psychology*. Toronto: Pearson, Allyn and Bacon, 2008.

Leone, C., and H. M. Wallace. "The Need for Closure and the Need for Structure: Interrelationships, Correlates, and Outcomes." *Journal of Psychology* 133, no. 5 (1999): 553–653.

Lesser, H. "The Socialization of Authoritarianism in Children." *High School Journal* 68 (1985): 162–66.

Lifton, Robert J. *Thought Reform and the Psychology of Totalism: A Study of "Brainwashing" in China*. New York: Norton, 1961.

Lipton, E. L., and A. Steinschneider. "Studies on the Psychophysiology of Infancy." *Merrill-Palmer Quarterly* 10 (1964): 102–17.

Lloyd, S. "Seth Lloyd." In *What We Believe but Cannot Prove: Today's Leading Thinkers on Science in the Age of Certainty*, edited by John Brockman, 55. New York: HarperCollins, 2006.

MacLeod, C. M. "Anxiety and Cognitive Processes." In *Cognitive Interference: Theories, Methods, and Findings*, edited by Irwin G. Sarason and G. R. Pierce, 47–76. New York: Erlbaum, 1996.

Macoby, E. E., and J. A. Martin. "Socialization in the Context of the Family: Parent-Child Interaction." In *Handbook of Child Psychology*, edited by P. H. Mussen, 1–102. New York: Wiley, 1983.

Macpherson, R., and K. E. Stanovich. "Cognitive Ability, Thinking Dispositions, and Instructional Set as Predictors of Critical Thinking." *Learning and Individual Differences* 17 (2007): 115–27.

Maddi, Salvatore R. *Personality Theories: A Comparative Analysis*. 4th ed. Georgetown, ON: Irwin-Dorsey, 1980.

Mahoney, M. J. "Publication Prejudices: An Experimental Study of Confirmatory Bias in the Peer Review System." *Cognitive Therapy and Research* 1 (1977): 161–75.

Malott, Richard W., K. Ritterby, and E. L. C. Wolf. *An Introduction to Behavior Modification*. Kalamazoo, MI: Behaviordelia, 1973.

Martin, B. M. "Scientific Fraud and the Power Structure of Science." *Prometheus* 10 (1992): 83–98.

Maslow, Abraham H. *The Farther Reaches of Human Nature*. New York: Viking, 1971.

———. *Motivation and Personality*. 2nd ed. New York: Harper and Row, 1970.

———. *Toward a Psychology of Being*. New York: Van Nostrand, 1962.

Maturana, Humberto R., and F. J. Varela. *The Tree of Knowledge: The Biological Roots of Human Understanding*. Boston: Shambhala, 1992.

May, Rollo. *The Cry for Myth*. New York: Norton, 1991.

———. *Freedom and Destiny*. New York: Dell Publishing, 1981.

———. *Love and Will*. New York: Norton, 1969.

———. *Man's Search for Himself*. New York: Norton, 1953.

———. *The Meaning of Anxiety*. New York: Norton, 1977.

———. *Psychology and the Human Dilemma*. New York: Norton, 1979.

McAdams, Dan P. *The Person: An Introduction to Personality Psychology*. 2nd ed. New York: Harcourt Brace, 1994.

McAdams, D. P. "A Psychology of the Stranger." *Psychological Inquiry* 5, no. 2 (1994): 145–48.

———. "What Do We Know When We Know a Person?" In *Pieces of the Personality Puzzle: Readings in Theory and Research*, edited by David C. Funder and D. J. Ozer. New York: Norton, 2004.

McAdams, D. P., and J. L. Pals. "A New Big Five: Fundamental Principles for an Integrative Science of Personality." *American Psychologist* 61, no. 3 (2006): 204–17.

McCrae, R. R. "Human Nature and Culture: A Trait Perspective." *Journal of Personality Research* 38, no. 1 (2004): 3–14.

———. "Personality Structure." In *Personality: Contemporary Theory and Research*, edited by Valerian A. Derlega, B. A. Winstead, and W. H. Jones, 192–216. Belmont, CA: Wadsworth, 2005.

———. "Social Consequences of Experiential Openness." *Psychological Bulletin* 120, no. 3 (2006): 323–37.

McCrae, Robert R., and P. T. Costa Jr. "A Five-Factor Theory of Personality." In *Handbook of Personality: Theory and Research*, ed. L. A. Pervin and O. P. John. New York: Guilford, 1999.

———. *Personality in Adulthood*. New York: Guilford, 1990.

———. *Personality in Adulthood: A Five-Factor Theory Perspective*. New York: Guilford, 2003.

———. "Personality Trait Structure as a Human Universal." *American Psychologist* 52 (1997): 509–16.

———. "The Stability of Personality: Observations and Evaluations." In *Current Directions in Personality Psychology*, edited by Carolyn C. Morf and O. Ayduk, 3–8. Upper Saddle River, NJ: Pearson Education, 2005.

———. "Toward a New Generation of Personality Theories: Theoretical Contexts for the Five-Factor Model." In *The Five-Factor Model of Personality: Theoretical Perspectives*, edited by Jerry S. Wiggins. New York: Guilford, 1996.

———. "Validation of the Five-Factor Model of Personality across Instruments and Observers." *Journal of Personality and Social Psychology* 52 (1987): 81–90.

McCrae, R. R., and O. P. John. "An Introduction to the Five-Factor Model and Its Applications." *Journal of Personality* 60, no. 2 (1992): 175–215.

McEwan, I. "Introduction." In *What We Believe but Cannot Prove: Today's Leading Thinkers on Science in the Age of Certainty*, edited by John Brockman. New York: HarperCollins, 2006.

McEwen, B. S. "Protective and Damaging Effects of Stress Mediators." *New England Journal of Medicine* 338 (1998): 171–79.

McGuire, M., and L. Tiger. "Close but Not Close Enough." *Social Science and Modern Society* 45 (2008): 159–61.

McQuaig, Linda. *All You Can Eat: Greed, Lust, and the New Capitalism*. Toronto: Penguin Canada, 2001.

Melnyk, G., ed. *Canada and the New American Empire: War and Anti-War.* Calgary: University of Calgary Press, 2004.

Michaels, Walter B. "Diversity's False Solace." *New York Times*, April 11, 2004, p. 14.

Mikulincer, M. "Adult Attachment Style and Information Processing: Individual Differences in Curiosity and Cognitive Closure." *Journal of Personality and Social Psychology* 72 (1997): 1217–30.

Milgram, Stanley. *Obedience to Authority: An Experimental View*. New York: Harper and Row, 1974.

Miller, D. T., and M. Ross. "Self-Serving Biases in the Attribution of Causality: Fact or Fiction?" *Psychological Bulletin* 82 (1975): 213–25.

Mischel, Walter. *Introduction to Personality*. 5th ed. Orlando, FL: Harcourt Brace Jovanovich, 1993.

———. *Personality and Assessment*. New York: Wiley, 1968.

———. "Personality Psychology Has Two Goals: Must It Be Two Fields?" *Psychological Inquiry* 5, no. 2 (1994): 156–58.

Mischel, W., Y. Shoda, and R. Mendoza-Denton. "Situation-Behavior Profiles as a Locus of Consistency in Personality." In *Current Directions in Personality Psychology*, edited by Carolyn C. Morf and A. Ozlem, 9–14. Upper Saddle River, NJ: Pearson Education, 2005.

Moghaddam, Fathali M., and A. J. Marsella, eds. *Understanding Terrorism: Psychosocial Roots, Consequences, and Interventions*. Westport, CT: Praeger, 2004.

Molfese, Dennis L., and V. J. Molfese. *Temperament and Personality Development across the Life Span*. Mahwah, NJ: Erlbaum, 2000.

Moskowitz, G. B. "Individual Differences in Social Categorization: The Influence of Personal Need for Structure on Spontaneous Trait Inferences." *Journal of Personality and Social Psychology* 65, no. 1 (1993): 132–42.

Murphy, S. T., and R. B. Zajonc. "Affect, Cognition, and Awareness: Affective Priming with Optimal and Suboptimal Stimulus Exposures." *Journal of Personality and Social Psychology* 64 (1993): 723–39.

Nakamura, H. "The Basic Teachings of Buddhism." In *The Cultural, Political, and Religious Significance of Buddhism in the Modern World*, edited by Heinrich Dumoulin and J. C. Maraldo, 3–34. New York: Macmillan, 1976.

Neisser, Ulric. *Cognitive Psychology*. New York: Appleton-Century-Crofts, 1967.

Nesse, R. M. "Evolutionary Psychology and Mental Health." In *The Handbook of Evolutionary Psychology*, edited by David M. Buss. Hoboken, NJ: Wiley, 2005.

Neuberg, S. L, and J. T. Newsom. "Personal Need for Structure: Individual Differences in the Desire for Simple Structure." *Journal of Personality and Social Psychology* 65, no. 1 (1993): 113–31.

Newberg, Andrew, and M. R. Waldman. *Why We Believe What We Believe.* New York: Free Press, 2007.

Nhat Hanh, Thich. *The Heart of the Buddha's Teaching.* Berkeley, CA: Parallax, 1998.

Nickerson, R. "On Improving Thinking through Instruction." In *Review of Research in Education,* edited by Ernst Z. Rothkopf, 3–57. Washington, DC, 1998.

———. "Why Teach Thinking?" In *Teaching Thinking Skills: Theory and Practice,* edited by Joan Baron and R. Sternberg, 27–40. New York: Freeman, 1987.

Niles, E., and S. J. Gould. "Punctuated Equilibria: An Alternative to Phyletic Gradualism." In *Models in Paleobiology,* edited by Thomas J. M. Schopf, 82–115. San Francisco: Freeman Cooper, 1972.

Norman, Donald A. *Emotional Design: Why We Love (or Hate) Everyday Things.* New York: Basic Books, 2004.

Norman, W. T. "Toward an Adequate Taxonomy of Personality Attributes: Replicated Factor Structure in Peer Nomination Personality Ratings." *Journal of Abnormal and Social Psychology* 66 (1963): 574–83.

Norris, Stephen P., and R. H. Ennis. *Evaluating Critical Thinking.* Pacific Grove, CA: Midwest Publications, 1989.

Nussbaum, Martha. "Patriotism and Cosmopolitanism." *Boston Review* 19, no. 5 (October–November 1994).

Obholzer, Anton. *Security and Creativity at Work.* Philadelphia: Brunner-Routledge, 2001.

Oltmanns, Thomas F., R. E. Emery, and S. Taylor. *Abnormal Psychology.* Toronto: Pearson Education Canada, 2002.

Over, David E. *Evolution and the Psychology of Thinking: The Debate.* New York: Psychology Press, 2003.

Overwalle, F. V., and C. Labiouse. "A Recurrent Connectionist Model of Person Impression Formation." *Personality and Social Psychology Review* 8 (2004): 28–61.

Oz, A. *How to Cure a Fanatic.* Princeton, NJ: Princeton University Press, 2002.

Packard, Vance. *The Status Seekers.* New York: William Petersen, 1959.

Peddle, Frank. *Thought and Being: Hegel's Criticism of Kant's System of Cosmological Ideas.* Lanham, MD: University Press of America, 1980.

Perry, Bruce D. "Childhood Experience and the Expression of Genetic Potential: What Childhood Neglect Tells Us about Nature and Nurture." *Brain and Mind* 3 (2002): 79–100.

———. *Maltreated Children: Experience, Brain Development and the Next Generation*. New York: Norton, 2007.

Perry, B. D., R. A. Pollard, T. L. Blakley, W. L. Baker, and D. Vigilante. "Childhood Trauma, the Neurobiology of Adaptation, and 'Use-Dependent' Development of the Brain: How 'States' Become 'Traits.'" *Infant Mental Health Journal* 16, no. 4 (1995): 271–91.

Pervin, Lawrence A. "Further Reflections on Current Trait Theory." *Psychological Inquiry* 5, no. 2 (1994): 169–78.

———. *The Science of Personality*. New York: Wiley, 1996.

Pervin, Lawrence A., and O. P. John. *Personality Theory and Research*. 7th ed. New York: Wiley, 1997.

Petty, R. E., and D. T. Wegener. "Attitude Change: Multiple Roles for Persuasion Variables." In *The Handbook of Social Psychology*, edited by S. T. Fiske, D. T. Gilbert, and G. Lindzey, 323–71. Boston: McGraw-Hill, 1998.

Phares, Vicky. *Understanding Abnormal Child Psychology*. Hoboken, NJ: Wiley, 2007.

Pianta, R. C., R. S. Marvin, and M. C. Morog. "Resolving the Past and Present: Relations with Attachment Organization." In *Attachment Disorganization*, edited by Judith Solomon and C. George, 379–98. New York: Guilford, 1999.

Pinel, John P. J. *Biopsychology*. 6th ed. Boston: Allyn and Bacon, 2006.

Pinker, Steven. *The Blank Slate: The Modern Denial of Human Nature*. New York: Penguin Putnam, 2002.

———. "The Decline of Violence." In *What Are You Optimistic About? Today's Leading Thinkers on Why Things Are Good and Getting Better*, edited by J. Brockman. New York: Harper, 2008.

———. *How the Mind Works*. New York: Norton, 1997.

———. *The Language Instinct*. New York: Morrow, 1994.

Pitcher, G. *The Death of Spin*. West Sussex, UK: Wiley, 2007.

Plomin, R., and A. Caspi. "Behavioral Genetics and Personality." In *Handbook of Personality: Theory and Research*, edited by Lawrence A. Pervin and O. P. John, 251–76. New York: Guilford, 1999.

Plomin, R. C., H. M. Chipur, and J. C. Loehlin. "Behavioral Genetics and Personality." In *Handbook of Personality: Theory and Research*, edited by Lawrence A. Pervin and O. P. John, 225–43. New York: Guilford, 1990.

Pomerantz, E. M., and M. M. Eaton. "Maternal Intrusive Support in the Academic Context: Transactional Socialization Processes." *Developmental Psychology* 37, no. 2 (2001): 174–86.

Popkin, Richard H. *The History of Skepticism: From Savonarola to Bayle.* New York: Oxford University Press, 2003.

Popper, Karl. *Conjectures and Refutations.* New York: Basic Books, 1963.

———. *The Open Society and Its Enemies: The Spell of Plato.* Princeton, NJ: Princeton University Press, 1971.

Post, J. M. "Terrorist Psycho-Logic: Terrorist Behavior as a Product of Psychological Forces." In *Origins of Terrorism: Psychologies, Ideologies, Theologies, States of Mind*, edited by Walter Reich. Baltimore: Johns Hopkins University Press, 1998.

Postman, Neil. *Conscientious Objections: Stirring Up Trouble about Language, Technology, and Education.* New York: Vintage, 1988.

Potkay, Charles R., and B. P. Allen. *Personality: Theory, Research, and Applications.* Monterey, CA: Brooks/Cole Publishing, 1986.

Presley, S. "Positive Steps to Becoming Less Vulnerable to Influence and Authority." *Free Inquiry* 15, no 1. (Winter 1994): 29.

Provine, R. R. "This Is All There Is." In *What Is Your Dangerous Idea?* edited by John Brockman. New York: HarperCollins, 2007.

Pyszczynski, T. "Why Do People Need Self-Esteem? A Theoretical and Empirical Review." *Psychological Bulletin* 130 (2004): 435–68.

Pyszczynski, T., J. Greenberg, and J. L. Goldenberg. "Freedom versus Fear: On the Defense, Growth, and Expansion of the Self." In *Handbook of Self and Identity*, edited by Mark R. Leary and J. P. Tangney, 314–43. New York: Guilford Press, 2003.

Pyszczynski, T., S. Solomon, and J. Greenberg. *In the Wake of 9/11: The Psychology of Terror.* Washington, DC: American Psychological Association, 2002.

Rahula, Walpola. *What the Buddha Taught.* New York: Grove, 1974.

Ratey, John J., and C. Johnson. *Shadow Syndromes: The Mild Forms of Major Mental Disorders That Sabotage Us.* New York: Bantam Books, 1998.

Ray, John. J. "Balanced Dogmatism Scales." *Australian Journal of Psychology* 26, no. 1 (1974): 9–14.

———. "The Behavioral Validity of Some Recent Measures of Authoritarianism." *Journal of Social Psychology* 120 (1983): 91–99.

———. "Book Review: *Enemies of Freedom* by R. Altemeyer." *Australian Journal of Psychology* 42 (1990): 87–111.

———. "Book Review: *Right-Wing Authoritarianism* by R. Altemeyer." *Australian Journal of Psychology* 35 (1983): 267–68.

———. "Defective Validity in the Altemeyer Authoritarianism Scale." *Journal of Social Psychology* 125 (1985): 271–72.

———. "The Development and Validation of a Balanced Dogmatism Scale." *Australian Journal of Psychology* 22, no. 3 (1970): 253–60.

Reich, Walter, ed. *Origins of Terrorism: Psychologies, Ideologies, Theologies, States of Mind.* Baltimore: Johns Hopkins University Press, 1998.

Reicher, S. D., and S. A. Haslam. "Rethinking the Psychology of Tyranny: The BBC Prison Study." *British Journal of Social Psychology* 45 (2006): 1–40.

Reiss, H. T., W. A. Collins, and E. Berscheid. "The Relationship Context of Human Behavior and Development." *Psychological Bulletin* 126, no. 6 (2000): 844–72.

Relethford, John H. *The Human Species: An Introduction to Biological Anthropology.* 5th ed. New York: McGraw-Hill, 2003.

Rhodes, N., and W. Wood. "Self-Esteem and Intelligence Affect Influenceability: The Mediating Role of Message Reception." *Psychological Bulletin* 111 (1992): 156–71.

Ricard, Mattieu. *Happiness: A Guide to Developing Life's Most Important Skill.* New York: Little, Brown, 2003.

Ridley, M. *Mendel's Demon: Gene Justice and the Complexity of Life.* London: Weidenfield and Nicolson, 2000.

Rizzolatti, G., and L. Craighero. "The Mirror-Neuron System." *Annual Review of Neuroscience* (2004): 169–192.

Roberts, B. W., and W. F. DelVecchio. "The Rank-Order Consistency of Personality Traits from Childhood to Old Age: A Quantitative Review of Longitudinal Studies." *Psychological Bulletin* 126 (2000): 3–25.

Robins, R. W., J. K. Norem, and J. M. Cheek. "Naturalizing the Self." In *Handbook of Personality: Theory and Research*, edited by Lawrence A. Pervin and O. P. John. New York: Guilford Press, 2003.

Rogers, Carl R. *Client-Centered Therapy: Its Current Practice, Implications, and Theory.* Boston: Houghton Mifflin, 1951.

———. "The Concept of a Fully Functioning Person." *Psychotherapy: Theory, Research, and Practice* 1, no. 17–26 (1963).

———. *On Becoming a Person: A Therapist's View of Psychotherapy.* Boston: Houghton Mifflin, 1961.

Rokeach, Milton. *Beliefs, Attitudes, and Values.* San Francisco, CA: Jossey-Bass, 1968.

———. *The Open and Closed Mind.* New York: Basic Books, 1960.

———. *Understanding Human Values: Individual and Societal.* New York: Free Press, 1979.

Rorty, Richard. "Universality and Truth." In *Rorty and His Critics*, edited by Robert Brandom, 1–30. Malden, MA: Blackwell, 2000.

Rose, Hilary, and S. Rose. *Alas, Poor Darwin: Arguments against Evolutionary Psychology.* New York: Harmony Books, 2000.

Rowe, D. C., and E. J. van den Oord. "Genetic and Environmental Influences." In *Personality: Contemporary Theory and Research*, edited by Valerian J. Derlega, B. A. Winstead, and W. H. Jones. Belmont, CA: Thomson Wadsworth, 2005.

Russell, Bertrand. *The Autobiography of Bertrand Russell: 1944–1967.* London: George Allen and Unwin, 1970.

Ruthven, Malise. *A Fury of God: The Islamic Attack on America.* London: Granta Books, 2004.

Ryan, R. M., and E. I. Deci. "On Assimilating Identities to the Self: A Self-Determination Theory Perspective on Internalization and Integrity within Cultures." In *Handbook of Self and Identity*, edited by Mark R. Leary and J. P. Tangney. New York: Guilford, 2003.

Ryckman, Richard M. *Theories of Personality.* 7th ed. Belmont, CA: Wadsworth, 2000.

———. *Theories of Personality.* 8th ed. Belmont, CA: Wadsworth/Thomson Learning, 2004.

Sartre, J. P. *Being and Nothingness.* New York: Simon and Schuster, 1943.

Saucier, G., and L. R. Goldberg. "The Language of Personality: Lexical Perspectives on the Five-Factor Model." In *The Five-Factor Model of Personality: Theoretical Perspectives*, edited by Jerry S. Wiggins, 21–50. New York: Guilford, 1996.

Saudino, K. J. "Moving beyond the Heritability Question: New Directions in Behavioral Genetic Studies of Personality." In *Current Directions in*

Personality Psychology, edited by Carolyn C. Morf and A. Ozlem, 57–64. Upper Saddle River, NJ: Pearson, 2005.

Saul, J. R. *Reflections of a Siamese Twin: Canada at the End of the Twentieth Century.* New York: Viking, 1997.

Scarr, Sandra. *Race, Social Class, and Individual Differences in I.Q.* Hillsdale, NJ: Erlbaum, 1981.

Schaller, M. B. C., J. Yohannes, and M. O'Brien. "The Prejudiced Personality Revisited: Personal Need for Structure and Formation of Erroneous Group Stereotypes." *Journal of Personality and Social Psychology* 68, no. 3 (1995): 544–55.

Schore, Allan N. *Affect Dysregulation and Disorders of the Self.* New York: Norton, 2003.

———. "The Experience-Dependent Maturation of a Regulatory System in the Orbital Prefrontal Cortex and the Origin of Developmental Psychopathology." *Developmental and Psychopathology* 8 (1996): 59–87.

———. "The Self-Organization of the Right Brain and the Neurobiology of Emotional Development." In *Emotion, Development, and Self-Organization*, edited by Marc D. Lewis and I. Granic, 155–85. New York: Cambridge University Press, 2000.

Schultz, P. Wesley, and A. Searleman. "Rigidity of Thought and Behavior: 100 Years of Research." *Genetic, Social and General Psychology Monographs* 128, no. 2 (2002): 165–209.

Serafini, Anthony. *The Epic History of Biology.* New York: Plenum, 1993.

Shaffer, David R. *Social and Personality Development.* 4th ed. Scarborough, ON: Nelson/Thomson Learning, 2000.

Sheldon, K. M., R. M. Ryan, L. Rawsthorne, and B. Ilardi. "Trait Self and True Self: Cross-Role Variation in the Big Five Traits and Its Relations with Authenticity and Subjective Well-Being." *Journal of Personality and Social Psychology* 73 (1997): 1380–93.

Sheng-yen. *Setting in Motion the Dharma Wheel: Talks on the Four Noble Truths of Buddhism.* Elmhurst, NY: Dharma Drum, 2000.

Shermer, Michael. "The Question of God: C. S. Lewis and Freud." Panel discussion. DVD. *Nova*, PBS, 2004.

———. *Science Friction: Where the Known Meets the Unknown.* New York: Henry Holt, 2005.

———. *The Science of Good and Evil: Why People Cheat, Gossip, Care, Share, and Follow the Golden Rule.* New York: Henry Holt, 2004.

————. *Why People Believe Weird Things: Pseudoscience, Superstition, and Other Confusions of Our Time*. New York: W. H. Freeman, 1997.

Siegel, Daniel J. *The Developing Mind*. New York: Guilford, 1999.

Skinner, B. F. *Science and Human Behavior*. New York: Macmillan, 1953.

Snelson, J. S. "The Ideological Immune System." *Skeptic* 4 (1993): 44–55.

Solomon, Judith, and C. George, eds. *Attachment Disorganization*. New York: Guilford, 1999.

————. "The Place of Disorganization in Attachment Theory: Linking Classic Observations with Contemporary Findings." In *Attachment Disorganization*, edited by Judith Solomon and C. George. New York: Guilford, 1999.

Solso, Robert L. *Cognitive Psychology*. 6th ed. Needham Heights, MA: Allyn and Bacon, 2001.

Soyinka, Wole. *Climate of Fear: The Quest for Dignity in a Dehumanized World*. New York: Random House, 2005.

Srivastava, S., O. P. John, S. D. Goslin, and J. Potter. "Development of Personality in Early and Middle Adulthood: Set Like Plaster or Persistent Change?" *Journal of Personality and Social Psychology* 85 (2003): 1041–53.

Sroufe, L. Alan. *Emotional Development: The Organization of Emotional Life in the Early Years*. Cambridge: Cambridge University Press, 1996.

Stagner, R. "Traits and Theoreticians." *Psychological Inquiry* 5, no. 2 (1994): 166–68.

Stanovich, Keith E. "Reasoning Independently of Prior Belief and Individual Differences in Actively Open-Minded Thinking," *Journal of Educational Psychology* 89 (1997): 342–58.

————. *The Robot's Rebellion: Finding Meaning in the Age of Darwin*. Chicago: University of Chicago Press, 2004.

Stern, Daniel N. *The Interpersonal World of the Infant*. New York: Basic Books, 1985.

Stern, J. *Terror in the Name of God: Why Religious Militants Kill*. New York: HarperCollins, 2003.

Sternberg, Robert J. *Thinking Styles*. Cambridge: Cambridge University Press, 1997.

Stokes, Philip. *Philosophy: One Hundred Essential Thinkers*. Toronto: Indigo Books, 2003.

Stroufe, L. A. "Attachment Classification from the Perspective of Infant-

Caregiver Relationships and Infant Temperament." *Child Development* 56 (1985): 1–14.

Sue, David, D. Sue, and S. Sue. *Understanding Abnormal Behavior*. 5th ed. Boston: Houghton Mifflin, 1997.

Suedfeld, P., and D. C. Leighton. "Early Communications in the War against Terrorism: An Integrative Complexity Analysis." *Political Psychology* 23 (2002): 585–99.

Suedfeld, Peter, K. Guttieri, and P. E. Tetlock. "Assessing Integrative Complexity at a Distance: Archival Analyses of Thinking and Decision Making." In *The Psychological Assessment of Political Leaders*, edited by J. M. Post, 246–70. Ann Arbor: University of Michigan Press, 2003.

Suedfeld, Peter, and P. E. Tetlock. "Individual Differences in Information Processing." In *Blackwell Handbook of Social Psychology: Intraindividual Processes*, edited by A. Tesser and N. Schwartz, 284–304. Oxford: Blackwell Publishing, 2003.

Swann, David. "Finding My Voice for Peace." In *Canada and the New American Empire: War and Anti-War*, edited by G. Melnyk, 113–25. Calgary: University of Calgary Press, 2004.

Tarnow, E. "Self-Destructive Obedience in the Airline Cockpit and the Concept of Obedience Optimization." In *Obedience to Authority: Current Perspectives on the Milgram Paradigm*, edited by Thomas Blass, 111–23. Mahwah, NJ: Erlbaum, 2000.

Tavris, C. and E. Aronson. *Mistakes Were Made (But Not by Me)*. Orlando, FL: Houghton Mifflin Harcourt, 2007.

Taylor, C. "Why Democracy Needs Patriotism." *Boston Review* 19, no. 5 (October–November 1994).

Taylor, D. M., and W. Louis. "Terrorism and the Quest for Identity." In *Understanding Terrorism: Psychosocial Roots, Consequences, and Interventions*, edited by Fathali M. Moghaddam and A. J. Marsella. Washington, DC: American Psychological Association, 2004.

Taylor, Donald M. *The Quest for Identity: From Minority Groups to Generation Xers*. Westport, CT: Praeger, 2002.

Tellegen, A., D. T. Lykken, T. J. Bouchard, K. J. Wilcox, N. L. Segal, and S. Rich. "Personality Similarity in Twins Reared Apart and Together." *Journal of Personality and Social Psychology* 54 (1988): 1031–39.

Tetlock, P. E., D. Armor, and R. Peterson. "The Slavery Debate in Antebellum America: Cognitive Style, Value Conflict, and the Limits of Compromise." *Journal of Personality and Social Psychology* 66 (1994): 115–26.

Thomas, Alexander, and S. Chess. *Temperament and Development*. New York: Brunner/Mazel, 1977.

Thompson, Mel. *Eastern Philosophy: Hinduism, Buddhism, Taoism, Confucianism, Jainism, Reincarnation, Nirvana, Zen, Vedanta, the Self, Yin/Yang, Ethics.* Chicago: NTC/Contemporary Publishing, 1999.

Thoreau, Henry D. *Walden and Essay on Civil Disobedience*. New York: Airmont Publishing, 1965.

Thorne, A. "Conditional Patterns, Transference, and the Coherence of Personality across Time." In *Personality Psychology: Recent Trends and Emerging Directions*, edited by David M. Buss and N. Cantor, 149–59. New York: Springer, 1989.

Tillich, Paul. *The Protestant Era*. Chicago: University of Chicago Press, 1947.

Todd, P. M., R. Hertwig, and U. Hoffrage. "Evolutionary Cognitive Psychology." In *The Handbook of Evolutionary Psychology*, edited by David M. Buss. Hoboken, NJ: Wiley, 2005.

Tolle, Eckhart. *A New Earth: Awakening to Your Life's Purpose*. New York: Penguin, 2005.

Trapnell, P. D. "Openness versus Intellect: A Lexical Left Turn." *European Journal of Personality* 8 (1994): 273–90.

Trungpa, Chögyam. *Cutting through Spiritual Materialism*, edited by J. Baker and M. Casper. Boston: Shambhala, 1973.

Tupes, E. C., and R. E. Christal. "Recurrent Personality Factors Based on Trait Ratings." *USAF ASD Tech. Rep.* No. 61–97 (1961).

Wallace, M. D., P. Suedfeld, and K. Thachuk. "Political Rhetoric of Leaders Under Stress in the Gulf Crisis." *Journal of Conflict Resolution* (1993): 94–107.

Waterman, A. S. "Identity in the Context of Adolescent Psychology." In *Identity in Adolescence: Processes and Contents*, edited by A. S. Waterman, 5–24. San Francisco: Jossey-Bass, 1985.

Waters, E., J. Wippman, and L. A. Stroufe. "Attachment, Positive Affect, and Competence in the Peer Group." *Child Development* 50 (1979): 821–29.

West, R. F., and K. E. Stanovich. "Is Probability Matching Smart? Associations between Probabilistic Choices and Cognitive Ability." *Memory and Cognition* 31 (1997): 243–51.

Westen, D., and A. K. Heim. "Disturbances of Self and Identity in Personality Disorders." In *Handbook of Self and Identity*, edited by Mark R. Leary and J. P. Tangney, 643–64. New York: Guilford, 2003.

Westen, D., P. S. Blagnov, K. Harenski, C. Kilts, and S. Hamann. "The Neural Basis of Motivated Reasoning: Am fMRI Study of Emotional Constraints on Political Judgment during the U.S. Presidential Election of 2004." *Journal of Cognitive Neuroscience* 18 (2006): 1947–58.

Westen, Drew. "Psychoanalytic Approaches to Personality." In *Handbook of Personality: Theory and Research*, edited by L. Pervin, 21–65. New York: Guilford, 1990.

Wheen, Francis. *How Mumbo Jumbo Conquered the World: A Short History of Modern Delusions.* New York: Perseus, 2004.

Widiger, T. A., and T. J. Trull. "Assessment of the Five-Factor Model of Personality." *Journal of Personality Assessment* 68 (1997): 228–50.

Wiggins, J. S., and J. L. Pincus. "Personality: Structure and Assessment." *Annual Review of Psychology* 43 (1992): 473–504.

Wilson, Edward O. *Consilience: The Unity of Knowledge.* New York: Knopf, 1998.

———. *On Human Nature.* Cambridge, MA: Harvard University Press, 1978.

Wilson, G. D. "The Psychology of Conservatism." In *The Psychology of Conservatism*, edited by Glenn D. Wilson, 3–16. New York: Academic Press, 1973.

Witkin, Herman A., and D. R. Goodenough. *Cognitive Styles: Essence and Origins.* New York: International Universities Press, 1981.

Wittgenstein, Ludwig. *On Certainty / Über Gewissheit.* Edited by G. E. M. Anscombe and G. H. von Wright. Oxford: Blackwell, 1969.

Wood, Julia T. *Communication Theories in Action: An Introduction.* Belmont, CA: Wadsworth/Thomson Learning, 2000.

Wright, Robert. *The Moral Animal: Why We Are the Way We Are.* New York: Vintage, 1994.

Yalom, Irvin D. *Existential Psychotherapy.* New York: Basic Books, 1980.

Zechmeister, Eugene B., and J. Johnson. *Critical Thinking: A Functional Approach.* Pacific Grove, CA: Brooks/Cole, 1992.

Zeilinger, A. "Going beyond Our Darwinian Roots." In *What Are You Optimistic About? Today's Leading Thinkers on Why Things Are Good and Getting Better*, edited by J. Brockman, 38. New York: Harper, 2007.

Zimbardo, P. G. "On the Ethics of Intervention in Human Psychological Research: With Special Reference to the Stanford Prison Experiment." *Cognition* 2 (1973): 243–56.

Zimbardo, P. G., M. Weisenberg, I. Firestone, and B. Levy. "Communicator Effectiveness in Producing Public Conformity and Private Attitude Change." *Journal of Personality and Social Psychology* 17, no. 33 (1965): 233–55.

Zimbardo, Philip G., and F. L. Ruch. *Psychology and Life*. Glenview, IL: Scott-Foresman, 1975.

Zuckerman, M. "The Psychophysiology of Sensation-Seeking." *Journal of Personality* 58 (1990): 313–45.

INDEX

ABOUT THE AUTHOR

JUDY J. JOHNSON, PhD, is a registered clinical psychologist and psychology professor at Mount Royal College, Calgary, AB, Canada. She has taught psychology to Palestinian students in Gaza during the intifadas of 1991 and 1992, to native women on the Sarcee Reserve, and to inmates and correctional officers in Canada's provincial and federal penitentiaries. She is the author of *Suicide Intervention Program: A Group Facilitator's Manual*, published by the Canadian Mental Health Association, Calgary, AB.

For further information, visit her Web site at www.dogmatism.ca.